WITHDF
UTSA Librarie

D0442808

RENEWALS 458-4574

Building Ethnic Collections

An Annotated Guide
for School Media Centers
and Public Libraries

Lois Buttlar   Lubomyr R. Wynar

Libraries Unlimited, Inc.
Littleton, Colo.

1977

Copyright ©1977 Libraries Unlimited, Inc.
All Rights Reserved
Printed in the United States of America

LIBRARIES UNLIMITED, INC.
P.O. Box 263
Littleton, Colorado 80160

LIBRARY
The University of Texas
At San Antonio

Library of Congress Cataloging in Publication Data

Buttlar, Lois, 1934-
   Building ethnic collections.

   Includes index.
   1. Minorities--United States--Bibliography.
I. Wynar, Lubomyr Roman, 1932-   joint author.
II. Title.
Z1361.E4B88   [E184.A1]   016.973'04   76-55398
ISBN 0-87287-130-4

TABLE OF CONTENTS

PREFACE

The upsurge of interest in ethnicity and the ethnic heritage in the past few years has resulted in the development of an ethnic curriculum in our schools and in renewed ethnic research by educators and scholars. On June 23, 1972, the President of the United States signed Public Law 93-318, also known as Educational Amendment of 1972 (Section 504), which provided for the establishment of an Ethnic Heritage Studies Program. The Congress of the United States emphasized the importance of the ethnic heritage studies in our elementary and secondary schools and noted that "in a multiethnic society a greater understanding of the contributions of one's own heritage and those of one's fellow citizens can contribute to a more harmonious, patriotic, and committed populace. It is further enacted in recognition of the principle that all students in the elementary and secondary schools of the Nation should have an opportunity to learn about the differing and unique contributions to the national heritage made by each ethnic group" (H. R. 14910). This acknowledgement of the pluralistic nature of American society was instrumental in the initiation of ethnic curriculum projects in American schools[1] and in the organization of special teachers' workshops that stressed the teaching of ethnicity. As a result, numerous new courses on ethnicity have already been introduced into the curriculum of many schools across the nation. At the same time, a number of educational organizations have directly contributed to the development of a conceptual framework within which ethnic studies courses can be implemented in the school curriculum. Organizations such as the National Educational Association (NEA), the Association for Supervision and Curriculum Development (ASCD), the National Council for Social Studies (NCSS), the Commission on Multicultural Education of the American Association of Colleges for Teacher Education, and many others have strongly endorsed the principle that it is essential for the school curriculum to provide multicultural education that reflects the cultural pluralism of American society. Thus, according to the Commission on Multicultural Education of the American Association of Colleges for Teacher Education, multicultural education

> affirms that schools should be oriented toward the cultural enrichment of all children and youth through programs rooted to the preservation and extension of cultural alternatives. Multicultural education recognizes cultural diversity as a fact of life in American society, and it affirms that this cultural diversity is a valuable resource that should be preserved and extended. It affirms that major educational institutions should strive to preserve and enhance cultural pluralism.[2]

---

[1] For a detailed analysis of recent ethnic projects, see *Title IX, Ethnic Heritage Project Analysis* (Chicago, Ill.: The Urban and Ethnic Education Section, Illinois Office of Education, 1975).

[2] "No One Model American," *Journal of Teacher Education* (Winter 1973), p. 265; quoted in Donna M. Gollnick, F. H. Klassen, and Joost Yff, *Multicultural Education and Ethnic Studies in the United States* (Washington, D.C.: American Association of Colleges for Teacher Education and ERIC Clearinghouse on Teacher Education, 1976), p. 9.

It is obvious that the development of library resources of ethnic materials, on both the elementary and secondary levels, is a process that parallels the development of a teaching curriculum. If a strong and well-balanced curriculum on ethnicity is to be maintained, there must also exist a strong and well-balanced library collection—for it is the school library media center and its holdings that form the firm base necessary for the development of strong and efficient teaching programs.[3] Since "the school library media specialist is the energizing force that powers the educational thrust of the instructional media program,"[4] her role in developing an ethnic print and non-print collection provides essential and indispensable support of the elementary and secondary ethnic curriculum.

Thus, keeping in mind the needs of school library media centers as well as the basic needs of teachers and other educators in the development of the ethnic curriculum, the authors undertook this project, whose purpose is to fill the existing gap in literature related to ethnicity. This guide, *Building Ethnic Collections: An Annotated Guide for School Media Centers and Public Libraries*, constitutes the most recent comprehensive reference tool in the area of ethnic studies as related to school media centers and the ethnic curriculum. It is designed to aid media specialists, librarians, teachers, and curriculum supervisors in their effort to establish a well-balanced media/library collection, to introduce multicultural educational curricula, and to acquaint all interested parties with the relevant materials on ethnicity and individual ethnic groups. Also, this guide will prove to be a valuable reference tool for public librarians interested in selecting print and non-print materials on ethnicity to serve the needs of the various age groups within their communities—particularly with respect to children and young adults. In addition, libraries within our community and junior colleges may find the listing of materials aimed at young adults and teachers to be a useful guide toward the expansion of their collections on ethnicity.

It is hoped, therefore, that by bringing together in one handy volume the basic reference and general print and non-print materials, this annotated guide will be widely used by the media specialists who are responsible for the organization of instructional materials and their integration in the instructional program, and by the teachers and curriculum supervisors who are responsible for developing ethnic courses within our schools.

The major role and objectives of this guide are as follows:

1) **Building Ethnic Print and Non-Print Collections**: to assist in the selection and purchase of necessary materials for school media centers supportive of the school curricula. Using this guide will help the media staff acquire the necessary ethnic materials. Information on the rental of certain audiovisual materials is also provided, thus enabling the media specialist to choose between purchasing or renting the material in question.

---

[3] L. R. Wynar submitted to the National Advisory Council on Ethnic Heritage during its hearings (Detroit, July 15, 1976) a number of recommendations concerning the role of school media centers and media specialists as well as librarians in the development of the ethnic media collections and ethnic curriculum. See L. R. Wynar, "Recommendations on Development of a Library Science Program and the Establishment of a National Ethnic Documentation Center," July 15, 1976 (typescript).

[4] Ruth Ann Davies, *The School Library Media Center: A Force for Educational Excellence*, 2nd ed. (New York: R. R. Bowker Co., 1974), p. 33.

2) **Curriculum Development and Classroom Instruction**: to help teachers and curriculum planners implement the multicultural educational curricula in elementary and secondary schools. In addition, this guide includes materials on methods of teaching ethnic courses, so it will be valuable to curriculum planners and instructors as they develop teaching strategies and course content.

3) **Reference Service**: media specialists, teachers, and public librarians can use this guide to provide better reference service related to ethnicity and individual ethnic groups. In this respect it may be useful in answering direct reference questions, and also in assisting students involved in the preparation of ethnic-related assignments.

In an effort to meet all the objectives of this publication, the compilers have attempted to 1) provide titles that are sources of materials (bibliographies, filmographies, discographies, and multimedia lists); 2) list titles that will help teachers and curriculum planners implement ethnic materials into the school program; and 3) list materials themselves.

The history, experience, and contributions of each group are presented in the non-fiction titles and the audiovisual materials sections; however, particular attention was also paid to fiction titles that take advantage of the child's ability to absorb, indirectly and unconsciously, the values and customs of another cultural heritage by identifying with the hero or main character in the story. It is hoped that not only the media specialists, librarians, and teachers, but also the students themselves will be able to consult this guide, in order to identify materials that will help them to discover a sense of identity with their own ethnic backgrounds, or to develop and expand their appreciation and understanding of others.

Lubomyr R. Wynar, Director
Program for the Study of Ethnic Publications
School of Library Science
Kent State University

July 1976

INTRODUCTION

Although bibliographies covering ethnic materials that are appropriate for use in the school curriculum do exist, the majority are either related to one particular minority group or are concerned with only a few ethnic groups. In some instances, bibliographies covering a wider spectrum of ethnic groups include out-of-print publications and give incomplete bibliographic information, two approaches that limit their reference value.[1] The present publication is planned to be a comprehensive annotated guide to available resources covering a broad spectrum of ethnic groups and ethnic topics in general; it is hoped that the guide will be used by librarians, media specialists, teachers, and students involved in ethnic studies.

METHODOLOGY

The titles included in this guide are based on a comprehensive literature survey and evaluation of ethnic publications in print. A small number of out-of-print titles have been included where the literature for a particular group is limited, since these titles can often be borrowed from another collection, and since the student, teacher, and/or media specialist should be aware of their existence.

Book titles were primarily identified through *Bibliographic Index* (1965-1976); *Cumulative Book Index* (1965-1976); *American Book Publishing Record* (1970-1976); *Library of Congress—Books: Subjects* (1950-1975); *Subject Guide to Books in Print* (1970-1976); and *Subject Guide to Children's Books in Print*, 6th ed. (Bowker, 1975). Special attention was also focused on current major bibliographies and reference publications. These important tools were identified through *American Reference Books Annual*, edited by Bohdan S. Wynar (Littleton, Colo.: Libraries Unlimited, 1970–); *Guide to Reference Books for School Media Centers*, by Christine L. Wynar (Littleton, Colo.: Libraries Unlimited, 1973;

---

[1] For instance, the recently published *Materials and Human Resources for Teaching Ethnic Studies: An Annotated Bibliography* (Boulder, Colo.: Social Science Education Resources, 1975) lacks sufficient bibliographic description of the titles included (does not include paging for the books nor prices for the books and films listed) and lacks essential information on film features (no indication whether they are black and white or color, length of time, 8mm or 16mm, etc.). Also, some of the materials included for individual ethnic groups are outdated and not representative.

Another recent publication, *American Ethnic Groups and the Revival of Cultural Pluralism*, 4th ed., by Jack F. Kinton (Mt. Pleasant, Iowa: Social Sciences and Sociological Resources, 1974), is not annotated and occasionally provides rather meager coverage of the literature concerning ethnic groups; other deficiencies include weak methodology and bibliographic incompleteness.

Neither of these publications contains any indices, a fact that further limits their usefulness as reference tools on ethnic studies.

1974-75 Supplement, 1976); and through contact with some of the major ethnic organizations and research centers. In addition, several ERIC literature searches were conducted and relevant titles were incorporated in this publication.

Other materials were chosen selectively on the basis of the following criteria:

1) availability of the media for purchase (currency)
2) quality and quantity of reviews appearing in standard media selection tools for school and public library materials, and inclusion in the Wilson Standard Catalogs (*Children's Catalog*, 12th ed., 1971– ; *Fiction Catalog*, 8th ed., 1971– ; *Junior High School Library Catalog*, 3rd ed., 1975– ; *Senior High School Library Catalog*, 10th ed., 1972– ; *Public Library Catalog*, 6th ed., 1973– ; and their supplements; and the *Elementary School Library Collection: A Guide to Books and Other Media*, 9th ed., Bro-Dart, 1974)
3) balancing the list with respect to representation of *kind of media*, and *grade level of materials*
4) the "classic" materials, or those whose appeal and usefulness have shown some permanence

The annotations provided in this guide are based, for the most part, on de visu examination, particularly for the print materials. The compilers also took into consideration reviews published in *Booklist* (American Library Association, 1905–); *Library Journal* (Bowker, 1876–); *School Library Journal* (Bowker, 1954–); *Book Review Digest* (Wilson, 1905–).

The audiovisual materials were, in some cases, included on the basis of reviews in *Previews: Non-Print Software and Hardware News Reviews* (Bowker, 1972–); *Film News: The International Review of AV Materials and Equipment* (Film News Company, 1941–); and *Booklist* (American Library Association, 1905–). Others were identified and/or previewed through the facilities of the Kent State University Department of Audiovisual Services, which has an excellent film rental library and a wide collection of producers' and distributors' catalogs; the *Library of Congress Catalog: Films and Other Materials for Projection* (Library of Congress, 1953–); and the *Elementary School Library Collection* (Bro-Dart Foundation, 1975 ed.).

The NICEM indexes were also utilized in the survey of audiovisual materials, including *Index to Educational Overhead Transparencies*, 3rd ed. (National Information Center for Educational Media, University of Southern California, 1973); *Index to Educational Videotapes*, 2nd ed. (1973); *Index to 8mm Motion Cartridges*, 3rd ed. (1973); *Index to Educational Records*, 3rd ed. (1975); *Index to 16mm Educational Films*, 5th ed. (1975); and *Index to 35mm Filmstrips*, 5th ed. (1975).

Some titles included in this guide do not appear in any of the above-mentioned sources. However, they were traced through various ethnic organizations that also serve as publishing agencies for the particular groups.

The collections of a number of libraries and research centers were used, including New York Public Library; Cleveland Public Library; Denver Public Library; Akron Public Library; University of Colorado Libraries; Case Western Reserve University Libraries; Libraries Unlimited, Inc., in Denver; Social Science Education Consortium in Boulder, Colorado; Program for the Study of Ethnic

Publications at Kent State University; numerous elementary and secondary media centers and public libraries in Ohio and Colorado; and the collection and interlibrary loan service of Kent State University Library. The coverage of 1976 imprints is limited to the first part of the year.

SCOPE

It is necessary to stress that this guide constitutes a selective listing of the English language materials on ethnicity and ethnic groups in the United States. The following groups are included:

American Indians	Irish Americans
Appalachian Americans	Italian Americans
Arab Americans	Japanese Americans
Armenian Americans	Jewish Americans
Asian Americans	Korean Americans
Basque Americans	Latvian Americans
Black Americans	Lithuanian Americans
British Americans	Mexican Americans
Chinese Americans	Norwegian Americans
Croatian Americans	Polish Americans
Cuban Americans	Puerto-Rican Americans
Czech Americans	Romanian Americans
Danish Americans	Russian Americans
Dutch Americans	Scotch and Scotch-Irish Americans
East Indian Americans	Serbian Americans
Estonian Americans	Slovak Americans
Filipino Americans	Slovenian Americans
Finnish Americans	Spanish-Speaking Americans
French Americans	Swedish Americans
German Americans	Swiss Americans
Greek Americans	Ukrainian Americans
Hungarian Americans	Welsh Americans

A separate chapter covers multi-ethnic materials—those pertaining to two or more ethnic groups. Besides materials related to individual ethnic groups, this guide includes general reference sources on ethnicity, general works on teaching methods and curriculum materials, general non-fiction titles (covering history, culture, sociology, and biography), and multi-ethnic audiovisual materials.

In regard to the *type* of materials, the bibliography includes books (reference, non-fiction, and fiction), curriculum publications, and audiovisual materials (films, filmstrips, slides, prints, transparencies, records, etc.). It should be pointed out that the materials covering the larger groups, such as Black Americans, American Indians, and Mexican Americans, are so abundant that it would be impossible to include all of them within this volume. However, special effort was made to provide comprehensive coverage of these groups.

Since additional titles are mentioned in the annotations, the guide includes a total of 2,873 titles, covered in 2,286 annotated entries.

ARRANGEMENT OF MATERIAL

This guide is arranged into two major parts, plus a directory of producers and distributors of audiovisual materials, an author index, a title index, and an audiovisual index.

The first part, General Titles on Ethnicity, consists of a section on reference sources, which includes guides, bibliographies, encyclopedic works, directories, and statistical sources that cover ethnic topics. This part also includes separate sections on teaching methodology and curriculum materials; non-fiction titles, which covers general studies on ethnicity (historical, cultural, sociological, and biography); literature; and audiovisual materials (multi-ethnic).

The second part is arranged alphabetically under individual ethnic groups with necessary cross references. Each section dealing with an individual ethnic group is arranged in five basic categories: 1) Reference Sources; 2) Teaching Methodology and Curriculum Materials; 3) Non-Fiction Titles (History, Culture, Sociology, Biography); 4) Literature and Fiction Titles (the term "Literature" here is intended to include folklore, tales, legends, poetry, fairy tales, and other forms of creative writing); 5) Audiovisual Materials.

The directory of producers and distributors of audiovisual materials is arranged in straight alphabetical order.

ENTRIES

Book entries provide complete bibliographical description, including author's name, title, place of publication, publisher, year, paging, and price. Also, the grade levels for which the title is best suited are indicated (e.g., "9-12," "3-6"); "T" designates a work for teachers or adults.

The ERIC publications include the ERIC ordering number.

Materials that are reprints have been so designated, and the original publisher and publication date are given.

Description of audiovisual materials includes title, type of medium, length of showing time, producer, date, and price. The producer's description has been followed for designating recordings, which may thus be described as records, discs, phonodiscs, etc. For 8mm and 16mm films the following abbreviations have been used: min. (minutes); sd. (sound); b&w (black and white); col. (color).

All print and non-print entries are annotated.

INDICES

This guide contains author, title, and audiovisual indices arranged in straight alphabetical order. Figures cited after the entries refer to the item number assigned to the title. The comprehensive table of contents serves as a subject index.

PART I

GENERAL TITLES ON ETHNICITY

REFERENCE SOURCES

Reference Guides and Bibliographies

1. Barton, Josef J. **Brief Ethnic Bibliography: An Annotated Guide to the Ethnic Experience in the United States.** Cambridge, Mass.: Press of the Langdon Associates, 1976. 52p. $2.75pa. (T)
An alphabetical listing of titles on ethnicity and individual ethnic groups is arranged in the following categories: general works, works about specific groups, literature, ethnic politics, journals and newsletters, ethnic press, reference works, bibliographies, archives and special collections. Statistical sources are also included. Author index and ethnic group index provided.

2. Carlson, Ruth Kearney. **Emerging Humanity: Multi-Ethnic Literature for Children and Adolescents.** Dubuque, Iowa: Wm. C. Brown, 1972. 246p. $3.95pa. (T)
The first part of this book discusses ethnic literature and criteria for its selection and use by teachers. The second part of the book is an annotated bibliography of literature on Africans, Black Americans, American Indians, and Mexican Americans. Arrangement is by age and grade level.

3. **Cartel: Annotated Bibliography of Bilingual Bicultural Materials.** Austin, Tex.: Dissemination Center for Bilingual Bicultural Education, 1973– . Monthly. $10.00/yr. (T)
Books, curriculum guides, and other multimedia educational materials published after 1967 on the Spanish-speaking, American Indians, French, Portuguese, Chinese, and Russians in the United States. Annotations give acquisition information; a list of publishers and distributors is included. Particular bibliographies in the series discuss ethnic families and children, guides for evaluating bicultural readers, textbooks, workbooks, dictionaries, folklore, and fiction. Emphasis is on bilingual sources.

4. Caselli, Ron, *et al.*, comps. **The Minority Experience–A Basic Bibliography of American Ethnic Studies.** Santa Rosa, Calif.: Sonoma County Superintendent of Schools, 1970. 61p. $3.15. ED 038221. (T)
Books and periodicals published between 1940 and 1969 are listed for teachers and students of American ethnicity. Covers Blacks, Mexican-Americans and American Indians; approximately 950 entries included.

5. Cohen, David, coordinator. **Multi-Ethnic Media: Selected Bibliographies in Print.** Chicago: Office for Library Service to the Disadvantaged, American Library Association, 1975. 33p. $2.00pa. (T)
A listing of bibliographies arranged in three sections: 1) bibliographic essays, 2) bibliographies, and 3) sources of information. Emphasis in the first section is on materials (books, pamphlets, and journal articles) that evaluate treatment of ethnic and minority groups in texts and books. Section two lists actual bibliographies that appear in articles, pamphlets and books, and the third section lists organizations, agencies, and publishers that are valuable sources of information on ethnicity in America. Highly selective.

6. **Curriculum Materials: A Selected Bibliography.** Sacramento, Calif.: California State Department of Education, Bureau of Intergroup Relations, 1975. 60p. free. (T)

Lists a sample of curriculum materials reviewed to test analysis instruments in the California Ethnic Heritage Program, 1974-1975. The major objective of the project was not to develop "a selective or comprehensive bibliography but to assess the relevance and effectiveness of the screening and analysis instruments" (Introduction). Includes 60 entries.

7. Dearman, Evalyn M. **Kaleidoscope: A Directory of Resource Materials for Ethnic Education, K-12.** Reno, Nev.: Research and Educational Planning Center, College of Education, University of Nevada, 1974. 145p. $4.00pa. (T)

An annotated bibliography of multimedia ethnic materials for teacher reference and student usage at the K-12 levels. Arrangement is alphabetical by author in six disciplines: social studies/history; reading; bilingual/dialect education; music; art; and mathematics. Grade levels are indicated. Audiovisual materials are listed at the end of each section. Groups covered are: Blacks, Spanish, American Indians, Orientals, Basques.

8. Dunfee, Maxine, ed. **Eliminating Ethnic Bias in Instructional Materials: Comment and Bibliography.** Washington, D.C.: Association for Supervision and Curriculum Development, 1974. 58p. $3.25. ED 096221. (T)

This bibliography is arranged in five sections: 1) A Rationale for a Pluralistic Society, 2) Evidence of Ethnic Bias in Instructional Materials, 3) Efforts to Change, 4) Resources for Educators, 5) Evaluating Your Textbooks for Racism, Sexism.

9. Gilmore, Dolores D., and Kenneth Petrie, comps. **People: Annotated Multiethnic Bibliography, K-12.** Rockville, Md.: Montgomery County Public Schools, 1973. 345p. $5.00pa. (T)

This bibliography is valuable for selecting multiethnic media for schools. Arrangement is by ethnic group (Asian, Jewish, Mexican, American Indian, Puerto Rican, other, and multi-ethnic). Subject headings used are: Heritage; In America; Art, Literature, Music, Customs; Biography, Fiction Sources, and Resources. Most entries are annotated. Grade levels are indicated.

10. Glancy, Barbara Jean. **Children's Interracial Fiction: An Unselective Bibliography.** Washington, D.C.: American Federation of Teachers, AFL-CIO, 1969. 124p. $1.00pa. (T)

An annotated bibliography of children's fiction books that have an interracial theme. Suggestions for eliminating racism and helping children to understand racial issues and problems are included.

11. Gollnick, Donna M., Frank H. Klossen, and Joost Yff. **Multicultural Education and Ethnic Studies in the United States.** Washington, D.C.: American Association of Colleges for Teacher Education and ERIC Clearinghouse on Teacher Education, 1976. (T)

Consists of two parts: multicultural education—a literature review; and bibliography of ERIC documents related to multicultural education in the United States.

There is no author or title index, which limits the reference value of this publication.

12. **Good Reading for the Disadvantaged Reader: Multi-Ethnic Resources.** Champaign, Ill.: Garrard, 1970. 201p. $4.25pa. (T)

Reading materials selected are those that will help the child develop his sense of ethnic identity and that have been graded for readability by Spache or Dale-Chall formulas. Ethnic groups included are Blacks, American Indians, Mexican Americans, Orientals, and Puerto Ricans. Author-title and title-author indexes.

13. Grambs, Jean Dresden. **Intergroup Education, Methods and Materials.** Englewood Cliffs, N.J.: Prentice-Hall, 1968. 199p. $2.95pa. (T)

Discusses intercultural education from three main aspects: Part I discusses the particular needs of minority group children; Part II suggests methods and materials to use, including role playing, pictures, and affective materials with suggested open-ended situations for discussion. Part III is a bibliography of textbooks, fiction and nonfiction books, and various adiovisual materials on the elementary and secondary levels as well as background resource materials for teachers.

14. Griffin, Louise, comp. **Multi-Ethnic Books for Young Children: Annotated Bibliography for Parents and Teachers.** Washington, D.C.: National Association for the Education of Young Children, 1971. 74p. $2.00pa. (T)

Approximately 600 books for preschool through elementary (grade 6) ages. Ethnic backgrounds covered are: American Indians and Eskimos, Appalachians, Blacks, Latin Americans, Asians, Jews, and other European groups. Also includes books for adult reference, the sources consulted for compilation of the bibliography, list of publishers. Bibliographic entries are briefly annotated and include grade level indication.

15. Haller, Elizabeth S., comp. **American Diversity: A Bibliography of Resources on Racial and Ethnic Minorities for Pennsylvania Schools.** Harrisburg: Pennsylvania State Department of Education, c1970, 1973. 237p. $9.87. (T)

The bibliography aims to help locate materials that emphasize the contributions of racial and ethnic groups for inclusion in the elementary and secondary history curriculums. Groups covered are Afro-Americans, American Indians, Jewish Americans, Mexican Americans, Oriental Americans, Pennsylvania Germans, Puerto Ricans, other Americans, and multi-ethnic groups. A separate list of audiovisual materials is included. Arrangement is alphabetical by author within the groups under topics such as social interpretation, history, biography, bibliographies and teacher resources, arts, and fiction. Grade level and price are included with bibliographic description. All entries are annotated. Two years after the first printing, a 71-page *1971 Supplement to American Diversity* was published; arrangement follows the original publication.

16.   Inglehart, Babette F., and Anthony R. Mangione. **The Image of Pluralism in American Literature: An Annotated Bibliography on the American Experience of European Ethnic Groups.** New York: Institute of Pluralism and Group Identity of the American Jewish Committee, 1974. 73p. $3.15pa. (T)

A selected, annotated bibliography on European immigrant and ethnic groups in America. Designed to help high school teachers develop an appreciation of cultural diversity. The 403 entries are divided into the following categories: anthologies, literature (fiction, drama, memoirs) of European groups in America, history, autobiographies, and criticism. Subject index. A similar title by these compilers is *Multi-Ethnic Literature: An Annotated Bibliography on European Ethnic Group Life in America* (American Jewish Committee, 1974. 62p. $3.15. ED 091701).

17.   Jackson, Anne, ed. **Contributions of Ethnic Groups.** Little Rock: Arkansas State Department of Education, 1970. 153p. $6.58. (T)

An annotated bibliography of 701 entries published between 1929 and 1970. Arrangement is classified (by subject and usage level); includes films and recordings recommended for use in the elementary and secondary schools. Author-title index.

18.   Janeway, William Ralph. **Bibliography of Immigration in the United States, 1900-1930.** Columbus, Ohio: H. L. Hedrick, 1934; reprint ed., San Francisco: R & E Research Associates, 1972. 105p. $6.00pa. (T)

A bibliography listing books, documents and periodical articles published between 1900-1930. Includes references on immigration history, causes, statistics, and laws. Also, the backgrounds and cultural heritages of many ethnic groups are presented in geographic divisions—e.g., North European, South European, Eastern European, Latin, Slavic, Asiatic, etc., and non-quota immigrants (from the Americas and island territories). Other topics are covered under social adjustment (family, education, arts, religion, politics, press, etc.) and race relations and assimilation. Outdated, but still useful for historical sources.

19.   Jenerette, Gay H. **Bilingual Bicultural Materials: A Listing for Library Resource Centers.** El Paso, Tex.: Cooley Model Bilingual Library Learning Resource Center, 1974. 80p. (T)

Lists materials for libraries and resource centers serving bilingual bicultural students on the elementary level. Materials included are slides, transparencies, filmstrips, records, kits, games and models, and books. Information given includes title, producer, publication date, type of medium, contents, price, source, suggested Dewey classification, grade level, and an evaluative recommendation for purchase consideration.

20.   Johnson, Harry A. **Multimedia Materials for Teaching Young Children: A Bibliography of Multi-Cultural Resources.** Storrs, Conn.: Connecticut University, National Leadership Institute—Teacher Education/Early Childhood, 1972. 27p. $1.85. (T)

Covers primary grade materials (films, filmstrips, recordings, audiotapes, photographs and study prints, multimedia kits, and books) which should be useful to educational programs attempting to provide curriculum materials of a pluralistic nature.

21. Keating, Charlotte Matthews. **Building Bridges of Understanding between Cultures**. Tucson, Ariz.: Palo Verde Publishing Company, 1971. 233p. $7.95.

Lists materials for children from pre-school through high school on Blacks, American Indians, Spanish-speaking, Asians and multi-ethnic groups in the United States. Chapters are also devoted to the countries from which these groups emigrated. One section is entitled "Books for Bilingual/Bicultural Children." Author and title indexes.

22. Kinton, Jack F. **American Ethnic Groups and the Revival of Cultural Pluralism: Evaluative Sourcebook for the 1970's**. 4th ed. Aurora, Ill.: Social Science & Sociological Resources, 1974. 205p. $9.95. (T)

A selective listing of books and articles on ethnic theory and individual groups. Arrangement is in six sections, one of which lists materials for about 25 individual groups. Other sections deal with racism and Blacks, a filmography, and other topics. A directory of research and cultural centers is included. The coverage is highly selective and not reliable.

23. Kolm, Richard, comp. and ed. **Bibliography on Ethnicity and Ethnic Groups**. Rockville, Md.: National Institute of Mental Health, Center for Studies of Metropolitan Problems, 1973. 250p. $2.85pa. (T)

Lists 1,681 references on "the situation of immigrant ethnic groups, their psychological adjustment and conditions affecting acculturation . . . patterns of ethnic behavior, family life, and communication structure," as indicated by the author in the preface. Annotated entries are included in one section; unannotated entries in another. Arrangement is alphabetical in each section. A subject index is provided.

24. Layer, Harold A. **Ethnic Studies and Audiovisual Media: A Listing and Discussion**. An Occasional Paper from ERIC at Stanford. Stanford, Calif.: Institute for Communication Research, Stanford University, 1969. 11p. $3.29. ED 031091. (T)

An audiovisual source list of 16mm films, audiotapes, filmstrips, sound filmstrips, videotapes, records, and transparencies that deal with the history and present experience of non-white minorities in the United States (Blacks, Asian-Americans, American Indians, Mexican-Americans, Spanish-speaking groups). Names and addresses of distributors are included. Entries are annotated.

25. Lightfoot, Jean H. **Multi-Ethnic Literature in the High School**. Washington, D.C.: Government Printing Office, 1973. 43p. $0.75pa. (T)

This reference guide for teachers is a collection of booklists that include titles recommended for promoting better understanding of and between ethnic groups in American society. Titles selected are appropriate for the senior high school level (grades 9-12). In addition to the bibliographical listings, this guide presents suggested activities for incorporation into an ethnic studies unit in the curriculum.

26. Nance, Elizabeth, *et al.* **A Community of People: A Multi-Ethnic Bibliography**. Portland, Ore.: Portland Public Schools, c1974, 1976. 140p. $5.00. (K-12)

A briefly annotated bibliography covering ethnic materials that are available in the elementary and secondary grade levels of the Portland Public Schools. Ethnic groups covered are Afro-American, Asian, Jewish, Mexican, Native-American, and Puerto Rican; a chapter entitled "Multi-Racial" is also included. Arrangement is by group in the following categories: Heritage, Collective Biography, Individual Biography, Poetry, Short Stories, Essays, Folklore, Fiction, Easy Fiction, Teacher's Background Reading, 16mm Films, Non-16mm Audiovisual. Entries are not provided for each category for every group. Dewey Decimal call numbers are provided for the entries in the Heritage category. Grade levels are indicated.

27. **Nassau County Educational Resources Center Catalog of Professional Materials: Multi-Ethnic Materials Collection.** Jericho, N.Y.: Nassau County Board of Cooperative Educational Services, 1971. 87p. $3.29. ED 070800. (T)

Lists professional resources available in the area of multi-ethnic studies by the Racial Ethnic Action Program (REAP) funded under Title III, Elementary and Secondary Education Act. Includes filmstrips, films, games, and print materials concerned with ethnic groups in the United States as well as methodology for implementing their use in the classroom.

28. Nichols, Margaret S., and Peggy O'Neill. **Multi-Cultural Materials: A Selective Bibliography of Adult Materials Concerning Human Relations and the History, Culture and Current Social Issues of Black, Chicano, Asian American and Native American Peoples.** Stanford, Calif.: Multicultural Resources, 1974. 40p. $2.00. (T)

A revised, enlarged edition of the California State Department of Education's *Bibliography of Multicultural Materials*, which is a highly useful list for curriculum planning. Includes ethnic materials in the areas of history and social sciences, biography, fiction, poetry, drama, art, and music. These authors have also jointly compiled a *Multicultural Bibliography for Pre-School through Second Grade: In the Areas of Black, Spanish-Speaking, Asian American, and Native American Cultures* (Multicultural Resources, 1972. $1.50).

29. Oaks, Priscilla. **Minority Studies: A Selective Annotated Bibliography.** Boston, G. K. Hall, 1975. 303p. $22.00. (T)

Highly selective bibliography that emphasizes American Indians, Black Americans, Mexican Americans, and Asian Americans. Many white ethnic groups are excluded, thus limiting the reference value of this publication. Overpriced.

30. **Portraits: Literature of Minorities; An Annotated Bibliography of Literature by and about Four Ethnic Groups in the United States for Grades 7-12.** Los Angeles, Calif.: Superintendent of Schools, Los Angeles County, 1970. 79p. ED 042771. Supplement, 1972. 71p. $3.29.

Provides an annotated bibliography of materials on Blacks, Mexicans, North American Indians, and Asians in the United States with suggestions for their use in the curriculum. Primarily intended for grades 7-12. Arranged under subject headings: fiction, poetry, prose, nonfiction, anthologies, background materials for teachers. Title and author indexes.

31.　Reid, Virginia M. **Reading Ladders for Human Relations.** Washington, D.C.:
　　　American Council on Education, 1973. 346p. $9.00; $3.95pa. (T)
This book was compiled to assist teachers, librarians, and others select materials
that would help children appreciate different cultures. Arrangement is alphabetical
within various reading levels. Entries are annotated and include works of fiction,
drama, poetry, and nonfiction. Over 1,000 books are included.

32.　Spache, George D. **Good Reading for the Disadvantaged Reader: Multi-
　　　Ethnic Resources.** Champaign, Ill.: Garrard Publishing Co., 1970. 201p.
　　　$4.25pa. (T)
This multimedia bibliography includes materials for teachers and other professional
resources as well as books graded for readability, special materials for bilingual
pupils and materials selected to help the child build his self-concept. Ethnic groups
covered include Blacks, American Indians, Eskimos and Alaskans, Mexican Americans,
migrant workers, Orientals, Puerto Ricans. Author and title indexes are provided.

33.　Tanyzer, Harold, and Jean Karl, comps. **Reading, Children's Books, and Our
　　　Pluralistic Society.** Newark, Dela.: International Reading Association,
　　　1972. 89p. $3.29. (T)
A selection of papers treating minority groups in children's literature. Included is a
list of bibliographies dealing with minority groups in books for children. The emphasis is on Blacks.

34.　Weed, Perry L., comp. **Ethnicity and American Group Life: A Bibliog-
　　　raphy.** New York: National Project on Ethnic America of the American
　　　Jewish Committee, Institute of Human Relations, 1972. 21p. $0.50pa. (T)
References to the political and social development and experiences of immigrants
in America are arranged by topics. Entries are not annotated, and references to
individual ethnic groups are limited.

35.　Weinberg, Meyer, comp. **The Education of the Minority Child: A Compre-
　　　hensive Bibliography of 10,000 Selected Entries.** Chicago: Integrated
　　　Education Associations, 1970. 530p. $10.95; $3.95pa. (T)
This comprehensive bibliography includes books, articles, dissertations, and congressional hearings concerned with the education of minority groups. Emphasis is
on Blacks, American Indians and Spanish-speaking groups. Arrangement is topical
in 24 sections.

36.　Wilson, Ruth Kearney. **Emerging Humanity: Multi-Ethnic Literature for
　　　Children and Adolescents.** Dubuque, Iowa: Wm. C. Brown, 1972. 246p.
　　　$3.95. (T)
Covers Blacks, American Indians, and Mexicans. Arrangement is by age level:
primary grade, intermediate grade, adolescent, and professional readings. Included
in this bibliography are teaching suggestions and selection criteria.

37.　Wolfe, Ann G., comp. **About 100 Books: A Gateway to Better Intergroup
　　　Understanding.** 7th ed. New York: Institute of Human Relations, Ameri-
　　　can Jewish Committee, 1972. 48p. $0.75pa. (T)

One hundred children's books published from 1969 to 1972 are listed. Many of the titles are about ethnic groups or are relevant to ethnic identity. Grades K-10 are covered here.

38.   Wynar, Lubomyr R., *et al.* **Ethnic Groups in Ohio with Special Emphasis on Cleveland.** Cleveland, Ohio: Cleveland State University, 1975. 254p. $6.50pa.
An annotated bibliography published as the first volume in a series of monographs on ethnic communities to be published by Cleveland State University as part of Ethnic Heritage Studies. Includes general reference sources and works on ethnicity as well as works dealing specifically with Ohio and/or Cleveland. Covers the 32 ethnic groups with the largest representation in Cleveland's population.

Encyclopedic Works, Handbooks, and Dictionaries

39.   Brown, Francis J., and Joseph S. Roucek, eds. **One America: The History, Contributions and Present Problems of Our Racial and National Minorities.** Englewood Cliffs, N.J.: Prentice-Hall, 1952; repr. ed., Westport, Conn.: Negro University Press, 1971. 717p. $24.50. (9-12, T)
Although this work is outdated, it is an excellent source for historical studies. The first part summarizes the general status of ethnic minorities in the United States. The second part studies individual groups with essays written by authorities in the field. The following sections describe the activities of the various minority groups, conflicts, education, and trends. Organizations, publications, and bibliography are appended. The work is indexed.

40.   Burnett, Bernice. **The First Book of Holidays.** New York: Watts, 1974. 87p. $3.45. (4-7)
Covers holidays and special celebrations of America's various ethnic groups as well as the standard holidays of all nations.

41.   **The Ethnic Chronology Series.** Dobbs Ferry, N.Y.: Oceana Publications, 1971– . $6.00cloth. (7-12, T)
According to the publishers, "this series was specifically designed as an introduction to reference materials for secondary school and community college students." Each publication constitutes a handbook covering one of the ethnic groups in the United States and contains a chronological section, documents, and selective bibliography. In many instances, the basic information provided for each ethnic group is not adequate, and bibliographies are rather limited. The description of each volume is provided in relevant sections covering individual ethnic groups.

42.   Moquin, Wayne, ed. **Makers of America.** Chicago: Encyclopaedia Britannica Corporation, 1971. 10 vols. $79.50. (7-12)
"The ten volumes of Makers of America contain some 731 'documents'—and in the broadest sense—by nearly as many different authors, reflecting and illustrating the ethnic diversity of the United States" (Introduction). Recommended for junior and high school libraries, this set includes topics about immigration, immigrants, ethnic groups, and minorities. The volumes are illustrated and the set includes an ethnic index, proper name index, topical index, author source index, and illustration

index. Volume titles are: 1) *The Firstcomers, 1536-1800*; 2) *Builders of a New Nation, 1801-1848*; 3) *Seekers after Freedom, 1849-1870*; 4) *Seekers after Wealth, 1871-1890*; 5) *Natives and Aliens, 1891-1903*; 6) *The New Immigrants, 1904-1913*; 7) *Hyphenated Americans, 1914-1924*; 8) *Children of the Melting Pot, 1925-1938*; 9) *Refugees and Victims, 1939-1954*; 10) *Emergent Minorities, 1955-1970*.

43. Santa Barbara County Board of Education. **The Emerging Minorities in America: A Resource Guide for Teachers.** Santa Barbara, Calif.: ABC-Clio Press, 1972. 256p. $11.95. (T)

Serves as a biographical dictionary of over 500 Blacks, Asians, Native Americans, and Mexicans in the United States. A chapter on each of the ethnic groups they represent is presented, with a bibliography of sources for studying the group. A section entitled "Teaching Strategies" is also included, with a list of concepts to be developed as well as a list of suggested learning activities. The appendix lists the immigrant or ethnic Americans by historical periods and by subject of occupational classification.

Directories

44. **Directory of Data Sources on Racial and Ethnic Minorities.** Washington, D.C.: Bureau of Labor Statistics, 1975. 83p. Bulletin No. 879. $1.50. (9-12, T)

Describes government publications that contain information, data, and statistics on racial and minority groups. Arrangement is in four sections: Black Americans, persons other than Black, persons of Spanish ancestry, and ethnic groups other than Spanish ancestry. The work is indexed.

45. Johnson, Willis L., ed. **Directory of Special Programs for Minority Group Members: Career Information Services, Employment Skills Banks, Financial Aid Sources.** 2nd ed. Garret Park, Md.: Garret Park Press, 1975. 400p. $8.50pa. (10-12, T)

Lists programs offered by over 700 national and local organizations, as well as federally sponsored programs. Includes sections on general employment opportunities and educational assistance programs, federal programs, women's programs, and college and university awards. Useful for student counselors and minority students.

46. U.S. Department of Commerce. **Directory of Minority Media.** Washington, D.C.: Government Printing Office, 1973. 89p. $1.25pa. (9-12, T)

Actually prepared for advertisement purposes, this minority directory lists minority newspapers, periodicals, and radio and television stations, and provides various minority statistics. Emphasis is on Black Americans.

47. Wynar, Lubomyr R., and Anna T. Wynar. **Encyclopedic Directory of Ethnic Newspapers and Periodicals in the United States.** 2nd ed. Littleton, Colo.: Libraries Unlimited, 1976. 256p. $15.00. (9-12, T)

The present directory covers publications of 63 ethnic groups arranged in 51 sections. It lists 977 publications, including multi-ethnic periodicals. Data provided include name of publication (with English translation), address, editor, language, sponsoring organization, frequency, price, circulation, and a description of the publication. The first edition of the *Encyclopedic Directory* (1972) was selected by the American Library Association as one of the best "Reference Books for 1972."

48.   Wynar, Lubomyr R., with the assistance of Lois Buttlar and Anna T. Wynar. **Encyclopedic Directory of Ethnic Organizations in the United States.** Littleton, Colo.: Libraries Unlimited, 1975. 414p. $19.50. (9-12, T)

A reference guide to 73 major ethnic groups in the United States. Organization name, address, telephone, officers, staff, founding date, branches, membership and dues, and the scope, nature, and purpose of the organization are indicated. Regular publications and conventions or meetings are also noted. Special requirements for membership in the organization and brief comments on the purpose, services, and activities of the membership are provided. Teachers and librarians searching for information on individual ethnic groups and their organizations will find basic data in this directory. Recommended for school libraries in *The Booklist* (July 15, 1976).

Statistical Sources

49.   Taeuber, Irene, and Conrad Taeuber. **People of the United States in the 20th Century.** Washington, D.C.: U.S. Bureau of the Census, Government Printing Office, 1971. 1046p. $5.75. (9-12, T)

Describes immigrants to the United States from 1820 to 1865 by country of origin and occupation. Includes various statistics by ethnic composition of the population by city or rural residence. Bibliographical references listed.

50.   U.S. Bureau of the Census. **Census of Population: 1970.** Series PC (2). **Subject Reports.** Series PC (2) 1–A. **National Origin and Language.** Washington, D.C.: Government Printing Office, 1973. 537p. $5.05pa. (9-12, T)

Statistics on population of foreign parentage and birth are cross-classified by social and economic characteristics. Population statistics also provided by states, regions, and cities.

51.   U.S. Bureau of the Census. **Current Population Reports.** Series P-20. **Population Characteristics.** Series P-20, No. 249. **Characteristics of the Population by Ethnic Origin: March 1972 and 1971.** Washington, D.C.: Government Printing Office, 1973. 35p. $1.25. (9-12, T)

Statistical data on the demographic and socioeconomic characteristics of persons from the following ethnic groups: English, Scotch or Welsh, French, German, Irish, Italian, Polish, Russian, Spanish. These groups comprise about 50 percent of the population; the other 50 percent is classified as "other."

52.   U.S. Bureau of the Census. **Reports.** (For school students) No. 15. **We the American Foreign Born.** Washington, D.C.: Government Printing Office, 1973. 14p. $0.40. (5-12, T)

Includes statistics, informational data, and discussion of the problems and future conditions of America's foreign born.

53.   U.S. Bureau of the Census. **Statistical Abstract of the United States.**
       Washington, D.C.: Government Printing Office, 1879– . Annual. $9.60pa.
       (7-12, T)
A compilation of statistical charts and tables covering the education, health, distribution, growth, age, sex, and various socioeconomic aspects of the population of the
United States. Statistics on immigrants, refugees, and displaced persons, passports,
quotas, and aliens by state of residence are included. Comparative historical data
on immigration are included in *Historical Statistics of the United States: Colonial
Times to 1970* (Bicentennial edition, 1976. 1200p. 2 parts. $26.00/set).

TEACHING METHODOLOGY AND
CURRICULUM MATERIALS

54.   Abrams, Grace, and Frances Schmidt. **Social Studies: Minorities in American
       Society.** Miami, Fla.: Dade County Public Schools, 1971. 51p. MF $0.65;
       HC $3.29. ED 063204. (T)
Describes and outlines a course that provides a historical view of ethnic, religious,
and social groups in American society. Emphasizes their contributions and problems. The unit of study can be adapted for grades 7-12. Topics covered are: 1)
types of minorities, 2) history, 3) causes of prejudice, 4) effects of prejudice, 5) role
of government at all levels, 6) role of volunteer organizations, 7) contributions of
minority groups, 8) progress in solving problems, 9) pluralism vs. melting pot
theory. Suggests a wide variety of student and teacher reference materials.

55.   Alloway, David N., and Francesco Cordasco. **Minorities and the American
       City: A Sociological Primer for Educators.** New York: McKay, 1970. 124p.
       $2.95pa. (T)
Emphasis is on urbanism and its special demands for education with respect to
minority groups.

56.   Banks, James A., ed. **Teaching Ethnic Studies: Concepts and Strategies.**
       Washington, D.C.: National Council for the Social Studies, 1973. 297p.
       $9.00; $7.20pa. (T)
The author contends that school curricula and textbooks often helped further
negative stereotypes and discrimination against ethnic minority groups. The
strategies presented here suggest ways teachers can build upon the ethnic group
experience and incorporate it into the social studies curriculum. Part One: Racism,
Cultural Pluralism, and Social Justice; Part Two: Teaching about Ethnic Minority
Cultures; Part Three: Teaching about White Ethnic Groups and Women's Rights.
Groups emphasized are Asians, Blacks, Chicanos, American Indians, and Puerto
Ricans. Each chapter includes a brief bibliography. Other titles by the author are
Ethnic Studies as a Process of Curriculum Reform (National Academy of Educa-
tion, 1975. $1.95); and *Multicultural Education: In Search of Definitions and Goals*
(Syracuse, N.Y.: National Academy of Education, 1974. $1.85).

57.   Banks, Samuel L. **Inquiry Techniques in Teaching a Multi Ethnic Social
       Studies Curriculum.** Baltimore, Md.: Baltimore City Public Schools, 1974.
       68p. $3.29pa. (T)

Provides the results of an in-service program on multi-ethnicity for teachers and administrators. Includes 1) methodology, lectures, demonstration, and lessons; and 2) a program approach to ethnic studies in the K-12 social studies curriculum.

58. Brown, Richard C. **Contemporary Social Science Curriculum, Man in America: Cultural Plurality.** Morristown, N.J.: Silver Burdett, 1974. 662p. $7.98. (T)

A curriculum design arranged in three individual units: 1) Immigrants to the United States; 2) What Is an American? 3) Civil Rights for All Americans. Ethnic groups included are: Germans, Austrians, Asians, Cubans, Puerto Ricans, Mexicans, Italians, Irish, Hungarians, Czechoslovakians, Polish, Russians, Scandinavians, and West Indians.

59. Carter, Yvonne, *et al.*, comps. **Aids to Media Selection for Students and Teachers.** Washington, D.C.: U.S. Office of Education, 1971. 82p. $1.00. Supplement, 1973. 67p. $0.95. (T)

This publication and its supplement give teachers, students, and librarians suggestions for selecting media, with a significant section in each entitled "Source of Multi-Ethnic Materials."

60. **Contributions of Black Americans, Indian Americans, Mexican Americans and Asian Americans to American History.** San Jose, Calif.: Santa Clara County Office of Education, 1970. 122p. $3.00. (T)

A teacher resource guide for social studies units (K-12) that study the roles and contributions of Blacks, Indians, and Mexicans in the United States. Emphasis is on their cultural, political, economic, and social development in the state of California. Bibliographies list print and audiovisual instructional materials to augment the units.

61. Davis, A. L., ed. **Culture, Class, and Language Variety: A Resource Book for Teachers.** Urbana, Ill.: National Council of Teachers of English, 1972. 222p. $5.75. (T)

A collection of essays for educators of multicultural students with emphasis on the disadvantaged and language problems. Examples of dialects are provided on an accompanying cassette.

62. Dawson, Martha E., and Patricia M. Markun, eds. **Children and Intercultural Education.** Washington, D.C.: Association for Childhood Education International, 1974. 72p. $2.95pa. (T)

This guide is in kit format with three individual booklets all designed to develop teacher awareness and sensitivity to ethnicity and student appreciation of cultural diversity through the curriculum.

63. Early Childhood Bilingual Education Project. **Early Childhood Bilingual Education.** New York: Modern Language Association, 1971. 187p. $4.00. (T)

This study on bilingual education includes a section entitled "Some Demographic Information on Minority Language Groups," curriculum materials, models, descriptions of programs, source lists, and bibliographies.

64. Edelman, Marshal, *et al.* **Minorities in America: Pilot Units for a Senior High School Elective**. Oakland, Calif.: Oakland Public Schools, 1969. 35p. $3.29. ED 053998. (T)
Sample pilot units for use in a high school course entitled "Minorities in America." Organizations, materials, and activities are suggested. Contents: The Multi-Ethnic Society; Minority Experience in America; Violence in America; Protest; Life in the Ghetto; and The Family.

65. Epstein, Charlotte. **Intergroup Relations for the Classroom Teacher**. Boston, Mass.: Houghton Mifflin, 1968. 214p. $2.95pa. (T)
Problems of human relations in the classroom are described in a variety of teaching circumstances and classroom compositions. Discusses how the subject of ethnicity can be integrated into the curriculum in various disciplines.

66. **Equal Rights: An Intergroup Education Curriculum**. Harrisburg, Pa.: Pennsylvania State Department of Education, Bureau of Curriculum Services, 1974. 247p. $11.40. (T)
The curriculum developed for Pennsylvania schools under Title IV of the Civil Rights Act of 1964 to promote "friendly and democratic relations between persons of different races, religions, national origins," etc.

67. Ethnic Heritage Studies Program. Curriculum Development Team. **What Is Ethnicity?** Cleveland, Ohio: Cleveland Public Schools, 1975. unp. n.p. (T)
The Cleveland Ethnic Heritage Studies Program is a joint effort by the Cleveland Public Schools and the Greater Cleveland Intercollegiate Council on Ethnic Studies to develop and implement ethnic studies materials for elementary and secondary classrooms in the Cleveland area. *What Is Ethnicity?* is designed for use in the junior and senior high schools. Goals, objectives, and interdisciplinary activities are outlined, and a series of colored 35mm slides narrated on a cassette tape are included in this overview unit. Others developed by this team are: *A Unit of Ethnic Poetry, Ethnic Literature, Why They Came, What They Encountered, Folklore: Heroes of Epic Literature, America Celebrates Fall, America Celebrates Winter, Ethnic Neighborhoods in Transition, Ethnic Foods*, and other materials.

68. **Evaluation Guidelines for Multicultural/Multiracial Education. Designed Primarily for Secondary Schools**. Arlington, Va.: National Study of School Evaluation, 1973. 57p. $3.29. (T)
Guidelines developed to help the secondary school educator to evaluate himself as a teacher of multicultural studies and to evaluate the programs implemented.

69. Feeley, Dorothy M. **Learning to Live in Today's World. Grade 1**. Stoneham, Mass.: Stoneham Public Schools, 1971. 18p. $3.29. ED 053009. (T)
Objectives for this first grade unit include: an awareness of the need to belong to different groups, and an understanding that different nationalities celebrate different holidays. Suggested group discussions, role playing, photographs, exhibits, field trips, art projects, films and filmstrips to accompany the unit are included. The extension of this program covers specific ethnic groups (Blacks, Chinese, American Indians, Puerto Ricans, Eskimos), with attention to their different

customs, in *Ethnic Groups in Our World Today. Grade 2* (1971. 29p. $3.29. ED 053010). The third year unit is entitled *Everybody Is Somebody. Grade 3* (1971. 35p. $3.29. ED 053011).

70.   **Fifth Grade Social Studies Unit and Student Readings.** Park Forest, Ill.: Park Forest Public Schools, 1970. 79p. $3.29. ED 062217. (T)

A resource unit with student readings is presented for the fifth grade level on the theme of America as a heterogeneous society of different racial, religious, cultural, and ethnic groups. Emphasis is on the immigration (causes, problems, and the immigration experience), discrimination, and contributions of the various groups. Includes list of books, filmstrips, films, and maps. A similar unit for the sixth grade focuses on the Mexican American: *Sixth Grade Social Studies Unit and Student Readings* (1970. 81p. $3.29. ED 048040).

71.   Finkelstein, Milton, Jawn A. Sandifer, and Elfreda S. Wright. **Minorities: USA.** New York: Globe Book Company, 1971. 406p. $5.95pa. (T)

A textbook presenting nine units for junior high and senior high school social studies curriculum on ethnic studies. An accompanying teacher's guide is a manual of discussion questions, activities, and print and non-print source materials. Films and filmstrips to develop each unit are listed at the back, with producers' names and addresses. Unit titles are: 1) American Indians, 2) Black Americans, 3) Mexican Americans, 4) Chinese Americans and Japanese Americans, 5) Catholic Americans, 6) Jewish Americans, 7) Puerto Ricans, 8) The Poor, 9) Minorities and Government.

72.   **First Grade Social Studies Unit.** Park Forest, Ill.: Park Forest Public Schools, 1970. 47p. $3.29. ED 048035. (T)

A primary-grade ethnic studies unit introducing the idea that many different kinds of families live in the United States and that they are alike in many ways and different in some. Learning experiences and activities, as well as multimedia instructional materials, are suggested. This same institution has also produced similar units for other grade levels—e.g., *Fourth Grade Social Studies Units and Students Readings* (1970. 68p. $3.29. ED 048039).

73.   Fisher, Norman, and Richard Kobliner. **Ethnic Studies: Elective Resource Bulletin. Junior High School, Intermediate School, High School.** Brooklyn: New York City Board of Education, 1970. 186p. $6.58. (T)

A five-month course of study providing activity guidelines as well as resource materials on cultural diversity. Specific ethnic groups studied here are: Chinese, Irish, Italian, Jewish. Provides the historical and sociological backgrounds of various minority groups and outlines the problems and adjustments they have had or are having to make. An appendix contains listings of organizations available for resources in ethnic studies.

74.   Gillespie, Margaret C., and A. Gray Thompson. **Social Studies for Living in a Multi-Ethnic Society.** Columbus, Ohio: Merrill, 1974. 304p. $8.50 text ed. (T)

Curriculum ideas for teaching and studying social studies in the United States at the elementary and secondary levels. Plans presented here are especially useful for individualized instruction, and a multi-level modular unit plan is suggested. Cultural diversity rather than the "melting pot" approach is taken.

75. Hadfield, Donald L. **Ethnic or Cultural Differences: A Suggested Approach to In-Service Training for Classroom Teachers.** St. Paul, Minn.: The Equal Educational Opportunities Section, State Department of Education, 1971. 37p. $3.29. (T)

This program was designed for teachers who wish to expand their knowledge of children of ethnic or minority backgrounds. Included is a one- to two-hour planning session guide for teachers of all grade levels and subjects, a leader training session, and four general meeting outlines. Includes objectives, planning suggestions, and evaluation criteria. A 72-entry bibliography, a list of Indian organizations and services, audiovisual resources, and a list of film distributors are included.

76. Halliburton, Warren J., and William Loren Katz. **American Majorities and Minorities: A Syllabus of United States History for Secondary Schools.** New York: Arno Press, 1970. 219p. $4.95; $2.95pa. (T)

The syllabus is divided into four major sections covering 38 curriculum units as follows: Units 1-3, Old World background; Units 4-19, American colonization to Reconstruction period; Units 20-33, Reconstruction through World War II; Units 34-38, Founding of the UN to Nixon's administration. The course is designed to fill an academic year, with each unit providing a framework for concepts to be developed, bibliographies for teachers and students, and suggested classroom activities.

77. **Hawaii's Immigrants. Social Studies. Secondary Education.** Honolulu: Hawaii State Department of Education, Office of Instructional Services, 1971. 64p. MF $0.65, HC $3.29. ED 053999. (T)

A packet prepared for developing the study of Hawaii's immigrants at the seventh-grade level. Objectives, instructions, and learning activities are all provided. Selected readings for students on Hawaii's immigrants (Chinese, Japanese, and other groups) are suggested.

78. Heath, G. Louis. **Red, Brown and Black Demands for Better Education.** Philadelphia, Pa.: Westminster Press, 1972. 216p. $4.76. (T)

Studies conditions existing in schools serving the American Indians, Spanish-speaking, and Black minority children. The need for a curriculum designed for the particular group and its culture is emphasized. The appendix contains topics requested by the minority students. A bibliography of materials for implementing ethnic needs into the curriculum is included.

79. Herman, Judith, ed. **The Schools and Group Identity: Educating for a New Pluralism.** New York: American Jewish Committee, Institute on Cultural Pluralism & Group Identity, 1974. 73p. $1.75pa. (T)

Indicates useful publications and materials for introducing ethnicity into the school program and curriculum. Defines the role of the school in developing an ethnic group identity and positive pupil self-image.

80. **Human Relations Education in Oklahoma Schools: A Curriculum Guide.** Oklahoma City: Oklahoma State Department of Education, Curriculum Division, 1971. 47p. $1.85. ED 091266. (T)

A guide for implementing minority and ethnic studies units into the curriculum of the Oklahoma Public Schools.

81. Hunter, William A., ed. **Multicultural Education through Competency-Based Teacher Education.** Washington, D.C.: American Association of Colleges for Teacher Education, 1974. 283p. $13.80. (T)

The result of a project which sought to identify needs common to all ethnic groups and diverse cultural situations. Groups emphasized in various sections of the book are: Blacks, Spanish-speaking (Puerto Ricans, Chicanos and Cuban Americans), and American Indians, with discussions of teacher competencies desirable for each group.

82. Kane, Frank, and Gary G. Baker. **Minorities and Prejudice in America.** Amherst, Mass.: Amherst College, 1966. 56p. $0.65. (T)

A high school unit on prejudices experienced by minorities, with manuals for students and teachers.

83. Kane, Michael B. **Minorities in Textbooks.** Chicago: Quadrangle Books, 1970. 148p. $5.95; $1.95pa. (T)

Examines the treatment of minorities in social studies textbooks from approximately 1950 to 1970. Groups studied are Jews, Blacks, American Indians, Orientals, Spanish-speaking. The appendix lists the 45 secondary school textbooks used in this study.

84. Kelly, Ernece B., ed. **Searching for America.** Urbana, Ill.: National Council of Teachers of English, 1972. 106p. $1.75. (T)

An evaluation of literature for the following groups: Blacks, Asians, Chicanos, American Indians. Materials are checked for racism and bias.

85. Kirkland, Hubert. **The Cultural Backgrounds of Americans: Grade Four, Unit Two, 4.2 Comprehensive Social Studies Curriculum for the Inner City.** Washington, D.C.: Office of Education, 1975. 64p. $3.32. (T)

The second unit of the grade four level of the Focus on Inner City Social Studies series. Unit I, Origin of Man, is followed by this study of man's cultural diversity in America. Included is a general introduction, teaching procedures and strategies, knowledge skill, behaviorial objectives, learning activities, and supplementary teacher and student resources.

86. Lohman, Joseph D. **Cultural Patterns in Urban Schools.** Berkeley: University of California Press, 1967. 210p. $3.95pa. (T)

Teachers from schools (elementary, junior high, and senior high) with large minority group populations have developed a manual to help educators, counselors, and administrators understand and cope with America's various subcultures. Concepts stressed are values, self-image, the school process, and its relation to life experience.

87. **Multicultural Education Guide for Grades 4, 5, and 8.** Millbrae, Calif.: Millbrae School District, 1970. 82p. $3.29. ED 051054. (T)

A resource guide for helping teachers incorporate ethnic group studies into the district's social studies at grades 4, 5, and 8. Five groups covered here are: Afro-Americans, American Indians, Chinese Americans, Japanese Americans, and Mexican Americans. Instruction materials and learning activities are outlined.

88. Public Issues Series/Harvard Social Studies Project. **The Immigrant's Experience: Cultural Variety and the "Melting Pot."** Columbus, Ohio: A.E.P. Education Center, 1967. $0.30/student. (T)

This study unit consists of case studies of immigrant life; problems of adjustment, acculturation, and assimilation are described. A teaching guide for use at the high school level is also available. Another study unit, *Religious Freedom: Minority Faiths and Majority Rule*, also discusses situations where minority group religious views conflict with the laws or norms of society.

89. **Roots of America.** Washington, D.C.: National Education Association, 1975. 189p. $4.50. (T)

A multi-ethnic curriculum resource guide for seventh to ninth grade social studies teachers. Part I discusses the rationale for teaching ethnic studies and the objectives to be accomplished; a brief basic ethnic studies bibliography covers the following groups: American Indian, Mexican, Blacks, Jews, Italians, Polish, Japanese, and Puerto Ricans. Part II is an outline of a curriculum model for each group, with suggested discussion questions and learning activities and projects. Appendix 1 is an essay entitled "Ethnicity and Education: Cultural Homogeneity and Ethnic Conflict," by Marvin Lazerson. Appendix II is: "Analysis of NEA/NJEA Ethnic Studies Programming Survey"; Appendix III contains 1974-75 Abstracts by State of Projects Funded by the Ethnic Heritage Studies Program, Title IX, ESEA. This unit was developed by the New Jersey Education Association in conjunction with the National Education Association, Ethnic Heritage Projects.

90. Stent, Madelon D., *et al.* **Cultural Pluralism in Education: A Mandate for Change.** New York: Appleton-Century-Crofts, 1973. 167p. $8.25. (T)

The authors contend that ethnic and cultural pluralism must be accepted as a positive force in education for long-overdue changes. Issues discussed and proposed are ethnic studies, bilingual education, and materials for teaching cultural pluralism.

91. Stone, James C., and Donald P. DeNevi, eds. **Teaching Multi-Cultural Populations: Five Heritages.** New York: Van Nostrand Reinhold Company, 1971. 488p. $5.95pa. (T)

The ethnic heritages of the Blacks, Puerto Ricans, Mexican Americans, American Indians, and Asian Americans are examined. Covers the cultural-historical view of the group, with a contemporary focus on family, social roles, and the child of that group in his U.S. educational setting. This is accomplished through a collection of essays by leading ethnic scholars and leading educators. The appendix contains an excellent comprehensive list of "Sources on the Education and Study of Multi-Cultural Populations." Included are discussions on how to integrate a school district's curriculum, bilingualism, etc.

92. **Teaching about Minorities in Classroom Situations: Resource Bulletin for Teachers in the Secondary Schools. Curriculum Bulletin, 1967-68 Series, No. 23.** Brooklyn: New York City Board of Education, Bureau of Curriculum Development, 1969. 122p. $2.00. (T)

This high school teaching guide has four objectives: 1) to help the pupil improve his self-image through an appreciation of his heritage, 2) to make the student aware of the contributions of the various ethnic groups, 3) to help him to realize that these groups are interdependent, and 4) to help him to develop skills in interpersonal relationships. Brief lesson outlines are given, and books and audiovisual materials are suggested.

93.   Tufts University. Lincoln Filene Center for Citizenship and Public Affairs. **The Development of Instructional Materials Pertaining to Race and Culture in American Life.** Medford, Mass.: Tufts University, Lincoln Filene Center, 1967. various paging. $20.40. (T)

The Center's final report to the U.S. Office of Education on the research and development of pilot instructional units and teaching strategies on racial and cultural diversity for elementary school levels. The bulk of the work consists of a series of appendices (A-J) in which topics such as the following are examined: "Race and Cultural Diversity: In American Life and American Education" and "The Treatment of Racial and Cultural Diversity and the Role of Negroes in a Selected Sample of K-6 Instructional Materials."

Audiovisual Materials

94.   **Ethnic Studies.** Multimedia kit. Boulder, Colo.: Social Science Education Consortium, Inc., 1975. $29.00. (T)

A multimedia kit containing an annotated bibliography of materials for teaching ethnic studies; a source book of teaching tips; an evaluative tool entitled *Ethnic Heritage Studies Materials Analysis Instrument*; and a filmstrip and cassette set entitled "What Is an Ethnic Group?" The bibliography, "Materials and Human Resources for Teaching Ethnic Studies," lists materials in three categories: curriculum materials, student resources, and teacher resources. It is highly selective and includes many out-of-print materials. Curriculum materials are rated on a scale according to specific evaluative criteria.

95.   **From Racism to Pluralism.** Multimedia kit. Council on Interracial Books, CIBC Resource Center, 1975. $32.50. (6-12, T)

This kit consists of an 18-minute sound and color 120-frame filmstrip with training kit and discussion guide available on a record (or cassette). It is suitable for use at the junior and senior high level and includes participants' materials for a group of 30. The teacher's, or leader's, reading materials include three booklets and a bibliography of suggested reading materials. The kit centers on problems of prejudice and racism and presents the concepts for problem solution and pluralistic appreciation.

NON-FICTION TITLES:
History, Culture, Sociology, Biography

96.   Abbott, Edith. **Historical Aspects of the Immigration Problem: Select Documents.** Chicago: University of Chicago Press, 1926; repr. ed., New York: Arno Press, 1969. 881p. $27.00. (T)

Original sources and documents (letters, diaries, and journals) that are concerned with the history of immigrations to America from Europe in the nineteenth century. Arrangement is chronological by subject heading. The author's *Immigration: Select Documents and Case Records* is an additional source.

97.   Beard, Annie E. S. **Our Foreign-Born Citizens.** 6th ed. New York: Crowell, 1968. 308p. $5.50. (6-10)
Twenty-three brief biographies of well-known immigrants with emphasis on their achievements in America.

98.   Behrens, June. **Who Am I?** Los Angeles: Elk Grove Press, 1968. 41p. $3.89. (K-2)
America's different ethnic and racial groups are introduced in a picture book for primary grades.

99.   Boggess, Louise. **Journey to Citizenship.** New York: Funk & Wagnalls, 1967. 110p. $3.95. (7-12)
A guide to the naturalization process covering immigration laws, alien entry into the United States, and other topics. Information about the immigration and naturalization services and a glossary are contained in the appendix.

100.   Brody, Eugene B., *et al.* **Minority Group Adolescents in the United States.** Baltimore, Md.: Williams and Wilkins Co., 1968. 243p. $8.25. (9-12, T)
Discusses the problems and adjustments that must be made by minority group young people, and also serves as a useful source of information on minority cultures.

101.   Carlson, Lewis H., and George A. Colburn, eds. **In Their Place: White America Defines Her Minorities, 1850-1950.** New York: Wiley, 1972. 353p. $5.50pa. (9-12)
An examination of racial views in American history. Includes presidential addresses, speeches by Congressional and Senate leaders, and articles in scholarly and popular media to survey white racism toward Indians, Blacks, Mexicans, Chinese, Japanese, Jews, and the New Immigrants.

102.   Coy, H. **The Americans.** Boston, Mass.: Little, Brown, 1958. 328p. $5.95. (7-9)
Relates the "story of people who built America: Puritans and Virginians, bound servants, German plain folk, The Scotch-Irish and Irish-Irish, Founding Fathers, mountain men, Texans, gold seekers, Yankee inventors, cotton planters, wheat farmers, slaves and freedmen, homesteaders, cowboys, captains of industry, labor leaders, Swedes, Italians, Slaves, scientists and engineers" (Foreword).

103.   Degler, Carl N. **Out of Our Past: The Forces That Shaped Modern America.** New York: Harper & Row, 1962, c1959. 484p. $12.50; $2.95pa. (10-12)
Questions the melting pot theory of assimilation of America's immigrants and examines the unique characteristics of each group that have influenced America.

104.   Demarest, David P., and Lois S. Lamdin, eds. **The Ghetto Reader.** New York: Random, 1970. 361p. $4.50pa. (7-12)
An anthology of readings on ghetto problems and alienation. Emphasis is on Black American history and experience.

105.   Dinnerstein, Leonard, and Frederick Cople Jabers, eds. **The Aliens: A History of Ethnic Minorities in America**. New York: Appleton-Century-Crofts, 1970. 352p. $4.95pa. (10-12, T)

Writings on various ethnic groups and their experience in America are arranged in four parts: 1) The Colonial Era, 2) The Young Republic, 3) The Industrial Transformation, 4) Ethnic Minorities in Contemporary America. Groups covered: American Indians, Germans, Blacks, Scandinavians, Irish, French, Jews, Polish, and Orientals.

106.   Dinnerstein, Leonard, and David M. Reimers. **Ethnic Americans: A History of Immigration and Assimilation**. New York: Dodd, Mead & Co., 1975. 184p. $4.50pa. (11-12, T)

A popular history of American immigration and assimilation. The emphasis is on non-English American ethnic groups. The period covered is the seventeenth century through the 1970s. A useful bibliographical index is included, as well as statistical tables on immigration to the United States.

107.   Eiseman, Alberta. **From Many Lands**. New York: Atheneum, 1970. 216p. $6.75. (5-9)

A history of immigration is presented through first-hand accounts recorded by American immigrants from Ireland, Germany, Scandinavia, Italy, China, Japan, as well as Jewish Americans. A bibliography of supplementary reading and an index are included.

108.   Faderman, Lillian, and Barbara Bradshaw. **Speaking for Ourselves: American Ethnic Writing**. 2nd ed. Glenview, Ill.: Scott, Foresman & Co., 1975, c1969. 615p. $5.95pa. (7-12)

A collection of writings by ethnic Americans from the following groups: Blacks, Orientals, Spanish, Jews, American Indians, Europeans, and Middle Easterners.

109.   Feldstein, Stanley, and Lawrence Costello, eds. **The Ordeal of Assimilation: A Documentary History of the White Working Class**. Garden City, N.Y.: Doubleday, 1974. 500p. $4.95pa. (10-12, T)

Covers the assimilation of the immigrant into American society from the first wave of immigration, adjustment to the new country, problems and prejudices, and ethnic communities to contributions to the American Labor Movement. Emphasis is on the European ethnic working class in America.

110.   Fellows, Donald K. **A Mosaic of America's Ethnic Minorities**. New York: John Wiley & Sons, 1972. 219p. $4.75pa. text ed. (9-12)

Discusses assimilation of Blacks, Mexicans, Indians, Chinese, Japanese, and Puerto Ricans. Factors influencing acculturation, Americanization and assimilation are examined (e.g., religion, economic conditions, educational opportunities, dispersion throughout the United States, and group customs). Student discussion questions are included at the conclusion of each unit. Bibliography and index included.

111.   Fermi, Laura. **Illustrious Immigrants: The Intellectual Migration from Europe, 1930-1941**. 2nd ed. Chicago: University of Chicago Press, 1971, c1968. 440p. $12.50; $3.95pa. (10-12)

Examines the intellectual immigration of the 1930s and early 1940s. Their reasons for leaving Europe, reactions to America, and their accomplishments in the new home are described. Discusses many individuals in the areas of science, art, music, and the literary world. An evaluation of their contributions and an analysis of the effect on Europe of this depletion of intellectuals is presented.

112.   Frazier, Thomas R., ed. **The Underside of American History: Other Readings.** New York: Harcourt Brace Jovanovich, 1974. 2 vols. $5.95pa. (9-12)

Readings on the experience of some of America's ethnic and minority groups are presented. Groups covered are American Indians, Blacks, Appalachians and poor whites, Chinese, Japanese, and Spanish-speaking groups.

113.   Glazer, Nathan, and Daniel P. Moynihan. **Beyond the Melting Pot: The Negroes, Puerto Ricans, Jews, Italians, and Irish of New York City.** 2nd rev. ed. Cambridge: Massachusetts Institute of Technology Press, 1970. 363p. $10.00 text ed.; $1.95pa. (11-12, T)

In this study of immigrant and ethnic groups in New York City, the unique characteristics that influence the Blacks, Puerto Ricans, Jews, Italians, and Irish are examined. Bibliographical notes and subject index are included. Another title edited by Glazer and Moynihan is *Ethnicity: Theory and Experience* (Harvard University Press, 1975. $15.00); a title authored by Glazer is *Ethnic Inequality and Public Policy: A "Critique of Affirmative Action"* (Basic Books, 1976. $10.95).

114.   Greeley, Andrew. **Why Can't They Be Like Us? America's White Ethnic Groups.** New York: Dutton, 1975, c1971. 223p. $6.95; $2.25pa. (10-12)

A study of white ethnic groups in America by a well-known sociologist. Emphasizes the new awareness being developed by white ethnic groups of their identity and heritage, in opposition to the historical melting pot theory.

115.   Greenleaf, Barbara Kaye. **America Fever: The Story of America's Immigration.** New York: Four Winds Press, 1970; repr. ed., New York: New American Library, 1974. 288p. $5.95; $1.95pa. (9-12)

Covers the history of all major ethnic groups in the United States and the problems and prejudices they encountered as immigrants, from Colonial days to the present.

116.   Handlin, Oscar. **Children of the Uprooted.** New York: Grossett & Dunlap, 1968. 551p. $3.95pa. (9-12)

A study of immigration in the United States, with emphasis on second and subsequent generations of immigrants to America. Their problems, conflicts between cultures and between generations within their ethnic group are covered. Examines the influence of the immigrants' offspring, their social status, political preferences, economic successes and ethnic group cohesiveness.

117.   Handlin, Oscar. **Immigration As a Factor in American History.** Englewood Cliffs, N.J.: Prentice-Hall, 1959. 206p. $4.95pa. (9-12)

Contributions of immigrants throughout America's history are examined, with emphasis on the forces that affected immigration quotas and restrictions. The reasons for leaving the homeland, the problems facing immigrants with respect to economic and social adjustment, political influences, and organizations of the various ethnic groups are discussed. A title on the recent immigrants in America is the author's *Newcomers: Negroes & Puerto Ricans in a Changing Metropolis* (Harvard University Press, 1959. $5.00). Another title is *Race and Nationality in American Life* (Doubleday, 1957. $1.95pa.).

118.   Handlin, Oscar. **A Pictorial History of Immigration.** New York: Crown, 1972. 344p. $12.50. (5-12)

Covers the arrival of the North American Indian, the early colonists, later waves of European immigration, and the Puerto Rican migration to the mainland. A topical bibliography and an index are included.

119.   Handlin, Oscar. **The Uprooted.** 2nd ed. Boston, Mass.: Little, Brown, 1973. 333p. $8.95; $3.95pa. (7-12)

A discussion of the contributions of immigrants, as well as their influence in shaping the growth and development of America. The problems of the immigrants, the adjustments they have had to make and cultural conflicts they have encountered are seen as an important factor in their response to America and America's reaction to these uprooted peoples.

120.   Hansen, Marcus Lee. **The Atlantic Migration, 1607-1860.** New York: Harper & Row, 1940, c1961. 386p. $3.25pa. (10-12, T)

A social history of the continuous wave of immigrants coming to the United States. Emphasis is on settlement, assimilation, and contributions. A similar title by the author is *The Immigrant in American History* (Harper & Row, 1941. $2.45pa.).

121.   Heaps, Willard A. **Story of Ellis Island.** Rev. ed. New York: Seabury, 1967. 152p. $6.95. (6-9)

Describes the processing station at Ellis Island in first-hand accounts, diaries, and interviews that stress the emotions and problems faced by the immigrant. Includes a list of sources and readings.

122.   Hirsch, S. Carl. **The Riddle of Racism.** New York: Viking, 1972. 222p. $5.50. (7-12)

Discusses the history of racism in America, with emphasis on the Blacks, American Indians, Chinese, and Japanese immigrants. Arrangement is a chronological description of events and incidents where racism has been prevalent.

123.   Hoff, Rhoda, comp. **America's Immigrants: Adventures in Eyewitness History.** New York: Henry Z. Walck, 1967. 156p. $5.00. (7-12)

Excerpts from the writings of 40 immigrants in the form of letters, poems, journals, advertisements and other documents reveal their feelings about the United States and their experiences in assimilation into American society.

124.   Huthmacher, J. Joseph. **A Nation of Newcomers: Ethnic Minorities in American History.** New York: Delacorte, 1969. 136p. $4.95. (7-12)

Analyzes the idea of "cultural pluralism" by a chronology of outstanding events or movements of various American ethnic groups. Groups included are the Irish, Italians, Chinese, Japanese, Puerto Ricans, and Blacks.

125.   Johnston, Johanna. **Who Found America?** Illus. by Anne Siberell. Chicago: Childrens Press, 1973. unp. $4.79. (1-4)

A chronological account of America's history and multi-ethnic heritage in the early days of its settlement. Groups and individuals prominent in exploration, discovery and settlement are described—e.g., Norsemen, Asiatics, Columbus, Ponce de Leon, the Pilgrims, Daniel Boone, etc. Another title by the author is *Together in America* (Dodd, Mead, 1965. $3.95).

126.   Katz, William Loren. **Minorities in American History: Early America, 1492-1812.** (Vol. I). New York: Watts, 1974. 88p. $4.95. (7-12)

This is the first of a six-volume series describing how minority groups have fared beginning with the American Indians shipped by Columbus to Spanish slave markets. The Blacks are also covered. Other volumes in the series are: Vol. 2, *Slavery to Civil War, 1812-1865* (1974); Vol. 3, *Reconstruction and National Growth, 1865-1900*; Vol. 4, *From the Progressive Era to the Great Depression, 1900-1929*; Vol. 5, *Years of Strife, 1929-1956*; Vol. 6, *Modern America, 1957 to the Present* (1975).

127.   Kennedy, John F. **A Nation of Immigrants.** Rev. and enl. ed. Introduction by Robert Kennedy. New York: Harper & Row, 1964. 111p. $7.27; $1.95pa. (7-12)

Traces the history of America's 40 million immigrants, their reasons for leaving their homelands, their experiences and contributions to American society, culture, and prosperity. Includes the text of President Kennedy's proposal to liberalize immigration statutes, a chronology of immigration, and a bibliography.

128.   LaGumina, Salvatore J., and Frank J. Cavaioli. **The Ethnic Dimension in American Society.** Boston, Mass.: Holbrook Press, 1974. 364p. $7.95pa. (9-12)

Social problems in America, the emergence of a cultural pluralism, and social roles are studied with respect to four American ethnic groups: Blacks, American Indians, Orientals, and Europeans.

129.   Leinwand, Gerald, ed. **Minorities All.** New York: Pocket Books, 1971. 191p. $0.95pa. (9-12)

Selected readings on America's multicultural heritages and the problems resulting from the interaction of various ethnic cultures.

130.   Levy, Eugene, and John Renaldo. **America's People.** Glenview, Ill.: Scott, Foresman & Co., 1975. 191p. $2.76pa. (7-12)

A text in the *Readings in American History* series, for the secondary level. Emphasis here is on cultural pluralism, immigration, assimilation, acculturation, and contributions of various groups. Some attention is given to racial prejudice and discrimination.

131.   Life International Editors. **Nine Who Chose America.** New York: Dutton, 1959. 190p. $5.50. (7-12)

A collection of brief biographies of well-known immigrants and their contributions to American life and culture. Included are Igor Sikorsky (Russian), Felix Frankfurter (Austrian), Dalip Saund (Indian), Gian Carlo Menotti (Italian), Irving Berlin

(Russian), Helena Rubenstein (Polish), David Dubinsky (Polish), Spyros Skouras (Greek), and Selman Waksman (Russian).

132. Mann, Arthur. **Immigrants in American Life.** Boston: Houghton Mifflin, 1974, c1968. 182p. $2.96pa. (7-12)
A collection of 53 essays portraying the causes, problems, and experiences relative to the various waves of immigration to America. Pros and cons about U.S. immigration policy are presented. Also discusses acculturation and assimilation.

133. Marden, Charles F., and Gladys Meyer. **Minorities in American Society.** 4th ed. New York: Van Nostrand, 1973, c1968. 486p. $1.95pa. (10-12)
Groups emphasized are Puerto Ricans, Japanese, Chinese, Blacks, American Indians, and Mexican Americans. Intergroup relations are examined with respect to religious and ethnic, as well as racial, minorities.

134. Neidle, Cecyle S. **Great Immigrants.** Boston: Twayne, 1972. 295p. $8.95. (7-12)
Portraits of twelve well-known immigrants to America are presented, including those of Albert Gallatin, John A. Robeling, John Peter Altgeld, Nikola Tesla, David Dubinsky, Herman Badillo, and others. Another collection of 65 autobiographical sketches collected by the author is *The New Americans* (Twayne, 1967. $7.00).

135. Novak, Michael. **The Rise of the Unmeltable Ethnics: Politics and Culture in the Seventies.** New York: Macmillan, 1971. 321p. $1.95pa. (11-12, T)
A well-known author on ethnic and minority studies, Novak examines the roles of the ethnic groups in political life, with emphasis on the white groups of European background.

136. Novotny, Ann. **Strangers at the Door: Ellis Island, Castle Garden and the Great Migration to America.** Riverside, Conn.: Chatham Press, 1971. 160p. $12.50. (10-12)
Surveys immigration to America in a photographic essay. Pictures are of immigrants in art and fiction, the Colonies, the Western frontier, well-known immigrants, and Ellis Island before and after 1907. Bibliography, appendix, and index included.

137. Peters, Barbara, and Victoria Samuels. **Dialogue on Diversity: A New Agenda for American Women.** Photographs by Bettye Lane. New York: Institute on Pluralism and Group Identity, 1976. 88p. $1.95pa. (9-12)
A collection of articles studying the roles of American women from a variety of ethnic, social, religious, and economic backgrounds. The opening article is entitled "The Challenge of the 'New Pluralism,' " by Nancy Seifer.

138. Raskin, Joseph, and Edith Raskin. **The Newcomers: Ten Tales of American Immigrants.** Illus. by Kurt Werth. New York: Lothrop, 1974. 126p. $4.59. (5-7)
Old diaries, court records, historical newspapers, and journals provide documentation for ten stories of early American immigrants. Several ethnic groups are represented, including the Blacks, British, Dutch, Corsican, Scotch, Jews, Germans, Norwegians, and Swedes.

139.   Stanek, Muriel. **How Immigrants Contributed to Our Culture.** Westchester,
       Ill.: Benefic, 1967. 96p. $3.89 text ed. (4-8)
Surveys the history and contributions of Jews, Japanese, Chinese, and Spanish-
speaking groups in the United States. The book also has been adapted to a filmstrip
by the same publisher ($6.00). Another title by Stanek and Clinton Hartmann is
Americans All: A Nation of Immigrants (1972. $3.80).

140.   Tripp, Eleanor B. **To America.** New York: Harcourt, Brace, Jovanovich,
       1969. 214p. $5.50; $2.85pa. (7-9)
A history of immigration to America from Mexico, Africa, Europe, and Asia.
Reasons for leaving the homelands are emphasized. Period covered is from 1630 to
1920. A bibliography is included.

141.   Wheeler, Thomas C., ed. **The Immigrant Experience: The Anguish of Becom-
       ing American.** New York: Penguin, 1971. 212p. $1.25pa. (7-12)
Nine essays reveal the problems, anxieties, prejudices, and adjustments that had
to be dealt with by immigrant and ethnic Americans. These personal narratives are
written by members of the Puerto Rican, Irish, Norwegian, Polish, English, Italian,
Jewish, Black, and Chinese ethnic groups in America.

142.   Wittke, Carl. **We Who Built America: The Saga of the Immigrant.** Cleve-
       land, Ohio: Case Western Reserve University, 1967. 547p. $7.95.
       (9-12, T)
An overview of the history of immigration in three parts: 1) the Colonial period,
2) the old immigration, 3) the new immigration and nativism. One chapter describes
the culture, contributions and occupations of the immigrants. Written by an outstanding historian.

143.   Wood, Leonard C., Ralph H. Gabriel, and Edward L. Beller. **America: Its
       People and Values.** 2nd ed. New York: Harcourt Brace Jovanovich, 1975.
       848p. $10.80; Teacher's manual, $3.30. (7-9)
Presents American history from the aspect of the people (American Indians, Blacks,
and other ethnic groups) that comprised the nation and their values that shaped and
developed it. Has accompanying student workbooks and teacher handbook ($1.50
and $2.49, respectively). The work is indexed.

144.   Wright, Kathleen. **The Other Americans: Minorities in American History.**
       Greenwich, Conn.: Fawcett Publications, 1973. 256p. $1.25pa.
       (6-10)
A history of America's various nationality groups from their historical background,
covering waves of immigration to America and their role in American society.

LITERATURE AND FICTION TITLES

145. Baron, Virginia Olsen, ed. **Here I Am!** Illus. by Emily Arnold McCully.
New York: Dutton, 1969. 159p. $4.95. (3-12)
An anthology of poems written by young people in some of America's minority groups.

146. Brooks, Charlotte, ed. **The Outnumbered: Stories, Essays, Poems about Minority Groups by America's Leading Writers.** New York: Dell, 1969.
172p. $4.50; $0.60pa. (6-10)
A collection of materials about various ethnic minority groups. Included are stories, essays, and poems by or about ethnic group members, such as Willa Cather, writing on the Czechs, selections by Malamud on the Jews, and William Saroyan, an Armenian author.

147. Brown, Dale, *et al.* **American Cooking: The Melting Pot.** New York: Time-Life, 1972. 208p. $7.95. (7-12)
Recipes from several American ethnic groups. Groups included are Italian, Jewish, Russian, Polish, and Puerto Rican. From the *Foods of the World* series.

148. Cavanah, Frances, ed. **We Wanted to Be Free.** Philadelphia: Macrae Smith, 1971. 207p. $5.95. (7-9)
An anthology of writings about immigrants, refugees, and minorities from the late nineteenth century to the 1960s. Ethnic groups included are Armenians, Austrians, Blacks, British, Chinese, Cubans, Czechs, Dutch, Germans, Greeks, Hungarians, Italians, Norwegians, Poles, Russians, and Spanish. An earlier work by the author for this age group is *We Came to America* (Macrae Smith, 1954. $5.79).

149. Chernoff, Dorothy A., ed. **Call Us Americans.** New York: Doubleday, 1968.
297p. $4.50; $1.98pa. (9-12)
The immigrant experience is told in short stories of high interest appeal. The traditions, food, clothing, customs of groups from various homelands are described.

150. Coffin, Tristam P., and Hennig Cohen, eds. **Folklore in America: Tales, Songs, Superstitions, Proverbs, Riddles, Games, Folk Drama, and Folk Festivals.** Garden City, N.Y.: Doubleday, c1966, 1970. 256p. $2.50.
(6-12)
Folk literature, folk speech, folk songs, and legendary figures are collected here. Ethnic origin is listed after each entry in the table of contents, and an index of ethnic groups and localities is helpful in locating examples of folklore for any specific group. Stories, songs, proverbs, riddles, games, and other folk literature have been compiled from the *Journal of American Folklore.*

151. Kherdian, David, ed. **Settling America: The Ethnic Expression of 14 Contemporary Poets.** New York: Macmillan, 1974. 126p. $6.95. (8-12)
Groups represented in this collection of ethnic poetry are Asians, Lebanese, Indians, Puerto Ricans, and Blacks.

152. Manning-Sanders, Ruth, comp. **Festivals.** New York: Dutton, 1973.
      188p. $5.95. (2-6)
Celebrations of various ethnic backgrounds are presented. Although the holidays
are described as they are celebrated in the foreign country, many of them have
carried over into the American ethnic community.

153. McDowell, Robert E., and Edward Lavitt, eds. **Third World Voices for
      Children.** Illus. by Barbara Kohn Isaac. New York: Third World Press (distr.
      by Viking), 1971. 149p. $5.95. (4-8)
Short stories, folk tales, poems, and songs from Africa, New Guinea, the West
Indies, Puerto Rico, and Black America arranged geographically. Illustrated with
pen and ink sketches.

154. Turner, Mary, ed. **We Too Belong: An Anthology about Minorities in
      America.** New York: Dell, 1969. $0.75pa. (5-8)
A collection of short stories, plays, poetry, and essays by well-known writers such
as Studs Terkel and Paul L. Dunbar.

AUDIOVISUAL MATERIALS (MULTI-ETHNIC)

155. **Accent on Ethnic America.** 6 filmstrips, 6 records (or cassettes), 6 teacher
      guides. Multi-Media Productions. $65.00/set with records; $75.00 with
      cassettes; 1 record, $12.95; 1 cassette, $14.95. (4-12)
A collection of photographs, art works, maps, charts, graphs, and cartoons all con-
cerned with the cultural heritages of America's ethnic groups. Titles include: *The
Chinese Americans*; *A Unique Heritage–The Polish American*; *Colonia–The Mexican
American*; *El Barrio: The Puerto Rican*; *Shtetl to Suburb: The American Jew*;
Italian Doesn't Mean Mafia: The Italian American. Teacher's manual includes
discussion questions and is available with the set or individual filmstrips.

156. **The American People: A Nation of Minorities.** 4 filmstrips, 4 cassettes.
      Educational Dimensions, 1974. $90.00. (7-12)
Titles include: *The Europeans*; *Indians and Orientals*; *The Blacks in America*;
Hispanic Peoples. Reasons the different groups immigrated to America, and their
contributions to American culture are the main topics.

157. **Celebrating the Peoples of the U.S.A.** 1 filmstrip, 1 disc, 1 manual. Friend-
      ship Press. $12.00. (3-6)
Discusses the various ethnic groups of the United States and their unique contributions to the nation's development.

158. **Children of Courage.** 5 filmstrips, 5 records (or cassettes), 1 teacher's
      guide. Spoken Arts. Set with records, $113.95; with cassettes, $126.95;
      1 filmstrip with record, $24.75; with cassette, $25.50. (3-8)
Five groups are described in an effort to help children develop both an ethnic pride
and/or an ethnic awareness. The set includes: *Donny's Star* (a boy's dream to become
the first Black astronaut); *Raquel & Perdido* (Puerto Rican children on the U.S.
mainland); *Pancho's Puppet* (a Mexican-American fantasy); *Whistling Boy* (an

American Indian legend); *Teru and the Blue Heron* (a Japanese boy in California).

159. **Culture Clashes: The Right to be Different.** 16mm film, 29 min., color, sd. Xerox Films, 1972. $350.00. (6-12)
Emphasis is on the differences between different ethnic, cultural, and religious groups in the United States and the importance of appreciating diversity. Examples in the film include the Amish people and the Oneida Community.

160. **Ellis Island.** 16mm film, 12 min., b&w. Films, Inc., 1972. $4.00 (rental). (7-12)
Part 3 in *The Americans: A Nation of Immigrants* series, this description of Ellis Island, the immigrant's first official contact with the United States, is narrated by Richard Basehart.

161. **Ethnic Heritage: A Living Mosaic.** 1 filmstrip, 1 cassette, workbook and teacher's guide. J. C. Penney Company, Educational and Consumer Relations Department, 1973. $5.23 (including tax). (5-8)
Examines the cultural heritages of the Japanese, Scandinavians, Mexicans, Jews, Africans, Irish, Amish, Puerto Ricans, Spanish, Italians, American Indians, and other groups. The contributions, values, arts and traditions of each group are stressed, with emphasis on student appreciation of America's cultural diversity and group understanding.

162. **The Ethnic Response: Parish/Neighborhood Survival.** 3/4" video cassette, 26 min., sd., color. David Peeler Productions, 1975. $175.00. (9-12)
This video cassette (also available as a 16mm film) was produced for the Catholic Conference on Ethnic and Neighborhood Affairs in cooperation with the National Center for Urban Ethnic Affairs. It discusses the changing role of the urban ethnic church, and as a documentary depicts the flavor of the immigrant era in America. Covers cultural pride in the ethnic communities, and neighborhood struggles against programs and agencies that destroy ethnic cohesiveness.

163. **Ethnic Studies: The Peoples of America.** Kit (4 color filmstrips, 2 cassettes; 18 cassettes). Educational Resources Division, Educational Design. (7-10)
Titles of the four filmstrips are: *Ethnic Groups in America* I & II, *Ethnic Foods*, and *Ethnic Holidays.* They present an overview. The 18 cassettes detail more of the ethnic group's impressions, problems and experiences in America. Titles include: *Irish Americans* I & II; *Polish Americans* I & II; *Scandinavian Americans*; *Black Americans* I & II; *German Americans* I & II; *Jewish Americans* I & II; *Mexican Americans* I & II; *Puerto Ricans*; *American Indians* I & II; *French Americans* I & II; *Greek Americans*; *Hungarian Americans*; *Russian, Ukrainian, Czech and Slovak Americans*; *Chinese Americans* I & II; *Japanese Americans* I & II. A listener review, summary comprehension exam, and teacher's guide are also provided. Preview is available.

164. **Family of Man.** Multimedia kit. Selective Educational Equipment, 1973.
A multimedia kit containing artifacts, study prints, filmstrips, cassettes, and booklets on the following topics: The Hopi Indian Family; The Japanese Family; An Ashanti

Family of Ghana; The Kibbutz Family in Israel; A Soviet Family in Moscow; A Quechua Family in Peru; and An Algonquin Indian Family.

165. **Folk Tales of Ethnic America.** 6 filmstrips, 3 records (or cassettes), 1 guide. Teaching Resources. Set with records, $72.00; with cassettes, $75.00; 1 filmstrip with record, $13.50; with cassette, $15.00. (K-6)

A collection of folk tales representative of America's diverse ethnic culture. Tales are from the following groups: African, Indian (East), Japanese, Mexican, Puerto Rican, and Alaskan.

166. **Forerunners of Equality: The Power That Built America.** 8 filmstrips, 4 records (or cassettes). Teaching Resources, 1975. Set with records, $94.00; with cassettes, $98.00; 1 filmstrip with record, $13.50; with cassette, $15.00. (K-6)

Describes several men of varying ethnic backgrounds and their contributions to America's development as a nation. Includes: *Lord Baltimore, Founder of Maryland*; *Peter Minuit, Founder of New York*; *Roger Williams, Founder of Rhode Island*; *William Penn, Founder of Pennsylvania*; *Dr. Goldberger, His Fight Against Disease*; *Paul Cuffe, A Black Man's Fight for Equality*; *Osceola, an Indian Leader's Fight for Justice*; *Thaddeus Kosciusko, Hero of Two Worlds*.

167. **The Golden Door.** 16mm film, 15 min., color. Macmillan Films, Inc., 1961. $150.00. (7-12)

An animated film on the hardships and adjustments faced by immigrants to America. Also gives a history of immigration with emphasis on quota systems and restrictions.

168. **Holidays and Festivals.** 1 filmstrip (color, cap. 30 fr.). Spirit Master, teacher's guide. Urban Media Materials, 1973. $9.95. (K-3)

Holidays of various religious and ethnic origin are described: St. Patrick's Day, Passover, Puerto Rican Parade, Afro-American Day, Chinese New Year, and many others.

169. **Holidays and Festivals in the City.** 4 filmstrips (color, 40-50 fr. each), 2 records (or cassettes). Miller Brody Productions, 1975. Set with records, $49.00; with cassettes, $53.00. (K-6)

Special ethnic celebrations and festivals are included in this presentation of major holidays.

170. **Holidays Your Neighbors Celebrate.** 16mm film, 10 min., color. Coronet, 1971. $5.50 (rental). (K-6)

Holidays of various American ethnic groups are described. National and religious celebrations are covered.

171. **The Huddled Masses.** 16mm film, 52 min., color, with teacher's guide. Time-Life Films, 1972. $600.00; $100.00 (rental). (7-12)

Produced in conjunction with BBC-TV and narrated by Alistair Cooke, this film is on the various ethnic groups comprising American society. Why they left Europe, Puerto Rico, etc., and the adjustments they had to make in the new world are considered. The film may be rented or purchased in two 26-minute episodes as well, at one-half the regular price. Preview is available.

172. **Immigrants in the City.** 16mm film, 11 min., b&w. Filmways, 1972. $4.00 (rental). (7-12)

Describes how American immigrants brought wealth to American cities by supplying a large industrial labor force. Part four of *The Americans: A Nation of Immigrants* series.

173. **Immigrants in the 19th Century.** 16mm film, 12 min., b&w. Films, Inc., 1972. $4.00 (rental). (7-12)

The social, political, and economic reasons for emigration from various European countries, Scandinavia, and China are covered. Part two in the series *The Americans: A Nation of Immigrants.*

174. **Immigration in America's History.** 16mm film, 11 min., b&w. Coronet, 1960. $4.00 (rental). (7-12)

A history of immigration to the United States from the Colonial period on. Groups covered are English, Irish, Germans, Chinese. Also discusses immigration laws.

175. **Immigration in the 20th Century.** 16mm film, 13 min., b&w. Films, Inc., 1972. (7-12)

U.S. immigration laws from 1920 to 1965. Part five in *The Americans: A Nation of Immigrants* series.

176. **Immigration: The Dream and the Reality.** 6 filmstrips (color, 62 fr. each), with 6 discs (or cassettes), 1 teacher's guide. Schloat Productions, 1971. Set with discs, $120.00; with cassettes, $138.00. (9-12)

A history of immigration to the U.S. in the following titles: *The Dream* (reasons for emigration); *The Reality* (difficulties experienced); *No Irish Need Apply* (job discrimination); *Little Italy* (exploitation under the Padrone system); *You Belong to Germany* (Nazi movement in the U.S.); *The Japanese Nightmare* (World War II relocation).

177. **Impressions of Prejudice.** 16mm film, 18 min., sd., color, teacher's guide. Guidance Associates, 1975. (7-12)

Blacks, whites, Jews and other ethnic groups are presented in this treatment of the impact of prejudice on people. The nature of prejudice and its effects are emphasized.

178. **The Inheritance.** 16mm film, 35 min., b&w, sd. Prod. by the Amalgamated Clothing Workers of America; distr. by Anti-Defamation League. $110.00. (7-12)

Immigration to America is studied with special attention to the changes faced by the various immigrant groups and the changes they helped to initiate in the development of America's economy and culture.

179.　**The Island Called Ellis.** 16mm film, 53 min., color. NBC; McGraw-Hill, 1966. $20.50 (rental). (7-12)

Forty million immigrants are seen from Ellis Island in New York Harbor, where they arrived and went through the processing procedures that began their experience in America.

180.　**Land of Immigrants.** 16mm film, 16 min., color. Churchill, 1966. $7.00 (rental). (4-12)

Attempts to show how American society has been influenced by the various ethnic groups that comprise it.

181.　**Living Together in America.** 24 pictures (color, 12¼" x 17") with teacher's manual. David C. Cook. $5.15. (K-6)

Pictures various ethnic groups engaged in daily life activities and customs. Titles, brief stories, or poems are provided in English and Spanish.

182.　**Minorities.** 5-16mm films, range: 13½-16 min., color or b&w, with teacher's guide. Coronet, 1972. Color, $175.00-$210.00; b&w, $87.50-$105.00 (rental available). (7-12)

Objectives of the series are to develop an ethnic awareness and identity among children, to develop an understanding of the reasons for immigration and the problems and discrimination faced by different minority groups. Titles included are: *Minorities: What's a Minority?*; *Minorities: From Africa, Asia and the Americas*; *Minorities: From Europe*; *Minorities: In the Name of Religion*; *Minorities: Patterns of Change.*

183.　**Minorities Have Made America Great.** Set I. 6 filmstrips with 6 records (or cassettes), 1 teacher's guide. Miller Brody Productions. Set with records, $120.00; with cassettes, $138.00. (5-12)

A set of filmstrips that treat the history, problems, and achievements of various American ethnic groups. Titles are: Negroes (Part 1), Negroes (Part 2); Jews, Germans, Italians.

184.　**Minorities Have Made America Great.** Set II. 6 filmstrips, 6 records, 1 teacher's guide. Warren Schloat Productions, Inc. Set with records, $120.00; with cassettes, $138.00. (5-12)

Set II covers American Indians, Puerto Ricans, Orientals, and Mexican Americans.

185.　**Minorities: Patterns of Change.** 16mm film, 13 min., sd., color. Coronet, 1972. $7.00 (rental) (7-12)

Compares the status of America's various minority groups of today with conditions in the past, emphasizing progress, problems, and the future outlook.

186.　**Minorities—USA.** 8 filmstrips, 8 phonodiscs (or cassettes). Globe Filmstrips, 1975. $96.00; $108.00 with cassettes. (7-12)

A set of filmstrips that teach cultural diversity and the concepts of discrimination and prejudice. Titles in the series include: *The American Dilemma* (stereotypes, prejudice); *Who Am I?* (American Indians); *A Piece of the Pie* (Blacks); *Executive Order 9066* (Japanese); *La Causa* (Mexicans); *Two Different Worlds* (Puerto Ricans); *To Breathe Free* (religious groups); *Bringing about Change* (freedom).

187.   **Minority Groups: Development of a Nation.** Cassette. Education Unlimited, 1972. $8.50. (7-12)
The following ethnic groups are introduced and studied on this tape: Negroes, Jews, Greeks, French, Welsh, Chinese, Dutch, Indians, Italians, Poles, Germans, Irish, Yankees, Japanese, Puerto Ricans, Armenians, Hungarians, and Mexicans.

188.   **Nation of Immigrants.** 16mm film, 52 min., sd., b&w. Prod: Metro-Media Producers Corp.; distr. by Films, Inc. $250.00 ($25.00 rental). (7-12)
Presents a historical survey of immigration to America, the immigrants' reasons for coming to America, the struggles, adjustments and problems of acculturation.

189.   **New Americans.** 4 transparency sets. Popular Science Co. $14.00. (4-12)
Titles in this series on American immigration are: *Immigrants Come to America*; *Our Cities Become Little Countries*; *Contributions of the Immigrants*; *Famous Immigrants.*

190.   **Peoples of America.** 4 filmstrips, 4 cassettes, teacher's guide. Educational Dimensions Corp., 1975. (6-8)
Titles in this set include: *An American Town, The First Settlers, America Grows Up*, and *The Melting Pot.* Themes stressed are America's cultural diversity, the history of immigrants from a variety of countries and backgrounds, and an appreciation of individuality.

191.   **Our Ethnic Heritage: Immigration, Migration, and Urbanization.** 6 filmstrips, 6 cassettes, teacher's guide. Current Affairs Films, 1975. $130.00 set; $22.00 each. (7-12)
A chronological history of ethnicity in America is told in the following titles: *Venturing Forth; Reaching Out; Building Dreams; Stirring the Pot; Can Everyone Be Satisfied; Shaping the Future.* Ethnic groups emphasized are the Italians, Irish, Slavs, Jews, Blacks, and Puerto Ricans.

192.   **Our Immigrant Heritage.** 16mm film, 32 min., color. McGraw-Hill, 1966. $12.50 (rental). (7-12)
Traces American immigration history from the first English colony at Jamestown to the arrival of Russian Jews in the twentieth century. Reasons for emigration, distribution of ethnic communities, occupational trends, and contributions are covered.

193.   **Story of America's People Today.** 8 filmstrips, 4 discs (or cassettes), 1 teacher's guide. Eye Gate House, 1972. Set with discs, $76.00; with cassettes, $78.00. (5-12)
Racial and immigrant groups that comprise America's population are studied, emphasizing assimilation, discrimination, and Americanization of second and third generation immigrants. Contents: *All Alike and All Different; The Old Ways and the New Ways; Being Black, Brown or Yellow; Being a Foreigner; Being a Puerto Rican; Being a Chicano; Being an Indian; The Third Generation.*

194. **They Came to America.** 4 filmstrips, 4 discs (or cassettes), teacher's guide. Audio-Visual Narrative Arts. $75.00 ($85.00 with cassettes). (7-12)
Four immigrants from Russia, Puerto Rico, England, and Ireland are described. Their life stories as immigrants, reasons for leaving their homeland, and their experience in the acculturation and Americanization process are related. The question of the melting pot theory as opposed to ethnic consciousness and awareness is raised.

195. **They Chose America.** 6 filmstrips, 6 cassettes, 1 listener's guide. Audio Visual Education Corp., 1975. $57.00. (7-12)
Personal accounts by 23 different ethnic Americans. Titles include: 1) *Conversations with Cuban Immigrants*; 2) *Conversations with Greek Immigrants*; 3) *Conversations with Japanese Immigrants*; 4) *Conversations with German Immigrants*; 5) *Conversations with Hungarian Immigrants*; 6) *Conversations with Scandinavian Immigrants*.

PART II

INDIVIDUAL ETHNIC GROUPS

AMERICAN INDIANS AND ESKIMOS

Reference Sources

Reference Guides and Bibliographies

196. **American Indians: An Annotated Bibliography of Selected Library Resources.** Minneapolis: Minnesota State Department of Education, University of Minnesota, 1970. 171p. $8.65. (K-12, T)
Items selected from an Indian point of view by the Library Services Institute for Minnesota Indians, with American Indians acting as consultants. Items are evaluated and grade levels are indicated. Arrangement is by type of material.

197. **An Annotated Bibliography of Young People's Fiction on American Indians.** Albuquerque, N.M.: Bureau of Indian Affairs Curriculum Bulletin No. 11, Language Arts Branch, Indian Education Resource Center, 1972. free. (K-12, T)
Titles in this bibliography are by tribe. A suggested grade level is indicated for stories. Another bibliography by this institution is a list of titles that have either been written or reviewed by American Indians, *An Annotated Bibliography of Young People's Books on American Indians.*

198. Association on American Indian Affairs. **Bibliography of Selected Childrens' Books about American Indians.** New York: Association on American Indian Affairs, 1969. price not indicated. (K-12, T)
This listing represents titles selected by American Indians with the intent of developing an awareness of the Indian culture historically and at the present time. A more extensive listing by this institute is entitled *Comprehensive Bibliography of Children's Books about American Indians.*

199. **Bibliography of Nonprint Instructional Materials on the American Indian.** Provo, Utah: Institute of American Indian Studies, Brigham Young University, 1972. 221p. $2.95pa. (K-12, T)
Approximately 1,400 audiovisual selections are arranged by title. Most materials were produced in the 1960s on the following subjects: Eskimos, pre-Columbian history, art, music, industry, tribal legends. Media description, producer, release date, grade, level, and synopsis are given.

200. **Books about Indians.** New York: Museum of the American Indian, 1972. 85p. $0.50. (K-12, T)
This list includes books available from the Museum as well as from publishers, which are considered to be the best titles available currently on the American Indian. Covers titles for juveniles and adults; the books for children have a suggested age range indicated. A revised edition was compiled by Frederick Dockstader in 1974 ($0.75pa.).

201.	Brown, Robert L., and Johnson Russell. **Catalogue of American Indian Teaching Materials: Films, Filmstrips, Tapes for Loan, Rental, Purchase.** Arcata, Calif.: Humboldt State University, 1972. 52p. $1.50. (K-12, T)
This annotated bibliography is arranged alphabetically by title. A subject index is provided for films. A list of distributors is included for convenience in ordering.

202.	Byler, Mary Gloyne, comp. **American Indian Authors for Young Readers: A Representative Bibliography.** New York: Association on American Indian Affairs, 1973. 30p. $1.00pa. (K-12, T)
A selected bibliography of books for children to read and also titles appropriate for storytelling. This work was published in a 1974 edition (Interbook Inc.) entitled *American Indian Authors for Young Readers: A Selected Bibliography.*

203.	Cane, Suzanne S., *et al.* **Selected Media about the American Indian for Young Children K-3.** Boston: Massachusetts Department of Education, 1970. 31p. $3.29. ED 048949. (K-3, T)
Books, records, films, and filmstrips are listed in this annotated bibliography available from Navajo Curriculum Center, Rough Rock Demonstration School, Chinle, Ariz. 86503. Titles are chosen because they are an accurate representation of the American Indian. Arrangement is by age level with adult background materials included.

204.	Goodman, R. Irwin. **Bibliography of Nonprint Instructional Materials on the American Indian.** Provo, Utah: Instructional Development Program for the Institute of Indian Services and Research, Brigham Young University, 1972. 221p. $2.95pa. (K-12, T)
Films (16mm and 8mm), film loops, filmstrips, slides, transparencies, maps, charts, tapes, records, prints, and multimedia kits are arranged alphabetically by title. Entries are annotated, and age and grade levels for recommended usage are indicated. Subject headings are given; subject index is provided. Also includes a directory of distributors for convenience in ordering materials.

205.	Harkins, Arthur M., *et al.* **Modern Native Americans: A Selective Bibliography.** Minneapolis: University of Minnesota, 1971. 131p. $6.58. (10-12, T)
Books, journal articles, research papers, etc., are included in this 1,500-entry bibliography of materials on the American Indian, published from 1927 to 1970.

206.	Hirschfelder, Arlene. **American Indian and Eskimo Authors: A Comprehensive Bibliography.** New York: Interbook Inc., 1974, c1973. 96p. $4.00pa. (7-12, T)
Describes about 400 books by Indian authors representing over 100 tribes. Materials included are anthologies, biographies, autobiographies, histories, and books on Indian customs and culture. Arrangement is alphabetical by author; there is a tribal index and a list of the Indian organizations sponsoring the publications included. An earlier work, entitled *American Indian Authors: A Representative Bibliography* (Association on American Indian Affairs, 1970. 45p. $1.00), is a list of books on different aspects of their history, culture, arts, and literature. It includes autobiographical sketches and a supplement of anthologies of Indian prose and poetry. Also includes a list of Indian periodicals. Arrangement is by tribe.

207. Marken, Jack W. **The Indians and Eskimos of North America: A Bibliography of Books in Print through 1972.** Vermillion: Dakota Press, University of South Dakota, 1973. 200p. $5.00pa. (9-12, T)
Publications about the Indians and Eskimos of North America are covered, with the exception of most fiction. Arrangement is alphabetical by author in the following divisions: bibliographies, handbooks, autobiographies, myths and legends, general books, reprints in American archeology and ethnology. Entries are not annotated, but complete bibliographic description is given, including price. A subject index is provided through which information on specific tribes can be located.

208. Murdock, George P. **Ethnographic Bibliography of North America.** 3rd ed. New Haven, Conn.: Human Relations Area File Press, 1960. 393p. $12.00; $6.75pa. (T)
This reference tool provides access to materials on even the smallest tribe or group. Arranged geographically by 15 major regions, it is subdivided by the tribes native to the region. A detailed table of contents provides a quick overview of tribal locations, and an index of tribal names is included.

209. Oklahoma State Department of Education. **A Guide for Teachers and Librarians with Suggestions for Teaching Indian Students.** Oklahoma City: The Department, 1972. 30p. free. (T)
Multimedia bibliography of books, pamphlets, films, filmstrips, newspapers, records, slide lecture kits, study prints, tapes, View Master reels, etc., on the American Indian.

210. Owen, Roger C., and James J. F. Deetz. **The North American Indians: A Sourcebook.** New York: Macmillan, 1967. 752p. $11.95. (4-12, T)
A collection of writings by outstanding authorities on the American Indian. Articles are arranged according to the geographic areas they discuss. A bibliography of additional readings, a bibliography of 250 educational films, and an author-subject index conclude the work.

211. Perkins, David, and Norman Tanis, comps. **Native Americans of North America.** Northridge, Calif.: California State University, Northridge, 1975. 558p. $12.00. (9-12, T)
A selective bibliography of books by and about American Indians in the United States, Canada, Mexico, and Central America. There are 3,500 entries in 21 subject areas including history, art, and anthropology. Entries are not annotated. An author-title index is included.

212. Revai, Loretta Z. **An Annotated Bibliography of Selected Books about American Indians for Elementary through High School Students.** New York: Columbia University, ERIC Clearinghouse on the Urban Disadvantaged, 1972. 69p. free. (K-12, T)
An annotated list of 293 titles that were written by or told to writers by American Indians and that relate the Indian's perspective. Covers pre-history to modern times. Grade level is indicated; prices are included. Categorical index classifies the works. The final section lists further sources on American Indian information and materials.

213.   Smith, Dwight, ed. **Indians of the United States & Canada: A Bibliography.**
       New ed. Santa Barbara, Calif.: ABC-Clio Press, 1974. 453p. $40.00. (T)
These 1,687 entries are annotated and arranged alphabetically by author in four
sections: 1) Pre-Columbian Indian History; 2) Tribal History, 1492-1920 (this section is alphabetical by tribe, by geographic area); 3) General Indian History,
1492-1900; 4) The Indian in the 20th Century. A list of periodicals surveyed for
abstracts and a list of abstracters is included. Indexed.

214.   Stensland, Anna L. **Literature by and about the American Indian: An
       Annotated Bibliography for Junior and Senior High School Students.**
       Urbana, Ill.: National Council of Teachers of English, 1973. 208p. $3.95pa.
       (7-12, T)
Designed for junior and senior high school students, this selected bibliography of
350 works by and about American Indians includes study guides to selected books
and condensed lists for a basic collection. Evaluative remarks and quotes from
reviews by Indian writers and researchers are included. A subject arrangement covers
myths; fiction; drama; biography; history; anthropology; modern life; music, arts,
and crafts; and aids for teachers. A section provides biographical sketches of
prominent Indian scholars and writers. Author and title indexes.

215.   Thomas, Sharon N. **Culture Based Curriculum for Young Indian Children.**
       Salt Lake City, Utah: Readers Enterprises, 1974. 342p. (T)
A collection of materials and relevant ideas for teaching Indian children or teaching
about them. Lesson plans for a curriculum unit are included. Stories, poems, songs,
and games are included as well as comprehensive listings of books and audiovisual
materials available.

216.   Ullom, Judith C. **Folklore of the North American Indians: An Annotated
       Bibliography.** Washington, D.C.: Government Printing Office, 1969.
       126p. $2.25. (K-12, T)
Materials selected in this annotated bibliography depict the spirit, poetry, and culture
of the American Indian accurately and with authenticity. These Indian writings present an insight into Indian traditions and values.

217.   U.S. Bureau of Indian Affairs. **Curriculum Bulletins 11 and 12, U.S.
       Bureau of Indian Affairs 1972-1973.** Washington, D.C.: Government Print-
       ing Office, 1973. 2 vols. free. (K-12, T)
Bibliographies of books recommended for increasing the American Indian's pride in
his identity are presented in these bulletins. Bulletin No. 11 is *An Annotated
Bibliography of Young People's Fiction on American Indians*, by Graustein and
Jaglinski. It includes titles arranged by tribe. Bulletin No. 12, *An Annotated
Bibliography of Young People's Books on American Indians*, by Sandra Fox, is a
supplement, adding both fiction and non-fiction titles with briefer annotations.

218.   Williams, Carroll W., and Gloria Bird. **Filmography for American Indian
       Education.** Santa Fe, N.M.: Zia Cine Inc., 1973. 201p. $5.00. (T)
Approximately 400 entries are arranged alphabetically by title. Entries include
running time, distributor, sale and/or rental price, date, and appropriate grade level.
The appendix lists films produced by the Bureau of Indian Affairs.

Encyclopedic Works and Dictionaries

219. Driver, Harold E. **Indians of North America.** 2nd ed. Chicago: University of Chicago Press, 1969. 632p. $6.85pa. (9-12)
An encyclopedic-type work that examines and analyzes the American Indian culture from pre-history. Covers patterns of housing, clothing, foods, religions, practices, education, property ownership, social grouping, tribal governments. Arrangement is by culture areas. Coverage is from an ethnological aspect. Maps and bibliography included; indexed.

220. Klein, Barry T., and Daniel Icolari, eds. **Reference Encyclopedia of the American Indian.** 2nd ed. Rye, N.Y.: Todd Publications, 1974. 2 vols. $30.00. (8-12, T)
Volume I (edited by Klein) includes government agencies, museums, libraries, associations, urban Indian centers, reservations and tribal councils, visual aids, schools, and publications. A comprehensive bibliography is arranged both alphabetically and by subject. Some of the 2,500 entries are annotated. Volume II (edited by Icolari) is a biographical who's who of American Indians and others prominent in Indian life and studies, with emphasis on their professional contributions.

221. Swanton, John R. **The Indian Tribes of North America.** Washington, D.C.: Government Printing Office, 1952; repr. ed., St. Clair Shores, Mich.: Scholarly Press, 1968. 726p. $15.00. (9-12)
Surveys the various North American Indian tribes with respect to their history and unique traditions. Tribal locations, some statistics, and a discussion of the background of tribal names are included. Arranged by states. Also includes Mexico and Central America. Maps and index included.

222. Tamerin, Alfred. **We Have Not Vanished: Indians of the Eastern U.S.** Chicago: Follett, 1974. 128p. $5.97. (5-9)
A reference source on the Indians along the eastern coast of the United States. Arranged by state. Information includes tribal histories, locations, population statistics, and economic and social conditions.

Handbooks, Guides, and Almanacs

223. Dennis, Henry C., comp. and ed. **The American Indian 1492-1970: A Chronology and Fact Book.** Dobbs Ferry, N.Y.: Oceana, 1971. 137p. $5.00. (7-12, T)
The first volume in the *Ethnic Chronology* series. A section entitled "Indians of the Past" gives biographical sketches of prominent Indian leaders. Indian wars, U.S. federal administrators of Indian affairs, museums, Indian organizations, and statistics on various topics are included. The appendices also contain a brief bibliography. Some non-print materials are also listed. Indexed.

224. **Federal and State Indian Reservations: An EDA Handbook.** Washington, D.C.: Government Printing Office, 1971. 428p. $3.75pa. (9-12)
This handbook is a valuable tool in schools that have in attendance Indian students who live on reservations. It provides facts and data on history, government, land status, population, occupational opportunities, the culture, location, climate, type of economy and facilities available at each of the different tribal reservations.

225. Kubiac, William J. **Great Lakes Indians: A Pictorial Guide.** Grand Rapids, Mich.: Baker Book House, 1970. 255p. $14.95. (9-12)
Oil painting reproductions and drawings enhance this comprehensive reference book of 25 Great Lakes Indian tribes. Arrangement is by tribal linguistic stock: Algonquin, Iroquois, and Sioux. Typical dwellings, tools, costumes, weapons, arts and crafts are described. A brief history of each tribe is also given. Maps and a bibliography are provided.

226. Marquis, Arnold. **A Guide to America's Indians, Ceremonies, Reservations, and Museums.** Norman: University of Oklahoma Press, 1974. 400p. $9.95; $4.95pa. (7-12, T)
A brief history of North American Indian tribes is presented in part one; emphasis is on arts, crafts, customs and ceremonies. Part two describes resorts and campgrounds available on Indian lands; part three lists names and addresses of museums and Indian associations (arranged geographically). Publications concerned with Indian affairs are also included. Illustrated.

227. Roessel, Robert A. **Handbook for Indian Education.** Los Angeles: Amerindian Publishing Co., 1974. price not indicated. (T)
A guide to help non-Indian educators understand the kinds of problems resulting from conflicts in cultures and how to cope with or solve them.

228. Schneider, Richard C. **Crafts of the North American Indians: A Craftsman's Manual.** New York: Van Nostrand Reinhold, 1974. 325p. $10.96; $6.95pa. (7-12, T)
A manual on American Indian leatherwork, pottery, basketmaking, beadwork, toys, and ceramics. Useful for art classes or general use. Well illustrated with step-by-step instructions. Could be used for activities accompanying units on American Indians, as it presents a concrete picture of Indian culture.

229. Terrell, John Upton. **American Indian Almanac.** New York: Crowell, 1974 ed. 494p. $15.00; $4.95 Apollo pa. ed. (5-12, T)
Emphasis is on the American Indian in the days prior to his contact with the white man. The ten geographic areas of the United States covered conform to various native American cultural areas. The author compares these areas with respect to social structures of these peoples, their ecologies, economics, climates, physical characteristics, value systems, arts, and political and religious systems. A selected bibliography and a glossary of names and terms are included in this handy one-volume reference tool. Indexed. Recommended for junior and senior high schools.

230.   U.S. Bureau of the Census. **Reports.** (For school students.) No. 12. **We the First Americans.** Washington, D.C.: Government Printing Office, 1973. 18p. $0.45. (5-12, T)

Statistics and other data that provide information on the history, experience, problems and social conditions of the American Indians in the United States.

231.   U.S. Bureau of the Census. **Census of Population: 1970.** Series PC (1). **Subject Reports.** Series PC (2) 1—F. **American Indians.** Washington, D.C.: Government Printing Office, 1973. 234p. (9-12, T)

Socioeconomic data and statistics on the American Indians are presented by regions, states, and urban areas in the United States.

232.   United States Commission on Civil Rights. **American Indian Civil Rights Handbook.** Washington, D.C.: Government Printing Office, 1972. 96p. free. (7-12, T)

This handbook explains to American Indians and Alaskan Eskimos living either on or off reservations their guaranteed rights and liberties. Discusses the freedom of speech, freedom of religion, freedom of the press, and the right to assemble, the right to due process, and legal protection. The appendix contains a directory of legal services offered.

233.   United States. Department of the Interior. **American Indian Calendar.** Washington, D.C.: Government Printing Office, 1974. unp. free. (4-12, T)

A calendar of American Indian celebrations, costumed ceremonies, dances, feasts or events of interest scheduled on or near Indian reservations. Entries are alphabetical by state, with individual events listed chronologically.

234.   United States. Department of the Interior. Bureau of Indian Affairs. **American Indians and Their Federal Relationship.** Washington, D.C.: Government Printing Office, 1972. 38p. free. (9-12, T)

This publication includes the names of all Indian tribes, bands, or groups for which the Bureau of Indian Affairs has definite responsibility. It also indicates Indian groups no longer entitled to Bureau services, lists public domain allotments, and is a directory of reporting agency offices and addresses for each area. Arrangement is alphabetical by state.

235.   United States. Department of the Interior. Bureau of Indian Affairs. **Answers to Your Questions about American Indians.** Washington, D.C.: Government Printing Office, 1970. 42p. free. (7-12, T)

A desk reference source book with questions and answers frequently asked about American Indians. Arrangement is in the following categories: The Indian People, The Legal Status of Indians, The Bureau of Indian Affairs, Indian Lands, The Economic Status of Indians, Indian Education, Law and Order on Reservations, and Indian Health. Included is a bibliography of selected reading, a special children's bibliography, and a list of Indian publications.

236.　U.S. Economic Development Administration. **Federal and State Indian Reservations and Indian Trust Areas.** Rev. ed. Washington, D.C.: Government Printing Office, 1974. 604p. $5.90pa. (9-12, T)

Information about Indian and Eskimo tribes is presented by state and reservation. Covers population, land status, history, culture, government, tribal economy, climate, transportation, community facilities, recreation, and vital statistics.

Non-Fiction Titles: History, Culture, Sociology, Biography

237.　Armstrong, Virginia Irving, comp. **I Have Spoken: American History through the Voices of the Indians.** Chicago: Swallow Press, 1971. 206p. $6.00; $2.95pa. (9-12)

Covers sources on Indian-white relationships from the earliest days of colonization and exploration in speeches, documents, excerpts from diaries, treaty records, and negotiations.

238.　Baldwin, Gordon C. **Indians of the Southwest.** New York: Putnam, c1970, 1973. 192p. $5.00; $2.55pa. (6-9)

About 20 Indian tribes are described, with emphasis on the Navajo. Each tribe's immigration, lifestyle, and culture are described. Meanings of Indian symbols, photographs, a glossary, a bibliography, and an index are included. Also useful are the lists of Indian museums, national parks, and monuments of the Southwest. The author has also written *How the Indians Really Lived* (Putnam, 1967) and *World of Prehistory* (Putnam, 1963) for slightly younger readers.

239.　Baylor, Byrd. **They Put on Masks.** Illus. by Jerry Ingram. New York: Scribner's, 1974. 48p. $5.95. (1-6)

Explains the reasons the Indians create masks and describes the masks of the different tribes (with colored illustrations). A well-written work which includes legends, songs, and poems useful for story telling in the lower grades and also for individual reading, as well as an excellent book on which to base art projects. The author's *Before You Came This Way* (Dutton, 1969) is also an appropriate Indian source for the primary grades, as is the well-reviewed book on Indian pottery and its uses in Indian culture, *When Clay Sings* (Scribner's, 1972).

240.　Bealer, Alex W. *Only the Names Remain.* Illus. by William Sauts Bock. Boston, Mass.: Little, Brown, 1972. 88p. $4.31. (6-10).

A history of the Cherokees and how they were forced off their land. Emphasis is on their peaceable ways, their willingness to adjust to the white settlers, and their tribe's unique culture and civilization. Their alphabet, their constitution, and their national newspaper are discussed.

241.　Bjorklund, Karna L. **Indians of Northeastern America.** Illus. by Lorence F. Bjorklund. New York: Dodd, 1969. 192p. $4.95. (7-12)

Algonquin and Iroquois Indians are emphasized in this picture of Northeastern American Indian culture and customs. Topics include historical backgrounds, dwellings, clothing, religion, ceremonies and celebrations, arts and crafts, and relations with white society.

242. Bonham, Barbara. **The Battle of Wounded Knee: The Ghost Dance Uprising.** Chicago: Reilly & Lee, 1970. 169p. $5.95. (6-8)
Only a few photographs and a rather slow-moving text, but useful because of the scarcity of material on this famous battle (for this age level).

243. Brandon, William. **The Last American: The Indian in American Culture.** New York, McGraw-Hill, 1973. 553p. $12.95. (9-12)
A history of the culture and contributions of the American Indians. This is a revision of the *American Heritage Book of Indians* (Simon & Schuster, 1961).

244. Bringle, Mary. **Eskimos.** New York: Watts, 1973. 87p. $3.45. (4-7)
Photographs and text describe the American Eskimo from his native origins, customs, foods, arts, religion, etc. Special attention is paid to encroaching civilization and the Eskimo's favorable and unfavorable reactions to changes in his lifestyle.

245. Brown, Dee. **Wounded Knee: An Indian History of the American West.** New York: Holt, 1974. 202p. $6.95. (6-9)
A condensed, simplified version of *Bury My Heart at Wounded Knee* (Holt, 1970) for younger readers. Portrays U.S. history in the West from the Indian's vantage point.

246. Brown, Vinson. **Great upon the Mountain: The Story of Crazy Horse, Legendary Mystic & Warrior.** New York: Macmillan, 1975. 169p. $5.95. (7-12)
A sensitive portrayal of a very dynamic and colorful Sioux Indian chief and personality.

247. Burnette, Robert, and John Koster. **The Road to Wounded Knee.** New York: Bantam, 1975. 384p. $1.95. (9-12)
A history of Indian and white relations prior to the 1973 incident at Wounded Knee. Some of the American Indian problems discussed are educational, political, or about ignored treaties and genocide. Emphasis is also on the new awareness of and interest in Indian religion.

248. Burnette, Robert. **The Tortured Americans.** New York: Prentice-Hall, 1971. 178p. $7.95. (9-12)
This modern-day leader of Indian people recommends a congressional investigation into tribal politics and calls for doing away with the Bureau of Indian Affairs.

249. Burt, Jesse, and Robert B. Ferguson. **Indians of the Southwest: Then and Now.** Illus. by David Wilson. Nashville, Tenn.: Abingdon Press, 1973. 304p. $8.95. (6-12)
The history and origins of the Choctaws, Chickawaw, Creek, Cherokee, and Seminole Indians are described. The Cherokee Trail of Tears, removal to Oklahoma territory, well-known Indian personalities, and the Indian in today's political and economic situation are discussed. The work is well documented with charts, maps, drawings, and photographs. Glossary, bibliography, and index included.

250. Cahn, Edgar S., ed. **Our Brother's Keeper: The Indian in White America.**
      New York: World Publishing, 1969. 193p. $3.95pa. (9-12)
A report of the Citizen Advocate Center on American Indian problems in health,
education, welfare, land ownership, and poverty.

251. Capps, Mary Joyce. **Yellow Leaf.** Illus. by Don Kueker. St. Louis, Mo.:
      Concordia, 1974. 119p. $1.75pa. (6-9)
Yellow Leaf is the true story of the author's great-grandmother who was abandoned
during the "Trail of Tears" march and taken in by a white trapper. She lived in his
cabin during the winter months and spent summers with a band of Indians, therefore learning the ways of two cultures.

252. Carlson, Vada, and Gary Witherspoon. **Black Mountain Boy: A Story of the
      Boyhood of John Honie.** Phoenix, Ariz.: O'Sullivan Woodside and Co.,
      1974. 80p. $3.50. (2-6)
This autobiography of John Honie, a Navajo medicine man, gives a realistic picture
of family life on a Navajo reservation.

253. Carpenter, Edmund. **The Story of Comoch the Eskimo.** New York: Simon
      & Schuster, 1968. 90p. $4.50. (5-8)
Compares the family lifestyle of Eskimos living near the Artic Circle with their
habits when they move to the mainland.

254. Clark, Ann Nolan. **Journey to the People.** New York: Viking, 1970. 128p.
      $4.50. (K-12, T)
The author describes her personal experiences teaching Indian children. She indi-
cates the differences between the American Indian's and the white man's culture and
values. She has written several titles for primary grades on American Indian children:
Little Indian Basket Maker (Melmont, 1957. $4.50); *Little Indian Pottery Maker*
(Melmont, 1955. $4.50); *Little Navajo Bluebird* (Viking, 1943. $3.57). For the
intermediate grades: *Medicine Man's Daughter* (Avon, 1973. $0.75); *Blue Canyon
Horse* (Viking, 1954. $4.53); *In My Mother's House* (Viking, c1969, 1972. $1.35pa.).

255. Correll, J. Lee, and Editha Watson, eds. **Welcome to the Land of the
      Navajo: A Book of Information about the Navajo Indians.** 3rd ed. Window
      Rock, Ariz.: Navajo Tribal Museum, 1972. 178p. (7-12, T)
Information about the Navajo Indian reservation, Navajo history and customs,
religion, arts and crafts, tribal government and programs, places of interest. A list
of books about the Navajos and items for sale at the Navajo Tribal Museum are
included.

256. Costo, Rupert. **Contributions and Achievements of the American Indian.**
      San Francisco: Indian Historian Press, 1972. $5.00pa. (7-12)
The author is an Indian and an authority on Indian history. He describes the civilization developed by the American Indian.

257. Council on Interracial Books for Children, ed. **Chronicles of American
      Indian Protest.** Greenwich, Conn.: Fawcett Premier, 1971. 373p.
      $1.25pa. (7-12)

These 31 documents written by and about American Indians are all concerned with their struggle for human and equal rights. Also provides notes of explanation about the sources.

258.   Coy, Harold. **Man Comes to America**. Boston, Mass.: Little, Brown, 1973.
       150p. $5.95. (5-9)
Describes how Indians and Eskimos arrived in America and how they lived in the days of pre-history.

259.   Debo, Angie. **A History of the Indians of the United States**. Norman:
       University of Oklahoma Press, 1971. 386p. $8.95. (9-12)
A comprehensive history of Indian and white relations from earliest records of their contact with early explorers and later settlers to contemporary situations.

260.   Deer, Ada, and R. E. Simon, Jr. **Speaking Out**. Chicago: Childrens Press,
       1970. 63p. $3.50; $1.00pa. (7-12)
Ada Deer, a half-breed Indian girl, tells in her autobiography how she overcame prejudice and helped her people speak out and have pride in their heritage.

261.   Deloria, Vine. **Custer Died for Your Sins**. New York: Collier-Macmillan,
       1969. 279p. $6.95; $1.25pa. (9-12)
Subtitled *An Indian Manifesto*, this work is a recounting of the exploitation of the Indian by the white man and a resume of conditions and attitudes existent in today's American Indian community. Other similar titles by the author are: *Behind the Trail of Broken Treaties* (Dell, 1974. $2.95pa.); *The Indian Affair* (Friendship Press, 1974. $2.50pa.); *We Talk, You Listen* (Dell, 1974. $0.95pa.).

262.   Dunn, Lynn P. **American Indians: A Study Guide and Sourcebook**. San
       Francisco, R&E Research Associates, 1975. 119p. $4.00pa. (10-12, T)
This study guide is one of a four-volume series on minorities in America (Asians, Blacks, Chicanos, and Indians), all treating the themes of identity, conflict, and integration/nationalism. Emphasis is on an interdisciplinary approach, as many of the sources suggested in the reading lists are from literature and other disciplines. A useful glossary of terms used by and about the American Indian is included.

263.   Erdoes, Richard. **The Sun Dance People: The Plains Indians, Their Past
       and Present**. New York: Knopf, 1972. 218p. $5.49. (5-12)
A history of the Plains Indians is presented with coverage given to recent years as well. Another title by this author on the Pueblo Indians is *The Pueblo Indians* (Funk & Wagnalls, 1968).

264.   Farquhar, Margaret. **Indian Children of America**. New York: Holt, Rinehart
       & Winston, c1964, 1972. unp. $3.27. (K-3)
Indians of four geographic areas are described, with emphasis on child-rearing customs and practices. Covers Indians of the Eastern Woodlands, the Great Plains, the Pueblos, and the Northwest Coast.

265. Felton, Harold W. **Ely S. Parker: Spokesman for the Senecas.** Illus. by
Lorence F. Bjorklund. New York: Dodd, 1973. 111p. $4.50. (7-9)
A biography of Ely S. Parker, a Seneca who studied law but was denied admission to
the bar because of his Indian ancestry. His contributions as an outstanding engineer,
lobbyist for Indian rights, and nineteenth century Commissioner of Indian Affairs
are highlighted.

266. Fish, Byron. **Eskimo Boy Today**. Photos by Bob and Ira Spring. Juneau:
Alaska Northwest Publishing Co., 1971. 61p. $6.95. (3-6)
Ten-year-old Gary Hopson's Eskimo name is Ahniksauk. He lives in Barrow, Alaska,
where the Eskimo way of life and environment are changing. The traditional Eskimo
homes, clothing, dances, folklore, and customs are described, as well as the new ways.

267. Forman, James. **The Life and Death of Yellow Bird**. New York: Farrar,
Straus & Giroux, 1973. 215p. $5.95. (7-12)
Yellow Bird is the descendant of one of the contemporaries of Sitting Bull and
Crazy Horse. Based on historical fact, Yellow Bird, a visionary, describes the Battle
of Little Bighorn, the death of Sitting Bull, Buffalo Bill, and the Wounded Knee
Massacre, among other outstanding events in American Indian history. Another
well-documented account is that of the Nez Percé Chief Joseph in *People of the
Dream* (Farrar, 1972. $0.95pa.) by the same author.

268. Fowler, Don D. **In a Sacred Manner We Live**. New York: Barre-Westover,
1972. 149p. $5.95pa. (9-12)
Photographs of the North American Indian by Rachel J. Homer chosen from the
author's 20-volume set, *The North American Indian*. Includes bibliographic note.

269. Fuchs, Estelle, and Robert J. Havighurst. **To Live on This Earth: American
Indian Education**. New York: Anchor, 1972. 390p. $8.95; $3.95pa. (T)
Studies American Indian education, covering the roles of students, teachers, educators and community leaders. Provides statistics on American Indian schools, and
evaluations of them.

270. Gallagher, H. G. **Etok: The Story of Eskimo Power**. New York: Putnam's,
1974. 288p. $7.95. (9-12)
Describes a young Inupiat Eskimo who is trying to reclaim land for the Eskimos.
Etok is a controversial figure, active in political protests, etc., on behalf of the
American Indian.

271. Georgakas, Dan. **Red Shadows: The History of Native Americans from
1600 to 1900, from the Desert to the Pacific Coast**. New York: Doubleday,
1973. 128p. $3.75; $1.45pa. (7-12)
Covers 300 years of the history of American Indians of the West. Arrangement is by
tribe, and each section relates that particular tribe's reaction to and interaction with
the whites. Tribal customs and ceremonies that are particular to a group or location
are described. A similar title covering Indians of the Eastern states to the Plains
states is *The Broken Hoop: The History of Native Americans from 1600 to 1890,
from the Atlantic Coast to the Plains* (Doubleday, 1973. $3.75; $1.45pa.).

272. Goble, Paul, and Dorothy Goble. **Brave Eagle's Account of the Fetterman Fight, 21 December 1866.** New York: Pantheon, 1972. 63p. $5.79. (4-9)
Brave Eagle, a teen-aged Sioux Indian, recounts an 1866 battle between the Plains Indians and the U.S. Army. The story is vivid and dramatic, with full-color illustrations by the author. Another work by the Gobles, which is equally authentic and exciting reading for children, is *Red Hawk's Account of Custer's Last Battle: The Battle of the Little Bighorn, 25 June 1876* (Pantheon, 1970).

273. Grant, Matthew G. **Crazy Horse: War Chief of the Oglala.** Illus. by John Keely and Dick Brude. Chicago: Childrens Press, 1974. 31p. $3.95. (2-4)
An easy-to-read biography of Chief Crazy Horse, who defeated General Custer at Little Big Horn.

274. Gridley, Marion E. **American Indian Tribes.** New York: Dodd, 1974. 192p. $5.50. (7-12, T)
A well-documented history of the major American Indian tribes, with brief biographies of outstanding chiefs and leaders. Other titles by the author for this age group are: *Indians of Today* (Indian Council Fire, 1970); *The Story of the Sioux* (Putnam's, 1972). An interesting collection of biographies is entitled *American Indian Women* (Hawthorn, 1974. $5.95). The lives of these Indian women cover a 300-year span of history. The author's *Contemporary American Indian Leaders* (Dodd, 1972. $4.95) covers such well-known leaders as Vine Deloria, Jr., and Henry Adams. A history for slightly younger readers is *Indian Tribes of America* (Hubbard, 1973. $4.95). Individual biographies are *Maria Tallchief* (Dillon, 1973. $3.95); *Pontiac* (Putnam's, 1970. $3.59); *Story of the Iroquois* (Putnam's, 1969); *Story of the Navajo* (Putnam's, 1971); *Story of the Seminole* (Putnam's, 1973); and *Story of the Sioux* (Putnam's, 1972). Written for the intermediate grades (3-6) these are $4.97 each.

275. Gurko, Miriam. **Indian America: The Black Hawk War.** New York: Crowell, 1970. 223p. $4.50. (7-9)
A history of the Black Hawk War in the early part of the nineteenth century, related from the Indian's viewpoint. Also discusses recent protests, developments, and the Indian's continued struggle for his rights.

276. Haverstock, Mary Sayre. **Indian Gallery: The Story of George Catlin.** New York: Four Winds, 1973. 229p. $7.95. (5-12)
This famous artist travelled among the Indians, preserving their culture in his paintings. This biography of Catlin is also a portrayal of the American Indian and is highlighted with reproductions of Catlin's work. Indexed.

277. Hays, Wilma P., and R. Vernon Hays. **Foods the Indians Gave Us.** Illus. by Tom O'Sullivan. New York: Washburn, 1973. 113p. $4.95. (6-9)
Foods that were popular with the American Indian and those the white man learned to cultivate from him are described. Some recipes such as "Succotash," "Aztec Chocolate Drink," and others are included.

278.   Henry, Jeanette. **Textbooks and the American Indian.** San Francisco: Indian Historian Press, 1970. 269p. $5.00. (K-12, T)
Over 300 textbooks were examined by a committee of the American Indian Historical Society to determine how the American Indians were represented for accuracy, amount of coverage, and contributions. Bibliography included.

279.   Heuman, William. **Famous American Indians.** New York: Dodd, 1972. 128p. $3.95. (7-10)
Biographical sketches of American leaders of the seventeenth, eighteenth, and nineteenth centuries. Included are such famous chiefs as Sequoyah, Sitting Bull, Crazy Horse, and Osceola.

280.   Hofsinde, Robert. **Indians at Home.** New York: Morrow, 1964. 96p. $3.78. (1-5)
The homes of Indians from different geographic locations are described and their unique types noted—e.g., the longhouse of the Iroquois, the Pueblo adobe, etc. A typical modern Indian home is also included. Other titles in print by this author and publisher for the elementary grades are: *Indian and the Buffalo, Indian Arts, Indian Beadwork, Indian Costumes, Indian Fishing & Camping, Indian Games & Crafts, Indian Hunting, Indian Medicine Man, Indian Music Makers, Indian Picture Writing, Indian Sign Language, Indian Warriors and Their Weapons, Indians on the Move, The Indian's Secret World.*

281.   Hoyt, Oldga. **American Indians Today.** New York: Abelard Schuman, 1972. 190p. $5.95. (7-11)
Describes the lifestyle of U.S. Indian tribes in current times, their relations with the government, and their attempts to obtain their civil rights and more federal aid.

282.   Jacobson, Daniel. **Great Indian Tribes.** Maplewood, N.J.: Hammond, 1970. 97p. $4.50. (6-10)
Covers about 25 North American Indian tribes. Arrangement is by geographic location, with emphasis on their histories and cultures. The style is popular; a brief bibliography and an index are provided. Another title by this author, describing the Assiniboine, Commanche, and Chippewa tribes, is *The Hunters* (Watts, 1974).

283.   Jones, Jayne C. **The American Indian in America.** Minneapolis, Minn.: Lerner Publications, 1973. 2 vols. $3.95ea. (5-10)
An overview of American Indian history from pre-historic times to the 1970s. The Indians' origins, contacts with the white man, and cultural heritage are discussed. Concludes with attention to the American Indians' influence and contributions.

284.   Jones, Louis T. **Amerindian Education.** San Antonio, Tex.: Naylor, 1972. 190p. $5.95. (7-12, T)
Surveys educational opportunities that have been available for American Indians at the college level and also the Bureau of Indian Affairs' role in education. Emphasis is on the need for vocational and technological training programs. Other titles by the author are *Indians at Work and Play* (Naylor, 1971. $6.95) and *So Say the Indians* (Naylor, 1970. $6.95).

285.   Josephy, Alvin M., comp. **Red Power: The American Indians' Fight for Freedom.** New York: McGraw-Hill, 1971. 259p. $6.95; $2.95pa. (7-12)
An anthology of contemporary articles, government reports and documents, speeches, and conference papers that reveal the American Indian's political and religious opinions and values.

286.   Kroeber, Theodore. **Ishi, Last of His Tribe.** New York: Bantam, 1973, c1964. 213p. $0.95pa. (7-12)
A historical biography of Ishi, the last member of the Yohi tribe of Indians, which had fled into hiding to avoid complete annihilation by the white settlers. A similar title is *Ishi in Two Worlds: A Biography of the Last Wild Indian in North America* (Berkeley: University of California Press, 1961. $2.45pa.).

287.   La Farge, Oliver. **A Pictorial History of the American Indian.** Rev. ed. New York: Crown, 1974. 288p. $9.95. (7-12)
La Farge has compiled a pictorial essay documenting Indian history and culture for young readers. Another title for school library use is a special edition of *The American Indian* (Golden Press, 1960. $6.95; $3.95pa.). Additional works of his are *Cochise of Arizona: The Pipe of Peace Is Broken* (Dutton, 1953. $4.50) and *Laughing Boy* (Houghton Mifflin, 1971. $2.45pa.).

288.   La Pointe, Frank. **The Sioux Today.** New York: Macmillan, 1972. 132p. $5.95. (7-12)
A collection of 24 sketches of young Sioux Indians and how they are reacting to their heritage. Compares their varying life styles in contemporary society.

289.   Levenson, Dorothy. **Homesteaders and Indians.** New York: Watts, 1971. 90p. $3.75. (4-6)
A picture of the relations and conflicts between the Indian and the early settlers of the American frontier. Illustrations, photographs and maps are included.

290.   Levine, Stuart, and Nancy O. Lurie. **The American Indian Today.** Baltimore, Md.: Penguin Books, 1972. 352p. $2.95pa. (9-12)
A discussion of American Indian identity and assimilation into white society. Provides statistics on national trends in Indian education, acculturation, employment, and relations with the government, the Bureau of Indian Affairs, and other agencies. Illustrations, maps, bibliography, and index are provided.

291.   Loh, Jules. **Lords of the Earth: A History of the Navajo Indians.** New York: Macmillan, 1971. 184p. $4.95. (7-12)
Describes the historical background of the Navajos, their culture, customs, and patterns of social behavior.

292.   Martin, Patricia. **Ekimos, People of Alaska.** Illus. by Robert Frankenberg. New York: Parents' Magazine Press, 1970. 64p. $4.59. (1-4)
Eskimo houses, food, hunting, customs, laws and everyday life are depicted. Another work by this author and publisher is *Indians: The First Americans* (1970. $4.59).

293. McGovern, Ann. **If You Lived with the Sioux Indians.** Illus. by Bob
Levering. New York: Four Winds Press, 1974. 88p. $5.95. (2-4)
A book of facts about the Sioux, their customs and lifestyle. The format is a
question- and-answer style. A glossary of terms is included.

294. McLuhan, T. C. **Touch the Earth: A Self-Portrait of Indian Existence.**
New York: Outerbridge & Dientsfrey, 1971. 185p. $6.95. (7-12, T)
Excerpts from speeches of American Indians, selected to present a history of the
American Indian experience, his values, and his responses to the decisions of the
white man.

295. Mitchell, Emerson Blackhorse. **Miracle Hill: The Story of a Navajo Boy.**
Norman: University of Oklahoma Press, 1967. 230p. $5.95. (5-8)
An interesting revelation of the bicultural experience of many contemporary young
Indians as they grow up in an Indian environment, then later enter a white man's
world. This is a young Navajo boy's autobiography.

296. Moquin, Wayne, ed. **Great Documents in American History.** New York:
Praeger, 1972. 418p. $4.95. (9-12)
This survey of Indian life and history is presented through a collection of articles
and speeches written by American Indians. It is divided into three sections: Part 1
contains epigraphs and quotations depicting tribal life; Part 2 contains records of the
Indian-federal government confrontations, and Part 3 contains writings on recent
twentieth century issues. A glossary of tribes and an index are included.

297. Morris, Richard B. **The First Book of the Indian Wars.** Illus. by Leonard
Everett Fisher. New York: Watts, 1959. 86p. $3.45. (4-6)
A history of the early conflicts between the Indians and the early settlers up to 1780.
Includes maps and an index.

298. Oswalt, Wendell H. **This Land Was Theirs: A Study of the North American
Indian.** 2nd ed. New York: Wiley, 1973. 617p. $14.95. (7-12)
Examines the North American Indian through the history and culture of ten tribes.
The author also describes the white man's response to and treatment of these Indian
tribes.

299. Phillips, Leon. **First Lady of America: A Romanticized Biography of
Pocahontas.** Richmond, Va.: Westover, 1973. 205p. $8.95. (6-9)
Describes Pocahontas's girlhood and abduction at the age of 16, her marriage, and
her death. Also provides an interesting picture of the early settlement of Jamestown
and the white man's relationships with the native Americans.

300. Roland, Albert. **Great Indian Chiefs.** New York: Macmillan, 1966. 152p.
$4.95. (6-12)
Nine portraits of famous American Indian chiefs include: Hiawatha, Pocahontas,
Philip, Pope, Pontiac, Macquinna, Tecumseh, Sequoyah, and Sitting Bull.

301. Shapp, Martha. **Let's Find Out about Indians.** Illus. by Peter Costanza.
New York: Watts, 1962. 42p. $3.45. (K-3)

A book of facts about American Indian customs and culture for the primary grades.

302. Showers, Paul. **Indian Festivals.** Illus. by Lorence Bjorklund. New York: Crowell, 1969. unp. $4.50. (K-3)
Indian festivals, holidays and sacred ceremonies of various American Indian tribes are described.

303. Sine, Jerry, and Gene Klinger. **Son of This Land.** Chicago: Childrens Press, 1970. 64p. $3.50; $1.00pa. (6-12)
An autobiographical account of a successful American Indian commercial artist. He points out the deprivations and prejudices faced by American Indian youth, but without resentment. A particularly poignant episode relates the death of his older brother because he could not obtain adequate medical treatment. Sine has accepted his Indian heritage and is proud of it.

304. Stirling, Matthew W. **National Geographic on Indians of the Americas.** Washington, D.C.: National Geographic Society, 1965, c1955. 432p. $7.50. (7-12)
The origins, customs, religion, arts, crafts, family roles and patterns, and tribal governments of American Indians are presented. Coverage is comprehensive—from pre-history to the mid-twentieth century. Included are 149 reproductions of paintings.

305. Szasz, Margaret. **Education and the American Indian: The Road to Self-Determination.** Albuquerque: University of New Mexico Press, 1974. 251p. $10.00. (T)
Ms. Szasz blames Congress, the Bureau of the Budget, and the Bureau of Indian Affairs for failures in Indian education. She presents a history of Indian education and notes changes brought about after 1960.

306. Terrell, John Upton, and Donna Terrell. **Indian Women of the Western Morning: Their Life in Early America.** New York: Doubleday, 1976. 194p. $2.95pa. (7-12)
Describes the lifestyle and role of Indian women in America at the time of the first contact with the white settlers and colonists.

307. Thompson, Hildegard. **Getting to Know American Indians Today.** Illus. by Shannon Stirnweis. New York: Coward McCann, 1965. 64p. $3.68. (3-5)
Emphasis is on contemporary lifestyle of American Indians on a Navajo reservation, but some coverage is also given to Hopi, Miccosukee, and Pueblo Indians.

308. United States. Bureau of Indian Affairs. **Indian and Eskimo Children.** Washington, D.C.: Government Printing Office, 1966. 48p. $4.75. (K-4)
Describes Indian children who live in pueblos, hogans, etc., as their ancestors did, as well as the life style of the contemporary urban Indians who have moved for employment, modern housing, etc.

309.   Vanderwerth, W. C., ed. **Indian Oratory: A Collection of Famous Speeches by Noted Chieftains.** Norman: University of Oklahoma, 1972. 300p. $8.95; $1.65pa. (9-12)
Speeches of 22 American Indian tribal chiefs are arranged chronologically from the mid-eighteenth century to the early twentieth century. A brief biography of each chief is also included.

310.   Vogel, Virgil J. **This Country Was Ours: A Documentary History of the American Indian.** New York: Harper and Row, 1972. 473p. $12.95. (10-12)
An objective approach to Indian-white relations using primary source documents to present a history of the American Indian. Arrangement is chronological. A comprehensive bibliography is included, as well as valuable appendix lists, such as "Famous Americans of Indian Descent." Indexed. The author has also written *The Indian in American History* (Integrated Education Associates, 1968).

311.   Voight, Virginia Frances. **Sacajawea.** Illus. by Erica Merkling. New York: Putnam's, 1967. 63p. $3.59. (K-4)
A simplified biography of a famous Indian woman married to one of the early explorers of the Lewis and Clark expedition. A list of Indian words and names is included.

312.   Warren, Mary Phraner. **Walk in My Moccasins.** Illus. by Victor Mays. Philadelphia, Pa.: Westminster, 1966. 157p. $4.75. (4-6)
The story of a Montana couple who adopt five American Indian children.

313.   Werner, Ben, Jr. **One Hundred One Things the Indians Made: And How They Made Them.** New York: Edmund Publishing Co., 1974. $4.95. (4-12)
This book is especially useful for children who love working with their hands, for art classes, or for making "props" for school dramatizations on the American Indian.

314.   Wissler, Clark. **Indians of the United States: Four Centuries of Their History and Culture.** New York: Doubleday, 1966. 336p. $7.95; $2.50pa. (9-12)
A book on Indian history and culture covering all geographic areas. The author is a well-known scholar on the American Indian.

315.   Wolf, Bernard. **Tinker and the Medicine Men: The Story of a Navajo Boy of Monument Valley.** New York: Random, 1973. 68p. $5.79. (4-7)
A pictorial essay of a six-year-old Navajo boy who wants to be a medicine man like his father. Provides information about the dual life styles of many American Indian children—e.g., life in a town public school and family life in a hogan home raising sheep and weaving rugs.

316.   Yellow Robe, Rosebud. **An Album of the American Indian.** New York: Watts, 1969. 87p. $4.95. (4-6)
Authored by the grand-niece of the famous Sioux Indian, Sitting Bull, this book describes Indian culture and problems in a child-oriented history of the Indian people.

Literature and Fiction Titles

317. Agle, Nan Hayden. **Princess Mary of Maryland.** Detroit: Gale Research, c1956, 1967. 108p. $4.00. (4-6)

An award-winning children's story of an Indian princess who came in contact with the white settlers of Colonial Maryland.

318. Allen, Leroy. **Shawnee Lance.** New York: Delacorte, 1970. 160p. $4.58. (3-7)

Daniel was adopted by the Shawnees after they killed his father. He learns to appreciate Indian skills and culture in an exciting story of conflict and war.

319. Allen, Terry D., ed. **The Whispering Wind: Poetry by Young American Indians.** New York: Doubleday, 1972. 128p. $4.95; $1.95pa. (7-12)

Authors of these poems were all participants in the writing program at the Institute of American Indian Arts, a combination high school and art institute. Their sensitive writing reflects their Indian culture and feelings about their identity. Another title that is a collection of Indian students' creative writings is *Arrow IV* (Pacific Grove Press, 1972), sponsored by the Bureau of Indian Affairs.

320. Arnold, Elliott. **The Spirit of Cochise.** New York: Scribner's, 1972. 183p. $5.95. (7-10)

Joe Murdock returns to his Apache Indian reservation from the war in Vietnam. He finds the white agent patronizing, prejudiced, and a cheat. He instigates reaction and indignation among the Indians, who then build their own store under his leadership. Another title for this age group, by the same author, is *Broken Arrow* (Hawthorn, 1954).

321. Balch, Glenn. **Indian Paint.** Illus. by Nels Hagner. New York: Scholastic Book Service, 1972. 244p. $2.28. (3-6)

This story of an Indian pony is a favorite theme for this age range. Other titles by this author are *Brave Riders* (Crowell, 1959) and *Indian Saddle-Up* (Peter Smith).

322. Belting, Natalia, comp. **Our Fathers Had Powerful Songs.** New York: Dutton, 1974. 32p. $4.95. (3-6)

Ten poems, derived from American Indian songs of various tribes, are illustrated in black and white drawings. They speak of the sun, moon, animals, spirits and forces of nature as they relate to the Indian. Other titles by the author are: *Whirlwind Is a Ghost Dancing* (Dutton, 1974), *Calendar Moon* (Holt, Rinehart & Winston, 1964), and *Silver Reindeer* (Holt, 1966).

323. Benedict, Rex. **Good Luck, Arizona Man.** New York: Yearling, 1974. 176p. $0.95pa. (4-7)

A half-breed Apache, Arizona Slim, was found and raised by the Apaches. He slyly manages to get the old chieftain to tell him where they found him. His search for his own identity leads him to hidden gold in a story that is both funny and suspenseful.

324.   Bierhorst, John, and Henry R. Schoolcraft, eds. **The Ring in the Prairie:
       A Shawnee Legend.** Illus. by Leo and Diane Dillon. New York: Dial
       Press, 1970. 48p. $4.95. (K-4)
Collage-style illustrations tell this romantic legend of a Shawnee warrior and the
daughter of a star. Similar titles by the authors are *Fire Plume: Legends of the
American Indians* (Dial Press, 1969) and *In the Trail of the Wind* (Farrar, 1971).

325.   Bonham, Frank. **Chief.** New York: Dutton, 1973, c1971. 215p. $0.95pa.
       (6-12)
Henry Crowfoot, the Santa Rosa Indian chief, goes to great lengths to get modern
conveniences, schools, stores, and medical treatment for his people.

326.   Borland, Hal. **When the Legends Die.** New York: Bantam, 1972, c1963.
       288p. $0.95. (9-12)
A picture of conflicting values and cultures is presented in this story of a young Ute
Indian boy who flees the reservation with his family when his father kills another
man. Thomas Black Bull returns to a primitive life style until a former rodeo star
helps him find himself. The story is set in Colorado around 1900.

327.   Brandon, William. **The Magic World: American Indian Songs and Poems.**
       New York: William Morrow & Co., 1971. 145p. $2.95. (7-12)
An anthology of songs, poems of joy, and poems of pain selected for their literary
beauty and quality.

328.   Bunting, Eve. **The Once-a-Year Day.** Illus. by W. T. Mars. Chicago:
       Childrens Press, 1974. 44p. $5.78. (3-6)
Once a year supplies are brought on a barge to 12-year-old Annie's Eskimo village.
Annie's everyday habits and what she wants to buy most from that barge shipment
contrast her lifestyle and values with that of the typical U.S. school child.

329.   Chandler, Edna W. **Almost Brothers.** Illus. by Fred Irvin. Chicago:
       A. Whitman, 1971. 128p. $3.50. (3-6)
Life in the rural Southwest, particularly among the Indian reservations and communities with poverty, unemployment, and cultural conflicts, is portrayed in this
story. Benjie, whose father is a Sioux Indian reservation doctor, finds it difficult
to be accepted in Arizona by the poor Indians or the Chicanos. Another title by
the author is *Charley Brave* (Whitman, 1971).

330.   Cone, Molly. **Number Four.** Boston, Mass.: Houghton Mifflin, 1972.
       134p. $4.85. (5-9)
Ben Turner is an American Indian high school senior who is not allowed to start an
Indian Culture Club because it would discriminate against whites. *Number Four*
refers to the fact that Ben is only the fourth Indian student to graduate from this
bigoted, small-town high school.

331.   Conklin, Paul. **Choctaw Boy.** New York: Dodd, 1975. 64p. $4.50. (4-6)
A clear picture of the Choctaw Indian heritage (games, food, and celebrations) is
interwoven into the daily life of this Indian boy living in a modern home and
attending a modern school.

332.   Cooper, James Fenimore. **Last of the Mohicans.** New York: Collier, 1964.
      378p. $0.65pa. (9-12)
Classic fiction about the American Indian, this 1964 edition is one of several books
by Cooper that are still popular. Other titles about Indians are *The Deerslayer*
and *Leatherstocking Saga.*

333.   Embry, Margaret. **Shadi.** New York: Holiday, 1971. 92p. $3.95. (7-10)
Shadi and her brothers and sisters live in a government-sponsored Indian boarding
school. When Shadi's father abandons them and her mother dies, Shadi and her
friend, Tom, devise a plan for him to sneak the baby sister that she had helped
deliver into the school. This sensitive portrayal of a young Navajo girl amost has
a counterpart in the author's story of a Navajo boy in *My Name Is Lion* (Holiday,
1970), for a slightly younger age group.

334.   Field, Edward, comp. and trans. **Eskimo Songs and Stories.** New York:
      Delacorte, 1973. 102p. $6.95. (3-7)
A collection of 34 Netsilik Eskimo songs and legends. Materials from Knud
Rasmussen's expeditions in the 1920s have been translated by the author and are
accompanied by sealskin stencil prints and lithographs.

335.   Fife, Dale. **Ride the Crooked Wind.** Illus. by Richard Cuffari. New York:
      Coward, 1973. 95p. $4.95. (5-10)
A Paiute Indian boy resists the white man's way of doing things in this story of
cultural diversities.

336.   Fry, Alan. **Come a Long Journey.** New York: Manor Books, 1972. 249p.
      $1.25pa. (9-12)
A sensitive story about two teen-aged boys, one white and one Indian, and the
relationship they develop on a canoe trip. The author's *How a People Die*
(Doubleday, 1970) is also revealing of Indian thought, history, and values.

337.   George, Jean Craighead. **Julie of the Wolves.** Illus. by John Schoenherr.
      New York: Harper & Row, 1972. 170p. $6.95. (7-12)
Julie Edward Miyax Kapugen is a 13-year-old Eskimo girl who escapes from an
arranged marriage with a dull-witted boy and tries to walk to San Francisco, where
she will live with her pen pal. Lost on the tundra, she learns to live with a pack of
wolves. This story of a young girl caught between two Eskimo cultures—the old
ways and the new ways learned from the whites—is a vivid picture of American
Eskimo life.

338.   Harris, Marilyn. **Hatter Fox.** New York: Bantam, 1974. 241p. $1.50pa.
      (9-12)
Hatter Fox is a teen-aged Navajo girl sent to a reformatory for stabbing an Indian
Bureau doctor. This story relates her painful rehabilitation by this doctor and is a
picture of Indian and white violence in their misunderstandings of each other, and
particularly of the Indian's frustration with the white system.

339.   Hodges, Margaret, reteller. **The Fire Bringer: A Paiute Indian Legend.** Illus. by Peter Parnall. Boston, Mass.: Little, Brown, 1972. 31p. $5.95. (2-4)
A version of the Promethean myth adapted from *The Basket Woman* by Mary Austin (Houghton, 1904). The story describes how fire was obtained when Coyote stole it from the Fire Spirits.

340.   Houston, James, ed. **Songs of the Dream People: Chants and Images from the Indians and Eskimos of North America.** Boston, Mass.: Atheneum, 1972. 83p. $5.95. (3-6)
The American Indian poetry presented here, arranged geographically, includes songs, chants, and poems from the Eastern Woodlands, Central Plains, Northwest Coast, and Eskimos. Drawings of Indian artifacts, pictographs, and other examples of Indian art are part of the author's illustrations. Other titles by James Houston for the primary grades are *Akvak: An Eskimo Journey* (Harcourt Brace Jovanovich, 1968. $4.50); *Ghost Paddle: A Northwest Coast Indian Tale* (Harcourt Brace Jovanovich, 1972. $4.50); *Kiviok's Magic Journey: An Eskimo Legend* (Atheneum, 1973. $5.25); *Wolf Run: A Caribou Eskimo Tale* (Harcourt Brace Jovanovich, 1971. $4.50).

341.   Jackson, Helen Hunt. **Ramona.** Abr. ed. New York: Scholastic Book Service, 1974. 349p. $1.25pa. (7-12)
This classic American novel has been made into three movie versions, a stage play, and a pageant. It is a story of culture conflict, drama, and romance set in Spanish and Indian California before it felt the white man's influence.

342.   Jones, Hettie, adapt. **The Trees Stand Shining: Poetry of the North American Indians.** New York: Dial Press, 1971. 32p. $4.95. (3-10)
The Caldecott Medal runner-up includes 32 poems, lullabies, prayers, and chants celebrating nature in the North American Indian oral tradition. Watercolor paintings (14 full page) are by Robert Andrew Parker. A collection of legends by this compiler is *Longhouse Winter: Iroquois Transformation Tales* (Holt, 1972. $5.29).

343.   Lampman, Evelyn. **The Years of Small Shadow.** New York: Harcourt Brace Jovanovich, 1971. 190p. $4.95. (4-6)
Small Shadow appreciates his Indian heritage after he is loaned out to serve a white lawyer who defended his father in a horse-stealing case. Other titles by the author for the same age group are *Cayuse Courage* (Harcourt Brace Jovanovich, 1970) and *White Captives* (Atheneum, 1975. $6.25).

344.   Levitas, Gloria, *et al.*, eds. **American Indian Prose and Poetry: We Wait in the Darkness.** New York: Putnam's, 1975. 325p. $5.33; $3.25pa. (7-12)
An anthology of American Indian writing and poetry divided chronologically into three sections: 1) pre-white man, 2) post-white man, and 3) today. Selections are further divided by geographical regions and tribes.

345.   Longfellow, Henry W. **Song of Hiawatha.** Illus. by Joan Kiddell-Monroe. New York: Dutton, 1959. 241p. $4.50. (4-8)

A children's version of this classic poem of a famous Indian woman in history. A grade 7-9 version was published by Hawthorn in 1966 ($3.95).

346.   Martini, Teri. **True Book of Indians**. Chicago: Childrens Press, 1954.
       46p. $4.95. (K-4)
Indian stories for primary children. A more recent title by this author is the story of Charlie and the special Sioux Indian lucky shirt he got from his grandfather, *The Lucky Ghost Shirt.*

347.   McDermott, Gerald, adapt. **Arrow to the Sun: A Pueblo Indian Tale**. New
       York: Viking, 1974. unp. $6.95. (K-4)
An excellent Indian legend for storytelling purposes done with outstanding color illustrations. It is also available as an animated film. Other titles by this author receiving good reviews are: *Anansi the Spider: A Tale from the Shanti* (1972) and *The Magic Tree: A Tale from the Congo* (1973).

348.   Miles, Miska. **Annie and the Old One**. Illus. by Peter Parnall. Boston,
       Mass.: Little, Brown, 1972. 44p. $5.95. (K-3)
A Newbery Honor Book, this is the story of a little Navajo Indian girl who finally comes to terms with her grandmother's approaching death.

349.   Momaday, M. Scott. **House Made of Dawn**. New York: Harper & Row,
       1968. 212p. $6.95. (10-12)
A Pulitzer Prize-winning novel about the life of a young Indian who finds his reservation life and values in conflict with the lifestyle he finds in the big city of Los Angeles.

350.   O'Dell, Scott. **Island of the Blue Dolphins**. Boston, Mass.: Houghton,
       1960. 184p. $3.95. (5-9)
An Indian girl is isolated on an island off the coast of California. Her story of survival is one of courage and dignity. Winner of the Newbery Medal.

351.   Quimby, Myrtle. **White Crow**. New York: Criterion Books, 1970. 254p.
       $5.95. (7-12)
A young half-Cherokee, half-white girl is torn between loyalty to both her parent heritages. This story of Oklahoma territory in the late nineteenth century is also a history of the government's treatment of Indians and the period of development of the United States.

352.   Richter, Conrad. **A Country of Strangers**. New York: Bantam, 1975,
       c1966. 169p. $1.25. (9-12)
The story of a white girl who was captured by the Indians and named Stone Girl. She is raised to think like an Indian; later, when she is forced to return to the white man's world, she and her half-breed son are rejected by her family. A fascinating story of culture conflicts for young people. Another story of a white child raised by Indians is the author's *Light in the Forest* (Knopf, 1966).

353. Rosen, Kenneth, ed. **Voices of the Rainbow: Contemporary Poetry by American Indians.** Illus. by R. C. Gorman and Aaron Yava. New York: Viking, 1975. 232p. $10.00. (6-12)

A collection of poetry by modern American Indians. The work of 21 different poets is represented here. Emphasis is on the current situation and contemporary life.

354. Sanders, Thomas Edward, and Walter W. Peek, comps. **Literature of the American Indians.** Riverside, N.J.: Glencoe Press, 1973. 534p. $10.95. (9-12)

An anthology of American Indian literature of both North and South American Indians and Eskimos arranged chronologically in eight categories. Each section has an introductory discussion on that group's origin and identity. Includes songs, legends, histories, stories, and oratory. The last section covers poetry, prose and selections concerned with protest movements. Ideal for small libraries where minority materials must be very limited.

355. Sandoz, Mari. **The Horsecatcher.** Philadelphia, Pa.: Westminster, 1957. 192p. $3.95. (6-9)

Young Elk, a Cheyenne, rebels against the war-like ways of a warrior tribe. This novel is a warm story full of insights into Indian thought, values, culture, and traditions.

356. Smucker, Barbara C. **Wigwam in the City.** Woodcuts by Gil Miret. New York: Dutton, 1966. 154p. $4.50. (4-8)

The story of an American Indian family who move to Chicago to earn a better living. The oldest brother is ashamed of his Indian heritage and runs away. His sister, Susan Bearskin, helps her family adjust to the new life style and problems of acculturation.

357. Witheridge, Elizabeth. **Just One Indian Boy.** New York: Atheneum, 1974. 218p. $6.25. (6-9)

A story of a young Indian boy and his need to find his place in contemporary society, the cultural conflicts he encounters, and problems of poverty. Help from a white teacher and Indian friend help Andy face his family problems and get schooling and the job he had always coveted.

Audiovisual Materials

358. **Airways to Learning.** 16mm film, 33 min., color. Bureau of Indian Affairs. (4-12)

Shows Eskimo life and villages in this description of how Eskimo, Indian, and Aleut Indian students are flown from isolated Alaskan villages to BIA boarding schools.

359. **The American Experience—Indians: The First Americans.** 50 study prints. 11" x 14" b&w prints, with text and teacher's guide. Scholastic Book Services, 1975. $19.50. (4-12)

Photos representing a wide range of Indian tribes, arts and crafts, historical incidents, and contemporary activities.

360. **The American Indian.** 1 filmstrip, 1 cassette. Universal Ed., $11.00. (4-8)
A picture of Indian culture and contributions to American society. Also covers cultural conflicts and problems. From the *Great Moments in American History* series.

361. **The American Indian.** 1 filmstrip, 1 cassette. Teaching Resources. $14.50. (5-10)
Describes recent American Indian movements of protest against inequalities. Also presents a survey of broken treaties in U.S.-Indian history. Set can also be purchased with record album for same price.

362. **The American Indian.** 6 cassettes (or tapes). Tapes Unlimited. Cassette set, $43.10; tape set, $37.10; individual cassettes, $7.50. (6-12)
Indian history is studied with respect to outstanding Indian personalities, cultural traditions, and contributions to American society. Titles in the series are: *Historical Background, Black Hawk–Sauk Chief, Cochise and Geronimo–Apache Chiefs.*

363. **The American Indian: A Dispossessed People.** 2 filmstrips, 2 records (or cassettes). Guidance Associates and the Associated Press, 1970. $41.50 (with records); $46.50 (with cassettes). (4-8)
The contemporary Indian who is no longer willing to accept the inferior conditions his people have endured is presented. The Bureau of Indian Affairs, treaties, reservations, Indian religion and culture, and problems of Indians living and working in urban areas are described.

364. **The American Indian: A Study in Depth.** 6 filmstrips with 6 records (or cassettes). Warren Schloat Production, 1969. Set with records, $120.00; with cassettes, $138.00. (4-8)
Titles in this study are: *Before Columbus*; *After Columbus*; *Growing Up*; *Religion*; *Arts and Culture*; *The American Indian Today*. The study is written by anthropologist Ethel Alpenfels.

365. **American Indian Art & Artifacts.** 25 slides, col. Sandak. Set $31.25. (4-12)
These colored slides picture Indian culture through examples of clothing, religious art, various well-known paintings, and examples of Indian arts and crafts from different tribes.

366. **The American Indian before Columbus.** 4 filmstrips, 2 cassettes (or records). Society for Visual Education, 1974. $47.75 ($16.50 each); with records, $45.00 ($15.00 each). (4-9)
A summary of the pre-Columbian Indians and the various Indian cultures prior to the sixteenth century. Includes the customs and culture of the burial and temple mound builders, the Hohokam, Anasazi Indians, the Toltec, Aztec, and Inca societies, and other Indians of the desert.

367. **American Indian Dances.** 1 record. Folkways Records, 1975. $8.95. (K-6)

These dances were selected from the Ethnic Folkways Library of Indian music by Ronnie and Stir Lipner. Notes describe the dances, steps and movements. Six or seven different Indian tribes are represented. Useful for music, language, or physical education classes.

368. **American Indian Gallery.** 60 posters. Class National Publishing, Inc. Set $24.60. (K-12)

This collection of 60 posters by John Carroll document the history and cultural contributions of the American Indians. A 200-word description is provided for each poster, and a teacher's guide gives suggestion for classroom use.

369. **American Indian Legends.** 12 study prints. Vanguard Visuals. Set $4.95. (K-2)

These posters each tell the story of an Indian legend, which is then printed on the reverse side.

370. **American Indian Music for the Classroom.** Kit with records (or cassettes). Canyon Records. Kit with records, $47.50; with cassettes, $52.50. (K-12)

This kit contains records, 20 study photographs, 20 spirit masters, a map, and a bibliography of related reading materials. It covers the cultural areas of various tribal regions in 27 songs. Songs are sung by Dr. Louis Ballard, who also interprets their cultural meanings.

371. **American Indian Myths.** 4 filmstrips, 4 records (or cassettes). Imperial Films, 1973. Set, $48.00 ($12.00 each); cassettes $51.80 ($12.95 each). (K-3)

A collection of folk stories on North American Indians for primary children. Titles include: *Glooskap and the Winter Giant*; *The Good Giants*; *Little Scar Face*; and *Why Turkeys Have Red Eyes*.

372. **American Indian Nature Legends.** 6 filmstrips, 3 cassettes. Troll Associates, 1974. $66.00. (K-6)

The Cherokee, Papago, Cheyenne, Iroquois, and Hopi Indian tribes are represented in this collection of Indian folklore. Titles include: *Thunder Spirits*; *Search for Buffalo*; *Stealing the Sun*; *Animal Mysteries*; *Creatures of the River*; and *Answering Universe*.

373. **The American Indian Speaks.** 16mm film, 23 min., color with teacher's guide. Encyclopaedia Britannica Educational Corp., 1973. $265.00 (rental available). (K-12)

Shows three Indian tribes (Muskogee Creek, Rosebud Sioux, Nisqually) and the ways in which the traditions of their cultures conflict with the white man's.

374. **The American Indian Today.** 2 filmstrips, 1 record, 1 teacher's guide. Teaching Resources, 1973. $23.00. (4-6)

The American Indian experience is presented in two titles: *The First Americans* and *Happily May I Walk*.

375. **The American Indians.** 1 filmstrip with ditto worksheets and teacher's guide. Urban Media. $9.95. (4-6)
The worksheets in this sheet have been designed for use with slow-learners or children who have poor or no English language ability.

376. **American Indians.** 24 transparencies with overlays. Creative Visuals, 1971. $50.00. (4-8)
These 24 transparencies are useful for studying American Indian biography and the contributions of such well-known Indians as Massasoit, Powhatan, Pocahontas, Sitting Bull, Cochise, etc.

377. **American Indians.** 1 cassette, 29 min. Educational Resources, 1973. $11.50. (6-12)
This cassette is from the *Ethnic Studies: The Peoples of America* series. It describes some of the early Indian-settler relationships, Indian reservation life, and some of the new protest and militant groups and their philosophies.

378. **American Indians and How They Really Lived.** 5 filmstrips. Troll Associates, 1970. Set, $35.00; individual filmstrips, $7.00. (3-7)
Indian crafts and customs are emphasized in this history arranged by tribal groups. Titles in the set: *Hopi and Navajo: People of the Southwest*; *The Seminoles of the South*; *The Crow: People of the Great Plains*; *The Chinook: Fishermen of the Northwest*; *The Iroquois: People of the Longhouse.*

379. **American Indians of the Southwest.** 6 filmstrips, 6 records (or cassettes). Coronet Instructional Films, 1972. Set, $47.50; with cassettes, $62.50. (2-4)
A description of the Southwestern American Indians with respect to their history, customs, religions, crafts, and current social and physical problems. Titles: *Who They Are*; *Their History*; *Their Homes*; *Their Handicrafts*; *Their Religions*; *Their Life Today.* A similar set is entitled *American Indians of the Southeast* (Coronet, 1972) and another group of 6 filmstrips and records is *American Indians of the North Pacific Coast* (Coronet, 1971).

380. **The Ancient American: The First Men.** 1 filmstrip, 1 record. Westwood, 1973. $20.00. (7-12)
Ancient Indian cultures of America are discovered through this filmstrip study. It traces their migration from Asia and their cultural development and surveys the customs, economies, etc., of various tribes. Other titles in this series: *The Ancient American: The Farmers*; *The Ancient Americans: The Builders*; and *The Ancient Americans: The Merging Cultures.*

381. **And Promises to Keep.** 16mm film, 22 min., color. Bureau of Indian Affairs. (4-12)
Describes the school system maintained by the BIA for American Indian children, and describes how laws make possible funds for improving facilities and learning.

382. **The Apache Indian.** Rev. ed. 16mm film, 10 min., color. Coronet. $140.00. (K-6)

This film on the ancient and modern American Indian cultures, with a description of modern ways of Indian protests, can be ordered for preview. It is accompanied by a teacher's guide. One of the few sources that discusses the new Indian movements on the primary level.

383. **Around Indian Campfires.** 10 cassettes. Troll, 1975. Set, $46.00; $4.90 each. (3-6)

Titles included in this series: *Indian Homes*; *Indian Tools*; *Indian Hunting*; *Indian Farming*; *Indian Customs*; *Indian Weapons*; *Indian Music*; *Indian Legends*; *Indian Family Life*; and *Indian Celebrations.*

384. **Bury My Heart at Wounded Knee.** 1 cassette. Voice Over Books. $6.95. (7-12)

A narration of Dee Brown's book by Henry Madden and Manu Tupou. Describes the conquest of the American West as the Indians saw it.

385. **Catlin and the Indians.** 16mm film, 24 min., color. NBC News. (7-12)

NBC has produced this film for the "Smithsonian Series" on the American Indians. Many of Catlin's outstanding portraits of American Indians are included.

386. **The Emerging Eskimo.** 16mm film, 15 min., color. Brayton-Kendall, 1972. $7.00 (rental). (7-12)

The Eskimos' origins, culture, and recent interaction politically and socially with the white man are examined.

387. **Eskimos of North America.** Kit. Instructo. $7.95. (4-8)

One filmstrip and transparencies and ditto masters for duplication comprise this kit picturing the culture of the North American Eskimo. Emphasis is on daily life, food, clothing, homes, etc.

388. **The First Americans: Culture Patterns.** 4 filmstrips with 4 discs (or cassettes). Warren Schloat Productions, 1974. Set, $80.00; with cassettes, $98.00. (9-12)

The set includes: *The Paleo-Indians*; *The Arctic; The Southwest;* and *The Mound Builders.*

389. **Geronimo Jones.** 16mm film, 21 min., color. Learning Corporation of America, 1970. (7-12)

Geronimo Jones is about a young Indian boy torn between two conflicting cultures on an Indian reservation in Arizona. It is the first title in *The Many Americans* series about children of different ethnic backgrounds.

390. **The Hopi Indians.** 16mm film, 10½ min., color, with teacher's guide. Coronet. $150.00. (3-9)

Presents the daily life and customs of the Hopi Indians. Also shows a Hopi wedding ceremony and some of their arts and crafts.

391. **How the Indians Discovered a New World.** 1 filmstrip, 1 record (or cassette). Current Affairs. $25.00; with cassette, $30.00. (7-12)
Traces the migration of the Indians from Asia during the Ice Age to North America. Shows the evolution of Indians from hunters to farmers, traders, craftsmen, etc.

392. **Indian Americans: Stories of Achievement.** 4 filmstrips, 4 discs (or cassettes). Walt Disney. $60.00; with cassette, $67.00. $18.00 and $20.00 each. (3-9)
Titles in this series: *Hiawatha, Father of a Democracy*; *Pocahontas, the Lady Ambassador*; *Ely S. Parker—Engineer, Soldier and Indian Spokesman*; and *Washakie, War Chief and Diplomat.*

393. **Indian Civil Rights Leaders.** 6 filmstrips, 6 records (or cassettes). Current Affairs, 1972. $90.00; with cassettes, $98.00. (9-12)
This series is in two parts. The first deals primarily with well-known Indian leaders, presenting their political views and comments on the American Indian situation on reservations and in other communities. Groups represented are the American Indian Movement, Native Americans United, the Alcatraz Indians. Part 2 includes leaders from the Taos, Pueblos, and a group attempting to save Indian fishing and hunting rights from white exploitation, the Protectors of Hunting and Fishing Rights.

394. **Indian Heritage.** 6 filmstrips. Troll. $42.00. (2-6)
This series for younger children is a simplified history of the American Indian experience. Includes: *Americans before Columbus*; *Indian Children*; *Indian Celebrations*; *Indian Legends*; *Indian Homes*; and *Indians Who Showed the Way.*

395. **Indian Life in North America.** 4 filmstrips, 4 records (or cassettes). Imperial Films, 1973. $48.00 set; $12.00 each; with cassettes, $51.80 set; $12.95 each. (4-8)
Titles in this series on the Grand Canyon and Pueblo Indians describe homes, economy, food, recreation, tribal rites and ceremonies, and daily activities. Cultural heritage is examined through a brief historical background and an examination of Indian wall paintings and carvings. Included are: *The Havasupai of the Grand Canyon* (Parts 1 and 2) and *The Pueblo Indians of the Southwest* (Parts 1 and 2).

396. **Indian People Who Demand Tomorrow.** Filmstrip with record (or cassette). Associated Press and Pathescope. $25.00. (4-6)
This set includes a teacher's guide and spirit masters for studying the future of the American Indian with respect to new demands for better living conditions, health care, education, etc.

397. **Indian Tribes.** 10 cassettes. Troll. $49.00; $4.90 each. (3-6)
Describes the different regional Indian tribes and tells how they differ in history, culture, and their Indian-white relationships.

398. **Indian Ways.** 1 filmstrip, teacher's guide. Denoyer-Geppert. $6.75. (K-3)
Pictures describing the Indian lifestyle and culture for the primary grades.

399. **The Indians among Us.** 2 cassettes. Key Records. $7.00 each. (4-8)
Parts 1 and 2 tell who the Indians were, where they lived, and their contributions to American society. Parts 3 and 4 describe the meanings and significance of different Indian ceremonies and discuss the conditions existing among the American Indians today.

400. **Indians before White Man.** 14 transparencies, 1 teacher's guide. Civic Ed. Service. $35.00. (7-12)
These colored transparencies describe the history, leadership, government, customs, traditions, rituals, and everyday life of the American Indians before contact with white society.

401. **Indians Have Helped to Build America.** Kit. Media Materials. $9.95. (4-7)
This kit contains a cassette, a spirit master for class duplication, and 35 students' books, all designed to study the contributions of the American Indians throughout history to modern culture.

402. **Indians of Early America.** 16mm film, 22 min., color, sd. Encyclopaedia Britannica Educational Corp. (6-12)
Activities and ceremonies from various representative tribes are enacted—e.g., a Sioux buffalo hunt, pottery making by the Pueblo Indians, and Iroquois death ceremonies.

403. **Indians of North America.** 5 filmstrips, 5 records (or cassettes). National Geographic Society, 1973. $67.50. (4-12)
Describes native Americans from ancient to present times. Emphasis is on their adjustment to, acceptance of, and rejection of white man's culture. Also covers customs, battles, treaties, and reservation life. Includes *The First Americans*; *The Eastern Woodlands*; *The Plains*; *West of the Shining Mountains*; *Indians Today*.

404. **Indians of the Western Hemisphere.** 20 filmstrips, 20 records (or cassettes). Ed. Services. $200.00; with cassettes, $240.00; Subset A, B, C, $70.00 each. (4-9)
Titles in this set include: *The First Americans*, *Geography*, *Ancient Indians*, *Archeology*, and *Indians Today* (Set A); *Three Great Civilizations*, *Indians of the Southeast*, *Indians of the Northeast*, *Indians of the Far North*, and *Indians of the Northwest* (Set B); *Indians of the Southwest*, *Indians of the Basin and Plateau*, *California Seedgatherers*, *Indians of the Plains*, and *Hawaiians* (Set C); *European Contact*, *Indians and the New Americans*, *Indian Removal*, *Indian Wars in the West*, and *Famous Indians*.

405. **Indians: Strangers in Their Own Land.** 2 filmstrips, 2 records (or cassettes). Narrative Arts, 1972. $35.00; with cassettes, $39.00. (5-12)
History of the American Indians including their migration to America, their various cultures and customs. Emphasis is on the Cherokees and their experiences with the Bureau of Indian Affairs (removal from their lands).

406. **Indians View Americans, Americans View Indians.** Kit. Educational Audio Visuals. $65.00. (7-12)

Role playing is done by using the materials and suggestions of this kit. The kit includes 2 filmstrips, 1 record, 21 spirit masters, an ethnography of two tribes, picture cards, and 25 student books. Titles of the units: *Red Men and White Men*; *The Black Hawk War and Cherokee Removal*; *The Sun Dance and Ghost Dance.*

407. **Introduction to the American Indian.** 1 cassette, worksheets, teacher's guide, 1 book. Wollensak. $9.95; book, $1.50 additional. (4-9)
The background and origin of the American Indian is traced.

408. **Lament of the Reservation.** 16mm film, 23 min., color, sd. McGraw-Hill Films, 1970. $9.35 (rental). (6-12)
Indian reservations are examined with respect to living conditions and the lifestyle of 600,000 residents of them. Emphasis is on mortality rates, suicide, poverty.

409. **Learning about Indians.** 4 filmstrips. Educational Development Corp., 1965. $28.00. (K-4)
Contains the following titles: *Learning about Indian Costumes*; *Learning about Indian Crafts*; *Learning about Indian Dances*; *Learning about Indian Houses.*

410. **Legal and Illegal—The Dispossession of the Indians.** 2 filmstrips, 1 record (or cassette). Multi-Media Productions, 1972. $14.95; with cassette, $16.95. (7-12)
Gives the white settlers' reasons and justification of the U.S. government for dispossessing the Indians from their lands during the westward movement.

411. **Matthew Aliuk: Eskimo in Two Worlds.** 16mm film, 18 min., color, with teacher's guide. Distr. Learning Corporation of America, 1973. $250.00 (rental, $20.00). (5-12)
An excellent picture of the way of life and problems facing the Eskimo in Anchorage and other cities, as well as those living in the northernmost villages.

412. **Navajo Arts and Crafts.** Super 8 loop, 3:40 min., color, with teacher's guide. Walt Disney, distr. by Doubleday. $23.50. (4-8)
This loop must be used with a Technicolor or Kodak projector. It describes Navajo leather work, pottery, beadwork, and jewelry making.

413. **Navajo Children.** 16mm film, 11 min., sd., b&w. Encyclopaedia Britannica Educational Corp. (K-8)
Relates the adventures of a Navajo boy and girl as they move from their winter home into a summer one with their family. Rug weaving and other aspects of their culture are also depicted.

414. **The Navajos of the 70's.** 16mm film, 16 min., color. Coleman, 1971. (5-12)
Studies the current conditions of the Navajos, as well as their history and future concerns.

415. **Our America, Background and Development: Early Indians and Their Culture.** Ed. by Edgar B. Wesley. Map. Denoyer-Geppert, 1966. $5.25. (4-10)

Illustrative symbols indicate the distribution of American Indians in the United States, their culture, housing, products, and other aspects of the American Indian communities on this instructional map.

416. **People of the Pueblos.** 16mm film, 20 min., color. Bureau of Indian Affairs. (4-12)

These Southwestern Indians are described with emphasis on how their history and culture have influenced their contemporary lifestyle.

417. **Red Sunday.** 16mm film, 28 min., color, sd., teacher's guide. Prod. Robert Henkel and James Graff for the Montana and North Dakota Bicentennial Comm.; distributed by Pyramid Films, 1975. $375.00; $30.00 (rental). (4-12)

A colorful description of the Battle of the Little Big Horn, with emphasis on the cultural conflicts existing and on the individuals and political situations that caused the incident. Narrated by John McIntire.

418. **Seminole Indians, Florida.** 10 slides, col. Photo Lab. $2.00. (4-12)

Scenes from everyday life, customs, work, recreation, of this Florida tribe are depicted.

419. **Sequoyah.** 16mm film, 15 min., color. Walt Disney Educ. $195.00. (7-9)

Sequoyah was a Cherokee who helped his tribe by setting down a written Indian language. He was also an excellent silversmith and craftsman. Also covers the Cherokee "Trail of Tears," their removal from their lands to Oklahoma.

420. **Sioux Legend.** 16mm film, 20 min., color, with teacher's guide. ACI Films Inc. $260.00. (rental available). (4-12)

Brief survey of life among the Sioux is dramatized by North Dakota Sioux Indians. Emphasis is on the culture before contact with the white society.

421. **Sounds of Indian America—Plains and Southwest.** 1 disc, 7 photographs. Indian House. $6.98. (2-12)

Recorded live at the 48th Inter-Tribal Indian Ceremonial, Gallup, New Mexico, this record includes: "Hopi Buffalo Dance," "Jemez Eagle Dance," "Zuni Rain Song," and many others.

422. **Southwest Indian Arts and Crafts.** 16mm film, 13½ min., color, sd. Coronet, 1973. $175.00 (rental available). (4-9)

Arts and crafts of the Southwestern Indians are presented clearly and with excellent photography. This film is useful for social studies units, history curriculum, or as stimulus for an art unit.

423. **Sun Dance People: The Plains Indians—Their Past and Present.** 2 filmstrips, 2 records (or cassettes). Random House, 1973. $24.95; $29.95 (with cassettes). (5-12)

Based on Richard Erdoes' book, *The Sun Dance People*, these materials are a historical overview of the life of the Plains Indians, as well as a portrait of contemporary life and activities. Indian culture, values, and roles within the community are described in the teacher's guide and portrayed in this excellent collection of photographs.

424.   **Treaties Made—Treaties Broken.** 16mm film, 18 min., color, sd. McGraw-Hill Films, 1970. $8.00 (rental). (6-12)
A review of the treaties that have been made by the U.S. government with the American Indian, and of the treaties that have been broken. Emphasis is on the disadvantaged situation of the American Indian and of unfair treatment to him. Specific tribe pictured here is the Nisqually Indian tribe of Washington.

425.   **United States. Bureau of the Census. 1970. Number of American Indians by Counties of the United States: 1970.** Map. Government Printing Office, 1973. (4-12)
The American Indian population in each county of the United States is presented on a 36" x 48" map. Distinctive color coding is useful for an overview picture of the concentration of Indian populations. A scale and key to the map are included.

426.   **White Man and Indian, the First Contacts.** 3 filmstrips, 1 record, teaching guide. Multi-Media Prod., 1970. $14.95; with cassette, $16.95. (7-12)
Examines the early contacts and relationships between the European settlers and the American Indians.

427.   **Why Did Gloria Die?** 16mm film, 27 min., color. Educational Broadcasting Corp.; distr. Indiana University Audio-Visual Center, 1973. $315.00 (rental, $11.50). (7-12)
A 27-year-old Chippewa Indian woman dies of hepatitis in Minneapolis. Bill Moyer narrates, questioning her untimely death and asking, in reviewing her life on the reservation and years of neglect, for more equality of opportunity for other American Indians.

AMISH. *See* **German Americans.**

APPALACHIAN AMERICANS

Reference Sources

428.   Dimitroff, Lillian. **An Annotated Bibliography of Audiovisual Materials Related to Understanding and Teaching the Culturally Disadvantaged.** Washington, D.C.: National Education Association, 1969. 42p. $0.75. (T)
Coverage of the culturally disadvantaged here includes several minority groups, but the people of Appalachia and migrants are emphasized. The bulk of this bibliography

includes films and filmstrips; also included are recordings and materials on the teaching strategy for the culturally disadvantaged.

429. Munn, Robert F. **The Southern Appalachians: A Bibliography and Guide to Studies.** Morgantown: West Virginia University Library, 1961. 106p. $5.00. (9-12, T)

An annotated bibliography of almost 1,100 items on Appalachia and Appalachians. Emphasis is on social and economic conditions of the mountain people. Subject arrangement.

Non-Fiction Titles: History, Culture, Sociology, Biography

430. Brooks, Maurice. **The Appalachians.** Boston, Mass.: Houghton Mifflin, 1965. 346p. $7.95. (7-12)

A study of the area that comprises the region called Appalachia. Emphasis is on the geographical, economic, and social conditions.

431. Campbell, John C. **The Southern Highlander and His Homeland.** New York: Russell Sage Foundation, 1921; repr. ed., Lexington: University Press of Kentucky, 1973. 405p. $3.45pa. (9-12)

A history of the people who settled the southern Appalachian highlands from the earliest pioneers. Their physical and social characteristics, their religion, education, and living conditions are described.

432. Caudill, Harry M. **Night Comes to the Cumberlands: Biography of a Depressed Area.** Boston, Mass.: Little, Brown, 1963. 394p. $8.50; $2.95pa. (10-12)

Mr. Caudill, a resident of the Cumberlands, writes often of his Appalachian countryside and the mountain people. A popular account of the history of the area is given here from early settlement to the 1960s.

433. Caudill, Rebecca. **My Appalachia.** New York: Holt, 1966. 90p. $4.95. (7-12)

The author reminiscences about the days in Appalachia before mining was allowed to spoil the natural beauty of the area, and before the area became such a serious poverty pocket.

434. Clark, Joe. **Tennessee Hill Folk.** Nashville, Tenn.: Vanderbilt University Press, 1972. unp. $7.95. (7-12)

A photographic history of Appalachia and its people—how they work, what they do for recreation, their customs and way of life.

435. Dykeman, Wilma. **Prophet of Plenty: The First Ninety Years of W. D. Weatherford.** Nashville: University of Tennessee Press, 1967. 263p. $6.50. (9-12)

A biography of an Appalachian mountain scholar and author who drew the nation's attention to the problems and social conditions of the hill people. His fight for educational opportunities for the Appalachians and his work at Berea College are documented in this personal account of his accomplishments on behalf of the Appalachians.

436. Eaton, Allen H. **Handicrafts of the Southern Highlands.** New York: Dover, 1973. 370p. $5.00pa. (7-12)
Arts and crafts typical of the mountain people give insights into their customs and culture.

437. Fetterman, John. **Stinking Creek.** New York: Dutton, 1970. 192p. $2.45pa. (10-12)
A portrait of a small mountain community in Appalachia, everyday life, and regional culture.

438. Ford, Thomas R., ed. **The Southern Appalachian Region: A Survey.** Lexington: University Press of Kentucky, 1962. 308p. $4.50pa. (10-12)
The study focuses on the social and economic conditions of the Appalachian people and specifically the problems of health, education, and employment. The author also examines the role of religion, and the culture and customs among the mountain people.

439. Glenn, Max E., comp. **Appalachia in Transition.** St. Louis, Mo.: Bethany Press, 1970. 156p. $4.95. (9-12)
Contains essays on various topics concerning the Appalachian people and their living conditions. Includes "The Appalachian-Urban Crisis," by S. C. Mayo, "Human Development Problems in Appalachia," by M. K. Appleby, and "How Religion Mirrors and Meets Appalachian Culture," by J. E. Weller, among others.

440. Hannum, Alberta P. **Look Back with Love: A Recollection of the Blue Ridge.** New York: Vanguard Press, 1969. 205p. $6.95. (9-12)
In these recollections the author emphasizes the isolation of the mountain people and describes how relatively untouched by progress they are. She presents the traditions that have been kept alive by the Appalachians and their unique culture and customs.

441. Hardin, Gail, and R. Conrad Stein. **The Road from West Virginia.** Chicago: Childrens Press, 1970. 63p. $3.50; $1.00pa. (7-12)
An autobiographical account of a high school girl who leaves her family in a West Virginia coal mining town after the grandmother died. Her story, told from her new home in Chicago, is a revealing picture of the hold of "the company" on the coal mining families and the strong influence of religion in the lives of the mountain people.

442. Horwitz, Elinor Lander. **Mountain People, Mountain Crafts.** Philadelphia, Pa.: Lippincott, 1974. 143p. $6.50; $2.95pa. (7-12)
A history of the traditions and techniques of mountain craftsmanship are presented in the words of the artist   and craftsman. Photographs illustrate musical instruments, toys and dolls, furniture, quilts, baskets, pottery, and also provide a picture of the life style of the Appalachians.

443.   Justus, May. **Children of the Great Smoky Mountains.** New York: Dutton, 1952. 158p. $4.00. (1-6)

A study of children in the Appalachian region shows their unique customs, culture, and lifestyle. Other titles for the elementary grades by this author are: *Holidays in No-End Hollow* (Garrard, 1969. $3.12); *Other Side of the Mountain* (Hastings, 1958. $3.95); and the *Complete Peddler's Pack: Games, Songs, Rhymes and Riddles from Mountain Folklore*, rev. ed. (University of Tennessee Press, 1967).

444.   Kahn, Kathy. **Hillbilly Women.** New York: Doubleday, 1973. 288p. $7.95. (9-12)

A collection of essays commenting on the deprivation in Appalachian mountain communities. The 19 women presented here are wives or daughters of miners or workers in the textile business, or workers who have left to work in urban areas. Emphasis is on exploitation of these women and other people by mine owners, unions, and politicians.

445.   Lee, Howard B. **My Appalachia.** Parsons, W. Va.: McClain Printing Co., 1971. $7.50. (9-12)

A description of the lifestyle of the residents of the Appalachian mountain communities, telling how the land and men have been exploited by the mining industry. Another title by the author is *Bloodletting in Appalachia* (McClain, 1969. $7.50).

446.   Meyers, Elisabeth P. **Angel of Appalachia: Martha Berry.** New York: Messner, 1968. unp. $4.29. (7-12)

A biography of a woman crusader who fought to solve the social problems in Appalachia.

447.   National Geographic Society. **American Mountain People.** Washington, D.C.: The Society, 1973. 198p. $4.75. (7-12)

The bulk of this work covers the Appalachian mountain people although some attention is also given to mountaineers of the Ozarks. Describes the homes, jobs, social conditions in Appalachia. Documented with photos and maps.

448.   Pearsall, Marion. **Little Smokey Ridge: The Natural History of a Southern Appalachian Neighborhood.** Birmingham: University of Alabama Press, 1959. 205p. $7.00. (9-12)

Studies not only the physical conditions of the Appalachians, but covers the traditions of the people, their superstitions and religious beliefs, and their adjustments to the outside world, as well as their isolation from it.

449.   Roberts, Bruce, and Nancy Roberts. **Where Time Stood Still.** New York: Crowell Collier, 1970. 114p. $6.95. (5-9)

A portrait of life in Appalachia and the people who live there. Numerous photographs and statistical accounts of poverty, unemployment rates, and descriptions of the living conditions are included. Traditions and problems of poor education are covered. The author captures the spirit of resignation and hopelessness of many of the people. Another title by Bruce Roberts is *A Portrait of Appalachia* (Macmillan, 1970. $6.95).

450. Sheppard, Muriel E. **Cabins in the Laurel.** Chapel Hill: University of North
Carolina Press, 1935. 311p. $7.25. (9-12)
Studies the isolated and unique communities of Appalachia as they are set apart
and as they differ from American society at large. The leisure activities, work,
values, and everyday living conditions are documented with the aid of many
photographs.

451. Shull, Peg. **The Children of Appalachia.** New York: Messner, 1969. 95p.
$3.95. (3-6)
Describes and documents with pictures the lives of three Appalachian mountain
families and their children's activities.

452. Surface, Bill. **The Hollow.** New York: Coward-McCann, 1971. 190p.
$5.95. (9-12)
The disadvantaged people of the Appalachian hills and hollows are examined.
Emphasis is on poverty and the economic situation and standards of living.

453. Toone, Betty L. **Appalachia: The Mountains, the Place, and the People.**
New York: Watts, 1972. 90p. $3.75. (5-8)
The first section of this book deals with the physical aspects of the land of
Appalachia, but the two following sections treat the Appalachians themselves.
Early settlers, the famous Hatfield-McCoy families, mountain legends, and the
lifestyle typical of children living in various sections of Appalachia are described.

454. Wigginton, Eliot, ed. **Foxfire Book.** New York: Doubleday, 1972. 384p.
$3.95pa. (7-12)
Articles selected from *Foxfire* magazine have been compiled to present a book of
text and pictures on the Appalachian people. Covers arts, crafts, folklore, and everyday customs of the region. *Foxfire Two* emphasizes spinning and weaving (Doubleday, 1973. $10.00; $4.50pa.); *Foxfire Three* was published in 1975 (Doubleday.
$4.95pa.).

Literature and Fiction Titles

455. Arnow, Harriette Simpson. **The Kentucky Trace.** New York: Knopf, 1974.
288p. $6.95. (9-12)
Leslie Collins was a soldier in the Revolutionary War. This story is one of history
and folklore of his life in the Appalachian Mountains.

456. Borland, Kathryn, and Helen Speicher. **Good-by to Stony Crick.** New
York: McGraw-Hill, 1975. 138p. $5.72. (4-6)
A boy from the Appalachian hills finds Chicago's urban culture a difficult adjustment from his countrified habits and culture. Rejected by his classmates and
teacher, he finds a friendship with another teacher, who is blind.

457. Caudill, Harry M. **The Senator from Slaughter County.** Boston, Mass.:
Little, Brown, 1974. 308p. $6.95. (7-12)
The story of a life of service to the Appalachian mountain people by a doctor-
turned-senator. The doctor's daily contacts present a vivid picture of Appalachian
conditions, lifestyles, and culture.

458. Caudill, Rebecca. **Did You Carry the Flag Today, Charlie?** New York:
Holt, 1966; Owlet Books, 1971. 94p. $1.65pa. (K-3)
Charlie longs to have the honor and prestige of carrying the flag for the group in his
kindergarten class. Other titles for this age group by the same author are *School
House in the Woods* (Holt, Rinehart & Winston, 1949. $3.07); *A Pocketful of
Cricket* (Holt, 1964. $3.50); and *Happy Little Family* (Holt, 1947. $2.95).

459. Chaffin, Lillie D. **Freeman.** New York: Macmillan, 1972. 152p. $4.95.
(5-8)
A 12-year-old boy lives with his grandparents in a small Appalachian coal mining
town. Told his parents were killed in an accident, he is not satisfied with this
explanation and searches for the truth. Another story set in a coal mining town in
Appalachia for this age group is the author's *John Henry McCoy* (Macmillan, 1971.
$4.95).

460. Clark, Billy C. **Sourwood Tales.** New York: Putnam's, 1968. 256p. $5.95.
(6-9)
A collection of 18 folktales based on mountain legend and superstitions of the
Appalachian people and communities.

461. Cleaver, Vera, and Bill Cleaver. **Where the Lilies Bloom.** Philadelphia, Pa.:
Lippincott, 1969. 174p. $3.95; 1974, pa. $1.25. (4-9)
Mary Call is a 14-year-old girl who tries to keep her family together after the father
dies. The children support themselves by wildcrafting—gathering medicinal plants
and herbs to sell—in this Appalachian community.

462. Credle, Ellis. **Down, Down the Mountain.** New York: Nelson, c1934, 1961.
$2.50. (K-3)
The poverty and lifestyle of many of the Appalachian mountaineer families are
typified in this story of Hetty and Hank and how they earn money for new shoes.
Another story for this age group by the author is *Johnny and His Mule* (Walck,
1946. $2.50).

463. Dykeman, Wilma. **Return the Innocent Earth.** New York: Holt, 1973.
428p. $8.95. (7-12)
Mountain feuds between families are the central theme of this novel. Other stories
about Appalachia by the author are *The Far Family* (Holt, 1966. $5.95) and *The
Tall Woman* (Holt, 1962. $5.50).

464. Hamner, Earl, Jr. **Spencer's Mountain.** New York: Dial Press, 1961, 1973.
247p. $6.95; $0.95pa. (7-12)
Clay-Boy takes the step away from the warmth and security of his large family and
Spencer's Mountain in Virginia to become a student at the university in Richmond,

Virginia. This story describes the Appalachian hill people and their patterns of living. Another popular title by this author is *The Homecoming* (Random, 1970. $4.95). The popular television series "The Waltons" is based on these titles by Hamner.

465.   Lenski, Lois. **Blue Ridge Billy**. Philadelphia, Pa.: Lippincott, c1946.
       203p. $5.82. Repr. ed. New York: Dell, 1967. $0.75. (4-6)
A colorful story of the music, arts, and culture of the Appalachian mountain people is told through the adventures of Billy Honeycutt and his fiddle.

466.   Miles, Miska. **Hoagie's Rifle-Gun**. Illus. by John Schoenherr. Boston,
       Mass.: Little, Brown, 1970. 40p. $5.95. (1-4)
A picture of the hill people's ways of life and how the poor families of Appalachia need to shoot their daily meat. Hoagie is an expert shot and when Old Bob, a familiar bobcat, beats Hoagie to a rabbit dinner, he takes a shot at him.

467.   Ogburn, Charlton. **Winespring Mountain**. New York: Morrow, 1973. 252p.
       $6.95. (7-12)
A story set in the coal mines of West Virginia and the conflict between generations. A son learns about life the hard way working in the mines.

468.   Scarborough, Dorothy. **A Song Catcher in Southern Mountains**. New York:
       AMS Press, 1937. 476p. $10.00. (7-12)
Subtitled *American Folk Songs of British Ancestry*, the author relates her experiences collecting this anthology of songs from among the Appalachians. Their contents reveal the British background of many highlanders, as well as their ideals and sentiments.

469.   Stephens, Mary Jo. **Witch of the Cumberlands**. Illus. by Arvis Stewart.
       Boston, Mass.: Houghton Mifflin, 1974. 243p. $4.95. (4-9)
Suspense, mystery, and a witch are a part of this Appalachian mountain story. Three youngsters stumble across a clue to an old mining mystery in this exciting story for the middle grades.

470.   Still, James. **Way Down Yonder on Troublesome Creek: Appalachian
       Riddles and Rusties**. Illus. by Janet McCaffery. New York: Putnam's,
       1974. unp. $3.96. (3-6)
Unfamiliar terms and sayings native to the mountain people, along with popular Appalachian riddles and jokes, are collected here.

471.   Stuart, Jesse. **A Jesse Stuart Reader**. New York: McGraw-Hill, 1963.
       310p. $4.95. (7-12)
A collection of poems, stories, and biographical sketches about the hill people of Appalachia. Another collection of short stories on Appalachian peoples, their traditions, background and culture is Stuart's *Come Back to the Farm* (McGraw-Hill, 1971. $6.95).

472.   Troughton, Joanna. **The Little Mohee: An Appalachian Ballad.** New York: Dutton, 1971. unp. $4.95. (1-3)
A Kentucky mountain ballad of Little Mohee, an Indian girl whose lover abandons her for his true love across the sea, but then returns to her. Words and musical score included. Can be sung to the tune of "On Top of Old Smokey."

473.   Williams, Vinnie. **Walk Egypt.** New York: Viking, 1964. 256p. $4.95. (7-12)
After her father dies, a young girl must bear the burden of raising the other children in the family. The story is set in the foothills of the Appalachian Mountains in northern Georgia, and is a vivid picture of "hillbilly" folklore and customs.

Audiovisual Materials

474.   **Appalachia: Rich Land, Poor People.** 16mm film, 59 min., b&w. National Educational Television. Released by Indiana University Audio-Visual Center, 1969. $10.00 (rental). (7-12)
Describes the land and people of Appalachia, with emphasis on the poverty, lack of employment, traditional ways of life.

475.   **Appalachian Heritage.** 16mm film, 55 min., color. Avco Corp. Released by Avco Embassy Pictures, 1968. $20.00 (rental). (6-12)
Life in the Appalachian region is described. Emphasized are the living and social conditions.

476.   **Appalachian Genesis.** 16mm film, 30 min., color. Appalshop Productions, 1971. $300.00; $45.00 (rental). (7-12)
Sponsored by the Appalachian Regional Commission, this film describes the social, economic, and political situation in Appalachia. It interviews young people discussing the coal mines, educational and job opportunities, recreational and health facilities, etc., available there.

477.   **Appalachian Woodcrafters.** 16mm film, 10 min., color, sd. Rockwell Company, 1970. $10.00 (rental). (6-12)
The woodworkers of Appalachia are seen in this excellent portrait of their art and craftsmanship.

478.   **Aunt Arie.** 16mm film, 18 min., sd., color, teacher's guide. Encyclopaedia Britannica Educational Corp. $220.00. (5-12)
An old mountain woman narrates the story of her life in North Carolina's Blue Ridge Mountains.

479.   **Aunt Molly Jackson.** 1 record (33 1/3rpm). Rounder Records. $3.50. (K-12)
Aunt Molly has recorded typical Appalachian music, and her songs provide a musical history of the area.

480. **The Blue Ridge: America's First Frontier**. 1 filmstrip with record (or cassette), teacher's guide. Lyceum. $18.00; with cassette, $21.00. (4-12)
The crafts, customs and culture of the Blue Ridge Mountain people are described and pictured.

481. **Coal Miner: Frank Jackson**. 16mm film, 12 min., b&w. Appalshop Productions, 1971. $120.00; $20.00 (rental). (5-12)
A biographical portrait of a man who has spent his life in the Appalachian coal mines.

482. **Foxfire**. 16mm film, 22 min., sd., color. McGraw-Hill, 1974. $8.50 (rental). (7-12)
Local history of the Appalachian region is explored by a school class in Rabun Gap, Georgia, with their English teacher, B. Eliot Wigginton. They developed a quarterly magazine about Appalachia called *Foxfire*.

483. **In the Good Old Fashioned Way**. 16mm film, 30 min., color. Appalshop Productions, 1973. $300.00; $30.00 (rental). (7-12)
Captures the impact and influence of the religion of the Appalachian people.

484. **In Ya Blood**. 16mm film, 20 min., b&w. Appalshop Productions, 1971. $200.00; $20.00 (rental). (7-12)
In this story a young boy must decide whether to work in the mines to buy a car that would impress his high school friends or whether to go to college and break the bondage to the mines that has enslaved his ancestors for generations.

485. **Judge Wooten and Coon-on-a-Log**. 16mm film, 10 min., b&w. Appalshop Productions, 1970. $100.00; $15.00 (rental). (K-12)
Appalachian customs and culture are depicted in this film record of a Fourth of July coon-on-a-log contest and a portrait of the typical mountaineer personality, Judge George Wooten, in a discussion of life in Appalachia.

486. **The Kentuckians. The Solid Bluegrass Sound of the Kentuckians**. 1 record. Melodeon MLP; distr.: Biograph. $5.98. (K-12)
Traditional bluegrass music of family songs, patriotic numbers and white gospel.

487. **Life in Rural America**. 5 filmstrips, 5 records (or cassettes), teacher's guide. National Geographic Society, 1973. $67.50/set. (5-12)
Appalachian life is seen through the eyes of a coal miner who can no longer work because of the black lung disease. Includes *The Family Farm*; *Cowboys*; *Coal Miners of Appalachia*; *Harvesters of the Golden Plains*; *Settlers on Alaska's Frontier*.

488. **The Mountain People**. 16mm film, 24 min., color. Wombat Prods. $315.00; $31.50 (rental). (9-12)
This Blue Ribbon award-winning film at the 17th Annual American Film Festival (1975) sponsored by the Educational Film Library Association is a documentary about the poor in Appalachia.

489.   **Old Time Mountain Guitar.** 33 1/3rmp record. Country Records, 1974.
       $4.98. (K-12)
The history of mountain music with typical selections of the Appalachian region are
presented. Includes the "Knoxville Blues" and the "Logan County Blues."

490.   **The Ramsey Trade Fair.** 16mm film, 20 min., color. Appalshop Produc-
       tions, 1974. $250.00; $25.00 (rental). (5-12)
A trade fair in a small coal mining town is filmed, showing the social nature of the
event and the mountain style of preaching and music that are a part of Appalachian
culture.

491.   **Todd: Growing Up in Appalachia.** 16mm film, 13 min., color. Learning
       Corporation of America, 1970. $7.00 (rental). (4-9)
Todd finds a purse with food stamps in this story of Appalachian children and
families. Because of his family's poverty and need, he is faced with a moral dilemma
when deciding the right thing to do. Poverty, social conditions, and the customs of
the daily routines and activities of these families are revealed through this story.

492.   **Tomorrow's People.** 16mm film, 25 min., color. Appalshop Productions,
       1973. $275.00; $30.00 (rental). (5-12)
Mountain culture in music and pictures is presented through old fashioned photographs. Dulcimer music, fiddlers, and square dancing comprise the typical scenes in
this portrait of Appalachian life.

ARAB AMERICANS

Non-Fiction Titles: History, Culture, Sociology, Biography

493.   Aswad, Barbara C. **Arabic Speaking Communities in American Cities.** New
       York: Center for Migration Studies of New York, Inc., and the Association
       of Arab-American University Graduates, Inc., 1974. 191p. $5.95pa. (10-12)
Arab-American communities are compared for language speaking, social status,
marriage outside of the ethnic group, and overall amount of Americanization or
acculturation to the society at large.

494.   Elkholy, Abdo A. **The Arab Moslems in the United States: Religions and
       Assimilation.** New Haven, Conn.: College and University Press, 1966.
       176p. $5.00; $1.95pa. (10-12, T)
This study compares the widely differing Arab American communities in Detroit,
Michigan, and Toledo, Ohio. Emphasis here is on the role religion has played in
isolation within the ethnic community or in contacts outside of the community.
A historical summary of the Arabs in America is also given.

495.   Hagopian, Elaine C., ed. **The Arab Americans: Studies in Assimilation.**
       Wilmette, Ill.: Medina University Press International, 1969. 111p. (10-12, T)

An extensive study on the Arab Americans who have settled in the United States and Canada, comparing them to immigrants from other ethnic groups with respect to the rate and degree of their adjustment and assimilation into American society.

496.   Hitti, Philip K. **The Syrians in America.** New York: George H. Doran Co., 1924. 139p. (10-12)

Traces the immigration of Syrians to America, and their experiences in the new homeland. The work is outdated but gives a good historical background of the problems of the Arab community, the social and educational patterns, and the churches in the Syrian communities.

497.   Kayal, Philip M., and Joseph M. Kayal. **The Syrians and Lebanese in America.** Boston, Mass.: Twayne, 1975. 260p. $12.50. (9-12)

With emphasis on religion and assimilation, this work begins with a discussion of Arab Christianity and a brief history of Syria and Lebanon in the Middle East. It examines reasons for immigration, and the Arab experience in America with respect to acculturation, group identity, and survival. A selected bibliography is included; indexed.

498.   Rizk, Salom. **Syrian Yankee.** New York: Doubleday, 1943. 317p. $4.95. (7-12)

A Syrian orphan writes of his experiences as an immigrant to America. Emphasis is on his problems and the difficulties of adjustment to a new life style and homeland.

Audiovisual Materials

499.   **Aladdin and the Magic Lamp.** 1 filmstrip, 1 record. Imperial Film Co., 1969. (2-6)

Based on a story from the *Arabian Nights*, this Arabian tale is a classic for children.

500.   **Ali Baba and the Forty Thieves.** 1 filmstrip, 1 record. Imperial Film Co., 1969. (2-6)

Another Arabian tale from the *Arabian Nights*, the story of Ali Baba is a favorite for children. This story has also been produced as a motion picture (McGraw-Hill, 1968). It is accompanied by a teacher's guide to help present background information about this story of Arabia. The film is 28 minutes, color, and sound.

501.   **Rajeb's Reward.** 1 filmstrip, 1 record. Jam Handy Organization, 1968. (2-6)

An Arabian fairy tale that illustrates the color and culture of the Arabian people. The story can be used to introduce a unit on Arabia, a study of Arabs in America for social studies, or as an isolated language arts or literature unit.

ARMENIAN AMERICANS

Teaching Methodology and Curriculum Materials

502.   Stone, Frank A. **Armenian Studies for Secondary Students: A Curriculum Guide.** Storrs: University of Connecticut, 1974. 55p. $5.15. ED 091303. (T)

A guide designed for a two- to six-week course for high school students studying Armenian history and culture. Its aim is to foster understanding of Armenian American peoples, their folklore, literature, music, culture, their religious, political and educational institutions, and their background history. The guide consists of the following seven units: 1) The Armenians in North America; 2) Sketches of Armenian History; 3) Armenian Mythology; 4) Voices of Fiction and Poetry; 5) Armenian Christianity; 6) Armenian Fine Arts; and 7) Armenian Political Aims. Includes instructional and resource materials for each unit.

Non-Fiction Titles: History, Culture, Sociology, Biography

503.   Chopourian, Giragos. **Our Armenian Christian Heritage.** Philadelphia, Pa.: Armenian Evangelical Union of America, 1962. 122p. $1.50. (7-9)

This history is designed to introduce Armenian youth to their cultural background and heritage. Covers the ancient Armenian people to the twentieth century immigration of Armenians to the United States and other countries. Emphasis is on the establishment of Christianity as the national religion of Armenia, the Armenians' struggle to preserve their religious beliefs and values, and the growth of the Armenian Protestant Church in America.

504.   Hogogrian, Rachel. **The Armenian Cookbook.** Illus. by Nonny Hogogrian. New York: Atheneum, 1971. 152p. $7.95. (4-12)

Recipes that have been favorites of Armenian American families. Includes a glossary of Armenian terms and a list of food supply sources for Near Eastern imports. However, most ingredients can be purchased locally.

505.   Malcom, M. Vartan. **The Armenians in America.** Boston, Mass.: The Pilgrim Press, 1919; San Francisco: R&E Research Associates, 1969. 142p. $8.00. (9-12)

Emphasis is on the Armenian as an immigrant and a contributor to American society and culture. A brief background history, including reasons for emigration, is included. Armenian-American religion, education, socioeconomic conditions, and their foreign language press in America are described.

506.   Mohakian, Charles. **History of Armenians in California.** San Francisco: R&E Research Associates, 1974. 92p. $8.00. (10-12)

This history of the Armenian communities in California describes their religious, social, and political institutions and organizations. Covers also the adjustments, problems, and adaptations to American society, and discusses economic and political patterns. Illustrations and maps included. This work is a reprint of the author's 1935 thesis.

507. Papajian, Rev. Sarkis. **A Brief History of Armenia.** Fresno, Calif.:
      Evangelical Union of North America, 1974. 134p. $2.00. (10-12)
A chronological view of Armenian history, the reasons for emigration, religious
customs, national and cultural characteristics.

508. Tashjian, James H. **The Armenians of the United States and Canada.** Boston,
      Mass.: Armenian Youth Federation, 1947; repr. ed., San Francisco: R&E
      Research Associates, 1970. 62p. $5.00. (9-12)
Part I covers the first immigration of Armenians in America, described from the
Colonial Records of Virginia, subsequent immigrations, and the dispersion of
Armenians in the United States and Canada. Part II examines Armenian-American
life with respect to occupations, prominent Armenians, political party preferences,
organizations, religion, education, cultural activities and outstanding contributions.

509. Yeretzian, Aram S. **A History of Armenian Immigration to America with
      Special Reference to Los Angeles.** San Francisco: R&E Research
      Associates, 1974. 78p. $8.00. (9-12, T)
A reprint of the author's 1923 thesis on Armenian immigration history. Special
attention is given to the Armenian community in Los Angeles and the process of
acculturation, adjustment, and other problems of the community members.

Literature and Fiction Titles

510. Cretan, Gladys Yessayan. **Because I Promised.** Illus. by Robert L. Jefferson.
      Nashville, Tenn.: Abingdon Press, 1970. 56p. $3.50. (1-3)
Small Sarkis resents being called "small" and tries to prove he is older and wiser.
Tending a flock of sheep for his friend leads him into a series of exciting adventures
and provides a picture of rural or peasant life in Armenia.

511. Cretan, Gladys Yessayan. **Sunday for Sona.** Illus. by Barbara Flynn. New
      York: Lothrop, 1973. 32p. $3.78. (2-4)
This is the story of Sona and her Armenian family living in San Francisco. Sona's
great desire to go sailing is in conflict with her family's ideals. When Sona sneaks
away with a friend to go sailing she is in for a few surprises.

512. Hogogrian, Nonny, reteller. **One Fine Day.** New York: Macmillan, 1971.
      unp. $4.95. (K-3)
An Armenian folktale in which an Armenian peasant woman chops off the tail of
the fox who steals her milk.

513. Hoogasian-Villa, Susie. **One Hundred Armenian Tales and Their Folkloris-
      tic Relevance.** Detroit, Mich.: Wayne State University, 1966. 602p. $11.95.
      (6-12, T)
Many of the stories in this collection are concerned with the Armenian ethnic community in Detroit, and their problems and experiences of adjustment and acculturation to American society.

514.	Hovhaness, Alan. **Armenian Folk Songs.** New York: C. F. Peters, 1963. 11p. (3-12)

A collection of 12 Armenian folk songs set to music for the piano or in instrumental settings. A useful addition to the social science curriculum as a motivating activity or introduction to the unit; can be used to teach folk dancing in the physical education curriculum.

515.	Saroyan, William. **My Name Is Aram.** New York: Harcourt, 1940. 220p. $3.95; Dell, $0.75pa. (7-12)

Short sketches and recollections of an Armenian-American who spent his youth in an Armenian community of Fresno, California.

516.	Tashjian, Virginia A. **Once There Was and Was Not.** Boston, Mass.: Little, Brown, 1966. 83p. $4.02. (K-4)

These folk tales are based on stories by H. Toumanian and are illustrated by Nonny Hogogrian, an Armenian-American artist. They reflect the life of the Armenian people. A similar title by this author and illustrator is *Three Apples from Heaven* (Little, Brown, 1971. $4.50) for just slightly older children.

Audiovisual Materials

517.	**The Armenian National Choral Society of Boston Presents a Concert of Armenian Music.** 1 record, 33 1/3 rpm. Armenian National Choral Society. (4-12)

Siranoush Der-Manuelian conducts sacred choruses and also folk songs sung in Armenian. Some Armenian dance music is also included.

518.	**The Heart of a Nation.** 16mm film, 30 min., color, sd. Armenian Relief Committee, 1973.

Features the historical development and present activities of the Armenian Relief Society.

ASIAN AMERICANS

See also **Chinese Americans, East-Indian Americans, Filipino Americans, Japanese Americans, Korean Americans.**

Reference Sources

519.	Duphiney, Lorna. **Oriental Americans: An Annotated Bibliography.** New York: ERIC Information Retrieval Center on the Disadvantaged, Teachers College, Columbia University, 1972. 24p. free. (T)

Lists materials on Oriental Americans published since 1960. Emphasis is on the social, economic, political, and educational problems and achievements of the Chinese and Japanese in the United States.

520. Engelberg, Linda, and Joan Hori. **Ethnic Groups in the United States: A Bibliography of Books and Articles of Groups in Hawaii and on the Mainland: Chinese, Filipinos, Hawaiians, Japanese, Koreans, Samoans.** Honolulu: University of Hawaii Libraries, 1972. 14p. free to libraries.
A checklist of the holdings on Asian Americans in the Sinclair Undergraduate Library, University of Hawaii.

521. Fujimoto, Isao. **Asians in America: A Selected Bibliography.** Davis, Calif.: University of California, Davis, Asian American Studies Division, 1971. 295p. (T)
An annotated bibliography on the Chinese, Japanese, and Filipinos in the United States. Over 800 entries are arranged alphabetically by author in two sections: books and articles.

522. Kitano, Harry H. L., comp. **Asians in America: A Selected Bibliography for Use in Social Work Education.** New York: Council on Social Work Education, 1971. 79p. $3.00pa. (T)
Chinese, Japanese, Korean, and Filipino Americans in the United States are covered in this annotated bibliography. Although much of the listing is too scholarly for use in public schools, the subject arrangement under each nationality group isolates useful studies on immigration, race and ethnic relations, and, for the Japanese, a section of titles on the evacuation and relocation; this arrangement could be helpful in junior and senior high schools.

523. U.S. Bureau of the Census. **Census of Population: 1970.** Series PC (2). **Subject Reports.** Series PC (2) 1–G. **Japanese, Chinese, and Filipinos in the U.S.** Washington, D.C.: Government Printing Office, 1973. 116p. $2.60. (9-12)
Data are provided on the Japanese, Chinese, and Filipinos in the United States by regions, states, cities, and rural areas. Mentions some socioeconomic statistics on the Hawaiians and Koreans as well.

524. U.S. Bureau of the Census. **Reports.** (For school students.) No. 13. **We the Asian Americans.** Washington, D.C.: Government Printing Office, 1973. 13p. $0.40. (5-12)
Includes statistics, information, progress, and problems of the Asians in America.

Teaching Methodology and Curriculum Materials

525. Dunn, Lynn P. **Asian Americans: A Study Guide and Source Book.** San Francisco: R&E Research Associates, 1974. 111p. $6.00. (9-12, T)
One of a four-volume series on American minorities (Blacks, Chicanos, Native Americans, and Asians) treating the themes of identity, conflict, and integration/ nationalism. Presents a chronological historical outline with notes and sources for further interdisciplinary reading. Includes a glossary of terms helpful in studying the Asian Americans and a bibliography.

Non-Fiction Titles: History, Culture, Sociology, Biography

526. Chan, J., *et al.*, eds. **Aiieee! An Anthology of Asian American Writers.**
      Washington, D.C.: Howard University Press, 1974. 200p. $7.95. (9-12)
A collection of writings by 17 Asian-American writers. Emphasis is on Chinese and
Japanese.

527. Goldberg, George. **East Meets West: The Story of the Chinese and Japanese
      in California.** New York: Harcourt Brace Jovanovich, 1970. 136p. $5.95.
      (7-12)
Traces the history of the Oriental in California with emphasis on the prejudice,
exclusion laws, segregation, and World War II evacuation of the Japanese. Goldberg also compares the adjustment and assimilation of the two groups.

528. Holland, Ruth. **The Oriental Immigrants in America.** New York: Grosset
      & Dunlap, 1969. 61p. $2.69. (4-6)
The Oriental groups in America are described, covering reasons for their immigration
to America and the discriminatory laws and treatment they endured.

529. Ignacio, Lemuel F. **Asian Americans and Pacific Islanders.** San Jose, Calif.:
      Philipino Development Associates, 1975. 150p. $6.95. (7-12)
Asian Americans and immigrants from the Pacific Islands are studied here with
respect to the reasons for their arrival in the United States, their experience, living
conditions, and treatment.

530. Lee, Ivy. **Profiles of Asians in Sacramento, Final Report.** Washington, D.C.:
      Department of Health, Education and Welfare, 1973. 65p. $3.29.
      ED 086774. (T)
This study attempts to 1) provide more data on the Asians, 2) determine social
services available, 3) discover what Asians consider the needs of their community,
4) compare attitudes and values across generations. Families of Chinese, Japanese,
and Filipino background were interviewed.

531. Melendy, H. Brett. **The Oriental Americans.** Boston, Mass.: Twayne, 1972.
      235p. $7.95; $2.95pa. (9-12)
An overview of the Chinese and Japanese immigrants in Hawaii and on the U.S. mainland. Covers their main contributions and the racial discrimination they experienced
as a group.

532. Palmer, Albert W. **Orientals in American Life.** New York: Friendship Press;
      repr. ed. San Francisco: R&E Research Associates, 1972. 212p. $10.00.
      (9-12, T)
Treats the Chinese, Japanese, Filipinos, and Hawaiians. For each group is given a
brief history of immigration, motives for it, and a record of their experience in the
United States. A breakdown of nationalities represented in Hawaii at the time is
given. As a missionary, the author emphasizes the role of the church in the acculturation of each group. Brief annotated book list and index provided.

533.   **Report to the Governor on Discrimination against Asians.** Olympia, Wash.:
       Washington State Commission on Asian-American Affairs, 1973. 124p.
       $3.29. ED 094068. (T)
Describes a public hearing conducted on March 3, 1973, by the Washington State
Asian American Advisory Council bringing attention to racism against Asians.
Testimony of experiences and observations was heard from Chinese, Filipino,
Japanese, and Korean Americans.

534.   Ritter, E., *et al.*, eds. **Our Oriental Americans.** New York, McGraw-
       Hill, 1965. 104p. $2.08 text ed. (10-12)
Describes the experiences of Orientals in the United States as immigrants—their
problems, areas of concentration, racial discrimination against them, and social and
economic conditions and opportunities. Main emphasis is on the Chinese.

535.   Tachiki, Amy, *et al.* **Roots—An Asian American Reader.** Los Angeles:
       University of California at Los Angeles, 1971. 345p. $6.95. (9-12)
A collection of essays relative to the Asian American experience. *Roots II—An All
New Asian American Reader* (1975. $5.50) is a reflection of the changing develop-
ment, problems, and directions of Asian communities in the United States.

Audiovisual Materials

536.   **Asian American People and Places.** 9 foldout stories with box. Japanese
       American Curriculum Project, Inc., 1975. $9.00. (3-6)
A collection of nine foldout stories with black and white photography depicting
Asian Americans and their experience in the United States.

537.   **Asian Fables.** 6 filmstrips, 6 records. AVI Associates, 1969; made by
       Joshua Tree Productions. (3-6)
Asian fables contained in this set are: *The Man Who Cut the Cinnamon Tree*;
Kantjil the Mouse Deer; *The Magic Leaf*; *One-Inch-Fellow*; *Koblookata*; and *The
Sandalmaker.*

538.   **Asian Folk Tales.** 6 filmstrips, 6 records, teacher's guide. Joshua Tree
       Productions. Released by International Book Corp., 1969.
These Asian folk tales depict the Asian customs and culture. Includes tales from
China, Indonesia, Vietnam, Japan, and India.

539.   **Chinese, Korean and Japanese Dance.** 16mm film, 28 min., color. Prod:
       Asia Society; Penn State AV Services. $11.20 (rental).
Chinese, Korean, and Japanese dances as performed in Asia and by Asian Americans
are filmed.

540.   **Families of Asia.** 6 filmstrips, 6 discs (or cassettes). Encyclopaedia
       Britannica Educational Corp., 1975. $83.95/set. (4-9)
Titles included are: *The Families of Hong Kong*; *Family of Bangladesh*; *Family of
India*; *Family of Japan*; *Family of Java*; *Family of Thailand.* Although these

selections are not about Asians in America, they are excellent background materials for understanding Asian cultural values and traditions.

541.   **Japanese-Americans and Chinese Americans.** 1 filmstrip, 1 record. Warren Schloat Productions, 1968. (5-10)
Discrimination against Japanese and Chinese in the United States is discussed.

542.   **Pieces of a Dream.** 16mm film, 30 min., color, sd. Visual Communications, n.d. $400.00; $25.00 (rental). (7-12)
An overview of the problems of Asian Americans in California, particularly in the field of agriculture.

AUSTRIAN AMERICANS. *See* **German Americans.**

BALTIC AMERICANS
(includes Estonians, Latvians, Lithuanians)

Reference Sources

543.   Balys, Jonas, comp. **Lithuania and Lithuanians: A Select Bibliography.** New York: Praeger, 1961. 190p. $5.00. (T)
A bibliography of 1,182 entries based on the Library of Congress holdings of materials on the Lithuanians and Lithuania. Arrangement is by subject; many publications are in English. Author and title index.

544.   **Encyclopedia Lituanica.** Boston, Mass.: Juozas Kapocius, 1970– . In progress. (7-12, T)
Four volumes were published (A–R inclusive) between 1970 and 1975 on Lithuanian history in Lithuania and America. Covers the land, the nation, and the state, major historical events, changes in social and economic structure, customs, religion, culture, language, folklore, literature, art, music, biography, organizations, and Lithuanian communities abroad. Arrangement is alphabetical by subject. Information on Lithuanians in America can be found under various headings, such as American, Amerika, Baltimore, Boston, Chicago (and other major cities), emigration, Lithuanian Roman Catholic Federation of America, Lithuanian American Council, etc.

545.   Karklis, Maruta, Liga Streips, and Laimonis Streips. **The Latvians in America 1640-1973: A Chronology and Fact Book.** Dobbs Ferry, N.Y.: Oceana, 1974. 151p. $6.00. (7-12)
A chronology of the Latvian Americans' experience in America with selected documents included. Covers from the settlement of Latvians in Delaware and Pennsylvania in 1640 to the 1970s. The appendices include statistical data on Latvians in the

United States, a list of Latvian American organizations, and a selected bibliography. The bibliography is arranged in the following categories: history, language and literature, articles, bibliographies, miscellaneous, Latvian periodicals. Name index.

546.   Parming, Marju Rink, and Tonu Parming. **A Bibliography of English-Language Sources on Estonia: Periodicals, Bibliographies, Pamphlets, and Books.** New York: Estonian Learned Society in America, 1974. 72p. $5.50. (9-12, T)

A list of 662 entries on sources useful in Baltic studies programs. Arrangement is by 14 major subject categories. Periodicals are covered in a separate section. Author index and short-title index included.

547.   Pennar, Joan, *et al.* **The Estonians in America, 1627-1975: A Chronology and Fact Book.** Dobbs Ferry, N.Y.: Oceana, 1975. 150p. $6.00. (7-12)

Part One is a chronology divided into three major sections: 1) The "Old Immigrants," The Period until 1922; 2) The Interwar Years 1922-1939 and the War Years 1940-1945; 3) The Arrival of the Refugees and Beyond: 1945-1975. A collection of documents relevant to Estonian American history comprises the second major part, and the appendix is a third section. The latter consists of six tables of Estonian population data, community centers, and Estonian-American organizations. Bibliographical aids and a name index are included.

Non-Fiction Titles: History, Culture, Sociology, Biography

548.   Armonas, Barbara. **Leave Your Tears in Moscow.** Philadelphia, Pa.: Lippincott, 1961. 222p. $3.95.

When a Lithuanian-American couple decided to visit the land of their heritage in the 1930s, they were unable to leave Lithuania to return to the United States as a family. Father and daughter were able to leave, but were not reunited with the wife and son for nearly 20 years, after years of effort and expense in attempting to seek the release of Mrs. Armonas and her son. She recounts those years of terror and hardship waiting in Lithuania.

549.   **Aspects of Estonian Culture.** Edited by Evald Uuslales. London: Boreas Publishing Co., 1961. 332p. (T)

Estonian culture is described in this collection of essays covering art, architecture, intellectual life, religion, and other topics. One, by Arvo Horm, is entitled "Estonians in the Free World."

550.   Greene, Victor. **For God and Country: The Rise of Polish and Lithuanian Ethnic Consciousness in America 1860-1910.** Madison: State Historical Society of Wisconsin, 1975. 202p. $17.50. (9-12, T)

Lithuanian Americans are examined in this work covering the Poles and Lithuanians with respect to their history, immigration, identity, and ultimate ethnic awareness. Emphasis is on the latter part of the nineteenth and early twentieth centuries.

551.   Kucas, Antanas. **Lithuanians in America.** Trans. by Joseph Boley. Boston,
         Mass.: Encyclopedia Lituanica, 1975. 349p. $6.00. (7-12)
This survey of Lithuanians in America covers Lithuanian background in the homeland, reasons for immigration, settlements in the East and Midwest, Lithuanian
parishes, the press, and Lithuanian organizations (religious, political, cultural,
economic, charitable). Illustrated with numerous photographs. Indexed.

552.   Raud, Villibald, comp. **Estonia: A Reference Book.** New York: Nordic
         Press, 1953. 158p. (7-12)
A history of Estonia and the Estonian culture and social and economic development.
Also covers the Estonian press, publications, arts and academic situation, organizations, religious preferences, educational facilities. A chapter deals with Estonians
in the United States and exile in other countries.

553.   Sirvaitis, Casimir Peter. **Religious Folkways in Lithuania and Their Conser-
         vation among the Lithuanian Immigrants in the United States.** Washington,
         D.C.: The Catholic University of America, 1952. 49p.
A study on acculturation among Lithuanian immigrants with special attention to
family festivals, devotions, church feasts and holy days, and other religious folkways
among the Lithuanians in the United States.

554.   Soby, James Thrall. **Ben Shahn—Paintings.** New York: Braziller, 1963.
         144p. $17.50. (7-12)
A biography of a famous Lithuanian artist, with illustrations of some of his well-
known paintings and other works. A similar title by the author is *Ben Shahn, His
Graphic Art* (Braziller, 1957. $12.50).

Literature and Fiction Titles

555.   Huggins, Edward, reteller. **Blue and Green Wonders and Other Latvian
         Tales.** Illus. by Owen Wood. New York: Simon & Schuster, 1971. 128p.
         $5.95. (3-6)
Ten Latvian stories plus a section at the end describing Latvian customs and culture.

556.   Sinclair, Upton. **The Jungle.** New York: Doubleday, 1906; repr. ed., New
         York: New American Library, 1973. 413p. $8.50; $0.60pa. (9-12)
The hero of this story of a Lithuanian immigrant's life in Chicago's stockyards
district is Jurgis Rudkus. Set at the turn of the century, this story tells of how he
became a convert to the ideals of socialism when he was unable to cope with the
economic and other problems and adjustments of immigrant life.

557.   Yakstis, Frank. **Translations by Frank Yakstis of Lithuanian Poetry.**
         Ozone Park, New York: Association of Lithuanian Workers, 1968.
         111p. (9-12)
Lithuanian life and culture is reflected in these poems translated by Frank
Yakstis.

558.   Zobarskas, Stepas. **Lithuanian Folk Tales.** 2nd enl. ed. College Park, Md.:
         University of Maryland, 1959. 240p. $4.50. (3-12)

A collection of popular Lithuanian folktales steeped in the culture and tradition of that country. Another collection compiled by the author is *Selected Lithuanian Short Stories* (Voyages, 1959. $5.00).

BASQUE AMERICANS

Reference Sources

559.   McCall, Grant. **Bibliography of Materials Relating to Basque Americans.** Reno: University of Nevada, 1968. 21p. (9-12, T)
This bibliography includes writings of a popular nature for general reading, as well as scholarly research and studies. It was compiled at the Desert Research Institute of the University of Nevada.

560.   Zane, Betsey A. **General Bibliography of English-Language Articles Relating to Basque History and Culture.** Reno: Basque Studies Program, University of Nevada, 1974. free. (9-12, T)
A comprehensive bibliography of periodical articles on Basque history and culture. Includes materials suitable for students at the elementary and secondary levels.

Teaching Methodology and Curriculum Materials

561.   Starrett, Gloria M., and June C. Gronert. **Basque Studies Curriculum Guide.** Reno: College of Education, University of Nevada, 1974. (T)
The College of Education at the University of Nevada sponsored a summer school course in teaching ethnic studies. This curriculum guide was developed for the fifth and sixth grades.

Non-Fiction Titles: History, Culture, Sociology, Biography

562.   Blaud, Henry C. **The Basques.** San Francisco: R&E Research Associates, 1974. 95p. $8.00. (9-12)
Studies the Basque community in the United States from a sociological perspective. Also includes a history of the experience of this ethnic group. A reprint of the author's master's thesis from the College of the Pacific (1957).

563.   Douglass, William A., and Jon Bilbao. **Amerikanauk: The Basques in the New World.** Reno: University of Nevada Press, 1975. (9-12)
A history of Basque immigration and the sheepherding communities they established in the northwestern United States. Another title by Douglass and Milton Da Silva is *Basque Nationalism* (University of Nevada, Basque Studies Program, 1971).

564.   Gallop, Rodney. **A Book of the Basques.** Illus. by Marjorie Gallop. Reno: University of Nevada Press, 1970. 298p. $7.00. (9-12)

An extensive examination of the Basques' language, arts, customs, folk literature, sports and dances. Some selected Basque music and songs, maps, and a bibliography are included.

565.   Laxalt, Robert. **Sweet Promised Land.** New York: Harper, 1957. 176p. (5-12)
A biographical portrait of the author's father, a Basque-American shepherd in Nevada, and his longings for his homeland in the Pyrenees.

566.   McCall, Grant Edwin. **Basque-Americans and a Sequential Theory of Migration and Adaptation.** San Francisco: R&E Research Associates, 1973. 86p. $7.00. (T)
Studies Basque immigration to the United States and adjustment and acculturation of Basque people to the American way of life. The work is a reprint of the author's 1968 thesis.

567.   McCullough, Sister Flavia M. **The Basques in the Northwest.** San Francisco: R&E Research Associates, 1974. 57p. $7.00. (9-12)
An overview of the Basque group in the northwestern part of the United States with emphasis on their unique culture, customs, and contributions. The work is a reprint of the author's 1945 thesis from the University of Portland.

568.   Reno Zazpiak-Bat Basque Club. **From the Basque Kitchen.** Reno: The Society, 1973. (4-12)
A cookbook of favorite Basque recipes sold at the annual North American Basque Festival sponsored by the Zazpiak-Bat Basque Club. Useful as a supplementary activity when studying the Basques as an ethnic group.

Fiction Titles

569.   Clark, Ann Nolan. **Year Walk.** New York: Viking, 1975. 208p. $6.95. (5-9)
Set in the early twentieth century in Idaho, this is the story of Kepa, a Basque shepherd boy. It provides a colorful picture of the Spanish Basques in America.

570.   Isasi, Mirim. **Basque Girl.** Illus. by Kurt Wiese. Glendale, Calif.: Griffin-Patterson, 1940. 249p. (5-9)
Basque life in the United States is seen through this story of a young Basque girl and the social and cultural customs of her environment. A similar title by the author and Melcena Burns Denny is *White Stars of Freedom* (Whitman, 1942), in which a young Basque American relates his adventures of migrating to California.

Audiovisual Materials

571.   **Basque Songs.** 1 record. (K-12)
Available from Louis M. Irigary, 155 Juniper Hill, Reno, Nevada.

572. **The Basques: Euzkadi.** 1 record. Folkway Records. (K-12)
Songs and dances of the Basque people. Some Christmas songs are included.
Sung and played by Juan Ônatibia.

BLACK AMERICANS

Reference Sources

Reference Guides and Bibliographies

573. Abajian, James, comp. **Blacks & Their Contributions to the American West: A Bibliography & Union List of Library Holdings through 1970.** Boston, Mass.: G. K. Hall, 1974. 487p. $29.50. (9-12, T)
Provides a listing of 4,300 sources of information on Blacks and their activities in the American West. Arrangement is by classification; includes books, articles, pamphlets, manuscript collections, archival holdings, and museum artifacts. Much attention is given to California and the Watts riot of 1965.

574. Atlanta University. **Black Culture Collection Catalog: United States Section . . . The Black Experience in America since the 17th Century.** Atlanta, Ga.: Bell & Howell Co., Micro Photo Division, 1974. 3 vols.
A Black library (on microform) of 6,000 titles. Most of the materials were originally from the collection of Henry P. Slaughter, a Black bibliophile. Volume 1 covers authors; Volume 2, titles; Volume 3, subjects.

575. Baker, Augusta, comp. **The Black Experience in Children's Books.** New York: Children's Services Division, New York Public Library, 1971. 109p. $0.50pa. (T)
This bibliography is a revision of *Books about Negro Life for Children* at the Countee Cullen Branch of New York Public Library. Books are for ages through 12, and are chosen for their ability to convey a positive image of the Black American and an understanding of his culture and identity. Arrangement is by country; about 250 titles are annotated.

576. Baxter, Katherine, comp. **The Black Experience and the School Curriculum; Teaching Materials for Grades K-12: An Annotated Bibliography.** Philadelphia, Pa.: Wellsprings Ecumenical Center, 1968. 52p. $2.00pa. (K-12, T)
Materials have been selected for their relevancy to the Black child. Arrangement is by category: Black history, social studies, readers, biography, fiction, poetry, teachers' guides, bibliographies, pictures, filmstrips, toys, etc.

577. **Bibliographic Survey: The Negro in Print.** Washington, D.C.: The Negro Bibliographic and Research Center, Inc. Vol. 1, No. 1– . May, 1965– . Bimonthly. $11.00/yr. $2.50/copy. (9-12, T)

Regular features of the periodical cover titles available on nonfiction, fiction, young readers, drama, music and poetry, periodicals, and a special feature. The special feature of the May 1971 anniversary edition is "Focus On: Black Studies Programs," which is a bibliography of basic materials divided into two levels: college and above; secondary and below.

578.   **Black Information Index.** Herndon, Va.: Infonetics, Inc., Vol. 1– . 1970– . Bimonthly. (6-12, T)
Guide to source information about minority culture, equal opportunity, civil rights, Black studies in this topically arranged bimonthly index to current data about Black Americans.

579.   **The Black Story: An Annotated Multi-Media List for Secondary Schools.** Rockville, Md.: Department of Educational Media and Technology, Montgomery County Public Schools, 1969. 97p. free. (9-12, T)
Books, periodicals, newspapers, pamphlets, art works, charts, pictures, filmstrips, kits, records, tapes, and transparencies are included in this list of media about Black Americans for high school students.

580.   Brignano, Russell C. **Black Americans in Autobiography: An Annotated Bibliography of Autobiographies and Autobiographical Books Written since the Civil War.** Durham, N.C.: Duke University Press, 1974. 118p. $6.50. (9-12, T)
Over 400 annotated entries comprise this bibliography of Black American autobiographies. A checklist of antebellum autobiographical works is appended. Supplementary indexes include a list of libraries where the works can be located.

581.   Cederholm, Theresa D. **Afro-American Artists: A Biobibliographical Directory.** Boston, Mass.: Boston Public Library, 1973. 348p. (7-12, T)
Black American artists and craftsmen are listed with titles of their works, awards, collections, and other biographical information. A comprehensive bibliography lists additional references to these and other Black artists.

582.   Chapman, Abraham. **The Negro in American Literature and a Bibliography of Literature by and about Negro Americans.** Oshkosh: Wisconsin Council of Teachers of English, Wisconsin State University, 1966. 135p. $2.00. (T)
Materials are arranged in the following categories: bibliographies; anthologies; fiction; poetry; drama; criticism; essays; autobiographies; biographies; music; folklore; art; education; reference sources; history and sociology; civil rights; press and journalism; religion.

583.   Chapman, Dorothy H. **Index to Black Poetry.** Boston, Mass.: G. K. Hall, 1974. 541p. $25.00. (7-12, T)
Indexes approximately 1,000 poems of Black and non-Black poets writing on the Black experience. Covers the period from the eighteenth century to the 1970s. Consists of three parts: title and first line index, author index, and subject index.

584.   Dodds, Barbara. **Negro Literature for High School Students.** Champaign, Ill.: National Council of Teachers of English, 1968. 157p. $2.70. (9-12, T)

A listing for teachers of American literature of Negro writers and books about Negroes. Arrangement is as follows: Historical Survey of Negro Writers; Works about Negroes; The Junior Novel; Biography; Classroom Uses of Negro Literature. A bibliography is included; indexed.

585. Downes, Patricia, comp. **Negroes in American Life: An Annotated Bibliography of Nonprint Media.** Rockville, Md.: Montgomery County Public Schools, 1971. 61p. $2.00; single copies free. (T)
A listing of audiovisual materials on Negroes in America arranged by media type: charts, film loops, filmstrips, games, kits, pictures, recordings, slides, transparencies. Criteria for selection included.

586. Fisher, Mary L., comp. **The Negro in America: A Bibliography.** 2nd ed. Cambridge, Mass.: Harvard University Press, 1970. 315p. $10.00; $4.95pa. (9-12, T)
Approximately 6,500 entries are arranged by broad subjects within the realm of Black American history, literature, art, biography, and politics. The period covered is primarily 1954 to 1970. The bibliography is a revision of Elizabeth W. Miller's 1966 work.

587. Hatch, James V. **Black Image on the American Stage: A Bibliography of Plays and Musicals 1770-1970.** New York: Drama Book Shop, 1970. 162p. $8.00. (9-12, T)
A list of plays written by Blacks, or containing Black characters, published over a 300-year period.

588. Irwin, Leonard B., comp. **Black Studies: A Bibliography for Use of Schools, Libraries and the General Reader.** Brooklawn, N.J.: McKinley, 1973. 122p. $8.50. (6-12, T)
A selective guide to Black American biography and history, literature and the arts, and other topics. Includes about 850 titles with brief annotations. Levels indicated are adult, young adult, and grades 6-10. Author and title indexes included.

589. Jackson, Miles M., ed. **A Bibliography of Negro History and Culture for Young Readers.** Pittsburgh, Pa.: University of Pittsburgh Press, c1968, 1969. 160p. $2.95pa. (5-12, T)
A 500-entry multimedia bibliography of books and audiovisual materials for young children. The foreword discusses the needs of Negro youth and the findings of the U.S. Riot Commission concerning early reader experiences. Arrangement is as follows: picture books, fiction, non-fiction, reference books, periodicals, and audiovisual materials. Appendices include lists of biographies and selection sources. Title-subject index and author index included.

590. Johnson, Harry Alleyn, ed. **Multimedia Materials for Afro-American Studies: A Curriculum Orientation and Annotated Bibliography of Resources.** New York: Bowker, 1971. 353p. $19.95. (9-12, T)
A selection of 8mm and 16mm films, filmstrips, records, tapes, slides, prints, transparencies, videotapes and print materials suitable for the elementary through senior high school levels. Producers, distributors, and publishers are listed. Books

are arranged alphabetically by author; nonprint media alphabetically by title. Part I emphasizes curriculum orientation; Part II, culture and contributions; Part III lists the nonprint materials. Indexed.

591.   Klotman, Phyllis R., *et al.* **The Black Family and the Black Woman, A Bibliography.** Bloomington: Indiana University Library, 1972. 107p. (9-12)
Although it is a bibliography of the holdings in the Indiana University Library, this listing includes children's literature and some audiovisual materials. Arrangement is in two major sections: 1) The Black Family, and 2) The Black Woman. Included are books, excerpts, articles and government publications on the historical and current materials.

592.   Koblitz, Minnie W. **The Negro in Schoolroom Literature: Resource Materials for the Teacher of Kindergarten through the 6th Grade.** New York: Center for Urban Education, 1966. 67p. $0.50. (T)
An annotated bibliography listing 250 books on the Negro arranged by broad subjects. Fiction and biography are also included. Materials are further subdivided by reading level. Includes background resource materials for teachers.

593.   Latimer, Bettye I., *et al.* **Starting Out Right: Choosing Books about Black People for Young Children, Preschool through Third Grade.** Madison: Children's Literature Review Board, Wisconsin State Department of Public Instruction, Division for Administrative Services, 1972. free. (T)
A list of 300 titles about Blacks examined by the Children's Literature Review Board. Included are their reasons for selecting or rejecting books for children about Blacks.

594.   McPherson, James M., *et al.* **Blacks in America: Bibliographical Essays.** New York: Doubleday, 1971. 430p. $8.95; $3.95pa.
A chronological and topical annotated guide to 6,000 titles on Black American history and culture. Part 1 covers racism; Parts 2-7 discuss social, economic, and political history. Part 8 covers literature and the arts. Author-title-subject index.

595.   Mills, Joyce White. **The Black World in Literature for Children: A Bibliography of Print and Non-Print Materials.** Atlanta, Ga.: School of Library Service, Atlanta University, 1975. 42p. $2.00pa. (T)
A multimedia listing of materials in age-level sections, subdivided by broad topics. Entries are arranged alphabetically by author, with brief annotations that are evaluative as well as descriptive. The bibliography is in three sections: grades 3-8; grades 9-13; adult levels. Materials included were published during 1974 and 1975.

596.   National Information Center for Educational Media. **Index to Black History and Studies—Multimedia.** 2nd ed. Los Angeles: University of Southern California, 1973. 260p. $19.50. (7-12, T)
Over 10,000 non-print titles on Black American history, experience, and achievements. Includes an index to subject headings, subject guide, alphabetical guide, and a directory of producers and distributors.

597.   Negroes in American Life: An Annotated Bibliography of Books for
       Elementary Schools. Rockville, Md.: Montgomery County Public Schools,
       Department of Educational Media and Technology, 1968. 74p. free. (T)
Evaluative annotations are included in this bibliography of titles on the American
Negro for the elementary school. A film list and teacher reference sources are
appended.

598.   New York Public Library. The Black Experience in Children's Audiovisual
       Materials. New York: New York Public Library, 1973. 32p. $1.00. (T)
A listing of audiovisual materials for children on Black Americans. Arrangement is
by type of media; included are records (and cassettes, tapes), films, filmstrips. Other
listings of print materials published by the library are *A Touch of Soul* (1970.
free) and *No Crystal Stair: A Bibliography of Black Literature* (1971. $2.00pa.).

599.   Porter, Dorothy B., comp. The Negro in the United States: A Selected
       Bibliography. Washington, D.C.: Government Printing Office, 1970. 313p.
       $3.25. (9-12, T)
Lists books that can be used in high school and undergraduate Negro history
courses. Arrangement is alphabetical by author under broad subject headings. Some
brief annotations are included. Author and subject index. Includes almost 1,800
entries. A similar title by the author is *Working Bibliography on the Negro in the
United States* (University Microfilms, 1969. $7.50).

600.   Powers, Anne. Blacks in American Movies: A Selected Bibliography.
       Metuchen, N.J.: Scarecrow Press, 1974. 157p. $6.00. (9-12, T)
A partially annotated listing of books, articles, and other materials on Blacks in
American films. Arrangement is by type of work. Periodical citations are under
subject categories. Includes a chronological listing and a filmography. Author and
subject index.

601.   Rollins, Charlemae. We Build Together: A Reader's Guide to Negro Life
       and Literature for Elementary and High School Use. Champaign, Ill.:
       National Council of Teachers of English, 1967. 71p. $1.95pa. (K-12, T)
A bibliography of Negro literature with discussion of trends in Black American folklore, biography, history, fiction, poetry, and non-fiction. Entries are annotated and
are arranged alphabetically by author in the following categories: picturebooks and
easy-to-read books, fiction, history, biography, poetry, folklore and music, science,
sports (non-fiction and fiction). A list of sources and a directory of publishers are
also included. Indexed.

602.   Rollock, Barbara. The Black Experience in Children's Books. New York:
       New York Public Library, 1974. 122p. $2.50pa. (K-12, T)
About 800 titles are annotated in this revised edition of Augusta Baker's bibliography. Selection policies are discussed and titles are arranged by geographical
division. Emphasis is on the United States, but South and Central America, Africa,
England, and other countries are also covered. Subdivisions for type of material
(picture books, biography, folklore, etc.) are provided. Author and title index.

603.   Salk, Erwin A., comp. and ed. **A Layman's Guide to Negro History**. New
        enl. ed. New York: McGraw-Hill, 1967. 196p. $6.95. (9-12, T)
Part one is entitled "A Fact Book on the History of the Negro People in the United
States"; Part two is "Bibliographies." The bibliographies cover print and non-print
materials for children and young adults—teaching materials and guides and various
subject bibliographies.

604.   Smith, Dwight L., ed. **Afro-American History: A Bibliography**. New ed.
        Santa Barbara, Calif.: ABC-Clio, 1974. 856p. $45.00. (9-12, T)
A selection of 3,000 abstracts of journal articles on Afro-American history.
Arrangement is alphabetical by author in six sections: 1) Traditions in Afro-American
Culture, 2) The Black Experience in Colonial America, 3) Slavery and Freedom, 4)
Reconstruction and Its Aftermath, 5) Afro-American Society in the Twentieth
Century, 6) The Contemporary Scene. A combined author, biographical, geographi-
cal, and subject index is followed by a list of Afro-American periodicals and a list
of abstracters.

605.   Sprecher, Daniel. **Guide to Films about Negroes**. Alexandria, Va.: Serina
        Press, 1970. 87p. $4.95pa. (T)
A brief synopsis of about 750 16mm films on Black culture, history, social problems,
and contributions in the United States and Africa. Arrangement is alphabetical by
title; length (running time), date, grade level are indicated. Source list included.

606.   Sturges, Gladys M., comp. **Professional Guide to the Afro-American in
        Print: A Bibliography of Current Works by and about the Black Man of
        America**. Normandy, Mo.: Afro-American Bibliographic and Research
        Center, 1969– . Semiannual.
An alphabetical listing of 450 books on the history of Black Americans. Entries are
annotated and include many titles on the current situation. Includes in the first
edition a descriptive list of current African literature.

607.   Treworgy, Mildred L., and Paul B. Foreman, eds. **Negroes in the United
        States: A Bibliography of Materials for Schools**. University Park:
        Pennsylvania State University Library Office, 1968. 93p. $2.50. (K-12, T)
An annotated multimedia bibliography of materials for classroom use. Emphasis is
on English, history, and civics books at the secondary level, but reference tools and
some materials on other minority groups are also included.

608.   Welsch, Erwin K. **The Negro in the United States: A Research Guide.**
        Bloomington: Indiana University Press, 1965. 142p. $2.25pa. (9-12, T)
A bibliographical essay arranged in four parts: Science, Philosophy and Race;
Historical and Sociological Background; The Major Issues Today; and The Negro
and the Arts. The appendix lists national and state Black organizations, as well as
Black periodicals. Subject index provided.

609.   Westmoreland, Guy F., Jr. **An Annotated Guide to Basic Reference Books
        on the Black American Experience**. Wilmington, Dela.: Scholarly
        Resources, 1974. 98p. $12.50. (9-12, T)
A selective listing of reference books on Black American history divided into two
major sections. Part one cites general reference sources; part two cites subject area

reference sources. The addendum includes recently published materials. Author, title, and subject indexes provided.

610. Whiteman, Maxwell. **A Century of Fiction by American Negroes, 1853-1952: A Descriptive Bibliography.** Philadelphia, Pa.: Albert Saifer, c1955, 1968. 64p. $10.00. (9-12, T)
A record of fiction by American Negroes as a guide for teachers and American literature students. Arrangement is alphabetical by author. A "Chronology" lists works by date and indicates whether they were published by a regular press or a Negro firm or were privately printed. Can be used with Frank Deodene's *Black American Fiction since 1952: A Preliminary Checklist* (Chatham Bookseller, 1970. $2.50pa.).

611. Williams, Ora. **American Black Women in the Arts and Social Sciences: A Bibliographic Survey.** Metuchen, N.J.: Scarecrow Press, 1973. 141p. $6.00. (9-12, T)
Over 1,000 entries of print and non-print materials on or by Black American women. Arrangement is alphabetical by author in subject categories: reference works, biography, anthologies, dramatic and literary works, and cultural studies. Includes selected portraits. Another bibliography on Black American women was recently published by Lenwood G. Davis: *The Black Woman in American Society: A Selected Annotated Bibliography* (Boston, Mass.: G. K. Hall, 1975. 159p. $17.00).

Encyclopedic Works and Dictionaries

612. Adams, Russell L., ed. **Great Negroes, Past and Present.** Illus. by Eugene Winslow. Chicago: Afro-American Publishing Co., 1969. 212p. $8.95; $5.95pa. (6-12)
An illustrated biographical dictionary of over 175 outstanding Black Americans with portraits. Arrangement is mainly by occupational categories: 1) African heroes, 2) early American, 3) science and industry, 4) business pioneers, 5) religion, 6) education, 7) literature, 8) theater, 9) music and 10) art. Each section includes a bibliography. A teacher's guide with suggestions for curricular use is provided. Portraits included.

613. **Afro-American Encyclopedia.** Martin Rywell, chief comp. and ed. North Miami, Fla.: Educational Book Publishers, 1974. 10 vols. $168.00. (9-12)
This work on Negro life and history covers the African experience in Africa, the West Indies, Canada, and Latin America, as well as the United States. Coverage ranges from popular topics and style to scholarly writing and interests. Articles are not signed, and no bibliography is included. Volume 10 contains a general index.

614. Baskin, Wade, and Richard N. Runes. **Dictionary of Black Culture.** New York: Philosophical Library, 1973. 493p. $15.00. (4-12)
A comprehensive biographical dictionary covering many aspects of Black life and culture in the United States. Although the depth of information for biographees is inconsistent, it is a valuable reference tool on Black subjects, places, and events. Alphabetical arrangement.

615.   Greene, Robert Ewell. **Black Defenders of America: 1775-1973.** Chicago:
        Johnson Publishing Co., 1974. 415p. $17.95. (7-12)
A biographical dictionary of Negro military personnel in U.S. wars, arranged in
chronological order from the Revolution to Vietnam. The appendixes contain
photographs, documents and statistics, and a bibliography. Name index.

616.   **International Library of Negro Life and History.** New York: Publishers
        Co., 1970. 10 vols. $138.75. (6-12)
An encyclopedia of the Black experience in America. Each volume is indexed and
each includes bibliographic references, illustrations, portraits, etc. Topics covered
are history, Black contributions, arts, literature, biographical data. The encyclopedia
is supplemented by the *International Library of Negro Life and History: Yearbook*
(1969– . Annual).

617.   Katz, William L., ed. **The American Negro: His History and Literature.**
        New York: Arno, 1969. 110 vols. Series 1, $610.50; Series 2, $610.00;
        Series 3 (1970), $322.00. (4-12)
Source material on the role of the Negro in American history from Colonial times
to date. Emphasis is on contributions in politics, economics, the development of the
United States, and the arts and literature.

618.   Rush, Theresa G., and Carol F. Myers. **Black American Writers Past &**
        Present: A Biographical & Bibliographical Dictionary. Metuchen, N.J.:
        Scarecrow, 1975. 2 vols. $30.00. (9-12)
A comprehensive dictionary of Black writers and works appropriate for a Black
studies curriculum. Entries are arranged alphabetically and include biographical
data, bibliographies, listings of the subject's publications, and critical studies.
Appendix I lists Black critics, historians, and editors; Appendix II lists non-Black
critics, historians, and editors. The volumes are illustrated.

619.   Spalding, Henry D., comp. and ed. **Encyclopedia of Black Folklore and**
        Humor. Middle Village, N.Y.: Jonathan David, 1972. 589p. $12.95. (7-12)
Black folklore in song, poetry, stories, and rhymes are included with a brief description of their context in Black American history and experience.

620.   Spradling, Mary Mace, ed. **In Black and White: Afro-Americans in Print;**
        A Guide to Afro-Americans Who Have Made Contributions to the United
        States of America. 2nd ed. Kalamazoo, Mich.: Kalamazoo Library System,
        1976. 505p. $10.00pa. (9-12, T)
A biographical index covering both living and deceased prominent Black Americans.
Included are Blacks who have made some significant achievement during the period
1619 to 1975.

621.   **Who's Who among Black Americans.** Edited by William C. Matney. North-
        brook, Ill.: Who's Who among Black Americans, 1976. 772p. $45.00.
This major biographical dictionary on Black Americans includes over 10,000
biographical sketches. It covers "leading executives and officials in government,
business, education, religion, journalism, civic affairs, fine arts, law, medicine, civil
rights, sports, contemporary art, music, theater, motion pictures, television and

those responsible for recent developments in science" (Preface). For retrospective biographical searches, see *Who's Who in Colored America: A Biographical Dictionary of Notable Persons of American Descent in America* (New York, Christian E. Burckel & Associates, 1950. 7 vols.).

Handbooks, Guides, and Almanacs

622.   **Black List: The Concise Reference Guide to Publications, Films & Broadcasting Media of Black America, Africa and the Caribbean.** Rev. ed. New York: Panther House, 1970, 1974. 289p. $17.00. (7-12)
Lists directories of mass media, Negro institutions and organizations. Emphasis is on colleges and universities as well as cultural organizations. Covers the United States, Africa, and the Caribbean.

623.   Burke, Joan M. **Civil Rights: A Current Guide to the People, Organizations and Events.** 2nd ed. New York: Bowker, 1974. 194p. $12.50. (9-12, T)
A source of biographical information on individuals and organizations involved in the Civil Rights movement from 1945 on. The appendices include a chronology of events and records of how U.S. Congressmen voted on civil rights legislation of the 1960s. A revision of the 1970 edition by A. John Adams.

624.   Ebony Editors. **Ebony Success Library.** Chicago: Johnson Publishing Co., 1973. 3 vols. $27.95. (6-12)
This reference source on Black Americans includes: Vol. 1, *One Thousand Successful Blacks*; Vol. 2, *Famous Blacks Give Secrets of Success*; Vol. 3, *Career Guide: Opportunities and Resources for You.*

625.   Ebony Editors and Doris E. Saunders. **The Ebony Handbook.** Chicago: Johnson Publishing Co., 1974. 553p. $20.00. (7-12)
A revision and expansion of the former *The Negro Handbook* (1966), covering vital statistics, historical and current events, education, crime, employment, housing, religion, professions, politics, press, arts, sports, obituaries, organizations, and institutions as they relate to the Black American. A handy, one-volume reference tool. Indexed.

626.   Garrett, Romeo B. **Famous First Facts about Negroes.** New York: Arno Press, 1972. 212p. $7.95. (7-12)
Brief essays on Blacks noted because they were the first of their race to make achievements in specific areas. Arrangement is by broad and then specific subjects. Individual name index provided.

627.   Hornsby, Alton. **The Black Almanac.** Rev. ed. Woodbury, N.Y.: Barron's, 1972. 212p. $7.25; $2.95pa. (7-12)
A chronological arrangement of the history and experience of Black Americans from 1619 to 1971. Includes outstanding news events, court decisions, deaths, contributions, and Civil Rights incidents and demonstrations. A bibliography and index are included.

628.   Ploski, Harry, and Ernest Kaiser. **Afro USA: A Reference Work on the Black Experience.** New York: Bellwether, 1971. 1110p. o.p. (6-12)
An updated and expanded version of the former *Negro Almanac* (1967). A good single-volume ready reference source providing statistics and historical and biographical information on the Blacks in the United States and other countries. A new edition of this work, *The Negro Almanac: A Reference Work on the Afro American* (1976; 1206p.; $59.95), was not available for examination.

629.   Sloan, Irving J. **Blacks in America, 1492-1970: A Chronology and Fact Book.** Dobbs Ferry, N.Y.: Oceana, 1971. 149p. $6.00. (7-12)
The first and second editions are published under the title of *The American Negro: A Chronology and Fact Book.* A broad chronology of events of import in American Negro history, a selection of critical documents, and a selected bibliography are the main sections of this work. Highly selective. Name index.

630.   U.S. Bureau of the Census. **Census of Population: 1970.** Series PC (2). **Subject Reports.** Series PC (2) 1−B. **Negro Population.** Washington, D.C.: Government Printing Office, 1973. 241p. $3.70.
Statistics on the Negro-American population with respect to social and economic conditions and characteristics are presented by U.S. regions, states, and some cities.

Directories

631.   Sanders, Charles L., and Linda McLean. **Directory: National Black Organizations.** New York: Afram Associates, 1972. 109p. $5.00pa. (9-12, T)
A directory of approximately 240 national Black organizations of a non-profit nature. Arrangement is alphabetical by subject category. Lists name, address, staff, officers, publications, awards, programs, and purpose of each organization.

632.   Schatz, Walter, ed. **Directory of Afro-American Resources.** New York: Bowker, 1970. 485p. $19.95. (9-12, T)
Lists Afro-American institutions and major collections of materials on Black Americans. Arrangement is geographic (by state and city) and the following information is provided: name of institution, address, phone, person in charge of collection, services, purpose, publications, description of the collection. Includes an index to directories and collections and an index to named personnel.

633.   Shockley, Ann A., and Sue P. Chandler, eds. **Living Black American Authors: A Biographical Directory.** Ann Arbor, Mich.: Bowker, 1973. 160p. $13.95. (9-12)
Biobibliographical information on Negro authors in American literature of the twentieth century is provided in this directory. Arrangement is alphabetical by author.

Teaching Methodology and Curriculum Materials

634. Aplen, Noretta, *et al.*, eds. **The Negro American: His Role, His Quest.** Cleveland, Ohio: Cleveland Public Schools, n.d. 246p. $3.75. (T)
Materials on Black studies created by the school system for implementation into the social studies curriculum at both the elementary and secondary levels. Bibliographies of suitable materials are included for each unit. A chronology of the Negro American experience in America is also included.

635. Banks, James A. **Teaching the Black Experience: Methods and Materials.** Belmont, Calif.: Fearon, 1970. 90p. $2.95pa. (K-12)
Methods, materials, and activities are suggested for developing a social studies unit studying the history and culture of Black Americans at the K-12 levels. Includes a discussion of racial attitudes on the part of teachers and students. Another title by the author is: *Teaching Ethnic Studies: Concepts & Strategies, 43rd Yearbook* (Washington, D.C.: National Council for the Social Studies, 1973. $6.00pa.).

636. Banks, James A., and Jean D. Grambs, eds. **Black Self-Concept: Implications for Education and Social Science.** New York: McGraw-Hill, 1972. 234p. $6.95; $2.95pa. (T)
A revision of *Negro Self-Concept* (1965), these essays are on racial prejudice, the Black protest movements, politics, and racism in American institutions, etc. Contributors are outstanding educators.

637. Broderick, Dorothy. **Image of the Black in Children's Fiction.** New York: Bowker, 1973. 215p. $13.25. (T)
Studies current as well as historical treatment of Blacks in about 100 children's books. Materials are analyzed for stereotypes and incidence of racism. Bibliographies included.

638. De Lerma, Dominique-René. **Black Music in Our Culture: Curricular Ideas on the Subjects, Materials & Problems.** Kent, Ohio: Kent State University Press, 1970. 263p. $7.50. (T)
Explores the role of Black music in America with particular attention to areas of education. Another title by the author, *Reflections on Afro-American Music* (Kent State University Press, 1971) and the former title were published as a result of national seminars on Black music at Indiana University.

639. Dell, Sister Norma. **Materials Handbook for Use with Primary Grades K-3.** Toledo, Ohio: Toledo Public Schools, Afro-American Resource Center, 1972. 47p. $2.00. (K-3, T)
A handbook of eight units with a teacher reference section and a listing of print and non-print materials. Items cover the 1960s and 1970s.

640. Dunn, Lynn P. **Black Americans: A Study Guide and Source Book.** San Francisco: R&E Research Associates, 1975. 112p. $6.00. (9-12)
Examines Black identity, conflict and integration/nationalism. Arrangement is in two-column pages with an outline appearing on one side and notes and sources of

documentation on the other. Includes a list of Blacks who have made contributions to American culture. A glossary is included as well as a bibliography.

641. Grambs, Jean Dresden, *et al.* **Black Image: Education Copes with Color: Essays on the Black Experience.** Dubuque, Iowa: W. C. Brown, 1972. 196p. $3.95pa. (T)
A collection of essays on the values and image of Black Americans found in textbooks and educational materials. Includes an annotated bibliography of multimedia materials for grades K-10 and for professional reading.

642. Katz, William Loren. **A Teacher's Guide to American Negro History.** Rev. ed. Chicago: Quadrangle Books, c1968, 1971. 192p. $6.95; $2.65pa. (T)
A curriculum resource guide for planning and developing a series of 15 units in a Black studies course. Emphasis is on Black history; a multimedia bibliography is included. References, teaching techniques, methods of evaluation, and sources of materials and collections are provided. Recommended for secondary school teachers.

643. MacCann, Donnarae M. **The Black American in Books for Children: Readings in Racism.** Metuchen, N.J.: Scarecrow, 1972. 230p. $6.50. (T)
A collection of 23 articles discussing the treatment of Blacks in children's literature published in the 1960s. Criteria for evaluating interracial books are included.

644. Roach, Mildred, and Marva Cooper. **Resource Manual for Black American Music.** Boston, Mass.: Crescendo, 1976. $17.50. (T)
This manual is useful for elementary and secondary school teachers in schools with large Black populations. Another title by the author is *Black American Music: Past and Present* (Crescendo, 1973. $7.50; $5.00pa.).

645. Sloan, Irving J. **Treatment of Black Americans in Current Encyclopedias.** Washington, D.C.: American Federation of Teachers, 1970. 32p. $1.00. (T)
An assessment of the treatment of Blacks in nine contemporary juvenile encyclopedias. The author also evaluates textbooks for both quality and quantity of Negro representation in *The Negro in Modern American History Textbooks: An Examination and Analysis of the Treatment of Black History in Selected Junior and Senior High School Level History Textbooks, as of September 1972,* 4th ed. (American Federation of Teachers, 1972).

646. Standifer, James, and Barbara Reeder. **Source Book of African and Afro-American Materials for Music Educators.** Washington, D.C.: Contemporary Music Project, Music Educators National Conference, 1972. 147p. $3.50. (T)
A bibliography of books, films, filmstrips, records, tapes, periodicals, and dissertations that emphasize poetry, dance, and the arts. This listing is useful for teachers involved in the music curriculum, as well as language arts.

647. **Teaching Black: An Evaluation of Methods and Resources.** Stanford, Calif.: Multi-Ethnic Education Resources Center, Stanford University, 1972. $4.00. (T)
Describes 40 curriculum units. Arrangement is by classroom type and grade level.

648. Turner, Darwin T., and Barbara Dodds. **Theory and Practice in the Teaching of Literature by Afro-Americans.** Urbana, Ill.: National Council of Teachers of English, 1971. 97p. $2.45pa. (T)
Teaching theory and selected reading lists of literature for high school and junior high school teachers. Also lists sources of multimedia teaching aids.

Non-Fiction Titles: History, Culture, Sociology, Biography

649. Adams, William, *et al.*, eds. **Afro-American Authors.** New York: Houghton Mifflin, 1971. 164p. $3.08 text ed. (9-12)
A selection from the works of Afro-American authors is compiled here. Adams has also compiled (with others) a series of collections of Afro-American literature, including *Afro-American Literature: Fiction* (1970); *Afro-American Literature: Nonfiction* (1970); *Afro-American Literature: Drama*; *Afro-American Literature: Poetry.* All are $3.08 in the text editions; accompanying teacher's guides are available.

650. Adoff, Arnold. **Malcolm X.** Illus. by John Wilson. New York: Crowell, 1970. 41p. $4.50; $1.25pa. (3-6)
A biography of a militant leader of the Black people who was assassinated in 1965. Emphasis is on Malcolm X's role in developing pride in the Black heritage and culture. Another title by the author is *Black on Black* (Macmillan, 1968. $5.95).

651. Alexander, Rae Pace. **Young & Black in America.** New York: Random, 1970. 139p. $3.90. (6-8)
An anthology of eight biographical narratives. Included are the personal experiences of Malcolm X, Jimmy Brown, and others.

652. Allen, James Egert. **The Negro in New York.** Jericho, N.Y.: Exposition, 1964. 94p. $5.00. (7-9)
Covers the Black history and experience in New York from the Colonial days (1625) to protest days (1964). Another title by the author is *Black History Past & Present* (Exposition, 1971. $7.50).

653. Alvarez, Joseph A. **From Reconstruction to Revolution: The Blacks' Struggle for Equality.** New York: Atheneum, 1971. 216p. $6.50. (7-12)
Treats the struggle of the Blacks in America from their freedom until the 1970s. Emphasis is on their long continual striving for equal rights.

654. Anderson, LaVere. **Saddles & Sabers: Black Men in the Old West.** Illus. by Herman Vestal. Champaign, Ill.: Garrard, 1975. 128p. $3.78. (6-9)
A survey of Black men's contributions and experiences in the development of the Western frontier.

655. Angeles, Peter A. **The Possible Dream: Toward Understanding the Black Experience.** New York: Friendship Press, 1971. 140p. $1.95pa. (7-12)
A collection of personal narratives, case histories, and statistical information

to document the Black experience in America. Topics discussed are housing, discrimination, employment, education, and Black image and identity.

656.   Aptheker, Herbert, ed. **A Documentary History of the Negro People in the United States.** New York: Citadel, 1951-1974. 3 vols. V. 1, $10.00; V. 2, $17.50; V. 3, $17.50; $4.95pa. (7-12)

A collection of documents giving a chronology and history of the Black experience in the United States. Volume 1 covers 1661-1910; Volume 2 covers 1910-1932; Volume 3 covers through 1945. Indexed. Other titles by the author are *Nat Turner's Slave Rebellion* (Humanities Press, 1966. $0.95pa.), *Afro-American History: The Modern Era* (Citadel Press, 1971. $7.95; $2.95pa.), and *To Be Free: Studies in American Negro History* (International, 1968. $2.95pa.).

657.   Bacon, Margaret Hope. **Rebellion at Christiana.** New York: Crown, 1975. 216p. $6.95. (7-12)

An account based on the writings of William Parker, a runaway slave, of how he and other runaways killed a white leader of slave owners and the trial that resulted. Well documented; indexed. Another biography by the author is *I Speak for My Slave Sister: The Life of Abby Kelley Foster* (Crowell, 1974. $5.50).

658.   Baker, Bettye F. **What Is Black?** New York: Watts, 1969. 45p. $3.95. (K-3)

A primary-aged picture book of things that are black. Pictures are chosen to give a positive image to the word—e.g., a black puppy, black candy, etc.

659.   Baldwin, James. **No Name in the Street.** New York: Dial, 1972. 197p. $6.95. (9-12)

The author, a well-known Black American writer, describes in a personal narrative his feelings about American racism. Other titles by Baldwin are: *The Fire Next Time* (Dial, 1963. $0.95pa.); *A Dialogue by James Baldwin and Nikki Giovanni* (Lippincott, 1973. $4.95).

660.   Banks, James A., and Cherry A. Banks. **March Toward Freedom: A History of Black Americans.** 2nd ed. Belmont, Calif.: Fearon, c1970, 1974. 148p. $5.20. (6-12)

A well-illustrated history covering Blacks from African background to the 1970s. Should be used as an introductory text.

661.   Bennett, Lerone, Jr. **The Challenge of Blackness.** Chicago: Johnson Publishing Co., 1972. 312p. $6.95. (7-12)

A collection of essays and speeches challenging all Americans to reconsider white values as the Blacks strive for social, political, and economic progress. Other titles by the author are *Pioneers in Protest* (Penguin, 1969. $2.95pa.); *Before the Mayflower: A History of Black America* (Johnson, 1969. $6.95); *Black Power U.S.A.: The Human Side of Reconstruction, 1867-1877* (Johnson, 1967. $6.95); and *Confrontation: Black & White* (Penguin, 1965. $3.50pa.).

662.   Berg, Jean Horton. **I Cry When the Sun Goes Down: The Story of Herman Wrice.** Philadelphia, Pa.: Westminster, 1975. 158p. $6.95. (5-9)

The biography of Herman Wrice, who rose from the world of gangs and ghettos to become an internationally famous urban leader.

663. Bergman, Peter M. **The Chronological History of the Negro in America.** New York: Harper & Row, 1969. 698p. $13.50; NAL, $1.50pa. (9-12)
A collection of chronologically arranged documents of Black history and culture including laws and court decisions, events, movements, and other relevant statistics. Bibliography and index included.

664. Billingsley, Andrew. **Black Families in White America.** New York: Prentice-Hall, 1968, 1969. 218p. $6.95; $2.45pa. (9-12)
An analysis of the social and economic discrimination the Blacks have faced in a white society. A similar title is *Black Families and the Struggle for Survival* (Friendship Press, 1974. $1.95pa.).

665. Bontemps, Arna. **The Story of the Negro.** 5th ed. Illus. by Raymond Lufkin. New York: Knopf, 1958, 1969. 243p. $5.69. (6-9)
A history of the Negro in America and his struggle for freedom from slavery to contemporary discrimination. Other titles by this author are *Famous Negro Athletes* (Apollo, 1970. $1.95pa.); *Great Slave Narratives* (Beacon Press, 1970. $2.95); *One Hundred Years of Negro Freedom* (Dodd, 1961. $6.00; Apollo, $1.95); and *We Have Tomorrow* (Houghton Mifflin, 1945. $3.95).

666. Boyle, Donald. **Toms, Coons, Mulattoes, Mammies, and Bucks: An Interpretive History of Blacks in American Films.** New York: Bantam, 1973. 260p. $12.50; $2.25pa. (9-12)
A history of Blacks in American films using the subject categories contained in the title of the work. It updates *The Negro in Films* by Peter Noble (1948), but the latter work is reviewed as a more solid interpretation.

667. Bracey, John H., Jr., August Meier, and Elliott Rudwick, eds. **The Afro-Americans: Selected Documents.** Boston, Mass.: Allyn & Bacon, 1972. 751p. $6.25pa. (9-12)
Primary sources on Black American history covering slavery, the Civil War, economic trends and opportunities, religion, ghettos, and relations with whites. Not indexed. Another title by the author is *Black Nationalism in America* (Bobbs-Merrill, 1969, 1970. $8.50; $4.00pa.).

668. Brimberg, Stanlee. **Black Stars.** New York: Dodd, 1974. 159p. $3.95. (5-7)
Brief excerpts about outstanding individuals in Black history, such as Harriet Tubman, Malcolm X, Martin Luther King, and others.

669. Brown, Claude. **Manchild in the Promised Land.** New York: Macmillan, $7.95; New American Library, 1965. 415p. $1.50pa. (6-12)
A description of the author's youth in Harlem and the pressures and influences of a culture of drugs, crime, and other slum problems.

670. Buckmaster, Henrietta. **Flight to Freedom: The Story of the Underground.** New York: Crowell, c1958, 1968. 217p. $6.95. (5-8)

Describes the slaves who escaped via the underground railroad and the people who were involved in it. Other titles by the author are: *Freedom Bound* (Macmillan, 1965. $5.95; $1.25 pa.); *Let My People Go* (Peter Smith, 1959. $5.50).

671. Burt, Olive W. **Black Women of Valor.** Illus. by Paul Frame. New York: Messner, 1974. 96p. $5.79. (5-7)
The work of four outstanding but little-known Black women is described. Included are: Juliette Derricotte, Maggie Mitchell Walker, Ida Wells Barnett, and Septima Poinsette Clark. The work also provides a list of 62 successful Black women.

672. Butcher, Margaret Just. **The Negro in American Culture.** 2nd ed. New York: Knopf, 1972. 313p. $7.95; $1.50pa. (9-12)
Examines the influence of Black American folk music, dance, and folklore in our society.

673. Butwin, Miriam, and Pat Pirmantgen. **Protest 2.** Minneapolis, Minn.: Lerner Publications, 1972. 223p. $4.95. (5-11)
Traces the Black Liberation Movement from the Civil War to the riot at Attica State Prison.

674. Carmichael, Stokely. **Black Power: The Politics of Liberation in America.** New York: Random House, 1967. 198p. $5.95; $1.95pa. (9-12)
An explanation of the goals, objectives, and philosophy of the Black Power movement. Contains a bibliography and an index.

675. Cavanah, Frances. **The Truth about the Man behind the Book That Sparked the War between the States.** Philadelphia, Pa.: Westminster, 1975. 187p. $6.95. (7-12)
The story of Josiah Henson, the slave who escaped to freedom and was the inspiration for the famous book *Uncle Tom's Cabin* and who devoted his life to helping his people attain their equal and human rights.

676. Chalk, Ocania. **Pioneers of Black Sport: A Study in Courage and Perseverance.** New York: Dodd, 1975. 300p. $7.95. (7-12)
Subtitled *The Early Days of the Black Professional Athlete in Baseball, Basketball, Boxing and Football*, this book is a history of Blacks in four major sports. Another title by the author is *Black College Sport* (Dodd, 1975. $8.95).

677. Chambers, Bradford, ed. **Chronicles of Negro Protest: Documenting the History of Black Power.** New York: Parents, 1968. 319p. $4.95. (1969. $0.95pa.). (7-12)
Protest feelings and movements are shown to have evolved from the unequal and prejudicial treatment of Negroes from Bible days to the 1960s.

678. Chisholm, Shirley. **The Good Fight.** New York: Harper, 1973. 206p. $6.95; $1.50pa. (9-12)
An account of Shirley Chisholm's Presidential campaign and her feelings about the future role of the minority groups politics and politicians. The appendixes contain

excerpts from Ms. Chisholm's writings and speeches. Another title by the author is *Unbought and Unbossed* (Houghton Mifflin, 1970. $5.95; $0.95pa.).

679. Christopher, Maurine. **America's Black Congressmen.** New York: Crowell, 1971. 283p. $8.95; $3.95pa. (1975 Apollo ed.). (7-12)
A collection of biographical sketches of Black-American Congressmen from the political pioneers of the early post-Civil War days to the elected representatives of 1970. A chronological list of Blacks in Congress is appended.

680. Clark, Margaret Goff. **Their Eyes on the Stars: Four Black Writers.** Champaign, Ill.: Garrard, 1973. 174p. $4.28. (5-9)
Black writers described here are Jupiter Hammon and George Moses Horton, 18th century poets; William Wells Brown, novelist and playwright; Charles Waddell Chesnutt, fiction writer.

681. Clarke, John. **Black Soldier.** Illus. by Harold James. New York: Doubleday, c1968, 1970. 144p. $3.95; $1.45pa. (7-8)
An account of the frustrations and humiliation suffered by a young Black soldier during World War II. Another title by the author is *Malcolm X: The Man and His Times* (Macmillan, 1970. $6.95).

682. Cleaver, Eldridge. **Soul on Ice.** New York: McGraw-Hill, 1970. 224p. $6.95; $0.95pa. (7-12)
Autobiography of a militant figure in the Black Americans' struggle for equal rights.

683. Clifton, Lucille. **The Black B C's.** Illus. by Don Miller. New York: Dutton, 1970. 48p. $3.95. (K-5)
Black history and contributions are spelled out in this book for younger children. Other titles by the author are: *The Boy Who Didn't Believe in Spring* (Dutton, 1973. $5.95); *Don't You Remember?* (Dutton, 1973. $5.50); *Good, Says Jerome* (Dutton, 1973. $5.95); and *All of Us Come Cross the Water* (Holt, 1973. $5.95).

684. Collier, James Lincoln. **Inside Jazz.** New York: Four Winds, 1973. 776p. $5.95. (6-12)
A history of jazz and the musicians who created, developed, and contributed to it. An annotated discography is included.

685. Coombs, Norman. **The Black Experience in America.** Boston, Mass.: Twayne, 1972. 250p. $7.95.
A history emphasizing attempts to colonize Negroes, the Blacks' struggle for self-improvement and equal rights. Covers Black achievements in the arts and the Harlem Renaissance.

686. Curtis, Richard. **The Life of Malcolm X.** Philadelphia, Pa.: Macrae Smith, 1971. 160p. $4.95. (7-9)
The evolution of Malcolm X's views on black and white relations is described.

687.   Cutler, John H. **Ed Brooke: Biography of a Senator.** Indianapolis, Ind.:
       Bobbs-Merrill, 1972. 430p. $12.00. (7-12)
A biography of the first Black senator after the Civil War. Includes his speeches,
appointments, and the newspaper coverage given to Mr. Brooke.

688.   David, Jay, and Catherine J. Greene, eds. **Black Roots: An Anthology.** New
       York: Lothrop, 1971. 224p. $5.50. (6-12)
A collection of essays by 20 Black Americans who describe their childhood lives
growing up in America. Authors include Floyd Patterson, Eartha Kitt, Roy
Campanella, Lena Horne, Langston Hughes, Claude Brown, Dick Gregory, Maya
Angelou, Anne Moody.

689.   Davis, Angela, *et al.* **If They Come in the Morning: Voices of Resistance.**
       New York: Third Press, 1971. 281p. $6.95. (9-12)
A collection of writings by Angela Davis, James Baldwin, George Jackson, and other
militant Blacks. Another title by Ms. Davis is: *Angela Davis: An Autobiography*
(Bantam, 1974. $8.95; $1.95pa.).

690.   Davis, Daniel S. **Marcus Garvey.** New York: Watts, 1972. 179p. $4.90. (7-10)
The story of a Black American who organized and led the Universal Improvement
Association, founded the *Negro World* newspaper and also a steamship company
owned and operated by Blacks, The Black Star Line. Another title by the author is
*Mr. Black Labor: The Story of A. Philip Randolph, Father of the Civil Rights Move-
ment* (Dutton, 1972. $7.50).

691.   Dekay, James T. **Meet Martin Luther King.** New York: Random House,
       1969. 89p. $3.77. (2-5)
This story of the life of Martin Luther King can be read to first graders and read by
children in grades two to five.

692.   Dobrin, Arnold. **Voices of Joy, Voices of Freedom.** New York: Coward,
       1972. 127p. $5.95. (5-9)
Short biographical narratives about prominent Blacks in the twentieth century.
Included are Marion Anderson, Sammy Davis, Jr., Lena Horne, Paul Robeson, and
Ethel Waters.

693.   Dorman, James H., and Robert R. Jones, eds. **The Afro-American Exper-
       ience: A Cultural History through Emancipation.** New York: Wiley,
       1974. 274p. $9.75; $4.95pa. (9-12)
Examines the values and philosophies as well as the incidents that shaped Black
American history.

694.   Douglas, William O. **Mister Lincoln and the Negroes: The Long Road to
       Equality.** New York: Atheneum, 1963. 237p. $4.95. (9-12)
Douglas attempts to give a social and historical interpretation to Abraham Lincoln's
philosophy of racial equality. Included are texts of some of the important documents concerned with the Black American struggle for civil rights.

695. Drisko, Carol, and Edgar A. Toppin. **The Unfinished March: The History of the Negro in the United States, Reconstruction to World War I.** New York: Doubleday, 1967. 118p. $3.75; $1.45pa. (6-9)
A history of the Blacks in America from the post-Civil War Reconstruction period to World War I.

696. Drotning, Phillip T., and Wesley South. **Up from the Ghetto.** New York: Cowles, 1969. 207p. $0.95pa. (9-12)
A collection of biographical narratives about people prominent in Black American history, politics, and the civil rights movement. Included are Shirley Chisholm; poet Gwendolyn Brooks; Richard Hatcher, mayor of Gary, Indiana; and others. Another title by Drotning is *Black Heroes in Our Nation's History* (Regnery, 1970. $6.95; $0.95pa.).

697. Du Bois, William Edward Burghardt. **A W. E. B. Du Bois Reader.** Ed. by Andrew G. Paschal. New York: Macmillan, 1971. 471p. $5.95. (9-12)
The selections in the collection are representative of Du Bois's entire writing career. Another title by the author is *The Souls of Black Folk* (Fawcett World, 1973. $1.25pa.).

698. Ducas, George, and Charles Van Doren, eds. **Great Documents in Black American History.** New York: Praeger, 1970. 321p. $12.50; $4.95pa. (9-12)
A collection of writings in the form of letters, speeches, essays, personal narratives, etc., by outstanding Black American leaders. Indexed.

699. Duckett, Alfred. **Changing of the Guard: The New Breed of Black Politicians.** New York: Coward, 1972. 126p. $4.00. (6-12)
Describes the new Black politicians who are becoming strong activist leaders in America.

700. Durham, Philip, and Everett Jones. **Adventures of the Negro Cowboys.** New York: Dodd, 1966. 143p. $4.50; $0.95pa. (8-12)
The contributions made by Black Americans in their seldom-discussed role as developers of the American West.

701. Ebony Editors. **Ebony Pictorial History of Black America.** Chicago: Johnson Publishing Co., 1971. 4 vols. $38.90. (4-12)
Titles in this history include: Vol. 1, *African Past to Civil War*; Vol. 2, *Reconstruction to Supreme Court Decision, 1954*; Vol. 3, *Civil Rights Movement to Black Revolution*; Vol. 4, *The 1973 Yearbook.*

702. Epstein, Sam, and Beryl Epstein. **Harriet Tubman, Guide to Freedom.** Illus. by Paul Frame. Champaign, Ill.: Garrard, 1968. 96p. $0.95pa. (3-6)
The story of Harriet Tubman as a runaway slave and the risks she took to help others find freedom via the underground railroad.

703.   Fax, Elton C. **Contemporary Black Leaders.** New York: Dodd, 1970.
        243p. $4.95; $1.95pa. (6-9)
Biographical sketches of 14 Black leaders including Malcolm X, Bayard Rustin,
Whitney Young, Coretta Scott King, Roy Wilkins, Thurgood Marshall, Floyd B.
McKissick, Fannie Lou Hamer, Charles Evers, Carl B. Stokes, Richard G. Hatcher,
Edward W. Brooks, Dr. Kenneth Clark, and Ruby Dee. Photographs included.

704.   Feelings, Muriel. **Jambo Means Hello: Swahili Alphabet Book.** Illus. by
        Tom Feelings. New York: Dial, 1974. 60p. $5.95. (5-12)
This picture book of African life and words has won several awards, including the
1975 Caldecott Honor Book award. A similar title by the author, of comparable
quality, is *Moja Means One: Swahili Counting Book* (Dial, 1971. $4.95).

705.   Feelings, Tom. **Black Pilgrimage.** New York: Lothrop, 1972. 72p. $6.95.
        (7-10)
Paintings and drawings by a Black artist including illustrations of over 70 Blacks.
Many were done in Brooklyn and depict the mood of the ghetto environment.
Although the author is leaving America to return to Africa, his pictures are arranged
in an excellent and moving chronology of the Black experience.

706.   Fenderson, Lewis H. **Daniel Hale Williams, Open Heart Doctor.** New York:
        McGraw-Hill, 1975. 128p. $4.72. (4-6)
An outstanding Black American surgeon who helped establish Provident Hospital
and Nursing School for Blacks. He was also a champion for racial equality. The
author has also written *Thurgood Marshall, Fighter for Justice.*

707.   Fishel, Leslie H., and Benjamin Quarles, eds. **The Black American: A
        Documentary History.** Glenview, Ill.: Scott, Foresman, 1970. 536p.
        $6.50 (brief); $8.50 (full). (9-12)
The history of the Black American is documented through newspaper accounts,
memoirs, speeches, travelogues, and other writings from Colonial America to the
1960s. Illustrations included; not indexed.

708.   Flynn, James J. **Negroes of Achievement in Modern America.** New York:
        Dodd, 1970. 272p. $4.50. (7-12)
Documents with photographs the life stories of 22 Black men and women who have
made significant contributions to contemporary America.

709.   Foner, Philip S. **The Voice of Black America.** New York: Simon &
        Schuster, 1972. 2 vols. 1215p. $3.25ea. (9-12)
Major speeches by Negroes in the United States from 1797 to 1971, with brief
biographical information on the speakers and a summary of the context of the
historical event in which the speech was made.

710.   Franklin, John Hope. **From Slavery to Freedom: A History of American
        Negroes.** 4th ed. New York: Knopf, 1974. 548p. $13.95; $6.95pa.
A basic history of Negro Americans from African origins to the perspectives of the
1970s. Illustrations, current statistics, and a bibliography are provided. Another title
by the author is *An Illustrated History of Black Americans* (Time-Life Books, 1970.
$7.95).

711. Frazier, Thomas R. **Afro-American History: Primary Sources.** New York: Harcourt, Brace & World, 1970, 1971. 280p. $5.95. (6-12)
Primary documents in a chronological arrangement. Includes statements made by prominent Black leaders. Emphasis is on the twentieth century. A brief historical introduction and bibliography included in each section. Another major work on Blacks by the author is *The Negro in the United States*, 2nd ed. (Macmillan, 1957. $10.95).

712. Friedman, Ina R. **Black Cop.** Philadelphia, Pa.: Westminster, 1974. 159p. $5.95. (7-10)
A biography of Tilmon B. O'Bryant, Assistant Chief of Police in Washington, D.C.

713. Fulks, Bryan. **Black Struggle: A History of the Negro in America.** New York: Delacorte, 1970. 368p. $5.95; $0.75pa. (6-12)
Covers all aspects of the Black experience in America with emphasis on the struggle for civil rights and equality.

714. Gayle, Addison, Jr. **Oak and Ivy: A Biography of Paul Laurence Dunbar.** New York: Doubleday, 1971. 175p. $4.50; $1.95pa. (7-12)
A well-written biography of the famous nineteenth century Black poet, not only describing his personal life, but pointing out how his work revealed the Black-white roles and relations of his time.

715. Goldman, Peter. **Civil Rights: The Challenge of the Fourteenth Amendment.** Rev. ed. New York: Coward, 1970. 120p. $4.00. (6-8)
A summary of the Blacks' struggle to obtain equal civil rights in America from the Emancipation Proclamation to the 1960s. Another title by the author is *Report from Black America* (Simon & Schuster, 1970. $6.95).

716. Goldston, Robert. **Negro Revolution: From Its African Genesis to the Death of Martin Luther King.** New York: Macmillan, 1968. 247p. $5.95. Teacher's manual, $0.60. (7-12, T)
A history of the Black man's protest against suppression and the quest for civil rights from its beginning to the death of Martin Luther King.

717. Goodman, M. C., and Kenneth Clark. **A Junior History of the American Negro.** New York: Fleet Press, 1969-70. 2 vols. $5.00 each; teaching manual, $0.50. (6-12, T)
A survey of the American Black experience with attention to some of the more prominent representatives of Black history, life, and culture. Volume 1 is entitled *Discovery to Civil War*; Volume 2 is *Civil War to Civil Rights War.*

718. Grant, Matthew G. **Harriet Tubman: Black Liberator.** Chicago: Childrens Press, 1974. 31p. $4.95. (2-4)
A biography for primary children on Harriet Tubman, runaway slave who helped 300 other slaves escape to freedom.

719. Gregory, Dick. **The Shadow That Scares Me.** Edited by James R. McGraw. New York: Doubleday, 1968. 213p. $4.95; $0.75pa. (9-12)

An analysis of the faults in American society with respect to racial problems. Other titles by Gregory are *Nigger* (McGraw-Hill, 1970. $2.12); *Up from Nigger* (Stein & Day, 1975. $8.95).

720.   Harris, Janet, and Julius Hobson. **Black Pride: A People's Struggle**. New York: McGraw-Hill, 1969. 160p. $4.95. (5-12)
Black power and patterns of Black protest are examined, with attention to Black leaders symbolic of the movement. Another title by Harris is *The Long Freedom Road* (McGraw-Hill, 1967. $4.72).

721.   Harris, Middleton, *et al.* **The Black Book**. New York: Random House, 1974. 198p. $5.95pa. (6-12)
A scrapbook covering 300 years of Black history in America recorded in photos, posters, recipes, news clippings, games, music, movies, advertisements, illustrations, and other unique items.

722.   Hasegawa, Sam. **Stevie Wonder**. Illus. by Dick Brude. Chicago: Childrens Press, 1974. 32p. $4.95. (4-7)
Portrays the family background and career of this popular Black musician. Other titles by the same publisher for this grade level are: *The Jackson Five*, by Charles and Ann Morse; *Roberta Flack* and *Aretha Franklin*, by James T. Olson; and *Duke Ellington: Ambassador of Music*, by Pamela Barclay.

723.   Haskins, James. **Ralph Bunche: A Most Reluctant Hero**. New York: Hawthorn, 1974. 134p. $6.95. (7-12)
A fine account of the first Black American to have an influential position in the state department, and winner of the Nobel Peace Prize in 1950. Other titles by the author are *Fighting Shirley Chisholm* (Dial, 1975. $5.95); *A Piece of the Power: Four Black Mayors* (Dial, 1972. $5.95); *Adam Clayton Powell: Portrait of a Marching Black* (Dial, 1974. $4.95); and *The Picture Life of Malcolm X* (Watts, 1975. $3.90).

724.   Hayden, Robert C. **Seven Black American Scientists**. Reading, Mass.: Addison-Wesley, 1970. 172p. $5.50. (7-9)
Prominent Black American scientists are covered here, including Benjamin Banneker, Daniel Hale Williams, Dr. Charles Drew, and G. W. Carver.

725.   Greenfield, Eloise. **Paul Robeson**. New York: Crowell, 1975. 33p. $4.50. (2-4)
A story of a famous Black artist and leader and the heritage of the Black people. Another title by the author is *Rosa Parks* (Crowell, 1973. $4.50).

726.   Griffin, Judith Berry. **Nat Turner**. Illus. by Leo Carty. New York: Coward-McCann, 1970. 62p. $3.99. (3-6)
The story of Nat Turner, leader of a slave rebellion, with emphasis on his youth and early experiences leading to his frustration and hatred of whites.

727.   Groh, George W. **The Black Migration**. New York: Weybright and Talley, 1972. 301p. $8.95. (9-12)

Traces the migrations of the Blacks after slavery and the response to his new urban environments.

728.   Grossman, Barney, and Gladys Groom. **Black Means.** New York: Hill and
         Wang, 1970. unp. $4.95. (K-4)
Positive images are given to the word black by describing and picturing pleasant things that are black.

729.   Haber, Louis. **Black Pioneers of Science and Invention.** New York:
         Harcourt Brace Jovanovich, 1970. 181p. $6.75. (5-12)
Covers the contributions in science and technology made by 14 Black Americans.

730.   Hamilton, Charles V. **The Black Experience in American Politics.** New
         York: Putnam's, 1973. 358p. $3.25. (10-12)
A collection of readings on: 1) programs relevant to the Black culture, 2) radical left politics, 3) attention to the role of the federal government in connection with Blacks.

731.   Hamilton, Virginia. **Paul Robeson: The Life and Times of a Free Black
         Man.** New York: Harper, 1974. 256p. $5.95. (9-12)
A sympathetic biography of Robeson, a former slave, actor, singer, and Communist sympathizer rejected by the Black people. Ms. Hamilton has also written *W. E. B. Du Bois: A Biography* (Crowell, 1972. $5.95).

732.   Haralambos, Michael. **Right On: From Blues to Soul in Black America.**
         New York: Drake, 1975. 187p. $5.33. (9-12)
The growth and development of Black music is traced. Special emphasis on the history of the blues.

733.   Heard, J. Norman. **Black Frontiersmen: Adventures of Negroes among
         American Indians.** New York: John Day, 1969. 128p. $3.95. (6-12)
Describes the experiences of two Black Americans and their relations with the American Indians, including a missionary and a Crow Indian chief.

734.   Holt, Deloris L. **The ABC's of Black History.** Illus. by Samuel Bhang, Jr.
         Los Angeles: Ritchie, 1971. unp. $4.50. (2-4)
Biographical sketches of famous Black Americans from the earliest period of America's development to the present. Attention is given to American Negroes often neglected in the field of children's literature.

735.   Hopkins, Lee Bennett. **Important Dates in Afro-American History.** New
         York: Watts, 1969. 188p. $4.90. (4-7)
A chronology of important events in Black history including important holidays and birth dates of Blacks who have made significant contributions to American society and/or the Black community.

736.   Howard, Thomas, ed. **Black Voyage: Eyewitness Accounts of the Atlantic
         Slave Trade.** Boston, Mass.: Little, Brown, 1971. 243p. $5.95. (6-12)

The impact of slavery on Americans is described through personal testimonies of slaves, traders, slave ship crewmen, and others.

737.   Hughes, Langston. **Famous American Negroes.** New York: Dodd, 1954. 147p. $3.95. (7-9)
Two collections of biographical sketches are the above title and *Famous Negro Heroes of America* (Dodd, 1958. $3.95).

738.   Hughes, Langston, Milton Meltzer, and E. Eric Lincoln. **A Pictorial History of Black Americans.** 4th rev. ed. New York: Crown, 1973. 377p. $4.95. (7-12)
Updates *A Pictorial History of the Negro in America* by including more details on the recent protest and civil rights movements. Also covers Black politics, achievements, problems in education, and recent developments in religion and the arts. Over 1,000 illustrations are included. Another title by the author is *The Book of Negro Humor* (Dodd, Mead, 1966).

739.   Jackson, Florence, and J. B. Jackson. **The Black Man in America.** New York: Watts, 1970-75. 6 vols. $3.90 each. (7-12)
The history of Black struggle, experience, and contributions in the arts, government, politics, and the struggle for civil rights is covered in this chronological set. Volume 1 covers 1619-1790; Volume 2, 1791-1861; Volume 3, 1861-1877; Volume 4, 1877-1905; Volume 5, 1905-1932; and Volume 6, 1932-1954.

740.   Jackson, Jesse. **Make a Joyful Noise Unto the Lord! The Life of Mahalia Jackson, Queen of Gospel Singers.** New York: Crowell, 1974. 160p. $5.50; $1.50pa. (5-9)
Describes the highlights of Mahalia Jackson's career as a gospel singer, her philosophies of life and contributions to the elimination of discrimination against Afro-Americans. Another title by the author is *Tessie* (Harper and Row, 1968; $4.95; $1.50pa.).

741.   Jackson, Jesse, and Elaine Landau. **Black in America—A Fight for Freedom.** New York: Messner, 1973. 112p. $5.29. (4-8)
An illustrated history of Blacks in America with emphasis on their struggle for civil rights and freedom from slavery, oppression, and discrimination. A list of outstanding Black Americans is included; the work is indexed.

742.   Johnston, Johanna. **A Special Bravery.** New York: Apollo, 1970. 94p. $0.95pa. (K-4)
A collection of narratives about Black Americans whose "special bravery" or achievements have earned them fame in American history. Other titles by the author are: *Paul Cuffe: America's First Black Captain* (Dodd, 1970. $4.50) and *Together in America* (Apollo, 1971. $1.95pa.).

743.   Jones, Hettie. **Big Star Fallin' Mama: Five Black Women in Black Music.** New York: Viking, 1974. 150p. $5.95. (7-12)
A history of the origin and characteristics of the blues and Black singers of the blues are described in biographical sketches of Ma Rainey, Bessie Smith, Mahalia

Jackson, Billie Holiday, and Aretha Franklin. Also included is an annotated list of other well-known Black women in music.

744.   Jordan, June. **Dry Victories.** New York: Holt, Rinehart & Winston, 1972. 80p. $5.50. (6-9)
Compares the status of the Blacks during different periods of U.S. history. Other titles by the author are *Fannie Lou Hamer* (Crowell, 1972. $4.50), *Who Look at Me* (Crowell, 1969. $8.50), and *Some Changes* (Dutton, 1971. $5.50; $2.95pa.). The latter titles are for young children.

745.   Katz, William Loren. **The Black West: A Documentary and Pictorial History.** Rev. ed. Garden City, N.Y.: Doubleday, 1971, 1973. 336p. $12.95; $5.59pa. (9-12)
This history of Black Americans is limited to their experience and contributions in the West. Other history texts by the author are *Eyewitness: The Negro in American History* (Pitman, 1967, 1974. $12.50; teacher's manual, $1.00), and *A History of Black Americans* (Harcourt Brace Jovanovich, 1973. $3.69).

746.   King, Martin Luther. **Why We Can't Wait.** New York: Harper and Row, 1964. 178p. $9.95. (9-12)
A description of Dr. King's campaign to obtain equal rights through non-violence. Other titles by Dr. King are *We Shall Live in Peace* (Hawthorn, 1968. $3.95), *Where Do We Go from Here? Chaos or Community* (Beacon Press, 1967. $7.95; $3.95pa.), and *Stride toward Freedom* (Harper and Row, 1955. $4.95; $0.75pa.).

747.   Klein, Aaron. **The Hidden Contributors: Black Scientists and Inventors in America.** Garden City, N.Y.: Doubleday, 1971. 203p. $4.95. (7-12)
A collection of brief biographies on Black scientists, doctors, and inventors, including some quite famous ones and others less well known.

748.   Lacy, Leslie Alexander. **Cheer the Lonesome Traveler: The Life of W. E. B. Du Bois.** New York: Dial, 1970. 160p. $5.95. (4-6)
An award-winning biography of W. E. B. Du Bois, Black leader and philosopher.

749.   Ladner, Joyce A. **Tomorrow's Tomorrow: The Black Woman.** New York: Doubleday, 1971. 304p. $2.50pa. (10-12, T)
A revision of the author's thesis from Washington University on Black women and Black families. A scholarly study, but included for its timeliness.

750.   Latham, Frank B. **The Dred Scott Decision, March 6, 1857: Slavery and the Supreme Courts "Self-Inflicted Wound."** New York: Watts, 1968. 54p. $3.95. (7-12)
The most famous slavery case in U.S. history is described here with a discussion of the events leading up to it, the Supreme Court trial, and the implications of the outcome. Another title by the author is: *The Rise and Fall of Jim Crow: The Long Struggle against the Supreme Court's Separate-but-Equal Ruling* (Watts, 1969. $3.90; $0.95pa.).

751.   Lawrence, Jacob. **Harriet and the Promised Land**. New York: Simon & Schuster, 1968. unp. $6.73. (2-4)
A picture book of Harriet Tubman's escape from slavery and her role in helping 300 Blacks to escape to the "promised land" of the North. The author has also illustrated this account with bold design and colors in the style of Picasso.

752.   Lerner, Gerda, ed. **Black Women in White America: A Documentary History**. New York: Random House, 1973. 630p. $12.95; $2.65pa. (9-12)
A compilation of letters, articles, and essays on the struggle of Black women in America to achieve recognition and equal rights. Includes biographical sketches and covers the Black woman's role and contributions.

753.   Lester, Julius. **To Be a Slave**. Illus. by Tom Feelings. New York: Dial, 1968. 160p. $3.95; $1.25pa. (5-9)
In this 1969 Newbery Honor Book, former slaves tell, in their own words, how it felt to be a slave. A chronological arrangement of their testimonies is included, with full-page illustrations. Another title by the author is *Black Folktales* (Grove Press, 1969. $1.95pa.).

754.   Lewis, Claude. **Benjamin Banneker: The Man Who Saved Washington**. New York: McGraw-Hill, 1970. 128p. $4.72. (4-7)
The story of a self-educated Black and his role in the nation's capitol building, and maker of the first clock in America.

755.   Lincoln, Charles Eric. **The Black Muslims in America**. Rev. ed. Boston, Mass.: Beacon Press, 1973. 302p. $12.50; $3.50pa. (9-12)
Studies and analyzes the history and objectives of the Black Muslim movement. Another title by the author is *The Negro Pilgrimage in America: The Coming of Age of Black America* (Praeger, 1969. $5.95).

756.   Logan, Rayford W. **The Negro in the United States. Vol. 1, A History to 1945: From Slavery to Second-Class Citizenship**. Magnolia, Mass.: Peter Smith, 1957. 168p. $5.50. (7-12)
A narrative, with documents included, on the history of Blacks in America. Covers outstanding individuals and institutions, legislation and court cases. Volume 2 in the series, by Logan and Michael R. Winston, is entitled: *The Ordeal of Democracy* (Peter Smith; $5.50). Also, Logan and Irving S. Cohen have written *The American Negro: Old World Background and New World Experience* (Houghton, 1970. $3.95pa.).

757.   Mapp, Edward. **Blacks in American Films: Today and Yesterday**. Metuchen, N.J.: Scarecrow, 1971, 1972. 278p. $8.50. (9-12)
Examines the role of Blacks in American films. Arrangement is chronological, and a bibliography is included.

758.   Maynard, Richard A. **The Black Man on Film: Racial Stereotyping**. Rochelle Park, N.J.: Hayden Book Co., 1974. 134p. $3.50pa. (10-12, T)
A collection of articles and discussions on stereotyping of Blacks in American films. Reasons for stereotyping and suggestions for eliminating it are excellent bases for student discussion.

759.   McCague, James. **The Road to Freedom: 1815-1900.** Champaign, Ill.: Garrard, 1972. 2 vols. $3.78 each. (5-9)
Traces the history of slavery in the United States in the early nineteenth century, the abolition movement, and the fate of Blacks after the Civil War. The first volume in this series is entitled *The Long Bondage, 1441-1815.*

760.   McCarthy, Agnes, and Lawrence Reddick. **Worth Fighting For: The History of the Negro in the United States during the Civil War & Reconstruction.** Illus. by Colleen Browning. New York: Doubleday, 1965. 118p. $3.75; $1.45pa. (6-9)
A history of the Negro during the Civil War and Reconstruction period especially designed for the slow reader at the junior high level.

761.   McElroy, Clifford D., Jr. **The House with 100 Lights.** New York: McGraw-Hill, 1971. unp. $4.95. (K-3)
New York City's Black children reveal, in their own language, how they feel about their physical surroundings. Black and white photos by Bonnie Unsworth help tell the story.

762.   McPherson, James. **Marching toward Freedom: The Negro in the Civil War, 1861-1865.** New York: Knopf, 1967. 181p. $3.95. (7-12)
Describes the role of the Black soldier in the Union Army as well as Black men and women who aided by serving as spies, nurses, messengers, etc. Another title by the author is *The Struggle for Equality* (Princeton University Press, 1967. $3.95); he also edited *The Negro's Civil War* (Pantheon, 1965. $7.95).

763.   Meltzer, Ida S. **Black History: Events in February.** Brooklyn, N.Y.: Book-Lab, Inc., 1972. $16.50 (set of thirty). (4-8)
Each title in this series consists of four softbound books, each of which is a feature story about the life of a famous black man or woman or an event in Black history, followed by a variety of activities to help develop vocabulary, word attack, comprehension, and writing skills. The books are written at fourth- and fifth-grade reading levels in an informal and readable style. An answer key is provided to enable self-checks and reviews. Teaching suggestions are included in a brief teacher's guide. Photographs and sketches are in black and white.

764.   Meltzer, Milton. **In Their Own Words: A History of the American Negro: Vol. 1, 1619-1865; Vol. 2, 1865-1916; Vol. 3, 1916-1966.** New York: Crowell, 1970. $5.95 ea.; $1.65 (Apollo pa. ed.). (9-12)
A three-volume series giving Black American history through excerpts from books, letters, interviews, government documents, articles, newspapers, and other writings by Blacks. Other titles for the intermediate grades are *Slavery I: From the Rise of Western Civilization to the Renaissance* (Regnery, 1970. $8.50) and *Slavery II: From the Renaissance to Today* (Regnery, 1972. $8.50).

765.   Meltzer, Milton, and August Meier. **Time of Trial, Time of Hope: The Negro in America, 1919-1941.** Garden City, N.Y.: Doubleday, 1966. 120p. $3.75; $1.45pa. (7-9)
The period between World War I and World War II is analyzed with respect to the

prevailing conditions among Black Americans. Covers the roles of federal agencies, and Black organizations such as the NAACP, Urban League, and others in the struggle for social and economic equality.

766.   Meriwether, Louise. **Don't Ride the Bus on Monday: The Rosa Parks Story.** Englewood Cliffs, N.J.: Prentice-Hall, 1973. unp. $4.95. (3-5)
Describes the situation in the South that triggered a major battle in the campaign for Black civil rights when Rose Parks refused to give up her seat on a bus. Another title by the author for the primary level is *The Freedom Ship of Robert Smalls* (Prentice-Hall, 1971. $4.95).

767.   Mitchell, Loften. **Black Drama: The Story of the American Negro in the Theatre.** New York: Hawthorn, 1970. 224p. $7.95; $2.45pa. (10-12)
An autobiographical history of the Negro in the American theater, with emphasis on the Harlem community and the Negro Renaissance of the 1920s.

768.   Morsbach, Mabel. **The Negro in American Life.** New York: Harcourt Brace & World, 1967, 1968. 273p. $7.50. (7-12)
This history of the American Negro includes brief biographical sketches of over 300 Black Americans. Includes maps and illustrations.

769.   Myrdal, Gunnar, *et al.* **An American Dilemma: The Negro Problem and American Democracy.** Rev. ed. New York: Harper and Row, 1962. 2 vols. $3.95 each pa. (T)
A thorough study of Black America first published in 1944, with a "Postscript Twenty Years Later" covering 1942 to 1962 in the 1962 edition. The study, well known for its accuracy and sociological relevance, was reprinted in 1975. A bibliography and index are included.

770.   Olsen, James T. **Muhammad Ali: I Am the Greatest.** Illus. by Harold Henriksen. Chicago: Childrens Press, 1974. 30p. $4.95. (3-4)
An understandable account of Ali's philosophies, religious views, and personal career in boxing. Includes many quotes by Ali.

771.   Orr, Jack. **Black Athlete: His Story in American History.** Introd. by Jackie Robinson. New York: Lion, 1969. 157p. $6.59. (6-12)
The story of the Black athlete in American baseball, football, basketball, boxing, golf, horseracing, and other sports.

772.   Parks, Gordon. **Born Black.** Philadelphia, Pa.: Lippincott, 1971. 192p. $10.00. (9-12)
Examines leaders and incidents during the decade of the 1960s civil rights and protest movements. Public reactions to the deaths of Martin Luther King and Malcolm X are studied. Photographs and essays on recent Black leaders are provided, as well as a photographic essay of a typical Black American family.

773.   Patterson, Lillie. **Martin Luther King, Jr.: Man of Peace.** Illus. by Victor Mays. Champaign, Ill.: Garrard, 1969. 96p. $3.58. (3-6)

The life of Martin Luther King, with an explanation of his philosophies and the values by which he lived and for which he died.

774. Peters, Margaret W. **The Ebony Book of Black Achievement.** Illus. by Cecil L. Ferguson. Chicago: Johnson Publishing Co., 1974. 90p. $5.50. (4-8)

A collection of biographical sketches of 21 Black American men and women who have made important contributions in various walks of life. Coverage is given to some individuals not included in other popular collections.

775. Petry, Ann. **Harriet Tubman: Conductor on the Underground Railroad.** New York: Washington Square Press, c1955, 1971. 227p. $3.95; $2.00pa. (7-11)

A well-reviewed account of Harriet Tubman's escape route on the underground railroad for over 300 slaves.

776. Pinkney, Alphonso. **Black Americans.** Englewood Cliffs, N.J.: Prentice-Hall, c1969, 1975. 242p. $8.95; $3.95pa. (9-12)

Surveys the Black American population with respect to its social institutions, patterns of stratification, assimilation, and behavior.

777. Radford, Ruby L. **Mary McLeod Bethune.** Rev. ed. Illus. by Lydia Rosier. New York: Putnam's, 1973. 61p. $3.96. (2-4)

An easy-to-read historical biography of Mary McLeod Bethune's accomplishments in the struggle for equality for Blacks.

778. Richardson, Ben Albert, and William A. Fahey. **Great Black Americans.** 2nd rev. ed. New York: Crowell, 1976. 344p. $7.50. (7-9)

A collection of biographical sketches on famous Black leaders such as Paul Robeson, Dick Gregory, James Baldwin, W. E. B. Du Bois, Malcolm X, Martin Luther King, Jr., Althea Gibson, Bill Russell. Emphasis is on contemporary leaders from a wide variety of backgrounds and professions.

779. Robinson, Jackie, with Al Duckett. **I Never Had It Made.** New York: Putnam's, 1972. 256p. $7.95. (9-12)

A moving account of the life of the first Black baseball player. It relates his struggles, achievements, racial prejudices encountered, personal tragedies, and admission to the Baseball Hall of Fame.

780. Rollins, Charlemae H. **Famous Negro Entertainers of Stage, Screen and TV.** New York: Dodd, 1967. 122p. $3.95. (7-12)

A history of the Black American in the entertainment world. Other titles by the author are: *The Christmas Gift* (Follett, 1963. $7.95); *Famous Negro Poets* (Dodd, 1970. $4.95); *They Showed the Way: Forty American Negro Leaders* (Crowell, 1964. $3.95).

781. Rowe, Jeanne A. **An Album of Martin Luther King, Jr.** New York: Watts, 1970. 72p. $4.90. (4-8)

A biography of Dr. Martin Luther King from his childhood to his death while active in the civil rights movement.

782. Rublowsky, John. **Black Music in America.** New York: Basic Books, 1971. 150p. $7.95. (9-12)
A history of the development of Black music in America from its earliest forms and beginnings. Emphasis is on ragtime, jazz, and rock-and-roll. A bibliography is included.

783. Rudeen, Kenneth. **Jackie Robinson.** Illus. by Richard Cuffari. New York: Crowell, 1971. 40p. $3.75. (4-12)
A biography of Jackie Robinson, the first Black man in major league baseball. Another sports biography by the author is *Wilt Chamberlain* (Crowell, 1970. $3.75).

784. Sanders, Ruby Wilson. **Jazz Ambassador: Louis Armstrong.** Illus. by John Solie. Chicago: Childrens Press, 1973. 79p. $6.00. (4-6)
A biography of Louis "Satchmo" Armstrong describes his early background, how he learned to play the cornet, and how he got into the entertainment world.

785. Schraff, A. E. **Black Courage.** Illus. by Len Ebert. Philadelphia, Pa.: Macrae, 1969. 158p. $5.97. (3-6)
The 21 Blacks described here all played courageous roles in the history and development of the Western states. Included are explorers, pioneers, miners, cowboys, and others.

786. Schultz, Pearle Henriksen. **Paul Laurence Dunbar: Black Poet Laureate.** Illus. by William Hutchinson. Champaign, Ill.: Garrard, 1974. 142p. $3.94. (4-7)
A biography of a Black American poet, his growing-up years, and a selection of some of his best-known dialect poems for children.

787. Seaberg, Stanley. **The Negro in American History.** New York: Scholastic Book Service, c1969, 1974. 2 vols. $1.25 each pa. (8-12)
A two-volume series on Black history and experience in America. Volume 1 is entitled *Which Way to Citizenship?*; Volume 2 is entitled *Which Way to Equality?*

788. Selby, Earl, and Miriam Selby. **Odyssey: Journey through Black America.** New York: Putnam's, 1971. 381p. $7.95. (9-12)
Interviews with over 400 Blacks from all ages and life styles record the experience of the contemporary Black community.

789. Simmons, Gloria M., Helene D. Hutchinson, and Henry E. Simmons. **Black Culture: Reading and Writing Black.** New York: Holt, Rinehart & Winston, 1972. 328p. $5.95pa. (9-12)
A collection of prose, poetry, and illustrations by Blacks divided into several major categories: The Beauty of Being Black; Language of Soul; Psyche of the White; Violated Self; Rage; Ideology; and Black Heritage.

790.   Spangler, Earl. **The Negro in America.** 4th rev. ed. Minneapolis, Minn.:
       Lerner, 1969. 93p. $3.95. (5-10)
A history of the Blacks in American life, with emphasis on their long struggle for
equal rights from Colonial days to the 1960s.

791.   Sterling, Dorothy, comp. **Speak Out in Thunder Tones: Letters and Other
       Writings by Black Northerners, 1787-1865.** New York: Doubleday, 1973.
       396p. $5.95. (8-12)
A history of free Blacks in the North during the years of slavery, the first title in a
three-volume series on the issues of the Black revolution prior to the Civil War
between 1787 to 1865. Other titles by the author are: *It Started in Montgomery:
A Picture History of the Civil Rights Movement* (Scholastic Book Service, 1974.
$2.00pa.), for younger children in the intermediate grades, and *Tear Down the
Walls: A History of the American Civil Rights Movement* (Doubleday, 1968.
$6.95), for junior high levels.

792.   Sterling, Dorothy, and Dr. Benjamin Quarles. **Lift Every Voice.** Garden
       City, N.Y.: Doubleday, 1975. 116p. $3.00; $1.45pa. (6-12)
The lives of Booker T. Washington, W. E. B. Du Bois, Mary Church Terrell, and
James Weldon Johnson.

793.   Sterling, Philip, and Rayford Logan. **Four Took Freedom.** Garden City,
       N.Y.: Doubleday, 1967. 116p. $3.75. (7-9)
The lives of Harriet Tubman, Frederick Douglass, Robert Small, and Blanche K.
Bruce.

794.   Sterne, Emma G. **They Took Their Stand.** New York: Crowell, c1968,
       1970. 238p. $4.50. (6-9)
A collection of biographical sketches about Southerners in the U.S. who dared to
stand up for the rights of Blacks. Other Black leaders in the civil rights movement are
covered in the author's *I Have a Dream* (Knopf, 1965. $5.39). Other titles are
Mary McLeod Bethune (Knopf, 1957. $5.39); *The Slave Ship* (original title: *The
Long Black Schooner*) (Scholastic, 1973. $0.95pa.).

795.   Stevenson, Janet. **The Montgomery Bus Boycott: December, 1955.** New
       York: Watts, 1971. 64p. $3.90. (7-12)
A demand by American Blacks to end segregation, in one of the earlier activities
of the civil rights movement. Titles on the subject by the author include *The School
Segregation Cases* (Watts, 1973. $3.90) and *Soldiers in the Civil Rights War*
(Reilly & Lee, 1971. $5.95), for grades 4-6.

796.   Stull, Edith. **Unsung Black American Heroes and Heroines.** Illus. by
       Ernest Crichlow. New York: Grosset and Dunlap, 1970. 72p. $2.95. (3-6)
A Black history emphasizing less familiar Black figures who have made important
contributions. Indexed.

797.   Sullivan, George. **Hank Aaron.** Illus. by George Young. New York:
       Putnam's, 1975. 61p. $3.96. (2-4)

A primary level biography of Hank Aaron, famous Black American baseball Home Run King.

798.   Swift, Hildegarde Hoyt. **North Star Shining: A Pictorial History of the American Negro.** Illus. by Lynd Ward. New York: Morrow, 1947. 44p. $3.98. (5-9)
An older but well-written pictorial history of the Negro in America. Each character tells, in verse, his role in the development of America.

799.   Taylor, Paula. **Coretta King: A Woman of Peace.** Chicago: Childrens Press, 1975. 31p. $4.95. (4-8)
Describes the wife of Dr. Martin Luther King, a noted civil rights leader in her own right.

800.   Tobias, Tobi. **Arthur Mitchell.** Illus. by Carole Byard. New York: Crowell, 1975. 33p. $4.50. (2-4)
The life and career of a Black male ballet dancer and founder of the Dance Theatre of Harlem.

801.   Toppin, Edgar A. **The Black American in United States History.** Rockleigh, N.J.: Allyn, 1973. 512p. $6.50. (9-12)
An overview of Afro-American history and a collection of 140 biographical portraits. A bibliography at the end of each chapter is included. Could also serve as a reference tool and a teacher's manual.

802.   Wade, Richard C., and Howard R. Anderson, eds. **The Negro in American Life.** Boston, Mass.: Houghton Mifflin, 1970. 261p. $3.96pa. (9-12)
Selected readings divided into two sections: Part 1, From Slavery to Citizenship 1619-1900; Part 2, Toward Full Equality since 1900.

803.   Walker, Alice. **Langston Hughes, American Poet.** Illus. by Don Miller. Ed. by Susan B. Weber. New York: Crowell, 1974. 33p. $4.70. (3-5)
A story of the life of Langston Hughes, emphasizing his childhood, family life, and youth. Another title by the author is *In Love and Trouble: Stories of Black Women* (Harcourt Brace Jovanovich, 1973. $6.50; $2.65pa.).

804.   Warren, Robert P. **Who Speaks for the Negro?** New York: Random House, 1965. 454p. $10.00. (6-12)
A study of the civil rights movement is the main emphasis here, with Black American history and biography included. Information has been gathered by taped interviews from Blacks involved in the struggle for equality.

805.   Washington, Booker T. **Up from Slavery.** New York, Bantam, c1933, 1970. 256p. $0.75pa. (6-9)
The story of this son of a slave who struggled for an education and became the founder of Tuskegee Institute and helped his people attain educations.

806. Wayne, Bennett, ed. **Black Crusaders for Freedom.** Champaign, Ill.:
Garrard, 1974. 168p. $4.48. (3-4)
Describes some of the leaders and their activities in the civil rights movement.

807. Werstein, Irving. **A Proud People: Black Americans.** Philadelphia, Pa.:
M. Evans, 1970. 192p. $4.95. (7-9)
Discusses stereotypes commonly associated with Black Americans and indicates the
contributions and accomplishments by those who have overcome hostility and
discrimination.

808. White, Anne Terry. **North to Liberty.** Champaign, Ill.: Garrard, 1972.
126p. $3.78. (4-8)
Describes the underground railroad and the stations, famous conductors, and
slaves that were involved in it. Another title by the author is *Human Cargo, the
Story of the Atlantic Slave Trade* (Garrard, 1972. $3.78).

809. Whitlow, Roger. **Black American Literature: A Critical History of the
Major Periods, Movements, Themes, Works, and Authors.** Chicago:
Nelson-Hall, 1973. 287p. $8.95. (10-12)
The traditions and movements that have been a part of Black literature and its
development are described, as well as the roles of numerous Black writers. A
1,520-entry bibliography of works by and about Black Americans is included.

810. Woodson, Carter Q., and Charles H. Wesley. **The Negro in Our History.**
12th ed. Washington, D.C.: Associated Publishers, 1972. 917p. (10-12)
The Negro in American history is covered from African origins and institutions,
foreign aggression, and slavery to early civil rights efforts, to freedom in the United
States, and accomplishments of the Negro thereafter. Numerous photographs and
illustrations are included.

811. Yates, Elizabeth. **Amos Fortune, Free Man.** Illus. by Nora S. Unwin. New
York: Dutton, 1955. 181p. $3.95. (5-12)
The story of a slave who purchased his freedom and then helped other Black Ameri-
cans attain theirs. A 1955 Newbery Medal winner.

812. Young, B. E. **The Picture Story of Frank Robinson.** New York: Messner,
1975. 63p. $5.29; $1.95pa. (4-8)
Numerous pictures and large print make this an easy-to-read biography with a high
interest level. It includes the story of major league baseball and Frank Robinson,
the first Black manager.

813. Young, Margaret B. **Black American Leaders.** New York: Watts, 1969.
120p. $3.90. (7-12)
Describes various Black American leaders prominent in the struggle for civil rights,
and political or governmental positions. Other titles by the author are: *The First
Book of American Negroes* (Watts, 1967. $3.90); *A Picture Life of Martin Luther
King, Jr.* (Watts, 1968. $3.90); and *A Picture Life of Thurgood Marshall* (Watts,
1971. $3.90).

Literature and Fiction Titles

See also fiction bibliographies in reference section.

814.   Adoff, Arnold, ed. **Brothers and Sisters: Modern Stories by Black Americans.** New York: Dell, c1970, 1975. 246p. $6.95; $0.93pa. (6-12)
A collection of short stories with selections by Langston Hughes, Ralph Ellison, Gwendolyn Brooks, James Baldwin, and many others. Adoff has also written *Black Is Brown Is Tan* (Harper and Row, 1973. $4.95) for the primary reader.

815.   Adoff, Arnold, ed. **My Black Me: A Beginning Book of Black Poetry.** New York: Dutton, 1974. 83p. $6.50. (5-12)
A collection of 50 poems by Black Americans. The main theme centers around Black awareness and pride in the Black identity. A similar title by the author is *Black Out Loud* (Macmillan, 1970. $4.95), a 1970 ALA Notable Children's Book. He has also compiled an anthology for the senior high level entitled *The Poetry of Black America: Anthology of the 20 Century* (Harper and Row, 1973. $9.89).

816.   Alexander, Martha. **Sabrina.** New York: Dial, 1971. 32p. $4.95. (K-3)
A picture book, illustrated by the author, about Sabrina, a little girl who finds cultural conflicts on her first day at nursery school. Other titles by the author are *The Story Grandmother Told* (Dial, 1969. $4.95) and *Bobo's Dream* (Dial, 1970. $4.95).

817.   Ambrose, Amanda, ed. **My Name Is Black: Anthology of Black Poets.** New York: Scholastic Book Service, 1975. 211p. $1.25pa. (7-12)
A collection of Black poetry chosen for junior and senior high school curriculum units.

818.   Armstrong, William H. **Sounder.** New York: Harper and Row, 1969. 116p. $4.79; $1.25pa. (6-12)
A Newbery Award winning story about the heartbreaking conditions of a poor Negro family in the rural South. Their dog, Sounder, is shot by the white authorities. A similar title by the author is *Sour Land* (Harper and Row, 1971. $4.95).

819.   Arnott, Kathleen. **African Myths and Legends.** New York: Walck, 1963. 211p. $4.00. (4-7)
A collection of 34 native tales including animal stories and folklore with moral lessons.

820.   Baker, Elizabeth. **Stronger Than Hate.** Illus. by John Gretzer. Boston, Mass.: Houghton Mifflin, 1969. 185p. $3.50. (7-12)
A story of five Black families and their integration experiences in an all-white town.

821.   Baker, Houston A., comp. **Black Literature in America.** New York: McGraw-Hill, 1971. 443p. $6.95. (6-12)
An anthology of Afro-American folklore and literature with biographical data about the authors.

822.	Bambara, Toni Cade, ed. **Tales and Stories for Black Folks.** New York:
	Zenith (Doubleday), 1971. 164p. $3.00; $1.75pa. (4-12)
A collection of short stories by well-known Black writers as well as college students
writing about life in the Black ghetto or problems of Black young people in the
South.

823.	Blue, Rose. **The Preacher's Kid.** Illus. by Ted Lewin. New York: Watts,
	1975. 52p. $5.95. (4-6)
The daughter of a minister, who decides not to join the Black community in opposition to busing, experiences conflicts between family and friends. When she attends
a new school she is met with unexpected hostility. Another story for slightly
younger children by the author is *Black, Black, Beautiful Black* (Watts, 1969.
$3.95).

824.	Bonham, Frank. **Cool Cat.** New York: Dutton, 1971. 151p. $4.95. (7-12)
A realistic story set in the ghetto street world of gangs and drugs. A similar title is
Durango Street (Dutton, 1965. $5.25), for which the author won an ALA Notable
Book award. Bonham also wrote *Hey, Big Spender!* (Dutton, 1972. $5.95),
The Mystery of the Fat Cat (Dutton, 1968. $1.25), and *The Nitty Gritty* (Dutton,
1968. $5.95).

825.	Bonsall, Crosby. **The Case of the Scaredy Cats.** New York: Harper and
	Row, 1971. 64p. $2.75. (K-4)
Bonsall has written a series of brief "mysteries" about young Black children in their
neighborhoods. Included are *The Case of the Hungry Stranger* (1963. $3.79), *The
Case of the Cat's Meow* (1965. $2.95), and *The Case of the Dumb Bells* (1966.
$2.75).

826.	Bontemps, Arna, ed. **American Negro Poetry.** New York: Hill and Wang,
	c1963, 1974. 197p. $2.95pa. (7-12)
A collection of Black poetry by a well-known and outstanding Black poet and
writer.

827.	Bontemps, Arna. **Lonesome Boy.** Illus. by Feliks Topolski. Boston, Mass.:
	Houghton Mifflin, 1967. 28p. $4.50. (5-9)
An illustrated poetic story about the adventures of a small Black boy who loved to
play his trumpet more than anything else.

828.	Brandon, Brumsic, Jr. **Luther from Inner City.** New York: Ericksson,
	1969. unp. $1.95. (1-4)
This well-known Black artist has drawn a series of cartoons about an opinionated
character named Luther. A sequel is *Luther Tells It As It Is* (Ericksson, 1970.
$1.95).

829.	Brooks, Gwendolyn. **Bronzeville Boys and Girls.** New York: Harper and
	Row, 1956. 40p. $3.95. (3-6)
A celebrated Black poet talks about city children and the emotions of children.
Other titles by the author are *Aloneness* (Broadside, 1971. $3.00; $1.00pa.),

Selected Poems (Harper and Row, 1963. $6.95; $2.25pa.), and *World of Gwendolyn Brooks* (Harper and Row, 1971. $10.00).

830.   Carlson, Natalie Savage. **Marchers for the Dream.** Illus. by Alvin Smith. New York: Harper and Row, 1969. 130p. $4.79. (4-7)
Bethany and her grandmother march in a demonstration for better housing. Other titles by the author are *Ann Aurelia and Dorothy* (Harper and Row, 1968. $4.95), and *The Empty Schoolhouse* (Harper and Row, 1965. $4.50).

831.   Cohen, Barbara. **Thank You, Jackie Robinson.** Illus. by Richard Cuffari. New York: Lothrop, 1974. 125p. $4.95. (4-7)
Sam is a fatherless white boy who helps his mother manage an inn. Their cook, Davy, is a Black man who takes Sam to the Brooklyn Dodgers game. Their mutual admiration of Jackie Robinson and baseball helps develop a special friendship.

832.   Cushman, Jerome. **Tom B. and the Joyful Noise.** Illus. by Cal Massey. Philadelphia, Pa.: Westminster, 1970. 110p. $4.25. (4-6)
A story of a little Black boy, jazz and the Preservation Hall musicians set in New Orleans.

833.   Desbarats, Peter. **Gabrielle and Selena.** Illus. by Nancy Grossman. New York: Harcourt Brace Jovanovich, 1968. 32p. $5.50; $0.95pa. (2-4)
Gabrielle and her black girl friend, Selena, decide to trade places and families. This humorous family story is also available as a film from BFA Educational Media.

834.   Dunbar, Paul Laurence. **The Complete Poems of Paul Laurence Dunbar.** New York: Apollo, 1969. 289p. $1.95pa. (7-12)
The works of one of the earliest Black poets to achieve wide recognition. Many poems are written in dialect.

835.   Evans, Mari. **JD.** Illus. by Kenneth Brown. Garden City, N.Y.: Doubleday, 1973. 64p. $4.50; $0.95pa. (4-6)
The story of JD, a 12-year-old Black boy growing up poor and fatherless in the squalor of the ghetto. How he develops his strengths and values makes good reading for the young reader. Other titles by the author are *I Am a Black Woman* (Morrow, 1970. $2.45pa.), *I Look at Me* (Third World, 1974. $3.95; $2.00pa.), and *Rap Stories* (Third World, 1974. $3.95; $2.00pa.).

836.   Giovanni, Nikki. **Gemini: An Extended Autobiographical Statement of My First Twenty-Seven Years of Being a Black Poet.** Indianapolis, Ind.: Bobbs-Merrill, 1971. 192p. $5.95; $1.75pa. (9-12)
A collection of autobiographical, political, and other essays of the author's feelings about her life and about being a Black poet. Some of her poems are in *Spin a Soft Black Song: Poems for Children* (Hill and Wang, 1971. $5.95), *Ego Tripping and Other Poems for Young People* (Lawrence Hill, 1973. $3.97), and *My House* (Morrow, 1972. $6.95).

837.   Hughes, Langston, and Arna Bontemps, eds. **The Book of Negro Folklore.** New York: Dodd, c1958, 1969. 624p. $3.45pa. (4-12)

Covers Negro folklore, animal tales and rhymes, stories from slavery, tales of superstition, magic and the supernatural, stories of preachers, sermons, prayers, and songs, as well as the popular prose and poetry of contemporary Harlem.

838. Fast, Howard. **Freedom Road.** New York: Bantam, 1944. 263p. $5.95; $1.95pa. (9-12)

A historical novel based on the post-Civil War South centered around Gideon Jackson and his struggle to become a leader of the Blacks and a member of Congress.

839. Fox, Paula. **The Slave Dancer.** Illus. by Eros Keith. Englewood Cliffs, N.J.: Bradbury, 1973. 176p. $5.95. (4-9)

A Newbery Medal-winning story of a young white boy who was shanghaied and forced to play music on a slave ship travelling to America.

840. Gaines, Ernest J. **The Autobiography of Miss Jane Pittman.** New York: Dial Press, 1971. 245p. $7.95. (6-12)

A fictionalized narrative of a Black woman who was freed from slavery with the Emancipation Proclamation. Her search for freedom and human rights is seen throughout a century of struggle. Another title by the author is *A Long Day in November* (Dial, 1971. $5.95; $0.95pa.).

841. Gorden, Nancy. **What Happened in Marston.** Illus. by Richard Cuffari. New York: Four Winds Press, 1971. 190p. $4.50. (4-9)

When an eighth-grade Black boy plans to enroll in an all-white school, the teachers and students try too hard to accept Joel and make the situation false and unnatural.

842. Graham, Lorenz. **Whose Town?** New York: Crowell, 1969. 246p. $4.95. (5-9)

A story of a Black family and racial prejudice in a town in the northern United States. David Williams, the son, is torn apart by the hostility of his community members, an attack by a white gang, and the murder of his friend.

843. Gray, Genevieve. **A Kite for Bennie.** Illus. by Floyd Sowell. New York: McGraw-Hill, 1975. 40p. $4.72. (K-3)

Bennie wants to fly a kite more than anything in this story of the life and language of the Black ghetto. Another family story by the author is *Send Wendell* (McGraw-Hill, 1974. $4.95).

844. Greene, Bette. **Philip Hall Likes Me: I Reckon Maybe.** Illus. by Charles Lily. New York: Dial, 1974. 144p. $5.95. (3-6)

Eleven-year-old Beth is attracted to the smartest boy in the class. A 1975 Newbery Honor Book and winner of other titles and awards.

845. Gregory, Susan. **Hey, White Girl!** New York: Norton, 1970. 221p. $5.95. (9-12)

A white girl, a senior in high school, finds she must move to a Black neighborhood on the West Side of Chicago. She relates her experiences and the feelings she developed toward her community and classmates.

846.   Grifalconi, Ann. **City Rhythms.** New York: Bobbs-Merrill, 1965. unp. $4.95. (K-3)
Jimmy finds the sounds of the city exciting on a hot summer day in the market, the subway, and other places he visits.

847.   Grossman, Mort. **A Rage to Die.** Philadelphia, Pa.: Westminster, 1973. 185p. $4.75. (9-12)
A high school riot involving the principal and a Black student leader whose interests and values are in conflict with a gang.

848.   Guy, Rosa. **The Friends.** New York: Holt, 1973. 203p. $5.95. (6-9)
Phyllisa, a Black from the West Indies, is rejected when her family moves to Harlem. Another title by the author is *Children of Longing* (Bantam, 1970. $4.50).

849.   Hamilton, Virginia. **M. C. Higgins, the Great.** New York: Macmillan, 1974. 288p. $6.95. (5-7)
This 1975 Newbery Medal winner is the story of a 13-year-old Black boy and his awareness of his self-image, the relationships to his family, his feelings about his home and environment, and thoughts about his future. Other titles by the author are *The Planet of Junior Brown* (Macmillan, 1974. $6.95) and *The House of Die's Drear* (Macmillan, 1970. $5.95; $1.25pa.).

850.   Hawkinson, John, and Lucy Hawkinson. **The Little Boy Who Lives Up High.** Chicago: Whitman, 1967. 32p. $3.75. (1-3)
The life of a little Negro boy who lives in a high-rise apartment is described in the adventures of his daily life. Ms. Hawkinson has also written *Days I Like* (Whitman, 1965. $2.95).

851.   Hildreth, Richard. **Memoirs of a Fugitive: America's First Antislavery Novel.** New York: Crowell, 1971. 210p. $4.50. (6-9)
The Slave, first published in 1836, has been abridged here by Barbara Ritchie into a more readable story of Archy and his slave experiences. Has historical value as the first novel to reveal the cruelty of slavery.

852.   Hill, Elizabeth. **Evan's Corner.** Chicago: Hult, 1967. unp. $5.95; $1.45pa. (K-3)
Evan finds a corner in his apartment that he can call his own and he furnishes it with all his personal collections and treasured items.

853.   Hughes, Langston, ed. **The Best Short Stories by Negro Writers.** Boston, Mass.: Little, Brown, 1967. 508p. $10.95; $2.95pa. (7-12)
A collection compiled by a famous Black American writer of what he considers outstanding stories written by Blacks.

854.   Hunter, Kristen. **The Soul Brothers and Sister Lou.** New York: Avon, 1969. 241p. $0.95pa. (4-8)
An ALA Notable Book and a Council for Interracial Books for Children award winner. This story describes how Lauretta forms a musical group in her Black

community. Another title by this author is *Guests in the Promised Land* (Scribner's, 1973. $5.95).

855.   Johnson, James Weldon, and J. Rosamond Johnson, eds. **The Book of American Negro Spirituals.** New York: Viking, 1969. 300p. $4.95. (4-12)
A collection of 120 spirituals edited by a Black American poet and a Black musician. Another title, a song composed to celebrate Abraham Lincoln's birthday in 1900, is often referred to as the Negro National Anthem. It is found in *Lift Every Voice and Sing* (Hawthorn, 1970. $4.95), and includes a piano arrangement for children.

856.   Jordan, June. **New Life: New Room.** Illus. by Ray Cruz. New York: Crowell, 1975. 53p. $6.70. (2-4)
The little boys in this Black family must accept a sister into their bedroom when a new baby joins the family. How their father helps them accept and adjust to this situation makes a warm and tender story for primary students.

857.   Katz, Bernard, and Jonathan Katz. **Black Woman: A Fictionalized Biography of Lucy Terry Prince.** New York: Pantheon, 1973. 269p. $5.97. (7-10)
A champion of Black women's rights, Lucy Terry Prince, was at one time a slave. The story is told of how Abijah Prince purchased his freedom because of her poetry writing. A bibliography documents the historical aspects of this novel.

858.   Keats, Ezra J. **Whistle for Willie.** New York: Viking, 1964. unp. $4.95; $0.95pa. (K-2)
Peter is having trouble learning to whistle, but eventually he can whistle for Willie, his dog, just as the other big boys do.

859.   Killens, John Oliver. **The Cotillion: Or One Good Bull Is Half the Herd.** New York: Trident Press, 1971. 256p. $6.50. (7-12)
A Black Harlem family in which the ambitious mother, a mulatto, is striving to move the daughter into society. The father is a warm and humorous character who feels secure in his Black identity. Other stories by the author are *Black Man's Burden* (Trident, 1970. $4.95) and *A Man Ain't Nothing But a Man* (Little, Brown, 1975. $5.95).

860.   Lester, Julius. **Long Journey Home: Stories from Black History.** New York: Dial, c1972, 1975. 126p. $4.95; $0.95pa. (7-12)
A collection of short stories that reveal the Blacks' struggle for emancipation from slavery, their courage, dignity, ingenuity, and sense of humor.

861.   Martin, Patricia Miles. **The Little Brown Hen.** New York: Crowell, 1960. 23p. $4.50. (K-3)
A little Black boy has a little brown hen for a pet. How he finds the hen when she gets lost is a warm and amusing story for primary grades.

862.   Mathis, Sharon Bell. **The Hundred Penny Box.** Illus. by Leo and Diane Dillon. New York: Viking, 1975. 47p. $5.95. (2-5)
Aunt Dew is 100 years old, and when she moves in with her son and his family

there are some conflicts and changes. Aunt Dew keeps a penny for every year she has lived in the hundred penny box, and she has a story for every penny.

863.   Mendoza, George. **And I Must Hurry for the Sea Is Coming In.** Englewood Cliffs, N.J.: Prentice-Hall, 1969. 32p. $3.95. (3-12)
A small boy of the Black ghetto dreams that his toy boat is a large ship entering the port. The story is told in a mood poem.

864.   Monjo, F. N. **The Drinking Gourd.** Illus. by Fred Brenner. New York: Harper and Row, 1969. unp. $3.43. (1-3)
Tommy discovers that his father is working with the underground railroad helping slaves to escape to freedom.

865.   Murphy, Barbara Beasley. **Home Free.** Illus. by Bill Murphy. New York: Delacorte, 1970. 88p. $4.95. (3-6)
A young Black boy and a young white boy experience the prejudices and racial discrimination existent in a small town in the South.

866.   Patterson, Lindsay, ed. **A Rock against the Wind: Black Love Poems.** New York: Dodd, 1973. 200p. $5.95. (9-12)
A collection of poems by such famous Black poets as Bontemps, Hughes, Cullen, and many others.

867.   Sharpe, Stella. **Tobe.** Chapel Hill: University of North Carolina Press, 1939. 125p. $4.95. (2-5)
The story describes the daily life and routines of a small Black boy in the rural South. Black and white photographs help tell the story.

868.   Shearer, John. **I Wish I Had an Afro.** New York: Cowles, 1970. 50p. $4.94. (3-9)
The youngest member of a Black family describes his Black American community and his longing for the popular hair style of his older brother.

869.   Shepard, Ray Anthony. **Sneakers.** New York: Dutton, 1973. 112p. $4.50. (4-6)
A Council on Interracial Books for Children award winner, this is the story of a Black boy's experience in an all-white school in Lexington.

870.   Stanford, Barbara D. **I, Too, Sing America: Black Voices in American Literature.** Rochelle Park, N.J.: Hayden Book Co., 1971. 308p. $6.85; $4.90pa. (9-12)
An anthology of American literature by Negro authors. Bibliographies are included. A similar title by the author is *Negro Literature for High School Students* (National Council of Teachers of English, 1968. $2.00).

871.   Steptoe, John. **Stevie.** New York: Harper and Row, 1969. unp. $4.95. (K-3)
A story of interracial prejudice and then acceptance among children, this title was selected as an outstanding interracial book by the Council on Interracial Books for

Children. Another title by the author is *My Special Best Words* (Viking, 1974. $6.95).

872. Stokes, Olivia P. **Beauty of Being Black: Folktales, Poems and Art from Africa.** Illus. by Karen Tureck. New York: Friendship Press, 1971. 63p. $2.50pa. (4-6)
A collection of folktales, poems, and short stories from Africa. Includes photographs and discussion of African art.

873. Taylor, Mildred D. **Song of the Trees.** Illus. by Jerry Pinkney. New York: Dial, 1974. 48p. $4.95. (K-3)
The story of eight-year-old Cassie and her family portrays Black family life in rural Mississippi during the Depression. Cassie feels threatened by a white man who chops down the trees on her family's land while her father is away.

874. Udry, Janice May. **Mary Jo's Grandmother.** Chicago: Whitman, 1970. unp. $4.25. (K-3)
Little Mary Jo is visiting her grandmother when the old lady falls down and hurts her leg. Mary Jo must help her and do the right thing in the situation.

875. Underwood, Mary. **The Tamarack Tree.** Boston, Mass.: Houghton Mifflin, 1971. 230p. $5.95. (5-9)
The attitudes of white superiority and prejudice prevalent in the 1830s are evident in this historical novel set around a Connecticut school for young women.

876. Wagner, Jane. **J. T.** Photographs by Gordon Parks. New York: Van Nostrand, 1969. 63p. $5.95; $0.95pa.
A story of a Black boy and the stray cat he befriended and named Bones. When Bones is killed the neighborhood grocer gives J.T. a new kitten and a job.

877. Wagner, Jean. **Black Poets of the United States: From Paul Laurence Dunbar to Langston Hughes.** Urbana: University of Illinois Press, 1973. 545p. $5.50pa. (9-12)
Analyzes Afro-American poetry published from 1890 to 1940. Emphasis is on the human experience in a more or less chronological order. Includes some biographical sketches and a bibliography.

Audiovisual Materials

878. **ABC's of Black History: Educational Multi-Media Program.** By Olivia Ward. Philadelphia, Pa.: Tandem Press, 1974. Pkg., $79.50. (T)
A series of teacher aids to help children learn language and Black history concurrently. The complete kit contains poster-sized alphabet cards with picture, name, and capital and lower-case letter of alphabet, with picture of Black figure related to the letter. A teacher's manual, songbook, and musical cassette are included.

879.   **Abolitionism.** Chart. Pitman, 1968. (4-8)
A large two-color chart for bulletin board display showing Black participants in the antislavery movement.

880.   **Afro-American Art.** 1 col. filmstrip, 1 record (or cassette). Educational Dimensions. $20.50; $22.50 with cassette. (5-8)
A discussion of Afro-American art forms and famous artists.

881.   **Afro-American History Fact Pack.** Multimedia kit. Afro-American House. $85.00. (5-9)
The Black man's contributions to America are covered in this kit. The accompanying teacher's guide is entitled "Highlights of Afro-American History." It surveys Black history from ancient East Africa and Egypt to the 1960s in the United States. Included are 60 2x2-inch color slides, 50 11x15-inch flashcards, a 141-frame filmstrip, a 33 1/3 rpm record album, and a 192-page guide. Lesson plans are also presented, and a bibliography is included.

882.   **Afro-American Literature: An Overview.** 2 filmstrips, 2 records (or cassettes). Educational Dimensions, 1968. $41.00; $45.00 (with cassettes). (7-12)
Studies Afro-American literature from the folk songs of slavery to modern protest and other contemporary music.

883.   **Afro-American Portfolios.** 24 study prints. Afro-American Publishing Company. (K-12)
This set of 24 11x14-inch study prints includes historical and modern Black American leaders in portrait. The text provides biographical information and covers Blacks in business, professions, government, arts, religion, education, science, and literature.

884.   **Afro-Americans Speak for Themselves.** 3 filmstrips, 3 records (or cassettes). Educational Dimensions Corp., 1969. $61.50; $67.50 (with cassettes). (7-12)
Voices of Malcolm X, Eldridge Cleaver, and others describe what it is like to be a Black American.

885.   **Akki: A Black Poet.** 16mm film, 25 min., sd., color. WKYC-TV; distr. by Films Inc. $275.00; $18.00 (rental). (7-12)
The streets of the city and also scenes from nature as seen through the eyes of a new Black poet. The poetry can be used in language arts or social studies curriculum.

886.   **American Negro Folk and Work Song Rhythms.** 1 record. Scholastic. (4-12)
Ella Jenkins and the Goodwill Spiritual Choir sing spiritual and work songs with the call-and-response pattern.

887.   **American Negro Pathfinders.** 6 filmstrips. Vignette Films, 1967. $48.00. (4-8)
Contributions of six outstanding Black Americans and their non-violent activities in the civil rights movement are covered. Included are *Dr. Ralph Bunche:*

Missionary of Peace; Justice Thurgood Marshall: Mr. Civil Rights; Gen. Benjamin O. Davis, Jr.: American Guardian; A. Philip Randolph: Elder Statesman; Dr. Mary McLeod Bethune: Courageous Educator; Dr. Martin Luther King, Jr.: Non-Violent Crusader.

888.   **American Negroes.** 8 filmstrips. Troll Associates, 1969. $56.00. (4-8)
Simple biographies chronicle the struggles and achievements of these famous American Negroes. Contents: Mary McLeod Bethune; George Washington Carver; Frederick Douglass; Martin Luther King, Jr.; Jackie Robinson; Sojourner Truth; Harriet Tubman; Booker T. Washington.

889.   **Amos Fortune, Free Man.** Multimedia kit. Miller-Brody, 1970. $0.95 paperback book; $4.50 hardcover book; record, $6.50; cassette, $7.95; 1 filmstrip, 1 cassette, teacher's guide, $22.00.
This multimedia kit can be purchased in various combinations. It is a Newbery Award-winning story of an African prince who was sold as a slave and later regained his freedom.

890.   **Anthology of Negro Poets.** 1 record. Folkways/Scholastic. (4-12)
An anthology of poetry, edited by Arno Bontemps, presenting the history and experience of Black Americans in music. Some poets represented are Gwendolyn Brooks, Langston Hughes, Countee Cullen, and others.

891.   **Autobiography of Miss Jane Pittman.** 16mm film, 110 min., sd., color. Produced by Robert Christiansen and Rick Rosenberg; distr. by Learning Corporation of America, 1974. $1,450.00 ($150.00 rental). (7-12)
The courageous and inspiring story of a Black women who narrates her recollections of the years of slavery, escape to the North, and her reactions to the civil rights movement during the 1960s. She recounts many experiences pertinent to Black American history in this autobiography of her 110 years of life.

892.   **Benjamin Banneker: Man of Science.** 16mm film, 9 min., sd., color. EBE. (4-10)
A story of the man who built the first wooden clock in American and who also salvaged the plans for Washington, D.C., and the nation's capitol building.

893.   **Biographies of Outstanding Black Americans.** Multimedia kit. Creative Visuals, 1973. 6 cassette tapes, $34.95; 56 transparencies, $140.00 ($4.50 each); 56 7½x9-inch study prints, $49.50. (4-10)
Biographical sketches of 56 outstanding Black Americans from all walks of life.

894.   **Black America: The Sounds of History.** 15 records. Miller Brody Productions. $79.00; $6.49 each. (5-9)
Afro-American history is recorded in music and narration in a chronological arrangement. Albums include: African Heritage; Black Cargoes; Slavery Takes Hold; Toward Freedom; Black Achievements; Civil War; Reconstruction; Separate and Unequal; Black Leadership; Harlem Renaissance; Blacks in the Depression; World War II and Beyond; Civil Rights Movement; Black Achievement; Black Spokesmen.

895.   **Black American Series.** 10 22x17-inch pictures. Eyegate House. (K-12)
Ten Black Americans are pictured, and text gives biographical information.
Includes Marian Anderson, Mary McLeod Bethune, Thurgood Marshall, and others.

896.   **Black American Wall Posters.** 12 2x3-foot; color posters, 1 teacher's
guide. Civic education Services. $47.50. (4-12)
Posters include literary personalities, entertainers, freedom leaders, athletes, and
Black Americans from other walks of life.

897.   **The Black Americans.** 24 cassettes (or tapes). ESP, 1974. $105.84;
$4.90 each. (4-12)
Titles in this series on the heritage and contributions of the Black American include
From Africa to America; *The Bonds of Slavery*; *Early Black Politics*; *The Blacks
Organize*; *Modern Black Politics*; *The New Black Image*; and others.

898.   **Black Americans in Government.** 5 filmstrips, 5 records, 5 color portraits.
McGraw-Hill, 1969. (4-8)
Workbooks and teacher's manuals are included with these filmstrips on the
biographies of five Black Americans prominent in American society.

899.   **Black and White: Uptight.** 1 super 8 mm film, 35 min., sd., color. Avanti
Films, Inc.; released by BFA Educational Media, 1969. $349.00. (7-12)
Discusses racial prejudice and inequalities for Blacks in education, economics, and
social areas.

900.   **Black Culture Program.** 8 filmstrips, 8 phonodiscs (or cassettes), teacher's
guide. Scholastic Magazines, 1973. $96.00; $112.00 (with cassettes).
(7-12)
The titles in this set survey Black cultural development in America. Biographical
sketches of Black Americans are included in the teacher's guide along with suggested
readings and activities for incorporation in the social studies, humanities, or language
arts curriculum. Included are Black Dance; Black Art; Black Religion, Pts. 1 and 2;
Black Poetry, Pts. 1 & 2; Black Music, Pts. 1 & 2.

901.   **The Black Experience.** 6 records, 1 guide. Spoken Arts, 1975. $39.50;
$6.98 each. (7-12)
Black-American history is protrayed through: Vinnie Burrows' *Walk Together
Children*, Vols. I and II; *The Dream Awake*; *Langston Hughes Reads and Talks
about His Poems*; *Voices of Protest*; Vols. I and II. The latter includes Martin
Luther King's "I Have a Dream" address.

902.   **The Black Experience in the Arts.** 4 filmstrips. Warren Schloat Productions.
$70.00; $85.00 (with cassettes). (7-12)
Four Black artists are interviewed: Dean Dixon, orchestra conductor; Charles
Gordone, playwright; James Earl Jones, actor; and Jacob Lawrence, painter.

903.   **The Black Experience Series.** 8 color prints. Wisdom Co., 1970. (5-8)
A portfolio of eight 19x25-inch silk screen reproductions of Black Americans,
with biographical information included in a teacher's manual.

904. **Black Heritage.** 28 cassettes, 35 activity booklets, teacher's manual. Imperial International Learning, 1975. $231.00; $8.75 each. (4-9)

These biographies of Black Americans emphasize their contributions. The teacher's manual summarizes each tape; student booklet answers questions and gives suggestions for further learning activities. Titles include: Sojourner Truth; Frederick Douglass; Sidney Poitier; Marian Anderson; Nat "King" Cole; Louis Armstrong; Benjamin O. Davis, Jr.; Asa Philip Randolph; Crispus Attucks; Dred Scott; Harriet Tubman; Martin Luther King, Jr.; Mary McLeod Bethune; Booker T. Washington; Jean Baptiste Pointe Du Sable; Matthew A. Henson; Ralph J. Bunche; Thurgood Marshall; Carl Stokes; Granville T. Woods; Paul Laurence Dunbar; James Baldwin; Charles Richard Drew; George Washington Carver; Jackie Robinson; Joe Louis; Althea Gibson; Jesse Owens.

905. **Black History.** 4 filmstrips, 4 phonodiscs (or cassettes). Library Filmstrip Center. $18.00; $20.00 (with cassettes) each. (4-12)

Four titles surveying Black history from pre-history in Africa to the protest and achievements that have spanned the years to 1970. Included are *Black History—Africa Past; Black History, 1492-1865; Black History, 1865-1915; Black History, 1915-1970.*

906. **Black History: Lost, Stolen or Strayed.** 1 Super 8mm film, 54 min., color, sd. Produced by CBS News; distr. by BFA Educational Media, 1968. $459.00. (4-12)

A history of Black Americans narrated by Bill Cosby. Special attention is paid to Black culture and Black contributions. The changing image of the Black man is also emphasized.

907. **The Black Man's Struggle.** 8 records (or cassettes). H. Wilson Corp., 1975. $52.00; $70.00 (with cassettes). (4-9)

Presents the history of the Black man from African origins and slavery to the Black power movements of 1970. Arranged in chronological narratives and dramatizations. Accompanied by a printed synopsis and a teacher's guide.

908. **Black Military Heroes.** 2 filmstrips, 1 record (or cassette), 1 teacher's guide. Multi-Media Productions. $16.95. (4-12)

The contributions of Black Americans serving in the military from Revolutionary times to the Vietnam War.

909. **Black Music in America.** 16mm film, 38 min., sd., color. Learning Corporation of America. (4-12)

A history of Black music in America, with many outstanding performers participating—e.g., Louis Armstrong, B. B. Kind, Leadbelly, Count Basie, and many others.

910. **Black on Black: Martin Luther King.** 16mm film, 4 min., color. Time/Life, 1971. (5-12)

Martin Luther King is shown making a speech on the night before his death. In the film he also explains his non-violent views and philosophies in the struggle for civil rights.

911.   **Black Pioneers in America.** 2 records (or cassettes). Caedmon. $6.98;
         $7.95 (cassette). (6-12)
Readings given are autobiographical selections taken from the works of famous
Black Americans such as Frederick Douglass, Charlotte Forten, W. E. B. Du Bois,
and others.

912.   **Black Poems, Black Images.** 6 filmstrips, 6 phonodiscs (or cassettes),
         guide. Warren Schloat Productions. $120.00; $138.00 (with cassettes).
         (9-12)
Outstanding Black American poets are included, with photography representative
of Black communities in the United States. Useful in history, social studies,
literature, poetry, or human relations classes. Titles in the set: *Childhood,
Womanhood, Manhood, Peace, The Past, The Present.*

913.   **Black Policeman (The Writing on the Wall).** 16mm film, 16 min., color,
         sd. (or video tape cassette). American Educational Films, 1974. $255.00;
         $25.00 (rental). (6-12)
A Black policeman worked hard during the riots in Washington, D.C., and finds he
has a surprisingly emotional reaction to the words "Kill the Nigger" written on the
police station walls. The film tells his story and provides excellent opportunity
for discussion on racism and prejudice.

914.   **The Black Revolution.** 8 filmstrips, 8 records (or cassettes), guide. Warren
         Schloat Productions. $120.00; $140.00 (with cassettes). (9-12)
The Black Revolution in America is studied through a series of dramatic debates
taped from William F. Buckley's TV forum. Topics cover Black separatism, the
Black Panthers, Black Power, and the ghetto community.

915.   **The Black Spectrum: Leadership Strategies in the Black Community.** 6
         filmstrips, 6 records, teacher's guide. Westinghouse Learning Corporation.
         (7-12)
Examines the different kinds of leadership within the Black community. Although
different views and philosophies are expressed by various leaders, the goal defined
is a common one. Julian Bond is the narrator.

916.   **Booker T. Washington.** 16mm film, 11 min., sd., color. BFA Educational
         Media. (4-8)
A biographical portrait of Booker T. Washington, founder of the Tuskegee Institute,
is presented through a dramatization using historical pictures and illustrations.

917.   **The Color of Justice.** 16mm film, 26 min., sd., color. Rediscovery Pro-
         ductions; Bill Buckley, 1971. $300.00; $50.00 (rental). (7-12)
Studies the important achievements of Thurgood Marshall with respect to the
attainment of justice for Black Americans in the courts of law. Covers various
Supreme Court decisions, the Ku Klux Klan, school integration in Little Rock,
Arkansas, other civil rights legislation, and a study of the U.S. Constitution.

918.   **Contemporary Black Artists.** 47 slides, study guide. Sandak. $58.75. (4-12)
A set of 47 slides based on an exhibition of 30 contemporary Black artists at

the Minneapolis Institute of Art. Includes biographical and critical data in the accompanying study guide.

919. **Contemporary Black Biographies.** 32 study prints, teacher's guide. Instructor Publications. $7.50. (3-9)

These 32 portraits of prominent Black Americans are 12x16-inch in size and include a biographical text and teacher's guide. Persons included are Marian Anderson, Althea Gibson, Ralph Bunche, Sammy Davis, Jr., Louis Armstrong, Malcolm X, and others.

920. **The Dream Awake: The Black Experience in America.** 7 filmstrips, 7 records (or cassettes). Spoken Arts. $179.97; $197.95 (with cassettes). (7-12)

Verse narration tells the story of the American Black from the days of slavery, covering Black cowboys, dissenters such as Frederick Douglass, Du Bois, and Marcus Garvey, to the marchers (Martin Luther King, Jr.) of the 1960s and then comtemporary poets and artists.

921. **Education and Religion.** 24 study prints, 11x14-inch. Afro-Am, 1969. $4.95. (4-12)

A collection of study prints with biographical data included on Blacks in education and religion. Some portrait subjects include: Alain Locke, Arthur Schomberg, Daniel Payne, Benjamin Mays, Father Divine, Adam C. Powell, Sr., and others.

922. **Equality: A Look at "The Dream."** 2 filmstrips, 2 records (or cassettes). Produced by Associated Press Prod. Co.: Scott Education; distr. by Prentice-Hall Media, 1975. $39.00. (9-12)

Records the Black Americans' struggles and achievements from the early civil rights movement activities of the 1950s up to the present. Describes progress in housing, education, politics, voting, Black organization, the Black image and other social areas. The voices narrating are those of contemporary Black leaders (Jesse Jackson, Marie Brookter, Charles Hamilton, Maynard Jackson, and Charles Evers).

923. **Evan's Corner.** 16mm film, 24 min., sd., color. BFA Educational Media. (3-6)

Based on the book by Elizabeth Starr Hill about a little Black boy who wants a place to call his own.

924. **First World Festival of Negro Arts.** 16mm film, 20 min., color. McGraw-Hill. (6-12)

A film documenting the festival of Negro arts held at Dakar in 1966, showing African music, dance, sculpture, and painting.

925. **Five Black Americans and Their Fight for Freedom.** 6 filmstrips, 6 records (or cassettes). Prod. by Paideia; distr. by BFA Educational Media, 1974. $78.00 ($13.00 each); $90.00 ($15.00 each) with cassettes.

A series of titles which present Black leaders in a chronological historical picture of their struggle for equality and civil rights.

926. **Four Hundred Years: Black History in America.** 5 filmstrips, 5 records (or cassettes). Educational Design. $87.50; $97.50 (with cassettes); $18.50 or $21.00 each. (4-12)

Black American figures are highlighted throughout this history of Black experience, status, culture, problems, and achievements. Includes *The Era of Black Slavery*; *The Black Man in the Late 19th Century*; *The Black Man in the Early 20th Century*; *The Black Revolution–Parts I and II.*

927. **Frederick Douglass: The House on Cedar Hill.** 16mm film, 17 min., sd., b&w. McGraw-Hill Films. (4-12)

An award-winning film telling the life story of Frederick Douglass and his work and accomplishments in the Black struggle for civil rights.

928. **A Gallery of Great Afro Americans.** 50 study prints. Pitman Publishing Corp. (K-12)

A series of 50 color portraits of historical figures in the Black American experience.

929. **George Washington Carver.** 16mm film, 12 min., sd., color. Artisan. (4-8)

A biogrpahical portrait of George Washington Carver, a famous Black American scientist and researcher.

930. **Glory of Negro History.** 1 record. Folkways Records, 1955. $5.98. (4-12)

A documentary of Negro history presented by Langston Hughes with the music, poetry, and voices of Booker T. Washington, Louis Armstrong, and others.

931. **Growing Up Black.** 4 filmstrips, 4 records (or cassettes). Warren Schloat Productions, 1969. $70.00; $85.00 (with cassettes). (4-9)

Five young Black people tell, in recorded interviews, what it is like to grow up Black in American society. A program guide is included in this set, which won an Honors Award in the American Film Festival. Can also be obtained from Miller Brody Productions for the same price.

932. **Harriet Tubman and the Underground Railroad.** 16mm film, 54 min., sd., b&w. McGraw-Hill Films. (4-10)

The story of Harriet Tubman's work helping slaves escape to the North via the underground railroad. Made for CBS television's "The Great Adventure" series.

933. **Heritage in Black.** 16mm film, 27 min., sd., color. Encyclopaedia Britannica, 1968. (5-12)

Emphasis is on Black American contributions to the growth and development of the nation throughout Black American history. Covers Crispus Attucks, Peter Salem, Harriet Tubman, Josiah Henson, Percy A. Julian, Malcolm X, Martin Luther King, Thurgood Marshall, and others.

934. **The Heritage of Africa.** 1 map. School Service. (K-12)

A 23x28-inch color map of the African continent depicting the various peoples and cultures of Africa.

935.   **Heritage of Afro-American History.** 9 filmstrips (captioned). Troll.
       $63.00. (5-10)
Nine captioned filmstrips visualize Black American history. Includes *From Africa
to the New World, 1000-1713*; *Life in the New American Colonies, 1713-1790*;
The Plantation System, 1790-1850; *From Abolition Movements to Civil War,
1850-1865*; *From Reconstruction to Jim Crow, 1865-1898*; *The Long Hard
Struggle, 1898-1942*; *Changing Currents of Civil Rights, 1942-1960*; *Years of
Challenge, 1960-Present*; *Leaders Who Left Their Mark.*

936.   **Heritage of Slavery.** 16mm film, 53 min., sd., color. Columbia Broadcast-
       ing System; distr. by BFA Educational Media, 1968. (7-12)
The effects of slavery on Americans, both Black and white, prior to the Civil War.
Also covers the numerous slave revolts in America.

937.   **The History of Black America.** 8 filmstrips, 8 records (or cassettes).
       Universal Education and Visual Arts. $68.00. (6-9)
A history of Blacks in America from their African origins to recent protest and
civil rights activities. Includes many biographical profiles. Titles include *The
African Past*; *Slavery and Freedom in the English Colonies*; *The Plantation South*;
Firebrands and Freedom Fighters; *From Freedom to Disappointment*; *New Leadership and the Turning Tide*; *Progress, Depression and Global War*; *Hope, Disillusionment and Sacrifice.*

938.   **The History of the Black Man in the United States.** 8 filmstrips, 4 records
       (or 8 cassettes), teacher's guide. Educational Audiovisual, 1970. $78.00;
       $108.00 (with cassettes). (4-12)
A general survey documenting Black American history from Colonial times to the
present, utilizing cartoons, photographs, paintings, drawings, etc. Titles include
The Colonial Period; *The Abolitionists*; *The Civil War*; *Reconstruction*; *Harlem
Renaissance*; *The Black Man in the Depression*; *Racism and the Kerner Commission
Report*; *Black Protest Movements.*

939.   **History of the Negro in America.** 16mm films, 20 min. ea., sd., b&w.
       McGraw-Hill; available from Educational Film Libraries. (6-12)
This history is covered in three films, narrated by James Earl Jones and made up of
old prints, paintings, and film footage. Part I: *1619-1860: Out of Slavery*; Part II:
1861-1877: Civil War and Reconstruction; Part III: *1877-Today: Freedom Movement.*

940.   **Hitch.** 16mm film, 90 min., sd., color. Mental Health Film Board. $900.00;
       $45.00 (rental). (7-12)
An award-winning film about a teen-aged Black boy, Hitch, who has moved to a
Harlem ghetto from the South. Fatherless, Hitch struggles to achieve a purpose and
identity and to overcome the frustrations of his helpless situation.

941.   **The Hurdler.** 16mm film, 16 min., sd., color. New York Times/Arno Press.
       (6-12)
A biography of Dr. Charles Drew, the Black American doctor and researcher who
worked with blood transfusions and established the first blood bank in the United
States.

942.   "I Have a Dream . . . " The Life of Martin Luther King, Jr. 16mm film,
        35 min., sd., b&w. BFA Educational Media. (4-12)
The highlights of Martin Luther King's career are shown in film footage taken
during the news reports of the Civil Rights Movement of the 1950s and 1960s.
His non-violent participation in boycotts, sit-ins, freedom rides, and other activities
is portrayed.

943.   Immigrant from America. 16mm film, 20 min., color, sd. Rediscovery
        Productions, Inc.; distr. by Bill Buckley, 1971. $225.00; $40.00 (rental).
        (9-12)
The film shows a class of students in a lively discussion of the problems facing
Black Americans as compared to those facing immigrants from other countries.
Emphasis is on equal civil rights.

944.   Immigrants in Chains. 16mm film, 11 min., sd., b&w. Films, Inc. $4.00
        (rental). (9-12)
Based on the John F. Kennedy book, *A Nation of Immigrants*, this film shows the
experience of the Blacks in America and all aspects of slavery from 1619 to 1863.
Part I of *The Americans: A Nation of Immigrants* series.

945.   Ivanhoe Donaldson. 16mm film, 57 min., sd., b&w. Macmillan, $350.00;
        $35.00 (rental). (9-12)
A documentary film describing the emergence of the civil rights movement and the
Civil Rights Act of 1964 and the Voting Rights Act of 1965, through connected
events and incidents in the deep South.

946.   Jazz: The Music of Black Americans. 4 filmstrips, 4 records (or cassettes).
        Educational Dimensions Corp., 1973. $82.00; $90.00 (with cassettes).
        (7-12)
Jazz forms provide the background to this history of Black American music.
Materials are written by Jim Earle and J. W. Deveir.

947.   Learn, Baby, Learn. 5 filmstrips. Miller Brody Productions. $42.00. (5-12)
These captioned filmstrips are based on advice from five outstanding Black Americans. Subjects are Gordon Parks, writer and filmmaker; Claude Brown, author of
Manchild in the Promised Land; Dr. James Comer, psychiatrist; Dr. Dorothy Brown,
surgeon and member of the Tennessee State Legislature; and Charles Lloyd, music
writer.

948.   A Letter to Amy. 16mm film, 7 min., sd., color. Weston Woods. (K-3)
The picture book by Ezra Jack Keats is made into a film about the little Black boy
who wants to invite a girl named Amy to his birthday party. The story is narrated
by Loretta Long.

949.   M. C. Higgins, the Great. Multimedia kit. Miller-Brody Productions,
        1975. $31.75; $33.75 (with cassettes); $13.90 records only. (6-9)
The kit contains two records (or cassettes) and three copies of the book by Virginia
Hamilton, *M. C. Higgins, the Great*. The story is a Newbery Honor Book about a
young Black boy.

950.   **A Man Named Charlie Smith**. 16mm film, 26 min., sd., b&w. Macmillan.
        $165.00; $12.50 (rental). (6-12)
In this autobiographical account, Mr. Charlie Smith tells of his experiences coming
to the United States on a slave ship in 1854, and of the treatment of Blacks in
America.

951.   **Martin Luther King, Jr.** 16mm film, 10 min., sd., color. Encyclopaedia
        Britannica. (6-12)
A summary of King's role in the civil rights movement and his philosophy of non-
violent means of attaining equality for his people. Other films about Mr. King by
this producer are *Martin Luther King—From Montgomery to Memphis* and *Martin
Luther King, Jr.: A Man of Peace.*

952.   **Martin Luther King, Jr.** 1 filmstrip, 1 7-inch record. Miller Brody Produc-
        tions, 1969. $14.00. (K-4)
A biography of Dr. Martin Luther King, Jr. from his childhood, his work in the
civil rights movement, receiving the Nobel Prize, to his untimely death in 1968.

953.   **Martin Luther King, Jr., A Musical Documentary**. 1 record. Scholastic.
        (5-12)
A 7-inch recording of children presenting highlights in the career of Dr. Martin
Luther King. Includes his famous "I've Been to the Mountaintop" speech.

954.   **Martin Luther King, Jr. Book Bag**. Kit. Childrens Press. $17.95. (K-3)
This kit contains books with a cassette, a resource card, and a book bag. Four copies
of an easy-reading picture book on the life of Martin Luther King, Jr., are coordin-
ated with the cassette tape. Packaged in a heavy-gauged clear plastic book bag.

955.   **Martin Luther King: The Man and the March**. 16mm film, 83 min., sd.,
        b&w. Indiana University Audio-Visual Center, 1968. $360.00; $19.50
        (rental). (7-12)
A documentary describing King's efforts at organizing the Blacks in the South in
the sixties.

956.   **The Matter with Me**. 16mm film, 15 min., sd., color. Monroe-Williams;
        released by Oxford, 1972. $6.35 (rental). (4-8)
A twelve-year-old Black boy is followed through his daily routines in the Black
ghetto community. A contrast of the affluence of the whites around him and the
poverty of his home. Music, but no narration.

957.   **Negro Folk Songs for Young People**. 1 record. Folkways/Scholastic.
        $6.98. (K-6)
Blues, spirituals, and Negro work songs are sung by Leadbelly (Huddie Ledbetter).

958.   **Negro History Week**. Multimedia kit. Association for the Study of Negro
        Life in History. (4-12)
A kit containing posters, biographical sketches, study prints, lesson plans, and
suggested activities for teaching Negro history. The kits are available for Negro History Week from the Association (1538 9th N.W., Washington, D.C. 20001).

959.   **The Negro Woman.** 1 record. Folkways/Scholastic. (6-12)
Seven Black women, including Sojourner Truth and Harriet Tubman, are studied through their writings, read by Dorothy Washington.

960.   **Negroes in Our History.** 24 study prints (11x14-inch). Afro-Am, 1969. $4.95. (4-12)
A collection of portraits of Black American leaders from slavery to contemporary personalities. A similar set of 24 pictures by this producer is entitled *Negroes of Achievement* (1969. $4.95).

961.   **Nothing But a Man.** 16mm film, 92 min., sd., b&w. Macmillan, 1974. $795.00; $65.00 (rental). (7-12)
In this award-winning film a young Black husband will not conform to the stereotyped image of the Black male in contemporary Alabama.

962.   **On Being Black.** 2 filmstrips, 2 records (or cassettes). Denoyer-Geppert Audio-Visuals. $39.00; $41.00 (with cassettes). (7-12)
Dr. William Grier narrates a personal view of the Black experience in the United States. The materials also provide a study of the Black heritage and customs.

963.   **On Freedom.** 16mm film, 26 min., sd., color. New York Times/Arno. (5-12)
A history of the civil rights movement and the people involved in it. Includes Martin Luther King, Governor Wallace, Governor Faubus, President Kennedy, the Ku Klux Klan, Mississippi Freedom Workers, and other groups and individuals.

964.   **Our Country, Too.** 16mm film, 30 min., sd., b&w. National Educational Television Film Service, 1966. $10.00 (rental). (9-12)
Life in the Black American community is observed by visiting Harlem, a debutante ball, a Black newspaper and radio station and other places of interest in the Black community.

965.   **Portrait in Black and White.** 1 Super 8mm film, 54 min., sd., color. CBS News; distr. by BFA, 1968. $239.00. (7-12)
Black and white Americans are interviewed in this survey of attitudes and problems of race in the United States.

966.   **Rush toward Freedom.** 8 filmstrips, 8 records (or cassettes), teacher's guide. Warren Schloat Productions. $120.00; $146.00 (with cassettes). (4-12)
The civil rights movement is described and narrated by Dr. Martin Luther King, Jr., George Wallace, Medgar Evers, J. F. Kennedy, and others. Titles include: *States against the Nation*; *Birth of Direct Action*; *The Non-Violent Creed*; *Give Us the Ballot*; *To Make Things Better*; *Over the Edge*; *Will It End?*; *Black Is Beautiful.*

967.   **Search for a Black Identity: Malcolm X.** 2 16mm films. Part I, 19 min., color; Part II, 15 min., color. Guidance Associates. (6-12)
A biographical sketch of Malcolm X, his personal views and philosophy. A text is included with the films.

968. **Search for a Black Identity: Martin Luther King, Jr.** 2 16mm films. Part I, 14 min., sd., color; Part II, 18 min., sd., color. Guidance Associates. (4-12)
The life story of Martin Luther King, Jr. is presented in this film with an accompanying text. Describes his cause and his death in Memphis.

969. **Shirley Chisholm: Pursuing the Dream.** 16mm film, 42 min., sd., color. Prod. by Tom Werner and Bob Denby; distr. by New Line Cinema. $500.00; $45.00 (rental). (7-12)
The story of the first Black Congresswoman and her campaign for the 1972 Presidential nomination.

970. **Slavery, Civil War and Reconstruction.** Multimedia kit. Current Affairs Film Company. (4-12)
This kit includes seven discs (or cassettes), and 20 study prints of subjects from Black American Civil War history and the periods immediately prior to and after. Pictures slave ships, scenes of slavery life, and other aspects of the period. Outstanding prominent Black writers contribute to a panel discussion presented on the recordings. Included are Arna Bontemps, Milton Meltzer, and others.

971. **Slavery, the Black Man and the Man.** 16mm film, 22 min., sd., color. Macmillan. $275.00; $20.00 (rental). (7-12)
Slavery scenes are intermingled with scenes from modern urban ghettos where Black youth are also slaves to racism, drug addiction, and inferior facilities and services.

972. **A Slave's Story: Running a Thousand Miles to Freedom.** 16mm film, 29 min., sd., color. Oberon Communications; Learning Corporation of America, 1972. $11.00 (rental). (6-12)
A true story of two slaves who escaped in 1848. Studies slavery in the South, master and slave relationships, and the conditions that led to the Civil War. The couple's great-granddaughter gives the introduction.

973. **Studies in the History of Black Americans.** 10 filmstrips, 10 records, 10 teacher's guides. Silver Burdett, 1970. $112.50. (7-12)
Surveys Black history with drawings, cartoons, newspapers, reproductions of woodcuts and engravings. Titles include: *African Ancestry*; *The American Revolution*; *Frederick Douglass*; *Black Participation in the Civil War*; *Reconstruction*; *Jim Crow and the "Progressives"*; *Broadening Perspectives*; *The Civil Rights Movement*; *Black Revolution.*

974. **They Have Overcome.** 5 filmstrips, 5 records (or cassettes), program guide. Warren Schloat Productions. $85.00; $100.00 (with cassettes). (6-12)
Presents the work of five prominent Black Americans and gives brief biographical sketches of their lives and contributions to the Black American community and to American society.

975. **A Ticket to Freedom.** 16mm film, 23 min., sd., color. Macmillan, 1968. $299.00; $13.50 (rental). (6-12)

Presents a review of the Plessy Case; in 1892 Homer Plessy sat in a railroad train seat reserved for whites. Covers the beginning of the struggle for civil rights.

976.   **To Kill a Mockingbird.** 2 records (or cassettes), 12 paperbacks. Miller Brody Productions. (7-12)

A narration of the Pulitzer Prize-winning novel by Harper Lee depicting the prejudices against Blacks in a small Southern town.

977.   **Twentieth Century Americans of Negro Lineage.** Pictomap. Friendship Press, 1969. $2.75. (4-12)

Black American leaders and those who have made outstanding contributions to American culture, history of the civil rights movement are pictured on this outline map of the United States.

978.   **We Shall Overcome.** 16mm film, 10 min., sd., b&w. Macmillan. $75.00; $8.50 (rental). (9-12)

A documentary of the prejudice and discrimination towards Black Americans and the workers in the civil rights movement that are working to eliminate it.

979.   **White Over Black.** 1 filmstrip, 1 record (or cassette), teacher's guide. Multi-Media Productions. $9.95; $11.95 (with cassette). (7-12)

Examines racial relations and the forces that have shaped and influenced racial prejudice in the United States.

980.   **William: From Georgia to Harlem.** 16mm film, 17 min., sd., color. Learning Corporation of America, 1970. $6.80 (rental). (5-9)

The story of a Southern Black boy who moves to New York City, where he seems out of place to his cousin. His courage and inner strength make him respected by a street gang, and he is accepted by the group.

BRITISH AMERICANS

See also **Scotch and Scotch-Irish Americans and Welsh Americans.**

Reference Sources

981.   Furer, Howard B., comp. and ed. **The British in America 1578-1970: A Chronology and Fact Book.** Dobbs Ferry, N.Y.: Oceana, 1973. 153p. $6.00. (9-12)

A chronology, selected documents, and a bibliography of materials concerning the English, Scotch-Irish, Scotch, and Welsh in America are presented in this seventh volume in the *Ethnic Chronology Series.* Also included is a list of British-American newspapers. Indexed.

Non-Fiction Titles: History, Culture, Sociology, Biography

982. Beck, Barbara L. **The Pilgrims of Plymouth.** New York: Watts, 1972. 89p. $3.45. (4-6)
A history of the early English settlers who made up the Plymouth Colony at Massachusetts Bay. Their homes, occupations, and customs are described, and a little information is given about the Scrooby Church in England, which they left.

983. Berthoff, Rowland T. **British Immigrants in Industrial America, 1790-1950.** Cambridge, Mass.: Harvard University Press, 1953; repr. ed. New York: Russell, 1968. 296p. $10.00. (9-12, T)
A history of English, Scotch, and Welsh immigration to America, with emphasis on their economic enterprise, and achievements. Discusses how language contributed to their early and successful assimilation.

984. Cates, Edwin H. **The English in America.** Minneapolis, Minn.: Lerner Publications, 1966. 70p. $3.95. (5-9)
This history of the English in America emphasizes the life style and customs established in the Colonies and the contributions and influence of outstanding Americans of English background.

985. Colby, Jean Poindexter. **Plimoth Plantation: Then and Now.** New York: Hastings, 1970. 128p. $5.95. (5-8)
A description of the Plimoth Plantation and the early British settlers' customs and life style. Discusses their reasons for leaving their homeland. Also describes the restoration of the original Plimoth Plantation as a national monument.

986. Coleman, Terry. **Going to America.** Garden City, N.Y.: Doubleday, 1972. 317p. $8.95; $2.50pa. (9-12)
A study of British immigration to America around the middle of the nineteenth century. Reasons for the move, the journey itself, response to new immigrants by the Americans, and the Industrial Revolution are all examined.

987. Elgin, Kathleen. **The Episcopalians: The Protestant Episcopal Church.** New York: McKay, 1970. 112p. $4.19. (4-6)
A history of the Episcopalians in America, with emphasis on the English colonists and their ties and conflicts with the Anglican Church. Provides good coverage of the role of religion in the American colonies and also includes an interesting list of famous American Episcopalians.

988. Erickson, Charlotte. **Invisible Immigrants.** Miami, Fla.: University of Miami Press, 1972. 531p. $17.50. (9-12, T)
The adaptation of English and Scottish immigrants in America during the nineteenth century is portrayed through letters and illustrations. Letters from immigrants are arranged in three categories: those in agriculture, those in industry, and those in the professional occupations.

989. Ettinger, Amos A. **James Edward Oglethorpe.** New York: Oxford University Press, 1936; repr. ed., Hamden, Conn.: Shoe String, 1968. 348p. $12.50. (9-12)

A biographical portrait of a British immigrant to the United States who was to become well known as an American philanthropist and soldier.

990. Faber, Doris. **The Perfect Life: The Shakers in America.** New York: Farrar, 1974. 215p. $6.95. (7-12)

Describes a Shaker colony that has remained in the United States and also presents the history of this group. Covers their immigration from England, their peak of communal living in the United States, their decline, and also the contemporary revival in their life style. A list of Shaker museums and collections is included. Documented with photographs and reproductions. Indexed.

991. Gompers, Samuel. **Seventy Years of Life and Labor: An Autobiography.** New York: Dutton, 1925; repr. ed., New York: Kelley, 1967. 2 vols. $27.50. (9-12)

This account of Samuel Gompers, British immigrant, is also an account of the labor movement in the United States and his role in it.

992. Grant, Neil. **The New World Held Promise: Why England Colonized North America.** New York: Messner, 1974. 96p. $5.79. (4-6)

English emigration to America is described. Covers such outstanding historical figures as Sir Walter Raleigh, Lord de la War, John Winthrop, and William Bradford. Describes the political and economic problems that motivated their migration and led to their prominent roles in colonizing the New World. Another title by this author for the same age level is *English Explorers of North America* (Messner, 1970. $3.64).

993. Groh, Lynn. **The Pilgrims: Brave Settlers of Plymouth.** Champaign, Ill.: Garrard, 1968. 95p. $3.68. (3-6)

A story of the Pilgrims and the first New England colony.

994. Harvey, Rowland H. **Samuel Gompers: Champion of the Toiling Masses.** Stanford, Calif.: Stanford University Press, 1935; repr. ed., New York: Octagon, 1973. 376p. $14.50. (10-12)

A biography of Gompers and the prominent part he played in the growth and development of the American Federation of Labor after he came to the United States from England.

995. Jacobs, W. J. **Roger Williams.** New York: Watts, 1975. 56p. $4.95. (4-6)

A biography of the founder of the Rhode Island Colony describing how his experiences during his youth in London helped him develop strong beliefs about religious freedom.

996. Morison, Samuel Eliot. **The Story of the "Old Colony" of New Plymouth, 1620-1692.** New York: Knopf, 1956. 296p. $3.50. (7-12)

English immigration to America is described, including reasons and motivations for leaving England, the temporary stay in Holland, the journey to America and settlements there. British influence is described with respect to the settlers' homes, clothing, religious services, government, politics, and educational facilities. Social behavior and standards in the colonies are also described.

997.   Norton, Mary Beth. **British Americans: The Loyalists.** Boston, Mass.: Little, Brown, 1972. 330p. $12.50. (4-12)
Describes the Tories in America who became refugees from the colonies after the Revolutionary War. These expatriates hoped for reunification of the two countries. Documented with photographs, illustrations, maps, cartoons, prints, etc.

998.   Powell, William S. **The North Carolina Colony.** New York: Macmillan, 1969. 154p. $4.50. (4-7)
America's English heritage is described. Walter Raleigh's influence in the early English colony of North Carolina is emphasized. Other well-known English-Americans are also covered.

999.   Shaw, Anna Howard. **The Story of a Pioneer.** Ed. by Rowena Keith Keys. New York: Harper & Bros., 1915; repr. ed., New York: Kraus Reprint Co., 1970. 291p. $18.00. (7-12)
This record of Dr. Shaw's life is also the record of the women's suffrage movement in the United States, as this determined woman of English background spent many years of her life working for this cause.

1000.   Smith, E. Brooks, and Robert Meredith, eds. **Pilgrim Courage.** Illus. by Leonard Everett Fisher. Boston, Mass.: Little, Brown, 1962. 108p. $4.95. (5-10)
This work was originally written by William Bradford and adapted by the editors for use in the public schools. These writings are from a first-hand account of episodes relating to the history of Plimoth Plantation and the early English settlers.

1001.   Sutton, Felix. **Sons of Liberty.** New York: Messner, 1969. 90p. $4.79. (4-6)
Emphasis is on the political contributions of the original British colonists and settlers around the time of the American Revolution. Biographical sketches of early patriots such as Paul Revere, Patrick Henry, and others are included.

1002.   Walsh, John E. **The Mayflower Compact, November 11, 1620: The First Democratic Document in America.** New York: Watts, 1971. 55p. $3.45. (7-9)
Reasons for the British Pilgrims' emigration from England to America (via Holland) are given; the journey and meetings aboard the Mayflower are described. The Mayflower Compact is also examined, and the experiences and influences of its signers in the New World are indicated.

1003.   Weslager, C. A. **English on the Delaware: 1610-1682.** New Brunswick, N.J.: Rutgers University Press, 1967. 303p. $7.50. (9-12)
The role of the English in the Delaware Valley is described, with emphasis on the important influence of the English language and institutions, which became

dominant in that area. States involved are Maryland, Virginia, New York, New Jersey, and Delaware.

1004.   Wilkie, Katharine E. **William Penn, Friend to All**. Champaign, Ill.: Garrard, 1964. 80p. $3.40. (2-5)
An Englishman who came to America to escape religious persecution is the subject of this book for primary and early intermediate grades. Describes how William Penn founded Pennsylvania and established a colony of English Quakers.

1005.   Williams, Selma R. **Kings, Commoners, and Colonists: Puritan Politics in Old New England, 1603-1660**. New York: Atheneum, 1974. 266p. $6.95. (8-12)
A history of the English settlers who established the Massachusetts Bay Colony with British principles and style of government.

Fiction Titles

1006.   Constiner, Merle. **Sumatra Alley**. Camden, N.J.: Nelson, 1971. 128p. $3.95. (5-7)
A historical novel about a 17-year-old boy who becomes involved with the British Redcoats and others loyal to the King of England.

1007.   Finlayson, Ann. **Greenhorn on the Frontier**. Illus. by W. T. Mars. New York: Frederick Warne, 1974. 209p. $4.95. (6-9)
A young British soldier and his sister, Sukey, settle in the frontier town of Pittsburgh. Life in the English colonies is described; Indian relations are also a part of the story. Though in the same vein as *Johnny Tremain*, the latter has a story line that is far superior.

1008.   Hall, Marjory. **The Other Girl**. Philadelphia, Pa.: Westminster, 1974. 185p. $5.25. (6-8)
A fictionalized account of an actual English-American family in colonial history. Quakers, Tories, bigotry, romance, and suspense are combined in this historical novel about a young British-American girl.

1009.   Haywood, Carolyn. **Primrose Day**. New York: Harcourt Brace Jovanovich & World, 1942. 200p. $5.50. (K-3)
A little British girl comes to the United States during World War II.

1010.   Latham, Jean Lee. **This Dear-Bought Land**. Illus. by Jacob Landau. New York: Harper and Row, 1957. 246p. $4.43. (6-12)
A novel of the English in Virginia and John Smith's role in the founding of Jamestown. David Warren, a 15-year-old immigrant from England to America, is the central character; his experiences typify those of many of the English settlers.

1011.   L'Engle, Madeline. **The Other Side of the Sun**. New York: Farrar, Straus & Giroux, 1971. 344p. $6.95; $1.25pa. (9-12)

A young bride from England comes to America to meet her husband's family. Something like an English gothic novel, the setting for this story is the post-Civil War South, with hints of witchcraft, voodoo, and intrigue.

1012. Levitin, Sonia. **Roanoke: A Novel of the Lost Colony.** New York: Atheneum, 1973. 213p. $6.25. (7-9)

A 16-year-old youth befriends an Indian in the first English settlement at Roanoke Island. How this "Lost Colony" disappeared is explained in an exciting and colorful account of the English in America, sixteenth century colonialism, and also the Indian culture of that time and location. Another title by this author for younger children (grades 3-7) is *Journey to America* (Atheneum, 1970. $4.25; $0.95pa.).

1013. Mayne, William. **The Jersey Shore.** New York: Dutton, 1973. 159p. $4.95. (5-7)

Arthur, a British boy, visits his aunt and grandfather, immigrants to New Jersey, in their New World home. Grandfather entertains Arthur with tales of days gone by.

1014. Rickards, Colin. **Bowler Hats and Stetsons.** San Francisco: R&E Research Associates, 1966. $4.00. (9-12)

A collection of stories of Englishmen in the wild West.

1015. Williamson, Joanne S. **The Glorious Conspiracy.** New York: Knopf, 1961. 211p. $3.00. (7-12)

In the early days of the American Republic a young boy escapes his hated apprenticeship in England and immigrates to New York City. He faces problems when his job on a Republican newspaper no longer exists because the paper is shut down by the government.

Audiovisual Materials

1016. **American Families: The Taylors.** 1 filmstrip, 1 record, 1 study guide. Coronet Instructional Films, 1971. (4-9)

A British American family is studied to see the social life, family customs, differences in the family's generations, and other interesting aspects of their English background.

1017. **The English Colonies.** 1 filmstrip, 1 teacher's guide, ditto masters. Urban Media Materials, 1973. (3-6)

The English colonies in the United States are studied, with emphasis on the influence of English culture and history on the colonies. This title is also available as a slide set of 20 2x2-inch slides.

1018. **The First Impact.** 16mm film, 52 min., color, 1 teacher's guide. Time/Life Films. $600.00; $100.00 (rental). 26 min. version: $300.00; $50.00 (rental). (7-12)

A British American, Alistair Cooke, tells his own first impressions and experiences as a student in America.

1019. **Jamestown—The First English Settlement in America.** 16mm film, 22 min., color. EBEC, 1958. $8.50 (rental). (7-12)
A drama of the founding of the first English settlement at Jamestown in 1607. England's influence on American culture and government is emphasized.

1020. **Life in the Early American Colonies.** 6 filmstrips, 3 cassettes. Troll. $66.00. (4-8)
Describes the customs of everyday life of the English settlers in the Plymouth Colony. Titles include: The Mayflower Experience; The Plymouth Plantation; Colonial Food; Colonial Shelter and Defense; Colonial Crafts; Religion, Education, Recreation.

1021. **Massachusetts—The Puritan Oligarchy.** 1 filmstrip, 1 record. Midwest Educational Materials, 1974. (7-12)
The social, religious, economic, and political influences of the English and Dutch Puritans on the Massachusetts Bay and Plymouth Colonies are examined.

1022. **The Mayflower Compact.** 1 record, 1 teacher's guide. Scholastic Audiovisuals. $6.50. (4-12)
The Mayflower Compact is an important document since it reveals the conditions of English government and society and their influence in the new homeland.

1023. **New England.** 4 filmstrips, 2 records, 4 scripts, 16 spirit master vocabularies. Filmstrip House. $35.00. (4-8)
The English background and influence in America is particularly emphasized in the first filmstrips in this set. Titles include: English Roots; Colonial Development; Becoming American; Urban Development.

1024. **The Pilgrim Adventure.** 16mm film, 53 min., color. McGraw-Hill, 1965. $20.50 (rental). (7-12)
Describes the religious conflict in the Church of England that caused a group of people to flee to Holland and later America. Topics covered are the journey to the United States, the Mayflower Compact, the first settlement at Plimoth Plantation in Massachusetts, and experiences there.

1025. **The Pilgrims.** 16mm film, 22 min., b&w. Encyclopaedia Britannica Films, 1954. $7.00 (rental). (5-12)
Studies the English Pilgrims, describing their problems in England, their stay in Holland, and the reasons for the ultimate search for a home in America.

1026. **Plymouth Colony: The First Year.** 16mm film, 16 min., color. Coronet, 1961. $7.00 (rental). (4-8)
Records the English settlers' first year at Plymouth. Emphasis is on religious conflicts of the Separatists, the Mayflower Compact, and the intermingling of the English life style with customs adapted from the Indians.

1027. **Story of the Pilgrims.** 16mm film, 28 min., color (2 reels). McGraw-Hill, 1955. $12.50 (rental). (4-8)

Reel 1 uses marionettes to dramatize the conflicts in England that motivated the Pilgrims' arrival in America. Reel 2 describes their life in America, English influences on our society, and the first Thanksgiving celebration. Reels can be rented or utilized separately.

CHINESE AMERICANS

See also Asian Americans.

Reference Sources

1028. Hansen, G. C., ed. **Chinese in California: A Brief Bibliographic History.** Portland, Ore.: Richard Abel & Co., Inc., 1970. 140p. $15.00. (9-12, T) This annotated bibliography of Chinese laborers in California also covers the role of the Chinese immigrants in the development of the West and the state of California. Arrangement is alphabetical by author.

1029. Tung, William L. **The Chinese in America 1820-1973.** Dobbs Ferry, N.Y.: Oceana Publications, 1974. 150p. $6.00. (7-12) A ready reference book covering in chronological order the history, important documents, acts, treaties, and judicial decisions concerning the Chinese in America. A bibliography on Chinese immigration is included, as are lists of Chinese American organizations.

1030. Young, Nancy E. **The Chinese in Hawaii: An Annotated Bibliography.** Honolulu: University Press of Hawaii, 1973. 149p. $4.00pa. (9-12, T) Lists a variety of materials available in Honolulu in an annotated bibliography providing source location. Includes both English and Chinese titles; arrangement is alphabetical by author.

Non-Fiction Titles: History, Culture, Sociology, Biography

1031. Char, Tin-Yuke, ed. **The Sandalwood Mountains: Readings and Stories of the Early Chinese in Hawaii.** Honolulu: University Press of Hawaii, 1974. 1368p. $12.00 text ed. (10-12) These writings, letters, family histories, etc., of Chinese immigrants to Hawaii describe customs of the Chinese culture that are becoming extinct on the American scene.

1032. Chinn, Thomas. **A History of the Chinese in California: A Syllabus.** San Francisco: Chinese Historical Society of America, 1969. 81p. (9-12) Outlines the history of the Chinese in California for use in teaching a unit on the Chinese experience in America. Includes suggested reading materials and bibliographical references, maps, and a survey of the history and activities of the Chinese Historical Society of America are included.

1033.   Chu, Daniel, and Dr. Samuel Chu. **Passage to the Golden Gate: A History of the Chinese in America to 1910.** New York: Doubleday, 1967. 117p. $3.95; $1.45pa. (6-9)
Describes exploitation of the Chinese in America during the 1800s in California, and the discriminatory legislation and treatment they encountered. Also discusses their contributions to American society.

1034.   Dowdell, Dorothy, and Joseph Dowdell. **The Chinese Helped Build America.** New York: Messner, 1972. 96p. $4.79. (3-6)
An overview of the Chinese in America emphasizing the experiences, achievements, contributions, and prejudicial treatment of the early immigrants. Arrangement is chronological, but a fictionalized account of an immigrant is included. American Chinatowns are also described.

1035.   Hsu, Francis L. K. **The Challenge of the American Dream: The Chinese in the U.S.** Belmont, Calif.: Wadsworth, 1971. 160p. $3.95pa. (10-12)
The Chinese in the United States are examined with respect to cultural conflict, group behavior, and adjustment.

1036.   Integrated Education Associates Editorial Staff. **Chinese Americans: School and Community Problems.** Evanston, Ill.: Integrated Education Associates, 1972. 76p. $1.25pa. (9-12, T)
A collection of articles by Chinese Americans on problems of their ethnic community. Topics covered are schooling, employment, language, community needs, care of the aged, and busing in Chinatown. School-related problems are emphasized and problems of the larger Chinatown areas such as San Francisco and New York City are discussed. Includes "Selected References on Asian-American School and Community Affairs."

1037.   Jones, Claire. **The Chinese in America.** Minneapolis, Minn.: Lerner Publications, 1973. 95p. $3.95. (5-11)
Covers the history of the Chinese immigrants to America, their experiences, contributions, and achievements. Popular presentation.

1038.   Kung, Shien-Woo. **Chinese in American Life.** Seattle: University of Washington Press, 1962; repr. ed., Westport, Conn.: Greenwood Press, 1973. 352p. $15.00. (9-12, T)
A history of Chinese immigration to the United States, and of the social and economic status of the Chinese Americans. Covers the contributions and achievements of outstanding Chinese in the United States, namely scholars, Nobel Prize winners, engineers, teachers, doctors, nurses, businessmen, etc. Includes a bibliography and an index.

1039.   Lowe, Pardee. **Father and Glorious Descendant.** Boston, Mass.: Little, Brown, 1943. 322p. $2.50.
An autobiographical account of the author's life in San Francisco's Chinatown. He tells his own experiences and recreates the life of his friends and family, particularly his father.

1040.　Lyman, Stanford M. **Chinese Americans.** New York: Random House, 1974. 213p. $3.95. (10-12)

This history of the Chinese in the United States begins with a brief overview of Chinese immigration. Included are reasons for coming to America, anti-Chinese discrimination and legislation, and Oriental racism in American business, schools, and other institutions. The latter part of the book deals with contemporary Chinatowns and their problems, their social and economic aspects, and their political impact on American society.

1041.　Miller, Stuart Creighton. **The Unwelcome Immigrant: The American Image of the Chinese, 1785-1882.** Berkeley: University of California Press, 1969. 259p. $3.25pa. (10-12, T)

Discriminatory treatment and prejudicial laws are emphasized in this history of the Chinese immigrant to the United States. The image of the Chinese American is traced from the eighteenth century on; the work also discusses the Chinese-American relations throughout the period studied. Bibliographical notes included; indexed.

1042.　Molnar, Joe. **Sherman: A Chinese-American Child Tells His Story.** New York: Watts, 1973. 48p. $0.95. (3-6)

Sherman lives in an all-white New York neighborhood where he is a 10-year-old second-generation Chinese American.

1043.　Nee, Victor G., and Brett De Bary Nee. **Longtime Californ': A Documentary Study of an American Chinatown.** New York: Pantheon Books, 1973. 410p. $10.00; $4.75pa. (9-12)

Contemporary Chinatown in San Francisco is discussed, with particular attention to the influences that caused and perpetuate its growth and development. Appendixes contain immigration laws; a map indicates communities of Chinese Americans in the United States.

1044.　Sung, Betty Lee. **The Chinese in America.** New York: Macmillan, 1972. 120p. $4.95. (5-7)

A history of the Chinese in America from the nineteenth century to the present. Emphasis is on anti-Chinese discrimination, Chinese accomplishments and contributions. Customs of family life, food, religious celebrations are also covered. A short bibliography and some illustrations are included. For older readers, the author has written *Mountain of Gold: The Chinese in the United States* (Macmillan, 1967. $6.95).

1045.　Weiss, Melford S. **Valley City: A Chinese Community in America.** Cambridge, Mass.: Schenkman Publishing, 1974. 269p. $8.95 text ed.; $5.95pa. (9-12)

A Chinese community is examined with special attention to social and economic assimilation. Distinctive Chinese-American cultural traits are indicated. A bibliography of additional reading references is included.

1046.   Wong, Jean H. "Chinese-American Identity and Children's Picture Books."
         Unpublished paper, 1971. 17p. $0.65. ED 067 663. (T)
A survey of children's books about Chinese and Chinese Americans indicates books
that contain stereotypes or over-generalizations about Chinese culture and traditions.
Books surveyed are on the K-3 reading level and arranged by theme. Outstanding
titles are indicated.

Literature and Fiction Titles

1047.   Bales, Carol A. **Chinatown Sunday: The Story of Lilliann Der**. Chicago:
         Reilly & Lee, 1973. 32p. $5.95.
A ten-year-old Chinese-American girl describes her family and their life in a Chicago
suburb.

1048.   Bulla, Clyde Robert. **Johnny Hong of Chinatown**. Illus. by Dong Kingman.
         New York: Crowell, 1952. 69p. $3.95. (2-4)
This story of a small boy in an American Chinatown depicts life and customs of the
Chinese-American community. Sad because he doesn't have any playmates his age,
Johnny Hong makes new friends in time for his birthday party.

1049.   Caen, Herb. **Cable Car and the Dragon**. Illus. by Barbara Byfield. New
         York: Doubleday, 1972. unp. $4.95. (2-4)
Describes San Francisco's Chinatown in an amusing story of Charlie, a cable car,
and Chu Chin Chow, a fire-breathing dragon.

1050.   Chang, Isabelle, reteller. **Tales from Old China**. Illus. by Tony Chen. New
         York: Random House, 1969. 67p. $3.50. (3-5)
A collection of traditional Chinese folk tales useful for story-telling in the primary
grades.

1051.   Chin-Yang, Lee. **The Flower Drum Song**. New York: Farrar, 1957. 244p.
         $3.50. (7-12)
The story of a Chinese immigrant who resists becoming Americanized in the New
World. The setting is San Francisco's Chinatown in the first half of the twentieth
century. Another title by the same author is *Lover's Point* (Farrar, 1958. $3.75).

1052.   Friedman, Frieda. **Sundae with Judy**. New York: Morrow, 1949. 192p.
         $4.75. (4-6)
Judy likes to wait on customers in her father's candy store, but she gets fat sampling
the merchandise. A story of New York's interracial neighborhoods and how Judy
befriends a girl from Chinatown.

1053.   Judson, C. I. **The Green Ginger Jar**. Illus. by Paul Brown, Boston, Mass.:
         Houghton Mifflin, 1949. 210p. $4.95. (4-7)
Chicago's Chinatown is the setting of this mystery of the ginger jar. The story gives
the reader a good background and insight into the life and customs of the Chinese-
American community.

1054. Keating, Norma. **Mr. Chu.** New York: Macmillan, 1965. 34p. $4.75.
(K-3)
Mr. Chu introduces Johnny, an orphan boy, to Chinese customs in his home in New York's Chinatown.

1055. LaPiere, Richard Tracy. **Where the Living Strive.** New York: Harper and Row, 1941. 346p. $2.50. (9-12)
A story of immigrant life set in the Chinese community of San Francisco. Chinese customs, values, and lifestyle during the last quarter of the nineteenth century and the first quarter of the twentieth are described.

1056. Lenski, Lois. **San Francisco Boy.** Philadelphia: Lippincott, 1955. 176p. $4.29. (4-6)
San Francisco's Chinatown is the setting of this story of two Chinese-American children, Mei Gwen and Felix, and their opposite reactions to life there. Typical situations in the community, the home and the Chinese language school are described.

1057. Martin, Patricia. **The Rice Bowl Pet.** Illus. by Ezra Jack Keats. New York: Crowell, 1962. unp. $4.50. (K-3)
The only pet Ah Jim is allowed to have is one small enough to fit into a rice bowl.

1058. Newman, Shirlee P. **Yellow Silk for May Lee.** Indianapolis, Ind.: Bobbs-Merrill Co., 1961. 128p. $3.25. (2-6)
May Lee saves her money for a long time to buy silk for a coveted first Chinese style grown-up dress. She pleases her family by her generous use of the silk.

1059. Niemeyer, Marie. **Moon Guitar.** Illus. by Gustave E. Nebel. New York: Watts, 1969. 151p. $2.63. (4-6)
Lee Su-Lin finds a moon guitar and a scroll painting in a mystery story that illustrates the conflict between generations in a Chinese-American family.

1060. Oakes, Vanya. **Willy Wong, American.** New York: Archway, 1951. 174p. $0.75pa. (4-6)
Willy Wong has conflicts with the American customs and his Chinese traditions and background. He learns to accept and enjoy both of his cultural heritages and wins many friends at school.

1061. Pinkwater, Manus. **Wingman.** New York: Dodd, Mead, 1975. 65p. $5.50. (9-12)
The story of a Chinese-American boy whose self-image is strengthened by his teacher after he has withdrawn into a world of fantasy. A sensitive portrayal of the feelings unique to all immigrant children who are self-conscious about their ethnic background.

1062. Reit, Seymour. **Rice Cakes and Paper Dragons.** Photos by Paul Conklin. New York: Dodd, Mead, 1973. 79p. $3.95. (2-5)
Marie-Chan attends a Chinese school in New York's Chinatown. Chinese customs, holidays, and family roles are emphasized.

1063.   Wong, Jade Snow. **Fifth Chinese Daughter.** New York: Harper and Row, 1950. 246p. $4.79. (7-12)
The story of a Chinese-American artist whose family opposed her desires to have a career as an artist. Another title by this author is *No Chinese Stranger* (Harper and Row, 1975. $8.95).

1064.   Wyndham, Robert, reteller. **Tales the People Tell in China.** Illus. by Jay Yang. New York: Messner, 1971. 92p. $5.64. (3-6)
A collection of 15 traditional Chinese folk tales, with background notes on the stories. The 14 Chinese proverbs also included give insight into Chinese customs and values.

1065.   Yep, Laurence. **Dragonwings.** New York: Harper and Row, 1975. 208p. $6.79. (6-9)
When he is eight-years-old, Moonshadow comes to the United States to join his father, a laundry operator and maker of fabulous kites. This is the story of San Francisco's prejudicial treatment of the Chinese Americans, a boy's wonderful adventure creating a flying machine with his father, and a vivid picture of Chinese customs and family life.

Audiovisual Materials

1066.   **American Families.** 1 filmstrip, 1 record. Coronet Instructional Films, 1971. (3-6)
A Chinese-American family is described with special emphasis on their religious, economic, and social activities. Also shows them as they respond and react to the community.

1067.   **The Changs Celebrate the New Year.** 1 filmstrip, 1 record. Encyclopaedia Britannica Corp., 1971. (3-6)
Shows the special holiday customs celebrated by a Chinese-American family living in a large urban area. Emphasis is on their cultural heritage and the problems they encounter maintaining their Chinese customs and adapting to their new country.

1068.   **The Chinese American—The Early Immigrants.** 16mm film, 20 min., color, 1 teacher's guide. Handel Film Corp., 1973. (6-12)
Describes Chinese immigration to the United States and the contribution of the Chinese Americans to their new country's economy and development. Also covers anti-Chinese discrimination and legislation. Emphasizes the period of gold mining and railroad construction in the United States.

1069.   **The Chinese American—The Twentieth Century.** 16mm film, 20 min., color, 1 teacher's guide. Handel Film Corp., 1973. (6-12)
The experiences of Chinese Americans during the twentieth century. Emphasizes prejudicial treatment and the contributions of the Chinese Americans.

1070.   **Chinese Americans.** Super 8mm film, 4 min., silent, color. Ealing Corp., 1970. $24.95. (6-12)

An American Chinatown, a Chinese festival, and other scenes typifying the lives of Chinese Americans are presented. Discusses the amount of assimilation into American society of the various generations among the Chinese families. The setting is a Chinese New Year's celebration.

1071. **The Chinese Forty-Niners.** 1 filmstrip, 1 cassette (or record), 1 teacher's guide. Multi-Media Productions. $11.95. (4-8)
Surveys the Chinese experience in the United States from immigration, discrimination, and prejudicial treatment to the Chinese American's contributions to California and America.

1072. **The Chinese—How We Got Here.** 1 videotape. Asian American Studies, Berkeley Unified School District. (5-10)
A tape prepared by Loni Ding, a Chinese-American, for the public schools in Berkeley, California, under the auspices of the Asian American Studies program of the Berkeley Unified School District.

1073. **Chinese New Year.** 1 videotape. Asian American Studies, Berkeley Unified School District. (5-10)
A tape prepared by Suzanne Joe available for use from the Berkeley Unified School District's Asian American Studies program.

1074. **Chinese Tales.** 4 filmstrips, 4 records (or cassettes). Warren Schloat Productions, 1974. $66.00; $78.00 (with cassettes). (3-12)
Typical Chinese customs and behavior can be found in these selections of folktales. The teacher's guide suggests follow-up ideas and activities for a social studies unit.

1075. **Ching Dao.** 1 filmstrip, 1 record (or cassette). Scott Education Division, 1970. (5-10)
New York's Chinatown is depicted showing the Chinese schools that the Chinese-American students attend to learn the Chinese language, history, and cultural heritage.

1076. **The Golden Mountain on Mott St.** 16mm film, 34 min., color. Columbia Boradcasting System; Association Films. $360.00. (9-12)
Discusses how the breakdown of family and Chinese traditions have been brought about by the second and third generation youth rebelling against maintaining Oriental customs and seeking to identify with the American way of life.

1077. **Kam Lee Comes to School.** Multimedia kit. Reader's Digest Services, Inc., Educational Division, 1967. $3.00; $2.25 (school price). (K-1)
Contents of the kit include a 64-page book, a lotto game for two to six players, and a teacher's manual with ideas and activities designed to help build appreciation of cultural diversity. The picture story book is the story of a little Chinese student in an inner city school.

1078. **The Oriental American.** 1 filmstrip, 1 record (or cassette). Miller Brody Productions. $14.50; with cassette, $17.50. (4-12)

Studies Orientals in America—their special problems, goals and achievements. From *The Other American Minorities* series.

1079.　**Siu Mei Wong: Who Shall I Be?** 16mm film, 18 min., color. Learning Corporation of America, 1970. $8.50 (rental). (4-12)
A young Chinese girl wants to take ballet lessons after school. Her father wants her to attend Chinese language class and preserve her cultural heritage. This story of culture conflict gives insights into the customs, goals, and values of the Chinese-American community.

1080.　**The Trouble with Chinatown.** 16mm film, 26 min., color. NBC Educational Enterprises, 1970. (7-12)
Analyzes the problems of the Chinese Americans living in isolated Chinatowns. Some of the new services to help solve their problems and to help them become assimilated into Western society and life are indicated—e.g., a bi-lingual professional program designed to help the Chinese community with housing, employment, family services, legal assistance, etc.

CROATIAN AMERICANS. *See* Yugoslav Americans.

CUBAN AMERICANS

See also Spanish-Speaking Americans.

Reference Sources

1081.　Valdes, Nelson P., and Edwin Liewen. **The Cuban Revolution: A Research Study Guide (1959-1969).** Albuquerque: University of New Mexico Press, 1971. 230p. $7.50. (9-12, T)
Contains approximately 3,500 entries on reference and general works on the Cuban Revolution. Covers Cuban history, culture, politics, and the Cuban exiles.

Non-Fiction Titles: History, Culture, Sociology, Biography

1082.　Fagen, Richard R., *et al.* **Cubans in Exile: Disaffection & the Revolution.** Stanford, Calif.: Stanford University Press, 1968. 161p. $5.95. (T)
Although this is basically a reference for teachers, some advanced high school students may be able to use the material in this work. The charts and graphs are not easy to interpret, but the work is objective and contains many facts about the Cuban Revolution and reasons for immigration to the United States. It covers the period between the late 1950s and the early 1960s, in the early days of Castro and Cuban refugee immigration.

1083.   Moncarz, Raul. **A Study of the Effects of Environmental Change on Human Capital among Selected Skilled Cubans.** Tallahassee, Fla.: Florida State University College of Arts and Sciences, 1969. 172p. $3.29. ED 053256. (9-12, T)

This study analyzes the skills and competencies the Cuban refugees had attained from their education prior to immigration, and the extent to which they could transfer their use in the United States. Interviews with Cubans in the United States are presented, with the following topics emphasized: legal status, self employment, retraining in the United States, education in United States schools and universities, age, sex, and others.

1084.   Roeg, Eleanor H. **The Occupational Adjustment of Cuban Refugees in the West New York, New Jersey, Area.** Bronx, N.Y.: Fordham University, 1970. 464p. $0.95pa. ED 051366. (9-12, T)

Attempts to determine whether Cuban refugees are aided in adjustment to the United States for forming close-knit communities, or whether economic class is significant in acculturation. Also the study attempts to determine whether governmental programs are effective in aiding adjustment.

1085.   Senior, Clarence. **Our Citizens from the Caribbean.** New York: McGraw-Hill, 1965. 122p. $1.96. (7-12)

Discusses various aspects of Cuban culture including education, economics, welfare, and social acceptance. Reasons for immigration to the United States are also covered.

1086.   Terzian, James. **Kid from Cuba: Zoilo Versalles.** Garden City, N.Y.: Doubleday, 1967. 142p. $3.95. (5-8)

A biography of Zoilo Versalles, Cuban American all-star baseball player for the Minnesota Twins in the 1960s. His birth and childhood in Cuba are included, but emphasis is on his baseball career.

Fiction Titles

1087.   Holland, Isabelle. **Amanda's Choice.** Philadelphia, Pa.: Lippincott, 1960. 152p. $4.50. (2-4)

The friendship between Santiago and Amanda is a story in which the Cuban-American relationship is portrayed.

Audiovisual Materials

1088.   **Cuba and Its Refugees.** 2 filmstrips, 1 cassette (or record), 1 teacher's guide. Society for Visual Education, 1973. $23.00; $21.00 (with record). (7-12)

Divided into two parts, this filmstrip presents good photographs of Cuba 14 years after Castro's revolution in Part I, The Island Country. The second part studies Miami's Cuban communities and the refugees who have made their home in the

United States. Emphasis is on their achievements, contributions, and their effect on the social, cultural, and economic life of the city of Miami.

1089.   **Cuba—From Friend to Foe.** Filmstrip, color. Scholastic Magazines, Inc. (5-12)
Events in Cuba since Fidel Castro came to power are described. Covers the reasons for refugees' immigrating to the United States and the evolution of the relationship of Cuba from a friendly to an unfriendly neighbor.

1090.   **Miami's Cuban Community.** Filmstrip, 1 phonodisc, 1 teacher's guide. Society for Visual Education, 1973. (4-10)
The community of Cuban refugees in Miami, Florida, is described. Cuban contributions and influences in the area are stressed.

CZECH AND SLOVAK AMERICANS

This section covers relevant materials on both
Czechs and Slovaks in the United States.

Reference Sources

1091.   Psencik, Leroy F. **Czech Contributions to the American Culture.** Austin: Texas Education Agency, 1970. 17p. $3.29. ED 053023. (T)
A bibliographic essay of books and journals on Czech culture, experience, and contributions to the United States.

Teaching Methodology and Curriculum Materials

1092.   Masters, Florence. **Curriculum Building: Ethnic Studies and the Community.** Cedar Rapids, Iowa: Kirkwood Community College, 1975. 18 units. $1.50. (T)
Model curriculum materials are designed for grades 7-14 (adaptable for grades K-6), with a concluding list of Czech values and attitudes. The Czech Ethnic Heritage Studies Program Model has two tracks: culture and language—further divided into clusters and modules. Module titles in the Culture Track are: Culture; Ethos; Ethnocentrism and Ethnicity; Culture and Personality; Czech Americans; An Historical Background; Czech Americans; Immigration Patterns; Music—Antonin Dvorak; Occupations in the New World—The Businessmen and Farmers of Cedar Rapids; Communications—The Czech Press in Cedar Rapids; Christmas—A Bohemian Christmas in Chicago; Poetry—"Silesian Woods"; Peter Bezruč.
        Titles in the Language Track include: Reading—Motýlkové; Dialogues—Student Guide; Dialogues—1) Nedělní Oběd; Zásnuby; Chlapu; 4) Přátelská návštěva, 5) Teta. Each track has a comprehensive instructional guide. The pattern for each module includes: objectives, concepts, references (print and non-print materials); activities; evaluation. Each track is accompanied by an instructional guide.

Non-Fiction Titles: History, Culture, Sociology, Biography

1093.   Andrlova, Marcela. **Children in Czechoslovakia.** New York: Sterling, 1969.
95p. $3.95. (4-8)
A photographic essay depicting games, holidays, food, folklore, studies, sports,
health care, and the duties and responsibilities in the home and community that are
familiar to the Czech child. Good background text for understanding the Czech-
American community.

1094.   Cada, Joseph. **Czech-American Catholics, 1850-1920.** Lisle, Ill.: Center for
Slav Culture, 1964. 118p. $2.00. (9-12, T)
A history of the religious activities of the Czech Catholic immigrants over a 70-year
period. Many Old Country traditions, customs and cultural traits are described, in
addition to those of the Czech Catholic Church.

1095.   Capek, Thomas. **The Czechs (Bohemians) in America.** Boston, Mass.:
Houghton Mifflin, 1920; repr. ed., New York: AMS Press, 1969. 278p.
$13.00. (7-12)
A history of Czech immigration and the status of the group in America with respect
to economic and social conditions. Covers the Czech customs, heritage, and tradi-
tions, and discusses the roles of religion, politics, etc., within the Czech community.
Also includes Czech contributions in the arts, literature, and other areas.

1096.   Červenka, R. W. **John Kohut and His Son Joseph.** Waco, Tex.: Texian
Press, 1966. 40p. $2.55. (7-12)
Mr. Cervenka writes a brief history of the Texas Czech pioneers. This account of
John Kohut and his son Joseph portray the adjustments, problems, and struggles
made by these immigrants in their new homeland.

1097.   Czechoslovak National Council of America, comp. **Panorama: A Historical
Review of Czechs and Slovaks in the United States of America.** Cicero,
Ill.: Czechoslovak National Council of America, 1970. 328p. (10-12, T)
A history of Czechs and Slovaks in the United States with emphasis on their social
and economic experience, and their contributions to American life. Biographies of
prominent Czechs and Slovaks are included.

1098.   Dvornik, František. **Czech Contributions to the Growth of the United
States.** Chicago: Benedictine Abbey Press, 1961. 108p. $1.00. (9-12, T)
This study of Czech immigration and Czech Americans concentrates on the Czechs
in the state of Texas, their adjustments, achievements, and outstanding contributions to the growth and development of the United States.

1099.   Gottfried, Alex. **Boss Cermak of Chicago.** Seattle: University of Washington Press, 1962. 459p. $6.50. (9-12)
Chicago's first and only foreign-born mayor, a Czech American, is portrayed in this
biography of Anton Joseph Cermak. His life story details his home life and his early
years as well as his career as a political leader. It also presents historical details
about the Czech immigrant's experience in the United States.

1100.   Polasek, Emily. **Albin Polasek: Man Carving His Own Destiny**. Jackson-
         ville, Fla.: Convention Press, Inc., 1970. 107p. $3.50. (7-12)
A biographical account of a Czech immigrant, Albin Polasek, who became a world
famous sculptor. Many photographs of his works are included.

1101.   Roucek, Joseph S. **The Czechs and the Slovaks in America**. Minneapolis,
         Minn.: Lerner Publications, 1967. 70p. $3.95. (5-11)
Czech and Slovak immigration to the United States and Czech and Slovak contributions to American culture are examined. Schools, churches, organizations, voting
trends, and Czech institutions are discussed. Also covers the impact and influence
of Czech and Slovak immigrants and their descendants on American culture and
society. Illustrated.

1102.   Schattschneider, Allen W. **Through Five Hundred Years: A Popular His-
         tory of the Moravian Church**. Winston Salem, N.C.: Comenius Press,
         1956. 146p. $1.25. (4-9)
Describes how the early Czech Protestants in the state of Texas established their own
church and religious denomination when settlers in Veseli (now Wesley in Washington
County) organized the Wesley Brethren in 1864. This group became a member of the
Union of the Bohemian-Moravian Brethren in Texas in 1903. The group's religious
history is also a picture of the early Czech immigrants' problems and struggles. The
most recent history of the Moravian church was written by J. T. Hamilton and
K. G. Hamilton, *History of the Moravian Church* (Winston-Salem, N.C.: Moravian
Church of America, 1967. 644p. $4.95. 10-12, T).

Literature and Fiction Titles

1103.   American Sokol Educational and Physical Culture Organization. **The Ameri-
         can Sokol Sings!** Berwyn, Ill.: The Organization, 1974. 120p. $5.00. (K-12)
The Czech musical heritage is perpetuated through these songs familiar to Czech
Americans. Included are traditional, folk, and popular Czech melodies, Czech
anthems and patriotic songs. Most have Czech translations; historical background
of the songs is given and there are biographies of two famous Czech songwriters.

1104.   Baca, Mary, comp. **Memorial Book and Recipes**. Taylor, Tex.: Merchants
         Press, 1957. 256p. $1.25. (4-12)
These recipes, bits of historical information, and photographs from the early Czech
community in Texas have been compiled by a Czech immigrant who was herself one
of the early Czechs and also a pioneer of the state of Texas.

1105.   Burg, Marie. **Tales from Czechoslovakia**. Chester Springs, Pa.: Dufour,
         1967. 125p. $3.95. (3-8)
A collection of folktales depicting favorite characters and customs from Czechoslo-
vakian folk history and tradition. Stories selected here are for the intermediate
grades into junior high school.

1106.   Cather, Willa. **My Antonia**. New York: Houghton, Mifflin, 1962. 266p.
         $5.00; $2.45pa. (7-12)

Antonia is a second-generation immigrant from Bohemia who, in spite of adverse family and economic conditions, makes a fruitful and rewarding life for herself in America. Her story is told by a family friend who admired her courage and spirit while she was managing the family farm in her early youth. The setting is in the Western prairie states in the early part of the twentieth century. An earlier title by the author is *Obscure Destinies* (Knopf, 1932).

1107. Chase, Mary Ellen. **Windswept.** New York: Macmillan, 1941. 440p. $7.95.
 (7-12)
A novel of a Czech American family in a Maine community overlooking the coast of the Atlantic Ocean. "Windswept" refers to the name of the Marston family home, and the story traces the generations of the family, their experiences, and their cultural contributions from the 1880s to 1939.

1108. **Czech and Slovak Short Stories.** Selected, translated, and with an Introduction by Jeanne W. Nemcova. London: Oxford University Press, 1967.
 296p. $3.50. (10-12)
A representative anthology covering both Czech and Slovak writers. Includes a valuable introduction.

1109. Drdek, Richard. **The Game.** Garden City, N.Y.: Doubleday, 1968. 142p.
 $2.95. (4-6)
A young Czech-American boy is raised in America by an affectionate uncle whose life style does not meet with the neighbors' approval.

1110. French, Alfred, comp. **Anthology of Czech Poetry.** Introduction by
 Rene Welleck. Ann Arbor: Department of Slavic Languages and Literatures
 of the University of Michigan, and Czechoslovak Society of Arts and
 Sciences in America, 1973. 372p. (Michigan Slavic Translations, no. 2).
 $4.50pa. (10-12)
A representative anthology of Czech poetry. Projected to be published in two volumes. The present volume covers the period from the fourteenth century through 1918. Well translated.

1111. Gág, Wanda. **Gone Is Gone.** New York: Coward, McCann & Geoghegan,
 1935. unp. $3.57. (K-3)
A Czech folktale about a man who thought his wife had the easiest role until he exchanged duties with her for a day.

1112. Haviland, Virginia. **Favorite Fairy Tales Told in Czechoslovakia.** Boston,
 Mass.: Little, Brown, 1966. 90p. $4.95. (K-6)
These five typical fairy tales are told by Czech-American parents to their children. These stories are reminiscent of the Czech heritage and background.

1113. Hlubucek, Theodore B. **Czech Family Sunday Dinner: A Play in One Act.**
 Cedar Rapids, Iowa: Czech Ethnic Heritage Studies, Kirkwood Community College, 1974. 26p. $1.50. (4-8)
A play with dialogue in both English and Czech is provided as a part of a curriculum package. The appended cultural notes give important insights into Czech culture

and traditions. The author was a Czech immigrant in the 1920s and was active in the Czech Dramatic Society in Cedar Rapids, Iowa.

1114.   Jacobs, Emma Atkins. **A Chance to Belong.** New York: Dell Publishing Co., c1953, 1966. 220p. $3.97. (7-9)
A young Czech American boy finds conflicts with loyalty to his parents and their Old Country ways and his desires to win acceptance and spend more time with the students in his high school classes. When Jan Karel meets Barbara, a relationship develops that helps him to bridge the gap between the old and new countries, his parents and his new friends.

1115.   Kafka, Franz. **Amerika.** Illus. by Emlen Etting. New York: New Directions, c1946, 1962. 299p. $1.75pa. (9-12)
The adventures and experiences of a young Czech immigrant from Prague. The book's emphasis is on the problems of adjustment in the new country.

1116.   Ness, Evaline. **Long, Broad & Quickeye.** New York: Scribner's, 1969. unp. $4.95. (K-3)
An adaptation of a Bohemian folk tale told by Andrew Lang. Illustrated by Ms. Ness. Suitable for storytelling at all ages, but reading level is for intermediate grades.

1117.   Perl, Lila. **Foods and Festivals of the Danube Lands.** Cleveland, Ohio: World Publishing, 1969. 280p. $6.50. (4-12, T)
Czech Americans describe the traditional festivals and foods of their ancestral background. Religious and other holidays are covered, and authentic Czech recipes are included.

Audiovisual Materials

1118.   **Czech Family Sunday Dinner: A Play in One Act.** Video cassette. Czech Ethnic Heritage Studies, Kirkwood Community College, 1974. $30.10. (3-8)
This play is dramatized by members of a Czech-American community. It portrays Czech-American family life typical in the 1920s and 1930s. The author was a Czech immigrant and active in the Czech Dramatic Society in Cedar Rapids, Iowa.

1119.   **The Pittsburgh Area: A Case Study.** 1 filmstrip, 1 record. Society for Visual Education, 1971. (4-8)
Describes the many Central European immigrants that make up the steel-making community of Pittsburgh. Emphasis is on the daily life and activities of a Slovak family.

DANISH AMERICANS

See also **Scandinavian Americans.**

Reference Sources
(*See* Reference Sources under Scandinavian Americans.)

Non-Fiction Titles: History, Culture, Sociology, Biography

1120.   Bille, John H. **A History of the Danes in America.** San Francisco: R&E
        Research Associates, 1971. 48p. (10-12, T)
Issued in 1896 as Volume 11 of the *Transactions of the Wisconsin Academy of Sciences, Arts and Letters*, this description of the largest Danish settlements in the United States covers communities in New York, Wisconsin, Utah, California, Illinois, and Iowa. Danish institutions, including churches, parochial schools, and cultural and other organizations are also discussed. Covers Danish assimilation into American society. A brief selected bibliography is included.

1121.   Meyer, Edith Patterson. **"Not Charity, But Justice": The Story of
        Jacob A. Riis.** New York: Vanguard, 1975. 172p. $5.95. (6-10)
The story of Jacob Riis, an immigrant from Denmark whose journalistic efforts to arouse urban social reforms in the late nineteenth and early twentieth centuries are well known.

1122.   Riis, Jacob A. **The Making of an American.** New York: Century, 1901;
        repr. ed., New York: Macmillan, 1970. $6.95. (9-12)
The life story of a famous Danish immigrant, newspaperman, writer, and reformer.

Literature and Fiction Titles

1123.   Hatch, Mary C. **Thirteen Danish Tales.** Illus. by Edgun. New York:
        Harcourt Brace Jovanovich, 1947. 169p. $3.75. (3-6)
A selection of 13 folk tales retold from the Jens Christian Bay collection. Useful for storytelling by the teacher in the lower grades. A similar title is *More Danish Tales* (Harcourt, 1949. $3.75).

1124.   Haviland, Virginia. **Favorite Fairy Tales Told in Denmark.** Illus. by Margot
        Zemach. Boston, Mass.: Little, Brown, 1971. 90p. $3.95. (3-6)
A collection of six fairy tales adapted for storytelling or for reading by children at the intermediate level. Includes "The Wonderful Pot," "Grayfoot," and others.

1125.   Kerr, Helen V. **Helga's Magic.** New York: Washburn Press, 1970. 87p.
        $3.50. (3-5)
When David and Deborah have Helga for a babysitter they experience some exciting adventures with her. Helga grew up on a farm in Denmark and the reader learns something of Danish life and customs, as well as special Danish Christmas celebrations.

Audiovisual Materials

1126.   **The Danish Field.** 1 filmstrip (71 fr.), 1 phonotape, 1 teacher's supplement. Institute of Texan Cultures, 1972.
Documents with recent and historical photographs the largest Danish settlement in Texas, located at Danevang. Presents Danish culture and traditions in the New World, as well as Danish-American contributions.

1127.   **The Danish Field.** 71 col. slides (2x2-inch), 1 phonotape.

DUTCH AMERICANS

Reference Sources

1128.   Brinks, Herbert, ed. **Guide to the Dutch-American Historical Collections of Western Michigan.** Grand Rapids and Holland, Mich.: Dutch-American Historical Commission, 1967. 52p. (9-12, T)
Lists five institutions in Western Michigan holding Dutch-American historical materials. The sources in Hope College, Calvin College, Western Theological Seminary, Calvin Theological Seminary, and the Netherlands Museum are given in a partially annotated bibliography. The combined archives include materials in newspapers, personal records, journals, church and educational publications, arranged by type. This is an important source for Dutch materials, since the Netherlands Museum has become a depository for many official documents concerned with the Dutch settlement in the early days of Holland, Michigan. Indexed.

1129.   Lagerway, Walter. **Guide to Netherlandic Studies: Bibliography.** Grand Rapids, Mich.: Calvin College, 1964. 164p. (T)
A revised and expanded edition of the U.S. Office of Education guide entitled *Guide to Dutch Studies*, prepared in 1961. Subjects in the topical arrangement include Dutch history, language, art, culture, economy, etc. One chapter covers the Dutch in the United States and another covers specific library resources for Netherlandic studies in the United States. Covers also the Dutch press and Dutch-American organizations.

1130.   Smit, Pamela, and J. W. Smit, comps. and eds. **The Dutch in America 1609-1970: A Chronology and Fact Book.** Dobbs Ferry, N.Y.: Oceana, 1972. 116p. $6.00. (7-12)
The fifth volume in the "Ethnic Chronology Series," this volume includes a chronology of the Dutch experience in American life, documents important to Dutch-American history, statistics on Dutch immigration, and a selected bibliography of books covering the topic. Indexed.

Non-Fiction Titles: History, Culture, Sociology, Biography

1131.   Bok, Edward. **The Americanization of Edward Bok**. New York: Scribner's,
         1920; repr. ed., New York: Scribner's (Norwood Editions), 1972. 461p.
         $19.50. (9-12)
The autobiography of a Dutch boy 50 years after his immigration to America.

1132.   Crouse, Anna, and Russel Crouse. **Peter Stuyvesant of Old New York**. Illus.
         by Jo Spier. New York: Random House, 1954. 184p. $3.87. (4-6)
Pictures home and community life of the Dutch families in colonial New Amsterdam
during the 1600s. Dutch traditions that have influenced American life, unique customs, and the Dutch heritage are part of this story of Peter Stuyvesant and his contributions to the Dutch colonies.

1133.   DeJong, Gerald F. **The Dutch in America, 1609-1974**. Boston, Mass.:
         Twayne Publishers, 1975. 326p. $9.95. (9-12, T)
This volume from the *Immigrant Heritage of America* series traces the history of
Dutch immigration and the experiences of these people in America. Coverage is
from colonial times to the present, with emphasis on the achievements of the Dutch
in America and their influence in government, politics, religion, labor, and the social
and cultural life of the country. Tables indicate the distribution of the Dutch population in the United States from 1790 to 1970 and compare the Dutch population in
the early settlements with that of the other European nationalities, and their distribution by state, etc. A selected bibliography is included. The work is indexed.

1134.   Dolson, Hildegarde. **William Penn**. New York: Random House, 1961.
         186p. $3.87. (3-7)
A biography of the influential colonist who was a leader of the Dutch settlement
that was the nucleus of the colony of Pennsylvania. He also aided many Dutch
Quakers in immigrating to America in the seventeenth and early eighteenth
centuries.

1135.   Emerson, Caroline D. **New Amsterdam, Old Holland in the New World**.
         Scarsdale, N.Y.: Garrard Publishing Co., 1967. 96p. $3.68. (3-6)
A story describing the Dutch colony established on Manhattan Island in 1647.
The customs and traditions of old Holland are portrayed in this picture of the early
Dutch settlers and their community lifestyle.

1136.   Hults, Dorothy. **New Amsterdam Days and Ways: The Dutch Settlers of
         New York**. New York: Harcourt Brace Jovanovich, 1963. 224p. $5.50.
         (4-6)
The life and customs of the Dutch in New Amsterdam (New York) are examined,
including the Dutch colony under Peter Stuyvesant's leadership and influence until
the English took over. Arrangement is chronological. Emphasis is on Dutch customs
in dress, food, religious preference, holiday celebrations, their educational methods,
and relations with the American Indians. A selected bibliography is included; the
work is indexed.

1137.   Janvier, Thomas A. **Dutch Founding of New York.** New York: Harper and Row, 1903; repr. ed., Port Washington, N.Y.: Kennikat, 1967. 218p. $6.00. (9-12)

Traces the Dutch experience in New Netherland and describes the influence the English-speaking colonies had on them. Also covers the reasons why the Dutch ultimately lost control of the government of this area.

1138.   Lane, Wheaton Joshua. **Commodore Vanderbilt: An Epic of the Steam Age.** New York: Knopf, 1942; repr. ed., New York: Johnson Reprint, 1973. 369p. $23.75. (9-12)

A biography of Commodore Vanderbilt, a Dutch American who made tremendous contributions to the shipping and railroad industry in American history.

1139.   Lobel, Arnold. **On the Day Peter Stuyvesant Sailed into Town.** New York: Harper and Row, 1971. unp. $4.95. (3-6)

Describes Peter Stuyvesant's arrival in America in 1647 and his political and other leadership and influence among the Dutch families of New Amsterdam.

1140.   McNeer, May Yonge. **The Hudson, River of History.** Champaign, Ill.: Garrard, 1962. 96p. $3.68. (4-7)

The Dutch settlement of New Amsterdam along the Hudson River is described. The roles of Peter Minuet and Peter Stuyvesant as early Dutch-American leaders of influence in America are examined.

1141.   Raesly, Elles Lawrence. **Portrait of New Netherland.** New York: Columbia University Press, 1945; repr. ed., Port Washington, N.Y.: Ira J. Friedman, Inc., 1965. 370p. $6.00. (9-12, T)

Records of the early Dutch colonists, religious and political leaders, etc., document this history of the early Dutch New Netherland. Emphasis is on religious, social, and political customs and institutions. Bibliography included; indexed.

1142.   Wabeke, Bertus H. **Dutch Immigration to North America 1624-1860.** Plainview, N.Y.: Books for Libraries, 1944. 160p. $12.25. (7-12, T)

A history of the Dutch immigration in the seventeenth, eighteenth, and nineteenth centuries, reasons for leaving the homeland for America, and adjustment to the new country. A bibliography of sources on immigration and early settlements is included.

1143.   Weslager, Clinton A. **Dutch Explorers, Traders and Settlers in the Delaware Valley.** Philadelphia: University of Pennsylvania Press, 1961. 329p. $10.00. (7-12, T)

The 350th anniversary of the discovery of Delaware Bay by Henry Hudson prompted this history of the early Dutch settlements on the Hudson. Appendices contain translations of documents relevant to the Dutch in America. Also covers relations with the American Indians, and early accounts of the social and political life of the settlers. A proper name index is included.

1144.   Widdener, Mabel C. **Peter Stuyvesant: Boy with Wooden Shoes.** Indianapolis, Ind.: Bobbs-Merrill, 1950. 190p. $2.95. (3-7)

A biography of a well-known immigrant from Holland and his life and contributions in the early days of America.

1145.   Zythott, Gerrit J. Ten. **The Dutch in America**. Minneapolis, Minn.:
        Lerner Publications, 1967. 98p. $3.95. (5-11)
A history of the Dutch in America beginning with the earliest explorers, then immigrants and early settlements. The author describes the physical and social atmosphere of New Netherland and indicates political, religious, and cultural contributions of the Dutch Americans. Some individuals who have made outstanding achievements are named, and places important in the history of the Dutch in America are discussed. Indexed.

Literature and Fiction Titles

1146.   Edmonds, Walter D. **The Matchlock Gun**. New York: Dodd, 1941. 50p.
        $5.50. (3-6)
When news of the French and Indian war reaches the little Dutch settlement in the Mohawk Valley, the men all leave their homes and families to assist in the battle. When Indians attack the home of young Edward, he uses the clumsy old matchlock gun to defend his family.

1147.   Ferber, Edna. **So Big**. New York: Doubleday, Doran & Co., c1924, 1951;
        repr. ed., Greenwich, Conn.: Fawcett World, 1973. 360p. $5.95; $0.95pa.
        (9-12)
A novel about a Dutch settlement in Illinois near the city of Chicago. The story centers around Selina De Jong, a teacher who marries a sober, hard-working Dutch farmer, and their son, "So Big."

1148.   Irving, Washington. **Rip Van Winkle and the Legend of Sleepy Hollow**. New
        York: Macmillan, c1925; repr. ed., New York: Scholastic Book Service,
        1971. 136p. $3.95; $0.85pa. (4-6)
Humorous and imaginative tales about the Dutch settlers on the Hudson in the early days of American colonization.

1149.   Moskin, Marietta. **Lysbet and the Fire Kittens**. New York: Coward, 1974.
        46p. $4.29. (1-3)
A beginning reader portraying Dutch colonial life in New Amsterdam. The story is of Lysbet, a little girl who forgets to feed her kittens, and the resulting consequences.

1150.   Spicer, Dorothy G. **Owl's Nest: Folk Tales from Freisland**. Illus. by Alice
        Wadowski-Bak. New York: Coward, 1968. 124p. $4.29. (3-8)
Seven tales from the northern region of the Netherlands provide insight into customs, values and folklore deities of the village people. Included are "The Singing Bell," "The Seven Wishes," "The Ring in the Porridge Bowl," and others.

Audiovisual Materials

1151. **Massachusetts—The Puritan Oligarchy.** 1 filmstrip, 1 record. Midwest Educational Materials, 1974. (7-12)
Examines the social, religious, economic, and political influence of the English and Dutch Puritans on the Massachusetts Bay and Plymouth Colonies.

1152. **The Matchlock Gun.** 1 filmstrip, 1 record. Miller-Brody, 1970. (4-8)
A true story based on the book by the same title by Walter D. Edmonds. A young boy in a small Dutch settlement must use the huge and heavy matchlock gun to defend his family from Indian attack.

1153. **The Mid-Atlantic.** Kit. Filmstrip House. $35.00. (4-8)
This multimedia kit contains 4 35mm filmstrips, 4 records, 4 scripts, and a study guide. It covers the history of the Hudson Valley, New York City, and the East Coast and their early Dutch settlements. Titles include *Our Dutch and Quaker Heritage*; *Later Immigration*; *Agriculture to Industry*; *Mid-Atlantic Megalopolis.* The first title is the only one strictly limited to Dutch-Americans.

EAST-INDIAN AMERICANS

See also Asian Americans.

Non-Fiction Titles: History, Culture, Sociology, Biography

1154. Bagai, Leona B. **The East Indians and the Pakistanis in America.** Minneapolis, Minn.: Lerner Publications, 1967. 63p. $3.95. (5-11)
A history of Americans from India, with emphasis on their contributions in science, education, the arts, and philosophy. Hindus, Sikhs, and Muslims are covered in this description of East Indians and Pakistanis and their experience in the United States. Indexed.

1155. Galbraith, Catherine Atwater, and Rama Mehta. **India: Now and through Time.** New York: Dodd, 1971. 148p. $4.95. (6-9)
A survey of India's historical and cultural past and the heritage of Indian Americans is presented by the wife of the former American Ambassador to India, John Kenneth Galbraith, and a former Foreign Service Officer.

1156. Lambert, Richard D., and Marvin Bressler. **Indian Students on an American Campus.** Minneapolis: University of Minnesota Press, 1956. 122p. $4.00. (11-12, T)
A sample of Indian students at the University of Pennsylvania is studied during the 1952-53 school year. Three aspects of the foreign student role (ambassador, student, tourist) are examined.

1157.   Rice, Edward. **Mother India's Children: Meeting Today's Generation in India**. New York: Pantheon, 1971. 176p. $5.99. (7-12)
Personal interviews with young Indians to describe their values and way of life. Some interviewees are: fisherman, farm wife, guru, elephant boy, office worker, and others. Hindus, Muslims, Sikhs, Brahmins, Parsi, and all castes have been described. The text and illustrations make this a good background source for studying India or Indian Americans.

1158.   Saund, D. S. **Congressman from India**. New York: Dutton, 1960. 192p. $3.50. (6-12)
Mr. Saund writes an autobiographical account of his life as a United States Congressman. He tells of his background in India, of his problems and struggles arriving in America at the age of 20, and of how he won a seat in Congress nearly 40 years later.

1159.   Shetty, Sharat. **A Hindu Boyhood**. Illus. by Mehli Gobhai. Philadelphia, Pa.: Lippincott, 1971. 59p. $3.95. (4-6)
Dr. Shetty recalls his boyhood in India, his family, and village life. A great deal of the book centers on the year he was nine years old in the summer of 1946.

Literature and Fiction Titles

1160.   Dolch, Edward W., and Margaret Dolch. **Stories from India**. Illus. by Gordon Laite. Champaign, Ill.: Garrard, 1961. 168p. $3.48. (2-8)
A collection of tales from the *Folklore of the World* series which displays Indic culture, customs, and values. Stories are suitable for reading at the intermediate grade level and for telling between grades 2 and 8.

1161.   Gobhai, Mehlli, reteller and illus. **Usha, the Mouse Maiden**. New York: Hawthorn, 1969. unp. $5.25. (K-3)
A tale of Indic folklore from the ancient Indian Panchatantra in which a mouse dropped into the hand of a praying sage by a hawk is changed into a baby girl. Because the baby girl (Usha) grows up to be so beautiful, a great search is launched for an appropriate husband for her.

1162.   Jacobs, Joseph. **Indian Fairy Tales**. Illus. by John D. Batten. New York: Dover, 1969. 255p. $4.50. (K-5)
A collection of 29 traditional Indian folk tales including the popular "The Tiger, the Braham, and the Jackal," "The Lion and the Crane," and "Why the Fish Laughed."

1163.   Mukherjee, Bharati. **The Tiger's Daughter**. Boston, Mass.: Houghton Mifflin, 1972. 210p. $5.95. (7-12)
A wealthy businessman in Calcutta decides to send his beautiful daughter, Tata, to Vassar for an education in America. This novel describes her experiences as an Indian-American student, her problems and adjustments, and her marriage to an American. A major emphasis of the book is her new awareness of the conditions in

India—the poverty and disease of the masses—and of the change in her response to her native land.

1164.   Shivkumar, K. **King's Choice.** Illus. by Yoko Mitsuhashi. New York: Parents, 1971. 40p. $4.95. (K-3)
A primary picture book with colorful Eastern scenes tells an Indian folktale where the fox, the leopard, and the vulture, courtiers of the lion king, try to trick the camel into making a meal of himself for the lion's dinner.

Audiovisual Materials

1165.   **Bhagabhai's Honesty.** 1 filmstrip, 1 phonodisc. Imperial Film Co., 1968. (3-6)
Translated from the original version of this well-known Hindu folktale, the filmstrip and accompanying recording relate an East Indian tale on honesty and its rewards. From the *Stories from Other Lands* series.

1166.   **How Death Came to Earth.** 16mm film, 14 min., sd., color. National Film Board of Canada; released in U.S. by Contemporary Films/McGraw-Hill, 1972. (3-8)
An ancient Indian folk tale is presented in cartoon style, telling the story of the beginning of life and death on earth and the continuous cycle involved.

1167.   **The Lion and the Rabbit.** 1 filmstrip, 1 phonodisc. Imperial Film Co., 1968. (3-6)
A Hindu tale about a rabbit who outsmarted a lion in a contest. This old Sanskrit fable is part of the *Stories from Other Lands* series.

1168.   **The Valiant Little Potter.** 1 filmstrip, 1 phonodisc. Xerox Films, 1973. (2-4)
A teacher's guide accompanies this filmstrip, adapted from the book by the same title by Erick Berry retelling an old Indian folktale. A little potter becomes famous for a mistake he makes.

ENGLISH AMERICANS. *See* **British Americans.**

ESKIMOS. *See* **American Indians.**

ESTONIANS. *See* **Baltic Americans.**

FILIPINO AMERICANS

See also Asian Americans and Spanish-Speaking Americans.

Reference Sources

1169.   Norell, Irene P. **The Literature of the Filipino American in the United States: A Selective and Annotated Bibliography.** San Francisco: R&E Research Associates, 1976. 200p. $8.00. (9-12, T)
General works and works on Asian Americans containing works of Filipino Americans, the Filipino American in the United States, Filipino immigration and exclusion, race and racism, social and economic conditions of the Filipino-American, Filipinos in the armed forces, and Filipinos as students are listed, with annotations.

Non-Fiction Titles: History, Culture, Sociology, Biography

1170.   Aquino, Valentin R. **The Filipino Community in Los Angeles.** San Francisco: R&E Research Associates, 1974. 81p. $7.00. (9-12)
A reprint of the author's 1952 thesis, this study examines the immigration, social and economic adjustment, and acculturation and assimilation of the Filipinos in Los Angeles, California.

1171.   Bulosan, Carlos. **America Is in the Heart.** New York: Harcourt Brace & Co., 1946. 326p. $3.45pa. (7-12)
A personal narrative about the author's experience as a Filipino American. Emphasis is on problems of adjustment and racial discrimination. Another title by the author is *Chorus for America: Six Philippine Poets* (Wagon & Star, 1942).

1172.   California. Department of Industrial Relations. **Facts about Filipino Immigration into California.** San Francisco: California Department of Industrial Relations, 1930; repr. ed., San Francisco: R&E Research Associates, 1972. 76p. $6.00. (10-12)
Facts and figures on Filipino immigration and population in California are included. Emphasis is on the effects of immigration on the state's economy and public reaction to the Filipino Americans.

1173.   Cariga, Roman R. **The Filipinos in Hawaii.** San Francisco: R&E Research Associates, 1974. 129p. $9.00. (9-12)
Studies the significance of Filipino immigration and migration to America in this description of the Filipinos in Hawaii. The work was originally the author's thesis in 1936.

1174.   Castillo, Lydia R., and Corazon A. Ponce. **Increasing Compatability between Educational Practices and the Educational Needs of Pupils Who Are Asian with Emphasis on Their Language and Cultural Needs.** San Francisco: San Francisco Unified School District, 1972. 52p. $3.29. ED 085450. (T)
This document is composed of eight different titles by scholars and educators on

the background of Filipinos in Hawaii, social problems of Filipinos on the mainland, Filipino cultural values, guidelines to help the Filipino child in the classroom, cultural and language differences, and acculturation of the Filipino immigrant. Reading lists entitled "The Philippine Culture and Heritage" are included.

1175.   Catapusan, B. T. **The Filipino Social Adjustment in the U.S.** San
        Francisco: R&E Research Associates, 1972. 124p. $7.00pa.
A reprint of the author's 1940 thesis on the social problems of adjustment, acculturation, language, and acceptance prevalent among the Filipino immigrants in the United States. Concentrations of Filipino-American populations are also indicated.

1176.   Lasker, Bruno. **Filipino Immigration to Continental United States and to
        Hawaii.** Chicago: University of Chicago Press, 1939; repr. ed., New York:
        Arno, 1969. 196p. $14.50. (10-12, T)
Describes the increase of Filipinos in the United States from 5,600 to 56,000 from 1920 to 1929, and the anti-Filipino discrimination and proposed legislation. Statistical data on Filipino immigration and case histories of the group's experience document this study.

1177.   Mariano, Honorante. **The Filipino Immigrants in the U.S.** San Francisco:
        R&E Research Associates, 1972. 98p. $7.00pa. (9-12)
A reprint of the author's 1933 thesis at the University of Oregon, this study of Filipino immigration includes a brief history and background of their life in the Philippines, causes and a statistical analysis of immigration to the mainland, and the economic and social life of the Filipinos in the United States. Anti-Filipino discrimination is also covered.

1178.   Provido, Generoso P. **Oriental Immigration from an American Dependence.**
        San Francisco: R&E Research Associates, 1974. 56p. $7.00. (9-12, T)
Filipino-American immigration is studied with respect to its role in American history and social change in America during the first part of the 20th century. The work is a reprint of the author's 1931 thesis.

1179.   Young, Nancy Foon. **Searching for the Promised Land.** Honolulu: Univer-
        sity of Hawaii, 1974. 101p. (10-12)
An examination of the Filipino history and experience in Hawaii. Another title by the author is *Ti Biag/Diay/Kampo Siete–Life in Camp Seven: The Story of a Filipino Family in Waimanalo, Hawaii* (General Education Branch, Honolulu Department of Education, 1974).

FINNISH AMERICANS

Reference Sources

1180.   Kolehmainen, John I. **The Finns in America: A Bibliographical Guide to
        Their History.** Hancock, Mich.: Finnish-American Historical Library,
        1947. 141p. (T)

The holdings of the Finnish-American Historical Archives at Suomi College are cataloged here. The majority of the titles are on the history of the Finnish in America, their immigration, experience, and contributions. Arrangement is topical in twelve different sections, each of which is introduced with a brief historical outline. Covers books, articles, newspaper articles, yearbook features, essays, etc., with English translations given for Finnish titles. Another title by the same author is *The Finns in America: A Student's Guide to Localized History* (New York: Teachers College Press, 1968. 42p. $1.50pa. 9-12, T).

Non-Fiction Titles: History, Culture, Sociology, Biography

1181.   Hoglund, Arthur William. **Finnish Immigrants in America, 1880-1920**.
Madison: The University of Wisconsin Press, 1960. 213p. $11.50. (9-12)
This study of the Finnish in America stresses family and customs of social behavior. Finnish-American organizations are also examined with special attention to their role in the Finnish community. Religious, political, fraternal, cultural, educational, social, temperance, and labor organizations are included. A comprehensive bibliography of materials on the Finns and their cultural heritage is provided.

1182.   Jalkanen, Ralph J., ed. **The Finns in North America: A Social Symposium**.
Hancock: Michigan State University Press, 1969. 224p. $7.50. (10-12)
A collection of essays published in recognition of the 75th anniversary of Suomi College. Some selected titles include: "The Riddle of Finnish Origin," by A. J. Toko; "The Kalevala and Finnish Culture," by L. Honko; "The Background of Finnish Emigration," by R. Kero; "A Survey of the Emigration from Finland to the United States and Canada," by T. Aaltio; "Finnish-Language Newspapers in the United States," by D. T. Halkola; "The Social Problems of the Finns in America," by E. E. Waisanen. Another title by the author is *The Faith of the Finns: Historical Perspectives of the Finnish Lutheran Church in America* (Michigan State University Press, 1972. $12.50).

1183.   Kolehmainen, John I., and George W. Hill. **Haven in the Woods: The Story of the Finns in Wisconsin**. Madison: State Historical Society of Wisconsin, 1951. 192p. $4.00. (7-12)
Finnish farming, mining, lumbering, and other economic practices in a Wisconsin community are described. Their co-ops, their religious preferences, and other Finnish-American institutions are discussed. The appendix data include statistics on Finnish immigration, distribution by county and city in the state of Wisconsin, and other relevant data.

1184.   Wargelin, John. **The Americanization of the Finns**. Hancock, Mich.: Finnish Lutheran Book Concern, 1924; repr. ed., San Francisco: R&E Research Associates, 1972. 185p. $9.00. (9-12)
A discussion of Americanization of an immigrant is presented in this study of the historical background of the Finns and reasons for their coming to the United States. Describes the Finnish settlements and geographic distribution, and studies how the Finns have earned a living, their preference in schools, churches, and

politics. The Finnish-American press is discussed, and contributions of the Finns in various walks of life are indicated. The work is indexed.

Literature and Fiction Titles

1185.   Adair, Margaret. **Far Voice Calling**. New York: Doubleday, 1964. 190p. $3.25. (4-6)
A Finnish fishing village on Oregon's Columbia River is the setting for this story of Toivo Jarvenin and Joe Whiskers, his pet sea lion.

1186.   Bosley, Keith, reteller. **The Devil's Horse**: **Tales from the Kalevala**. New York: Pantheon, 1971. 148p. $3.95. (4-7)
The author retells this version of the Finnish national epic and its wizards and heroes of the North.

1187.   Bowman, James. **Tales from a Finnish Tupa**. Illus. by Laura Bannon. Chicago: A Whitman, 1936. 273p. $4.50. (5-9)
A collection of tales from a translation by Aili Kilehmainen. Includes the internationally known Finnish tale, "Who Was Tricked?," and others.

1188.   Miller, Helen. **Kirsti**. New York: Doubleday, 1964. 262p. $1.98. (6-10)
This is the story of 16-year-old Kirsti Junnola, whose family is Finnish. Immigrants to the United States, they have settled in a community in Idaho. When Kirsti wants to marry a boy who is not of Finnish background, both of their families are upset.

1189.   Stong, Phil. **Honk, the Moose**. New York: Dodd, Mead & Co., 1935. 80p. $3.95. (4-6)
An amusing tale of two Finnish-American boys and a moose. The setting is in a small mining town in Minnesota where Finnish and other Scandinavian immigrants live and are employed.

1190.   Tokoi, Oskari. **Sisu: Even through a Stone Wall**. With an introduction by John Kolehmainen. New York: Speller, 1957. 252p. $6.00. (7-12)
An autobiography of the author, who came to America in the nineteenth century. He worked as a miner until he made a large enough strike to return to Finland. There he became active in politics and eventually became the first premier in Finland. Tokoi was also editor of a Finnish newspaper in America, where he later returned to live.

Audiovisual Materials

1191.   **The Magic Pot**. 1 filmstrip, 1 phonodisc. Cooper Films and Records, 1969. (2-6)
A Finnish folktale about a magic pot that overflows with enough soup to make the people in the village worry about a flood. A teacher's guide is included to suggest uses for this adapted tale in the language arts curriculum, or as an activity to add interest to a social studies unit on the Finnish peoples.

1192. **Who Was Tricked?** 1 filmstrip, 1 phonodisc. Educational Enrichment
Materials, 1969. (2-5)
A Finnish folktale from the *Folktales of Different Lands* series which describes a
farmer's son who is tricked into selling his cow for very little. When the farmer's
son finds a way to turn his misfortune into profit, the trick is on the other man.
James Bowman and Margery Bianco have written a book by the same title, illustrated by John Faulkner (Whitman, 1966. $3.25).

FRENCH AMERICANS

Reference Sources

1193. Blaney, Robert, comp. **French/Français: Mountain Plains Educational
Media Council Film Rental Catalog.** 1973. 12p. $2.00. ED 100173. (T)
A list of films about the French or France that appear in the "1973-75 Mountain
Plains Educational Media Council Film Rental Catalog." These films can be
rented from the Bureau of Educational Media, University of Colorado, Stadium
Building, Boulder, Colorado 80302. The list is comprised of 104 annotated entries.

1194. Pula, James S., comp. and ed. **The French in America, 1488-1974: A
Chronology & Fact Book.** Dobbs Ferry, N.Y.: Oceana, 1975. 154p.
bibliog. index. (Ethnic Chronology Series, Number 20). $6.00.
Consists of three major sections: chronology, documents, and bibliography. The
bibliography is highly selective and is limited to books.

Teaching Methodology and Curriculum Materials

1195. Dube, Normand. **Chez Nous: Ma Famille (At Our House: My Family).**
Washington, D.C.: Division of Bilingual Education, 1972. 31p. $1.85.
ED 100130. (K-3)
An elementary French reader designed for use in a bilingual program. Includes
songs, poems, illustrations, and vocabulary lists.

1196. Lambert, Wallace E. **Culture and Language as Factors in Learning and
Education.** Bellingham: Western Washington State College, 1973. 54p.
$3.15. ED 096820. (T)
A paper presented at the Annual Learning Symposium on "Cultural Factors in
Learning" (Western Washington State College, Nov. 1973) and at the Annual Con-
vention of the Teachers of English to Speakers of Other Languages (Denver,
Colorado, March 1974). It discusses similarities and differences among ethno-
linguistic groups. The authors contend that the linguistic distinctiveness of a particular ethnic group is part of its members' personal identity. Covers results of work with
adolescent French-American students in Maine and French-Canadian students.

Non-Fiction Titles: History, Culture, Sociology, Biography

1197.   Abodaher, David J. **French Explorers of North America**. New York:
         Messner, 1970. 96p. $3.95. (3-6)
Brief biographical sketches of the French explorers including Champlain, Duluth,
Joliet, Marquette, LaSalle, and Cartier. Describes how their explorations and early
settlements influenced the development of America, and their individual contributions to American history. The work includes maps and is indexed.

1198.   Bishop, Claire Huchet. **Lafayette, French-American Hero**. Champaign, Ill.:
         Garrard, 1960. 80p. $3.40. (2-5)
The biography of Marquis de Lafayette and his contributions to America in the
eighteenth century.

1199.   Burt, Olive. **John Charles Fremont: Trail Marker of the Old West**. New
         York: Messner, 1955. 192p. $3.34. (6-12)
The "Pathfinder" was a French immigrant who later played a prominent role in the
fight against slavery. The French influence and contribution toward opening the
Western United States is described.

1200.   Eccles, William John. **France in America**. New York: Harper and Row,
         1972. 297p. $8.95; $4.95pa. (7-12)
Documents the rise and fall of the French empire in the United States and Canada
and the Franco-British war. Also covers the French influence in America from the
earliest part of the sixteenth century to the latter part of the eighteenth. Particular
attention is given to the French colonists and early settlements.

1201.   Fosdick, Lucian J. **The French Blood in America**. New York: F. H.
         Revell; repr. ed., Baltimore, Md.: Genealogical Publishing, 1973. 448p.
         $14.00. (9-12, T)
Studies the French Huguenots, their reasons for leaving France, and their unsuccess-
ful attempts to establish colonies in America. Their early settlements at Plymouth,
New Amsterdam, and Virginia are also described.

1202.   Hirsch, Arthur H. **The Huguenots of Colonial South Carolina**. Durham,
         N.C.; repr. ed., Hamden, Conn.: Shoe String Press, 1973. 338p. $12.50.
         (7-12)
A comprehensive study of the French Protestant Huguenots who settled in South
Carolina during the Colonial period. Emphasis is on churches, religious, political,
and economic activities, and the influence of the French Huguenot customs and
culture in American life. Also discusses the assimilation of the Huguenot families
into American society at large. A selected bibliography included; indexed.

1203.   Kershaw, Doug. **Louisiana Man: The Doug Kershaw Songbook**. Edited by
         Robin Nelson. New York: Macmillan, 1971. 144p. $6.95; $2.95pa. (K-12)
An autobiographical sketch as well as a collection of Cajun songs of the French. The
sounds of the Louisiana bayous and the French flavor and influence are heard and
felt in this folk music.

1204.   Kunz, Virginia Brainard. **The French in America**. Minneapolis, Minn.:
        Lerner Publications, 1966. 94p. $3.95. (7-10)
An illustrated volume tracing the history of the French in America from the days
of the early French explorers, the early French and Indian relationships, and the
French settlers who pioneered various territories of the United States. Includes
reasons for French immigration to the new country with attention to religious
persecutions and the French Revolution. The influence of the French heritage
in America is also discussed, and some prominent French-Americans and their outstanding contributions or achievements are described. Popular presentation.

1205.   Parkman, Francis. **LaSalle and the Discovery of the Great West**. Boston,
        Mass.: Little, Brown, 1897; repr. ed., Williamstown, Mass.: Corner House,
        1968. 483p. $12.50. (6-12)
A biographical sketch of LaSalle is included in this historical study of the pioneers
in America. It also examines the influence of the French Jesuits who lived and
worked among the Indians. Emphasis is on the French explorations and settlements around the Great Lakes and the Western territories. Other titles on the same
subject by the author are *France and England in North America*, a nine-volume set
published by Ungar ($95.00) and *The Jesuits in North America* (repr. by Corner
House, 1970. $12.50).

1206.   Post, Lauren C. **Cajun Sketches from the Prairies of Southwest Louisiana**.
        Baton Rouge: Louisiana State University, 1974, c1962. 215p. $6.95. (7-12)
Brief sketches describe the French influence and heritage of the Cajun people of
Southern Louisiana. The persistence of the French culture and French language are
indicated.

1207.   Syme, Ronald. **Cartier: Finder of the St. Lawrence**. Illus. by William
        Stobbs. New York: Morrow, 1958. 95p. $4.14. (4-6)
The biography of a French explorer who charted and mapped much of the virgin
land in America. Emphasis is on his founding of the St. Lawrence and his relations
with the native American Indians. Includes maps. The author has written other
biographical sketches on French explorers: *Champlain of the St. Lawrence*
(Morrow, 1952. $4.95) for the junior and senior high school levels; *LaSalle of the
Mississippi* (Morrow, 1953), also for the secondary student; and *Marquette and
Joliet: Voyages on the Mississippi* (Morrow, 1974. $4.50), which is another title
for the intermediate grades (4-6). Two titles that span the intermediate and junior
high levels are: *Fur Trader of the North: The Story of Pierre de la Verendrye*
(Morrow, 1973. $4.32) and *Frontenac of New France* (Morrow, 1969. $4.95).

1208.   Williams, Barry. **Struggle for North America**. New York: McGraw-Hill,
        1967. 96p. $4.12. (4-8)
Although much of the emphasis in this book is on the French and Indian wars and
on the French in Canada, it does give some attention to the early French colonists
and their influence. It includes brief biographical sketches of French Americans
and their contributions and achievements.

Literature and Fiction Titles

1209.   Canfield, Kenneth. **Selections from French Poetry**. Illus. by Tomi Ungerer. Irvington-on-Hudson, N.Y.: Harvey, 1965. 191p. $4.89. (9-12)
A collection of French poems especially selected for the high school and college young adult. Arrangement is in a bilingual format, with the French version appearing on the facing page. The volume can be useful in the French language class as well as in the literature or social studies curriculum. Brief biographical notes on the poets and their works are included. Indexed.

1210.   Cather, Willa. **Death Comes for the Archbishop**. New York: Knopf, 1927. 303p. $6.50. (9-12)
A novel about a French priest, set in the mid-nineteenth century in Santa Fe, New Mexico. The story relates the life and death of this French-American priest who became archbishop.

1211.   Coatsworth, Elizabeth. **The Fair American**. New York: Macmillan, 1940. 132p. $3.95. (3-7)
Sally and Andrew, two children on board *The Fair American*, help in the rescue of a little refugee of the French Revolution.

1212.   Erdman, Loula. **Room to Grow**. New York: Dodd, 1962. 242p. $3.50. (7-12)
The Danton family emigrated from France to the Panhandle of Texas. The French customs, the French heritage, and cultural influence on the Southwestern United States are described.

1213.   Field, Rachel. **Calico Bush**. Illustrated by Allen Lewis. New York: Macmillan, 1966. 201p. $4.95; $0.95pa. (7-9)
Maggie Ledoux emigrated from France as a bond servant to a pioneer family in the state of Maine at the time of the French and Indian War. This story, which shows her adjustments in her new home, is a portrayal of a way of life and way of immigration taken by many newcomers to America.

1214.   Hays, Wilma Pitchford. **The Open Gate: New Year's 1815**. Illus. by Carolyn Cather Tierney. New York: Coward, 1970. 64p. $3.49. (2-4)
The French colony in New Orleans is described in this story of two young friends: one an American boy, and the other, a Creole girl. The story is set in Louisiana during the War of 1812.

1215.   Hodge, Jane Aiken. **Savannah Purchase**. New York: Doubleday, 1971. 205p. $5.95; $1.25pa. (9-12)
This historical novel has two French Americans as its main characters. They are refugees to their new home after being exiled from France during the period of Napoleon.

1216.   Lenski, Lois. **Bayou Suzette**. Philadelphia, Pa.: Lippincott, 1943. 207p. $4.82. (3-6)

This story of ten-year-old Suzette Durand portrays family life in the bayou country of Louisiana. French customs, dialect, and the culture of the Bayou French are described. The illustrations highlight events of local color (e.g., the Mardi Gras, etc.).

1217.   Massignon, Genevieve. **Folktales of France**. Trans. by Jacqueline Hyland. Chicago: University of Chicago Press, 1968. 315p. $9.95. (6-12)
This collection of approximately 70 French folktales is arranged by geographical regions. Notes are included to explain local peculiarities in version or rendition. Includes an "Index of Motifs," "Index of Tale Types," and a general index.

1218.   Peck, Robert Newton. **Fawn**. Boston, Mass.: Little, Brown, 1975. 143p. $5.95. (6-12)
Fawn is the son of a French Jesuit in America during the 1750s. His grandfather was a Mohawk Indian, and in the frontier wars of the French, English, and Indians, Fawn is torn between conflicting identities and cultural heritages.

1219.   Pundt, Helen. **Spring Comes First to the Willows**. New York: Crowell, 1963. 231p. $4.50. (7-12)
Anna's parents are French immigrants, and she finds their values in conflict with those of her new classmates when they move to an affluent neighborhood and she changes high schools. She comes to realize that, in spite of their different cultures, her father's ideals and values are good and she is proud of her parents and their background.

Audiovisual Materials

1220.   **The French and Indian Wars: Road to the American Revolution?** 2 film-strips, 1 disc (or cassette). Multi-Media Productions. $16.95/set. (9-12)
Discusses the role of the French in the early development of the United States and the importance of this role in fostering attitudes favoring independence.

1221.   **The French Contribution to the Birth of the United States**. 3 filmstrips, 6 cassettes; also available in French version: 3 filmstrips, 6 cassettes, teacher's guide. ALEP. Bilingual version: $94.75; French or English only, $59.95 each. (3-12)
A set of sound filmstrips examining French contributions to the political and philosophical ideas that led to America's thrust for independence. The English version is geared for use in grades 3-12; the French version is suitable only for the senior high level (grades 9-12).

1222.   **French Explorations in the New World**. 16mm film, 11 min., color and b&w. Coronet, 1956. (6-12)
Soldiers, explorers, and missionaries of French nationality influenced the early development of America. How they left their influence on its cultural development is studied here. Cartier, Marquette, Joliet, and others are described, and their individual achievements and contributions are indicated.

1223.   **French Influences in North America**. 16mm film, 11 min., color. Coronet
         Films, 1951. (6-12)
The French settlers' permanent contributions to the United States are described.
Emphasis is on their cultural contributions to American language, clothing,
architecture, religion, and arts.

GERMAN AMERICANS

Reference Sources

1224.   Furer, Howard B., ed. **The Germans in America, 1607-1970: A Chronology
         and Fact Book**. Dobbs Ferry, N.Y.: Oceana, 1973. 153p. $6.00. (7-12)
A book for ready reference in three sections: a chronology of Germans in America
covering their immigration history from Jamestown in 1607 to 1970; a selection of
documents relevant to the German American history; and a bibliography of
materials on the German-American culture and experience. Materials included in
this listing are useful at both the elementary and secondary levels. Indexed.

1225.   Meynen, Emil. **Bibliography on German Settlements in Colonial North
         America**. Detroit: Gale, 1966. (Repr. of 1937 ed.). 636p. $20.00. (T)
Approximately 8,000 entries are included in this comprehensive bibliography on
the German settlements in North America. Emphasis is on the Colonial period,
but all aspects of German-American life are covered. Books, newspapers, articles,
essays, addresses, speeches, pamphlets are included in this listing. Arrangement is
both topical and geographical. Covers the period from the early seventeenth
century to 1935.

1226.   Tolzmann, Don Heinrich. **German-Americana: A Bibliography**. Metuchen,
         N.J.: Scarecrow Press, 1975. 384p. $15.00. (10-12, T)
A bibliography of works on German-American history, literature, and culture,
most of which were published between 1941 and 1973. Only a few items are
annotated; some entries indicate library location. All major bibliographies, general
histories, German-American organizations, historical and literary societies, periodicals and newspapers, book stores, printers, and schools are included.

Non-Fiction Titles: History, Culture, Sociology, Biography

1227.   Beidelman, William. **The Story of the Pennsylvania Germans**. Easton, Pa.:
         Express Book Co., 1898; repr. ed., Detroit: Gale, 1969. 254p. $10.00.
         (9-12, T)
A history of the German immigrants who settled in Pennsylvania. Special emphasis
is given to their reasons for leaving their homeland, their origins and background,
and their dialects.

1228.   Billigmeier, Robert Henry. **Americans from Germany: A Study in Cultural Diversity**. Belmont, Calif.: Wadsworth, 1974. 129p. $4.95pa. (9-12)
A history of the experience of the German immigrants in America, with emphasis on the degree and rate of assimilation of this group in comparison to other nationality groups. The groups are also compared with respect to social, economic, and political behavior and other aspects of their experience in America.

1229.   Brand, Millen. **Fields of Peace: A Pennsylvania German Album**. New York: Dutton, 1973. 158p. $3.95. (6-12)
An authentic portrayal of the non-commercialized Pennsylvania "Dutch" country. Many photographs, by George A. Tice, depict the quaint customs and the culture of the descendants of German immigrants.

1230.   Cunz, Dieter. **They Came from Germany: The Story of Famous German Americans**. New York: Dodd, Mead, 1966. 178p. $3.50. (6-8)
Presents a survey of German immigration to America, some sketches of prominent German-Americans (e.g., John Peter Zenger, John Jacob Astor, Carl Schurz, Wernher von Braun, etc.), and a bibliography on Germans in America. Another title by this author is *Maryland Germans: A History*. (Kennikat, 1971; reprint of 1948 ed. $17.50).

1231.   Davis-DuBois, Rachel, and Emma Schweppe, eds. **Germans in American Life**. New York: Nelson & Sons, 1936; repr. ed., New York: Books for Libraries, Inc., 1972. 180p. $11.50. (9-12)
The German participation in American political, social, and economic life is described. German-American culture and unique customs are also included. Outdated, but useful for its comprehensive historical coverage.

1232.   Flach, Vera. **A Yankee in German America: Texas Hill Country**. San Antonio, Tex.: Naylor, 1973. 176p. $6.95. (6-12)
A description of life in the early German community of the Texas hill country. Married for 50 years to a German American, the author traces the history of the German community, customs, and culture to the present day, indicating the community's influence on the region and German contributions to society.

1233.   Gay, Kathlyn. **The Germans Helped Build America**. New York: Messner, 1971. 96p. $4.50. (4-8)
Causes of immigration, early history and life in America, and contributions of German Americans are covered. Illustrated with drawings and some historical photographs.

1234.   Hofer, Jesse W. **An Amish Boy Remembers, from Behind Those Fences**. San Antonio, Tex.: Naylor, 1973. 225p. $8.95. (7-12)
The author reviews his boyhood isolated by the Amish religion, German language, and clothing of his ancestors, who had originated a closed community. Emphasis is on the culture, customs, and problems he experienced because of his German heritage.

1235.   Holland, Ruth. **German Immigrants in America: Their Culture and Contri-**
         butions in the New World. New York: Grosset and Dunlap, 1969. 61p.
         $2.69. (6-12)
An overview of the history of German immigration to and settlement in America
from Colonial times to World War II Nazi hysteria. Describes the contributions of
German Americans in many areas and walks of life.

1236.   Kunz, Virginia B. **Germans in America.** Minneapolis, Minn.: Lerner,
         1966. 86p. $3.95. (5-11)
This history of the Germans in America includes a brief account of their life in
Germany and describes their reasons for immigration to the United States, the
experiences and adjustments they had to make, the contributions they made to the
development of America, and unique aspects of the German cultural heritage.
Some of the most outstanding German Americans and their achievements are
indicated (e.g., Dwight D. Eisenhower, John D. Rockefeller, Wernher von Braun,
and others).

1237.   Luebke, Frederick C. **Bonds of Loyalty: German Americans during**
         World War I. DeKalb, Ill.: Northern Illinois University Press, 1974.
         366p. $10.00; $3.00pa. (11-12, T)
Studies the anti-German discrimination and hostilities against German Americans
during World War I. The author terms these hostilities as the culmination of post-war
ethno-cultural struggles. Illustrated with cartoons of the times. Bibliography
included; indexed. Another title by this author is *Immigrants and Politics: The*
Germans of Nebraska, 1880-1900 (University of Nebraska Press, 1969. $9.95).

1238.   Naylor, Phyllis R. **An Amish Family.** Illus. by George Armstrong.
         Chicago: J. Philip O'Hara, 1974. 160p. $5.95. (6-12)
The Stolzfus family of the Amish community in Pennsylvania is described. Rules
governing Amish life are referred to as the Ordnung, and some of these rules,
such as shunning (disciplining members of the community), are described. The
book provides many colorful illustrations and much informative data about these
German Americans.

1239.   O'Connor, Richard. **The German-Americans: An Informal History.**
         Boston, Mass.: Little, Brown, 1968. 484p. $10.00. (9-12)
A study of the German immigrants to the United States, the German colonies, and
later German-American settlements and communities. Distribution of Germans,
their degree of assimilation into American society, and the influence of the German
cultural heritage are examined. Bibliography included; indexed.

1240.   Rippley, La Vern. **Of German Ways.** Illus. by Henning B. Jensen.
         Minneapolis, Minn.: Dillon Press, 1970. 301p. $6.95. (9-12)
German history in America is included in this study of German culture, which
examines reasons for immigration to the new land and various aspects of the German
heritage. Emphasis is on the arts, language, holidays, customs, folklore, and legend.

1241.   Spaulding, E. Wilder. **The Quiet Invaders.** New York: Frederick Ungar,
         1968. 324p. $8.00. (9-12, T)

The Austrian element in the United States is discussed here as separate from the German-American group, with which they are usually identified. The Austrians are labelled "the quiet invaders" here because of their more rapid assimilation into American society. Their important political, economic, scientific, artistic, and literary contributions are covered, as well as their contribution to the entertainment world. Also included is an overview of their Habsburg background and reasons for the Austrian immigration to America. An index of persons is given.

1242.   Stevens, S. K. **The Pennsylvania Colony**. New York: Crowell-Collier, 1970. 133p. $5.95. (5-8)
Describes the early settlers of Pennsylvania, who were mainly German Americans. Particular attention is given to the German Mennonites (Pennsylvania Dutch), other uniquely German aspects of the Pennsylvania Colony and the German contributions to American state and federal government, as well as their assistance in expanding the American frontier.

1243.   Stoudt, John J. **Sunbonnets and Shoofly Pies: A Pennsylvania Dutch Cultural History**. South Brunswick, N.J.: A. S. Barnes, 1973. 272p. $25.00. (7-12)
Describes customs, traditions, culture, and contributions of the settlers of German background in the Pennsylvania Dutch communities of Pennsylvania. Covers economic patterns and conditions, art, literature, humor, medicine, and religious traditions. Illustrated.

1244.   Tutt, Clara. **Carl Schurz, Patriot**. Madison: State Historical Society of Wisconsin, 1966, c1960. 107p. $3.00. (4-12)
A biography of Carl Schurz, a German immigrant who became a leading abolitionist, defender of human rights, and later the first immigrant to be elected to the United States Senate.

1245.   Wittke, Carl F. **German Americans and the World War**. Columbus: Ohio State Archaeological and Historical Society, 1936; repr. ed., New York: J. S. Ozer, 1974. 223p. $10.95.
A discussion of the effect of World War I on the Germans in the United States, the ambivalent feelings toward them, and in particular the plight of the German press in the United States during that period. Other titles by the author are *German Language Press in America* (Haskell, 1972; repr. of 1957 ed. by the University of Kentucky Press; $18.95) and *Germans in America: A Student's Guide to Localized History* (New York: Teachers College, 1967. 26p. $1.50pa.).

Literature and Fiction Titles

1246.   Baker, Betty. **The Dunderhead War**. New York: Harper, 1967. 206p. $4.79. (6-9)
A lively and humorous story of Uncle Fritz, a German immigrant, who fights as a volunteer in the war against Mexico. His nephew, 17-year-old Quincy, and he have some exciting experiences together.

1247.   Benary-Isbert, Margot. **The Long Way Home**. Trans. from the German
        by Richard and Clara Winston. New York: Harcourt Brace Jovanovich,
        1959. 280p. $5.95. (7-9)
Thirteen-year-old Christoph Wegener escapes from East Germany and comes to the
United States. He lives with an ex-G.I., spends time in New York, Chicago, and a
ranch in California. His adjustments to American culture and the influence of his
German background are an interesting portrayal of the situation of the later
refugees and immigrants.

1248.   Good, Merle. **Happy as the Grass Was Green**. Scottdale, Pa.: Herald Press,
        1971. 156p. $3.95; $0.95pa. (9-12)
A fictionalized examination of the customs, values, religion, and culture of the
Pennsylvania Dutch Mennonites. The story centers around a radical student from a
New York university who visits Lancaster County to attend the funeral of a friend
killed during a student demonstration. Other titles by this author are *Hazel's
People* (Pillar Books, 1975. $1.25pa.); *People* (Herald Press, 1974; $2.95pa.); and
These People Mine (Herald Press, 1973. $1.25pa.).

1249.   Hoff, Carol. **Johnny Texas**. Illus. by Bob Meyers. Chicago: Follett,
        c1950. 149p. $4.98. New York: Dell, 1967. $0.75pa. (4-7)
As German immigrants in the big land of Texas, Johnny and his father adapt quickly
to their new life, but the old habits and customs are missed by Mama.

1250.   Jordan, Mildred. **Proud to be Amish**. Illus. by W. T. Mars. New York:
        Crown, 1968. 144p. $3.95. (4-6)
Although Katie longs for some of the things taboo to her Pennsylvania Dutch community members, she is proud of her Amish heritage. This story depicts the unique
social and religious customs of the German Mennonites in America.

1251.   Kraus, George, illus. **The Lord Is My Shepherd**. New York: Windmill
        Books, 1971. unp. $2.95. (K-2)
Scenes from Amish life are depicted by folk illustrations in a hand-lettered text of
the Twenty-Third Psalm for small children.

1252.   Mannix, Daniel. **The Healer**. New York: Dutton, 1971. 224p. $6.95. (9-12)
When Billy moves in with his old uncle in rural Pennsylvania he is not impressed by
his uncle's reputation as a wizard who can heal with his plants and herbs. The novel
reveals some of the more primitive Pennsylvania German beliefs in hexes, hex
signs, and the supernatural.

1253.   Milhous, Katherine. **Appolonia's Valentine**. New York: Scribner's, 1954.
        28p. $4.46. (3-5)
A story of children in an old-fashioned one-room schoolhouse in the German
Mennonite community making valentines with traditional Pennsylvania Dutch
designs.

1254.   Richter, Conrad. **The Free Man**. New York: Knopf, 1943. 147p. $5.95.
        (7-12)

An exciting story of a German immigrant youth who was forced by swindlers to become an indentured servant. The setting is in Philadelphia just prior to the Revolution. How he escapes to the Pennsylvania Dutch country and wins his freedom makes a tale of great interest and suspense.

1255.   Rowland, Florence Wightman. **Amish Wedding**. Illus. by Dale Pagson. New York: Putnam's, 1971. 60p. $3.69. (K-3)
A portrayal of the Amish people, their religious customs and ceremonies is presented through an account of a traditional Amish wedding. Roles of the bride, groom, and their close relatives are described.

1256.   Selz, Irma. **Katy, Be Good**. New York: Lothrop, 1962. unp. $3.25.
Many surprises are in store for Katy, a little Amish girl who is used to the plain and quaint ways of her community. Her visit to a friend in New York finds her discovering television, air conditioning, escalators in the big department stores, and many other fascinating things for the first time. Another title by the author about the Amish community is *Wonderful Nice!* (Lothrop, 1960).

1257.   Singmaster, Elsie. **I Heard of a River: A Story of the Pennsylvania Germans**. New York: Holt, 1948. 209p. OP. (6-12)
In this story Hannes, a German-Lutheran boy, escapes religious persecution and economic conditions in Europe to join a band of Swiss Mennonites. The group immigrates to William Penn's colony in the United States and is promised freedom and new opportunity in a new settlement on the Susquehanna River.

1258.   Tobenkin, Elias. **The House of Conrad**. New York: Frederick A. Stokes Co., 1918; repr. ed., New York: Gregg, 1971. 375p. $12.50. (10-12)
Three generations of a German immigrant family are the central characters in this novel of one man's dreams for his family. Gottfried Conradi immigrates to America in 1868 and has great aspirations for "The House of Conrad." The story portrays the problems and adjustments made by the German immigrants during the process of Americanization that was typical in the late nineteenth century.

1259.   Van Woerkem, Dorothy. **The Queen Who Couldn't Bake Gingerbread**. Illus. by Paul Galdone. New York: Knopf, 1975. unp. $5.50. (K-3)
An adaptation of a German folktale for the primary grades. Useful for storytelling in kindergarten and for easy-reading in the early grades.

1260.   Weik, Mary Hays. **A House on Liberty Street**. Illus. by Ann Grifalconi. New York: Atheneum, 1973. 71p. $4.50. (5-10)
This is the story of Louis Kranz, who immigrates to America from Germany in 1848. It is a memoir of the author's grandfather, whose glorious dreams of America did not materialize but who nevertheless kept on struggling to attain what he valued. The story is a picture of the social, political, and economic conditions faced by newcomers to the country, as well as an account of their role in shaping its future.

1261.   Williamson, Joanne S. **And Forever Free**. New York: Knopf, 1966. 197p. $5.39. (7-10)
The problems, adjustments, and role of the German immigrant in the nineteenth

century are portrayed in this story of Martin, a 15-year-old orphan boy who comes to live with his uncle in New York. The story also gives an excellent historical background of the area in the 1860s when, just prior to the Civil War, Martin helps a runaway slave.

Audiovisual Materials

1262.   **The American Immigrants: A German Settler's View.** 1 filmstrip, 1 record (or cassette), 1 teacher's guide. Multi-Media Productions. $11.95. (4-8)
A German immigrant woman recounts the experiences of her family when they left Bavaria in 1845. She discusses the effects of the Civil War and other historic events on the German-American community.

1263.   **Berks the Beautiful.** 16mm film, color. Prod. by Samuel L. Schulman Productions. Pennsylvania Dutch Travel Association, 1968. (4-12)
The customs, historic sites, folk festivals, food, clothing, houses, etc., of the Pennsylvania Dutch farm people in Berks County, Pennsylvania, are described.

1264.   **The Cat Spring Germans.** 1 filmstrip, 1 phonotape. Institute of Texan Cultures, 1971. (6-12)
Traces the history of the development of Cat Spring, Texas, from the days of its earliest German immigrant settlers. Their successful agricultural methods and experimentation are noted, as well as their contributions to the history and settlement of this community with respect to cultural and economic achievements. This presentation is also available as a set of 72 color slides with an accompanying teacher's supplement.

1265.   **City in the Wilderness.** 16mm film, 28 min., sd., color. Doubleday Multimedia. (4-12)
Describes reasons for German Moravians' migration to Pennsylvania from their homeland, their relationships with the American Indians, their religious preferences and practices, and their community life. Pressures of Americanization and acculturation are also indicated.

1266.   **Coming of the Pennsylvania Germans.** Slide set. Visual Aids Section, State Library, Harrisburg, Pennsylvania. Free loan. (5-9)
A slide set depicting the arrival of the early German settlers in Germantown and other counties in Pennsylvania. The set may be borrowed by writing to the State Library, Harrisburg, Pennsylvania 17126.

1267.   **German Americans.** Multimedia kit. Field Educational Publications, 1972. (4-8)
This kit consists of a filmstrip, record, a set of study prints, and a teacher's manual. It depicts the unique heritage of the Germans in the United States and is based on the book, *The American Adventure.*

1268.   **Germans.** 1 filmstrip, 1 record, 1 teacher's guide and transcript. Warren
        Schloat Productions, 1966. (4-9)
German Americans and their outstanding achievements and contributions to the
growth and development of America are indicated in this history of German immigration and settlement in the United States. Covers the period from 1638 to the mid-
1900s. Prominent individuals described are Baron Von Steuben, Carl Schurz, Horace
Mann, Dwight D. Eisenhower, and several others. This title is from the *Minorities
Have Made America Great* series.

1269.   **The Old Order Amish.** 16mm film, 32 min., color. Prod. by Vedo Films.
        Available from Pennsylvania State AV Services, University Park,
        Pennsylvania. $11.00 (rental). (7-12)
The Old Order Amish are studied, with emphasis on the influence of their religious
convictions and their German heritage in their daily lifestyle.

1270.   **Pennsylvania: Arts and Crafts of the Pennsylvania Germans.** Slide set.
        Visual Aids Section, State Library, Harrisburg, Pennsylvania. Free loan.
        (5-12)
A German settlement is depicted. Homes and furnishings are emphasized. Includes
the eighteenth century homes of the Millbach and Stiegel families and pictures of
the early iron works villages. May be borrowed from the State Library, Harrisburg,
Pennsylvania 17126.

1271.   **Pennsylvania Dutch Folk Songs.** 1 record (33 1/3 rpm). Folkway Records.
        (K-12)
George Britton sings and plays on the guitar some of the old folk songs of the
Pennsylvania German community.

1272.   **The Sights and Sounds of the Kutztown Folk Festival.** 16mm film, 24
        min., color. Prod. by Roy Productions. Pennsylvania Folklife Society,
        1969. (4-12)
The crafts, foods, clothing, and customs for which the Kutztown, Pennsylvania,
Folk Festival is famous are displayed in this filmstrip.

1273.   **A Way of Life.** 16mm film, color. L. Bauer, Jr., 1970. (4-12)
The quaint and unique customs and cultural activities of the daily lifestyle of the
Amish and Mennonite families of the Pennsylvania Dutch community are shown in
this film. Their religious values and special ceremonial traditions are a major aspect
of their culture.

1274.   **World Myths and Folktales: Siegfried and the Jealous Queen.** 1 filmstrip,
        1 phonotape (or cassette). Globe Filmstrips; released by Globe Book Co.
        and Coronet Instructional Media, 1976. (2-6)
The German folktale about Siegfried and the jealous queen depicts values and
customs inherent in the German culture.

GREEK AMERICANS

Reference Sources

1275.   Cutsumbis, Michael N. **A Bibliographic Guide to Materials on Greeks in the United States, 1890-1968.** Staten Island, N.Y.: Center for Migration Studies, 1970. 100p. $4.50pa. (T)
This bibliography is arranged in 12 sections as follows: books; articles; works of fiction; publications dealing with the Greek Orthodox Church in America; unpublished works; almanacs, guides, and directories; Greek-American serials currently published; Greek-American serials suspended; fraternal publications; parish and archdiocesan materials; manuscript collections; and research in progress.

Teaching Methodology and Curriculum Materials

1276.   Massialas, Byron G. **A Project in Multicultural Learning: Greek-American Contributions to American Society.** Tallahassee: The Florida State University, 1975. 221p. (price not indicated). (T)
The first comprehensive curriculum unit on Greek Americans and their contribution to American culture and society.

Non-Fiction Titles: History, Culture, Sociology, Biography

1277.   Burgess, Thomas. **Greeks in America: An Account of Their Coming, Progress, Customs, Living and Aspirations.** Boston, Mass.: Sherman, French & Company, 1913; repr. ed., New York: Arno Press, 1970. 256p. $12.00. (9-12)
A well-documented source of information on Greek immigration and the Greek experience in the United States. Topics covered in this historical survey are: the exodus from Greece, early hardships, immigration from 1891 to 1913, industrial development, institutional development, their religion, life in the cities, mill towns and great West, and famous American Greeks. Although outdated, this is valuable historical material. A bibliography is included.

1278.   Christowe, Stoyan. **My American Pilgrimage.** Boston, Mass.: Little, Brown, 1947. 264p. $2.50. (9-12)
A warm and humorous sketch of the author's first five years in America as a Greek immigrant. Achievements, problems, adjustments are all a part of the picture.

1279.   Constantelos, Demetrios J. **The Greek Orthodox Church: Faith, History, and Practice.** New York: The Seabury Press, 1967. 127p. $1.95pa. (9-12)
The basic philosophy and teachings of the Greek Orthodox Church are explained, with coverage of its history and role and influence in America. The traditional practices and attitudes of the church help the reader understand the attitudes and behavior of the Greek Americans. Bibliography included.

1280.   Fairchild, Henry Pratt. **Greek Immigration to the United States.** New
         Haven, Conn.: Yale University Press, 1911. OP. (T)
Greek immigration to the United States, reasons for leaving the homeland, the conditions upon arriving in the new country, and the adjustments made by the
immigrants are discussed in this volume. Also considers the effects of the emigration on the native country. A bibliography is included.

1281.   Georgas, Demitra. **Greek Settlement of the San Francisco Bay Area.** San
         Francisco: R&E Research Associates, 1974. 60p. $7.00. (10-12)
A reprint of the author's 1951 thesis studying the role and importance of the
Greek-Americans in settling and developing the West. Particular attention is paid
to the Greek-American community in the San Francisco Bay area.

1282.   Jones, Jayne. **Greeks in America.** Minneapolis, Minn.: Lerner Publications
         Co., 1969. 78p. $3.95. (5-10)
The geography, historical background, and other aspects of the Greek heritage are
presented. Greek immigration to America and the life of the Greeks in America
are also described. Problems, adjustments, accomplishments of note, and outstanding
contributions of the Greek-American community are discussed. Individuals such as
Harry Mark Petrakis, Alex Karas, etc., are described.

1283.   Leber, George J. **The History of the Order of Ahepa.** Washington, D.C.:
         The Order of Ahepa, 1972. 588p. $10.00. (9-12)
This publication celebrates the 50th anniversary of the American Hellenic Educational Progressive Association. It gives a history of Greek immigration to America
and traces the distribution of Greeks throughout the United States. Describes
Greek-American contributions to American society, and activities designed to main-
tain the Greek national heritage in the United States. A chronology of activities
and conventions of the Association are also recorded, with photographs of officers
and members. Name index included.

1284.   Panagopoulos, E. P. **New Smyrna: An Eighteenth Century Greek Odyssey.**
         Gainesville: University of Florida Press, 1966. 207p. $7.50. (9-12)
The British attempt to develop an early Greek colony in the United States is
described. Greek population in Florida is discussed, with particular attention to the
community at New Smyrna.

1285.   Saloutos, Theodore. **The Greeks in the United States.** Cambridge, Mass.:
         Harvard University Press, 1964. 445p. $15.00. (8-12, T)
A history of Greeks in America beginning with the reasons for their emigration from
Greece. Early years and the immigrant experience in the United States are described
with attention to economic conditions, social status, and political preferences. The
role of the two world wars is discussed; conditions affecting assimilation and
acculturation are also examined. Illustrations, bibliography, and index included.
Other titles by the author are *Greeks in America* (Teachers College Press, 1967.
$3.95; $1.50pa.) and *They Remember America: The Story of Repatriated Greek-
Americans* (University of California Press, 1956).

1286.   Vlachos, Evangelos C. **Assimilation of Greeks in the United States.** New
         York: International Publications Service, 1969. 287p. $9.50. (9-12, T)
This is a publication of the author's Ph.D. dissertation from Indiana University in
1964. It studies three generations of Greek Americans with respect to their assimilation and the emerging Greek-American culture and its influence on the Greek community. Topics considered and analyzed are: vocations, organizations, politics,
education, language, religion, and family life.

1287.   Xenides, J. P. **The Greeks in America.** New York: George H. Doran
         Company, 1922. 160p. $8.00.
Greek background and history are presented, along with the experience of the
immigrants and their descendants in America. Describes customs and aspects of
the cultural heritage that are unique to Greek Americans. Political, economic,
social, and religious conditions in Greece and then in America are described. The
degree of Greek acceptance of the American way of life and acceptance of the
Greeks by other Americans is also discussed. The appendix includes a list of Greek
newspapers. A bibliography and index is provided.

Literature and Fiction Titles

1288.   Brandenberg, Aliki. **The Eggs: A Greek Folk Tale.** New York: Pantheon,
         1969. unp. $3.95. (K-3)
A humorous tale, retold and illustrated by Aliki Brandenberg, about an innkeeper
who tries to take advantage of another man's honesty. His attempt to make himself
a large profit is thwarted by an equally sly lawyer.

1289.   Demetrios, George. **When Greek Meets Greek.** Boston, Mass.: Houghton
         Mifflin, 1947. 245p. $11.75. (7-12)
A collection of short stories about Greeks in the Old World and the New. Greek
immigrants who settled in Boston are characters in some of the 25 stories in this
volume.

1290.   George, Harry S. **Demo of 70th St.** Illus. by Robert Quackenbush. New
         York: Walck, 1971. 151p. $4.75. (5-6)
Demo, whose real name is Demosthenes Demetracopoulos, is a Greek-American boy
of immigrant parents. Living in New York City, his adventures provide a good picture of Greek customs, values, and family life.

1291.   Green, Roger L. **Old Greek Fairy Tales.** Illus. by Ernest Shepard. New
         York: Roy, 1969. 186p. $3.95. (4-6)
A collection of 16 myths told in modern idiom. The tales revolve around the
characters of Perseus and the Gorgon, Midas, Orpheus, and others.

1292.   Haviland, Virginia. **Favorite Fairy Tales Told in Greece.** Illus. by Nonny
         Hogrogian. Boston, Mass.: Little, Brown, 1970. 90p. $3.25. (3-6)
A collection of eight favorite fairy tales of supernatural and natural beings. Greek
values and customs are evident, but these Greek tales are universal in appeal.

1293.   Newfeld, Rose. **Beware the Man without a Beard and Other Greek Folk Tales.** Illus. by Marjorie Auerbach. New York: Knopf, 1969. 74p. $3.95. (3-7)
Nine Greek folk tales are presented here for independent reading at the intermediate-grade level, or for storytelling at the primary and intermediate levels.

Audiovisual Materials

1294.   **Jason and the Argonauts.** 16mm film, 104 min., sd., color. Morningside Worldwide Pictures; released by Columbia Pictures Corp., 1963. (3-6)
A classic Greek myth told here for the intermediate grade level in the elementary school.

1295.   **Jason and the Golden Fleece.** 1 filmstrip. Hulton Educational Publications, 1969. (3-6)
A story in pictures of the classic Greek myth about Jason and the Golden Fleece.

HUNGARIAN AMERICANS

Reference Sources

1296.   Bakó, Elemér. **Guide to Hungarian Studies.** Stanford, Calif.: Hoover Institute Press, 1973. 2 vols. $35.00. (T)
A bibliography of international scope arranged in broad subject categories on Hungarian studies. A chapter is devoted to "Hungary and the United States" and includes many materials on the Hungarians in America. The bibliography is annotated.

1297.   Bognar, Desi K., ed. **Hungarians in America: A Biographical Directory of Professionals of Hungarian Origin in the Americas.** Mount Vernon, N.Y.: AFI Company, 1973. 239p. $16.50. (9-12, T)
This directory lists names, addresses, and the professional occupations of Hungarians in America. It includes other brief biographical information.

1298.   Szeplaki, Joseph. **The Hungarians in America, 1583-1974: A Chronology and Fact Book.** Dobbs Ferry, N.Y.: Oceana Press, 1975. 152p. $6.00. (7-12)
Includes a chronology, documents, and bibliography related to the Hungarian experience in the United States. A list of Hungarian societies, churches, and presses is included.

Non-Fiction Titles: History, Culture, Sociology, Biography

1299.   Bihaly, Andrew. **Journal of Andrew Bihaly**. Ed. by Anthony Tuttle. New
         York: Crowell, 1973. 300p. $6.95. (9-12)
Abandoned by his mother and left in a Hungarian monastery to escape harm from
the Nazis in World War II, Bihaly somehow was able to come to the United States
as a young adult. He kept a diary of his life in Manhattan, and his desperate
attempts to find love and to fight long-time feelings of rejection are recorded.

1300.   Bursten, Martin A. **Escape from Fear**. Syracuse, N.Y.: Syracuse University
         Press, 1958; repr. ed., Westport, Conn.: Greenwood, 1973. 224p. $12.50.
         (9-12)
A collection of episodes, quotes, stories, and notes based on interviews with
Hungarian refugees who escaped to the United States and other areas of the free
world, particularly Austria, after the 1956 revolution.

1301.   Fishman, Joshua A. **Hungarian Language Maintenance in the United
         States**. Bloomington: Indiana University Research Center for Language
         Sciences, 1966. 58p. $5.00pa. (10-12, T)
A survey of Hungarian immigration to the United States documented with census
data from 1870 to 1960. Describes how the maintenance of the Hungarian language
has been positively or negatively affected by the world wars, the Hungarians'
institutions and organizations, and their efforts to preserve the language. A
selected bibliography is included.

1302.   Gracza, Rezsoe, and Margaret Gracza. **The Hungarians in America**.
         Minneapolis, Minn.: Lerner Publications, 1969. 76p. $3.95. (5-11)
A chronology of the history of the Hungarians in America is presented from the
days of the early explorations of Leif Ericson's crew, which is said to have
included one Hungarian. The various waves of immigration are described and famous
Hungarians throughout the period are discussed. Individuals of outstanding achievement and those who have made contributions to American society are indicated.
Many photographs document the work. Indexed.

1303.   Konnyu, Leslie. **Hungarians in the U.S.A.: An Immigration Study**.
         St. Louis, Mo.: The American Hungarian Review, 1967. 86p. $5.50;
         $4.25pa. (9-12)
This study of Hungarian immigration describes the different waves of immigration
and the political, economic, social, and cultural significance of each. Conditions
in the homeland at the time of each immigration and the background of the immigrant groups are described, and there is discussion of Hungarian distribution in the
United States and the press, churches, communities, organizations, institutions,
and contributions of the Hungarian Americans. A bibliography, maps, photographs, are included. Name index. Another title by the author is *A History of
American Hungarian Literature* (Cooperative of American Literature, 1962).

1304.   Lengyel, Emil. **Americans from Hungary**. Philadelphia, Pa.: Lippincott,
         1948; repr. ed., Westport, Conn.: Greenwood Press, 1974. 319p. $15.25.
         (9-12)

A history of the Hungarians in America with emphasis on their migrations within Europe and the United States; the impact of the Industrial Revolution, world wars, and the Depression on the group; and the noteworthy Hungarian Americans who contributed to American culture and society. A title for slightly younger children, at the upper elementary and junior high level, is the author's *The Land and People of Hungary*, rev. ed. (Lippincott, 1972. $5.95. 6-9).

1305. Michener, James. **Bridge at Andau.** New York: Random House, 1957. 270p. $5.95. (10-12)
The bridge at Andau is the bridge over which thousands of Hungarian refugees fled during the 1956 revolt against the communists. Their story is told through a series of interviews with refugees who escaped into Austria.

1306. Myers, Hortense. **Joseph Pulitzer: Young Journalist.** Indianapolis, Ind.: Bobbs-Merrill, 1975. 200p. $3.50. (3-7)
A biography of a famous Hungarian-American journalist and his contributions to the field, as well as his struggles to achieve success.

1307. Souders, D. A. **The Magyars in America.** New York: George H. Doran Co., 1922; repr. ed., San Francisco: R&E Research Associates, 1969. 149p. $8.00. (9-12)
Describes Hungarian immigration and the social and economic conditions typical of the Hungarian Americans since they came to America. Problems of adjustment, the role of the Eastern Orthodox Church in the Hungarian-American community, and the accomplishments and achievements of well-known Hungarians are discussed. The appendixes include a discussion of Americanization, a selected listing of Hungarian publications in the United States, and a bibliography. The work is indexed.

1308. Weinstock, S. Alexander. **Acculturation and Occupation: A Study of the 1956 Hungarian Refugees in the U.S.** (Publication of Research Group for Migration Problems, no. 8). The Hague: M. Nijhoff, 1969. 127p. $16.20. (10-12, T)
Examines the acculturation of the Hungarian refugees of the 1956 revolution with respect to sex, religion, occupation, language maintenance, education, personality, leisure activity, reasons for immigration, family and friendship patterns, participation in politics, and life goals. Data were collected through interviews; bibliography included.

1309. Xantus, John. **Letters from North America.** Translated from Hungarian by Theodore and Helen Schoenman. Detroit, Mich.: Wayne State University Press, 1975. 198p. $13.95. (9-12)
The first of two volumes on the author's experiences in America. Xantus was a political refugee from Hungary and the letters translated here were written to his family in Hungary.

Literature and Fiction Titles

1310. Lewiton, Mina. **Elizabeth and the Young Stranger.** Eau Claire, Wisc.:
        Hale, 1961. 133p. $2.75. (7-12)
Elizabeth makes friends with a young Hungarian refugee girl. Her friends in her
New England town remain aloof to the new girl, and her father disapproves of her
new friendship.

1311. Manning-Sanders, Ruth. **The Glass Man and the Golden Bird: Hungarian
        Folk and Fairy Tales.** Illus. by Victor G. Ambrus. New York: Roy, 1968.
        194p. $5.95. (4-6)
A collection of Hungarian folktales appropriate for reading at the intermediate
grade levels. Translations use the modern British idioms. Useful for reading aloud
to primary children.

1312. Remenyi, Joseph. **Hungarian Writers and Literature: Modern Novelists,
        Critics, and Poets.** Edited with an Introduction by August J. Molnar. New
        Brunswick, N.J.: Rutgers University Press, 1964. 512p. $12.00. (10-12)
Covers the Hungarian writers and poets of the nineteenth and twentieth centuries.
Also contains an important introductory historical survey of Hungarian literature,
special essays of English translation, and Hungarian humor.

1313. Leader, Ninon A. M. **Hungarian Classical Ballads and Their Folklore.**
        Cambridge, Mass.: Cambridge University Press, 1967. 367p. $12.50.
        (10-12)
The comprehensive study of Hungarian classical ballads. Contains a historical
survey of Hungarian ballad research as well as a comprehensive bibliography,
indexes of motifs, and ballad titles. An important work for the study of Hungarian
folklore.

Audiovisual Materials

1314. **Immigrants.** 16mm film, 30 min., b&w. Made by National Broadcasting
        Co., released for public educational use in the United States through
        U.S. Office of Education. (6-12)
A Hungarian refugee family is sponsored by a Catholic agency in their emigration
to the United States. The film portrays their adjustments, problems, their general
experiences and their sentiments and attitudes toward their new homeland. This
title is also available in a 35mm filmstrip.

1315. **Now We Are Free.** 16mm film, 26 min., b&w. Made by Hearst Metrotone
        News. U.S. Information Agency, 1957. Released for public educational
        use in the United States through U.S. Office of Education. (4-12)
Traces the emigration of a Hungarian refugee family crossing the border into
Austria, to Camp Kilmer in New Jersey, and to the community in the Midwest in
which they eventually made their new home.

1316.   **Out of Hungary to Freedom.** 16mm film, 19 min., b&w. U.S. Information
        Agency, 1957. Made by Hearst Metrotone News. Released for public
        educational use in the United States through the U.S. Office of Education.
        (6-12)
Describes the refugees of the 1956-57 revolution in Hungary and tells how the
refugees left the country via Austria for new homes. Depicts Vice-President Nixon
visiting Austrian refugee camps. Shows scenes of Hungarian immigrants who chose
to make their homes in the United States and how they became adjusted to
American society.

1317.   **The Story of the Hungarian American.** 1 filmstrip, 1 teacher's manual.
        Eye Gate House, 1966. (The Story of America's People, Series 1, no. 1).
        (5-10)
A brief survey of the early history of Hungarians, including explorers, in America.
The Hungarian Americans' role in American military service during the Revolutionary and Civil Wars is discussed. Also covers contributions and achievements of
the Hungarians in the United States.

IRISH AMERICANS

Reference Sources

1318.   Eager, Alan R. **A Guide to Irish Bibliographic Materials.** London: The
        Library Association, 1964. 392p. (T)
A bibliographic index of materials for use in studying the Irish and/or the Irish in
America. Bibliographies, catalogs, periodicals (and their indexes), monographs, and
unpublished papers are included.

1319.   Griffin, William D., ed. **The Irish in America, 550-1972: A Chronology and
        Fact Book.** Dobbs Ferry, N.Y.: Oceana, 1973. 154p. $6.00. (7-12)
A ready-reference volume of the Irish immigration and culture in America. The
first part of the book is a chronology of events relevant to the Irish in America
from 550 to 1972. The second section is a series of documents pertaining to Irish
history in the United States, and the concluding section is a bibliography of materials on the Irish Americans. Statistical tables and immigration records are also
included. Indexed.

Non-Fiction Titles: History, Culture, Sociology, Biography

1320.   Abodaher, David J. **Rebel on Two Continents: Thomas Meagher.** New
        York: Messner, 1970. 190p. $3.50. (7-8)
The biography of an Irish patriot who immigrated to America and ultimately
became Governor of Montana.

1321.   Adams, William Forbes. **Ireland and the Irish Emigration to the New World from 1815 to the Famine**. New Haven, Conn.: Yale University Press, 1932; repr. ed., New York: Russell and Russell Publishers, 1960. 444p. $16.00. (9-12)
Describes Irish migrations with respect to the history of Ireland, England, and the United States. Also discusses the conditions that prompted emigration and provides maps and statistical tables for immigration from 1815 to the mid-nineteenth century.

1322.   Birmingham, Stephen. **Real Lace: America's Irish Rich**. New York: Harper and Row, 1973. 322p. $10.00; $1.75pa. (9-12)
Wealthy Irish-American families are described here, including the Kennedys, Fords, and others in New York and California. Particular attention is given to how these families became rich and attained their high social and economic status.

1323.   Blanshard, Paul. **Irish and Catholic Power: An American Interpretation**. Boston, Mass.: Beacon Press, 1953; repr. ed., Westport, Conn.: Greenwood Press, 1972. 375p. $16.75. (9-12)
Irish Catholic influence in the United States is described, with a background history of the church in Ireland as well. Irish Catholicism has been studied with respect to the Irish American's politics, education, moral standards, marriage partners, etc.

1324.   Broehl, Wayne G. **The Molly Maguires**. Cambridge, Mass.: Harvard University Press, 1964. 409p. $15.00. New York: Chelsea House, 1970. $2.45pa. (11-12)
Describes an Irish secret society of coal miners called the Molly Maguires. This group, organized in Pennsylvania in the latter part of the 1800s, was an attempt at unionization with a plan to murder the mine bosses. This work is a history of the labor conditions faced by many of the Irish Americans who found employment in the mines.

1325.   Byrne, Stephen. **Irish Immigration to the United States: What It Has Been and What It Is**. New York: Catholic Publication Society, 1873; repr. ed., New York: Arno, 1969. 165p. $5.00.
Part 1 of this title in the *American Immigration Collection Series* (No. 1) covers the role of the Irish American as an immigrant, describing specific problems, dangers, and responsibilities faced. Part 2 is a demographic survey of Irish Americans in the United States. Arrangement is by state and territory; statistics on the Irish population in general and on those that are Catholics are provided.

1326.   Clark, Dennis. **The Irish in Philadelphia: Ten Generations of Urban Experience**. Philadelphia, Pa.: Temple University Press, 1974. 284p. $12.50. (9-12)
Describes the adjustments made in the acculturation process of the Irish in Philadelphia, particularly of those who came from rural environments. Also compares the treatment and status of the Irish Catholics in Philadelphia with those who settled in Boston.

1327.   Duff, John B. **The Irish in the United States**. Belmont, Calif.: Wadsworth, 1971. 87p. $3.50. (7-12)
This title in the *Minorities in American Life* series examines the Irish experience in the United States. It describes the adjustments, problems, and achievements of Irish Americans. Attention is given to the reasons for immigration from Ireland, early settlements in America, the economic and political contributions, the role and influence of the Catholic Church, and areas in which assimilation was apparent, as well as those in which it was lacking.

1328.   Evans, E. Estyn. **Irish Folk Ways**. Boston, Mass.: Routledge & Kegan Paul, 1966. 324p. $13.25; $6.50pa. (7-12)
Describes Irish customs and traditions including home and family life, building styles, and other aspects of the Irish heritage that are a part of American society.

1329.   Graves, Charles P. **Father Flanagan, Founder of Boys Town**. Illus. by William Hutchinson. Champaign, Ill.: Garrard, 1972. 95p. $3.58. (3-6)
A portrait of a compassionate Irish-American priest who started a home for orphaned, delinquent, and homeless boys. His work with them grew into the internationally known "Boys Town."

1330.   Greeley, Andrew M. **That Most Distressful Nation: The Taming of the American Irish**. Chicago: Quadrangle, 1973. 281p. $8.95; $2.95pa. (10-12)
A sociological study of the Irish experience in the United States which includes the historical background and the conditions prompting emigration from Ireland. Covers Irish-American family life, social and economic struggles and status, the Irish political and religious preferences, and other aspects of the Irishman's life and role in American society.

1331.   Hale, Edward E. **Letters on Irish Emigration**. Boston, Mass.: Phillips, Sampson and Company, 1852; repr. ed., New York: Books for Libraries, 1972. 64p. $8.75. (10-12)
Letters that described the conditions facing the Irish immigrant, as well as the conditions in his homeland, and the hardships crossing the ocean, were originally published in the *Daily Advertiser* in Boston. Appearing in the mid-nineteenth century, these letters aimed at creating better treatment and more help for the newly arrived Irish-American immigrants. Includes statistics on the Irish-American population.

1332.   Handlin, Oscar. **Boston's Immigrants: A Study of Acculturation**. Rev. and enl. ed. Cambridge, Mass.: Harvard University Press, 1959. 382p. $12.00. (T)
Describes the Irish Americans in Boston and the adjustment of the illiterate, unskilled immigrants to a city where culture and high society were well esteemed. Immigration statistics and the acculturation of the Irish in political, economic, religious, and social areas is examined. A biography by the author about a prominent Irish-American is *Al Smith and His America* (Little, Brown, 1958. $5.00; $2.95pa.).

1333.   Harmon, Maurice, ed. **Fenians and Fenianism.** Seattle: University of
         Washington Press, 1970. 101p. $4.95; $1.95pa. (11-12)
These essays describe the Fenian movement in Ireland and in New York and its
effect on Irish and Irish-American political and cultural life, particularly literature.
Also some of the essays in the collection deal with the relationship of the Catholic
Church and the Fenians.

1334.   Johnson, James E. **The Irish in America.** Minneapolis, Minn.: Lerner
         Publications, 1966. 78p. $3.95. (5-11)
This history of the Irish heritage in America covers life in Ireland during the 1800s,
emphasizing the 1850s when immigration to America was gaining momentum.
Also covered are the Catholic Church, the Irish in the American West, the Fighting
Irish, and Irish political leaders in the United States. Irish contributions and some
biographical sketches of outstanding Irish Americans are included. Indexed.

1335.   Levine, Edward M. **Irish and Irish Politicians: A Study of Social and Cul-
         tural Alienation.** South Bend, Ind.: University of Notre Dame Press, 1966.
         241p. $7.95. (10-12, T)
Describes the influence of Irish Americans in politics in the United States, with
attempts to give some explanations for the dominating role played by this ethnic
group. Some factors considered are: social isolation, religion, social acceptance or
lack of it. Chicago politics are given particular attention, and the future role of the
Irish Americans is also studied.

1336.   Maguire, John Francis. **Irish in America.** London: Longmans, Green &
         Co., 1868; repr. ed., New York: Arno, 1969. 653p. $18.50. (7-12)
The contributions of early Irish immigrants are studied in this history of the Irish
ethnic group in the United States. Emphasis is on social and economic status, anti-
Irish discrimination, the growth of Catholicism in America, the Irish in the labor
force, and the role of the woman in society.

1337.   McDonnell, Virginia B. **The Irish Helped Build America.** New York:
         Messner, 1969. 96p. $3.95. (3-6)
Reasons for Irish immigration to America and a history of the Irish experience in
the United States are presented. The Irish-American's role in American life and
contributions to the development of transportation, industry, the arts, literature,
education, entertainment, politics, and the military are indicated. Outstanding
Irish-Americans are also noted, and the influence of the Irish on Catholicism in the
United States is discussed.

1338.   McGee, Thomas D'Arcy. **A History of the Irish Settlers in North America.**
         Boston, Mass.: P. Donahoe, 1852; repr. ed., New York: Jerome S. Ozer,
         1971. 240p. $9.95. (9-12)
Relates how the Irish helped in the development of the United States. Excerpts
from letters and documents are arranged chronologically to document events and
experiences in Irish-American settlements and communities.

1339.   Murphy, Gene, and Tim Driscoll. **An Album of Irish Americans.** New
         York: Watts, 1974. 87p. $4.90. (5-8)

An illustrated history of the Irish in America. Includes their motivations for leaving Ireland, the problems they faced when they got to the new land, etc. Photos and cartoon drawings document the portrayal of the Irish community in America, with emphasis on the important role of religion and the Church, the Irish contributions to American society, and their economic and political roles.

1340.   O'Brien, Michael J. **A Hidden Phase of American History: Ireland's Part in America's Struggle for Liberty**. New York: Devin-Adair Co., 1919; repr. ed., Baltimore, Md.: Genealogical Publishing Co., 1973. 533p. $24.75. (9-12)

The contributions of the Irish in the Revolutionary War are noted here, as well as the names of Irish-Americans who signed the Declaration of Independence. The appendix includes a list of officers and enlisted men of Irish descent. Other records of the Irish in America by this author are *The Irish at Bunker Hill* (Devin-Adair Co., 1969. $10.00) and *The Irish in America* (Genealogical, 1965. $5.00).

1341.   O'Donovan, Jeremiah. **Irish Immigration in the United States: Immigrant Interviews**. Pittsburgh, Pa.: the author, 1864; repr. ed., New York: Arno-New York Times, 1969. 382p. $11.50. (9-12)

A personal narrative in which O'Donovan describes first-hand interviews with fellow Irish immigrants. The background history of conditions they faced in Ireland and their early experiences in the United States are covered. Some family names and genealogical data are also included.

1342.   O'Grady, Joseph P. **How the Irish Became Americans**. Boston, Mass.: Twayne, 1973. 190p. $7.95. (9-12)

A history of the Irish in America for the last 300 years. Examines the question of whether the Irish used political leverage to make their strength. Assimilation of the Irish into the mainstream of American society is also covered.

1343.   Potter, George. **To the Golden Door**. Westport, Conn.: Greenwood, 1960, 1974. 631p. $25.75. (7-12)

Describes the conditions in Ireland that prompted two million Irishmen to immigrate to the United States. Also covers the voyage to America, early settlements, the social and economic conditions experienced in the New World, Irish involvement in the Civil War, and the growth of the Catholic Church in the United States as it relates to Irish immigration.

1344.   Shannon, William V. **The American Irish**. New York: Macmillan, 1966. 484p. $9.95; $4.95pa. (1974). (7-12)

A background history of conditions in Ireland and the large waves of immigration to the United States. The cultural heritage of the Irish-Americans is examined, with an indication of the Irish influence and achievements in the social, political, economic, literary, religious, and other fields. Presents biographical sketches of outstanding Irish immigrants and their descendants, including President John F. Kennedy.

1345. Tansill, Charles Callan. **America and the Fight for Irish Freedom, 1866-1922: An Old Story Based upon New Data**. New York: Devin-Adair Co., 1957. 489p. $10.00. (10-12)
Discusses the secret societies organized by Irish-Americans with the intent of helping Ireland attain freedom. Leaders of this kind of movement and their contributions are indicated.

1346. Walker, Mabel Gregory. **The Fenian Movement**. Colorado Springs, Colo.: R. Myles Co., 1969. 215p. $5.95; $2.95pa. (10-12)
Describes the Fenian Brotherhood, organized for the purpose of promoting freedom and independence for Ireland. Covers also the impact this had on Ireland and the support and opposition it received within the United States from the government and other groups.

1347. Webb, Robert N. **America Is Also Irish**. New York: Putnam's, 1973. 128p. $3.89. (5-9)
Surveys the history of the Irish in America, social acceptance or rejection of them, their religious values, and their contributions. Includes biographical sketches of well-known Irish Americans in the arts and professions. Statistics on the Irish-American population are included; indexed.

1348. Wittke, Carl F. **The Irish in America**. Baton Rouge: Louisiana State University Press, 1956; repr. ed., New York: Teachers College, 1969. 319p. $1.50pa. (9-12)
A classic work on the Irish-American experience, culture and image in the United States. It describes the economic situation faced by unskilled immigrants who became the labor force that developed several American industries. The Irishman's role in politics, literature, drama, etc., is also indicated.

Literature and Fiction Titles

1349. Condon, Richard. **Mile High**. New York: Dial, 1970. 364p. $1.25pa. (9-12)
A humorous story of an Irish-American who gets the idea of initiating Prohibition and then makes a fortune on bootlegging. He builds himself a "mile-high castle" in New York.

1350. Danaher, Kevin. **Folktales of the Irish Countryside**. Illus. by Harold Berson. New York: David White, 1970. 103p. $4.95. (5-9)
A collection of amusing and entertaining Irish folktales that have been written down by members of the Irish Folklore Commission as they remember hearing or having them told to them. An important feature is a glossary of Irish terms and dialect words.

1351. Farrell, James T. **Judgement Day**. New York: Vanguard, 1935; repr. ed., New York: Avon, 1973. 465p. $1.25pa. (10-12)
This is the last story in a trilogy of the life story of Studs Lonigan, a young Irish-American immigrant in Chicago. Other titles in the series are *Young Lonigan* and *The Young Manhood of Studs Lonigan.*

1352.   Fenton, Edward. **Duffy's Rocks**. New York: Dutton, 1974. 198p. $5.95.
        (5-8)
Timothy Brennan is a young Irish American who is searching for his father. Irish
family and community life are portrayed in this novel.

1353.   Green, Kathleen. **Philip and the Pooka and Other Irish Fairy Tales**. Illus.
        by Victoria De Larrea. Philadelphia, Pa.: Lippincott, 1966. 93p. $3.39.
        (4-6)
A collection of ten original Irish fairy tales full of the humor and imaginative
"little people" that typify Irish stories.

1354.   Mercier, Vivian, ed. **Great Irish Short Stories**. New York: Dell, c1964,
        1971. 384p. $0.95pa. (7-12)
A collection of Irish stories consisting of classic favorites as well as the less familiar.
The arrangement is in two sections. Part one is comprised of ancient tales and folk-
lore; part two is comprised of the typical short story.

1355.   O'Connor, Edwin. **The Last Hurrah**. Boston, Mass.: Little, Brown, 1956,
        1970. 427p. $7.95; $1.50pa. (Bantam). (10-12)
Written with warmth and humor, this story set in an Irish community covers, to a
certain extent, the social and political history of Boston. Campaigns, election
nights, city bosses, and an Irish wake are some of the scenes painted. Another novel
by the author tells the story of an Irish-American priest: *The Edge of Sadness*
(Little, Brown, 1961).

1356.   Shura, Mary Francis. **Shoe Full of Shamrock**. Illus. by N. M. Bodecker.
        Boston, Mass.: Atheneum, 1965. 64p. $3.59. (3-6)
Davie O'Sullivan gets his secret wish when he meets a magic leprechaun in New
York City's Central Park.

1357.   Stolz, Mary. **Noonday Friends**. New York: Harper and Row, 1965. 182p.
        $4.79. (3-7)
A warm family story set in New York. Twins Franny and Jim react to their poverty
and deal with it in different ways in this story of Irish-American children.

1358.   Sullivan, Peggy. **O'Donnells**. Illus. by Mary Stevens. Chicago: Follett,
        1956. 160p. $3.99. (3-6)
The experiences and problems of an Irish-American family and their neighbors
in Kansas City are the background of a warm, sometimes humorous, and sometimes sentimental story. The setting is around the turn of the century in a community of first- and second-generation immigrants.

Audiovisual Materials

1359.   **The American Immigrants: The Irish Experience.** 1 filmstrip, 1 record (or cassette), 1 teacher's guide. Multi-Media Productions. $11.95. (4-8)
Set in New York around 1859, this filmstrip is about a 12-year-old Irish boy's description of his life in an Irish-American community. The filmstrip also describes the kinds of employment typical of immigrants working on the railroads, and portrays the ambitions, goals, social acceptance, and education typical of Irish immigrants of the time.

1360.   **Irish Americans.** Film loop. Ealing. $24.95. (4-10)
Depicts Irish Americans wearing the traditional green at a St. Patrick's Day parade. Also depicts this ethnic group as they are absorbed into American society in various aspects of life, and as they contribute to America's industry, economy, culture, arts, etc.

ITALIAN AMERICANS

Reference Sources

1361.   Cordasco, Francesco. **The Italian-American Experience: An Annotated and Classified Bibliographical Guide.** New York: Burt Franklin & Co., 1974. 179p. $14.50. (9-12, T)
This guide is arranged by various areas of study—e.g., 1) bibliographies and archives, 2) Italian emigration to America, 3) Italian-American history and regional studies, 4) sociology of Italian-American life, 5) political and economic context. The appendix, entitled "Casa Italiana Educational Bureau Publications" includes "The Casa Italian Educational Bureau—Its Purpose and Program"; "The Italians in America," by Leonard Covello; "Italian Population in New York," by William B. Shedd, and "Occupational Trends of Italians in New York City," by John J. D'Alesandre. These studies include population maps and tables. The work is indexed. Another reference title by Cordasco and Salvatore La Gumina is *Italians in the United States: A Bibliography of Reports, Texts, Critical Studies and Related Materials* (New York: Oriole Editions, 1972. 137p. $20.00. 9-12, T).

1362.   Diodati, C. M., J. Coleman, and J. F. Valletutti. **Writings on Italian-Americans.** New York: Italian American Center for Urban Affairs, Inc., 1975. 70p. (9-12, T)
This bibliography of the Italian-American immigrant experience and the Italian-American as contributor to American society is partially (and briefly) annotated. Arrangement is alphabetical by author under various chapter topics—e.g., The History of the Italian Americans, Influences Affecting the Immigrant, Italian Americans in the Arts, Italian Americans in Business, Italian American Laborers, Italian Americans in Politics, Italian American Scholars, Italian American Literature and Personalities, Periodicals, Theatre and Cinema. Indexed.

1363.   LoGatto, Anthony F., ed. **The Italians in America, 1492-1972: A Chronology and Fact Book.** Dobbs Ferry, N.Y.: Oceana, 1972. 149p. $6.00. (7-12)

This fourth volume in the *Ethnic Chronology Series* is a handy one-volume ready reference tool. It is arranged in three major sections: a historical chronology, important documents relevant to the history of the Italians in the United States, and various appendices containing a list of outstanding Italian Americans, a list of Italian-American newspapers and periodicals, and a selective bibliography and list of audiovisual media.

Teaching Methodology and Curriculum Materials

1364.   South East Michigan Regional Ethnic Heritage Studies Center. **Elementary Unit in Italian Ethnic Studies.** Detroit: South East Michigan Regional Ethnic Heritage Studies Center, 1975. 26p. Free. (T)

An eight-week unit developed in a teacher workshop training program to provide teachers and curriculum specialists with materials for teaching about Italian Americans at the upper elementary level. It can also serve as a useful model for study of other ethnic cultures. Each lesson includes the desired objectives and suggested activities and resources.

Non-Fiction Titles: History, Culture, Sociology, Biography

1365.   Amfitheatrof, Erik. **The Children of Columbus, an Informal History of the Italians in the New World.** Boston, Mass.: Little, Brown, 1973. 371p. $8.95. (7-12)

Traces the experience of the Italians in the United States by use of mini-biographies. Emphasis is on the contributions of the Italian Americans in various aspects of the country's growth and development. Coverage is thorough; style is popular narrative.

1366.   Child, Irvin L. **Italian or American: The Second Generation in Conflict.** New Haven, Conn.: Yale University Press, 1943; repr. ed., New York: Russell & Russell, 1970. 206p. $11.00. (11-12, T)

Generation gaps between the Italian immigrants and their children are described. Accent is on social, family, and religious life. Also discusses conflicting values and identifies specific examples.

1367.   Churchill, Charles W. **The Italians of Newark: A Community Study.** New York: Arno, 1975. 173p. $13.00. (11-12, T)

At the time the author conducted this study for his doctoral thesis from New York University in 1942, the Italians in Newark were about 80,000 in number. He provides a history of this Italian-American community and the results of data compiled from interviews with 700 Italian-American members of it. Emphasis is on work and occupations, family life, religion, political life, organizations, recreational activities, social life, and education.

1368.   Clark, Francis E. **Our Italian Fellow Citizens in Their Old Homes and Their New.** Boston, Mass.: Small, Maynard & Co., 1919; repr. ed., New York: Arno, 1975. 217p. $14.00. (7-12)
Portrays the Italians as an immigrant group, describing the rate and degree of their Americanization and assimilation into American society. The author also emphasizes the positive aspects of the Italians in America, their contributions and achievements.

1369.   Coe, Douglas. **Marconi: Pioneer of Radio.** New York: Julian Messner, 1943. 272p. $3.95. (5-12)
A fictionalized biography of a great Italian-American inventor. Good to use with students interested in science and engineering. Includes black and white illustrations and a selected bibliography.

1370.   Cordasco, Francesco, and Eugene Bucchioni. **The Italians: Social Backgrounds of an American Group.** Clifton, N.J.: Augustus Kelly, 1974. 598p. $19.95. (10-12)
A sourcebook of documents and materials from Italian Americans and major resource centers and depositories. Topics included are those concerned with Italian immigration, social conditions in the Italian-American communities (health, education, employment, etc.) and the Italian sentiments about and reaction to the new homeland. Tables, maps, photographs are provided. Bibliographies and an index are included.

1371.   Corsi, Edward. **In the Shadow of Liberty: The Chronicle of Ellis Island.** New York: Macmillan, 1935; repr. ed., New York: Arno, 1969. 321p. $11.00. (7-12)
The story of an immigrant from Italy who became the U.S. Commissioner of Immigration at Ellis Island.

1372.   Covello, Leonard. **The Social Background of the Italo-American School Child: A Study of the Southern Italian Family Mores and Their Effect on the School Situation in Italy and America.** Edited by Francesco Cordasco. Leiden: E. J. Brill, 1967; repr. ed., Totowa, N.J.: Rowman, Littlefield, 1972. 488p. $25.00. (T)
This work is the author's 1944 doctoral dissertation at New York University in which he studied the immigrant child and the educational program of a large city school. Because his work was 10 years in preparation, and because he discusses not what the school did for the Italian child, but what it did not do, it is still useful for teachers and scholars studying the needs of the child from the Italian cultural background.

1373.   D'Angelo, Pascal. **Son of Italy.** New York: Macmillan, 1924; repr. ed., New York: Arno, 1975. 185p. $11.00. (9-12)
An autobiographical narrative in which an Italian immigrant of 1910 tells how he was exploited as a laborer in his early days in America, and of all the other problems and struggles, both economic and social, in adapting to a new land and achieving some of his dreams.

1374.   DeConde, Alexander. **Half-Bitter, Half-Sweet: An Excursion into Italian-American History.** New York: Scribner's, 1972. 466p. $12.50. (10-12)
Traces the Italians' earliest encounters in America from Columbus on. Italian discrimination among the immigrants is discussed, as are Italian nationalism in America, political preferences, and relations between Italy and America. Major sources in Italian history are evaluated. A selected bibliography is included; indexed.

1375.   Ehrmann, Herbert. **The Case That Will Not Die.** Boston, Mass.: Little, Brown, 1969. 576p. $12.50.
The famous Sacco-Vanzetti case, in which two Italian Americans are the defendants, is described here by the author, who served as junior counsel for the defense in the last two years of trial. Ehrmann also indicates how political pressures interrupted the legal process. Another title in a similar vein is his *Untried Case: The Sacco-Vanzetti Case and the Morelli Gang* (Vanguard, 1960. $7.95).

1376.   Ets, Marie H. **Rosa: The Life of an Italian Immigrant.** Foreword by Rudolph J. Vecoli. Minneapolis: University of Minnesota Press, 1970. 254p. $7.50. (7-12)
The life of Rosa Cavalleri, an immigrant from Italy, is a revealing picture of Italian social life and customs, and the adjustments and problems of the newcomers to America from that country.

1377.   Foerster, Robert F. **Italian Emigration of Our Times.** Cambridge, Mass.: Harvard University Press, 1919; repr. ed., New York: Russell & Russell, 1968. 556p. $15.00. (10-12)
Analyzes the causes of emigration from Italy, and traces the emigrants to the various countries, including the United States, into which they settled. Also describes their contributions to American economy and society and the areas in which they found employment and earned a living.

1378.   Gallo, Patrick J. **Ethnic Alienation: The Italian Americans.** Rutherford, N.J.: Fairleigh Dickinson, 1974. 254p. $10.00. (10-12)
Studies the Italian subsociety that Gallo contends persists in spite of the process of assimilation. He further studies assimilation with respect to occupation, residence, and income, and covers political preferences of Italian Americans in light of their ethnicity and religious background.

1379.   Gambino, Richard. **Blood of My Blood: The Dilemma of the Italian-Americans.** New York: Doubleday, 1974. 350p. $5.33. (9-12)
Discusses from a personal standpoint the background of the immigrants from Italy to the United States. Gambino describes Italian-American culture and the problems of identity that subsequent second- and third-generation Italian Americans have.

1380.   Grossman, Ronald P. **The Italians in America.** Minneapolis, Minn.: Lerner Publications, 1966. 62p. $3.95. (5-9)
A brief history of the Italians in America is provided. Emphasis is given to contributions of the Italian Americans. Individuals who have made outstanding achievements in various areas are indicated (e.g., sports, literature, arts and sciences, and

the entertainment field). Italians in the years before the mass migrations, such as explorers, missionaries, and early settlers, are also described.

1381.   Iorizzo, Luciana J., and Salvatore Mondello. **The Italian-Americans.** Boston, Mass.: Twayne, 1971. 273p. $7.50. (10-12)
Studies the assimilation and acculturation of Italians into American society and their role in agriculture, viniculture, politics, the arts, and other areas.

1382.   Jackson, Stanley. **Caruso.** New York: Stein & Day, 1975. 302p. $3.95pa. (6-12)
A biography of the life and career of Enrico Caruso. It tells of his Italian background and traces his successful career in New York's Metropolitan Opera.

1383.   Kaufman, Mervyn. **Fiorella La Guardia.** Illus. by Gene Szafran. New York: Crowell, 1972. 33p. $3.75. (2-4)
A biography of Fiorella La Guardia, an Italian-American immigrant who was elected mayor of New York City and served three consecutive terms. Covers his early life, his family, and his service in politics.

1384.   Kobler, John. **Capone: The Life and World of Al Capone.** New York: Fawcett World, 1972. 409p. $1.95pa. (10-12)
Interesting material on the chief of Chicago's underworld in the 1920s.

1385.   LaGumina, Salvatore J. **An Album of the Italian-American.** New York: Watts, 1972. 85p. $4.95. (4-10)
Describes the immigration and traces the history of Italian Americans, discussing where the immigrants settled, how they earned a living, their churches, arts, customs, sports, political views, and the social and cultural organizations in America's "Little Italys." Also, the accomplishments of prominent Italians in the United States from the fifteenth century to the present are indicated. Another title by the author is *Vito Marcantonio: The People's Politician* (Dubuque, Iowa: Kendall/Hunt, 1969), for junior and senior high levels.

1386.   Lopreato, Joseph. **Italian Americans.** New York: Random House, 1970. 204p. $3.95pa. (9-12)
A study of Italian-American history, starting with the reasons for their immigration from Italy to America, their problems of adjustment and acceptance in their new home and society, and their unique cultural habits and institutions.

1387.   Mangano, Antonio. **Sons of Italy. A Social and Religious Study of the Italians in America.** New York: Missionary Education Movement of the United States & Canada, 1917; repr. ed., New York: J. S. Ozer, 1971. 234p. $11.50. (10-12)
A social and religious study of the Italians in America. Topics covered are Italian colonies in America compared to life in the Old Country; religious backgrounds, including a description of the Protestant churches as well as the Roman Catholic; the Italian American as a citizen; assimilation; and Italian contributions. Indexed.

1388. Mangione, Jerre. **America Is Also Italian**. New York: Putnam's, 1969.
126p. $3.49. (6-9)
A junior-high level history of Italian-American immigration and the problems of
adjustment, economic difficulties, and other experiences of the immigrants.
Characteristics of the Italians as a group and accomplishments of many individuals
are indi*ated.

1389. Mann, Arthur. **La Guardia**. New York: Lippincott, 1959. 384p. $6.50.
(7-12)
An interesting biography of Mayor Fiorella La Guardia who served three terms in
New York City in the 1930s and 1940s. His Italian-American background, family
life, and political career are covered.

1390. Mariano, John Horace. **The Italian Contribution to American Democracy**.
Boston, Mass.: The Christopher Publishing House, 1921; repr. ed., New
York: Arno, 1975. 317p. $19.00. (9-12)
Examines socioeconomic conditions of the Italians in America during the early
years of the twentieth century. Topics considered are population distribution,
occupations, health standards, child labor, housing conditions, immigration restrictions, literacy, citizenship, social welfare, Italian organizations, and group characteristics. The work is a revision of the author's dissertation at New York University in
1921. Another reprint by this author is *The Italian Immigrant and Our Courts*
(Arno, 1975; c1925).

1391. Marinacci, Barbara. **They Came from Italy: The Stories of Famous Italian
Americans**. New York: Dodd, 1967. 246p. $3.75. (6-9)
Nine biographical sketches of Italian Americans are presented with a brief chapter
on Italian-American history and emigration to the United States. Individuals
included are: Henri de Tonti, Philip Mazzei, Constantino Brumidi, Luigi Palmadi
Cesnola, Francesca Xavier Cabrini, Arturo Toscanini, A. P. Giannini, Fiorella
La Guardia, and Enrico Fermi. Bibliography provided.

1392. Militello, Pietro. **Italians in America**. Philadelphia, Pa.: Franklin
Publishing, Locust, 1973. 59p. $4.95. (9-12)
A brief study of the Italian-American community of Philadelphia, Pennsylvania.
The Italian-American heritage, traditions, customs, and social cohesiveness are
examined, as well as the economic trends and other traits of the group.

1393. Moquin, Wayne, and Charles Van Doren. **A Documentary History of the
Italian Americans**. New York: Praeger, 1974. 443p. $15.00; $4.95pa.
(9-12)
A collection of newspaper and journal articles, letters, and special papers to document the history of the Italian experience in the United States. Arrangement is
chronological from the days of Christopher Columbus on.

1394. Musmanno, Michael A. **The Story of the Italians in America**. New York:
Doubleday, 1965. 300p. $5.95. (7-12)
A study of the contributions of the Italians to American life and society. The
author, who was judge of the Pennsylvania Supreme Court at the time of this writing,

documents his text with pictures. He discusses the famous trial of two Italian Americans, Sacco and Vanzetti, for which he served as a defense counsel. Individuals mentioned range from Christopher Columbus to popular contemporary individuals in all walks of life, such as Joe DiMaggio.

1395.　Panunzio, Constantine M. **The Soul of an Immigrant.** New York: Macmillan, 1928; repr. ed., New York: Arno, 1969. 329p. $7.50. (9-12)
This autobiography of an Italian immigrant describes how he came to the United States, how he found his first job, his problems and unfortunate imprisonment, his struggles for an education, the naturalization and Americanization processes. The author feels that his story is more or less typical of that of Italian immigrants.

1396.　Rolle, Andrew F. **The Immigrant Upraised: Italian Adventurers and Colonists in an Expanding America.** Norman: University of Oklahoma Press, c1968, 1970. 391p. $6.95; $3.95pa. (10-12)
This study of the Italians in America covers those who settled in the Western territories during frontier and pioneer life. Another title by the author in a more general vein is *The American Italians: Their History and Culture* (Wadsworth, 1972. $3.95pa.).

1397.　Rose, Philip M. **The Italians in America.** New York: Doran, 1922; repr. ed., New York: Arno Press, 1975. 155p. $9.00. (7-12)
This study, undertaken to point out "the social, economic, and religious background" of the Italian-American immigrant community, is arranged in six main sections: 1) The Background in Italy; 2) Immigration and Economic Conditions of Italian Americans; 3) Social Conditions and Educational Forces among Italian Americans; 4) Religious Conditions among Italian Americans; 5) Problems of Religious Leadership; 6) Conclusions and Recommendations. Appendixes have statistics on settlement houses; a bibliography is included.

1398.　Sandler, Gilbert. **The Neighborhood.** Baltimore, Md.: Bodine, 1974. 93p. $5.95; $3.95pa. (10-12)
Relates the story of Baltimore's "Little Italy." Includes a history of the community, and examines the customs, traits, and acculturation of the various generations of the Italian immigrants who settled there.

1399.　Schiano, Anthony, and Anthony Burton. **Solo: Self-Portrait of an Undercover Cop.** New York: Dodd, 1973. 247p. $6.95. (7-12)
An American of Italian descent, Anthony Schiano, was once a member of the Italian gang, The Dukes, but he was later decorated by Mayor Lindsay with the Combat Cross for his work as a courageous and outstanding New York detective.

1400.　Schiavo, Giovanni Ermenegildo. **Italian-American History. Vol. I.** New York: Vigo, 1947; repr. ed., New York: Arno, 1975. 604p. $36.00. (9-12)
An anthology of three individual monographs. The first is a survey of Italian music and musicians in America from Colonial times; the second is a dictionary of musical biography; and the third is an in-depth treatment of Italian-American public officials in the United States from the seventeenth century to the mid-twentieth.

Volume II is entitled *The Italian Contribution to the Catholic Church in America* (Vigo, 1949; Arno, 1975. $64.00). Other studies by this author are *The Italian in America before the Civil War* (Arno, 1975, c1934. $23.00); *The Italians in Chicago: A Study in Americanization* (Arno, 1975, c1929. $15.00); *The Italians in Missouri* (New York: Arno, 1975, c1929. $14.00); and *Four Centuries of Italian American History* (Vigo, 1961. $25.00).

1401.   Shapp, Charles, and Martha Schapp. **Let's Find Out about Christopher Columbus.** New York: Watts, 1964. 44p. $3.90. (K-3)
The story of Christopher Columbus and his struggle to get his tiny fleet of three ships, The Nina, The Pinta, and the Santa Maria, across the ocean.

1402.   Tomasi, Lydio F., ed. **The Italians in America: The Progressive View, 1891-1914.** Staten Island, N.Y.: Center for Migration Studies of New York, 1972. 221p. $4.95. (11-12)
A collection of essays on a variety of topics covering the four million Italian immigrants who came to America between 1880 and 1915. Economic conditions, health and social welfare, jobs, politics, rate of assimilation, etc., are all discussed.

1403.   Tomasi, Silvano M., and Madeline H. Engel. **The Italian Experience in the United States.** Staten Island, N.Y.: Center for Migration Studies, 1970. 239p. $8.00; $4.95pa. (9-12)
A collection of essays that study Italian immigration and the experience of this group in America. Italian culture, customs, and problems of adjustment are covered. Emphasis on the post-war years. Studies the ethnic school and the Italian church as well as three generations of Italians in New York City.

1404.   Ulin, Richard Otis. **The Italo-American Student in the American Public School: A Description and Analysis of Differential Behavior.** New York: Arno, 1975. 201p. $15.00. (T)
A reprint of the author's doctoral thesis at Harvard University in 1958, this volume is a sociological study of acculturation among Italian-American public school students. School performance is studied, as are family patterns and the degree to which Old Country attitudes still affect the Italian-American child with respect to his education.

1405.   Williams, Phyllis H. **South Italian Folkways in Europe and America.** With an introduction by Francesco Cordasco. New Haven, Conn.: Yale University Press, 1938; repr. ed., New York: Russell & Russell, 1969. 216p. $8.50. (9-12)
Subtitled *A Handbook for Social Workers, Visiting Nurses, School Teachers, and Physicians*, this volume gives an account of the social, health, and welfare conditions among the Italian Americans in the 1920s and 1930s.

Literature and Fiction Titles

1406.   Angelo, Valenti. **Golden Gate.** New York: Viking Press, 1939; repr. ed., New York: Arno, 1975. 273p. $15.00. (5-9)
Nino, an Italian immigrant, is the hero of this story of what America represented

and was like to the immigrant in the early years of the twentieth century. Another title by the author is *Bells of Bleecker Street* (Viking, 1949), which is also a novel about a small boy living in the United States.

1407.   Benasutti, Marion. **No Steady Job for Papa.** New York: Vanguard, 1966. 243p. $7.95. (7-10)
This story centers around Rosemary, an Italian-American girl in Pennsylvania and her family. Papa and Mama were immigrants, and Papa found work where he could doing seasonal jobs. Rosemary has to help support the family and does so by working in the mills, writing, and eventually going to business college. It is a story of Italian community life, and it covers interactions with other groups, as Rosemary eventually marries a young Irishman.

1408.   Caruso, Joseph. **The Priest.** New York: Macmillan, 1956. 214p. $3.50. (9-12)
A story of Sicilians set in the Italian-American community of Boston's West End. Religious customs and behavior influenced by the Roman Catholic Church are portrayed.

1409.   Cimino, Maria. **The Disobedient Eels and Other Italian Tales.** Illus. by Claire Nivola. New York: Pantheon, 1971. unp. $3.50. (3-6)
A collection of 17 humorous short stories which make good individual reading, or popular storytelling material for teacher use. The illustrations give an Italian "Old Country" atmosphere.

1410.   D'Agostino, Guido. **Olives on the Apple Tree.** New York: Doubleday, 1940; repr. ed., New York: Arno, 1975. 302p. $17.00. (9-12)
A vivid description of Italian immigrant life in America is seen through the eyes of a young Italian. The process of assimilation is a major theme along with the conflicts in values, culture, and acceptance by the rest of the society. Other titles by the author are *Hills Beyond Manhattan* (Doubleday, 1942) and *My Enemy, the World* (Dial, 1947).

1411.   De Capite, Raymond. **A Lost King.** New York: McKay, 1962. 213p. $3.75. (9-12)
The story of an Italian-American boy growing up in the "Little Italy" of Cleveland, Ohio, where immigrants and their descendants worked as laborers. Another story by De Capite along the same vein is his *The Coming of Fabrizze* (McKay, 1960).

1412.   De Paola, Tomie, reteller. **Strega Nona.** Englewood Cliffs, N.J.: Prentice-Hall, 1975. unp. $6.95. (K-3)
An Italian folktale about a magic pasta pot which belongs to Strega Nona (grandmother witch). The magic pot makes enough pasta to feed the whole village, but when everyone is full the pot will not stop.

1413.   Di Donato, Pietro. **Christ in Concrete.** Indianapolis, Ind.: Bobbs-Merrill, c1939, 1975. 311p. $6.95; $3.95pa. (10-12)
Twelve-year-old Paul's father is killed when a building collapses, and Paul must follow in his father's steps as a bricklayer and support his mother and seven

younger brothers and sisters. The story is a picture of Italian-American construction workers—their customs, economic problems, and their religious piety. *Christ in Concrete* is a sequel to *Three Circles in Light* (Messner, 1960).

1414.   Forgione, Louis. **The River Between.** New York: Dutton, 1928; repr. ed., New York: Arno, 1975. 254p. $13.00. (9-12)
A story of immigrant life in an Italian settlement on the edge of the Palisades above the Hudson River. Oreste and his father, old Demetrio, who is slowly going blind, are prosperous Italian-American building contractors. Family relationships, problems of adjustment typical of the Italian immigrants, and the drive for success are all themes.

1415.   Granger, Peg. **After the Picnic.** New York: Lothrop, 1967. 159p. $4.95. (7-12)
A story of high school seniors and the indecision many of them face upon graduation. Dudley Anson's problem is complicated because of her interest in Rocco, an Italian-American boy, who is treated and thought of as a foreigner.

1416.   Hammontree, Marie. **Giannini: Boy of San Francisco.** Indianapolis, Ind.: Bobbs-Merrill, 1956. 192p. $3.50. (6-9)
Giannini is caught between two cultures, and as an Italian American he finds both comfort and embarrassment in the Old Country ways of his immigrant parents. This is a story of a youngster growing up and searching for values and identity.

1417.   Mangione, Jerre. **Mount Allegro.** Boston, Mass.: Houghton Mifflin, 1943; repr. ed., New York: Crown, 1972. 292p. $5.95. (7-12)
The author, of Sicilian descent, records the memories of his childhood in Rochester's "Little Italy," known as Mount Allegro. It is a warm, humorous collection of sketches and anecdotes on Italian social activities, education, and religion.

1418.   Pagano, Jo. **Golden Wedding.** New York: Random House, 1943; repr. ed., New York: Arno, 1975. 300p. $17.00. (9-12)
Traces the adventures of Luigi Simone from the little village in Italy from which he emigrated, to a mining community in Colorado, to Utah where he married Marcella, and finally to California, where he lives with his family when they celebrate their 50th wedding anniversary. According to the author, the history of Luigi's life was "the history of an era" and of many other Italian-American families. Other fiction by the author about Italians is a collection of short stories, *The Paisanos* (Little, Brown, 1940).

1419.   Panetta, George. **Shoeshine Boys.** Illus. by Joe Servello. New York: Grosset & Dunlap, 1971. 99p. $4.59. (3-6)
Tony Aoccaccio and his friend, MacDougal, enter into a business partnership shining shoes. This is a story of Italian-American young people. Another title for the elementary age group by the author is *Sea Beach Express* (Harper and Row, 1966. $4.43). For the older student the author has written *We Ride a White Donkey* (Harcourt, 1944).

1420.   Politi, Leo. **A Boat for Peppe**. New York: Scribner's, 1950. unp. $4.95.
         (K-3)
A picture book about a little Italian-American boy in California. Living among the
village fishermen, Peppe wants a boat of his own.

1421.   Puzo, Mario. **The Fortunate Pilgrim**. New York: Lancer, c1965, 1971.
         301p. $1.25pa. (9-12)
This tale of Italian immigrant life is also a portrayal of New York's West 30s in the
second quarter of the twentieth century. A picture of the Italian-Americans in the
underworld is the popular *The Godfather* (Fawcett World, 1973. $1.75pa.).

1422.   Ruddy, Anna C. (Christian McLeod, pseud.). **The Heart of the Stranger**:
         A Story of Little Italy. New York: F. H. Revell Co., 1908; repr. ed., New
         York: Arno, 1975. 221p. $13.00. (7-12)
The story of Anna Ruddy, who worked with Italian immigrant families in New
York and young people. She established The Home Garden for young Italians in
East Harlem in 1901. Her experiences, such as learning Italian to communicate with
these young people, are fictionalized in a series of sensitive portraits.

1423.   Villa, Silvo. **The Unbidden Guest**. New York: Macmillan, 1923; repr. ed.,
         Freeport, N.Y.: Books for Libraries, 1970. 282p. $11.25. (9-12)
Traces through brief sketches the life of an Italian boy, Carletto, who immigrates to
America. Many events in Italian history, as well as aspects of Italian-American
culture, are described within the narrative. Although he becomes wealthy and
successful in his new country, Carletto is always reminiscing about beautiful native
Italy.

Audiovisual Materials

1424.   **American Families: The de Stefanos**. 1 filmstrip, 1 phonodisc (or cassette),
         1 study guide. Coronet Instructional Films, 1971. (4-8)
Follows the daily activities of an Italian-American family and the customs of their
cultural heritage. The father is shown at his job, the mother in the home, and the
family is viewed together in the activities of a Sunday evening.

1425.   **Ghettos**. 1 filmstrip, 1 teacher's guide. Jones and Osmond; released by
         Modern Learning Aids, 1968. (3-6)
The first section of the filmstrip describes an Italian peasant family as they immigrate to the United States, the ocean journey in steerage, their entrance into Ellis
Island, New York, and their final settlement with the husband hunting a job. The
second section traces the activities of the mother living and providing for the family
in the ghetto while her husband is working in the West. Captions at the elementary
grade level are supplied.

1426.   **Italian Americans**. 1 Super 8mm film loop, 4 min. (silent), color. BFA .
         Educational Media. (5-9)
Four generations of Italian Americans from New York's "Little Italy" are

pictured in small family scenes during a traditional Sunday dinner gathering. Study questions are included.

1427.   **Italian Doesn't Mean Mafia: The Italian American.** 1 filmstrip, 1 cassette. Multi-Media Productions, Inc., 1972. (6-12)
From the *Accent on Ethnic America Series* this filmstrip is designed to give a positive view of the Italian-American ethnic group, with emphasis on their cultural heritage and contributions to American society.

1428.   **An Italian Family: Life on a Farm.** 16mm film, 21 min., sd., color. Encyclopaedia Britannica Educational Corp., 1975. $290.00. (3-9)
A good film for comparing the simple rural lifestyle of an Italian family in its native homeland with the large urban ghettoes where most Italian Americans have found employment and have made their New World homes.

JAPANESE AMERICANS

See also **Asian Americans.**

Reference Sources

1429.   Gefvert, R. H. **American Refugees: Outline of a Unit of Study about Japanese Americans.** Los Angeles: American Friends Service Committee. Committee on Educational Materials for Children, 1943. 59p.
A bibliography of materials for children in the elementary and secondary grades. A curriculum unit for studying the Japanese in the United States is included, but it is outdated. Entries in the bibliography are useful for historical materials and for materials on the treatment of the Japanese during World War II.

1430.   Herman, Masako, ed. **The Japanese in America, 1843-1973: A Chronology and Fact Book.** New York: Oceana, 1974. 152p. $6.00. (7-12)
A chronology of 130 years of the Japanese experience in the United States, emphasizing the immigrants and the World War II evacuation and relocation. Selected documents on those experiences and other events important in the history of the Japanese-Americans are included in the second section of the book. The various appendices contain census data, lists of relocation centers, Japanese-Americans and their World War II military service, prominent individuals in education, writers, Japanese-American newspapers and organizations, and a selected bibliography.

1431.   Ichioka, Yuji, *et al.*, comps. **A Buried Past: An Annotated Bibliography of the Japanese American Research Project Collection.** Berkeley: University of California Press, 1974. 227p. $10.00. (T)
A catalog of the UCLA Research Library's materials on Japanese immigration and history. Arrangement is by 18 subject categories, with an introductory historical summary in each division. Covers about 1,500 sources, including many government documents.

1432.   Matsuda, Mitsugu. **The Japanese in Hawaii: An Annotated Bibliography.**
Rev. ed. Honolulu: University Press of Hawaii, 1975. 320p. $6.00. (10-12, T)
This new edition has been revised and indexed by Dennis M. Ogawa and Jerry Y.
Fujioka. There are over 800 annotated entries of English titles, arranged by sub-
ject. Japanese titles also have annotations in English. An earlier bibliography by
the author is entitled *The Japanese in Hawaii, 1868-1967: A Bibliography of the
First Hundred Years* (University of Hawaii, 1968).

Teaching Methodology and Curriculum Materials

1433.   Fukuda, K., and T. Kashima. **A Guide for Teaching and Understanding
the History and Culture of Japanese Americans.** San Diego, Calif.: San
Diego Unified School District, 1972. price not indicated.
A guide for teaching the history and culture of Japanese Americans. A glossary of
terms, a bibliography, and statistical charts of Japanese-American population and
occupational trends are included.

1434.   Japanese American Citizens League. Advisory Council to the Ethnic
Heritage Project. **The Experience of Japanese Americans in the United
States: A Teacher Resource Manual.** San Francisco: Japanese-American
Citizens League, 1975. 191p. price not indicated. (T)
This instructional manual includes a history of the Japanese in America and a narrative of their contemporary experience in the United States. This section covers
immigration and anti-Japanese legislation and discrimination, the evacuation and
relocation with specific court cases related to it, contemporary social issues within
the Japanese community, Third World efforts and contributions, and many other
topics. The second section includes notes on instructional activities for the following grade levels: K-3, 4-6, 7-8, and 9-12. An annotated bibliography and an
annotated multi-media materials list follows. An annotated listing of resource
materials concludes the manual.

1435.   **Japanese and Japanese American Activities.** San Francisco: The Bay Area
Learning Center Teacher Learning Center and the Japanese American
Committee on Education, 1975. price not indicated. (K-8)
A curriculum guide for elementary and junior high school teachers. The guide is
divided into two parts: 1) Japanese cultural characteristics, with materials and
activities suggested for the K-6 grade level; 2) Japanese-American contributions,
history, and the contemporary issues, situation and interests. This study is designed
to cover the intermediate and early junior high school grades.

Non-Fiction Titles: History, Culture, Sociology, Biography

1436.   Bailey, Pearl. **City in the Sun.** Los Angeles: Westernlore Press, 1971. 222p.
$7.95. (9-12)
The city described here is Poston, Arizona, where a relocation camp for the
Japanese Americans living on the West Coast during World War II was established.

The social and economic status of the Japanese living on California's Terminal Island, Fish Harbor, is described, as well as the assembly center at the old Santa Anita race track, where the residents of this California community were temporarily housed.

1437.   Boddy, E. Manchester. **Japanese in America.** San Francisco: R&E
         Research Associates, 1970. (Repr. of 1921 ed.). 171p. $8.00. (7-12)
A discussion of the social and economic conditions of the Japanese, with 19 biographical sketches of first-generation Japanese immigrations and their contributions to the United States.

1438.   Bosworth, Allan R. **America's Concentration Camps.** New York: Norton,
         1967. 283p. $8.50. (9-12)
A discussion of the significance of the relocation, with reference to the fact that our laws still allow for a repetition of it. The roles of the Japanese Citizens League, the California press, and Lt. Gen. John L. De Witt are discussed. A chronology of the evacuation under the War Relocation Authority program, photographs, a bibliography, and an index are included.

1439.   Broek, Jacobus ten, Edward N. Barnhart, and Floyd W. Watson. **Prejudice,**
         War and the Constitution. Berkeley: University of California Press, 1954.
         408p. $7.50; $4.50pa. (9-12)
Part I presents the history of anti-Oriental sentiments on the West Coast; Part II is the complete record of the World War II evacuations from the exclusion areas. It also considers the constitutional dimension of this historic event. Part III deals with the role of the courts and discusses the basic questions of citizens' rights and war powers.

1440.   Conrat, Maisie, and Richard Conrat. **Executive Order 9066.** Cambridge,
         Mass.: MIT Press, 1972. 100p. $4.95pa. (6-12)
A photographic essay revealing anti-Japanese sentiments and the depths and diversity of emotions triggered by the order which authorized the evacuation of Japanese Americans from the West Coast military areas after the bombing of Pearl Harbor during World War II. Photographs are by Dorothea Lange.

1441.   Conroy, Hilary, and T. S. Miyakawa, eds. **East across the Pacific.** Santa
         Barbara, Calif.: ABC-Clio, 1972. 340p. $15.00. (9-12)
Japanese immigration and assimilation are examined in a collection of essays arranged in four general sections: Historical Essays—Hawaii and the Pacific Islands; Historical Essays—Mainland North America; From History to Sociology; and Sociological Essays.

1442.   Cross, Jennifer. **Justice Denied: A History of the Japanese in the United**
         States. New York: Scholastic Book Service, 1972. 128p. $2.00pa. (4-8)
One of the *Firebird Library* books on ethnic studies, this paperback discusses the problems and prejudices experienced by the Japanese Americans in the United States.

1443.   Daniels, Roger. **Concentration Camps USA: Japanese Americans and World War II.** New York: Holt, Rinehart & Winston, 1972. 188p. $5.59; $3.50pa. (9-12)
A discussion of the civilian, political, and military pressures that led to the decision for the World War II evacuation of the Japanese from their West Coast homes. Also describes the administration of the relocation program and discusses the constitutional legality of the order. A bibliographical note on sources and an index are included. Other titles discussing prejudicial treatment of Japanese Americans are the author's *The Politics of Prejudice* (Peter Smith, 1966. $2.95), and *The Decision to Relocate the Japanese Americans* (Lippincott, 1975. $3.25).

1444.   Dowdell, Dorothy, and Joseph Dowdell. **The Japanese Helped Build America.** New York: Messner, 1970. 96p. $4.79. (4-8)
Traces the experiences of the Sugimoto family, who emigrated from Japan to America in 1895. Their Pacific Ocean voyage, employment and social discrimination, family life, education, religious life, and observation of holidays and ceremonies are described.

1445.   Girdner, Audrie, and Anne Loftis. **The Great Betrayal: The Evolution of the Japanese Americans during World War II.** New York: Macmillan, 1969. 562p. $12.95. (9-12)
This reference source traces the history of the Japanese in America and the events preceding the World War II evacuation. The relocation and resettlement into society are also covered. A chapter entitled "Twenty-Five Years Later" attempts to assess the effects of the evacuation on the Japanese Americans of today. Attention is given to population, employment, education, intermarriage, and assimilation. Appendices contain documents and notices pertinent to the relocation. A bibliography and index are included.

1446.   Goldberg, George. **East Meets West.** New York: Harcourt Brace Jovanovich, 1970. 144p. $5.95. (7-12)
Traces the history of the Oriental in California, with special emphasis on the prejudice, exclusion laws, segregation, and World War II evacuation of the Japanese. Goldberg discusses the more complete assimilation of the Japanese (as compared to the Chinese) and the World War II evacuation and dispersed relocation.

1447.   Hosokawa, Bill. **Nisei: The Quiet Americans.** New York: Morrow, 1969. 522p. $10.95; $3.95pa. (7-12)
The author tells how and why the Japanese came to the United States, describes their treatment as a minority group, and emphasizes the impact of World War II on their experience. He discusses the relocation to internment camps after Pearl Harbor and the efforts of the Nisei to prove their loyalty to America. About 100 photographs document the text. Indexed.

1448.   Houston, Jeanne Wakatsuki, and James D. Houston. **Farewell to Manzanar.** New York: Houghton Mifflin, 1973. 192p. $5.95. (7-12)
The 25 years that have elapsed since her girlhood internment at Camp Manzanar have helped the author to understand the impact of that period on her life. This

first-hand account is a revealing picture of Japanese Americans' personal reactions to the enforced changes in their family roles and life styles, and how they increased racial tensions and prejudicial discrimination for them for many years.

1449. Ichihashi, Yamato. **Japanese in the United States.** Stanford, Calif.: Stanford University Press, 1932; repr. ed., New York: Arno Press, 1969. 426p. $13.00. (9-12)
Subtitled *A Critical Study of the Problems of the Japanese Immigrants and Their Children*, this volume studies assimilation, acculturation, and discrimination among the Japanese Americans prior to World War II. Another title by this author is *Japanese Immigration: Its Status in California* (Marshall Press, 1915; repr. ed., Ozer, 1971. $5.95).

1450. Inouye, Daniel. **Journey to Washington.** Englewood Cliffs, N.J.: Prentice-Hall, 1967. 297p. $5.95. (6-10)
An autobiography of Daniel Inouye and his family's immigration to Hawaii from Japan. Covers his childhood, his participation in World War II, and his political career as United States Senator from Hawaii.

1451. Ito, Kazuo. **Issei.** (English Edition). Seattle, Wash.: Japanese American Community Services, 1973. 987p. (7-12)
Biographical narrative of the Issei generation of Japanese in America, covering their immigration, their early days of pioneering, and discriminatory treatment. Personal accounts, Issei poetry, and a chronology of U.S.-Japan events are included.

1452. Japanese American Curriculum Project. **Japanese Americans: The Untold Story.** New York: Holt, Rinehart & Winston, 1971. 161p. $3.60. (3-6)
Traces the history of Japanese immigrants in the United States, telling of their contributions to the economy and culture. Also discusses the prejudice and repressive measures directed against the Japanese during World War II. Illustrated; bibliography included.

1453. Kitagawa, Daisuke. **Issei and Nisei: The Internment Years.** New York: Seabury Press, 1967. 174p. $3.95. (9-12, T)
A relocation center chaplain presents the problems of the Japanese Americans before, during, and after the World War II internment in temporary camps. He also discusses the roles of the church and other social agencies or citizens' committees in the Japanese experience. Personal vignettes and photographs help give the feeling and flavor of the Japanese-American community.

1454. Kitano, Harry L. **Japanese Americans: The Evolution of a Subculture.** Englewood Cliffs, N.J.: Prentice-Hall, 1969. 186p. $6.95; $3.95pa. (9-12)
Characteristics of three generations of the Japanese in America are examined (the Issei, Nisei, and Sansei generations) with emphasis on the experience of the Japanese in finding ways of adapting to conflict within their own ethnic group. The arrangement is chronological, with sections on pre-war, wartime, and post-war events. The achievements and contributions of the Japanese and their unique culture and institutions are also covered.

1455.   Leathers, Noel L. **Japanese in America.** Minneapolis, Minn.: Lerner Publications, 1967. 70p. $3.95. (5-11)
This history of Japanese immigration and experience in America emphasizes the effect of World War II on the lives of the Japanese Americans. It also stresses their great contributions in the fields of agriculture, industry, and the professions. Discrimination and prejudice against the group is discussed. Documented with photographs; indexed.

1456.   Mizumura, Kazue. **If I Were a Cricket.** New York: Crowell, 1973. 32p. $4.50. (K-3)
A primary science book with outstanding art. The author and illustrator is a Japanese American who has also written other primary titles with excellent learning content: *If I Built a Village* (Crowell, 1971. $4.50); *If I Were a Mother* (Crowell, 1973. $4.50).

1457.   Myer, Dillon S. **Uprooted Americans.** Tucson: The University of Arizona Press, 1971. 360p. $8.50; $5.95. (9-12)
Covers the historical background of the Japanese in the United States up to the World War II evacuation, life in the relocation centers, and the out-of-center relocation program. A summary chapter considers such topics as evacuee property, constitutional questions, court cases, and legal aspects, and provides a resume of crucial decisions made. Appendices contain final recommendations of the Western Defense Command, executive orders, public laws, documents, and statistics relevant to the evacuation and relocation.

1458.   Ogawa, Dennis, ed. **From Japs to Japanese: The Evolution of Japanese American Stereotypes.** Berkeley, Calif.: McCutchan Publishing Co., 1971. $1.75. (9-12)
Outlines the evolution of the image of the Japanese American from the negative "Jap" to a positive image of the Japanese ethnic group. Another title dealing with the Japanese in Hawaii is the author's *Jan Ken Po, the World of Hawaii's Japanese Americans* (Japanese American Research Center, 1974. $6.95).

1459.   Okimoto, Daniel I. **American in Disguise.** New York: Walker/Weatherhill, 1971. 206p. $7.50. (7-12)
The author of this personal narrative was born in the Santa Anita Assembly Center. Although he discusses the internment during World War II, he emphasizes the lifestyle and circumstances of the Japanese that made them so tolerant of discrimination, so compliant to military orders, and model internees. Foreword is by James Michener.

1460.   Petersen, William. **Japanese Americans.** New York: Random House, 1971. 268p. $3.95pa. (10-12)
This coverage of the Japanese experience in America concentrates on their cultural patterns and social relationships. Anti-Japanese laws and exclusionist policies serve as background to the section on the World War II internment. A bibliography of 260 entries on Japanese immigration and life in America is included; indexed.

1461.   Sagara, Peter. **Written on Film.** Chicago: Childrens Press, 1970. 64p.
         $2.25; $0.75pa. (4-8)
An autobiography of Peter Sagara, a Japanese-American. Emphasis is on the World
War II discrimination and enforced evacuation. A freelance photographer, Sagara
tells how he overcame problems and eventually owned his own studio and profitable
business.

1462.   San Mateo City School District. Japanese American Curriculum Project.
         "The Japanese Americans." **The Bay Leaf** (February 1970). (K-6)
This issue of *The Bay Leaf* gives an elementary level min-course on Japanese-
American contributions. It also includes articles on a Japanese-American festival
and explains Japanese terms and some vocabulary words.

1463.   Smith, Bradford. **Americans from Japan.** Philadelphia, Pa.: Lippincott,
         1948; repr. ed., Westport, Conn.: Greenwood, 1974. 409p. $16.75. (7-12)
This account of the Japanese in America is done in a popular, highly readable style.
It covers the Japanese in Hawaii on the various plantations, religious life, education,
the move to urbanization, racial tensions, and the effect of Pearl Harbor. The
second half of the book deals with the U.S. mainland, with much attention to the
World War II internment in relocation camps, as well as a general history.

1464.   Sone, Monica Ito. **Nisei Daughter.** Boston, Mass.: Little, Brown, 1953.
         238p. $6.95. (6-12)
An autobiographical narrative of life divided between two cultures. Six-year-old
Monica comes to terms with the fact that she is Japanese and different from her
other friends in America. She relates attending Japanese language class after public
school, and when Pearl Harbor is attacked her family's life in a relocation camp is
described. She paints a revealing picture of the Japanese-American character, culture,
and sentiments through this story of her childhood, college years, and young
adulthood.

1465.   Thomas, Dorothy Swaine. **The Salvage.** Berkeley: The University of
         California Press, c1952, 1975. 637p. $22.50. (9-12)
Sequel to *The Spoilage*, published in 1946. "Salvage" refers to the Japanese Americans who migrated from the War Relocation Centers to the Midwest or East during
1943 and 1944 to resettle and improve their social and economic status. Official
evacuee censuses, transcripts of transfers and permits, participant observation, and
interviews with resettlers in the Chicago area provide primary data. A statistical
appendix with 29 tables, an index, and a glossary are included.

1466.   Thomas, Dorothy Swaine, and Richard S. Nishimota. **The Spoilage.**
         Berkeley: The University of California Press, c1946, 1969, 1974. 388p.
         $14.25; $2.45pa. (9-12, T)
An analysis of changes in behavior and attitudes of Japanese Americans at certain
relocation centers during World War II. This first volume analyzes the experiences
of the Issei and the Nisei generations who relinquished citizenship to return to
Japan (termed the "spoilage"). "The Life History of a 'Disloyal,' " a subject index,
and a name index are included.

1467.   Tobias, Tobi. **Isamu Noguchi, the Life of a Sculptor**. New York: Crowell, 1974. 42p. $5.95. (3-6)
The life and struggles of Isamu Noguchi, a Japanese-American sculptor, are described. The details of his career give insights into the world of modern art as well.

Literature and Fiction Titles

1468.   Bonham, Frank. **The Burma Rifles: A Story of Merrill's Marauders**. New York: Crowell, 1960. 260p. $4.95. (6-10)
A Nisei soldier, who volunteered for the army after being evacuated from his California home to an internment camp, is determined to show his loyalty to America. Working for the army's language school, he is shipped to India to become one of the famous Merrill's Marauders. Another title by the author is *Mystery in Little Tokyo* (New York: Dutton, 1966. 125p. $5.95. 3-7).

1469.   Buck, Pearl. **The Hidden Flower**. New York: John Day, 1952. 308p. $1.50pa. (7-12)
A Japanese war-bride married to an American of Virginia aristocracy realizes that family rejection and cultural conflicts make her marriage impossible. When she returns to Japan she leaves her small son with an American woman, a doctor.

1470.   Cavanna, Betty. **Jenny Kimura**. New York: Morrow, 1964. 224p. $4.75. (5-10)
When a Japanese girl comes all the way from Japan to visit her Japanese-American grandmother in the United States she has mixed feelings about her two cultural heritages.

1471.   Charyn, Jerome. **American Scrapbook**. New York: Viking, 1969. 177p. $4.95. (10-12)
A novel that reveals the effects of the relocation of the Japanese Americans. The story is about the Tanaka family; the format is designed so that each of the six members of the family narrates a separate chapter.

1472.   Christopher, Matt. **Shortstop from Tokyo**. Illus. by Harvey Kidder. Boston, Mass.: Little, Brown, 1970. 121p. $4.50. (4-6)
A baseball story of conflict and the aspirations of two players, one a Japanese-American boy, in securing the exciting shortstop position on the team.

1473.   Haugaard, Kay. **Myeko's Gift**. Illus. by Dora Ternsi. New York: Abelard-Schuman, 1966. 160p. $3.95. (3-7)
A story of a young girl from Japan, her reactions to life in the United States, the problems of adjusting to her new American school and finding new friends.

1474.   Hawkinson, Lucy Ozone. **Dance, Dance Amy-Chan!** Chicago: Albert Whitman, 1964. unp. $3.95. (K-3)
Story and pictures depict a Japanese-American folk festival celebration where the young children can learn the traditional dances of Japan and also find out more about the history of their cultural heritage.

1475.   Irwin, Wallace. **Letters of a Japanese Schoolboy.** New York: Doubleday, 1909; repr. ed., New York: Gregg, 1969. 370p. $13.50. (9-12)
A collection of letters that relate a Japanese immigrant's sometimes naive, and often humorous, experiences and impressions of America.

1476.   Lewis, Richard, ed. **In a Spring Garden.** Illus. by Ezra Jack Keats. New York: Dial, 1965. 32p. $4.95. (4-8)
A collection of haiku poems all describing a day in spring from the early morning to an evening goodnight from a firefly.

1477.   Means, Florence Crannell. **The Moved Outers.** Boston, Mass.: Houghton Mifflin, 1945. 154p. $5.95. (7-9)
A novel of the discriminatory treatment given to Japanese Americans during World War II, this is the story of Sue Cordova and her family. It relates the fear, shock, bitterness, and confusion of a young teenager who is popular in school. She is one day a member of a respected business-owning family, and the next worrying about her father's arrest and confiscation of the family's property. Her reactions to and experiences during relocation in a camp for the war duration are also a part of the narrative.

1478.   Okada, John. **No-No Boy.** Rutland, Vt.: Charles E. Tuttle, 1957. 308p. $4.75. (7-12)
A young Nisei's strong feelings of Japanese nationalism made him refuse the draft into the U.S. Army. After release from prison camp after the war, he is rejected by the community. This is the story of his struggle for acceptance.

1479.   Politi, Leo. **Mieko.** Illus. by the author. San Carlos, Calif.: Golden Gate, 1969. unp. $4.79. (3-7)
A revealing picture of the Japanese traditions that are still practiced in the Japanese community of Los Angeles is given in this story of Mieko, a Nisei girl. She works very hard to learn all about the Japanese ceremonies and traditional arts in order to surprise her parents by winning the title of Queen of the Ondo Parade.

1480.   **Sojourner IV.** Berkeley, Calif.: Berkeley High School Asian Writer Project, 1974. 152p. $2.50pa. (9-12)
Stories, poems, drawings, and photographs by students and parents dealing with the experience of the Japanese Americans. A section on American women of Asian background is also included.

1481.   Sugimoto, E. I. **A Daughter of the Samurai.** New York: Doubleday, 1926; repr. ed., Rutland, Vt.: Charles E. Tuttle, 1966. 314p. $8.95. (7-12)
This is the story of a daughter of the Samurai of feudal Japan who came to America and had to transcend hundreds of years of change in one generation to fit into Japanese-American life and culture.

1482.   Uchida, Yoshiko. **The Birthday Visitor.** Illus. by Charles Robinson. New York: Scribner's, 1975. 30p. $5.95. (2-4)
A picture book with watercolors adding the flavor and atmosphere of the

Japanese-American community. It tells the story of a Japanese family in the 1930s and of little Emi's seventh birthday.

1483. Uchida, Yoshiko. **Journey to Topaz.** New York: Scribner's, 1971. 149p. $5.95. (5-10)
This novel is based on the author's experiences living in a World War II Relocation Center in Topaz, Arizona. She relates the horrors of evacuation, and the fears, resentments, material losses, and inconveniences suffered by the Japanese Americans through the eyes of 11-year-old Yuki, as well as the fun, new friends, and excitement that children found in the situation.

1484. Uchida, Yoshiko. **The Promised Year.** New York: Harcourt, Brace & Co., 1959. 192p. $6.50. (4-6)
Keiko visits her Japanese-American aunt and uncle for a year. Coming from Japan, she is faced with many problems of adjustment, and the story of her experiences tells the reader something about the attitudes and problems faced by the Japanese in the United States. Other titles for this middle grade level are the author's *Magic Listening Cap; More Folk Tales from Japan* (Harcourt, 1955. $1.25pa.); *Mik and the Prowler* (Harcourt, 1960); and *New Friends for Susan* (Scribner's, 1951).

1485. Uchida, Yoshiko. **Samurai of Gold Hill.** Illus. by Ati Forberg. New York: Scribner's, 1972. 119p. $5.95. (5-8)
The Wakamatsu Colony was established in Gold Hill, California, by a small group of Japanese Americans. This story of Koichi, a Japanese immigrant of the late nineteenth century, shows the prejudices, oppressions, and problems the group experience. Japanese customs, religious ceremonies, festivals and arts, and contributions to American agriculture are told.

1486. Yashima, Mitsu, and Taor Yashima. **Momo's Kitten.** New York: Viking, 1961. 33p. $3.50. (K-3)
Momo is a little Japanese-American girl who finds and befriends a small kitten. When the kitten grows up, it becomes the mother of five more small kittens. Another picture book by the author is *Umbrella* (Viking, 1958. $4.95; $0.95pa.), in which Momo gets an umbrella for a birthday present and can't wait for rain so she can use it.

1487. Yoshida, Jim, and Bill Hosokawa. **The Two Worlds of Jim Yoshida.** New York: Morrow, 1972. 256p. $6.95. (8-12)
A Japanese-American boy returned to Japan to visit and while there was drafted into the Japanese army. When he eventually returned to the U.S., he wanted to regain his American citizenship so badly that he served with the U.S. forces in Korea. He contrasts his life in America and Japan in a fictionalized autobiography of his two life styles and cultures. He describes the customs that have become a part of the Japanese-American community.

Audiovisual Materials

1488. **Cane Camp**. 16mm film, 20 min., color. William J. Sollner. Released by Solfilm International, 1972. (5-12)
Describes the Japanese immigrants who came to work in the sugar cane industry in Hawaii during the nineteenth century. Their contributions to America's fiftieth state are emphasized.

1489. **Children of the Inner City**. 6 filmstrips, 3 records (or cassettes), 1 teacher's guide. Society for Visual Education, 1970. $49.50; $55.00 (with cassettes). (2-6)
Six groups are covered in this series of ethnic cultures in the inner city. The title that deals with the Japanese is *Cynthia: Japanese American Girl*. It covers home, school, religious, and community activities through a series of photographs, which attempt to present everyday life of the members of the Japanese-American community.

1490. **East/West Activities Kit**. Multimedia kit. Visual Communications. $5.00. (4-12)
This kit includes four large work sheets with 12 different activities, games, poetry, language, etc. A teacher's guide is included for inclusion of this kit into the curriculum unit studying Japanese Americans.

1491. **Fence at Minidoka**. 16mm film, 30 min. KOMO Television, Seattle, Washington. free. (4-12)
The World War II camp at Minidoka, Idaho, is visited by a third-generation Japanese-American television reporter. The film is available through the Public Affairs Manager, KOMO TV, 100 Fourth Ave. North, Seattle, Washington 98109. The film is loaned free for the cost of the postage.

1492. **Grandma Lives in Our House**. 16mm film, 9 min., color. King Screen Productions, 1970. (5-10)
Japanese-American family structure and roles are depicted through the activities of a young girl and her grandmother. Other members of the family—brothers, sisters, parents, and grandparents—are also introduced.

1493. **Guilty by Reason of Race**. 16mm film, 51 min., color. NBC Educational Enterprises, 1972. $500.00; $25.00 (rental). (6-12)
This TV documentary on the Japanese-American community traces the history of their prejudicial treatment and resulting experiences in America, such as the World War II evacuation and relocation. The constitutional rights of the Japanese Americans are under scrutiny in this report.

1494. **Haiku: The Mood of Earth**. 2 filmstrips, 2 phonodiscs (or cassettes). Lyceum, 1971. $33.00; $36.00 (with cassettes). (4-8)
Examples of haiku poetry accompanied by beautiful photographs. Narration is based on the book by Ann Atwood. Excellent teaching activity for studying Japan and Japanese Americans in social science or language and literature curriculum units.

1495.   **Issei, Nisei, Sansei.** 16mm film, 30 min., b&w. New Jersey Public Broadcasting. $250.00; $30.00 (rental). (7-12)
A documentary for television on the Japanese American community of Seabrook, New Jersey.

1496.   **Issei: The First Fifty Years.** 16mm film, 17 min., b&w. Asian American Studies Center. $133.00; $30.00 (rental plus $3.00 postage). (7-12)
A chronicle of the exploitation of the Japanese immigrants known as the Issei generation. A teacher's manual is also available for using this film on the secondary level.

1497.   **The Japanese American.** 16mm film, 30 min., color, with study guide. Handel Film Corp., 1974. $30.00 (rental). (6-12)
Describes the Japanese ethnic group in the United States and gives a history of U.S.-Japanese relations. Covers discriminatory treatment and the World War II relocation of Japanese-American citizens, outstanding achievements in business, agriculture, and other enterprises.

1498.   **The Japanese American Experience.** Slide presentation. Ms. Amy Uno Ishii, 1801 North Dillion St., Los Angeles, California 90026.
A slide presentation on the evacuation and internment during World War II is available for rent from the above person. For persons in the Los Angeles area a guest classroom speaker is available to provide a personal account of life in the relocation centers.

1499.   **Japanese American Relocation, 1942.** Multi-media kit. Olcott Forward, Inc., 1970. $65.00. (3-8)
This kit includes two filmstrips (black and white) and one 33 1/3 rpm record, a teacher's guide, pre-printed spirit masters, picture cards, and reading books. It is adaptable for various elementary grade levels. It is a documentary portrayal of the evacuation of the Japanese-Americans from their West Coast homes during World War II to remain in relocation centers throughout the duration of the war. It describes the effects of this procedure on the individuals and on the Japanese community, as well as on the Japanese image. Events leading to the government's decision to relocate the Japanese are also summarized.

1500.   **JACL Workshop I: The Japanese in America.** Multimedia kit. Prod. by Don Estes, San Diego, JACL Headquarters and Visual Communications, 1974. Price varies.
This kit was produced in a workshop under the auspices of the Japanese American Citizen's League. It includes a research guide, the historical outline, a slide presentation, and an annotated bibliography on the experience of the Japanese in the United States. Another title by the same producer is *JACL Workshop II: The Camp Experience*, which contains a chronology of the evacuation, a research guide, a slide presentation, a bibliography, and maps of the various relocation camp sites.

1501.   **Japanese Americans: An Inside Look.** 2 filmstrips, 1 record (or cassette), teacher's guide. Japanese American Curriculum Project in cooperation with Multi-Media Productions, 1973. $17.95; $19.95 (with cassette). (4-8)

Describes the exploitation of the Japanese minority group in the United States as compared to that of the Blacks, Mexican Americans, and American Indians. Concepts on racism, prejudice, and citizenship are explained. The teacher's manual indicates methods of incorporating these materials into the curriculum at various grade levels.

1502. **Japanese-Americans and Chinese-Americans.** 1 filmstrip, 1 phonodisc (33 1/3 rpm), teacher's guide. Warren Schloat Productions, 1968. (4-8)
Problems of adjustment and assimilation of the Japanese and Chinese in American life are examined. Prejudices and discriminatory treatment are shown as part of the struggle by these groups for acceptance into American society.

1503. **Japanese Folk and Fairy Tales.** Record (or cassette). CMS, 1967. $5.95; $7.95 (cassette). (4-8)
Some of the more popular Japanese folk and fairy tales are narrated by Christine Price. Titles include: "Urashima," "The Miraculous Tea-Kettle," and "Momotaro, Son of the Peach."

1504. **Just Like Me.** 16mm film, 8 min., color. Oakland Unified School District (Oakland, California). (K-6)
A film designed to prompt children to consider their individual differences and to value their individuality, instead of treating someone who is different with prejudice and discrimination.

1505. **Manzanar.** 16mm film, 15 min., color. Visual Communications. $200.00; $25.00 (rental). (6-12)
This autobiographical account of a man who lived in the relocation center as a boy describes his feelings, experiences, conditions, and the atmosphere of the camp.

1506. **Minority Youth: Akira.** 16mm film, 15 min., color. Stuart Roe. Released by BFA Educational Media, 1971. $195.00; $7.00 (rental). (5-12)
A Japanese-American boy is the subject of this film. He explains how it feels to be a part of the Japanese culture and community and yet also live daily in American society. Japanese customs and traditions are revealed in his narration.

1507. **Nisei: The Pride and the Shame.** 16mm film, 30 min., b&w. CBS News. Available from the Japanese American Citizens League, 1965. $150.00; $10.00 plus postage (rental). (7-12)
Originally part of the CBS "20th Century" series narrated by Walter Cronkite, the film gives an overview of the evacuation from the West Coast during World War II and relocation in camps. Recounts the motivations for the decision to relocate the Japanese and Japanese-Americans and their experiences and reactions to it.

1508. **Prejudice in America: The Japanese Americans.** 4 filmstrips, 2 records (or cassettes). Multi-Media Productions, 1972. $29.90; $33.90 (with cassette). (9-12)
Winner of the 1972 Award of the ALA, this set traces the history of anti-Japanese sentiments in the United States by studying the way various American institutions

reacted to the Japanese Americans during World War II and how they used their influence to help or discriminate against them.

1509.   **Rainbow Origami.** Kit. Yasutomo & Co. $2.50. (4-12)
This kit includes varying sizes of origami sheets in 10 colors, with 113 sheets per package. It includes easy directions for beginners, with full illustrations and samples. An outstanding activity for a unit on the Japanese American history, culture, art, etc.

1510.   **Relocation of Japanese-Americans: Historical Background.** Multimedia kit. Zenger Productions, released by Social Studies School Service, 1971. (6-12)
This kit includes a black and white filmstrip, one record, guide, and study prints with materials written by Harry Kitano of the Japanese-American community. It traces the Japanese immigrants' adjustment to American life, the discriminatory treatment and prejudices they experienced, and their successful economic and agricultural enterprises.

1511.   **Relocation of Japanese Americans: Right or Wrong?** Multimedia kit. Zenger Productions; available from Japanese American Citizens League. $29.00; $31.00 (with cassettes). (5-10)
These two filmstrips by Dr. Harry Kitano are accompanied by two records (or cassettes), 10 documentary 11x14-inch photographs, and a teacher's guide. They question the legality and morality of the World War II evacuation and relocation of the Japanese-American citizens. Also includes the government's explanation for the decision in light of wartime hysteria.

1512.   **Tales from Japan.** 8 sound filmstrips, 8 phonodiscs (or cassettes). Coronet, 1971. $60.00; $80.00 (with cassettes). (K-6)
Folk tales new and old are told through puppets, paper sculptures, and collages, with a background of Japanese music. Each is introduced with haiku poetry. They provide an excellent source for materials that give the flavor of Japanese art, literature, and culture.

1513.   **Traditional Folk Dances of Japan.** 1 record. Folkways, 1952. $7.95. (5-9)
The music recorded here includes traditional Bon dance festival tunes, Buddhist ritual chants, legends and stories about animals.

1514.   **Urashima Taro: A Japanese Folktale.** Filmstrip, record (or cassette). Guidance Associates, 1971. $16.00; $18.00 (with cassette). (3-6)
The story of Taro, a young fisherman who rescues a tortoise and is invited to visit the Dragon-King, is accompanied by Japanese koto music.

1515.   **Wataridori: Birds of Passage.** 16mm film, 30 min., color. Visual Communications. $400.00; $25.00 (rental). (6-12)
Portrays the present and past experiences of three surviving first-generation, or Issei, Japanese immigrants. Their accounts provide a picture of the early Japanese in the United States—their sentiments and feelings about their new country and their status there.

JEWISH AMERICANS

Reference Sources

1516.   **The American Jewish Experience: A Graded, Annotated Bibliography for Grades 7-12.** Part Two. Cleveland, Ohio: Educational Research Council of America, 1972. 23p. $0.50. (T)
An annotated bibliography of titles recommended by the Educational Research Council of America and the American Association of Jewish Education on the Jews in America. Materials selected stress the Jewish cultural heritage as well as the experience of this group in the United States. Materials are for the junior high and senior high levels and indicate the specific grade level (7-12).

1517.   **American Jewish Year Book.** New York: The Jewish Publication Society of America, 1900– . $13.95. (6-12, T)
The Jews in the United States and other countries are covered in this annual publication. In the United States, articles appear under the following section headings: Civic and Political; Communal; Demographic. A section of special articles includes "Library Resources for Jewish Studies in the United States" (Volume 75). Included also are lists of Jewish organizations in the United States and other countries, and Jewish communities in other countries. The yearbook also features obituaries and directories, periodicals and monthly calendars with Jewish holidays, sabbaths, festivals, and feasts indicated. Indexed. Indispensable reference work.

1518.   Anti-Defamation League of B'nai B'rith. **Teaching about Jews and Judaism: Bibliographic and Audio-Visual Aids.** New York: Anti-Defamation League of B'nai B'rith, n.d. free. (T)
A bibliography of print and non-print materials arranged in the following categories: American History; Anti-Semitism; World History; Geography and Current Events; Israel; Religion and Culture; Literature.

1519.   **Encyclopaedia Judaica.** New York: Macmillan, 1972. 16 vols. $500.00. (4-12, T)
An illustrated encyclopedia of over 25,000 articles plus maps, charts, tables, and diagrams. It gives comprehensive coverage of the Jewish history and experience in America. Emphasis is on problems and achievements of the Jews as well. Detailed bibliographies are appended to the articles.

1520.   **Encyclopedia of Zionism and Israel.** Edited by Raphael Patai. New York: Herzl Press/McGraw-Hill, 1971. 2 vols. $39.50.
Emphasis is on Israel, from the second half of the nineteenth century to the present. Extensive coverage is also given to Zionism. Contains approximately 3,000 signed articles.

1521.   Goldberg, Mark. **Jewish Studies in the Secondary School: Materials and Sources, 1881-1917: The Great Migration.** Stony Brook, N.Y.: State University of New York, Stony Brook, 1972. 17p. $0.65 MF; $3.29 (ED 058143). (7-12, T)

An annotated bibliography of sources on a variety of disciplines, including history, sociology, short stories, novels, essays, letters, reportage, etc., on all aspects of Jewish immigration and experience in America, particularly New York City, where the largest Jewish community exists. All of the printed sources are contained in the New York City Public Library and most are available on interlibrary loan. Materials selected are appropriate for use at the secondary level (junior and senior high school grades).

1522.   Marcus, Jacob R. **An Index to Scientific Articles on American Jewish History**. New York: KTAV, 1971. 240p. $17.50. (9-12, T)
An author, title, and subject index to 13 major publications on American Jewish history in effect from 1884-1968. English-language publications indexed include *American Jewish Year Book* and *Jewish Quarterly Review*, among others.

1523.   National Council on Jewish Audio-Visual Materials. **The Jewish Audio-Visual Review**. New York: American Association for Jewish Education, 1973. (T)
Films on Jewish history and culture are described in this filmography, arranged by subject. Categories include Jewish history, religion, festivals, ethnic studies, and others.

1524.   Rosenbloom, Joseph R. **A Biographical Dictionary of Early American Jews: Colonial Times through 1800**. Lexington: University of Kentucky Press, 1960. 175p. $10.00. (6-12, T)
A reference tool for studying the early period of American Jewish history. The author estimates that approximately 80 percent of Jews in America before 1800 are included in this alphabetical arrangement of biographical descriptions.

1525.   Schlesinger, Benjamin. **The Jewish Family: A Survey and Annotated Bibliography**. Toronto, Canada: University of Toronto Press, 1971. 175p. $7.50. (T)
Fiction and non-fiction references depicting Jewish family life are presented. Includes publishers and addresses.

1526.   Sloan, Irving J., ed. **The Jews in America 1621-1970: A Chronology and Fact Book**. Dobbs Ferry, N.Y.: Oceana Press, 1971. 151p. $6.00. (7-12)
About one-third of this third volume in the *Ethnic Chronology Series* is devoted to a historical chronology of the Jewish-American experience. Pertinent documents are another major section, and the appendices contain a selected bibliography, population statistics (by state), audio materials, a list of Jewish organizations, and American Jewish newspapers and periodicals.

1527.   **Who's Who in World Jewry**. 3rd ed. by I. Carmin Karpman. New York: Pitman, 1972. 999p. $45.00. (6-12, T)
A biographical dictionary of over 10,000 biographical sketches of prominent Jews in America and other countries. Data include name, country of residence, place of origin, date of birth, education, achievements, publications.

Teaching Methodology and Curriculum Materials

1528. Mersand, Joseph, and Elie Wiesel. **Teachers' Study Guide: Jewish Legends. The Image of the Jew in Literature.** New York: B'nai B'rith, 1969. 29p. free. (T)
Excerpts from a lecture on Jewish legends are followed by suggestions for classroom activities; discussion topics related to the study of Jewish legend are included. A four-week model instructional unit for the 12th grade is presented.

1529. Ruderman, Jerome. **Jews in American History: A Teacher's Guide.** New York: Anti-Defamation League of B'nai B'rith, 1974. 224p. $5.00. (T)
A guide for teaching a curriculum unit on Jews in the United States at the secondary level. Attention is given to Jewish history and experience.

Non-Fiction Titles: History, Culture, Sociology, Biography

1530. Alofsin, Dorothy. **America's Triumph: Stories of American Jewish Heroes.** Illus. by Louis Kabrin. New York: Books for Libraries, 1949. 312p. $15.25. (7-12)
A collection of short biographical sketches and incidents involving Jewish history and contributions in America.

1531. Baron, Salo W. **Steeled by Adversity: Essays & Addresses on American Jewish Life.** New York: Jewish Publication Society of America, 1971. 729p. $9.00. (11-12, T)
A chronological arrangement of articles in three sections: "Gradual Unfolding, 1654-1879"; "Climax of Immigration, United States 1880-1914"; "Twentieth Century Problems." One chapter is entitled "Cultural Pluralism of American Jewry." Indexed.

1532. Butwin, Frances. **The Jews in America.** Minneapolis, Minn.: Lerner Publications, 1969. 107p. $3.95. (5-11)
Describes the Jewish experience in America from the earliest colonists to the present. Causes for emigration from various areas of Europe, the major Jewish communities of New York, and brief biographical sketches are presented. Prominent Jews in the fields of science, arts, music, theater, literature, government, business, and industry are indicated.

1533. Chyet, Stanley F., ed. **Lives & Voices: A Collection of American Jewish Memoirs.** Philadelphia, Pa.: Jewish Publication Society of America, 1972. 388p. $6.50. (7-12, T)
A popular, readable collection of memoirs from the American Jewish Archives, containing: "Prelude to America," "Con Brio," "Deep in the Heart of Texas," "A Hoosier Rabbinate," "A Philadelphia Childhood," "The End of an Era," "Father Was a Rabbi," "Anchors Aweigh," "From Rovno to Dorchester." Indexed.

1534. David, Jay (pseud.). **Growing Up Jewish.** Edited by Bill Adler. New York: Pocket Books, div. of Simon and Schuster, 1969. 341p. $0.95pa. (7-12)

A collection of personal narratives describing the Jewish customs and traditions observed among Jewish religious, social, and educational groups in the United States. Incidents related range from immigrant problems to the advantages of the rich Jewish cultural heritage.

1535.   Doroshkin, Milton. **Yiddish in America: Social & Cultural Foundations.**
         Rutherford, N.J.: Fairleigh Dickinson, 1970. 281p. $12.00. (10-12)
In this social history the author attempts to define the term Jew; he also examines the restratified Jewish community as the working class decreased, studies the early immigrants and Eastern European immigration, and the development of Yiddish language and literature. Other major sections discuss the social role of the Yiddish press and Jewish organizations. The appendixes list immigration statistics, newspaper circulations, and organizational memberships. Includes an extensive bibliography; indexed.

1536.   Fast, Howard. **Haym Salomon: Son of Liberty.** New York: Julian Messner,
         c1941, 1968. 243p. $4.79. (7-12)
A fictionalized biography of a Jewish immigrant from Poland and the role he played in the American Revolution. Another title by the author is *The Jews: Story of a People* (Dial, 1969. $7.50).

1537.   Feingold, Henry L. **Zion in America.** New York: Twayne, 1974. 357p.
         $5.95pa. (9-12)
A summary of the Jewish experience in America from Colonial times to the present. Chapters discuss the Old World background, the Jewish role in the colonial economy, the Revolution, politics, labor, and foreign affairs. Other topics covered are the German Jews, East European Jews, Reform Judaism, Zionism, Jewish organizations, World War II, and the American Jewish condition in the 1970s. Bibliography and index included.

1538.   Fishman, Priscilla, ed. **The Jews of the United States.** New York:
         Quadrangle/The New York Times Book Co., 1973. 302p. $8.95. (9-12)
Describes the three main waves of Jewish immigration and how these new Jewish Americans affected the domestic history of the United States. The arrangement is chronological and covers many topics in great detail, such as the largest Jewish community in history in New York, Jewish organizations and religious institutions, labor unions, and the Jewish role and image in literature. Current trends and philosophies in the Jewish-American community are also examined.

1539.   Gartner, Lloyd P., ed. **Jewish Education in the United States.** New York:
         Teachers College, 1970. 224p. $6.95; $2.75pa. (11-12, T)
A collection of essays on the Jewish educational experience in the United States from the late 1700s to the early 1960s. Gartner's introduction includes a bibliographic essay on sources of research in the area.

1540.   Gilbert, Arthur, and Oscar Tracov. **Your Neighbor Celebrates.** New York:
         KTAV, 1957. 118p. $4.00. (3-8)
The origin of American Jewish holidays and the way they are celebrated is presented with particular emphasis on customs involving Jewish children. A glossary of Hebrew words is included, as well as numerous full-page photographs.

1541.   Glanz, Rudolf. **Studies in Judaica Americana**. New York: KTAV, 1970.
         407p. $16.95. (9-12, T)
Jewish immigration, Jewish economic trends (particularly peddling), community
histories, Jews in literature, early American humor, and social conditions are among
the topics covered in this collection of essays on the German Jew in the United
States. Other titles by the author are *The Jew in Early American Wit and Graphic
Humor* (KTAV, 1973. $15.00); *The Jew in Old American Folklore* (KTAV, 1961.
$10.00); *The Jewish Female in America: Two Female Generations, 1820-1929*,
Vol. 1 (KTAV, 1970. $15.00).

1542.   Glazer, Nathan. **American Judaism**. Rev. ed. Chicago: University of
         Chicago Press, 1972. 210p. $7.95. (10-12, T)
An excellent presentation of a chronological history of American Judaism from
1654 to the 1960s. Covers the German and East European immigrations, Jewish
American religion, Reform and Conservative Judaism, the Jewish revival, and
Jewish religious institutions. Indexed.

1543.   Golden, Harry, and Richard Goldhurst. **Travels through Jewish America**.
         New York: Doubleday, 1973. 276p. $7.95. (9-12)
An overview of the Jewish American ethnic communities in Cleveland; Hartford;
Pittsburgh; New York; Charleston, West Virginia; Savannah; Waltham,
Massachusetts; Chicago; Los Angeles; and St. Louis. Covers immigrant life,
politics, religion, economics, education, and a variety of other topics. Presented
in a popular style, the work gives both the history and the flavor of Jewish culture
and life.

1544.   Goldhurst, Richard. **America Is Also Jewish**. Illus. by Judith Leeds. New
         York: Putnam's, 1972. 128p. $3.64. (6-12)
A warm and colorful account of the Jewish-American experience in the United
States. It covers historical aspects and includes quotations from famous
Jewish-Americans.

1545.   Goldstein, Sidney, and Calvin Goldscheider. **Jewish Americans: Three
         Generations in a Jewish Community**. Englewood Cliffs, N.J.: Prentice-
         Hall, 1968. 274p. $3.95pa. ED 061394. (9-12)
Studies assimilation and acculturation in the Jewish community of Providence,
Rhode Island, as they are related to social change and generation change. Also
gives a general overview of Jewish migration to America and a demographic and
sociological analysis of population growth and composition, distribution, migration,
fertility, mortality, family structure, socioeconomic status, and religious identification. Research methods used are described in the appendix.

1546.   Gordon, Albert I. **Jews in Suburbia**. Boston, Mass.: Beacon Press, 1959;
         repr. ed., Westport, Conn.: Greenwood, 1973. 264p. $12.00. (10-12)
Describes how the advent of the suburbs has affected Jewish life in America (and
vice versa). Specific Jewish-American communities are described from data
collected as well as the author's impressions.

1547.   Handlin, Oscar. **American Jews: Their Story**. New York: Anti-Defamation
         League, 1966. 48p. (5-10)
A brief pictorial history of the Jewish experience and contributions to United
States history and culture.

1548.   Heitzmann, William R. **American Jewish Voting Behavior: A History and
         Analysis**. San Francisco: R&E Research Associates, 1975. 121p. $8.00.
         (10-12)
An interpretation of voting research conducted in this attempt to record the history
and analyze the political activity of Jews in the United States.

1549.   Janowsky, Oscar I., ed. **American Jew**. New York: Harper and Row, 1942;
         repr. ed., Freeport, N.Y.: Books for Libraries, 1973. 322p. $13.25. (9-12)
A composite portrait of the cultural, economic, religious, and educational life of
American Jews. Covers anti-Semitism, Jewish-American history, Zionism, and
contacts outside the Jewish community. Janowsky also wrote *The American Jew:
A Reappraisal* (Jewish Publication Society of America, 1964. $6.00); and *The
Education of American Jewish Teachers* (Beacon Press, 1967. $8.50).

1550.   Kahn, Roger. **The Passionate People: What It Means to be a Jew in America**.
         New York: International Publications Service, 1969. 350p. $7.50. (9-12)
A description of the Jewish-American identity through brief character sketches
(based on interviews) and short historical episodes. The book covers Jewish religion,
philanthropy, and scholarship, and discusses the disproportionate number of Jews
in the professions, arts, law, entertainment, medicine, education, and publishing.

1551.   Karp, Abraham. **The Jewish Experience in America**. New York: KTAV,
         1969. 5 vols. $59.50. (9-12, T)
A chronological arrangement of the Jewish history and experience in America.
Volume titles are: Vol. I, *The Colonial Period*; Vol. II, *In the Early Republic*;
Vol. III, *The Emerging Community*; Vol. IV, *The Era of Immigration*; Vol. V,
At Home in America. Articles by outstanding scholars of American Jewish historiog-
raphy were selected from the *Publications of the American Jewish Historical Society*
and arranged, edited, and introduced by Mr. Karp. Illustrations and index in each
volume.

1552.   Karp, Deborah. **Heroes of American Jewish History**. New York: KTAV,
         1972. 155p. $4.75. (5-12)
Post-Biblical Jewish thought and history are surveyed. The work includes biographical sketches of prominent writers and philosophers, along with quotations from
some of their writings. The book contains many photographs, a glossary of terms,
and an index.

1553.   Kripke, Dorothy K. **Let's Talk about the Jewish Holidays**. Illus. by Naomi
         Kitov. New York: Jonathan David Publishers, 1970. 52p. $3.95. (K-4)
Describes eleven different Jewish holidays including two seldom covered: Independence Day and Tisha B'Av. Includes background history.

1554.   Kurtis, Arlene H. **The Jews Helped Build America**. New York: Messner,
          1970. 95p. $4.64. (4-6)
A fictitious Russian Jewish family is described in order to present the history of
Jewish immigration, assimilation, and acculturation in the United States. Family
life, occupational trends, and the Jewish ethnic community customs are
emphasized. Contributions to American life are also discussed.

1555.   Leonard, Oscar. **Americans All**. Illus. by Ellen Simon. New York: Behrman
          House, 1944. 232p. $4.50. (4-8)
Benny is told by his grandfather of the Jews' role in the discovery and development
of America.

1556.   Levine, Naomi, and Martin Hochbaum. **Poor Jews: An American Awaken-
          ing**. New Brunswick, N.J.: Transaction Books, 1974. 206p. $12.95;
          $3.95pa. (10-12)
These essays give a different picture of the Jews than the typical one of a middle
and upper-middle class affluent group. Another image of Jews is portrayed in
these writings dealing with Jews, urban poverty, and a lower socioeconomic stratum
of American society.

1557.   Levinger, Lee J. **History of the Jews in the United States**. New York:
          Union of American Hebrew Congregations, c1961, 1970. 570p. $4.90
          textbook; $1.75 workbook. (6-10)
A junior high school history textbook of the history and experience of the Jews in
the United States. Covers Jews who came to America as colonists and their contributions to the development of the nation. Also discusses the later waves of immigration, Judaism, Jewish organizations, anti-Semitism, and post-World War II trends
among American Jews in education, labor, defense and other aspects of American
culture.

1558.   Lotz, Philip H., ed. **Distinguished American Jews**. New York: Association
          Press, 1945; repr. ed., Freeport, N.Y.: Books for Libraries, 1970. 107p.
          $9.00. (7-12)
A collection of biographical sketches about prominent Jews in various walks of
life. Music, nursing, military, religion, writing, acting, and other vocations and
professions are represented.

1559.   Madison, Charles A. **Eminent American Jews: 1776 to the Present**. New
          York: Ungar, 1971. 460p. $10.00. (10-12)
Fifteen Jewish Americans are presented in these biographical sketches. Personalities
chosen are from business, science, medicine, law, journalism, labor, and politics,
covering a span of almost 200 years of American history.

1560.   Meltzer, Milton. **Remember the Days: A Short History of the Jewish
          American**. New York: Doubleday, 1974. 114p. $3.95; $1.75pa. (9-12)
A history of Jews in America from their arrival during Colonial days to the post-
World War II immigration of Eastern European Jews. Also discusses Zionism,
Jewish militants, anti-Semitism and outstanding Jewish philanthropy.

1561.   Ribalow, Harold U., ed. **Autobiographies of American Jews.** Philadelphia,
         Pa.: Jewish Publication Society, 1965. 496p. $6.00. (7-12)
These memoirs cover the period from 1880 to 1920, during which the Jewish
American community underwent many changes. The autobiographical sketches
include descriptions of Jewish-American communities, Zionism, Jewish unions,
rabbinical careers, lives of Jewish writers, the assimilation process, and other
topics.

1562.   Rieger, Shay. **Our Family.** New York: Lothrop, 1972. 64p. $5.95. (5-12)
The author's illustrations and photos of her sculptures portray the life and experience of her Jewish immigrant relatives, who came to the United States just before
the turn of the century. Family life and customs of the Jewish-American community are depicted.

1563.   Rosen, Bernard Carl. **Adolescence and Religion: The Jewish Teenager in
         American Society.** Cambridge, Mass.: Schenkman, 1965. 203p. $4.95.
         (9-12, T)
A study of Jewish identity and the move of Jewish-American adolescents away from
a fairly homogeneous group to one of greater variety as they increase contact with
non-Jews. The author differentiates between abandonment of an ethnic custom or
behavior pattern and a change in attitude or values. Emphasis is on Jewish youth
with respect to religious practices and values.

1564.   Sanders, Ronald. **The Downtown Jews: Portraits of an Immigrant Genera-
         tion.** New York: Harper and Row, 1969. 477p. $10.00. (9-12)
Politics, including socialist and anarchist ideologies, labor unions, the Yiddish press
and language, and the theater are among the topics presented in this description of
Jewish-American life in Manhattan's Lower East Side. Another title by the author
is *Reflections on a Teapot, a Personal History of a Time* (Harper and Row, 1972).

1565.   Schappes, Morris U., ed. **Documentary History of the Jews in the United
         States.** New York: Schocken Books, 1971. 766p. $6.95. (9-12)
This collection of documents is arranged chronologically to present a history of the
Jews in America. The writings reflect both how the Jews lived and thought of them-
selves, and how the contemporary non-Jews thought and wrote about them.

1566.   Schoener, Allon. **Portal to America: The Lower East Side, 1870-1925.**
         New York: Holt, Rinehart & Winston, 1967. 256p. $5.95pa. (9-12)
Old photographs and correspondence from the early Jewish press in New York
describe the life of the Jewish immigrant. His daily life, living conditions, typical
methods and types of employment, and adjustment to America are included.

1567.   Selzer, Michael, ed. **Kike: Anthology of Anti-Semitism.** New York: New
         American Library, 1972. 231p. $3.95pa. (9-12)
A collection of writings that trace the development of anti-Semitism in the United
States from the early days of the Dutch colonials to the present. Anti-Semitism in
legislation, politics, and social institutions is covered.

1568.   Shapp, Martha, and Charles Shapp. **Let's Find Out about Jewish Holidays.**
        Illus. by Marvin Friedman. New York: Watts, 1971. 48p. $3.90. (K-3)
Jewish holidays and ceremonies are described, including Sabbath, Simchath,
Torah, Rosh Hashanah, Yom Kippur, Succoth, Hanukkah, Purim, Passover, and
others.

1569.   Sklare, Marshall. **America's Jews.** New York: Random House, 1971.
        234p. $3.95. (9-12)
Includes a social history of Jews as an American ethnic group including social and
demographic characteristics, family roles and relationships. The study of the Jewish
community emphasizes typical community and social services; Jewish education is
also examined. Concluding chapters discuss intermarriage, and relations with Israel.
Indexed. These patterns are explored to a greater degree in *Jews: Social Patterns
of an American Group* (Free Press, 1958. $10.95). Other titles by the author are
The Jew in American Society (Behrman House, 1974. $12.50) and *Jewish Commun-
ity in America* (Behrman House, 1974. $12.50).

1570.   Strober, Gerald S. **American Jews—Community in Crisis.** New York:
        Doubleday, 1974. 297p. $7.95. (10-12)
An outline of the problems faced by the American Jewish community, as well as
an evaluation of the strengths and weaknesses it possesses. Both domestic and
international problems are considered, and an analysis of the Jewish community
of the future is projected.

1571.   Suhl, Yuri. **An Album of the Jews in America.** New York: Watts, 1972.
        89p. $4.95. (4-9)
Traces Jewish immigration to America and concentrates on the contributions of the
Jewish communities in America. The Jewish experience is covered, including
discrimination and other problems. Includes a list of prominent twentieth century
Jewish Americans with accompanying photographs.

1572.   Walden, Daniel, ed. **On Being Jewish: American Jewish Writers from
        Cohan to Bellow.** Greenwich, Conn.: Fawcett World Publications, 1974.
        480p. $1.75pa. (9-12)
A collection of writings on Jews in America and the American Jewish experience.
Some are sad and thought-provoking, some extremely funny, but all reflect the
Jewish immigrant's hopes, dreams, and problems, or those of his descendants.
Commentary by the editor is provided.

1573.   Washington Post Company and Stephen D. Isaacs. **Jews and American
        Politics.** New York: Doubleday, 1974. 302p. $8.95. (10-12)
A history of Jews in American politics in a popular, readable style based on interviews with Jewish-American scholars and politically involved Jews. The Jew as a
radical, a liberal, an intellectual, a financial contributor, and a voter is discussed.
Bibliography included; indexed. A similar but more advanced monograph on the
same topic was written by Nathaniel Weyl, *The Jew in American Politics* (New
Rochelle, N.Y.: Arlington House, 1968. 375p. $6.95).

Literature and Fiction Titles

1574. Asch, Sholem. **The Mother.** New York: Horace Liveright, 1930; repr. ed.,
        New York: AMS Press, 1970. 351p. $8.75. (7-12)
The color and atmosphere of Jewish immigrant life is caught in this story of a
family from Poland. This sentimental novel describes the mother as the center of
the family's life. After her death they are lost, but eventually the older daughter
returns to help raise the younger children.

1575. Cahan, Abraham. **The Rise of David Levinsky.** New York: Harper and
        Row, 1917. 529p. $4.45. (9-12)
The story of a 20-year-old Jewish immigrant from Russia who studied the Talmud
in Jewish seminary before becoming a peddler in a New York ghetto. His struggles
to obtain success portray the problems of the immigrants.

1576. Chapman, Abraham, ed. **Jewish-American Literature: An Anthology.** New
        York: New American Library, 1974. 727p. $1.95. (7-12, T)
The literature of American Jews is included in this anthology of fiction, poetry,
autobiography, and criticism. Includes all writers of Jewish or partially Jewish
descent.

1577. Cohen, Barbara. **The Carp in the Bathtub.** Illus. by Joan Halpern. New
        York: Lothrop, 1972, 1975(pa.). 48p. $4.59; $0.75pa. (2-4)
Two Jewish children try to keep alive the carp their mother buys to make gefilte
fish for Passover. They keep the fish in the bathtub until it is time to prepare the
special holiday dishes. This is a story of Jewish family life set in New York during
the 1930s.

1578. Cone, Molly. **A Promise Is a Promise.** Illus. by John Gritzer. Boston,
        Mass.: Houghton Mifflin, 1964. 153p. $5.95. (7-9)
Ruthy feels left out when her family is the only one in their neighborhood without
Christmas decorations. A neighbor helps her to accept her Jewish heritage and
identity. Other titles by the author for the primary grades are *Purim* (Crowell,
1967. $4.95); *Stories of Jewish Symbols* (Bloch, 1975. $3.50); *Jewish Sabbath*
(Crowell, 1966. $4.95); and a biography of a famous Jewish-American, *Leonard
Bernstein* (Crowell, 1970. $4.50).

1579. Fineman, Irving. **Hear, Ye Sons!** New York: Longmans, Green & Co.,
        1933; repr. ed., New York: Arno Press, 1975. 306p. $19.00. (9-12)
A portrait of a successful Jewish immigrant who, as a senior citizen, relates the
story of life in the Jewish ghettos of two countries, Poland and America. His
story gives the reader insights into the Jewish heritage and tradition, family customs
and values.

1580. Gerson, Corrine. **The Closed Circle.** New York: Funk & Wagnalls, 1968.
        122p. $3.50. (3-7)
A sixth-grade girl experiences prejudice and rejection in a Pennsylvania school and
community. But gradually the other girls are helped to include persons of different

ethnic or religious backgrounds. Description of a Chanukah party provides insights into Jewish family and cultural life.

1581.   Gold, Michael. **Jews without Money.** Woodcuts by Howard Simon. New York: Liveright Books, 1930; repr. ed., New York: Avon Books, 1968. 309p. $0.95pa.
A classic collection of short stories about Jews and Jewish-American culture, family life, and customs. Most are set on the East Side of New York City.

1582.   Grossman, Mort. **The Summer Ends Too Soon.** Philadelphia, Pa.: Westminster Press, 1975. 159p. $5.50. (6-12)
The story of Diane, a Gentile girl and Marc, a Jewish boy, and the conflicts, negative reactions, and prejudices they encounter as a result of their romance.

1583.   Hample, Stoo. **Blood for Holly Warner.** New York: Harper and Row, 1967. 187p. $3.79. (7-10)
A Jewish teenager, Howie Coleman, experiences anti-Semitic discrimination and learns to accept the Jewish identity of his ethnic heritage. He also begins to appreciate the struggles and problems of his parents and to accept them as people in their own right.

1584.   Konigsburg, E. L. **About the B'nai Bagels.** New York: Atheneum, 1969, 1973. 172p. $5.50; $0.95pa. (3-7)
The story of a Jewish American family with two sons, twelve-year-old Mark, and Spencer, a junior in college. Family activities, Jewish holidays and customs, and a mother who becomes involved in Little League baseball are all a part of the story.

1585.   Lewiton, Mina. **Rachel and Herman.** Pictures by Howard Simon. New York: Watts, 1957. 202p. $3.45. (4-8)
A Jewish family in New York moves from Downtown to Uptown and the children must adjust to a new school, new teacher, new public library, and new friends. Uncle Boris from Chernovinsk adds excitement to their activities.

1586.   Little, Jean. **Kate.** New York: Harper and Row, 1971. 162p. $4.95; $1.25pa. (5-8)
A story of Jewish family life and the problems a young Jewish American girl has in accepting and understanding her Jewish identity.

1587.   Madison, Winifred. **Becky's Horse.** New York: Four Winds, 1975. 152p. $5.95. (4-8)
A pre-World War II story of a Jewish-American family. The family worries about the persecution of their European relatives. The children, self-consciousness over their mother's foreign accent and other problems, are typical of many ethnic or immigrant groups. Another title by the author is *Max's Wonderful Delicatessen* (Little, Brown, 1972. $5.95).

1588.   Malamud, Bernard. **The Assistant.** New York: Farrar, 1957. 246p. $6.95; $2.25pa. (9-12)

260 / Jewish Americans

The assistant is second-in-command in a Jewish family's grocery store. The story is set in New York's Jewish ghetto. The family has many economic and other problems. The only son dies, and the store is losing money because the assistant is stealing. When the owner dies, the assistant takes over the store. Other Jewish novels by the author and this publisher are *The Fixer* (1966. $6.95; $1.25pa.); *The Malamud Reader* (1967. $6.95); and *Pictures of Fidelman* (Simon & Schuster, 1969, 1975. $1.75pa.).

1589.   Moskin, Marietta. **Waiting for Mama.** Illus. by Richard Lebenson. New York: Coward, 1975. 91p. $5.95. (3-5)
Becky, the seven-year-old daughter in a Jewish immigrant family, describes their voyage to the United States, their worries and problems of adjustment living in New York, and the tension that builds as they wait for Mama to be allowed to join them from Russia.

1590.   Neville, Emily Cheney. **Berries Goodman.** New York: Harper and Row, 1965. 178p. $5.50; $1.50 pa. (5-9)
A family story of anti-Semitic feelings, prejudices, discrimination, and hostility experienced by children in a New York Jewish community.

1591.   Potok, Chaim. **My Name Is Asher Lev.** Greenwich, Conn.: Fawcett World, 1972. 369p. $7.95; $1.95pa. (8-12)
Asher Lev is born of a Hasidic heritage in Brooklyn. With talents and aspirations to become an outstanding painter, he is faced with the Hasidic rejection of the worth of the artist and he is torn between his gift and his cultural heritage.

1592.   Ross, Leonard Q. **The Education of Hyman Kaplan.** New York: Harcourt, 1937; repr. ed., Harcourt, 1968. 144p. $0.75pa.
A New York City night class in Americanization is the setting of this Jewish-American novel about Hyman Kaplan. A series of humorous sketches deal with his efforts to speak the English language correctly. An additional collection of stories is found in *Return of Hyman Kaplan* (Harper and Row, 1949; $10.00).

1593.   Sachs, Marilyn. **Peter and Veronica.** Illus. by Louis Glanzman. Garden City, N.Y.: Doubleday, 1969. 174p. $4.50. (4-7)
Peter, a Jewish American boy, wants his parents to allow him to invite his Gentile friend, Veronica, to his Bar Mitzvah. This is not only a story of a Jewish family and their customs, but a story of growing up and early boy-girl relationships.

1594.   Schecter, Ben. **Someplace Else.** New York: Harper and Row, 1971. 167p. $4.50. (3-6)
Although the writing style is a little slow-moving for this age level, the story is concerned with many aspects of Jewish-American family life and religious traditions in this story of a pre-teenaged boy.

1595.   Segal, Lore. **Tell Me a Mitzi.** Illus. by Harriet Pincus. New York: Farrar, Straus & Giroux, 1970. 40p. $4.95. (K-3)
The adventures of Mitzi and Jacob are the basis of this story of a Jewish-American

family. Highlights of the book are Mitzi's secret plan to visit her Grandma, and baby brother Jacob's role in stopping the president's parade.

1596.   Suhl, Yuri. **Eloquent Crusader: Ernestine Rose.** New York: Messner, 1970. 191p. $3.50. (7-12)
The story of Ernestine Rose, a crusader against anti-Semitism in Europe and America. She also was active in the battle against slavery in the South and in the early days of the women's movement in the North.

1597.   Taylor, Sydney. **All-of-a-Kind Family.** Illus. by Helen John. Chicago: Follett, 1951. 188p. $4.95. (4-6)
The all-of-a-kind family refers to five daughters of a Jewish-American family as they grow up in a Jewish ghetto on New York's East Side. Other books in the series are *All-of-a-Kind Family Downtown* (1972); *All-of-a-Kind Family Uptown* (1958); and *More All-of-a-Kind Family* (1954). The titles also picture Jewish family and religious customs and festivals.

1598.   Tobenkin, Elias. **Witte Arrives.** New York: Frederick A. Stokes Co., 1916; repr. ed., Upper Saddle River, N.J.: Gregg, 1969. 304p. $9.50. (9-12)
The story of young Emil, a Russian-Jew who has emigrated with his family from Russia. The process of adjustment and acculturation is described as the story unfolds and traces Witte's experiences working his way through high school and the university. He becomes a reporter in Chicago, marries a Gentile girl, and is forced into intimate interaction with non-Jewish American society.

Audiovisual Materials

1599.   **Albert Einstein.** Filmstrip, with accompanying script. New York, Jewish Education Committee of New York. $7.50. (4-9)
The story of Albert Einstein and the historical events of his life-time as well as his contributions to American society.

1600.   **America—I Love You.** 16mm film, 30 min., b&w. Israel Broadcasting Service. Made and released in the U.S. by Shalom Productions, 1973. (7-12)
An English-language documentary about Jews in America—subtitles are in Hebrew. Interviews and compares two families, one of which is a Jewish-American family that has been assimilated into American life and society.

1601.   **American Families: The Mandels.** 1 filmstrip, 1 phonodisc (or cassette). Coronet Instructional Films, 1971. (4-8)
This is a story of a family of Jewish descent. Their daily activities and lifestyle are described, with emphasis on Sabbath Eve celebrations, the father's job, and the children's community project.

1602.   **An American Girl.** 16mm film, 28 min., b&w. Prod. by Dynamic Films, 1958. Distr. by Macmillan. $165.00; $10.00 (rental). (5-12)

A young American girl experiences and exposes the racial prejudice and anti-Semitism of the members of her small home town.

1603.　**The American Jew.** 140 color slides, 1 cassette. TR Productions; distr. by American Jewish Historical Society. $12.50 (rental). (6-12)
An overview of Jewish American history from the first immigrants to contemporary times.

1604.　**Between Two Eternities.** 16mm film, 30 min., b&w. Distributed by the National Academy for Adult Jewish Studies of the United Synagogue of America. $8.50 (rental). (6-12)
A biographical presentation of the life of Solomon Schecter—teacher, scholar, and one of the most influential leaders in the development of Conservative Judaism in the United States.

1605.　**The Gift.** 16mm film, 30 min., b&w. Distributed by the National Academy for Adult Jewish Studies of the United Synagogue of America. (7-12)
A biographical narrative of the life of Judah Touro, an outstanding religious figure in the Jewish American community. Points out how Touro liberated his slave and discusses the meaning and various aspects of freedom.

1606.　**The Golden Years.** 16mm film, 14 min. Sponsored and distributed by the Federation of Jewish Philanthropies of New York. (9-12)
An outstanding example of Jewish philanthropical activity and concern with social problems, this film tells the story of a senior citizen, a tailor who was unemployed but still able to make a contribution to society. Describes the function of a workshop vocational center operated for elderly handicapped men and women by an employment and guidance agency connected with the Federation of Jewish Philanthropies of New York.

1607.　**Hasidim (Lubavitch-Chabad).** 16mm film, 29 min., color. Applause Productions. Released by Vedo Films, 1972. (6-12)
Describes the New York Hasidic community with emphasis on its history, practices, and ceremonies. Special religious customs and traditions are also apparent. A discussion of why the Hasidim have survived, grown, and influenced other Jews is also included.

1608.　**Isaac Mayer Wise: Master Builder of American Judaism.** 1 filmstrip. Produced and distributed by the Commission on Jewish Education, Union of American Hebrew Congregations. $7.50. (4-9)
The life story of a famous religious leader and his efforts on behalf of Reform Judaism in America. His struggles, outstanding incidents, and his successful establishment of major religious institutions are indicated.

1609.　**Jewish Americans.** Super 8mm film loop, 4 min., color. Ealing Corp., 1970. (5-12)
The story centers around a woman from the suburbs who goes into the Jewish ghetto of the city to visit her parents. Family life, customs, traditions, values stressing education, and other Jewish-American trends are indicated other than religious ties.

1610. **The Jews in America.** 2 filmstrips. Produced and distributed by the Jewish Education Committee of New York. $7.50 each. (6-9)
These filmstrips provide a history of the Jewish experience in America, with emphasis on the arrival of the first Jewish immigrants, their role in the Revolutionary War, the Westward movement to California, Jewish participation in the Civil War, the later immigrations from Eastern Europe, and the establishment of Jewish religious, social, and educational institutions. Describes Jewish cultural contributions to American society and communal activities in the American Jewish community.

1611. **Jews in America.** 2 filmstrips, 1 record (or cassette). Anti-Defamation League of B'nai B'rith, 1974. $35.00; $40.00 (with cassette). (5-8)
Tells the story of the Jews in America, with emphasis on their immigration and early experience and contributions. Their later interaction with the American Indians and the Blacks as a minority group is described. The struggles and achievements, history and values are all included in these two titles: Part I, *The Ingathering*; Part II, *Inside the Golden Door.*

1612. **My Name Is Asher Lev.** 1 cassette. Voice Over Books. $6.95. (7-12)
A dramatization of the novel by Chaim Potok about a Jewish painter who is a member of the Orthodox Jewish faith. Jerry Orbach does the narration of this story which is a revealing portrait of Jewish life within the Orthodox community.

1613. **The Pugnacious Sailing Master.** 16mm film, 30 min., b&w. Distributed by the National Academy for Adult Jewish Studies of the United Synagogue of America. $8.50 (rental). (7-12)
A biographical presentation of the life of Uriah P. Levy, a Jewish American whose influence and activity brought about abolition of corporal punishment in the United States Navy. The film is also a good springboard for a discussion of anti-Semitism.

1614. **The Question of Life.** 16mm film, 30 min., color. WKYC-TV, 1974. (7-12)
The life style and customs of a Jewish immigrant from Russia are compared to his way of life in the Old Country. Also discusses problems of the Jewish-American community, and the process of adjustment and assimilation.

1615. **Rabbi Stephen S. Wise: A Twentieth Century Prophet.** 1 filmstrip, 1 record. Sponsored and distributed by the Commission on Jewish Education, Union of American Hebrew Congregations. $7.50 (filmstrip); $2.00 (record). (5-8)
A series of highlights from the life of Rabbi Wise, a leader in the American Jewish community in the areas of religion, Zionism, and culture. Rabbi Wise is also indicated as an active leader in social reform against social problems and evils.

1616. **Rendezvous with Freedom.** 16mm film, 37 min., color. ABC-TV. Released by Macmillan Films, 1974. (6-12)
The immigration and history of Jews in the United States from the days of the earliest settlers to their response to the social issues of today.

1617. **Shtetl to Suburb: The American Jew.** 1 filmstrip, 1 cassette. Multi-Media Productions, 1972. (4-8)

A filmstrip from the *Accent on Ethnic America Series* describing the Jewish experience in the United States and including problems and contributions.

1618.   **300 Years: Memorable Events in American Jewish History.** 1 filmstrip, 1 record. Distributed by the Commission on Jewish Education, Union of American Hebrew Congregations. $7.50 (filmstrip); $2.50 (record). (5-8)

A history of the Jewish-American community in America with emphasis on religious institutions and the participation of the Jews in westward expansion through settlement and exploration.

1619.   **To Be As One.** 16mm film, 31 min., b&w. Distributed by Jewish Center Lecture Bureau, National Jewish Welfare Board. $15.00 (rental). (6-12)

An insight into the Jewish-American community is given through this description of the Jewish Community Center program program's history and activities.

1620.   **Verdict on Survival.** 16mm film, 10 min., color. United Jewish Welfare Fund. Made by Robert Story Productions. Released by Jewish Federation-Council of Greater Los Angeles, 1971. (6-12)

Although it is a fund-raising film for the United Jewish Welfare Fund, this film describes some of the problems of Jews in Los Angeles and some of the issues of concern to them and to Jews all over the world. A major emphasis of the film is the problem posed by the Soviet intervention in the Middle East as it affects the nation of Israel.

KOREAN AMERICANS

See also **Asian Americans.**

Reference Sources

1621.   Gardner, Arthur L. **The Koreans in Hawaii: An Annotated Bibliography.** Honolulu: University of Hawaii Press, 1970. 83p. $3.50pa. (9-12, T)

An annotated bibliography of published and unpublished books, writings, biographies, autobiographies, poetry, etc. Titles are in Korean, but annotations are in English.

1622.   Kim, Hyung-chan, and Wayne Patterson, comps. and eds. **The Koreans in America 1882-1974: A Chronology & Fact Book.** Dobbs Ferry, N.Y.: Oceana, 1974. 147p. $6.00. (6-9)

A ready-reference fact book in three main sections: chronology, documents, bibliography. The chronology indicates significant dates and events in the Korean-American experience in the United States. Documents included deal with Korean-American history, immigration, and the role of the church in America. The selected bibliography is of a very limited nature. Name index included.

Teaching Methodology and Curriculum Materials

1623. Lee, Peter H. **Korean Literature, Topics and Themes.** New York: American Council of Learned Societies, 1965. 152p. $6.08. (11-12, T)
A text developed for the U.S. Office of Education to study Korean prose and poetry. It includes a comparative chronology of Korean and Western literary figures and events, a glossary, bibliographies, and indexes.

Non-Fiction Titles: History, Culture, Sociology, Biography

1624. Buck, Pearl. **Welcome Child.** New York: John Day, 1963. 96p. $3.95. (K-3)
A personal photographic narrative of a young Korean girl who is adopted by an American family. She describes how it feels to be in an alien culture and how she adjusts during the process of acculturation.

1625. Givens, Helen L. **The Korean Community in Los Angeles.** San Francisco: R&E Research Associates, 1974. 60p. $7.00. (10-12)
This reprint of the author's 1939 thesis is a study of the Korean Americans in Los Angeles, California. Emphasis is on the Korean's part in community life.

1626. Johnson, Doris. **Su An.** Chicago: Follett, 1968. 30p. $3.95. (4-12)
A Korean orphan adopted by an American couple describes her feelings and experiences.

1627. Kang, Younghill. **East Goes West.** New York: Scribner's, 1937. 401p. (7-12)
An autobiographical account of the author's arrival in America and his adjustment to life in America and Western living.

1628. Koh, Kwang Lim. **Koreans and Korean-Americans in the United States.** New Haven, Conn.: East Rock Press, 1974. 137p. $5.00. (9-12)
Summarizes three conference proceedings (1971-1973) held at Central Connecticut State College at the Center for Area and Interdisciplinary Studies on Koreans and Korean-Americans. The subjects included "Problems and Perspectives of Koreans and Korean-Americans" and "Korean Tradition in American Context."

1629. Lee, Don Chang. **Acculturation of Korean Residents in Georgia.** San Francisco: R&E Research Associates, 1975. 91p. $8.00. (10-12)
Describes the acculturation and Americanization of Koreans in a Korean community in Georgia. Also provides a history of the group and their socioeconomic experience in the United States.

Literature and Fiction Titles

1630. Baron, Virginia Olsen, adapt. **Sunset in a Spider Web: Sijo Poetry of Ancient Korea.** New York: Holt, 1974. unp. $4.95. (4-12)
Sijo poems are different from the haiku, which is so often introduced into the school

curriculum, and are perhaps closer to poetry as Americans know it. It involves use of counterpoint and anti-theme and is excellent material for language arts curriculum integrated with the social sciences. The vocabulary and illustrations convey the flavor and atmosphere of the Korean culture and aesthetic sense.

1631.   Im, Bang, and Yi Ryuk. **Korean Folk Tales: Imps, Ghosts and Fairies.** Tr. by James S. Gale. Portland, Vt.: Charles E. Tuttle, 1963. 233p. $2.20pa. (6-12)

These folk tales have been handed down by the Korean people for centuries and have the religious backgrounds of Taoism, Buddhism and Confucianism. These 13 short stories give some insight into the ancient Korean culture and value system.

1632.   Lee, Peter H. **Anthology of Korean Poetry from the Earliest Era to the Present.** Comp. and tr. by Peter H. Lee. New York: John Day, 1964. 196p. $6.25.

A Unesco collection of representative works, Korean series; the revised edition is *Poems from Korea: A Historical Anthology* (1973. $7.50).

1633.   Waybill, Marjorie Ann. **Chinese Eyes.** Illus. by Pauline Cutrell. Scottdale, Pa.: Herald Press, 1974. unp. (K-2)

A first-grade Korean girl suffers discrimination and teasing from her classmates because she is adopted and her eyes are not like those of her American mother.

Audiovisual Materials

1634.   **Korean Folk Dances.** 16mm film, 25 min., sd., color. Produced by University of Washington School of Music Archives; distr. by University of Washington Press. $280.00. (9-12)

Presents the Chul t' a gi or Rope Dance, and the colorful Farmers' Dance called nong ok.

1635.   **Southern Korea.** 1 filmstrip. Imperial Films, 1967. $7.00. (4-8)

A background on the culture and peoples of southern Korea, from a set of six filmstrips entitled *Our World Neighbors: Asia and the Pacific.*

LATVIAN AMERICANS. *See* **Baltic Americans.**

LITHUANIAN AMERICANS. *See* **Baltic Americans.**

MEXICAN AMERICANS

See also Spanish-Speaking Americans.

Reference Sources

Reference Guides and Bibliographies

1636.   Aceves, Edward A. **Resource Materials for Teaching Mexican-Chicano Culture: Grades K-6.** San Diego, Calif.: Office of Materials Development, San Diego City Schools, 1973. 403p. $6.00. ED 097 138. (T)
Basic materials for teaching the Mexican/Chicano culture in grades K-6 are divided into nine sections: 1) Calendar of Cultural Events, 2) Classroom Activities, 3) Arts and Crafts, 4) Dances, 5) Songs, 6) Proverbs, Poems, Rhymes, Limericks, Tongue Twisters, and Riddles, 7) Games, 8) Holidays and Celebrations, and 9) Historical and Contemporary Mexican/Chicano Personalities. Includes English, Spanish, and bilingual materials. Intended to be used with recording entitled "Estudiantina 'El Cid' de Calexico." Indexed.

1637.   Baird, Cynthia, comp. **La Raza in Films: A List of Films and Filmstrips.** Oakland, Calif.: Oakland Public Library, 1972. 68p. free. (T)
Lists 270 films and filmstrips on the Spanish-speaking in the United States as well as the Third World in Latin America, and the Mexican. Includes a directory of sources for the materials.

1638.   Barrios, Earnest, comp., *et al.* **A Resource Guide for Teaching Chicano Studies in Junior and Senior High Schools.** San Diego, Calif.: Office of Materials Development, Education Center, San Diego City Schools, 1969. 222p. $3.35. ED 080 223. (T)
This resource guide for junior and senior high school teachers includes materials and information on history, sociology, anthropology, literature, and Mexican-American contributions in music, art, and drama. Another bibliography by Barrios is *Bibliografia de Aztlan: An Annotated Chicano Bibliography* (San Diego State College, 1971).

1639.   **Chicano Children's Literature, Annotated Bibliography.** Comp. by E. A. Martinez. Rohnert Park, Calif.: Sonoma State College, 1972. 41p. $0.65; $3.29. ED 075 158. (4-12, T)
An annotated bibliography of 249 books on Chicanos for children, published between 1938 and 1972. Selections were made on the basis of 1) realistic characters, 2) attitudes, 3) modern viewpoints, 4) lack of bias, and 5) literary merit.

1640.   Conwell, Mary K., and Pura Belpre. **Libros en Espanol: Annotated List of Children's Books in Spanish.** New York: New York Public Library, 1971. 52p. $0.50. (4-12, T)
An excellent bibliography for selecting materials for Spanish-speaking children. Annotations are in Spanish and English, and a list of sources is included.

1641.   Cortes, Carlos E. **Mexican American Bibliographies.** New York: Arno, 1974.
            236p. $22.00. (9-12, T)
Contains five retrospective bibliographies on the Mexican American in the United
States. Included are: *The Mexican Immigrant: An Annotated Bibliography* (The
Council on International Relations, 1929. 21p.), compiled by Emory S. Bogardus;
Mexicans in the United States: A Bibliography (Division of Labor and Social Infor-
mation of the Pan American Union, 1942; 14p.), compiled by Robert C. Jones;
*Spanish-Speaking Americans and Mexican Americans in the United States: A
Selected Bibliography* (Bureau for Intercultural Education, unp.), compiled by Lyle
Saunders; *Materials Relating to the Education of Spanish-Speaking People in the
United States: An Annotated Bibliography* (University of Texas, 1959. 75p.), com-
piled by George I. Sanchez and Howard Putnam; *The United States-Mexican Border:
A Selective Guide to the Literature of the Region* (Official Journal of the Rural
Sociological Society, Vol. 25, June 1960, No. 2. 236p.), compiled by Charles C.
Cumberland.

1642.   Duran, Pat Herrera, and Roberto Cabello-Argendono, comps. **The
            Chicana: A Bibliographic Study.** Los Angeles: California University,
            Chicano Studies Center, 1973. 51p. $0.65 MF; $3.29 HC. (7-12, T)
A partially annotated bibliography of 281 books, documents, papers, articles,
theses, dissertations, films, and newspapers published between 1923 and 1972.
Materials selected are concerned with the Mexican-American woman's culture,
education, and socioeconomic background.

1643.   Dwyer, Carlota Cardenas de. **Chicano Literature: An Introduction and an
            Annotated Bibliography.** Austin, Texas: Depts. of English and American
            Studies, 1974. 23p. $0.75 MF; $1.50 HC. (9-12, T)
An annotated bibliography divided into the following sections: novels, short story
collections, Chicano anthologies, multi-ethnic anthologies, literary criticism, and
bibliographies. Reading level and knowledge of Spanish required are indicated.

1644.   Feeney, Joan V. **Chicano/Special Reading Selection.** ERIC, 1972. 72p.
            $0.65 MF; $3.29 HC. (6-12, T)
A bibliography of approximately 350 entries of materials on the Mexican American
culture divided into age-level divisions: pre-school and primary, intermediate and
advanced. Selected titles include information on arts, crafts, cooking, dances and
custumes, stories of the Spanish explorers, Mexican travels, life in early California,
Mexican folklore and poetry, Chicano family life, migrant workers, life in the
barrios, and biographical information about prominent Mexican-American leaders
throughout their history in the United States.

1645.   Garza, Ben, *et al.* **Chicano Bibliography. Education . . . The Last Hope of
            the Poor Chicano.** Davis, Calif.: Movimento Estudiantil Chicano de Aztlan,
            California University Library, 1969. 56p. $0.65 MF; $3.29 HC. ED
            034642. (9-12, T)
A bibliography prepared for Chicano studies programs. The materials selected (900
sources) describe the Chicano heritage, history, and prehistory. Contemporary problems
of health, nutrition, employment, working conditions, education, and civil rights from
1829 to 1969 are covered.

1646.   Heathman, James E., and Cecilia J. Martinez. **Mexican American Education—A Selected Bibliography**. Las Cruces, N.M.: Education Resources Information Center, New Mexico State University, 1969. 58p. ED 031352. $0.65 MF; $3.29 HC. (7-12, T)
Documents on Mexican American education indexed and abstracted in *Research in Education* are included in this bibliography. All 156 of the entries represent materials published since 1965. Citations are indexed by subject under ERIC descriptor terms. This bibliography has been updated by David M. Altus in a 206-page supplement published in 1971 for $2.50. Materials in it emphasize academic achievement of Mexican Americans, bilingual education, and teaching English as a second language. *Supplement no. 2* was compiled by Albert D. Link (GPO, 1972. 345p. $2.50); *Supplement no. 3* was a 294-page bibliography published in 1973, and *Supplement no. 4* was compiled in 1974 (National Educational Laboratory Publishers, 1974. 166p. $7.00). These bibliographies provide cumulative coverage of Mexican American education and materials available through *Research in Education* and *Current Index to Journals in Education*.

1647.   Hernandez, Luis F. **The Mexican Americans: A Selected and Annotated Bibliography**. Stanford, Calif.: Stanford University, Center for Latin American Studies, 1969. 139p. $2.25pa. (9-12, T)
An annotated bibliography of 274 selected entries describing outstanding studies on the Mexican American. Emphasis is on the contemporary situation and conditions; entries are signed by contributing staff members of the Center for Latin American Studies. Arrangement is alphabetical by author in two sections: Bibliographies and Resource Information; Books and Articles. Subject index included.

1648.   Jordan, Lois B. **Mexican Americans: Resources to Build Cultural Understanding**. Littleton, Colo.: Libraries Unlimited, 1973. 265p. $8.50. (6-12, T)
A multimedia bibliography for junior-high-school-age and up of materials on the Mexican American. It covers the following topics: the Mexican heritage; the Mexican American today, the arts and literature, biography, and fictional stories about Mexican Americans. Over 1,000 entries are annotated with evaluative comments. Grade level is indicated. Appendixes present information on Mexican Americans who have achieved success in American life (sports, entertainment, government); a directory of the Chicano Press Association; lists of Mexican-American periodicals and newspapers; Mexican-American organizations; and general references that include Mexican Americans. Author and title indexes.

1649.   Meier, Matt S., and Feliciano Rivera. **A Bibliography for Chicano History**. San Francisco: R&E Research Associates, 1972. 96p. $5.00; $3.00pa. (9-12, T)
A chronological arrangement of materials covering each of the major historical periods of the Mexican in the United States. It includes books, government publications, periodical articles, pamphlets, theses, and dissertations. Three topical divisions are also included: Labor and Immigration; Civil Rights; and Mexican American Culture. A bibliography of bibliographies is also included.

1650.   Nogales, Luis G., ed. **The Mexican American: A Selected and Annotated Bibliography.** 2nd ed. Stanford, Calif.: Stanford University Bookstore, 1971. 162p. $2.00. (7-12, T)
Includes 474 annotated entries on the Chicano, with emphasis on his goals and aspirations. Arrangement is alphabetical; books, articles, government documents, and dissertations are included. Chicano publications are appended. Subject index.

1651.   Talbot, Jane Mitchell, and Gilbert R. Cruz. **A Comprehensive Chicano Bibliography 1960-1972.** Austin, Tex.: Jenkins Publishing Co., 1973. 375p. $9.50. (9-12, T)
A bibliography of monographs, articles, government documents, theses, and dissertations written by or about the Chicanos from 1960 to 1972. A list of Chicano newspapers and periodicals is included. Arrangement is by subject (history, education, health, economics, literature, music), and only a few entries are annotated. One section is devoted to audiovisual materials. Author index and "cross index" included.

1652.   Trejo, Arnulfo D. **Bibliografia Chicana: A Guide to Information Sources.** Detroit, Mich.: Gale, 1975. 193p. $18.00. (T)
A bibliography covering reference works and materials on the humanities, social sciences, and applied sciences. A directory of newspapers and a publishers' index are also included. Trejo follows an alphanumeric system used by Winchell in her *Guide to Reference Sources.* It overlaps to a certain extent Jordan's *Mexican Americans* (Libraries Unlimited, 1973), Cortes' *American Mexican Bibliographies* (Arno, 1974), and others.

1653.   Trueba, Harry T. **Mexican-American Bibliography: Bilingual Bicultural Education.** ERIC, 1973. 26p. $0.65 MF; $3.29 HC. (T)
A total of 306 books and articles published between 1919-1973 are listed in this bibliography of Mexican Americans and bilingual bicultural education. It is divided into three major sections: 1) social sciences, 2) education, and 3) bibliographies.

Almanacs and Dictionaries

1654.   **The Chicano Almanac.** San Antonio: Texas Institute for Educational Development, 1973. 242p. $2.50. (4-12, T)
An almanac of general information about the 67 Texas counties with the highest Chicano population concentrations. Arrangement is alphabetical by county, with statistical information on agriculture, mineral resources, geography, economy, population characteristics, educational systems, and other sociological data.

1655.   Vasquez, Dr. Librado Keno, and Maria Enriqueta Vasquez. **Regional Dictionary of Chicano Slang.** Austin, Tex.: Jenkins Publishing Co., 1975. 111p. $8.95. (5-12, T)
Slang dialects spoken in the Southwest are given in this comprehensive list of regional speech variants. Includes Chicano/Hispano-American phrases, a bibliography, proverbs and sayings, riddles, Chicano folk medicine and folk songs. Indexed.

Teaching Methodology and Curriculum Materials

1656. Angel, Frank. **Program Content to Meet the Educational Needs of Mexican Americans.** Las Cruces, N.M.: Educational Resources Information Center, New Mexico State University, 1968. 21p. $0.92. ED 017 392. (T)
A description of the requirements of a sound program for teaching Mexican-American students. Emphasis is on language, cognitive development, affective development, inter-group relations, and occupational education training programs.

1657. Cabrera, Arturo Y. **A Study of American and Mexican-American Culture Values and Their Significance in Education.** San Francisco: R&E Research Associates, 1972. 359p. $7.00pa. (T)
Examines how Mexican-American students are affected in their learning process and academic achievement by conflicting cultural values. This is a significant study for planning curriculum outlines in schools of Mexican American populations. The appendix also lists recommendations for a bilingual program and gives a basic oral vocabulary for Spanish-speaking children prior to the development of reading ability. This work was originally the author's Ed.D. thesis from the University of Colorado in 1963. Another title by Cabrera is **Emerging Faces—The Mexican Americans** (William C. Brown, 1971. $2.95).

1658. Carter, Thomas P. **Preparing Teachers for Mexican American Children.** Las Cruces, N.M.: ERIC/CRESS, National Education Association and New Mexico State University, 1969. 16p. $1.00. ED 025 367.
A discussion of the insights and understandings needed by teachers of Mexican American children in a cross-cultural classroom situation.

1659. **Casa De La Raza: Separatism or Segregation—Chicanos in Public Education.** Hayward, Calif.: Southwest Network, 1974. 134p. $2.00. (T)
A description of the Casa de la Raza, a K-12 school operated for 125 Mexican-American children from September 1971 to June 1973 as part of the Berkeley Unified School District's Experimental Schools Program. Also discusses the bilingual curriculum adopted to foster academic achievement through a family culture and language environment. The events that led to the closing of the school on charge of non-compliance with the 1964 Civil Rights Act are also examined.

1660. Dunn, Lynn P. **Chicanos: A Study Guide and Sourcebook.** San Francisco: R&E Research Associates, 1975. 122p. $6.00. (9-12)
Historical and chronological treatment in outline form is used to develop the theme in each section: Part One, Chicano Identity; Part Two, Chicago Conflict; Part Three, Chicano Integration and Nationalism. Includes lists of Chicanos prominent in civic and political activities, and other important figures. A glossary of terms used by or about Chicanos is provided, as well as a bibliography of sources for teachers and students.

1661. Duran, Livie Isauro, and Bernard H. Russell. **Introduction to Chicano Studies: A Reader.** New York: Macmillan, 1973. 385p. $5.95. (11-12, T)
A reader divided into three main sections: Part I, "Yesterday"; Part II, "Today"; Part III, "Tomorrow." Individual readings cover many topics including the Mexican

American heritage, culture, education, politics, migrant workers, and the Chicano image. Each section includes a list of suggested readings, and the book concludes with a list of magazines and newspapers, a list of annotated bibliographies, and a glossary of Mexican-American terms.

1662.   Escobedo, Arturo. **Chicano Counselor.** Lubbock, Tex.: Trucha Publications, Inc., 1973. 211p. $6.50. (T)
The problems of Chicano students at the secondary level are described, as well as the cultural conflicts they encounter.

1663.   Garber, Malcolm. **Classroom Strategies: Culture and Learning Styles.** Albuquerque, N.M.: Southwestern Cooperative Educational Laboratory, 1968. 34p. $1.80. ED 025 364. (T)
The learning style of Mexican-American children as it relates to their cultural heritage is examined. Classroom strategies are discussed concerning the teaching of various subjects; tests of measurement are also considered in this discussion of environmental factors as they affect the Mexican child's learning.

1664.   Gorena, Minerva, comp. **Information and Materials to Teach the Cultural Heritage of the Mexican American Child.** Austin, Tex.: Education Service Center Region 13, 1972. 288p. $0.65 MF; $9.87 HC. ED 081 516. (T)
Supplementary historical and cultural materials designed for a bilingual program at the K-3 level. Major topics in the information section include historical background, an overview of Mexico, places to see, games, dances, legends, fables, stories, and units for teaching the Mexican-American cultural heritage. A bibliography, a list of materials used by the regional bilingual program, and sources for the same were also included.

1665.   Hernandez, Luis. **A Forgotten American: A Resource Unit for Teachers on the Mexican American.** New York: Anti-Defamation League of B'nai B'rith, 1969. 56p. $0.75. (T)
A chronological outline of Mexican history and culture, a brief bibliography, and suggested activities for the social studies teacher are included in this resource unit on Mexican Americans. Topics for discussion are provided for older students.

1666.   Johnson, Henry Sioux, and William J. Hernandez-M. **Educating the Mexican American.** Valley Forge, Pa.: Judson Press, 1970. 384p. $6.95. (T)
A collection of readings by leading Mexican-American educators discussing the historical and cultural perspective of education for Mexican Americans, and suggesting recommendations for change in the curriculums and programs of U.S. schools attended by large Mexican-American populations. Indexed.

1667.   Litsinger, Dolores Escobar. **The Challenge of Teaching Mexican American Students.** New York: American Book Co., 1973. 222p. $7.95. (T)
Discusses the characteristics of the Mexican American student and the attitudes of teachers and students. Also proposes special teaching stragegies and programs to meet the needs of Mexican-American pupils. The challenge of bilingual-bicultural

education and how teachers can be educated to meet it is also presented. A bibliography is included as well as a list of state programs for migratory children. Indexed.

1668.   Martinez, Frank, *et al.* **Bilingual/Bicultural Education Models. Final Report.** Springfield, Va.: National Technical Information Service, 1973. 176p. $3.00. ED 080 261. (T)
A report in English and Spanish presenting bilingual and bicultural program models for education in the Mexican-American community. Topics covered are: 1) Conflects and Problems: The Chicano Experience; 2) Discrepancy between Theory and Practice; 3) Definition of the Need for Bilingual/Bicultural Education in the Northwest; 4) Administration and Classroom Teaching; and 5) The Main Issue: The Principle of Community Control Versus the Principle of Experimental Controlled Variation.

1669.   **Mexican and Mexican American Literature for the Junior High School: Short Story, Novel, Biography.** San Jose, Calif.: San Jose Unified School District, 1970. 86p. $1.50. ED 039 066. (T)
A curriculum guide for the junior high school teacher containing six short stories, one novel, and three biographies. Lesson plans to accompany the materials, suggested activities, vocabulary terms, and background information are all included in the guide. A similar guide for this level covers poetry, essay, and drama (ED 039 067). These same curriculum guides have also been prepared for the high school level (ED 039068 and ED 039069).

1670.   Rivera, Feliciano. **A Mexican American Source Book.** Menlo Park, Calif.: Educational Consortium of America, 1971. 200p. $6.00. (T)
A study outline of the history of Mexican Americans including 32 full-page prints from *A Portfolio of Outstanding Americans of Mexican American Descent*, excerpts and reprints of other works on the Mexicans in the United States, and a bibliography of books, articles, magazines, newspapers, and audiovisual materials.

1671.   U.S. Commission on Civil Rights. **Mexican American Education Study.** Washington, D.C.: Government Printing Office, 1971-1973. Reports 1-5. $1.50 each. (T)
A four-year study of Chicano education in the Southwest with data on conditions in schools attended by Chicanos, educational practices in these schools, and educational achievement of Mexican American students. Other official reports by the Commission are *Mexican Americans and the Administration of Justice in the Southwest* (1970); *Ethnic Isolation of Mexican Americans in the Public Schools of the Southwest* (1971); *Teachers and Students: Differences in Teacher Interaction with Mexican American and Anglo Students* (1973); and *Toward Quality Education for Mexican Americans* (1974).

1672.   Wilson, Jeannette. **Our Hispano Heritage.** Cortez, Colo.: Montelores Studies Center, 1969. 67p. $3.29. ED 067 170. (T)

An elementary level (grades 3-6) curriculum unit with suggested activities for presenting the historical development of the Spanish-speaking Americans in the Southwest. An annotated bibliography is included.

Non-Fiction Titles: History, Culture, Sociology, Biography

1673.   Acosta, Oscar Zeta. **The Revolt of the Cockroach People.** New York: Bantam, 1974. 258p. $7.95; $1.95pa. (9-12)
A Chicano lawyer accuses Americans of racism in courts, churches, schools, and hospitals against the Mexican Americans. He describes his growing-up years as a Mexican-American searching for cultural identity in *The Autobiography of a Brown Buffalo* (Straight Arrow Press, 1972. $3.50).

1674.   Acuna, Rodolfo. **Occupied America: The Chicano Struggle toward Liberation.** Scranton, Pa.: Canfield Press, 1972. 282p. $5.50. (9-12)
Part 1 describes the U.S. conquest of the Southwest during the 1800s in a historical overview of the conquest of Mexico, the Mexican American War, and colonization of the Southwest. Part 2 relates the experiences of the Chicanos during the 1900s, including migration patterns, legislation and education, religion, and Chicano efforts at unionization. Subject indexed. Other titles by the author are: *A Mexican American Chronicle* (American Book Co., 1971. $3.68); *The Story of the Mexican Americans: The Men and the Land* (American Book Co., 1969. $4.75).

1675.   Armas, Jose. **La Familia de la Raza (The Family of the Race).** Albuquerque, N.M.: RAZA Associates, 1972. 38p. $1.50. (9-12, T)
Chicano family values, customs, life styles, and language are discussed in this publication on the Chicano family, covering 1) the family role in the Chicano movement, 2) the emerging identity of La Raza today, 3) the future of La Raza amid a changing Anglo-dominated society, 4) concepts of Chicanismo, 5) Anglo-Chicano contrasts of family values and perspectives, and 6) implications of future shock on La Raza.

1676.   Bernard, Jacqueline. **Voices from the Southwest: Antonio Jose Martinez, Elfego Baca, Reies Lopez Tijerina.** New York: Scholastic Book Services, 1972. 128p. $3.95; $2.00pa. (5-9)
Mexican-American leaders of the Chicano movement and activists in the struggle to retain land in the Southwest are described in these brief biographies.

1677.   Blawis, Patricia Bell. **Tijerina and the Land Grants: Mexican Americans in Struggle for Their Heritage.** New York: International, 1971. 189p. $6.95; $2.65pa. (9-12)
The leader of the Alianza and of the Mexican Americans' struggle for the return of their native lands is described in a sympathetic vein.

1678.   Bogardus, Emory S. **The Mexican in the United States.** Los Angeles: University of California Press, 1934; repr. ed., New York: Arno and the New York Times, 1970. 126p. $6.00. (10-12)

A history and background of the Mexican in the United States, covering such topics as community and camp life, family, health conditions, labor, industry, poverty, crime, recreation, morals, religion, art, child welfare, citizenship, adult education, second-generation immigrants, and laws relating to entry into the U.S. and repatriation. The bibliography provided includes brief annotations.

1679.   Briggs, Vernon M. **Chicanos and Rural Poverty.** Baltimore, Md.: Johns Hopkins, 1973. 81p. $6.00; $1.95pa. (9-12)
Covers the rural Mexican in the Southwest and his economic problems. Lacking workman's compensation and related benefits, the farm worker is depicted as an exploited socioeconomic group member.

1680.   Brischetto, Robert, and Tomas Arciniega. **Inequalities in Educational Opportunity and the Chicano: A Study of School Systems in the Southwest. Final Report.** El Paso: Texas University, 1973. 318p. $0.65 MF; $13.16 HC. ED 082 935. (T)
An examination of educational inequalities for Mexican Americans in the Southwest based on a survey of 1,166 public schools and 636 school superintendents in Arizona, California, Colorado, New Mexico, and Texas. Inequalities found in educational resources and services based on ethnic composition of the school district are indicated, with important implications for legislation and policy-making concerning the Mexican-American student.

1681.   Burma, John, ed. **Mexican Americans in the U.S.: A Reader.** Cambridge, Mass.: Schenkman, 1970. 487p. $5.95pa. (11-12)
A collection of 41 essays on the culture and heritage of the Mexicans in the United States. Other topics covered are prejudice, the Chicano image, education, economics, family, religion, politics, economics, acculturation and assimilation, health and general living conditions.

1682.   Carranza, Eliu. **Pensamientos en Los Chicanos: A Cultural Revolution.** Berkeley, Calif.: California Book Co., Ltd., 1969. 58p. $2.00. (9-12)
A collection of essays on the Chicano movement and demand for equal rights. Authors are outspoken in their rejection of Anglo culture and value system.

1683.   Carter, Thomas P. **Mexican Americans in School: A History of Educational Neglect.** New York: College Entrance Examination Board, 1970. 235p. $4.75. (T)
A history of Mexican-American education is compiled from interviews. Three factors—the nature of the local society, the school, and the subculture—are identified as interacting to contribute to the overall unsuccessful school record of Mexican Americans.

1684.   Casavantes, Edward J. **A New Look at the Attributes of the Mexican American.** Albuquerque, N.M.: Southwest Cooperative Educational Laboratory, 1971. unp. $2.25. (T)
An essay for teachers on distinguishing Chicano characteristics from "the culture of poverty" and on the heterogeneity of the Chicanos as a group.

1685.   Castro, Tony. **The Emergence of Mexican America.** New York: Dutton,
         1974. 320p. $9.95; $3.95pa. (8-12)
A chronology of the Mexican-American history and experience, with emphasis on
the protest movements of the 1960s and 1970s. Documented with photographs.
Gives opinions on the activities and influence of such leaders as Cesar Chavez,
Reies Tijerina, Corky Gonzales, Jose Angel Gutierrez, and others.

1686.   Cortes, Carlos E., ed. **The Mexican American.** New York: Arno, 1974.
         21 vols. $495.00 set. (7-12)
A 21-volume study of the Mexicans in the United States, covering all aspects of
Mexican history, immigration, and culture. Other titles by the author are: *Church
Views of the Mexican American* (Arno, 1974. $38.00); *Education and the Mexican
American* (Arno, 1974. $30.00); *The Mexican American & the Law* (Arno, 1974.
$20.00); *Mexican Labor in the United States* (Arno, 1974. $26.00); and *The New
Mexican Hispano* (Arno, 1974. $30.00), all reprints in *The Mexican American*
series.

1687.   Day, Mark. **Forty Acres: Cesar Chavez and the Farm Workers.** New York:
         Praeger, 1971. 222p. $6.95. (7-12)
"Forty acres" refers to the headquarters of Cesar Chavez in Southern California.
A priest, missionary to the Spanish-speaking migrant farm workers, describes Chavez
and the non-violent protest movement. Much emphasis is also given to La Huelga.

1688.   de Burciaga, Cecilia Preciado, *et al.* **Toward Quality Education for Mexi-
         can Americans: Mexican American Education Study.** Washington, D.C.:
         Commission on Civil Rights, 1974. 281p. $9.87. ED 086 407. (T)
The sixth and final report of the MAES (Mexican American Education Study)
discusses specific educational problems of Mexican-American children in the Southwest and recommends action to alleviate them. It also suggests three basic principles
for reform: 1) Mexican American culture, language, and history should be inherent
and integral parts of the educational process; 2) Mexican Americans should be
represented in decision-making policies; 3) all levels of government should reorder
their budget priorities to implement the given recommendations.

1689.   De Garza, Patricia. **Chicanos: The Story of the Mexican Americans.** New
         York: Messner, 1973. 96p. $5.29. (3-6)
An overview of 400 years of Mexican-American history, covering the initial Spanish
settlement of the Southwest, the Gold Rush and the Mexican American, migrant
farm workers, "wetbacks," anit-Mexican discrimination, Indian relations, and contemporary protest groups. The format is a series of fictionalized accounts. Biographical information on prominent Mexican Americans is presented. Many photographs are included.

1690.   De Leon, Nephtali. **Chicanos: Our Background and Our Pride.** Denver,
         Colo.: Totinen Pub. Co., 1972. 95p. $2.60. (10-12)
A history of the Mexicans in America from the time of the Aztecs. Includes a
discussion of Aztec and Spanish heritage, Mexico's revolutions, Mexican-American
culture, education and the Chicano movement. Other titles by the author, published
in 1972 by Trucha Publications, are *Chicano Poet* ($3.00); *Coca Cola Dream* ($1.00);

Five Plays ($3.50); and *I Will Catch the Sun* ($2.00). The latter title is for the fifth and sixth grade level; the others are for the junior and senior high school levels.

1691. Dobrin, Arnold. **New Life–La Vida Nueva: The Mexican Americans Today.** New York: Dodd, Mead, 1971. 109p. $4.50. (7-12)
A history of the Mexican-American immigration, with emphasis on the problems of prejudice, education, and civil rights. Emphasis is on the Mexican as a migrant farm worker. Describes roles of Ricardo Montalban, Cesar Chavez, and others in providing equal opportunities for Mexican Americans.

1692. Dunne, John Gregory. **Delano.** New York: Farrar, 1967, 1971. 202p. $7.95; $2.95pa. (6-12)
The author gives a personal report on the Delano grape strike and its impact on the San Joaquin Valley communities. The activities of both sides, the employers and the laborers, are described and evaluated.

1693. Forbes, Jack D. **Aztecas Del Norte: The Chicanos of Aztlan.** New York: Fawcett, 1973. 336p. $0.95pa. (10-12)
A study of the Indian heritage of the Mexican Americans of the Southwest, covering Mexican American history from the time of the Aztecs. Major topics are: the Tollecayotl and Mexicayotl backgrounds; the northward movement; discrimination in the Southwest; Mexican self-identity; religion; education; La Raza Unida and other movements toward organization.

1694. Franchere, Ruth. **Cesar Chavez.** Illus. by Earl Thollander. New York: Crowell, 1970. 42p. $4.50; $1.25pa. (2-5)
The biography of this Mexican-American leader active in the Chicano struggle for an improved economic status. Also describes his role in initiating the famous grape boycott.

1695. Fusco, Paul, and George D. Horwitz. **La Causa: The California Grape Strike.** Intro. by Cesar Chavez. New York: Macmillan, 1970. 158p. $7.95; $3.95pa. (5-12)
A photographic essay by Fusco with a text by Horwitz giving the story of the well-known huelga (strike) against the grape growers of Delano, California. The account is a revealing portrait of the poverty and inadequate living conditions of the Mexican-American migrant worker.

1696. Galarza, Ernesto. **Barrio Boy.** South Bend, Ind.: University of Notre Dame Press, 1971. 275p. $7.95; $3.95pa. (7-12)
An autobiographical account of a Mexican family who immigrated to California. It is a revealing portrait of the problems of adjustment and acculturation they faced and also of the Mexican family roles and customs. Other titles by the author are *Merchants of Labor: The Mexican Bracero Story* (McNally & Loftin, 1964. $2.95); *Mexican Americans in the Southwest* (McNally & Loftin, 1969. $3.95); *Poemas Pe-Que Pe-Que-Nitos* (Educational Consortium of America, n.d. $1.25); and *Rimas Tontas* (Educational Consortium of America, 1972. $1.40).

1697.   Garcia, Ernest F., and George Shaftel. **Mexican American Heritage.** Palo
        Alto, Calif.: Fearon, 1972. $5.60. (7-12)
A social studies text designed for the junior and senior high school levels describing
the heritage, culture, experience, and contributions of the Mexican Americans.
Another title by Garcia is *Chicano Cultural Diversity* (1974. $1.50. ED 091 375).

1698.   Garcia, F. Chris. **Political Socialization of Chicano Children: A Comparative
        Study with Anglos in California Schools.** New York: Praeger, 1973.
        255p. $16.50. (T)
This study attempts to determine whether the Chicano child's orientation toward
the American political system is different from that of the Anglo child, and what the
implications are of a distinctive socialization for the future role of the American
political system. Anglo and Mexican American children give responses to questions about their government and environment at grades 3, 5, 7, and 9. Includes
a description of the interviewing technique and bibliographical notes. Another title
by the author is *La Causa Politica: A Chicano Politics Reader* (University of Notre
Dame, 1973. $14.95; $4.95pa.).

1699.   Gomez, David F. **Somos Chicanos: Strangers in Our Own Land.** Boston,
        Mass.: Beacon Press, 1973. 204p. $8.95. (9-12)
The author, a Catholic priest and a Chicano activist, presents a history of his people
and an analysis of their reaction to their experience in the United States. Implications for the future are also indicated. He describes family life in the Mexican
American community and the social discrimination and struggles faced by the
young Chicano as he grows up.

1700.   Gonzalez, Nancie L. **Spanish-Americans of New Mexico: A Heritage of
        Pride.** Albuquerque: University of New Mexico Press, c1967, 1969. 246p.
        $7.95. (8-12)
Compares the Mexican population of New Mexico with other Spanish-speaking
populations in the United States. The heritage and culture of the early conquista-
dores are described with respect to language, race, the social system, voluntary
associations, effects of urbanization and change. A concluding chapter discusses
activism in New Mexico during the late 1960s. Bibliography included.

1701.   Grebler, Leo, Joan W. Moore, and Ralph C. Guzman. **Mexican American
        People: The Nation's Second Largest Minority.** New York: Free Press,
        1970. 800p. $14.95. (9-12, T)
A study of the socioeconomic status of Mexican Americans in selected Southwestern
cities is made from census data, interviews, observations, and published and unpublished materials. Chapters include: Socioeconomic Conditions; The Individual in the
Social System; The Role of Churches; Political Interaction; Summary and Conclusions; Appendices. Books, pamphlets, government publications, articles, unpublished
materials, and bibliographies are listed in an extensive bibliography.

1702.   Haddox, John. **Los Chicanos: An Awakening People.** Pictures by Jose
        Cisneros. El Paso, Tex.: Western Press, 1970. 44p. $2.00. (7-12)
A popular-style history of the Chicanos. Documented with pictures. Covers the
recent movements and organization among the Mexican Americans.

1703.   Heins, Marjorie. **Strictly Ghetto Property: The Story of Los Siete De La Raza.** Berkeley, Calif.: Ramparts, 1972. 324p. $7.95; $2.95pa. (7-12)
Biographical sketches of seven Mexican-American teenagers charged with the killing of a policeman in the Mission District of San Francisco in 1969 are revealing pictures of their home environments in the ethnic barrio.

1704.   Heller, Celia S. **New Converts to the American Dream? Mobility Aspirations of Young Mexican Americans.** New Haven, Conn.: College & University Press, 1972. 287p. $7.50; $2.95pa. (T)
This volume is concerned with the problems of Mexican-American youth, their goals and skills for upward mobility. Questionnaires were utilized to identify socioeconomic background, detect ambitions, and discover whether or not the young person subscribed to success-related values. Education and IQ are also studied as a means of upward mobility. Another title by the author is *Mexican American Youth: Forgotten Youth at the Crossroads* (Random House, 1966. $2.95pa.).

1705.   Lamb, Ruth S. **Mexican Americans: Sons of the Southwest.** Claremont, Calif.: Ocelot Press, 1970. 198p. $5.95pa. (7-12)
A chronological history of the Chicano in the Southwest with emphasis on civil rights and political activities. A comprehensive bibliography is included, with entries arranged under subject headings. One heading, "The Mexican American in Children's Literature," includes 76 references. Indexed.

1706.   Laundes, Ruth. **Latin Americans of the Southwest.** St. Louis: McGraw-Hill, 1965. 104p. $3.95. (6-12)
Discusses assimilation and acculturation of the Chicano in the Southwest. Also traces the history of the Spanish-speaking peoples and their cultural background in Mexico.

1707.   Ludwig, Ed, and James Santibanez, eds. **The Chicanos: Mexican American Voices.** Baltimore, Md.: Penguin Books, 1971. 286p. $1.50. (7-12)
A collection of writings and excerpts from writings of fiction and non-fiction by such well-known Mexican Americans as Cesar Chavez, Reies Lopez Tijerina, Joan Baez, and others. Emphasis of the selections is on interaction with the Anglo community, particularly of Southern California.

1708.   Manuel, Herschel T. **Spanish-Speaking Children of the Southwest; Their Education and the Public Welfare.** Austin: University of Texas Press, c1965, 1970. 222p. $7.50; $2.25pa. (T)
A survey of the problems of Mexican Americans in the realm of education. Emphasis is on cultural conflicts, discrimination, language problems, lack of facilities and the attendance records of children of migrant farm workers.

1709.   Martin, Patricia Miles. **Chicanos: Mexicans in the United States.** Illus. by Robert Frankenberg. New York: Parents' Magazine Press, 1971. 64p. $4.59. (2-5)
Written in the style of an easy reader for primary children, this book gives the history of Mexican Americans, the Spanish conquest in the homeland, and the

northward movement of the "Mestizos." It details immigration across the Rio Grande for work and the migrant labor camps where many found employment. Also discusses urban "barrios," Chicano culture, bilingualism, discrimination, prominent Chicano figures, and cultural contributions.

1710.　Martinez, Elizabeth Sutherland, and Enriqueta Longeaux y Vasquez. **Viva La Raza!: The Struggle of the Mexican-American People.** New York: Doubleday, 1974. 353p. $4.95. (10-12)
The Chicano version of America's discovery and historical events involving Mexican-Americans are discussed by two activist leaders in the Chicano movement. Emphasis is on exploitation of the Chicanos and their contributions to American culture.

1711.　Martinez, Rafael. **My House Is Your House.** New York: Friendship Press, 1964. 127p. $2.50pa. (7-12)
A book on the cultural contributions and heritage of the Mexican Americans. Pictures and other illustrations depict family life and daily activities.

1712.　McWilliams, Carey. **North from Mexico: The Spanish Speaking People of the U.S.** New York: Lippincott, 1949; repr. ed., New York: Greenwood Press, 1968. 320p. $11.25. (10-12)
A history of the Mexican-American culture including the origin of the Mexican American, exploitation by whites and border attacks, the Mexican-American War, and economic opportunities. Also covers the role of the Mexican-American in developing the Western frontier, the Mexican-American influence in Southwestern culture, foods, architecture, clothing; other contributions are indicated, and recent labor disputes and riots are also described. Another title by the author is *The Mexicans in America* (Teachers College Press, 1968. $1.50pa.).

1713.　Meier, Matt S., and Feliciano Rivera. **The Chicanos: A History of Mexican Americans.** New York: Hill and Wang, 1972. 302p. $8.95; $2.45pa. (7-12)
Describes the Chicanos in the United States from their Indian heritage in Mexico to the current movements. Covers discriminatory treatment, language, everyday life, religion, and other aspects of the Mexican-American culture. Includes a glossary, bibliographic notes, maps, and an index. Another title by the authors is *Readings on La Raza* (Hill and Wang, 1974. $8.95; $3.50pa.).

1714.　Molnar, Joe. **Graciela: A Mexican-American Child Tells Her Story.** New York: Watts, 1972. n.p. $6.90. (4-8)
Graciela is a 12-year-old Mexican-American girl whose family earns a living as migrant crop pickers. She tapes a description of their life style, hopes, aspirations, and problems. Photographs of her family help document her story.

1715.　Moquin, Wayne, and Charles Van Doren, eds. **A Documentary History of the Mexican Americans.** New York: Bantam, 1972. 399p. $1.50pa. (7-12)
A collection of 65 essays chronicling the history of Mexicans in the United States. The latter selections cover the Chicano movements of today. A bibliography is included in addition to many famous and significant documents in the development of the Mexican-American heritage.

1716. Morin, Raul. **Among the Valiant: Mexican Americans in World War II and Korea.** Alhambra, Calif.: Borden, 1966. 280p. $6.00. (9-12)
Discusses the two million Mexican Americans who served in the military during World War II and the Korean conflict. Emphasis is on the role of the military in increasing identity with the United States and assimilation, the treatment of the Mexican Americans, and some of their outstanding contributions as soldiers. Also discusses the development of the Mexican Americans as a political force and voice.

1717. Nava, Julian, and Michelle Hall. **Mexican American Profiles: Bilingual Biographies for Today.** Walnut Creek, Calif.: Aardvark Media, Inc., 1974. 116p. $3.50. (7-9)
Brief biographies of 26 Mexican Americans from various walks of life and life styles. Emphasis is on their contributions to the Mexican American community and American society. An index by state of origin or residence, and a list of sources for additional information are included. Other titles by Julian Nava are *The Mexican American in American History* (American Book Company, 1973. $7.95; $3.95pa.); *Mexican Americans: A Brief Look at Their History* (Anti-Defamation League of B'nai B'rith, 1970. $0.75pa.); *Mexican Americans: An Anthology of Basic Readings* (American Book Co., 1973. $4.95); *Mexican Americans: Past, Present and Future* (American Book Co., 1969. $2.79); and *Mexican Americans Today* (Xerox Educational Publications, 1973).

1718. Nelson, Eugene. **Huelga: The First Hundred Days of the Great Delano Grape Strike.** Delano, Calif.: Farm Workers Press, 1966. 122p. $1.50. (7-12)
A chronology of the events and activities of the famous grape strike of the 1960s. The viewpoint here is sympathetic to the Mexican-American agricultural workers.

1719. Pablano, Ralph. **Ghosts in the Barrio: Issues in Bilingual-Bicultural Education.** San Rafael, Calif.: Leswing Press, 1973. 374p. $5.95. (T)
A collection of essays on issues in bilingual-bicultural education by Chicano educators. Some are personal narratives, others scholarly research representing a left-to-right political view. All are aimed at individuals who deal with Chicano students or those interested in Chicano language, culture, and goals.

1720. Pinchot, Jane. **The Mexicans in America.** Minneapolis, Minn.: Lerner Publications, 1973. 99p. $3.95. (5-11)
A popular history of the Mexican Americans in the United States, their reasons for coming, problems of language and acculturation. Also discusses some outstanding Mexican-American personalities and their contributions to society.

1721. Prago, Albert. **Strangers in Their Own Land: A History of Mexican Americans.** New York: Four Winds, 1973. 226p. $5.95. (7-12)
This history of Mexican Americans emphasizes the recent years and includes sketches of the lives of some of the more militant leaders (Juarez, Gonzales, Chavez, and others). However, it also indicates some efforts in the past at achieving equal social, civil, economic, and political rights for the Mexican Americans.

1722.   Quirarte, Jacinto. **Mexican American Artists.** Austin: University of Texas
         Press, 1973. 149p. $12.50. (7-12)
Covers Mexican-American artists from the earliest days of the colonial mission
artists to those of the present day. Compares artistic styles, accomplishments of the
artists, and their contributions to ethnic consciousness.

1723.   Rendon, Armando B. **Chicano Manifesto.** New York: Collier, 1971.
         337p. $7.95. (9-12)
Describes conditions in the Mexican-American community that have resulted in
demands for change and an end to discrimination in numerous areas. Also describes
the current revolt of Mexican Americans against the Anglo system of life, presenting
in this manifesto, a statement of purpose and destiny with respect to the future
role of Chicanos in America.

1724.   Rosaldo, Renato, *et al.* **Chicano: The Evolution of a People.** Minneapolis,
         Minn.: Winston Press, 1973. 461p. $7.00. (9-12)
A collection of 51 essays on the history of the Mexicans in the United States.
Emphasis is on the Southwest and on the Chicanos as a political and social voice.
Twenty-three of the contributors are of Mexican-American background.

1725.   Ruiz, Jesse N. **El Gran Cesar.** Menlo Park, Calif.: Educational Consortium
         of America, 1973. unp. $2.95. (4-8)
A photographic essay on the life and adventures of a Mexican-American boy in the
barrio. The text, in both English and Spanish, describes the Mexican culture and
heritage. Style is that of an elementary reader.

1726.   Santillan, Richard. **La Raza Unida.** Los Angeles: Tlaquilo Publications,
         1973. 179p. $2.25. (10-12)
Proposes the establishment of La Raza Unida Party as a voice for political influence
and activity of Chicano leaders. Santillan discusses the role of this party in the continued struggle of the Mexican Americans for equal political and social rights.

1727.   Simmen, Edward, ed. **Pain and Promise: The Chicano Today.** New York:
         New American Library, 1972. 348p. $1.25pa. (7-12)
Gives the historical background of the Chicano and a summary of his present
problems and concerns in a series of essays, book excerpts, and views expressed in
recently published articles on the Mexican American. Writers contributing are
Anglos and Chicanos. Another collection of papers on the subject by the author is
The Chicano: From Caricature to Self Portrait (New American Library, 1971.
$1.25pa.).

1728.   Steiner, Stan. **La Raza: The Mexican-Americans.** New York: Harper and
         Row, 1970. 418p. $10.00; $2.75pa. (7-12)
The author interviewed, and often quotes, Mexican Americans in this history of
their background and experience in the U.S. A lot of attention is given to militant
movements, such as Tijerina and his struggle to retain land for the Chicanos, the
farm workers efforts to organize, and others. The barrio community of Los
Angeles is also described.

1729.   Tebbel, John, and Ramon Eduardo Ruiz. **South by Southwest: The Mexican-American and His Heritage.** Illus. by Earl Thollander. New York: Doubleday, 1969. 122p. $3.95. (5-9)
Presents the history of Mexico and Mexican-American relations. Discusses the part the Mexican Americans played in the development of the Southwestern states. Touches also on discrimination against the Mexican immigrant.

1730.   Terzian, James, and Kathryn Cramer. **Mighty Hard Road: The Story of Cesar Chavez.** New York: Archway, 1972. 146p. $3.95; $0.75pa. (6-12)
A biography of Cesar Chavez, a prominent Mexican American leader, for young people. Describes the living conditions of the Mexicans in the United States and their struggle for a better life and equalities in employment, education, and other areas.

1731.   Weiner, Sandra. **Small Hands, Big Hands: Seven Profiles of Chicano Migrant Workers and Their Families.** New York: Pantheon, 1970. 55p. $4.41. (4-10)
Interviews were the source of data for these seven biographical sketches of Chicano migrant farmers and their families in California. Their living conditions, attitudes, stamina, and hopes for a better life are still revealed in these profiles. Black and white photographs document their stories.

1732.   White, Florence M. **Cesar Chavez: Man of Courage.** Illus. by Victor Mays. Champaign, Ill.: Garrard, 1973. 96p. $3.58; $0.95pa. (3-5)
A biography of the life of a prominent Mexican-American leader, Cesar Chavez. Chavez organized the National Farm Workers Association, the first union for migrant workers.

Literature and Fiction Titles

1733.   Adams, Ruth. **Fidelia.** Illus. by Ati Forberg. New York: Lothrop, 1970. unp. $4.75. (1-4)
Fidelia, a second grader, wants to play an instrument in the orchestra as her older brother and sister do. She solves her problem by constructing her own "cigar box" violin in this warm story of a Mexican-American family.

1734.   Alurista, Alberto. **Nationchild Plumaroja.** San Diego, Calif.: Toltecas en Aztlan, Centro Cultural de la Raza, 1972. $2.10. (10-12)
An illustrated collection of poems written by Chicanos in the language of the youth of today.

1735.   Anaya, Rudolfo. **Bless Me, Ultima.** Berkeley, Calif.: Quinto Sol Publications, 1972. 248p. $3.75. (10-12)
This novel won the Premio Quinto Sol Literary Award. Set in New Mexico, it is a historical novel of the Mexican-American people and heritage, supernatural happenings and murder.

1736.   Barrio, Raymond. **The Plum Plum Pickers**. New York: Canfield Press, 1971. 201p. $7.00; $2.75pa. (10-12)
A protest novel in sympathy with the Chicano migrant crop pickers. Set in Santa Clara County, California, the story is told through a series of character portraits including the migrant camp foreman, the employer, a family of farm workers, and the single laborers.

1737.   Beckett, Hilary. **Rafael and the Raiders**. Illus. by Leonard Shortall. New York: Dodd, Mead, 1972. 127p. $3.95. (4-8)
When 13-year-old Rafael visits his Mexican American cousins in New York, he finds a visit to the art museum unusually exciting. A thief attempts to use Rafael as her cover, but he later helps to capture the gang of thieves.

1738.   Behn, Harry. **Two Uncles of Pablo**. New York: Harcourt, Brace & World, 1959. 96p. $4.95. (5-9)
This story of a Mexican-American family revolves around Pablo and the appreciation he develops for his two uncles.

1739.   Bishop, Curtis. **Fast Break**. Philadelphia, Pa.: Lippincott, 1967. 192p. $5.95; $3.50pa. (7-10)
A young Mexican-American high school basketball star, Rene Alvarez, finds resentment among his team members. This is also a story of friendship between a Chicano and an Anglo boy.

1740.   Blue, Rose. **We Are Chicano**. Illus. by Bob Alcorn. New York: Watts, 1973. 58p. $4.95. (4-6)
A picture of the problems of a 12-year-old Chicano student in an all-white school, as well as family conflicts. Included also is a portrayal of the life style of migrant farm workers.

1741.   Bolognese, Don. **A New Day**. New York: Delacorte, 1970. 32p. $4.95. (K-3)
A Christmas story of the nativity with Mexican characters, Jose and Maria, assuming the leading roles. Migrant farm workers traveling south, they must find shelter for Maria, who is pregnant. Maria's baby is born in a gas station.

1742.   Bonham, Frank. **Viva Chicano**. New York: Dutton, 1970. 180p. $5.50. (7-12)
Keeny is a young Chicano accused of the attempted murder of his brother. He is sent to a home for boys after running away, and his story is told by his parole officer. Keeny's living conditions have helped him to become hostile.

1743.   Cardenas, Leo. **Return to Ramos**. Illus. by Nilo Santiago. New York: Hill and Wang, 1970. 54p. $2.77. (5-7)
Chita leads the other Chicano students in a boycott of the community high school. When her father intervenes, Anglos and Chicanos begin to talk things over together and solve some of their cultural conflicts and misunderstandings.

1744.   Chavez, Albert C., ed. **Yearnings: Mexican American Literature.** West
         Haven, Conn.: Pendulum Press, 1972. 134p. $1.75. (10-12)
A collection of contemporary writings by Chicano authors. These selections
appeared in a Mexican-American journal, *Con Safos.*

1745.   Chavez, Angelico. **From an Alter Screen, El Retablo: Tales from New
         Mexico.** New York: Books for Libraries, 1957. 119p. $9.00. (8-12)
A collection of seven folktales that have come down through the centuries. Father
Chavez was a Catholic chaplain during World War II and all of his stories have a
religious flavor.

1746.   Cox, William R. **Third and Goal.** New York: Dodd, Mead, 1971. 182p.
         $3.95. (6-10)
A story combining football, racial prejudice, and Mexican-American family life and
customs. Other titles by the author for this age group are: *Trouble at Second Base*
(Dodd, 1966. $4.50) and *Chicano Cruz* (Bantam, 1972. $0.95pa.).

1747.   Diaz, Paul, *et al.* **Up from El Paso.** Chicago: Childrens Press, 1970. 63p.
         $3.50. (6-12)
The author tells his life story from his boyhood in El Paso, as a migrant crop worker
in California, his army experiences, and the poverty that kept him struggling to get
his education. Diaz was the first Mexican American in the area to be appointed a
police-sergeant. In his present position as Health and Safety Inspector for Salinas,
he helps the Spanish-speaking find employment opportunities.

1748.   Dunne, Mary Collins. **Reach Out, Ricardo.** New York: Abelard-Schuman,
         1971. 159p. $4.95. (4-7)
This story of Ricardo Torres, the son of a migrant farm laborer, is a revealing
portrait of the socioeconomic status of this group of Mexican Americans in the
United States. It also shows the inner conflicts of a young adolescent boy.

1749.   Ets, Marie Hall. **Bad Boy, Good Boy.** New York: Crowell, 1967. 49p.
         $4.50. (2-4)
Roberto is considered bad because he plays alone in the streets all day. After he is
sent to a day-care center, he learns to write and speak English. He sends a touching
letter to his mother, and she returns to the home. After this Roberto is called a
good boy. Another title for the elementary child is *Gilberto and the Wind*
(Viking, 1963. $4.95; $0.95pa.).

1750.   Flores, Joseph A., ed. **Songs and Dreams.** West Haven, Conn.: Pendulum
         Press, 1972. 137p. $1.75. (10-12)
A collection of Chicano literature and poetry useful for the high school curriculum
and for social studies units on Mexican-American or Chicano literature.

1751.   Foster, Ed. **Tijanos.** Illus. by Bill Negron. New York: Hill and Wang, 1970.
         48p. $2.77. (4-6)
The historical battle of the Alamo is fictionalized and told from the viewpoint of an
11-year-old Mexican American whose father fought on the side of the Texans.

1752.   Fulle, Suzanne G. **Lanterns for Fiesta.** Illus. by John R. Gibson.
         Philadelphia, Pa.: Macrae, 1973. 134p. $5.75. (4-6)
A Mexican-American family story situated among migrant workers of East Texas.
Twelve-year-old Juanita wants an education and is determined to achieve her goal
in spite of discouraging circumstances.

1753.   Galbraith, Clare K. **Victor.** Illus. by Bill Commerford. Boston, Mass.:
         Little, Brown, 1971. 48p. $4.95. (2-4)
Victor is a child of two cultures—the Anglo world at school, and the Mexican-
American and Spanish-speaking world of his home and family. This situation
presents many problems for him, but when Parents' Night is held at school a
pleasant solution is provided. A glossary of some Mexican-American terms is
included.

1754.   Gee, Maurine H. **Chicano, Amigo.** Illus. by Ted Lewin. New York:
         Morrow, 1972. 96p. $6.59. (3-5)
Kiki and Marc are friends, but when Marc is teased about his "Chicano" friend the
relationship is jeopardized. An earthquake brings about a solution to the problem.

1755.   Gonzales, Rodolfo. **I Am Joaquin.** New York: Bantam Pathfinder Editions,
         1972. 122p. $1.25. (7-12)
This epic poem gives an historical portrait of the Chicano heritage from the pre-
Columbian days to the Mexican problems as immigrants and in contemporary
American society. Describes the plight of the Mexican Americans and the social
and economic discrimination they have faced.

1756.   Hamilton, Dorothy. **Anita's Choice.** Illus. by Ivan Moon. Scottsdale, Pa.:
         Herald Press, 1971. 96p. $1.95pa. (4-8)
Anita Hernandez is a 14-year-old migrant farm worker whose family moves to
Indiana. The story reveals the discrimination, uprootings, and heartaches that
young people of migrant families experience.

1757.   Heuman, William. **City High Five.** New York: Dodd, Mead, 1964. 176p.
         $3.95. (6-10)
This story for basketball enthusiasts features Mike Harrigan and his friend Pedro
Martinez, a Mexican-American student in a bicultural community.

1758.   Hitte, Kathryn. **Mexicali Soup.** New York: Parents Magazine, 1970. unp.
         $6.95. (K-3)
Mama, a Mexican-American immigrant, makes a delicious spicy soup, but her children become self-conscious of their different cultural background and eating customs
in their new urban environment. They start objecting to the garlic and other
ingredients. When Mama omits all the objectionable spices and vegetables, the
children find the soup tasteless and disappointing. A warm and amusing story of
cultural conflicts and Mexican-American family life.

1759.   Hood, Flora. **One Luminaria for Antonio: A Story of New Mexico.**
         Berkeley, Calif.: Putnam's, 1966. 46p. $3.96. (3-5)

A little Chicano boy loves the Mexican Christmas tradition of lighted luminarias. Set in New Mexico, this is the story of Mexican-American family life and customs, particularly around the Christmas holidays.

1760. Jackson, Helen Hunt. **Ramona.** Boston, Mass.: Little, Brown, 1939; repr. ed., New York: Avon, 1975. 249p. $6.50; $1.75pa. (6-12)
Ramona grows up in an aristocratic Mexican family during the nineteenth century in what is now California. This is a story of Mexican and Spanish customs of the time, as well as a tale of romance.

1761. Krumgold, Joseph. **And Now Miguel.** Illus. by Jean Charlot. New York: Crowell, 1953; repr. ed., New York: Apollo, 1970. 245p. $4.50; $1.65pa. (5-10)
Miguel watches for a chance to prove himself a man working as a sheepherder in the Mexican-Indian culture of New Mexico.

1762. Laklan, Carli. **Migrant Girl.** New York: McGraw-Hill, 1970. 144p. $4.95. (7-9)
Sixteen-year-old Dacey and her family are migrant workers experiencing the poverty, hard work, and hopelessness of their living conditions. Juan, a young Mexican American, tells them about Cesar Chavez and the hope he has brought to the migrant workers of California.

1763. Lopez, Norbert C. **King Pancho and the First Clock.** Illus. by Marianne Gutierrez. Fayetteville, Ga.: Oddo Publishing, 1968. 32p. $4.75; $1.75pa. (2-7)
A Mexican story written and illustrated by Mexican Americans about the race between the turtle and the rabbit.

1764. Madison, Winifred. **Maria Luisa.** Philadelphia, Pa.: Lippincott, 1971. 187p. $4.43; $1.95pa. (5-10)
When a 12-year-old Chicano girl goes to live with her aunt in San Francisco, she is faced with problems of adjustment, school problems, and language difficulties. The story portrays the conflicts faced by Chicano children in an Anglo society.

1765. Mireles, Florecita. **Carlitos.** Illus. by Nephtali De Leon. Lubbock, Tex.: Trucha Publications, 1972. $2.00. (K-4)
A fantasy told to Mexican American children about Carlitos, a little toad who floats down the river on a piece of tortilla.

1766. O'Dell, Scott. **Child of Fire.** Boston, Mass.: Houghton Mifflin, 1974. 213p. $6.95. (7-12)
A dramatic novel about a teenaged Mexican American boy, Manuel, and his realtionship with Delaney, a juvenile parole officer. Mexican culture, bull fights, drugs, ghetto gangs, farm workers' strikes, and abortion are all a part of this story.

1767. Ortego, Philip, ed. **We Are Chicanos: An Anthology of Chicano Literature.** New York: Washington Square Press, 1973. 330p. $1.25. (7-12)
A collection of writings by and about Chicanos including essays, folklore, poetry, a

play, short stories, and an excerpt from "The Plum Plum Pickers," a novel by Raymond Barrio. The materials in this anthology cover Mexican American history and problems.

1768.   Politi, Leo. **Pedro, the Angel of Olvera Street.** New York: Scribner's, 1946. unp. $5.95. (K-3)
Pedro plays the part of an angel in a Mexican-American Christmas celebration. A Caldecott Medal-winning picture book by the author is *Song of the Swallows* (Scribner's, 1949); other titles are *The Mission Bell* (Scribner's, 1953. $5.95), *Lito and the Clown* (Scribner's, 1964. $3.25), and *Juanita* (Scribner's, 1948. $2.50).

1769.   Paredes, Americo, and Raymundo Paredes. **Mexican American Authors.** New York: Houghton Mifflin, 1972. 152p. $2.20. (8-12)
An anthology of Mexican American writings including folklore, stories, poetry, and a play. Only one story was written by a non-Mexican, but he writes under a Spanish-name pseudonym.

1770.   Rivera, Tomas. . . .**Y No Se Lo Trago La Tierra . . . And the Earth Did Not Part.** Berkeley, Calif.: Quinto Sol, 1971. 177p. $3.75. (7-12)
A bilingual reader containing a collection of prize-winning stories on Mexican-American culture and interests.

1771.   Roldan, Fernando. **The Kite.** Illus. by Hector F. De Leon. Lubbock, Tex.: Trucha Publications, 1972. $2.00. (4-6)
The story of Juanito, a Mexican-American boy, and his adventures at school and with his kite.

1772.   Roy, Cal, reteller. **The Serpent and the Sun: Myths of the Mexican World.** New York: Farrar, 1972. 119p. $5.95. (4-6)
Twelve Mexican myths have been retold for children in order to depict the history, culture, religious life and heritage of Mexican-Americans. Illustrated.

1773.   Salinas, Luis Omar, and Lillian Faderman, eds. **From the Barrio: A Chicano Anthology.** San Francisco: Canfield Press, 1973. 154p. $3.50. (7-12)
A collection of writings by Chicano authors, including essays, poetry, fiction, drama. Arrangement is in two sections: those of a political theme, and those of a miscellaneous, but non-political expression. A brief autobiographical sketch is included for each writer.

1774.   Schaefer, Jack. **Old Ramon.** Boston, Mass.: Houghton Mifflin, 1960. 102p. $10.00. (5-7)
Old Ramon, of Mexican heritage, is a wise old shepherd. He gains a young boy's respect by teaching him some secrets of nature and ways of the animals.

1775.   Summers, James L. **Don't Come Back a Stranger.** Philadelphia, Pa.: Westminster Press, 1970. 186p. $4.95. (6-12)
The relationship between an Anglo and a Mexican-American student is described in

this story of college and campus life. Another title for junior high students is *You Can't Make It by Bus* (Westminster, 1969. $3.95).

1776. Taylor, Theodore. **Maldonado Miracle**. New York: Doubleday, 1973. 189p. $4.95. (5-10)
When Jose sneaks across the U.S. border from Baja California, he unexpectedly finds himself in a camp for migrant workers. Although the story is humorous and has a surprise ending, it is a good picture of conditions faced by the migrant workers, many of whom are Mexican Americans.

1777. Valdez, Luis, and El Teatro Campesino. **Actos**. Fresno, Calif.: Cucaracha Press, 1971. 145p. $2.50. (9-12)
A collection of plays that could be performed or read at the high school level. All are concerned with the Chicano experience and are written by young Chicanos.

1778. Valdez, Luis, and Stan Steiner, eds. **Aztlan: An Anthology of Mexican American Literature**. New York: Knopf, 1972. 410p. $2.45pa. (10-12)
Various writings, arranged chronologically by subject, include poems, essays, dramas, stories, government documents, and some personal correspondence by and/or about Mexican Americans.

1779. Vasquez, Richard. **Chicano**. New York: Doubleday, 1970. 376p. $7.95; repr. ed., New York: Avon, 1971. $1.25pa. (9-12)
A novel about four generations of the Mexican-American Sandoval family. The immigrants' problems of adjustment, minority group discrimination, family life, and romance are all a part of the story. Setting is the Latin barrio of Los Angeles.

1780. Whitney, Phyllis. **A Long Time Coming**. New York: David McKay Company, 1954; repr. ed., New York: New American Library, 1976. 256p. $1.25. (5-12)
Christie's father owns the canning factory where a group of migrant Mexican-American workers are employed. She finds herself in the middle of a controversial and discriminatory situation.

1781. Young, Bob, and Jan Young. **Across the Tracks**. New York: Messner, 1958; repr. ed., New York: Pocket Books, 1972. 192p. $3.50; $0.75pa. (6-9)
A popular Mexican-American high school student is faced with the problem of lack of tolerance and cultural understanding between Chicano and Anglo students. Betty Ochoa, a Chicano girl, comes to appreciate her Mexican heritage and helps the Anglos and Chicanos accept each other.

Audiovisual Materials

1782.   **American/Mexican Stories.** 4 filmstrips, 4 cassettes, teacher's guide.
        Educational Dimensions. $66.00. (K-3)
Story titles in this set include *A Folk Tale of Mexico*; *Mexican-American in the
Southwestern Barrio*; *The Living Cesar Chavez*; *The Mexican-American Heritage.*

1783.   **Arts and Crafts of Mexico: Part 1. Pottery and Weaving.** 16mm film,
        14 min., b&w or color. Encyclopaedia Britannica Educational Corp.,
        1961.
The heritage of Mexican-Americans is displayed in this film on the ancient crafts
of pottery making and weaving. The second part of the film, entitled *Basketry,
Stone, Wood, and Metals*, is an 11-minute b&w or color film showing embroidery,
basketry, onyx carving, wood carving, and metal works.

1784.   **A Better Life.** 16mm film, 37 min., sound, color. Motion Picture Prod.
        Div., Sandia Corp., 1973. (4-12)
Mexican Americans and Indians are examined, with emphasis on the problems of
racial discrimination and prejudice. Education for these minority groups is also
discussed.

1785.   **Change: Education and the Mexican American.** 16mm film, 57 min., sound,
        b&w. Extension Media Center, Film Distribution, University of California,
        Berkeley. (9-12, T)
Covers the high school walkouts in Los Angeles during 1968. Dr. Julian Nava and
other educators discuss education for the Mexican American and changes that have
been and must be made.

1786.   **Chicano.** 16mm film, 23 min., color. BFA Educational Media, 1971.
        $10.50 (rental). (9-12, T)
Describes the goals of the Chicano movement and Mexican-American organizations
in response to discrimination in educational, social, and economic opportunities for
the Chicano community.

1787.   **Chicano.** 16mm film, 27 min., sound, color. McGraw-Hill Contemporary
        Films, 1971. (5-12)
Describes Mexican Americans in various walks of life and different roles in American society. Traditional Mexican music is in the background, and interviews have
been taped and recorded to show the sentiments, aspirations, and demands of the
Chicano.

1788.   **Chicano from the Southwest.** 16mm film, 15 min., color. Encyclopaedia
        Britannica Educational Corp., 1970. $7.00 (rental). (5-9)
A typical rural Mexican-American family moves from Texas to Los Angeles and
must adjust to urban life and Anglo culture. Their values, customs, and cultural
conflicts are seen as the family adjusts and seeks employment.

1789.   **The Culture of the Mexican-Americans.** 1 filmstrip. Educational Film-
        strips, 1973. $7.50. (4-9)

A captioned filmstrip on Mexican-American traditions, culture, and heritage. Also produced in Spanish, *La Cultura de los Norteamericanos de Origin Mexicano.* This filmstrip can also be purchased with a cassette instead of captions and includes a teacher's manual for $12.00.

1790. **Education and the Mexican-American.** 16mm film, 57 min., sound, b&w. University of California, University Extension Department of Urban Affairs. Distr. by University of California Extension Media Center, Berkeley, 1969. (6-12, T)

Part I presents the viewpoint of students, educators, attorneys, and others involved in the education of the Mexican American in the Los Angeles area. Part II is a panel discussion of some of the issues raised by the participants of Part I.

1791. **Educational Needs of Chicanos.** Audio tape. Pacifica Tape Library. (T)

This tape, narrated by Arturo Cabrero, discusses bilingualism, discriminatory treatment of Mexican Americans, and some educational programs that would be beneficial or would meet the particular needs of the Chicano student.

1792. **Fiesta.** 16mm film, 8 min., sd., color. Sutherland Learning Associates, 1972. (K-3)

Two Mexican-American children organize a fiesta to celebrate their grandfather's birthday. Narration is in Spanish and English; many Mexican religious and family customs are portrayed.

1793. **The Hands of Maria.** 16mm film, 15 min., sound, color. Prod. by Southwestern Educational Films, Inc.; distr. by RMI Film Productions, 1968. (5-12)

A documentary film on the arts and crafts of the Rio Grande Valley of New Mexico. The pottery of Maria Martinez, a Mexican-American craftsman, is pictured, along with the historical background of her skills and techniques.

1794. **Harvest of Shame.** 16mm film, 58 min., sd., b&w. Prod. by CBS News; distr. by McGraw-Hill/Contemporary Films. (6-12)

A documentary film originally shown on CBS as an Edward R. Murrow report. It depicts the plight of the migrant farm workers in the United States—the majority of whom are Mexican Americans—and the economic and social conditions under which they must live and work.

1795. **How's School, Enrique?** 16mm film, 18 min., color. Frager Cahil; distr. by AIMS, 1970. $8.00 (rental). (5-12)

Fourteen-year-old Enrique is a junior high school student in the Mexican-American barrio. This film follows him through the activities of a school day, through classrooms and his responses and relations to his teachers, and vice versa. The pressures, problems, and cultural conflicts that deter his obtaining a quality education are indicated.

1796. **Huelga.** 16mm film, 52 min., sd., color. Prod. by King Film Productions; distr. by McGraw-Hill/Contemporary Films, 1967. (6-12)

A chronology of the events of the first year of the grape strike at Delano, California.

Mexican-American leaders in the struggle for economic equality are indicated, and the influence and role of the National Farm Workers' Association in bettering living conditions for migrant workers are discussed.

1797.   **I Am Joaquin.** 16mm film, 20 min., sd., color. El Teatro Campesino.
         Released by George Ballis Association, 1970. (7-12)
This is a dramatization of an epic poem about the Mexican-American farm workers' struggle against economic exploitation and oppression. Photographs by George Ballis depict the essence of the poem by Rudolfo Gonzalez, entitled *I Am Joaquin.*

1798.   **Mexican-American: An Examination of Stereotypes.** 8 cassettes, teacher's
         guide. Prod. by Henry Olguin; distr. by BFA Educational Media. (10-12, T)
These tapes analyze Mexican-American stereotypes and the stereotyping of Anglos by the Mexican Americans. Covers the origin of stereotyping, how it develops and is perpetuated, and the effects it has on both groups.

1799.   **Mexican-American Culture: Its Heritage.** 16mm film, 18 min., sd., color.
         Prod. and distr. by Communications Group West, 1970. (4-12)
Ricardo Montalban narrates this portrayal of the music and dance of the Mexican tradition and heritage. The costumes, clothing, and spirit of the Mexican people are captured in this film on their cultural heritage. The film gives information on the arts and dance relating them to the history of the Mexican American peoples and indicates how their traditions have influenced the development of the Southwestern United States.

1800.   **A Mexican American Family.** 16mm film, 16 min., sd., color. Prod. and
         distr. by Atlantic Productions, Inc., 1970. (4-10)
An American family of Mexican descent is interviewed and filmed in the Southwest. Activities within the Mexican-American community, family values and customs, and the problems of existing within a bicultural world.

1801.   **Mexican-American: Heritage and Destiny.** 16mm film, 29 min., sd., color.
         Prod. and distr. by Handel Film Corporation, 1971. (4-12)
Contributions and achievements of the Mexican Americans in art, law, education, recreation, athletics, architecture, sports, and entertainment. The film is narrated by Ricardo Montalban.

1802.   **Mexican American: Heritage and History.** 16mm film, 18 min., sd., color.
         Prod. and distr. by Communications Group West. (4-12)
A historical perspective of the contributions of the Mexican Americans to the Southwestern United States. Emphasis is on music and art. The film, narrated by Ricardo Montalban, is also available in Spanish.

1803.   **The Mexican American Speaks: Heritage in Bronze.** 16mm film, 20 min.,
         sd., color. Encyclopaedia Britannica Educational Corporation, 1973. (7-12)
Describes the cultural heritage of the Mexican American in the Southwest. Also covers the new awareness, La Raza movements and ethnic pride in the cultural traditions.

1804. **Mexican-Americans.** 1 filmstrip, 1 record. Warren Schloat Productions, 1968. (4-8)
A history of the Mexicans in the United States from the early days of colonization and settlement of the Southwest. Also includes information about the efforts at organization among the migrant farm workers and La Huelga, the famous grape pickers' strike at Delano, California.

1805. **Mexican Americans.** Multimedia kit. Field Educational Publications. (6-12)
This kit, part of the *American Adventure* series, includes a long filmstrip (121 frames), a record, a teacher's manual, and a study print on the history, assimilation, and culture of the Mexican Americans. The unit also covers the movements of the 1960s and 1970s and discusses the identity conflicts of the Mexican-American people, particularly the youth.

1806. **Mexican-Americans: An Historic Profile.** 16mm film, 29 min., sd., b&w. By Maclovic Barraza, Chairman of the Board of the Southwest Council of La Raza. Anti-Defamation League of B'nai B'rith, 1971. (6-12)
A chronological history of the Mexican American from the days of the Spanish Conquest. Emphasis is on the twentieth century and current political and economic protests and movements towards equal rights. Film from historical archives and old photographs help document this history.

1807. **Mexican Americans in Texas History.** 12 transparencies, 10x12-inch, 1 teacher's manual. Creative Visuals, 1971. $28.50 set; $3.00 each. (5-10)
Emphasis is on the history and contributions of Mexican Americans in Texas in this series of portraits. The teacher's manual also includes biographical sketches of Mexican-American men and women who have been significant in the development of the United States.

1808. **Mexican-Americans: Invisible Minority.** 16mm film, 38 min., color. Prod. by National Educational Television and Radio Center; distr. by Indiana University Audio-Visual Center, 1969. (7-12)
Reveals the poverty and inequalities that Mexican Americans have been struggling against. Features several prominent individuals in the current protest movement, such as Cesar Chavez, Reies Tijerina, Corky Gonzales, and others.

1809. **Mexican-Americans: Viva La Raza!** 16mm film, 54 min., sd., b&w, teacher's guide. CBS News. Released by McGraw-Hill, n.d. (6-12)
Protest movements and political and social problems of the Mexican Americans are depicted. Emphasis is on the Los Angeles, California, area.

1810. **Mexican Ceramics.** 1 Super 8mm film loop, 18 min., sd., color. Prod. by Randall and Townsend; distr. by Bailey Film Association, 1966. (4-12)
Different types of pottery are described in this film loop, from the methods of making the very earliest low-fire pottery to the beautiful high-fired multi-color pottery made by the Mexican Americans of today.

1811.   **Mexican Dances, Pts. I & II.** 16mm film, 18 min., sd., color, teacher's
        guide. Prod. by Associated Film Services; distr. by Aims Instructional
        Media Services. $245.00 each; $25.00 each (rental). (4-12)
The Ballet Folklorico Estudiantil of Lincoln High School in Los Angeles performs
Mexican-American dances to Mexican music in this film depicting one aspect of
the Mexican-American culture.

1812.   **Mexican Folk Songs.** Cassette (or reel tape), 30 min. Prod. by Pennsylvania
        Department of Public Instruction; distr. by the National Center for Audio
        Tapes, Bureau of Audiovisual Instruction, University of Colorado, 1965.
        (4-12)
Mexican folk songs are sung and played on instruments native to the Mexican heritage and tradition.

1813.   **Mexican Foods—The American Way.** 16mm film, 14 min., sd., color.
        Prod. by Gebhardt Mexican Foods Company; distr. by Modern Talking
        Pictures Service, n.d. (4-12)
Preparation of Mexican foods, in an Americanized style, is depicted in this history
of Mexican-American cooking. Recipes are given and can be copied down and used
as a special extracurricular activity in a unit on the Mexican-American culture.

1814.   **Mexican or American.** 16mm film, 17 min., sd., color. Distr. by Atlantis
        Production, Inc., 1970. (6-12)
A Mexican-American family is studied to get a picture of the conflicts they face
living in a bicultural world. Family structure and roles and family customs in the
Mexican-American community are also observed.

1815.   **Migrant.** 16mm film, 53 min., sd., color. Prod. and distr. by NBC Educa-
        tional Media, 1971. (5-12)
A positive view of the Mexican-American migrant family is seen through the eyes
of the daughter, Angie. However, the poverty and undesirable living conditions of
the community are seen, in spite of the fact that the parents give their children
warmth and security.

1816.   **North from Mexico.** 16mm film, 20 min., sd., color. Prod. by Center for
        Mass Communication of Columbia University Press; distr. by Greenwood
        Press, 1971. (6-12)
A film adaption of Carey McWilliams' book of the same title on the history of the
Mexicans in the United States. Coverage begins with Coronado's explorations into
North America in 1540 and continues to the socioeconomic movements of protest
among the Chicanos of today.

1817.   **Olivia: Mexican or American?** 16mm film, 12 min., sd., color, teacher's
        study guide. Dimension Films; released by Churchill Films, 1973. (7-12)
An open-ended discussion for classroom use on the study of the problems of the
Mexican Americans can be initiated through the story of Olivia, who seeks to
identify with Anglos and rejects her Mexican background.

1818.　**A Portfolio of Outstanding Americans of Mexican Descent**. 37 study prints, 11x14-inch portraits. Social Studies School Service, 1970. $7.50 set. (K-12)

A set of 37 black and white portraits with biographical sketches is presented. The text is bilingual (English and Spanish). Individuals portrayed include historical figures and important leaders in the Chicano movement, as well as Mexican Americans who have made outstanding contributions to American society.

1819.　**La Raza, the Mexican Americans**. 24 filmstrips, 12 discs, teacher's guide. Multi-Media Productions. $235.00 set. (6-10)

A four-part set of filmstrips with each part providing two lessons. A teacher's manual covers the whole set. Each part may be purchased individually. The titles give chronological coverage of the history of the Mexican Americans in the United States. Part I is *The Mexican Heritage*; Part II is *The Pioneer Heritage*; Part III is *Conflict of Cultures*; and Part IV is *The Awakening*. The last part deals with the background and development of the social and political movement of La Raza.

1820.　**Salazar Family: A Look at Poverty**. 16mm film, 14 min., sd., b&w. Prod. and distr. by the University of California, Media Extension Center, Berkeley, 1970. (7-12)

A portrait of a Mexican-American family and the problems they face—poverty and lack of educational, social, and economic opportunity. Each member of the family is studied to see the effects of poverty on each.

1821.　**Schlitz Mexican-American Historical Calendar**. Calendar. The Joseph Schlitz Brewing Company. $1.00 (free to schools and non-profit organizations). (K-12)

Pictures outstanding Mexican Americans in the history of the United States and describes their contributions and achievements. The calendar is bilingual (English and Spanish). Each day of the month indicates an historical event of significance in the Mexican-American chronology.

1822.　**Strangers in Their Own Land: The Chicanos**. 16mm film, 16 min., sd., color. ABC Media Concepts, 1971. (7-12)

Hope Ryden narrates the events in the town of Phair, Texas, that emphasized public discrimination and prejudicial treatment of the Mexican Americans in the community.

1823.　**Viva La Causa—the Migrant Labor Movement**. 2 filmstrips, 2 records (or cassettes). Denoyer-Geppert Audio-Visuals, 1971. $39.00; $41.00 (with cassettes). (8-12)

California Mexican-American migrant farm workers attempt to organize a union to collect better pay and improve their living and working conditions. Cesar Chavez' efforts are described, and migrant workers and union organizers are interviewed. This title is also offered in a 16mm film version produced and distributed by Denoyer Geppert Company (1971).

1824.   **Voice of La Raza.** 16mm film, 60 min., sd., color. Distr. by William
        Graves Productions. (7-12)
An overview of the Mexican American in the United States, with emphasis on his
social and economic problems and the movements to better his situation. The film
is narrated by Anthony Quinn.

1825.   **Walk the First Step.** 16mm film, 28 min., sd., color. KCET; released by
        Indiana University Audio-Visual Center, 1973. (10-12, T)
The role of the Mexican-American Opportunity Foundation training program is
described, with emphasis on its job counseling and placement services as well as
classes offered in Mexican-American history.

1826.   **We Came from the Valley.** 16mm film, 28 min., sd., color. Vought
        Aeronautics, 1971. (10-12)
The Vought Aeronautics Aerospace Company describes its programs of training
unskilled Mexican-American workers to work in its Dallas plant.

1827.   **Why? La Basta: Chicano Moratorium at Laguna Park.** 16mm film, 12
        min., sd., color. Prod. and distr. by Cintech Productions, 1971. (10-12)
Describes the riot of August 1970 when Ruben Salazar, a Mexican American, was
killed in an East Los Angeles Mexican barrio. The events that led up to the riot and
the effects on the Mexican American community are studied.

1828.   **Yo soy Chicano.** 16mm film, 59 min., sd., color. KCET; released by
        Indiana University Audio-Visual Center, 1972. (8-12)
Presents a history of the Mexican migration to the United States by dramatizing
major events in Mexican history and by filming interviews with well-known
Mexican-American leaders. The discussion centers around problems that face this
ethnic minority group.

NORWEGIAN AMERICANS

See also **Scandinavian Americans.**

Reference Sources
(*See* Reference Sources under Scandinavian Americans.)

Non-Fiction Titles: History, Culture, Sociology, Biography

1829.   Andersen, Arlow W. **The Norwegian Americans.** New York: Twayne,
        1975. 280p. $7.50. (7-12)
Traces Norwegian migration to the United States and covers the history of the
Norwegian-American experience. Emphasis is on religion, education, economic
opportunities, Norwegian institutions, and other aspects of Norwegian-American
culture. Primarily concerned with areas of heavy Norwegian population—Illinois,

Iowa, Wisconsin, and Minnesota. A bibliography and index are provided. Other titles by the author are *The Immigrant Takes His Stand: The Norwegian-American Press and Public Affairs, 1847-1872* (Greenwood, 1973 reprint; $10.75) and *The Salt of the Earth: A History of Norwegian-Danish Methodism in America* (Pantheon, 1962, o.p.).

1830.   Bergmann, Leola N. **Americans from Norway.** New York: Lippincott,
         1950; repr. ed., Westport, Conn.: Greenwood, 1973. 324p. $15.00. (7-12)
A history of the Norwegian immigration to America, the experience of the Norwegian community in the United States and the contributions and cultural achievements of this group. Biographical sketches of outstanding Norwegian Americans are included. Bibliographical sources and index provided.

1831.   Blegen, Theodore Christina. **Grass Roots History.** Minneapolis: University
         of Minnesota Press, 1947; repr. ed., Port Washington, N.Y.: Kennikat,
         1969. 266p. $10.00. (9-12)
This history of the Norwegian immigrants on the American frontier, prepared by an outstanding historian, was constructed from letters written by the immigrants to friends and relatives in their homeland. Emphasis is on everyday experiences and their social and cultural activities. A similar title by the author is *Land of Their Choice: The Immigrants Write Home* (University of Minnesota Press, 1955). An additional work, *Norwegian Migration to America: 1825-1860* (Arno, 1969. $12.50) and a companion volume, *Migration to America: The American Transition* discuss the expansion of Norwegian immigration and the reasons for leaving the homeland, as well as the part the immigrant played in developing America.

1832.   Hillbrand, Percie V. **The Norwegians in America.** Minneapolis, Minn.:
         Lerner Publications, 1967. 79p. $3.95. (5-10)
Norwegian history in America is covered, with emphasis on the earliest immigrants and their settlements including the Viking sailors. Some Norwegians are noted for their outstanding achievements or talents in various fields; contributions of the group as a whole are also indicated. Illustrated.

1833.   Holland, Ruth. **Vikings of the West: The Scandinavian Immigrants in
         America.** Pictures by H. B. Vestal. New York: Grosset, 1968. 61p. $1.95pa.
         (6-12)
Describes some of the voyages of the Vikings and the areas of the American West in which they settled. Covers their contributions to American expansion and development.

1834.   Larson, Laurence M. **The Changing West and Other Essays.** Northfield,
         Minn.: Norwegian-American Historical Association, 1937; repr. ed.,
         Freeport, N.Y.: Books for Libraries Press, 1968. 180p. $10.50. (7-12)
Essays dealing with the Norwegians in America include: "The Changing West," "The Norwegian Element in the Field of American Scholarship," "Tellef Grundysen and the Beginnings of Norwegian-American Fiction," and "The Norwegian Element in the Northwest," among others.

1835.　Lovoll, Odd. **A Folk Epic: The Bygdelag in America.** Northfield, Minn.:
　　　　Norwegian-American Historical Association, 1975. 326p. $8.50. (10-12)
Organizational life of Norwegian Americans is discussed, with particular emphasis
on the groups formed by the early immigrants. The origin, peak, services and
activities, and demise of Norwegian-American organizations are described.

1836.　Nelson, Clifford, and Eugene L. Fevold. **The Lutheran Church among
　　　　Norwegian Americans.** Minneapolis, Minn.: Augsburg Publishing House,
　　　　1960. 2 vols. $12.50. (10-12)
A history of the Lutheran Church among Norwegian Americans sheds light on their
social, religious, and moral behavior. Prominent early Norwegian immigrants are
noted for their work in the church and among the Norwegian communities.

1837.　Norlie, Olaf Morgan. **History of the Norwegian People in America.**
　　　　Minneapolis, Minn.: Augsburg, 1925; repr. ed., New York: Haskell, 1972.
　　　　602p. $22.95. (9-12)
The Norwegian experience in the United States is traced from the days of the
earliest Norse explorers to the time of publication.

1838.　Roinestad, Soren C. **A Hundred Years with the Norwegians in the East
　　　　Bay.** Oakland, Calif.: n.p., 1963; repr. ed., San Francisco: R&E Research
　　　　Associates, 1970. 108p. $5.00pa. (9-12)
Although this history studies the Norwegians only in the San Francisco Bay Region
of California, it covers a one-hundred-year period of Norwegian social, cultural,
religious, economic, and institutional life.

1839.　Sundby-Hansen, Harry. **Norwegian Immigrant Contributions to America's
　　　　Making.** New York: The International Press, 1921; repr. ed., San Francisco:
　　　　R&E Research Associates, 1970. 170p. $8.00. (7-12)
Written for the America's Making Exhibit and Festival in New York (October 29-
November 12, 1921), this volume was designed to educate the public about the
achievements of citizens from Norway. Emphasis is on Norwegian culture, customs,
and types of foods and clothing, etc.

1840.　Ylvisaker, Erling. **Eminent Pioneers: Norwegian American Pioneer
　　　　Sketches.** Minneapolis, Minn.: Augsburg Press, 1934; repr. ed., Freeport,
　　　　N.Y.: Books for Libraries, 1970. 162p. $11.50. (7-12)
Sketches of the events, culture, and people that pioneered America in the
Norwegian immigrant communities.

Literature and Fiction Titles

1841.　Archer, Marion F. **There Is a Happy Land.** Chicago: Whitman, 1963. 160p.
　　　　$3.95. (3-6)
The story of a family of Norwegian immigrants, the problems they encounter, and
the adjustments they must make living in Midwestern America.

1842.   Asbjørnsen, Peter C. **The Squire's Bride: A Norwegian Folktale.** New York: Atheneum, 1975. unp. $5.95. (K-3)

A rich squire wants to marry a beautiful but poor girl. Her father is also anxious for this alliance, but the girl outwits all their plans to make her marry against her will. Another title by the author is *Norwegian Folk Tales* (Viking, 1961. $4.00).

1843.   Bojer, Johan. **The Emigrants.** Translated by A. G. Jayne. New York: Century, 1924; repr. ed., Westport, Conn.: Greenwood, 1974. 351p. $15.00. (9-12)

A family of Norwegian pioneers are the central characters. The story traces their activities from their home in Norway to their new home in North Dakota's Red River Valley. The parents intend to save money and eventually return to Norway, but their children become more and more assimilated into American culture and they realize that their life is in America.

1844.   Cather, Willa. **O Pioneers.** New York: Houghton, c1941, 1962. 308p. $2.65pa. (7-12)

A story of the Bergsen family, Norwegian immigrants on the Nebraska prairies. Their difficulties in adjusting to a new country, a new way of earning a living, a new language, and new customs are described. The Norwegian family life, heritage, and influence in this country are also seen in this narrative.

1845.   Dahl, Borghild. **Homecoming.** New York: Dutton, 1953, 1960. 251p. $4.50. (6-12)

Lyng Skoglund is a second-generation Norwegian living in Minneapolis. She rebels against the old Norwegian customs of her home and family and wants to be Americanized and do the things her American friends do. When she graduates from the University of Minnesota she wants to teach and tries to attain for the Norwegian children in her classes the advantages of an American education. The story is a picture of the conflict between cultures, the problems of second-generation immigrations and of the Norwegian customs and culture in particular. Another title by the author is *Good News* (Dutton, 1966).

1846.   D'Aulaire, Ingri, and Edgar P. D'Aulaire. **Norse Gods and Giants.** Garden City, N.Y.: Doubleday, 1967. 154p. $7.95. (3-6)

The adventures of Thor, Freya, Loki, the Valkyries, and others in the world of Norse mythology. The volume is well illustrated and is useful as a reference volume and for reading or storytelling. Another title by the author is *Ola* (Doubleday, 1939. $3.95).

1847.   Forbes, Kathryn. **Mama's Bank Account.** New York: Harcourt, Brace & Co., c1943, 1975. 204p. $3.95; $0.95 (Scholastic) pa. (7-12)

A collection of short stories about a Norwegian immigrant family. The setting is San Francisco in the early 1900s. The characters are warm, sentimental, and humorous; they reflect the amusing situations as well as the problems of immigrant families.

1848.   Havighurst, Walter, and Marion Havighurst. **Song of the Pines.** New York: Holt, 1949. 205p. $3.27. (6-12)

Nils Thorson, a knife grinder, struggles to earn a living in America, to learn the language, and to be accepted by others in his new homeland. Another title by the authors is *High Prairie* (1944).

1849.   Hong, Edna Hatlestad, and Howard Hong. **Muskego Boy.** Illus. by Lee
          Mero. Minneapolis, Minn.: Augsburg, c1943, 1971. 96p. $3.50. (3-6)
The story of a young Norwegian-American boy living in the rural Scandinavian community on one of the Midwestern swamp and lake regions where these farmers and woodsmen from the Old Country often settled. Norwegian customs, traditions, and values are a part of this story, as well as the Norwegian contribution to the development of America's frontier.

1850.   Rolvaag, Ole Edvart. **The Boat of Longing.** New York: Harper & Bros.,
          1921; repr. ed., Westport, Conn.: Greenwood Press, 1974. 304p. $13.00.
          (7-12)
When Nils Vaag leaves Norway and immigrates to America, he writes enthusiastic letters home to his parents. When times get hard, he no longer writes home and his parents are sick with worry. His father sets out to find Nils, but is turned back at Ellis Island because he is not sponsored by an American. On the ship going home he hears of two sons who made it good in America. He invents a success story of Nils to tell his wife. Other titles about Norwegians in America by the author are *Giants in the Earth* (Harper, 1927. $5.95); *Peder Victorious* (Harper, 1929; o.p.); *Pure Gold* (Harper, c1930; repr., Greenwood, 1973. $13.50); *Their Father's God* (Harper, 1931; repr. ed., Greenwood, 1974. $13.75); and *The Third Life of Per Smevik* (Dillon, 1971. $5.95).

Audiovisual Materials

1851.   **The Dahl House: Norwegian Texans of Bosque County.** 1 filmstrip, 1
          phonotape. Institute of Texan Cultures, 1970.
Presents the family life and activities of Norwegian immigrants who have settled on farms in Texas. The same title is also available as a slide set (76 color 2x2-inch slides with accompanying phonotape), by the same producer.

PENNSYLVANIA-DUTCH. *See* **German Americans.**

POLISH AMERICANS

See also **Slavic Americans.**

Reference Sources

1852.   Bolek, Francis, ed. **Who's Who in Polish America: A Biographical Directory of Polish-American Leaders and Distinguished Poles Resident in the Americas.** New York: Harbinger House, 1943; repr. ed., New York: Arno, 1970. $23.50. (7-12, T)
About 5,000 biographical sketches of living and deceased Polish Americans. Arrangement is by occupation and geographical area. The author has also compiled *Polish American Encyclopedia* (Polish American Encyclopedia Committee, 1954).

1853.   Hoskins, Janina W., comp. **Polish Books in English, 1945-1971.** Washington, D.C.: GPO, 1974. 163p. $1.55pa.
Includes over 1,000 entries. According to the compiler, "This record of translated Polish works in the fields of the humanities and social sciences is designed to help the American reader to become acquainted with Polish cultural, political, economic and historic development" (Preface). Alphabetical arrangement. Covers books and pamphlets published in Poland or outside Poland during the period 1945-1971.

1854.   Maciuszko, Jerzy J. **The Polish Short Story in English: A Guide and Critical Bibliography.** Detroit, Mich.: Wayne State University Press, 1968. 473p. $15.00.
Lists over 600 titles from 1884 through 1960. All entries are annotated. Very valuable bibliography for students of Polish literature. Another important title is Boleslaw Taborski, *Polish Plays in English Translation: A Bibliography* (New York: Polish Institute of Arts and Sciences in America, 1968. 79p. $2.50pa.).

1855.   Renkiewicz, Frank, ed. **The Poles in America, 1608-1972: A Chronology and Fact Book.** Dobbs Ferry, N.Y.: Oceana, 1973. 128p. $6.00. (7-12)
A historical chronology, selected pertinent documents and appendices containing statistical tables of the distribution of Poles by state, Polish-American fraternal statistics, publications, institutions, and a selected bibliography are present in this one-volume ready reference aid.

1856.   Zurawski, Joseph W. **Polish American History and Culture: A Classified Bibliography.** Chicago: Polish Museum of America, 1975. 218p. index. $4.75pa.
Lists over 1,600 entries covering Polish-American history, Polish political, social, economic, and cultural life. The compiler also provides separate chapters on "Polish American Biographical Accounts," "Polish Americans in U.S. Novels," "Polish American Poetry," "Polish American Theatre," and other subjects that reflect the Polish experience in this country. Publications in the Polish language are excluded. An author index concludes this interesting volume. Zurawski's compilation will serve as a useful reference tool for reference librarians as well as for individuals interested in the Polish ethnic community in the United States.

Non-Fiction Titles: History, Culture, Sociology, Biography

1857.   Abodaher, David J. **Warrior on Two Continents: Thaddeus Kosciuszko.**
        New York: Julian Messner, 1968. 192p. $3.50. (7-12)
Kosciuszko is described as a warrior who not only led the Polish Insurrection in his
homeland in 1794, but, after immigrating to America, fought again for freedom as
a general in Washington's army. A similar biography by the author is *Freedom
Fighter: Casimir Pulaski* (Messner, 1968. $3.50).

1858.   Abrahall, Clare. **The Young Marie Curie.** New York: Roy Publishers,
        1961. 128p. $3.25. (5-12)
A biography of the childhood days and young adulthood of Marie Curie, born
Marie Sklodowska, an outstanding woman scientist of Polish descent.

1859.   Bakanowski, Adolf. **The Polish Circuit Rider.** Cheshire, Conn.: Cherry
        Hill Books, 1971. 49p. $2.00pa. (9-12)
Memoirs of the early Polish settlement in Texas and the influence of the Catholic
Church in the community. This work has been translated and annotated by Marion
Moore Coleman.

1860.   Buczek, Daniel. **Immigrant Pastor.** New York: The Kosciuszko Founda-
        tion, 1973. 184p. $2.95. (9-12)
The life of the Right Reverend Monsignor Lucyan Bojnowski of New Britain,
Connecticut, and his work and contributions to the people of a Polish-American
community. A bibliography is included.

1861.   Coleman, Arthur Prudden. **Wanderer's Twain.** Cheshire, Conn.: Cherry
        Hill Books, 1964. 111p. $5.00. (9-12)
Memoirs on Helena Modjeska and Henryk Sienkiewicz and their experiences and
reactions to the United States.

1862.   Fox, Paul. **The Poles in America.** New York: George H. Doran Company,
        1922; repr. ed., New York: Arno, 1970. 143p. $6.00. (7-12)
Part I deals with the conditions in Poland at the time many Poles left to come to the
United States, as well as a brief overview of Poland's history. Part II covers the
distribution of Polish immigrants and their descendants in the United States.
Covers their economic, social, religious, and institutional life and other aspects of
Polish-American culture.

1863.   Haiman, Mieczyslaw (Miecislaus). **Polish Pioneers of Virginia and
        Kentucky.** Chicago: Polish Roman Catholic Union of America, 1937; repr.
        ed., San Francisco: R&E Research Associates, 1970. 84p. $5.00. (9-12)
Describes the early Polish-American settlers of the states of Virginia and Kentucky,
indicating outstanding families. Emphasis is on their contributions to the development of America's frontier and their social, religious, and community life.
Another history of the Polish-American experience by the author is *Polish Past in
America, 1608-1895* (Polish Museum of America, 1975. $4.75). Other reprints
of his works are *Polish Pioneers of California* (R&E Research Associates, 1970.
$5.00); *Poles in the Seventeenth and Eighteenth Centuries* (R&E Research

Associates, 1970. $5.00); and *Kosciuszko in the American Revolution* (Gregg, 1972. $10.00).

1864. Lerski, Jerzy Jan. **A Polish Chapter in Jacksonian America: The United States and the Polish Exiles of 1831.** Madison, Wisc.: University of Wisconsin Press, 1958. 242p. $11.50. (10-12)
Describes the pro-Polish sympathy in the United States when Poland rose against Russia in 1830, and the law that President Andrew Jackson signed establishing a Polish community in Illinois.

1865. Milosz, Czeslaw. **The History of Polish Literature.** New York: Macmillan, 1969. 544p. $14.95.
A comprehensive, scholarly survey of Polish literature from its beginnings through 1966. The author also discusses Lithuanian, Byelorussian, and Ukrainian literatures as they relate to Polish writings. The same author also published an important anthology, *Postwar Polish Poetry* (Garden City, N.Y.: Doubleday, 1965. 199p. $4.95), which includes an English translation of 90 poems by 21 outstanding Polish poets.

1866. Pilarski, Laura. **They Came from Poland: The Story of Famous Polish Americans.** New York: Dodd, 1970. 179p. $4.50. (6-12)
Polish immigration to America is covered from the seventeenth century to the present. Emphasis is on the contributions in arts, science, politics, and sports of well-known Polish Americans, including those who were military men in the American Revolution.

1867. Przygoda, Jacek. **Texas Pioneers from Poland: A Study in Ethnic History.** New York: The Kosciuszko Foundation, 1971. 171p.
The Poles in Texas differed in that they established a semi-rural community, whereas the typical Polish immigrant found his work and life in a large urban and industrial area. This study describes the history and experience as well as the contributions of the Poles in Texas.

1868. Sandberg, Neil C. **Ethnic Identity and Assimilation: The Polish American Community.** New York: Praeger, 1974. 88p. $12.50. (9-12)
Studies an urban Polish-American community in Los Angeles and its social status in relation to other ethnic groups. Emphasis is given to the process of assimilation.

1869. Wood, Arthur E. **Hamtramck, Then and Now: A Sociological Study of a Polish-American Community.** New Haven, Conn.: College and University Press, 1955; repr. ed., New York: Octagon Books, 1975. 253p. $12.00. (9-12)
Hamtramck is a small Polish community within the Detroit urban area. Polish culture, generational conflicts, and the Polish family are studied over a period of three decades. Special attention is given to the Polish ethnic vote as a political force.

1870. Wytrwal, Joseph. **The Poles in America.** Minneapolis, Minn.: Lerner Publications, 1969. 84p. $3.95. (5-11)

A brief survey of the land and history of Poland as well as a more thorough discussion of the Poles in America, their individual contributions, and their reasons for coming to a new homeland. Other titles by the author are *America's Polish Heritage: A Social History of the Poles in America* (Endurance, 1961. $6.75) and *The Poles in American History and Tradition* (Endurance, 1969. $6.75).

Literature and Fiction Titles

1871.   Algren, Nelson. **The Neon Wilderness.** Garden City, N.Y.: Doubleday,
          1947; repr. ed., Magnolia, Mass.: Peter Smith, 1969. 286p. $4.25. (9-12)
A collection of short stories of the Polish-American community in Chicago.
Describes the hardships, physical and spiritual, of life on Chicago's West Side during
the days of acculturation and Americanization of the Polish immigrants and their
descendants. Other titles by the author are *Never Come Morning* (Harper, 1942)
and *The Man with the Golden Arm* (Doubleday, 1949. $3.95).

1872.   Burt, Katherine N. **Strong Citadel.** New York: Scribner's, 1949; repr. ed.,
          New York: New American Libraries, 1975. 281p. $0.95pa. (9-12)
A proud aristocratic family in Philadelphia is a part of this story of Katia Polenov.
The daughter of Judge Evarts learns through harsh disillusionment that a simple
peasant girl can be wise and understanding.

1873.   Chase, Mary Ellen. **A Journey to Boston.** New York: W. W. Horton &
          Co., 1965. 114p. $3.95. (9-12)
A story centering around the lives of Polish farmers in the Connecticut Valley and
reflecting the old European customs and culture. A young Polish-American boy is
the central character.

1874.   De Angeli, Marguerite. **Up the Hill.** New York: Doubleday, c1942, 1970.
          88p. $3.95. (4-8)
The son of this Polish-American family wants to be an artist, but his father
feels he should follow in the tradition of the other men in their Pennsylvania
mining town and seek financial security as a miner. The story centers around how
the son manages to convince his father to send him to art school.

1875.   Eichelberger, Rosa. **Bronko.** New York: Morrow, 1955. 192p. $0.95pa.
          (4-6)
A story of a Polish refugee who, trying to adjust to urban life in New York City,
finds that life in the new world can be a great adventure. The author has also
written *Call Me Bronko* (Scholastic Book Service, 1972. $0.95pa.) for the
intermediate-grade level).

1876.   Estes, Eleanor. **The Hundred Dresses.** Illus. by Louis Slobodkin. New
          York: Harcourt Brace Jovanovich, 1974. 80p. $5.95; $1.50pa. (4-8)
Wanda always wore the same dress to school, but bragged that she had one hundred
dresses at home. She did, in fact, have a talent for designing, and she had one
hundred pictures of costumes of her own creation.

1877.   Fast, Howard M. **The Proud and the Free**. Boston, Mass.: Little, Brown, 1950. 311p. $0.95. (9-12)
A historical novel about a Polish-American, Sergeant Stanislaus Prukish, during the revolt of the 11th Regiment of the Pennsylvania Line, January 1, 1781. The story is recalled and retold by another sergeant of the line, Jamie Stuart.

1878.   Gacek, Anna Zajac. **Polish Folk Paper-Cuts**. Minneapolis, Minn.: Heritage Resource Center, 1969. price not indicated.
Useful for integrating Polish studies units into the social studies, or art curriculum.

1879.   Janney, Russell. **The Miracle of the Bells**. New York: Prentice-Hall, c1946, 1973. 497p. $1.50pa. (Avon). (7-12)
A story set in Hollywood about a Polish-American girl from Pennsylvania who is about to become a big star when she meets with an untimely death. Her publicity man, who is also in love with her, returns to her hometown in Pennsylvania and experiences the "miracle of the bells."

1880.   Kelly, Eric P. **The Trumpeter of Krakow**. New York: Macmillan, c1929, 1966. 208p. $3.95. (5-7)
This Newbery Award-winning story is set in ancient Krakow, where a trumpeter played a hymn in the old tower every hour on the hour. The color and traditions of old Poland in the fifteenth century are passed on to young readers in this adventure story.

1881.   Krawczyk, Monica. **If the Branch Blossoms and Other Stories**. Minneapolis, Minn.: Polanie, 1950. unp. $2.75. (9-12)
A collection of short stories that are favorites in the Polish-American community there.

1882.   Lenski, Lois. **We Live in the North: Short Stories**. Philadelphia, Pa.: Lippincott, 1965. 152p. $3.59. (K-3)
A collection of short stories for primary children discussing various aspects of acculturation and adjustment in the United States for a Polish-American family.

1883.   Roberts, Cecil. **One Small Candle**. New York: Macmillan, c1942, 1970. 284p. $4.75. (9-12)
A story of a Polish pianist, Paul Korwienski, who marries an American movie star just prior to World War II. The story is set in Florida and Europe.

1884.   Schenker, Alexander M., ed. **Fifteen Modern Polish Short Stories: An Annotated Reader and a Glossary**. New Haven, Conn.: Yale University Press, 1970. 186p. $8.50; $3.75pa.
A collection of 15 short stories by contemporary Polish authors. Each short story includes an editor's introduction, with brief biographical information and a short comment on his writings.

1885.   Sienkiewicz, Henryk. **Western Septet**. Cheshire, Conn.: Cherry Hill Books, 1973. 161p. $5.00. (9-12)

These stories of the American West and the people that settled it are written by a Polish author, Henryk Sienkiewicz, author of *Quo Vadis.*

1886.   Tomczykowska, Wanda. **Polish Christmas Traditions and Legends.** Oakland,
        Calif.: Polish Arts and Culture Foundation, 1972. 24p. (K-12)
A description of Polish Christmas traditions and legends with typical Christmas dinner menus, religious practices, activities of the children, folk beliefs, and Christmas proverbs. Included also are carols, giving English translations as well as Polish words.

1887.   Vogel, Joseph. **Man's Courage.** New York: Knopf, 1938. 312p. o.p. (9-12)
Adam Wolak emigrates from Poland to America with the dream of owning his own farm, but the conditions of urban life in the city for the many immigrants who had to find work as skilled laborers finally wear him down. With his dream given up, he loses courage and hope.

1888.   Wisniowski, Sygurd. **Ameryka 100 Years Old: A Globetrotter's View.**
        Cheshire, Conn.: Cherry Hill Books, 1972. 125p. $5.00pa. (9-12)
Stories of love, adjustment, loneliness, and life on the American frontier. Includes "Langenor," a tale of Polish Americans settling the American West.

1889.   Wojciechowska, Maria. **Till the Break of Day.** New York: Harcourt Brace
        Jovanovich, 1972. 156p. $5.95. (7-12)
The author, a Polish-American and Newbery Medal winner, describes her family's escape from Poland at the onset of World War II. Their journeys throughout Europe and their experiences enroute to their new home are covered in this fictionalized narrative. The story is subtitled *Memories: 1939-1942.*

1890.   Zand, Helen S. **Polish Proverbs.** Scranton, Pa.: Polish American Journal,
        1961. 59p.
A collection of Polish proverbs that are representative of Polish culture. Gives both English and Polish versions of the proverbs.

Audiovisual Materials

1891.   **Immigrant America.** 2 filmstrips, 1 phonodisc, teacher's guide. Sunburst
        Communications, 1974. (4-10)
Life as an immigrant in New York City and the coal mines of Pennsylvania in the early 1900s is contrasted to the Mexican and Polish communities of today in Chicago.

1892.   **The Immigrant Experience: A Long, Long Journey.** 16mm film, 31 min.,
        sd., color, with study guide. Learning Corporation of America, 1973.
        $12.50 (rental). (5-12)
Studies the Polish immigrants in the United States through the experiences of a Polish family in the early 1900s. An interview with the grandfather compares that generation's opportunities with those available for his grandchildren.

1893.   **Panna Maria: First Polish Colony in Texas.** 1 color filmstrip, 1 phonotape.
Institute of Texas Culture, 1970.
The Polish settlements in Texas are described from the days of the early immigrants through development of their current status. This material is also available as a slide set.

1894.   **Polish Heritage.** 1 record. The Kosciuszko Foundation.
The Schola Moderna, a Polish-American chorus, sings selections of traditional Polish music and historical events.

1895.   **Trumpeter of Krakow.** 1 cassette tape. Educational Record Sales. (4-9)
A dramatization of Eric P. Kelly's classic story about the trumpeter of the ancient city of Krakow. The story is a Newbery Award winner for children.

1896.   **A Unique Heritage: The Polish American.** 1 filmstrip, 1 cassette. Multi-
Media Productions, 1972.
A filmstrip presenting the customs, traditions, contributions, and experience of the Polish-Americans in the United States. From the *Accent on Ethnic America* series.

PUERTO RICAN AMERICANS

See also **Spanish-Speaking Americans.**

Reference Sources

Reference Guides and Bibliographies

1897.   Cordasco, Francesco, *et al.* **Puerto Ricans on the United States Mainland:**
A Bibliography of Reports, Texts, Critical Studies and Related Materials.
Totowa, N.J.: Rowman and Littlefield, 1972. 146p. $12.50. (9-12, T)
Materials on the Puerto Rican experience on the island and the mainland, including reasons for migration and resultant problems, are covered here. Coverage is fairly comprehensive, in a subject arrangement. Emphasis is on educational and sociological problems. The work is indexed. Other bibliographies by Cordasco are *The Puerto Rican Experience: A Sociological Sourcebook* (Rowman and Littlefield, 1972. $10.00) and *The Puerto Ricans: Migration and General Bibliography* (Arno, 1975. $22.00).

1898.   Hill, Marnesba D., and Harold B. Schlarfer. **Puerto Rican Authors: A**
Bibliographic Handbook. Metuchen, N.J.: Scarecrow, 1974. 267p. $7.50.
(T)
The literature and life of Puerto Rican culture are represented by 251 authors of Puerto Rican descent. Emphasis is on diplomacy, island politics, law, medicine, and literature.

1899.   Jablonsky, Adelaide, comp. **The Education of Puerto Rican Children and Youth: An Annotated Bibliography of Doctoral Dissertations.** ERIC/IRCD Doctoral Research Series, Number 6. New York: Columbia University, ERIC Clearinghouse on the Disadvantaged, 1974. 39p. ED 090 054. $0.75 MF; $1.85 HC. (T)

A compilation of dissertations on the education of Puerto Rican children that resulted from the research funded as a result of ESEA titled programs of 1965. Arrangement is in three sections: "Studies of Puerto Rican Students on the Mainland"; "Comparisons of Puerto Rican Students with Those of Other Ethnic Groups"; and "Studies of Schools and Students in Puerto Rico." Index lists by subject, author, and institution.

1900.   New York Public Library. **Borinquen: A Bilingual List of Books, Films and Records on the Puerto Rican Experience.** 3rd ed. New York: New York Public Library, 1974. 41p. $3.00. (9-12, T)

Updating a bibliography originally published in 1963, entitled *Puerto Rico*, this listing includes materials on the Puerto Rican experience in nine different sections: General Works, History, Social Sciences, Language, The Arts, Biography, Films, Records, and Literature.

1901.   Vivo, Paquita, ed. **The Puerto Ricans: An Annotated Bibliography.** New York: Bowker, 1973. 299p. $15.50. (9-12, T)

A comprehensive bibliography (over 2,600 sources) on Puerto Ricans. Arrangement is in four sections: books, pamphlets and dissertations; government documents; periodicals; and audiovisual materials. Entries are annotated and are arranged alphabetically by subject within each section. Emphasis is on history, culture, education, music, science, and social conditions of the Puerto Rican experience. Author, subject, and title indexes provided. Another comprehensive bibliography is *Annotated Selected Puerto Rican Bibliography*, by E. R. Bravo (New York: Columbia University, 1972. $5.00).

1902.   Zirkel, Perry Ann. **Puerto Rican Pupils: A Bibliography.** West Hartford, Conn.: Hartford University, College of Education, 1973. 67p. $3.29. (T)

A resource list for teachers and educators organized in four sections: 1) books including children's literature and lists in Spanish and English; 2) audiovisual materials; 3) self-contained research studies; 4) periodical articles that list bibliographies for and about Puerto Rican students. Another listing from the University of Hartford compiled by the same author is *A Bibliography of Materials in English and Spanish Relating to Puerto Rican Students* (1971).

Handbooks, Guides, and Almanacs

1903.   Cordasco, Francesco. **The Puerto Ricans 1493-1973: A Chronology and Fact Book.** Dobbs Ferry, N.Y.: Oceana, 1973. 137p. $6.00. (7-12, T)

A chronology, documents section, and bibliography of materials relating to the Puerto Rican experience on the U.S. mainland. The chronology lists dates and events important in the historical development of Puerto Rico and its relation to the United States. The title is useful as a one-volume ready-reference tool. The relationship of the U.S. with Puerto Rico is covered in "Report of the United

States—Puerto Rico Commission on the Status of Puerto Rico" (1966). The bibliography is annotated.

1904.   U.S. Bureau of the Census. **Census of Population: 1970.** Series PC (2).
         Subject Reports. Series PC (2) 1—E. **Puerto Ricans in the U.S.** Washington,
         D.C.: Government Printing Office, 1973. 158p. $2.35. (7-12)
Statistics on various socioeconomic aspects of Puerto Rican life in the United States
are included by state, region, and some cities. Housing characteristics also tabulated.

Teaching Methodology and Curriculum Materials

1905.   Aran, Kenneth, *et al.* **Puerto Rican History and Culture: A Study Guide
         and Curriculum Outline.** New York: United Federation of Teachers,
         1973. 151p. $4.00 (T)
Resource units developed by teachers on Puerto Rican history and culture at the
7-12 grade levels. Suggested teaching techniques (class discussion, interviews,
debate, and research) for the following units are included: 1) identity, 2) migration, 3) adjustment to urban life, 4) influence of Spanish rule on Puerto Rico,
5) influence of U.S. on Puerto Rico, 6) family customs and values, 7) geographic
and economic forces, 8) Puerto Rican culture, 9) religion. Also includes an
annotated bibliography.

1906.   Battle, Ana, *et al.* **The Puerto Ricans: A Resource Unit for Teachers.** New
         York: Anti-Defamation League of B'nai B'rith, 1972. 65p. $1.25.
A resource unit for teachers arranged in five chapters covering Puerto Ricans: 1)
background, 2) migration to the mainland, 3) problems, 4) cultural values, 5)
students and education. It also includes a bibliography, an annotated list of audiovisual materials, and a list of "Sources of Information."

1907.   Cordasco, Francesco, and Eugene Bucchioni. **The Puerto Rican Community
         and Its Children on the Mainland: A Source Book for Teachers, Social
         Workers and Other Professionals.** Metuchen, N.J.: Scarecrow Press, 1972.
         465p. $11.00. (T)
A collection of readings on various aspects of Puerto Rican culture: the family,
conflict and acculturation, schools on the mainland, and historical background. The
author attempts to understand the Puerto Rican experience to provide effective
education for Puerto Rican children and youth. A bibliography by Cordasco and
Leonard Covello is included in the appendix: "Studies of Puerto Rican Children in
American Schools." Other titles by the co-authors of this source book are *Education
Programs for Puerto Rican Students* (Jersey City Board of Education, 1971. $3.29)
and *The Puerto Ricans and Educational Opportunity: An Original Anthology*
(Arno, 1975 rep. $12.00).

1908.   **The Puerto Rican Experience: An Educational Research Study.** Trenton,
         N.J.: Puerto Rican Congress of New Jersey, 1974. 54p. $3.15. (T)
This study of 21 public school districts with large Puerto Rican enrollments focuses
on the educational needs of the Puerto Rican students, assimilation, bilingual/
bicultural education, educators' attitudes toward Puerto Rican children, and paren-
tal involvement.

1909.   **Puerto Rican Studies: Related Learning Materials and Activities in Social Studies for Kindergarten, Grade 1 and Grade 2.** Curriculum Bulletin Number 6, 1972-73 Series. Brooklyn: New York City Board of Education, Bureau of Curriculum Development, 1973. 246p. $3.00. (T)
A list of teaching materials and suggested activities at the primary level for curriculum units on Puerto Rican culture and heritage. Covers Puerto Rican customs, values, and contributions. Includes a bibliography of books and audiovisual materials for children, as well as reference materials for teachers.

1910.   Wall, Muriel, comp. **Audio-Visual Aids to Enrich the Curriculum for the Puerto Rican Child in the Elementary Grades, Part 1 and 2.** New York: CUNY, Hunter College, 1971. 33p. $0.75 MF; $3.29 HC. ED 049 659. (T)
A two-part bulletin containing a variety of sources of audiovisual aids and instructional materials for use with Puerto Rican children in the elementary school. Part 1 is a short article on listening skills and information on the classroom use of the tape recorder, plus an annotated list of records and tapes, a list of "Read-with-Me Recordings" and addresses of distributors of sheet music, records, and tapes. Part 2 contains additional lists of films and filmstrips and other bilingual instructional materials.

Non-Fiction Titles: History, Culture, Sociology, Biography

1911.   Abramson, Michael. **Palante: Young Lords Party.** New York: McGraw-Hill, 1971. 159p. $3.95pa. (7-12)
A photographic essay of the Puerto Rican revolutionary movement is written by the Young Lords Party and Michael Abramson. Personal interviews, photographs, and writings of members of the New York Puerto Rican community are included.

1912.   Allyn, Paul. **The Picture Life of Herman Badillo.** New York: Watts, 1972. 48p. $3.90. (2-4)
A simple text is included in this picture story of the first Puerto Rican to be a voting member of the United States Congress.

1913.   Babin, Maria T. **Puerto Rican Spirit: Their History, Life and Culture.** New York: Macmillan, 1971. 180p. $1.95pa. (9-12)
Although emphasis is on the island culture, this work does present the heritage, traditions, literature, and arts of America's Puerto Rican citizens. Includes a bibliography.

1914.   Bean, Charles S. **My Name Is Jose.** Chicago: Franciscan Herald, 1974. 136p. $4.95. (4-9)
A study of the Puerto Ricans on the U.S. mainland is done through the narration of Jose, a young Puerto Rican American. Problems of adjustment and acculturation, and other socioeconomic aspects are told in a way children can understand.

1915.   Brahs, Stuart J. **An Album of Puerto Ricans in the United States.** New York: Watts, 1973. 84p. $4.90. (4-6)
An objective picture of the Puerto Rican life style on the mainland—the problems and social adjustments that are mandatory in the Puerto Rican community.

Also indicates the strong feelings and some of the militant emotions expressed by this group.

1916.   Cooper, Paulette, ed. **Growing Up Puerto Rican.** New York: Arbor House, 1972. 216p. $6.95. (7-12)
A collection of personal narratives and case histories compiled from taped interviews with Puerto Ricans on the U.S. mainland. Describes problems of adjustment, discrimination, poverty, language, and inequalities in other areas.

1917.   Fitzpatrick, Joseph P. **Puerto Rican Americans: The Meaning of Migration to the Mainland.** Englewood Cliffs, N.J.: Prentice-Hall, 1971. 215p. $6.95; $3.95pa. (9-12)
Examines reasons for Puerto Rican migration to the mainland and studies Puerto Rican identity and unique aspects of their culture. Also discusses problems of adjustment in housing, church, and parishes, and discrimination because of the diversity in skin color.

1918.   Kurtis, Arlene Harris. **Puerto Ricans: From Island to Mainland.** New York: Messner, 1969. 96p. $3.95. (4-8)
A history of the Puerto Ricans from the days of Spanish rule to their present relationship with the United States. Puerto Ricans on the U.S. mainland are also discussed, with attention to their problems and the Puerto Rican identity.

1919.   Larsen, Ronald J. **The Puerto Ricans in America.** Minneapolis, Minn.: Lerner Publications, 1973. 87p. $3.95. (5-10)
Describes Puerto Rican immigration to the mainland and life in the Puerto Rican communities there. Emphasis is on the Puerto Rican cultural heritage and its influence on American society.

1920.   Lewis, Oscar. **A Study of Slum Culture: Backgrounds for La Vida.** New York: Random, 1968. 240p. $7.95. (9-12)
Housing, educational achievements, occupations, family income, and migration patterns of the Puerto Ricans are all studied in this comparison of the social conditions of this group in San Juan and New York City. Another title by the author is *La Vida: A Puerto Rican Family in the Culture of Poverty—San Juan and New York* (Random, 1966. $12.50; $2.95pa.).

1921.   Lopez, Alfredo. **The Puerto Rican Papers: Notes on the Re-emergence of a Nation.** Indianapolis, Ind.: Bobbs-Merrill, 1973. 383p. $8.95; $3.95pa. (9-12)
Examines the revolutionary activity begun toward independence of the island of Puerto Rico and political autonomy in the United States. Provides insights into the oppression and poverty of Puerto Ricans in the United States and into some of the aspects of their culture.

1922.   Mapp, Edward. **Puerto Rican Perspectives.** Metuchen, N.J.: Scarecrow Press, 1974. 171p. $6.00. (7-12)
A collection of essays arranged under four categories: 1) education, 2) the arts, 3) the Puerto Rican community, and 4) the Puerto Rican individual.

1923.   McCabe, Inger. **A Week in Henry's World: El Barrio.** New York: Crowell-
        Collier, 1971. unp. $4.50. (K-2)
This story of Henry, who lives in a New York Puerto Rican neighborhood called
El Barrio, is a vivid picture of the social conditions existing for many Puerto Rican
families in one of Harlem's ethnic communities.

1924.   Mercer, Charles. **Roberto Clemente.** Illus. by George Loh. New York:
        Putnam, 1974. 58p. $3.96. (2-4)
An easy-to-read biography of this famous Puerto Rican American baseball player
from his childhood to his exciting career days and generous acts of charity.

1925.   Mohr, Nicholasa. **El Bronx Remembered.** New York: Harper, 1975. 256p.
        $5.95. (7-12)
A collection of 12 sketches of Puerto Rican migrants in New York's "El Bronx"
ethnic community. The stories typify problems and atmosphere of the Spanish-
speaking ghetto.

1926.   Molnar, Joe. **Elizabeth: A Puerto-Rican-American Child Tells Her Story.**
        New York: Watts, 1975. 48p. $4.90. (4-6)
Based on tape-recorded conversations, *Elizabeth* is the story of a Puerto Rican girl
in East Harlem—her school, home, and community.

1927.   Nash, Veronica. **Carlito's World: A Block in Spanish Harlem.** Illus. by
        David K. Stone. New York: McGraw-Hill, 1969. unp. $3.83. (2-4)
New York's Spanish Harlem is seen in this story of Carlito, a Puerto Rican American
child.

1928.   Padilla, Elena. **Up from Puerto Rico.** New York: Columbia University Press,
        1958. 317p. $12.00. (9-12)
A study of Puerto Ricans in Manhattan covers topics from an anthropological and
sociological interest. Describes family customs and roles and cultural values.

1929.   Senior, Clarence. **Strangers—Then Neighbors: From Pilgrims to Puerto
        Ricans.** Chicago: Quadrangle, 1965. 128p. $1.65pa. (7-12)
Studies the adjustment problems of immigrants and the rates of assimilation for
various ethnic groups, with main emphasis on the Puerto Ricans. The foreword is
by Hubert H. Humphrey. Other titles by the author are *Our Citizens from the
Caribbean* (McGraw-Hill, 1965. $1.96) and *Puerto Ricans* (Watts, 1965. $2.95).

1930.   Shearer, John. **Little Man in the Family.** New York: Delacorte, 1972. unp.
        $5.95. (4-8)
A photographic essay comparing the everyday life style, hopes, and plans of David
Roth, a white boy from an affluent suburban neighborhood, and Lilo (Louis)
Berrios, an inner-city Puerto Rican youth. The text is recorded from taped interviews.

1931.   Simon, Norma. **What Do I Say?** Chicago: Whitman, 1967. unp. $4.25. (K-3)
Traces the daily activities of Manuel, a Puerto Rican immigrant who is trying to learn
English. This English/Spanish version of his story gives words and pictures centered
around his nursery school and home.

1932.   Thomas, Piri. **Down These Mean Streets**. New York: New American Library, 1971. 352p. $1.25pa. (9-12)

An autobiographical narrative of Thomas's life in Spanish Harlem. Prejudice, discrimination, identity, and other problems facing the Puerto Rican American on the mainland are covered. A sequel to this book is the author's *Savior, Savior, Hold My Hand* (Doubleday, 1972. $1.95pa.), and another title devoted to the prison term of Piri Thomas is *Seven Long Times* (Praeger, 1974. $7.95).

1933.   Wagenheim, Kal. **A Survey of Puerto Ricans on the U.S. Mainland in the 1970s**. New York: Praeger, 1975. 133p. $13.50. (T)

A recent survey of Puerto Rican culture, customs, history, contributions, and overall experience in the United States in a textbook version suitable for the secondary school level. A biography by the same author for use at the junior and senior high school levels is entitled *Clemente!* (Praeger, 1973. $6.95); it is a good description of the life of this hero of Puerto Rican youth and his famous baseball career.

Literature and Fiction Titles

1934.   Alegria, Ricardo E., ed. **The Three Wishes: A Collection of Puerto Rican Folktales**. Illus. by Lorenzo Homar; trans. by Elizabeth Culbert. New York: Harcourt, 1969. 128p. $5.50. (K-6)

A collection of 23 folktales that have been popular among Puerto Rican children for over 400 years. Can be used for storytelling on the primary level, and individual reading in the upper elementary levels.

1935.   Babin, Maria Teresa, and Stanley Steiner. **Borinquen: Anthology of Puerto Rican Literature**. New York: Random, 1974. 515p. $2.65. (7-12)

A collection of folklore, stories, poems, essays, letters, and other writings by Puerto Ricans spanning a period of 400 years of history and culture.

1936.   Barth, Edna Day. **The Day Luis Was Lost**. Illus. by Lilian Obligado. Boston, Mass.: Little, Brown, 1971. 58p. $4.50. (2-4)

Luis has just moved to New York from Puerto Rico. All of the adventures he experiences walking to school the first day make an interesting story at the third-grade reading level.

1937.   Belpre, Pura. **Santiago**. Illus. by Symeon Shimin. New York: Warne, c1961, 1971. 31p. $4.95. (1-5)

Santiago's lonesomeness for his native Puerto Rico is compounded by the loss of Salina, his pet hen left behind in Puerto Rico. This story of life in New York's Spanish-speaking community can also be obtained in a Spanish edition.

1938.   Binzen, Bill. **Carmen**. New York: Coward-McCann, c1969, 1970. unp. $4.49. (K-2)

A story told in text and photographs about a little Puerto Rican girl who is lonely until she makes a friend in her new neighborhood. A story by the author about a small Puerto Rican boy is entitled *Miguel's Mountain* (Coward-McCann, 1969. $4.69).

1939.   Blue, Rose. **I Am Here. Yo Estoy Aqui.** New York: Franklin Watts, 1971.
         48p. $4.33. (K-4)
A picture story about a little Puerto Rican girl who must begin a new school in a
new homeland where she is unable to speak English and understand what is going on.

1940.   Bouchard, Lois. **The Boy Who Wouldn't Talk.** New York: Doubleday,
         1969. 77p. $3.50. (2-5)
Carlos misses the beautiful scenery of his home in Puerto Rico, his family, and his
old friends. He has a difficult time adjusting to urban New York. Learning to speak
English is such a problem he decides to communicate by drawing pictures. His
rebellion is cured when he meets a blind boy and wants to talk to him.

1941.   Buckley, Peter. **I Am from Puerto Rico.** New York: Messner, 1971. 128p.
         $4.95. (4-7)
Freddy narrates the story of his return to Puerto Rico after living in New York
City. He works in the sugar cane fields and must readjust to rural life after living
in the accelerated pace of the city.

1942.   Burchard, Peter. **Chito.** Photos by Katrina Thomas. New York: Coward-
         McCann, 1969. unp. $3.86. (2-4)
Chito is having a difficult time adjusting to urban New York's Spanish Harlem after
rural Puerto Rico. The noise and crowds frighten him, but a new friend, Juan, helps
him to feel at home.

1943.   Burchardt, Nellie. **A Surprise for Carlotta.** Illus. by Ted Lewin. New York:
         Watts, 1971. 128p. $4.95. (3-5)
A warm family story of life in a New York Puerto Rican neighborhood. The story
centers around the experiences of eight-year-old Carlotta.

1944.   Colman, Hila. **The Girl from Puerto Rico.** New York: Morrow, 1961.
         222p. $5.95. (7-9)
Felicidad and Carlos Marquez convince their mother that the family should move
to New York after their father dies in Puerto Rico. Their experiences are a picture
of the adjustments and problems they must make and face.

1945.   Felt, Sue. **Rosa-Too-Little.** Garden City, N.Y.: Doubleday, 1950. unp.
         $4.50. (K-3)
When she can finally print her own name, Rosa gets a long-awaited library card of
her own.

1946.   Figueroa, Pablo. **Enrique.** Illus. by Bill Negron. New York: Hill & Wang,
         1970. 57p. $2.77. (4-8)
Enrique has been warned by a medium about a murderer in his new home in New
York's Puerto Rican ghetto. How this prophecy came true is an exciting tale of
suspense in this story of Puerto Rican family life and culture.

1947.   Heuman, William. **City High Champion.** New York: Dodd, Mead, 1969.
         156p. $3.95. (5-9)
Hostility toward Puerto Ricans by the basketball team's star player, Tex, has a bad

influence on Pedro's game. How the problem is solved is an exciting sports story for the intermediate and junior high grades.

1948.   Keats, Ezra Jack, and Pat Cherr. **My Dog Is Lost!** New York: Crowell, 1960. unp. $3.95. (K-3)
Juanito is a little Puerto Rican boy in New York City who loses his dog. New friends help him to find the missing animal. The last page of this picture book lists Spanish words and phrases and their English translation.

1949.   Kesselman, Wendy Ann, and Norma Holt. **Angelita.** New York: Hill & Wang, 1970. unp. $4.95. (K-4)
A story of a Puerto Rican immigrant girl and some of the changes she has to face in her new home in New York. New friends at school and a favorite rag doll help her to make the adjustment and learn to like her new home.

1950.   Lewiton, Mina. **That Bad Carlos.** Illus. by Howard Simon. New York: Harper and Row, 1964. 175p. $4.79. (2-6)
A story of a Puerto Rican boy's reluctance to leave his home for New York, his dreams of a new bike. The problems he encounters—and creates—make an interesting story for the elementary school reader.

1951.   Lexau, Joan. **Maria.** Illus. by Ernest Chrichlow. Eau Claire, Wisc.: Hale, 1967. unp. $4.95. (2-4)
This story of a birthday is a picture of Puerto Rican family customs and foods. Maria Rivera receives a longed-for doll because of the love and sacrifice of her parents. Another title by the author for this age group is *Jose's Christmas Secret* (Dial, 1963. $3.50).

1952.   Mann, Peggy. **How Juan Got Home.** Illus. by Richard Lebenson. New York: Coward-McCann, 1972. 94p. $4.95. (2-6)
Juan receives a one-way plane ticket to New York from his uncle. The big city, language difficulties, and the strangeness of the children he meets add to his homesickness. But his success on the stickball team helps him adjust to his new home. A picture of Spanish Harlem seen through the eyes of a ten-year-old boy. An additional title by the author is *Street of the Flower Boxes* (Coward-McCann, 1966. $3.86).

1953.   Melendez, Carmello, with R. E. Simon, Jr., and Emmet Smith. **A Long Time Growing.** Chicago: Childrens Press, 1970. 64p. $3.50; $1.00pa. (6-12)
Carmello Melendez and his mother search for his father, who abandoned them in Puerto Rico. They find him in East Chicago, Indiana, but life is still not rosy. Carmello overcomes family, language, and financial problems to study to become a medical x-ray technician.

1954.   Plenn, Doris Troutman. **The Green Song.** New York: McKay, 1954. 128p. $3.50. (K-4)
Puerto Rican culture is seen through the adventures of Pepe, a little tree frog who journeys from Puerto Rico to live in New York City. The tale also reveals the adjustment problems faced by Puerto Ricans on the mainland.

1955.   Shotwell, Louisa R. **Magdalena**. Illus. by R. Lilian Obligado. New York: Viking, 1971. 124p. $5.95. (4-6)
A story set in a Puerto Rican neighborhood in Brooklyn centered around the school and family activities of Magdelena and her friends. Cultural contrasts are revealed as well as the problems of immigrant youth.

1956.   Sonneborn, Ruth. **Friday Night Is Papa Night**. Illus. by Emily A. McCully. New York: Viking, 1970. unp. $3.95. (K-2)
Because the father of this Puerto Rican immigrant family must work two jobs in order to provide for them, the children only see him on Friday evenings. This they call Papa Night, and they help their mother prepare food and clean all day. The story centers around the Papa Night when Carlos, Ricardo, Peter, and Manuela are all ready and waiting but their father does not come. Other titles by the author are *Seven in a Bed* (Viking, 1968. $3.95) and *The Lollipop Party* (Viking, 1967. $3.75).

1957.   Talbot, Toby. **I Am Maria**. Chicago: Regnery, 1969. 31p. $4.50. (2-5)
Maria is a little girl who has just migrated from Puerto Rico to New York. Confined to a wheelchair, Maria experiences a fall and is rescued by a neighbor. This helps her overcome her reluctance to speak English and to accept her new home in New York City. Another title by the author is *Thomas Takes Charge* (Lothrop, 1966. $4.50).

1958.   Thaler, Susan. **Rosaria**. New York: McKay, 1967. 117p. $3.25. (5-8)
Rosaria Mendez lives in New York's Puerto Rican ghetto. Her brother Carlos is full of hatred, defiance, and frustration because of the circumstances of the family and ghetto life. When the father deserts the family, Rosaria is beginning to feel the rejection faced by many teenagers in similar situations.

1959.   Thomas, Dawn C. **Mira, Mira**. Illus. by Harold L. James. Philadelphia, Pa.: Lippincott, 1970. 44p. $3.95. (K-3)
Ramon is an immigrant from Puerto Rico who is overwhelmed by the many new changes in his life style and environment. The story describes his plane trip, his reaction to his new home in a high-rise apartment, and the snow he has never seen before. Another story of a Puerto Rican family is the author's *Pablito's New Feet* (Lippincott, 1973. $4.95).

1960.   Weiner, Sandra. **They Call Me Jack: The Story of a Boy from Puerto Rico**. New York: Pantheon, 1973. 60p. $5.49. (3-7)
This story is about a 10-year-old Puerto Rican boy, Jacinto, his home and his family. He compares his New York life style to customs of his home in Luquillo. His house, food, school, physical environment, and family life are all described. Told in the vernacular.

Audiovisual Materials

1961.   **Ain't Gonna Eat My Mind!** 16mm film, 34 min., sd., color. Carousel Films, 1973. (9-12, T)
Educational and social problems in New York's Puerto Rican and other ghettos are examined.

1962.   **American Families: The Garcias.** 1 filmstrip, sd., 1 phonodisc (or cassette). Coronet Instructional Films, 1971. (4-9)
The Garcias, a family of Puerto Rican descent, are described as the father and grandfather go to work, the mother cares for the children at home, and the older children go to school in their Puerto Rican community.

1963.   **El Barrio: The Puerto Rican.** 1 filmstrip, 1 cassette. Multi-Media Productions, Inc., 1972. (5-9)
A filmstrip from the *Accent on Ethnic America* series, accompanied by a teacher's guide. Covers Puerto Rican history, experience, and contributions on the United States mainland.

1964.   **The Batistas Buy a Store.** 1 filmstrip, 1 phonodisc, 1 teacher's guide. Encyclopaedia Britannica Educational Corp., 1971. (3-6)
Shows the problems of language and cultural conflict experienced by a Puerto Rican family who have come to the mainland to seek a better way of life and improved economic conditions.

1965.   **El Blocke.** 16mm film, 43 min., sd., b&w. Cinepueblo Productions, 1972. (6-12)
The activities that go on in a block within the Puerto Rican ghetto of New York City are described throughout the period of one summer season. Includes Puerto Rican customs and traditions of their cultural heritage.

1966.   **Chiquitin and the Devil: A Puerto Rican Folktale.** 1 filmstrip, 1 disc (or cassette), teacher's guide. New York Guidance Association, 1973. $17.50; $19.50 (with cassette). (3-6)
A Puerto Rican folktale in which a little boy saves his family from hunger and starvation by out-tricking the devil. Narrated by Rita Moreno.

1967.   **Distinguished Puerto Ricans and Historical Monuments.** 25 14x19-inch study prints. Urban Media. $27.50. (4-8)
Puerto Rican Americans who have made outstanding contributions or have become well known in American history are pictured here; biographical sketches are presented in either English or Spanish.

1968.   **Harlem Crusader.** 16mm film, 29 min., sd., b&w. National Broadcasting Co.; released by Encyclopaedia Britannica Films, 1966. (7-12)
Dean Murrow, social worker for the American Friends Service Committee, lived among the Puerto Ricans in New York's Spanish Harlem for five years. He reports about his experiences there and life among Puerto Rican Americans.

1969.   **I Am a Puerto Rican.** 1 filmstrip, 1 phonodisc. Scott Education Division, 1970. (4-9)
The problems, adjustments, and daily routines of a Puerto Rican school child in New York City are compared to those of a child in his native Puerto Rico. Emphasis is on language differences and the desire to be accepted in America and still retain identification with the Puerto Rican cultural heritage.

1970.   **An Island in America.** 16mm film, 28 min., sd., color. Anti-Defamation
         League of B'nai B'rith; released by DMS Productions, 1972. (6-12)
A description of Puerto Rican communities in the United States is narrated by
Raul Julian. He describes social, cultural and economic conditions and also
discusses the island background of the people. The problems in education (such
as learning English as a second language) are discussed. Congressmen Herman
Badilo, Joseph Monserrat, and other Puerto Ricans are interviewed.

1971.   **Manuel from Puerto Rico.** 16mm film, 14 min., sd., color. Encyclopaedia
         Britannica Educational Corp., 1968. $7.00 (rental). (4-10)
A little boy from Puerto Rico moves to New York and must make many adjustments in school and his new community.

1972.   **Miguel: Up from Puerto Rico.** 16mm film, 15 min., sd., color. Learning
         Corporation of America, 1970. $7.80 (rental). (4-8)
Miguel earns a dollar by translating for the Spanish-speaking customers in a
neighborhood store in this portrayal of everyday life in a New York Puerto Rican
community. A teacher's guide is provided with this film from the *Many Americans*
series.

1973.   **Nelson Albert Rolon.** 16mm film, 11 min., sd., b&w. Douglas Darnell,
         1970. (6-12)
A documentary of East Harlem, with a Puerto Rican boy describing how he feels
about his own identity, his self-image, and conditions in the Puerto Rican ghetto.

1974.   **Nine Artists of Puerto Rico.** 16mm film, 20 min., sd., color. Organization
         of American States, n.d. (7-12)
This film, available in English or Spanish narration, takes the viewer to the studios
of nine artists of Puerto Rican extraction. Included are views of Lorenzo Homar,
Julio Rosado del Valle, Jose Alicea, Rafael Ferrer, Olga Albizu, and Rafael
Villamil.

1975.   **Puerto Rican Americans.** Super 8mm film loop, 4 min., silent, color.
         Ealing Corp., 1970. (4-8)
A brief overview of the Puerto Rican community of New York and some of the
outstanding cultural traditions and the economic conditions.

1976.   **Puerto Ricans.** 1 cassette. Educational Resources, 1973. $11.50. (6-12)
Traces the history of Puerto Ricans from subjects of Spain to citizens of America.
From the series entitled *Ethnic Studies: The Peoples of America.*

1977.   **Puerto Ricans.** 2 filmstrips, 2 phonodiscs, teacher's guide and script.
         Warren Schloat Productions, 1968. (4-12)
These filmstrips, part of the *Minorities Have Made America Great* series, cover
Puerto Rican migration to the mainland and the process of acculturation experienced by these relocated Americans. Also covers problems of economic opportunity,
identification, and social acceptance.

1978.   **Puerto Rico.** 16mm film, 55 min., sd., b&w. CBS Television; released by
        McGraw-Hill, 1957. (6-12)
A documentary study taken from the CBS program "See It Now" on the island of
Puerto Rico and the reasons why so many Puerto Ricans migrated to New York
City. It also covers the effects of the migration on the Puerto Ricans and on the
homeland they left behind. A similar film is *Puerto Rico: Homeland* (16mm film,
9 min., color, sd. Released by Sterling Educational Films, New York, 1972).

1979.   **Puerto Rico and the Puerto Ricans.** 2 filmstrips, 2 phonodiscs, teacher's
        guide. Urban Media Materials, 1969. (4-8)
The people of Puerto Rico are examined as they live on the island and as they live
in the urban areas of New York and other large cities. Covers adjustments, employment trends, and contributions they have made.

1980.   **Strangers in Their Own Land: The Puerto Ricans.** 16mm film, 14 min.,
        sd., color. ABC News; released by ABC Media Concepts, 1971. (6-12)
Describes the function of the Puerto Rican Family Institute in New York City, run
for and by Puerto Rican Americans. The film is accompanied by a teacher's guide
for help in clarifying the role of the Institute and for stimulating discussion.

1981.   **The Way It Is.** 16mm film, 50 min., sd., b&w, teacher's study guide.
        Adelphia University School of Social Work; made and released by Synchco
        Films, 1970. (6-12)
A social service agency assists a family with problems experienced in the Puerto
Rican ghettos of New York.

1982.   **The World of Piri Thomas.** 16mm film, 60 min., sd., color. National Educa-
        tion Television and Radio Center; released by Indiana University Audio-
        visual Center, 1968. (6-12)
A description of life in the Puerto Rican ghetto in New York's Harlem is presented
by Piri Thomas, author of *Down These Mean Streets* and *Savior, Savior, Hold My
Hand*, two stories centered in the Spanish-speaking community.

ROMANIAN AMERICANS

Reference Sources

1983.   Wertsman, Vladimir, comp. and ed. **The Romanians in America 1748-
        1974: A Chronology and Fact Book.** Dobbs Ferry, N.Y.: Oceana, 1975.
        118p. $6.00. (7-12)
Three major sections are presented, including 1) a chronology of events pertinent
to Romanian American history, 2) a collection of related documents, and 3) the
appendix. The latter locates Romanian American communities and lists organizations, art collections, and Romanian language courses in American universities. The
Romanian alphabet is presented, along with some Romanian proverbs and recipes,

and immigration statistics are included. A bibliography and index is provided. The only comprehensive bibliography on Rumanians in English was prepared by Stephen Fischer-Galati, *Rumania: A Bibliographical Guide* (U.S. Library of Congress, 1963. Reprinted by Arno Press).

Non-Fiction Titles: History, Culture, Sociology, Biography

1984.   Galatzi, Christine Avghi. **A Study of Assimilation among the Roumanians in the United States**. New York: Columbia University Press, 1929; repr. ed., New York: AMS Press, 1968. 282p. $15.00. (9-12, T)
Traces the establishment of the Romanians in the United States, their characteristics, the process of social assimilation, and economic adaptation. The work, originally the author's 1929 Ph.D. thesis at Columbia University, is primarily useful for historical purposes. Appendix I is "A Study of One Hundred Roumanian Families in Chicago." Appendix II lists Romanian organizations. A bibliography and index are included.

1985.   Neagoe, Peter. **Time to Keep**. New York: Coward-McCann, 1949. 281p. o.p.
Autobiographical memoirs of the author's boyhood in Romania among the peasant people, many of whom later immigrated to America, as he did. Neagoe is an outstanding Romanian-American writer. His first novel, entitled *Easter Sun*, was published in 1934; it is also full of Romanian folklore and legend.

1986.   Ravage, Marcus Eli. **An American in the Making: The Life Story of an Immigrant**. New York: Harper, 1917; repr. ed., New York: Dover, 1971. 265p. $3.00pa. (9-12)
The author, an immigrant from Vaslui in Romania, describes the poverty and also the spirit of adventure and ambition that prompted him to leave his homeland for New York. He describes the life of an alien in the New World, the first job, the struggles, heartaches, and achievements.

1987.   Stan, Anisoara. **The Romanian Cook Book**. New York: The Citadel Press, 1969. 229p. $2.00. (4-12)
A collection of 450 popular and traditional Romanian dishes. The recipes vary from simple to complicated and can be used at various grade levels for a related activity in the ethnic studies curriculum. Another title by the author which describes Romanian folklore, customs, costumes, holiday celebrations, and foods is *They Crossed Mountains and Oceans* (William-Frederick Press, 1947).

1988.   Vasilu, Mircea. **Which Way to the Melting Pot?** New York: Doubleday, 1963. 309p. $4.95. (9-12)
A former Romanian embassy secretary in Washington resigned his diplomatic position to marry an American girl and become a U.S. citizen. He struggles to learn English, and art, and becomes familiar with American ways.

Literature and Fiction Titles

1989.   Manning, Olivia. **Romanian Short Stories**. New York: Oxford University
         Press, 1971. 335p. $5.50. (7-12)
A collection of favorite Romanian short stories with an introduction by Olivia
Manning.

1990.   Popa, Eli. **Romania Is a Song: A Sample of Verse in Translation**. Detroit,
         Mich.: America Pub. Co., 1967. 160p. $4.00. (9-12)
Romanian and Romanian-American poets are described in brief biographical
sketches. Some of their works are also included.

1991.   Rudolph, Marguerita. **The Magic Egg and Other Folk Stories of Rumania**.
         Illus. by Wallace Tripp. Boston, Mass.: Little, Brown, 1971. 71p. $4.95.
         (K-3)
A collection of six Romanian folk stories, featuring "The Magic Egg," "The
Partridge, the Fox and the Hound," and other animal stories.

Audiovisual Materials

1992.   **Romanian Popular Melodies from Indiana Harbor and Chicago**. 1 record.
         Columbia Album No. 31042F (or Victor, No. V-19020).
Many immigrants from Romania settled in the industrial communities of Chicago and
Indiana Harbor. Music of their community is played by John Hatiegan and his
orchestra.

1993.   **Pipes of Pan, Romanian Shepherd Pipe Solos**. 1 record. Decca Album
         (No. A-119).
Typical music of the Romanian shepherd is played by George Stefanescu.

1994.   **Romanian Rhapsody No. 1 in A Major (Op. 11)**. 1 record album. RCA
         Victor (DM-830).
A famous work by the world-renowned Romanian composer, George Enesco,
performed by the National Symphonic Orchestra. Conductor is Eugene Ormandy.
The flip side has *Romanian Rhapsody No. 2 in D Major (Op. 11)* performed by the
National Symphony Orchestra with Hans Kindler conducting.

1995.   **The Romanians**. 16mm film, 18 min., color, sd. Public Media Inc.
         Released by Films Incorporated, Wilmette, Ill. 1969.
Describes the life, culture and work of Romanian people.

RUSSIAN AMERICANS

See also **Slavic Americans.**

Reference Sources
(*See* Reference Sources under Slavic Americans.)

Non-Fiction Titles: History, Culture, Sociology, Biography

1996.   Antin, Mary. **The Promised Land**. Boston, Mass.: Houghton, Mifflin, c1912, 1969. 373p. $2.65pa. (7-12)
An autobiographical story of a young immigrant woman from Russia who views her life in America as the experience of a new or different person. Her loneliness, determination, problems of adjustment, are combined into a sensitive account set around the turn of the century.

1997.   Argus, Mikhail Konstantinovich, and Mikhail Jeleznov. **Moscow-on-the-Hudson**. New York: Harper and Bros., 1951. 182p. o.p.
Describes the Russian settlement on the Hudson River in New York. Argus, a former writer for the largest Russian newspaper in the United States, describes the culture, customs, and experiences of the Russian Americans.

1998.   Chevigny, Hector. **Russian America: The Great Alaskan Venture, 1741-1867**. New York: Viking, 1965. 274p. $5.95. (9-12)
Describes the early influence of Russians in America during the exploration and development of Alaska in the eighteenth century. Discusses the fur trade and the Russian-American Company, which also made explorations in the Northwest and California.

1999.   Davis, Jerome. **The Russian Immigrant**. New York: Macmillan, 1922; repr. ed., New York: Arno, 1969. 219p. $7.00. (8-12)
A description of the problems of the Russian immigrant in American life during the early years of the twentieth century. Includes a discussion of what America has or has not done to help the Russians in the process of adjustment and assimilation. Another title by the author is the *Russians and Ruthenians in America: Bolsheviks or Brothers* (George H. Doran, 1922).

2000.   Eubanks, Nancy. **The Russians in America**. Minneapolis, Minn.: Lerner Publications, 1973. 94p. $3.95. (5-11)
A history of Russian immigration to the United States, with particular attention to early settlements in Alaska. Reasons for leaving the Russian homeland, the living conditions existent among the early settlers, and unique aspects of their Russian culture and customs are covered. The various waves of Russian immigration are explained and the Russian contributions to America are described. Many individual biographical sketches of those well known in the arts, sciences, government, etc., are included.

2001.   Hatch, Flora Faith. **The Russian Advance Into California**. San Francisco:
        R&E Research Associates, 1971. 72p. $7.00. (9-12)
Originally presented as the author's thesis at the University of California at Los
Angeles, this study is a history of the Russians in California and their settlement at
Fort Ross. Their reasons for coming and their influence in America are examined.
A bibliography is given at the conclusion of this study.

2002.   Pierce, Richard A., ed. **Russia's Hawaiian Adventure, 1815-1817**. Berkeley,
        University of California Press, 1965. 245p. $5.50. (9-12)
Early expedition to Hawaii and settlements there by the Russians are described.
Another early record of exploration is the author's *Rezanov Reconnoiters California,
1806* (San Francisco: The Book Club of California, 1972).

2003.   Posell, Elsa Z. **Russian Composers**. Boston, Mass.: Houghton Mifflin,
        1967. 192p. $4.25. (4-6)
Biographical portraits of Russian composers whose music has been widely performed
in America and is a part of American life. Includes Prokofieff, Stravinsky,
Tchaikovsky, and many others. Another similar title for the junior high level is
Russian Authors (Houghton Mifflin, 1970. $4.25), also by Posell.

2004.   Sallet, Richard. **Russian-German Settlements in the United States**. Fargo:
        North Dakota Institute for Regional Studies, State College Station, 1974.
        207p. $9.50. (10-12)
Studies the Russian-Germans in the United States, particularly those who settled
in the prairie states. A section entitled "Place Names of German Colonies in Russia
and the Dobrudga" is by Armand Bauer. Bibliography and index included.

2005.   Simirenko, Alex. **Pilgrims, Colonists and Frontiersmen**. New York: Free
        Press, 1964. 232p. $7.50. (9-12)
A study of Russians in Minneapolis, presented as the author's Ph.D. dissertation
at the University of Minnesota (1961). Covers the founding of the Russian community in Minneapolis in 1880, and the changing patterns in class, status, and
power as seen by analyzing occupation, residential status, voting behavior,
economics, participation in the professions, and church allegiance. The pilgrims
are the first generation immigrants, the colonists are the second generation conserva-
tives, and the frontiersmen are the second-generation radicals. Various charts
portray statistics on different aspects of acculturation.

2006.   Thompson, Robert A. **The Russian Settlement in California**. Oakland,
        Calif.: Biobooks, 1951; repr. ed., San Francisco: R&E Research Associates,
        1973. 50p. $3.00. (9-12)
An illustrated history of the founding of Fort Ross, a Russian settlement in California in 1812. Reasons for the coming of the Russians and reasons for their abandonment of the settlement in 1841 are included.

2007.   Yarmolinsky, Avrahm. **A Russian's American Dream**. Lawrence: University
        of Kansas Press, 1965. 147p. $4.00. (9-12)
A memoir on William Frey (the adopted name of Vladimir Konstantinovich Geins)
son of a Russian general who came to America with his young wife in 1868. It

324 / Russian Americans

describes their life in several rural commune and communist groups in the United States. Other titles by the author are *Treasury of Great Russian Short Stories* (Macmillan, 1944. $9.75); and *Treasury of Russian Verse* (Books for Libraries, 1949; $16.00).

Literature and Fiction Titles

2008.   Afanes'ev, Aleksandr, coll. **Russian Fairy Tales**. Translated by Norbert
        Guterman. New York: Pantheon, 1973. 662p. $12.95. (K-12)
Classic Russian folk tales and fairy tales are collected and translated here. Reading level is approximately fourth grade and up, but the stories are suitable for reading aloud to the primary grade children. A commentary on the stories, illustrations, and other bits of Russian history lend authenticity to this comprehensive selection of stories.

2009.   Angoff, Charles. **Journey to the Dawn**. Cranbury, N.J.: A. S. Barnes, 1951.
        421p. $5.95. (9-12)
Volume 1 of a trilogy on the problems, achievements, and joys of a Russian immigrant family. Though they experience hardships and disappointments, they are delighted with the freedoms and opportunities of their new homeland. Other volumes in the series are *In the Morning Light* (Beechhurst, 1952. $5.95) and *The Sun at Noon* (Beechhurst, 1955. $5.95).

2010.   Budberg, Marie, and Annabel Williams-Ellis. **Russian Fairy Tales**. New
        York: Warne, 1967. 272p. $4.95. (3-6)
The humor and culture of Russian life are revealed in this collection of literature for intermediate grades. Illustrated.

2011.   Bullard, Arthur. **Comrade Yetta**. New York: Macmillan, 1913; repr. ed.,
        Upper Saddle River, N.J.: Gregg, 1969. 448p. $12.50. (9-12)
Yetta Tayefsky comes to America as a little immigrant girl. Her work in a sweat shop is typical of that of many immigrant children. The story details her life and shows how she became a union organizer.

2012.   Clark, Margery. **Poppy Seed Cakes**. Illus. by Maud and Miska Petersham.
        New York: Doubleday, 1924. 158p. $4.95. (2-4)
Two Russian immigrants, Andrewshek and Erminka, become acquainted when they find they are neighbors in New York in their new homeland.

2013.   Norton, Miriam, ed. **A Harvest of Russian Children's Literature**. Berkeley:
        University of California Press, 1966. 600p. $16.50. (K-12)
Stories, poems, and excerpts of longer works in Russian are translated into English. Arrangement is by age level. Illustrations are reproduced from the original Russian editions. Such well-known authors as Chekhov, Turgenev and Chukovsky are included. Critical and explanatory notes on the selections are provided. Another title by this editor is *The Moon Is Like a Silver Sickle: A Celebration of Poetry by Russian Children* (Simon and Schuster, 1972. $4.95).

2014.　Papashvily, George, and Helen Papashvily. **Anything Can Happen.** New York: Harper, 1945. 202p. $5.17. (7-12)
A collection of incidents in the life of the Papashvilys, an immigrant couple from the province of Georgia in Russia. The Papashvilys look on their experience of adjustment and acculturation with a warm sense of humor. The story also describes their activities in farming, sculpting, etc. Papashvily relates the story of his return to the community of his birth fifty years later in *Home and Home Again* (Harper and Row, 1973. $5.95).

2015.　Williams, Jeanne. **Winter Wheat.** New York: Putnam's, 1975. 157p. $6.95. (4-6)
When the Czar made demands that conflicted with their religion, this Mennonite family came to the United States in the nineteenth century. This is the story of their immigration and life on the Kansas frontier.

Audiovisual Materials

2016.　**Ivan Ivanovich: Life in a Russian Family.** 16mm film, 29 min., sd., color. American Broadcasting Co. Released by McGraw-Hill Book Co., New York, 1968.
Portrays the daily life of a Russian family in the city.

2017.　**Life in Rural America.** 5 filmstrips with 5 phonodiscs (or cassettes), teacher's guide. National Geographic Society, 1973. $67.50 per set. (5-12)
A part of this series describes rural life on the Alaskan frontier and the Russians that settled there. Attention is given to a Russian sect that sought refuge there known as the Old Believers. Russian culture and traditions have been preserved in the village of Nikolaevsk. The title of this filmstrip is *Settlers on Alaska's Frontier.*

2018.　**The Soviet Union: Epic Land.** 16mm film, 29 min., sd., color. Encyclopaedia Britannica Educational Corp., Chicago, Ill., 1971.
Provides general background on the Soviet Union, its people, and its political and economic development.

SCANDINAVIAN AMERICANS

See also **Danish Americans, Norwegian Americans, and Swedish Americans.**

Reference Sources

2019.　Furer, Howard B. **The Scandinavians in America, 986-1970: A Chronology and Fact Book.** Dobbs Ferry, N.Y.: Oceana, 1972. 152p. $6.00. (7-12)
A chronological history of the experiences of the Swedes, Danes, and Norwegians in the United States, selected documents relevant to the history of these Scandinavian-American groups, and a bibliography are presented. Only the bibliography

section treats the groups individually; books and journal articles are included. Indexed.

Non-Fiction Titles: History, Culture, Sociology, Biography

2020.   Babcock, Charles Kendric. **The Scandinavian Element in the U.S.** Champaign: University of Illinois, 1914; repr. ed., New York: Arno Press, 1969. 223p. $6.50. (10-12)
A discussion important for its historical information on why the Scandinavian groups left their homelands to come to America. Settlements in America are described, with particular attention to the traits of this ethnic group, their social and religious institutions, their values and beliefs with respect to morality, education, family life, and freedom. Their adjustments and problems in becoming Americanized are also described. Their contributions to the development of American land and economy are indicated.

2021.   Grant, Matthew G. **Leif Ericson: Explorer of Vinland.** Chicago: Childrens Press, 1974. 31p. $3.95. (1-3)
A brief biography for primary readers of Leif Ericson as a Viking explorer.

2022.   Malmberg, Carl. **America Is Also Scandinavian.** New York: Putnam's, 1970. 126p. $4.29. (6-8)
This examination of Scandinavians in America stresses the reasons why the Swedes, Danes, and Norwegians were assimilated more rapidly than other groups. Attention is also given to their language, social and religious preferences, and individual and group contributions.

2023.   Mulder, William. **Homeward to Zion: Mormon Migration from Scandinavia in the U.S.** Minneapolis: University of Minnesota Press, 1957. 375p. $10.00. (9-12)
Describes the role played by the Scandinavians in the development of the Mormon Church in the United States. The study is documented by historical records and personal narratives found in diaries and correspondence of Scandinavian immigrants.

2024.   Nelson, O. N., ed. **History of the Scandinavians and Successful Scandinavians in the United States.** Minneapolis, Minn.: O. N. Nelson & Company, 1904; repr. ed., New York: Haskell. 2 vols. in 1. $39.95. (9-12)
A collection of essays on Scandinavians in the U.S., covering immigration, characteristics, religion and religious institutions, education and schools, organizations, and biographical portraits.

2025.   Skardal, Dorothy Burton. **The Divided Heart: Scandinavian Immigrant Experience through Literary Sources.** Preface by Oscar Handlin. Lincoln: University of Nebraska Press, 1974. 393p. $20.00. (10-12, T)
The literature of the Norwegian, Swede, and Dane in the United States is analyzed and discussed in this work. Emphasis is on immigration and the problems of adjustment, acculturation, and assimilation as they are expressed in Scandinavian literature. A useful source of titles concerning Scandinavian Americans.

Literature and Fiction Titles

2026. Craigie, W. A. **Scandinavian Folklore**. New York: Gordon Press, 1896; repr. ed., Detroit: Singing Tree, 1970. 554p. $34.95. (7-12)
Illustrations of the traditional beliefs of the Northern peoples are included in this work on Scandinavian folklore.

2027. Jones, Gwyn. **Scandinavian Legends and Folk-Tales**. Illus. by Joan Kiddell-Monroe. New York: Walck, 1956. 222p. $6.00. (4-6)
Traditional tales from the various countries of Scandinavia and Iceland are authentically retold. Included are old favorites, as well as some of the less familiar sagas. Arrangement is by category: "Princes and Trolls," "Tales from the Ingle-Nook," "From the Land of Fire and Ice," "Kings and Heroes." Illustrated.

2028. Sperry, Margaret, trans. and adapt. **Scandinavian Stories**. New York: Watts, 1971. 288p. $5.88. (4-6)
A collection of 29 short stories from the Scandinavian countries of Sweden, Denmark, Finland, Lapland, and Iceland. Illustrations are included in these stories for the intermediate grade level.

Audiovisual Materials

2029. **The Mysterious Lufte-Folk**. 1 filmstrip, 1 phonodisc. Walt Disney Educational Media Co., 1975.
A Scandinavian folk tale about two brothers, one of whom comes to possess the magic treasure of the Lufte-folk while the other is lost in a storm. A teacher's guide accompanies this filmstrip, which is adaptable for various age levels in the elementary curriculum.

SCOTCH AND SCOTCH-IRISH AMERICANS

See also **British Americans.**

Reference Sources
(*See* Reference Sources under British Americans and Irish Americans.)

Non-Fiction Titles: History, Culture, Sociology, Biography

2030. Black, George Fraser. **Scotland's Mark on America**. New York: The Scottish Section of "America's Making," 1921; repr. ed., San Francisco: R&E Research Associates, 1972. 126p. $7.00. (9-12)
Covers emigration to the American colonies and indicates prominent Scots and their families, with particular attention to persons in government, the military, professions, the church, industry, and journalism. Scottish societies in the United States are also described.

2031. Bobbe, Dorothie. **New World Journey of Anne Mac Vicar**. New York: Putnam's, 1971. 127p. $3.86. (5-9)

A true story based on the journal of Anne Mac Vicar, wife of a young officer whose Scottish regiment was sent to the British-American colony of South Carolina in the 1750s. She writes her impressions of the New World and the struggles of the early settlers.

2032. Clark, Electa. **Cherokee Chief, the Life of John Ross**. Illus. by John Wagner. New York: Crowell-Collier, 1970. 118p. $4.95. (5-8)

This Scottish-American, who became a leader of the Cherokee Indian tribe and eventually led them on their famous "Trail of Tears" journey, is described in this biographical portrait. The work also provides an interesting historical picture of the early settlements in Georgia and the Oklahoma territory.

2033. Dickson, R. J. **Ulster Emigration to Colonial America, 1718-1775**. Boston, Mass.: Routledge and Kegan Paul, 1966. 320p. $11.50. (9-12)

Describes the conditions in Ireland that prompted the Scotch-Irish to leave Ulster and immigrate to America. Their religious beliefs, the voyage across the Atlantic, and their life in the United States are all covered. Maps and bibliography included.

2034. Dines, Glen. **John Muir**. New York: Putnam's, 1974. 64p. $3.96. (2-4)

A biography of the life of John Muir, an outstanding conservationist. Coverage is given to the years of his youth and his immigration to America from Scotland.

2035. Ford, Henry J. **The Scotch-Irish in America**. Princeton, N.J.: Princeton University Press, 1915; repr. ed., New York: Arno, 1969. 607p. $15.00. (9-12)

This history of the Scotch-Irish in the United States explains how the Scotch-Irish became labelled by that designation. In addition to a discussion of their historical background and experience in the United States, the appendices provide interesting and informative essays: "Ireland at the Time of the Plantation"; "The Scottish Undertakers"; "The Making of the Ulster Scot"; "Statement of Frontier Grievances"; "Galloway's Account of the American Revolt"; and "The Mecklenburg Resolves."

2036. Graham, Ian. **Colonists from Scotland**. Ithaca, N.Y.: Cornell University Press, 1956. 213p. $6.00. (6-12)

Scottish immigration to America is covered, with emphasis on reasons for leaving the homeland, settlements in America, and the role of the Scots in the development of their new country.

2037. Henderson, Nancy Wallace. **The Scots Helped Build America**. New York: Messner, 1969. 96p. $3.95. (3-6)

A chronological history of the Scots in America, following a group of immigrants who settle in North Carolina. Famous Scotch-Americans are indicated and a reference list of persons of Scottish descent is included.

2038. Johnson, James E. **The Scots and Scotch-Irish in America**. Minneapolis, Minn.: Lerner Publications, 1966. 86p. $3.95. (5-11)

The history and contributions of the Scotch and the Scotch-Irish are covered, with an explanation of the term Scotch-Irish and the Scotch people who immigrated to America via Ulster, Ireland. Prominent personalities and their specific achievements are indicated, including the soldiers in the American Revolution of Scottish descent.

2039.   Leyburn, James. **The Scotch-Irish**. Chapel Hill: University of North
        Carolina Press, 1962. 377p. $8.95.
A social history of the Scotch-Irish in America, covering the background in Scotland, the migration to the Plantation of Ulster in 1610 and thereafter, and the eventual move to America. Specific Scotch-Irish settlements in Pennsylvania, Virginia, the Carolinas, and the South are described. Scotch-Irish culture on the frontier, the Presbyterian Church, and the role of the Scotch-Irish in American politics are examined. Appendix I defines the name "Scotch-Irish" and Appendix II lists "Important Events in Scottish History."

2040.   Malone, Mary. **Andrew Carnegie: Giant of Industry**. Illus. by Marvin
        Besunder. Champaign, Ill.: Garrard, 1969. 95p. $3.58. (3-5)
A fictionalized biography of a Scotch-American immigrant who found opportunity in America to make a fortune in the steel industry. Other similar biographies about Mr. Carnegie are Gerald Kurland's *Andrew Carnegie: Philanthropist and Early Tycoon of the Steel Industry* (Sam Har Press, 1972. $2.29; $0.98pa.), and Katherine B. Shippen's *Andrew Carnegie and the Age of Steel* (Random, 1957). The former is for the junior and senior high school levels; the latter is for the intermediate grades.

2041.   Meyer, Duane. **The Highland Scots of North Carolina 1732-1776**. Chapel
        Hill: University of North Carolina Press, c1957, 1961. 218p. $7.50;
        $0.50pa. (1968). (10-12)
Reasons for the emigration of Scottish highlanders to America in the eighteenth century are included in this history of the Scots in the U.S. colony of North Carolina at Cape Fear. The voyage to America, the early customs, culture, and experience of this group, and their role in the American Revolution are covered. Maps, figures, notes, bibliography, and index are included.

2042.   Reid, Whitelaw. **The Scot in America and the Ulster Scot**. New York:
        Macmillan, 1912; repr. ed., San Francisco: R&E Research Associates,
        1970. 56p. $5.00. (9-12)
Consists of the material given in addresses before the Edinburgh Philosophical Institution in 1911 and the Presbyterian Historical Society at Belfast in 1912. Particular attention is given to the Scotch and the Scotch-Irish in the United States in the nineteenth and early twentieth centuries.

2043.   Stevenson, Robert Louis. **From Scotland to Silverado**. Cambridge, Mass.:
        Harvard University Press, 1966. 287p. $3.95. (9-12)
This well-known Scottish-American writer tells the story of his voyage from Scotland to California, and his impressions of life as an immigrant. It includes sketches he has written about the land and people of California.

2044.   Veglohn, Nancy. **Buffalo King, the Story of Scotty Philip**. Illus. by Donald
        Carrick. New York: Scribner's, 1971. 180p. $5.50. (4-8)
The life of James "Scotty" Philip is reenacted in this story of the Scottish immigrant in America. His experiences as a farmer, gold prospector, and crusader to save
the American buffalo are told.

Literature and Fiction Titles

2045.   Aldrich, Bess Streeter. **A Lantern in Her Hand**. New York: Scholastic Book
        Service, c1928, 1968. 307p. $0.95pa. (7-12)
Abbie Deal is the center of this novel about Scotch settlers in the Midwest. A pioneer
mother, she raises her family and helps develop a new land.

2046.   Armstrong, William H. **The Mac Leod Place**. New York: Coward, 1972.
        188p. $5.95. (6-12)
Seven generations of Scotch Americans had lived on the Mac Leod place in the Blue
Ridge Mountains. This story is about the Mac Leod family and centers around Tor,
a young boy.

2047.   Crook, Beverly. **April's Witches**. Austin, Tex.: Steck-Vaugh, 1971. 219p.
        $3.25. (6-9)
Orphaned April Mackenzie goes to live with her Scottish ancestors, who live in a
Scottish-style castle in the backwoods country of Maryland.

2048.   Dodge, Constance W. **The Dark Stranger**. Philadelphia: Pennsylvania
        Pub. Co., 1940. 439p. o.p. (9-12)
A historical novel centered around the experiences of a Scottish immigrant in the
New World.

2049.   Gray, Elizabeth J. **Meggy McIntosh**. New York: Doubleday, 1930. 274p.
        o.p. (9-12)
A good history of the Scottish immigrants in America is a part of this story of a
young Scotch girl who ran away from home and sailed to the United States. The
story takes place in the latter part of the eighteenth century.

2050.   Lofts, Nora. **Blossom Like the Rose**. 2nd ed. New York: Knopf, c1939,
        1973. 363p. $1.25pa. (9-12)
A historical novel of a young Scotch boy, wealthy, but crippled and bitter, who
came to America as an immigrant. It is a tale of intense human drama and romance.

2051.   Nic Leodhas, Sorche, reteller. **Thistle and Thyme: Tales and Legends from
        Scotland**. Illus. by Evaline Ness. New York: Holt, Rinehart and Winston,
        1962. 143p. $3.27. (4-6)
Scottish legends of humor and suspense are retold from memory by the author,
herself a Scottish-American. A previous work by the same author is *Heather and
Broom: Tales of the Scottish Highlands* (Holt, 1960. $3.07).

2052. Wilson, Barbara K. **Scottish Folk-Tales and Legends.** Illus. by Joan Kiddell-Monroe. New York: Walck, 1954. 207p. $6.00. (3-6)
A variety of tales about animals, legendary figures, and knights, as well as fairy tales, are collected here for reading to or by primary and intermediate-aged children.

Audiovisual Materials

2053. **Barbara Allen.** 1 filmstrip. Brunswick Prod.; released by Educational Record Sales, 1969.
A captioned picture representation of the famous Scottish ballad, "Barbara Allen."

2054. **Scotland: The Highlands.** 16mm film, 18 min., sd., color. International Film Bureau, Chicago, Ill., 1970. (8-12)
Provides information on the geography of the Scottish Highlands and its economic development. Historical development of the Scottish people is presented in *Scotland—The Proud and the Brave* (16mm film, 95 min., color, silent. Douglas Productions, Detroit, Mich., 1967).

SERBIAN AMERICANS. *See* Yugoslav Americans.

SLAVIC AMERICANS

See also Czech and Slovak Americans, Polish Americans, Russian Americans, Ukrainian Americans, and Yugoslav Americans.

Reference Sources

2055. Roucek, Joseph S. **American Slavs: A Bibliography**. New York: Bureau of Intercultural Education, 1944. 49p. (Reprinted by the author, 1970; $2.50pa.).
Although this bibliography is outdated, it is useful for retrospective history of the Slavs in America. Books, articles, and pamphlets on the Bulgarians, Czechs, Slovaks, Poles, Russians, Ukrainians, and Yugoslavs are included. Histories, biographies, autobiographies, novels, and children's stories are represented.

2056. Roucek, Joseph S., ed. **Slavonic Encyclopaedia**. New York: Philosophical Library, 1949; repr. ed., Port Washington, N.Y.: Kennikat, 1969. 4 vols. $65.00. (7-12)
Covers important developments in the history of the Slavic peoples, including those who have immigrated to America. All important topics have subdivisions dealing

with the different Slavic nations (e.g., Slovenes, Slovaks, Croats, Poles, Ukrainians, etc.). Although outdated, the work is excellent for Slavic background history, for studies of the great immigration period, and for brief biographical sketches of outstanding Slavic Americans.

Non-Fiction Titles: History, Culture, Sociology, Biography

2057.　Balch, Emily. **Our Slavic Fellow Citizens.** New York: Charities Publication Committee, 1910; repr. ed., New York: Arno, 1969. 536p. $20.00. (10-12)

The situation of the Slavs in Europe before they immigrated to the United States is described, with attention to their reasons for leaving the homeland and the cultural developments they had attained there. The second half of the book is an overview of the Slavic experience in America. Statistics, maps, and charts document their history. A bibliography and an index are included. A useful source for historical studies and for those pertaining to the Slav as an immigrant.

2058.　Edwards, Charles E. **The Coming of the Slav.** Philadelphia, Pa.: Westminster Press, 1921; repr. ed., San Francisco: R&E Research Associates, 1972. 148p. $8.00. (9-12)

Slavs in the United States are discussed, with particular attention given to those Slavic peoples who joined the Presbyterian Church in America. The role of the Church among these immigrant groups and its mission work is examined.

2059.　Greene, Victor R. **The Slavic Community on Strike: Immigrant Labor in Pennsylvania Anthracite.** Notre Dame, Ind.: University of Notre Dame Press, 1968. 260p. $8.95. (10-12, T)

A study of the Slavic peoples of Europe who immigrated to America and found employment in the anthracite coal fields of eastern Pennsylvania. Covers the role of the Slav in labor organization; strikes and lockouts are described. Differences in attitude by the old and new Slavic immigrants are also pointed out.

2060.　Meler, Vjekoslav. **The Slavonic Pioneers of California.** San Francisco: The Slavonic Pioneers of California, 1932; repr. ed., San Francisco: R&E Research Associates, 1968. 101p. $7.00. (9-12)

Published on the occasion of the Diamond Jubilee, 1857-1932, of the Slavonic Mutual and Benevolent Society of San Francisco, this collection of essays on Slavs in California records their history, experience, and contributions. Slavic groups described are the Yugoslavs and Russians; many articles are about all of the southern Slavs or all of the northern Slavs. Their background history in the Old World is also included. Outstanding Slav immigrants are indicated, and outstanding Slav churches are pictured. The work is illustrated with photographs and maps.

2061.　Miller, Kenneth D. **Peasant Pioneers.** New York: Council of Women for Home Missions and Missionary Education Movement, 1925; repr. ed., San Francisco: R&E Research Associates, 1970. 200p. $10.00. (9-12)

An interpretation of the Slavic peoples' history and experience in the United States, including their European background, their socioeconomic life, their religious and other institutions, and cultural heritage.

2062.   Pehotsky, Bessie O. **The Slavic Immigrant Woman.** Cincinnati, Ohio:
        Powell and White, 1925; repr. ed., San Francisco: R&E Research Associates,
        1970. 117p. $7.00. (10-12)
Emphasis is on the change of life style and role that many of the Slavic immigrant
women had to face when they came to America. The process of adjustment and
acculturation is described, as well as the work they accomplished in the church
and in other Slavic-American organizations. Special attention is given to the Russian
woman in America and her background in Russia.

2063.   Sestanovich, Stephen N., ed. **Slavs in California.** Oakland, Calif.: Slavonic
        Alliance of California, 1937; repr. ed., San Francisco: R&E Research
        Associates, 1968. 136p. $7.00. (9-12)
This history of the experience of the Slavs in California includes such chapter titles
as "The Slavonic Peoples: Their Place in History," "Assimilation Works Both
Ways," "Financial Standing of Slavs in California," "Political Activity of Slavs in
California," "Social Problems of Slavs," "Russian Contributions to California Life,"
"Poles in Los Angeles," "Jugoslavs in Oakland, San Francisco, and Los Angeles,"
and others.

2064.   Warne, Frank J. **The Slav Invasion and the Mine Workers: A Study in
        Immigration.** Philadelphia, Pa.: Lippincott, 1904; repr. ed., New York:
        Ozer, 1971. 211p. $8.95. (10-12)
A study of the Slav immigrants in America and their role in the development of the
United Mine Workers of America labor organization.

Literature and Fiction Titles

2065.   Lord, Albert, ed. **Slavic Folklore: A Symposium.** Philadelphia, Pa.:
        American Folklore Society, 1956. 132p. $3.50pa. (9-12, T)
Essays on folktales, epics, lyric songs, rituals, customs, and beliefs as well as the
dance are presented here. Sample chapter headings include: "Harvest Festivals
among Czechs and Slovaks in America," "Dance Relatives of Mid-Europe and
Middle America: A Venture in Comparative Choreology," "Some Social Aspects
of Bulgarian Folksongs."

2066.   Naake, John Theophilus. **Slavonic Fairy Tales.** London: H. S. King & Co.,
        1874; repr. ed., New York: Gordon Press, 1972. 272p. $35.00. (7-12)
A collection of Slavonic tales translated from the Russian, Polish, Serbian, and
Bohemian languages.

SLOVAK AMERICANS. *See* **Czech and Slovak Americans.**

SLOVENIAN AMERICANS. *See* Yugoslav Americans.

SPANISH-SPEAKING AMERICANS

See also Cuban Americans, Mexican Americans, and
Puerto Rican Americans.

Reference Sources

2067. Baird, Cynthia, comp. **La Raza in Films: A List of Films and Filmstrips.**
Oakland, Calif.: Latin American Library, Oakland Public Library, 1972.
68p. Free. (9-12, T)
A filmography of 270 English and Spanish language films and filmstrips. Entries are
annotated and provide price and distributor. A directory of distributors is also
included. Three sections are provided: 1) background on Mexico and Latin America;
2) Spanish-speaking in the United States; 3) Third World in Latin America.

2068. **Bibliography of Spanish Materials for Children K-6, 7-12.** Sacramento:
California State Department of Education, Bureau of Publications, 1971.
40p. (T)
An annotated bibliography of Spanish materials for public school children on both
the elementary and secondary levels. Arrangement is alphabetical by author, within
broad grade levels.

2069. Conwell, Mary K., and Pura Belpre. **Libros en Español: An Annotated List
of Children's Books in Spanish.** New York: Office of Branch Libraries, New
York Public Library, 1971. 52p. $0.50. (T)
Children's books in Spanish are by type of book: picture books; young readers;
books for the middle age; books for older boys and girls; folklore, myths, and
legends; songs and games; bilingual books; books for learning Spanish; anthologies.
Annotations are provided in Spanish and English. Sources are listed; author and
title index provided.

2070. Harrigan, Joan. **Materiales Tocante Los Latinos.** Denver: Colorado Department of Education, 1967. 40p. $2.00. (T)
A bibliography of materials on Spanish Americans arranged in six sections: 1) a
general reading list, 2) bilingual materials, 3) bibliographies, 4) professional
materials, 5) newsletters and periodicals, 6) a publishers directory. The bibliography
is updated by *More Materiales Tocante Los Latinos* (1969).

2071. **Hispanic Americans in the United States. A Selective Bibliography, 1963-
1974.** Washington, D.C.: Department of Housing and Urban Development,
1974. 31p. $1.85 HC; $0.65 MF. ED 096 089. (T)

A listing of 328 books, reports, articles, and bibliographies on Hispanic Americans in the United States. Covers general historical background and insights into educational, economic, and social adjustment. Arrangement is in three sections: 1) general background, 2) Mexican Americans, 3) Puerto Ricans and other Caribbean Spanish-speaking peoples. An author index by item number is provided.

2072.   **Libros en Venta.** 2nd ed. Buenos Aires, Bowker Editores S.A.; distr. New York: R. R. Bowker, 1974. 2v. bibliog. index. $54.00.

The first complete revision since 1964, the second edition of *Libros en Venta* records approximately 120,000 titles currently available in Spanish from publishers in 24 countries. It is arranged in three main parts: Author, Titulo, and Materia. Most complete entries appear in the author section, where the elements are author's name, title, occasionally pagination, price, and publisher. The "Materia" section is a classified list arranged by Dewey.

2073.   Natella, Arthur A., Jr., comp. and ed. **The Spanish in America, 1513-1974: A Chronology and Fact Book.** Dobbs Ferry, N.Y.: Oceana, 1975. 139p. $6.00. (7-12)

A ready reference book in the *Ethnic Chronology Series* arranged in three major sections: 1) a chronology of events relevant to the Spanish history and experience in America; 2) a collection of documents including treaties with Spain; and 3) a bibliography of books, articles and dissertations, which includes a listing of English and a listing of Spanish titles. Indexed.

2074.   Ortiz, Ana Maria, comp. **A Bibliography on Hispano America History and Culture.** Springfield: Illinois State Commission on Human Relations, Department of Education Services, 1972. 35p. $0.65; $3.29. ED 080 270. (T)

The 145 entries in this bibliography cover materials written between 1945 and 1969 designed for children, students, teachers, librarians, and parents. Arrangement is in the following sections: 1) introduction (in English and Spanish); 2) general history and culture; 3) the Puerto Rican experience; 4) the Chicano-Mexican American experience; 5) story books for children. Recommendations for book purchasing are included in the addendum.

2075.   Sanchez, George I., and Howard Putnam. **Materials Relating to the Education of Spanish-Speaking People in the United States: An Annotated Bibliography.** Austin: Texas University, Institute of Latin American Studies, 1959. 40p. $1.50. ED 041 680.

Concerned with the education of Spanish-speaking people in the United States. Emphasis is primarily on Mexicans and Puerto Ricans. The bibliography consists of 882 entries listing books, articles, bulletins, pamphlets, curriculum outlines, bibliographies, and unpublished theses and dissertations. Materials included were published between 1923 and 1954. Subject index provided.

2076.   **The Spanish Speaking in the United States: A Guide to Materials.** Washington, D.C.: Cabinet Committee on Opportunity for the Spanish Speaking, 1971; repr. ed., Detroit, Mich.: Blaine Ethridge Books, 1974. 175p. $16.50. (9-12, T)

Contains over 1,300 entries on Mexican Americans, Puerto Ricans and Cuban refugees and their role, contributions, problems, and experiences in the United States. Emphasis is on Mexican Americans; some entries are annotated.

2077.   U.S. Bureau of the Census. **Census of Population: 1970**. Series PC (2). **Subject Reports**. Series PC (2) 1–D. **Persons of Spanish Surname.** Washington, D.C.: Government Printing Office, 1973. 153p. $2.55. (9-12)
Population statistics for persons with Spanish surnames are given by city and place in five Southwestern states. Information given is taken from socioeconomic data and surveys of housing trends and characteristics.

2078.   U.S. Bureau of the Census. **Current Population Reports**. Series P-20. **Population Characteristics**. Series P-20, No. 250. **Persons of Spanish Origin in the United States: March 1972 and 1971**. Washington, D.C.: Government Printing Office, 1973. 37p. $1.25. (9-12)
Cities of the Southwest are surveyed for data and information about persons of Spanish origin. Cross-classified by demographic, social, and economic characteristics.

2079.   U.S. Bureau of the Census. **Reports**. (For school students.) No. 6. **Nosotros**. Washington, D.C.: Government Printing Office, 1973. 19p. $0.45.
Persons of Spanish origin are surveyed to obtain information about their social and economic status in the United States. Other pertinent statistics also included.

Teaching Methodology and Curriculum Materials

2080.   Archuleta, Lena, comp. **The Rodeo and Cattle Industry–Its Rich Spanish-Mexican Heritage: A Bilingual-Bicultural Resource Booklet for Teachers, Pre-School through Grade Six**. Denver, Colo.: Denver Public Schools, 1973. 35p. $0.75 MF; $1.85 HC. ED 100 735. (T)
Teacher resource material describing the Spanish-Mexican contribution to the cattle industry, rodeo, and cowboy culture. Background material, resources, and activities for developing a bilingual-bicultural educational course are included. Primary, intermediate, and upper grades are covered. Spanish songs, poems, and riddles are included as well as a varied selection of learning activities for each grade level.

2081.   Ceja, Manual Valencia. **Methods of Orientation of Spanish-Speaking Children to an American School**. San Francisco: R&E Research Associates, 1973– . 57p. $8.00pa. (T)
This reprint of a 1957 thesis at the University of Southern California provides a plan for a program to integrate Spanish-speaking children into the public schools of the Westmorland School District. Describes the unique needs of Spanish-speaking children in an American school and methods of orienting Spanish-speaking children used previously and by other districts. A bibliography is also included.

2082.   **A Total Immersion in the Hispano Culture**. Denver, Colo.: Adams County School District 12, 1970. 103p. $6.58. (T)
A thermofaxed book designed to help teachers motivate students to become acquainted with and involved in all phases of the Hispano culture: Spanish, Latin,

Mexican American, and the Native American. Objectives, teaching and learning
strategies, concepts to be developed, suggested experiences and correlated units,
activities, visual aids, and a bibliography are provided.

2083.	Way, Robert V. **Adapting the Curriculum of an Elementary School to
Serve the Language Needs of Spanish-Speaking Children.** San Francisco:
R&E Research Associates, 1974. 51p. $7.00. (T)
This reprint of a 1948 thesis is relevant to the needs of inner-city Spanish-speaking
children as well as to the needs of the rural school children of the Southwest.

Non-Fiction Titles: History, Culture, Sociology, Biography

2084.	Alford, Harold J. **The Proud Peoples: The Heritage and Culture of Spanish
Speaking Peoples of the United States.** New York: New American Library,
1973. 325p. $1.75pa. (9-12, T)
A history of the heritage and culture of the Spanish-speaking in the United States.
Covers the period of Spanish exploration to the present. The subject is discussed
in five major sections: studying the Spanish Americans as explorers, settlers,
rancheros, migrants, and militants. Biographical sketches of prominent Spanish
Americans are included. A bibliography and index are provided.

2085.	American Ethnological Society. **Spanish-Speaking People in the United
States.** Edited by June Helm. Seattle: University of Washington Press,
1968. 215p. $4.00pa. (9-12, T)
Addresses, essays, and lectures are included in these proceedings of the 1968
annual meeting of the American Ethnological Society, which was concerned with
a discussion of the Spanish Americans in the United States. Some bibliographies
are included, and other reports also have implications for the classroom teacher.

2086.	Axford, Roger W. **Spanish-Speaking Heroes.** Midland, Mich.: Pendell
Publishing, 1973. 85p. $3.95. (5-12)
A collection of biographical sketches of 23 outstanding Spanish-speaking heroes
in the fields of government, education, labor, sports, and the performing arts.
Included are Cesar Chavez, Roberto Clemente, Joseph M. Montoya, Dennis Chavez,
and others.

2087.	Bandelier, Adolph F. **The Gilded Man and Other Pictures of the Spanish
Occupancy of America.** New York: Appleton, 1893; repr. ed., New York:
AMS Press, 1974. 302p. $18.00. (9-12)
A collection of articles on the early Spanish explorations and settlements in
America and their influence in the development of the Southwestern United
States. Particular attention is given to the history of New Mexico.

2088.	Bernard, Jacqueline. **Voices from the Southwest: Antonio Jose Martinez,
Elfego Baca, Reies Lopez Tijerina.** New York: Scholastic, 1973. 128p.
$3.95. (6-9)
Three leaders of the Spanish-speaking people of the Southwest are described, with
emphasis on how they helped their people attain their rights for education, land
ownership, etc.

2089.   Bunker, Robert, and John Adair. **First Look at Strangers**. New Brunswick, N.J.: Rutgers University, 1959. 151p. $6.00. (10-12)
A description of the intercultural problems and differences in a cross-cultural exchange between Anglo educators, administrators and sociologists and the Spanish-speaking communities of the Southwest. How these problems were resolved and the process of acculturation among these Spanish Americans as they enter a modern society is also examined.

2090.   Burma, John H. **Spanish-Speaking Groups in the United States**. Durham, N.C.: Duke University Press, 1954; repr. ed., Detroit, Mich.: Blaine Ethridge, 1974. 214p. $12.00. (10-12)
This reprint includes a new preface by the author and gives historical information on the Chicanos, Hispanos, and Puerto Ricans in the United States. Emphasis is on their political preferences, progress, economic conditions, and family life. Some coverage is given to Filipino Americans. The Los Hermanos Penitentes (Penitent Brothers), a political-religious society, is described in the appendix. A bibliography is also included.

2091.   Eiseman, Alberta. **Mañana Is Now; The Spanish-Speaking in the United States**. New York: Atheneum, 1973. 184p. $6.25. (5-10)
Mexican Americans, Puerto Ricans, and Cubans in the United States are described, with emphasis on their historical backgrounds and experiences as a part of American society. They are also compared with the Oriental and European ethnic groups. The study is documented with photographs. Indexed.

2092.   Glubok, Shirley. **Art of the Spanish in the United States and Puerto Rico**. New York: Macmillan, 1972. 48p. $6.95. (4-8)
Describes in text and photos by Alfred Tamarin the strong and rich influence the Spanish people had on American architecture in the U.S. mainland and the island of Puerto Rico. Spanish customs and life style are depicted through the examples of forts, churches, furniture, household articles, and religious and legendary statues.

2093.   Gonzalez, Nancie L. **The Spanish-Americans of New Mexico: A Heritage of Pride**. Albuquerque: University of New Mexico Press, 1969. 246p. $7.95; $3.95pa. (10-12)
New Mexico leads the Southwest in percentage of Spanish-speaking peoples, with nearly 30 percent of its population being Spanish Americans. This study of New Mexico's Spanish heritage covers the language, race, culture, early settlements, and social systems of the Spanish-speaking peoples. The latter includes family, community, La Raza, and bicultural patterns. Spanish associations, changes and urbanization, and activism of the 1960s are also examined. A bibliography and index are included.

2094.   Manuel, Herschel T. **Spanish-Speaking Children of the Southwest: Their Education and the Public Welfare**. Austin: University of Texas Press, 1965. 222p. $7.50 ; $2.25pa. (T)
A book addressed to educators on the problems of education for Spanish children in the United States. Emphasis is on cultural conflicts, language, poverty, and

migrant parents. The appendix tables chart distribution of Spanish population in the states of the Southwest. Index included.

2095.   Perales, Alonso S. **Are We Good Neighbors?** San Antonio, Tex.: Artes
        Graficas, 1948; repr. ed., New York: Arno, 1974. 298p. $16.00. (9-12)
A collection of essays, addresses, court cases, dialogues, newspaper clippings, letters, and other items that reflect discrimination against Latin Americans in the United States.

2096.   Samora, Julian, ed. **La Raza: Forgotten Americans.** South Bend, Ind.:
        University of Notre Dame Press, 1966. 218p. $7.95; $2.50pa. (9-12)
A collection of papers by well-known authorities on the Spanish-speaking population is divided into the following chapters: I) History, Culture and Education; II) The Role of the Christian Church; III) Leadership and Politics; IV) The Migrant Worker; V) The Right to Equal Opportunity; VI) Community Participation and the Emerging Middle Class; VII) Demographic Characteristics. The work is indexed.

2097.   Spanish Institute, Inc. **Hispanic Influences in the United States.** New York:
        Interbook, 1975. 60p. $2.00. (9-12)
Papers presented at a seminar on "Hispanic Influences in the United States" held at the Spanish Institute in New York City in 1974. Attention is given to congresses on the Spanish language in the United States. Bibliography references are included.

2098.   Wright, James Leitch. **Anglo-Spanish Rivalry in North America.** Athens:
        University of Georgia Press, 1971. 257p. $10.00. (9-12)
Surveys English-Spanish confrontations in the United States, with emphasis on Spain's attitudes toward English settlement in areas of predominantly Spanish population. The period covered is the early days of exploration and colonization to 1821. Maps and bibliography included.

Literature and Fiction Titles

2099.   Campa, Arthur L. **Treasure of the Sangre de Cristos: Tales and Traditions
        of the Spanish Southwest.** Norman: University of Oklahoma Press, 1963.
        223p. $6.95; $2.95pa. (6-12)
A collection of folk tales ranging from stories of the Spanish explorers, to gold mining days and the present situation in the Spanish Southwest.

2100.   Cervantes, Saavedra Miguel de. **The Adventures of Don Quixote de la
        Mancha.** Illus. by Warren Chappell. New York: Knopf, 1960. 307p.
        $3.50. (4-8)
Although not a story of ethnic America, this Spanish novel, adapted by Leighton Barret, is a classic in the school curriculum. It follows the adventures of the renowned Don Quixote. The above edition is from the *Easy Reader* series. An additional title is *The Exploits of Don Quixote* (Walck, 1960. $5.50).

2101.   Forbes, Harrie Rebecca Piper. **Mission Tales in the Days of the Dons.**
        Chicago: A. C. McClurg & Co.; repr. ed., Freeport, N.Y.: Books for
        Libraries, 1970. 344p. $11.50. (9-12)

A collection of short stories about Spanish America in the early days of settlement. Nine full-page illustrations by Langdon Smith are included.

2102. Lawaetz, Gudie. **Spanish Short Stories, 1972.** New York: Penguin, 1966-1972. 214p. $1.95pa. (7-12)
A collection of Spanish short stories translated into English. Explanatory notes define words and terms unintelligible to non-Spanish or Latin American readers. "Bibliographical Notes on the Authors" and "Notes on Spanish Texts" are appended. An earlier volume, edited by Richard H. Olmsted and Raymond L. Grisner (Ronald Press, 1942. $5.50), is the first volume in this two-volume series designed for high school use.

2103. Lenski, Lois. **Vaquero Pequeno: Cowboy Small.** New York: Walck, 1960. 48p. $3.95. (K-3)
A small boy's life on a ranch caring for his horse and rounding up and branding cattle is described. The text is in both English and Spanish, which is helpful for Spanish-speaking children who are just learning to read and communicate in English.

2104. Nason, Thelma C. **No Golden Cities: A Saga of the First Permanent Settlement in America.** Illus. by Paul Williams. New York: Macmillan, 1971. 154p. $4.50. (5-8)
A historical novel about the first permanent settlement in America. Twelve-year-old Cristobal is a sixteenth century Spanish explorer's son and a part of the exciting party that claimed New Mexico for the Spanish king.

2105. Ormsby, Virginia. **What's Wrong with Julio?** Philadelphia, Pa.: Lippincott, 1965. unp. $3.79.
An easy-to-read book about a boy who is homesick for his mother and father. Illustrations (by the author) include both the English and the Spanish word for the objects depicted.

2106. Price, Eugenia. **Don Juan McQueen.** New York: Lippincott, 1974. 384p. $8.95; Bantam, 1975. $1.75pa. (7-12)
A novel of the early Spanish settlements and rule in the area of the South that is now Florida. Don Juan McQueen spent most of his life as an aide to the governor of Florida under Spanish rule rather than stay in Georgia with his family and face debtor's prison. This historical novel is one of romance and tragedy, as well as a picture of Spanish life and influence in Florida, particularly St. Augustine.

2107. Resnick, Seymour, and Jeanne Pasmantier, eds. **An Anthology of Spanish Literature in English Translation.** New York: Frederick Ungar, 1958. 2 vols. $17.00. (9-12)
Volume 1 covers the Medieval period, the Renaissance, and the Golden Age. Volume 2 covers the eighteenth through twentieth centuries. The introduction outlines Spanish poetry, prose and drama, and each selection is preceded by a brief biographical and critical sketch about the author.

2108.   Schwartz, Kessel, ed. **Introduction to Modern Spanish Literature.** New
        York: Twayne, 1968. 336p. $7.95. (7-12)
An anthology of Spanish fiction, poetry and essay. A 37-page introduction presents a history of Spanish literary and cultural contributions from the Middle Ages
to the twentieth century. A brief biographical and critical sketch of the author and
his works precedes each selection.

2109.   Turnbull, Eleanor L. **Ten Centuries of Spanish Poetry.** Baltimore, Md.:
        Johns Hopkins Press, 1969. 452p. $14.95; $3.95pa. (9-12)
An anthology of Spanish poetry in English translation from its beginnings to the
mid-twentieth century. Some translations have been reprinted from The Hispanic
Society of America's publication *Translations from Hispanic Poets* and other
similar publications. Arrangement is chronological; brief biographical sketches
introduce each poet.

2110.   Wellwarth, George E., ed. **The New Wave Spanish Drama.** New York: New
        York University Press, 1970. 321p. $10.00; $3.95pa. (9-12)
An anthology of seven Spanish plays that are useful for dramatization by Spanish
language classes, or for reading and understanding the Spanish cultural heritage
and values. Includes "The Best of All Possible Worlds" and "The Hero," both by
Antonio Martinez Bellesteros, "The Man and the Fly" and "The Jackass," both by
Jose Ruibal, and others.

Audiovisual Materials

2111.   **Francisco Bravo: Doctor, Banker, Civic Leader.** 1 filmstrip, 1 phonodisc
        (or cassette). AVI Associates; released by FBA Educational Media, 1974.
        (4-12)
This filmstrip from the *Spanish-American Leaders of 20th Century America* series
is a biographical portrait of Francisco Bravo and his accomplishments and
contributions.

2112.   **Hispanic Cultural Arts.** 16mm film, 25 min., sd., color. Denver Public
        Schools; produced for ETV on Channel 6 KRMA. (5-12)
From the *Cultural Understanding* series, this film traces the Spanish heritage and
influence in American language, art, music, and dance. Two other films in the
series are: *Hispanic Heritage* and *Hispanic Life in the City.* The films are accompanied by an elementary teacher's guide.

2113.   **History and Contributions of the Spanish and Why We Should Recognize
        These Contributions.** Video tape, 60 min. Prepared by Horacio Ulibarri,
        Colorado Department of Education.
This tape on the Spanish-American and his contributions is also available on an
audio tape with accompanying color slides.

2114.   **Latino: A Cultural Conflict.** 16mm film, 21 min., sd., b&w. Oxford Films,
        1972. $210.00; $25.00 (rental). (7-12)
San Francisco's Mission District is filmed using the story of Mauricio, an immigrant
from El Salvador, and his problems in school, with the law, and in obtaining a job.

Not a picture of the Latin-American community; rather, it reveals the problems of cultural conflict and the need for help in the Spanish-speaking ghettos.

2115.   **Luis Quero Chiesa: Culture of a Proud People.** 1 filmstrip, 1 phonodisc (or cassette), teacher's study guide. AVI Associates; released by BFA Educational Media, 1974. (6-12)
A part of the *Spanish American Leaders of 20th Century America* series, this filmstrip presents a biography of a Spanish-American author and artist who overcame poverty and inadequate educational opportunities to make outstanding contributions to the United States.

2116.   **New Spain in America.** 1 filmstrip, teacher's guide, and ditto masters. Urban Media Materials, 1973. (5-9)
Indicates areas of the United States with large Spanish-speaking populations and shows the Spanish influence in America. A slide set by the same title is also available.

2117.   **Spanish-American Leaders of the 20th Century.** 8 filmstrips, 4 discs, teacher's study guide. AVI Associates; released by BFA Educational Media, 1974. (4-8)
These eight filmstrips are biographical portraits of famous Spanish-American leaders in various walks of life. Included are Cesar Chavez, Henry Gonzales, Luis Quero Chiesa, Leopold Sanchez, and Jose Feliciano.

2118.   **Spanish Influence in the United States.** 16mm film. Coronet, 1948. $4.00 (rental). (5-12)
Areas of Spanish concentration in the United States in Florida, California, and the Southwest are described. The Spanish traditions as they affected American culture (food, clothing, language, architecture, and religion) are examined.

2119.   **Spanish-Speaking Americans.** 12 study prints (11x14-inch) color, 24 study prints (11x14-inch) b&w. Audio-Visual Enterprises, 1972. $15.00. (K-12)
Biographical sketches of 36 prominent Spanish-speaking Americans are included on these portraits by Paul Rodriguez. Included are Vikki Carr, Anthony Quinn, Romana Banuelos, Lee Trevino, Jose Ferrer, and others. The text discusses their career highlights.

2120.   **Spanish Speaking People Have Helped to Build America.** 1 multi-media kit. Media Materials. $9.95. (4-7)
The materials contained in this kit consist of 1 cassette tape, 1 spirit master, 35 student books and a teacher's guide. The emphasis is on the contributions of Spanish Americans to U.S. culture and life. Music, art, and foods are described.

2121.   **The Voice of La Raza.** 16mm film, 53½ min., sd., color. Office of Economic Opportunity. Made and distributed by William Greaves, Inc., 1971. (6-12)
An award-winning film describing the problems of the Spanish-American community of the United States. The film is narrated by Anthony Quinn, who also participates

in enacting problems of job discrimination and economic frustration. Emphasis is on Mexican and Puerto Rican Americans.

2122.   **What Can You Do?** 16mm film, 26 min., sd., color. National Audiovisual Center, 1974. (7-12)
Encourages Spanish-speaking Americans to pursue careers in the professions (doctors, dentists, nurses, health care professions, and technicians) with descriptions of recent graduates who are entering these fields.

2123.   **Who Needs You?** 16mm film, 11 min., sd., color. Distr. by AIMS Instructional Media Services, 1971. (5-10)
A Spanish-American boy discovers that his friends will respect him and his heritage when he is able to appreciate his background and take pride in the culture and customs of his ancestors.

SWEDISH AMERICANS

See also **Scandinavian Americans.**

Reference Sources

2124.   Ander, Oscar Fritiof. **The Cultural Heritage of the Swedish Immigrant: Selected References.** Rock Island, Ill.: Augustana College Library, 1956. 191p.
Swedish immigrants in America—their historical background, experience, customs, and contributions—are covered in this comprehensive bibliography. Arrangement is in ten sections: Bibliography of Bibliographies; Background of Swedish Emigration; America Books; Emigrant Guide Books; Swedish Immigrants in American Life; Church and Education; Religious and Secular Literature; Art, Music, and the Theater; Newspapers, Periodicals, and Annuals; and Archive Materials.

Non-Fiction Titles: History, Culture, Sociology, Biography

2125.   Barton, H. Arnold, ed. **Letters from the Promised Land: Swedes in America, 1840-1914.** Minneapolis: University of Minnesota Press, 1975. 344p. $16.50. (9-12)
The Swedish immigrants tell their own story of life in America—the voyage, Swedish settlements, social, economic, religious, and educational customs, and institutions. The process of acculturation and adjustment is also covered. Arrangement is chronological; emphasis is on contributions in the development of farming, agriculture, and other aspects of the American economy. Selected bibliography and index.

2126.   Benson, Adolf B., and Naboth Hedin. **Swedes in America, 1638-1938.** New
         Haven, Conn.: Yale University Press, 1938; repr. ed., New York: Haskell,
         1969. 614p. $29.95. (9-12)
Swedish contributions to America over a period of 300 years are indicated. A brief
historical background of Swedish immigration, religious life and education, and the
immigrants' life style in America are all described. Another title by the author on
the subject is *Americans from Sweden* (Lippincott, 1950).

2127.   Billdy, Ruth Bergin. **Pioneer Swedish-American Culture in Central Kansas.**
         Lindsborg, Kans.: W. A. Linder, 1965. 163p. $5.00. (9-12)
A history of the Swedes in Kansas, their early settlements, contributions and experience. Their story is also a record of the history of McPherson County, Kansas.

2128.   Dowie, J. I., and E. M. Espelie, eds. **Swedish Immigrant Community in
         Transition: Essays in Honor of Dr. Conrad Bergendoff.** Rock Island, Ill.:
         Augustana, 1963. 246p. $5.95. (10-12)
A collection of 15 papers covering Swedish immigration, Americanization and
acculturation. Problems of language, Bergendoff's career and life as a Swedish-
American, and other aspects of immigrant life in general are described. One essay is
entitled "Bibliography of the Published Writings of Dr. Conrad Bergendoff, 1918-
1963."

2129.   Franchere, Ruty. **Carl Sandburg: Voice of the People.** Illus. by Victor Mays.
         Champaign, Ill.: Garrard, 1970. 144p. $3.94. (5-9)
A biography of America's great Swedish-American poet including a lot of fictionalized
dialogue and well documented with interesting photographs.

2130.   Hillbrand, Percie V. **The Swedes in America.** Minneapolis, Minn.: Lerner
         Publications, 1966. 80p. $3.95. (5-11)
Presents a background of Swedish history and the reasons why the Swedes left their
homeland. The years of immigration and life in the New World are then described. The
last section of the book, the major part, describes Swedish contributions to American
life and culture. Outstanding Swedish Americans are indicated.

2131.   Janson, Florence E. **Background of Swedish Immigration, 1840-1930.** New
         York: Arno, 1970. 517p. $21.50. (9-12)
The economic, social, and political causes of the Swedish immigration to America
are described. The character of the immigrant during the various periods of immigration is also considered—with respect to his reactions to the U.S. and the new
nation's response to the Swede as an immigrant. Attention is given to agencies in
the United States that encouraged and helped Swedish Americans. The work was
the author's 1931 thesis at the University of Pennsylvania.

2132.   Longo, Lucas. **Carl Sandburg: Poet and Historian.** Edited by Steve
         Rahmas. Charlotteville, N.Y.: SamHar Press, 1971. 30p. $2.29; $0.98pa.
         (7-12)
An interesting view of America's famous poet of Swedish background is given in this
story of his life and work. A similar title for younger children (grades 3-7) is Grace
Melin's *Carl Sandburg: Young Singing Poet* (Bobbs-Merrill, 1973. $3.50).

2133. Reed, H. Clay. **The Delaware Colony.** New York: Crowell-Collier, 1970. 131p. $4.50. (5-8)
The Delaware Colony is described, with particular emphasis on the Swedish immigrants who established this settlement known as "New Sweden." Swedish customs and traditions transported to and transplanted in America are indicated. Of particular interest is the Swedish-style log cabin, which became popular in America. Illustrated with drawings and numerous photographs.

2134. Rogers, W. G. **Carl Sandburg, Yes: Poet, Historian, Novelist, Songster.** New York: Harcourt Brace Jovanovich, 1970. 212p. $5.95. (7-12)
A biography of the Swedish-American poet, with photographs and a map. Describes his hometown and his Swedish immigrant parents and family, and chronicles the highlights of his writing career.

2135. Stephenson, George M. **Religious Aspects of Swedish Immigration: A Study of Immigrant Churches.** New York: AMS Press, 1932; repr. ed., New York: Arno, 1969. 542p. $16.50. (10-12)
Describes the religious groups that developed in Sweden as a result of the rigid rule of the state church in the nineteenth century, and the reasons some of these groups decided to immigrate to America. Some of the more outstanding leaders are mentioned with respect to the role of these religious groups of Swedish Americans in their new homeland.

Literature and Fiction Titles

2136. Bjorn, Thyra Ferre. **Papa's Wife.** Old Tappan, N.J.: Fleming Revell, c1955, 1973. 305p. $0.95pa. (7-12)
Papa's wife meets him when she applies for a job as his housekeeper. The family later migrates to America where they raise their children and continue in the traditions and customs the family had known in their Swedish parsonage. Sequels to the story are *Papa's Daughter* (Holt, Rinehart & Winston, 1958. $4.95; $0.95pa.) and *Mama's Way* (Holt, 1959. $4.50).

2137. Budd, Lillian. **Land of Strangers.** Philadelphia, Pa.: Lippincott, 1953. 369p. (7-12)
Two young Swedish immigrants find problems of adjustment in their new homeland. This is the story of Carl and Ellen, their daughter, and neighbors.

2138. De Angeli, Marguerite. **Elin's Amerika.** New York: Doubleday, 1941. 96p. $3.50. (4-6)
Elin lived in the first Swedish colony in America in this story of pioneer days and activities in Delaware. The book portrays family customs and celebrations introduced to the United States from Sweden.

2139. Haviland, Virginia. **Favorite Fairy Tales Told in Sweden.** Illus. by Ronni Solbert. Boston, Mass.: Little, Brown, 1966. 92p. $3.95. (2-6)
A collection of six favorite humorous fairy tales that are traditionally told in Sweden. Colorful illustrations appear on almost every page, making this attractive to both primary and intermediate children.

2140.   Judson, Clara Ingram. **They Came from Sweden**. Illus. by Edward C.
         Caswell. Boston, Mass.: Houghton, Mifflin, 1942. 214p. (5-8)
Native Swedish customs brought to the United States are described in the story of
this Swedish-American family and their hardships, struggles, and contributions to
America's development.

2141.   Lindquist, Jennie. **Golden Name Day**. Illus. by Garth Williams. New York:
         Harper, 1955. 247p. $5.79; $1.50pa. (3-6)
Swedish customs in this story of a New England Swedish-American community are
evident. When Nancy must go to live with her grandparents during her mother's ill-
ness, she becomes familiar with the foods, daily life, traditions, and folklore of her
Swedish background. Other titles by the author that describe many Swedish holiday
customs are *Little Silver House* (Harper, 1959. $5.79) and *The Crystal Tree* (Harper
and Row, 1966. $5.79), which describes a rural Swedish-American community of
the 1900s.

2142.   Moberg, Vilhelm. **The Emigrants**. Trans. by Gustaf Lannestock. New York:
         Simon and Schuster, 1951; repr. ed., New York: Popular Library, 1971.
         366p. $1.25pa. (7-12)
Set in the middle of the nineteenth century, this is the story of a Swedish family
who leave their homeland and immigrate to New York. Reasons for their move,
the trip across the Atlantic, and life in New York as immigrants are described.
This is the first volume in a trilogy; other titles relating the experiences of this
Swedish-American family are *Unto a Good Land* (Simon and Schuster, 1954) and
Time on Earth (Simon and Schuster, 1965. $4.50).

2143.   Norris, Gunella B. **Feast of Light**. Illus. by Nancy Grossman. New York:
         Knopf, 1967. 126p. $4.59. (4-7)
Ten-year-old Ulla is an immigrant from Sweden who experiences the stigma of being
different from her native-born American peers. Her language difficulties and
trouble at school make her adjustment to her new home very painful.

2144.   Nyblom, Helena. **Witch of the Woods: Fairy Tales from Sweden**. Illus. by
         Nils Hald. Trans. by Holger Lundbergh. New York: Knopf, 1968. 209p.
         $4.50. (3-6)
Witches, princes and princesses, and trolls are the subjects of these 11 fairy tales
from Sweden.

2145.   Turngren, Ellen. **Hearts Are the Fields**. New York: McKay, 1961. 183p.
         $3.50. (7-12)
The story of Nils and Lovissa Enberg and the problems they have as parents and
immigrants. Their adjustment to the ways of their new country, the conflicts
between generations, the Americanization of the children, and the problems of
marriage are the themes. This novel is a sequel to *Shadows Into Mist* (McKay,
1958). Another Swedish-American family story by the author is *Listen My Heart*
(McKay, 1956. $3.95).

Audiovisual Materials

2146. **Christmas in Noisy Village.** 1 filmstrip, 1 cassette, teacher's guide. Viking, 1973. $12.50. (K-2)
From the picture book by the same title, by Astrid Lindgren, this filmstrip shows Swedish Christmas customs and traditions in colorful illustrations.

2147. **Many Wishes of a Dog.** 1 filmstrip, 1 phonodisc. Xerox Films, 1975. (K-4)
A favorite Swedish folk tale is presented for use with primary grade children. An accompanying poster and teacher's guide can also be purchased.

2148. **Nail Soup.** 1 filmstrip, 1 phonodisc. Educational Enrichment Materials, 1969. (K-6)
A traditional Swedish folk tale based on the book by Harve Zemach and illustrated by Margot Zemach. How to make soup from a nail is told by a sly tramp passing through the village.

2149. **Swedes in America.** 16mm film, 16 min., sd., b&w. U.S. Office of War Information. Distr. by U.S. National Archives and Records Service. $45.25; $7.50 (rental).
Features contributions of Swedes to American culture and society, with an emphasis on Minnesota. Narrated by Ingrid Bergman.

SWISS AMERICANS

Non-Fiction Titles: History, Culture, Sociology, Biography

2150. Billigmeier, Robert, and Fred Picard, eds. **The Old Land and the New: The Journals of Two Swiss Families in America in the 1820's.** Illus. by Hans Erni. Minneapolis: University of Minnesota Press, 1965. 281p. $7.50. (10-12)
An account of the journey to and across America by the families of Johannes Schweizer and Jakob Ruttinger. Informal records describe their early impressions of America, the colonies, the churches, and other aspects of Swiss-American life in the new homeland.

2151. Douty, Esther M. **Under the New Roof: Five Patriots of the Young Republic.** Chicago: Rand McNally, 1965. 288p. $4.50. (7-12)
An autobiographical sketch of Albert Gallatin, a Swiss immigrant who became Secretary to the Treasury under President Jefferson, is presented. Four other biographies are included.

2152. Eshleman, H. Frank. **Historic Background and Annals of the Swiss and German Pioneer Settlers of Southeastern Pennsylvania and of Their**

Remote Ancestors. Lancaster, Pa.: the Author, 1917; repr. ed., Baltimore, Md.: Genealogical Pub. Co., 1969. 386p. $12.50. (11-12)
A history of the Swiss and German settlers of southeastern Pennsylvania, particularly those of the German-Swiss Mennonite, Amish, or Anabaptist faith. Information has been compiled from original records and sources. Emphasis is on the religious reasons for their immigration from their homeland.

2153.   Josephy, Alvin M., Jr. **The Artist Was a Young Man: The Life Story of Peter Rindisbacher (1806-1834).** New York: Abrams, 1970. 102p. $12.50. (9-12)
A biography of the Swiss-American artist Peter Rindisbacher, with reproductions of many of his works. The story describes his immigration to St. Louis by way of Canada; both his career and his personal background are covered.

2154.   Lienhard, Heinrich. **From St. Louis to Sutter's Fort 1846.** Edited by Erwin G. and Elizabeth Gudde. Norman: University of Oklahoma Press, 1961. 204p. $3.95. (10-12)
Translation of sketches from Lienhard's dairy, kept during his trip to California at the time of the gold rush. The author made the trip with his friend, who was also a Swiss immigrant.

2155.   Lurie, Edward. **Louis Agassiz: A Life in Science.** Chicago: University of Chicago Press, 1960. 449p. $12.00. (9-12)
A biographical portrait of Louis Agassiz, Swiss-American scientist of the nineteenth century, and his role in the development of science and technology in America.

2156.   Rickenbacker, Edward V. **Rickenbacker.** Englewood Cliffs, N.J.: Prentice-Hall, 1967. 458p. $8.95; $1.25pa. (7-12)
An autobiography of a Swiss-American who received fame and notoriety as a race-car driver, pilot, and businessman, and who was the founder of Eastern Airlines Company.

2157.   Todd, Vincent Hollis, ed. **Christoph Von Graffenried's Account of the Founding of New Bern.** Raleigh: North Carolina State Department of Archives and History, 1920; repr. ed., Spartanburg, S.C.: Reprint Co., 1973. 434p. $18.00. (9-12)
A history of the Swiss in North Carolina and the founding of the Swiss-American colony at New Bern.

2158.   Von Grueningen, John P. **The Swiss in the United States.** Madison, Wisc.: Swiss-American Historical Society, 1940; repr. ed., San Francisco: R&E Research Associates, 1973. 153p. $8.00. (9-12)
Studies Swiss communities in the United States. Economic trends, typical treatment of the Swiss, their church, their local newspapers, their language and speech, and their role in the textile and other industries as well as United States labor are all examined.

Literature and Fiction Titles

2159.   Duvoisin, Roger. **Three Sneezes and Other Swiss Tales**. New York: Knopf, 1941. 245p. $5.99. (4-6)
A collection of Swiss folk tales and nature legends representing all of the different Swiss provinces. The stories are divided into "Swiss French Tales" and "Tales from German Switzerland." Illustrated by the author.

2160.   Spyri, Johanna. **Heidi**. Illus. by Greta Elgaard. New York: Macmillan, 1962. 284p. $4.95. (2-6)
A classic story for children about a little girl who lives in the Swiss Alps with her grandfather. Although not a story about Swiss Americans, this well-known story is typical of Swiss family customs, values, and activities. It first became popular in the United States in the 1920s and is still available in numerous editions as a long-time children's favorite.

SYRIAN AMERICANS. *See* Arab Americans.

UKRAINIAN AMERICANS

See also **Slavic Americans.**

Reference Sources

2161.   Shtohryn, Dmytro M., ed. **Ukrainians in America: A Biographical Directory of Noteworthy Men and Women of Ukrainian Origin in the U.S.A. and Canada**. Champaign, Ill.: Association for the Advancement of Ukrainian Studies, 1975. 424p. $20.00. (10-12, T)
This publication constitutes the first comprehensive biographical directory of noted Ukrainians in North America. Arranged in straight alphabetical order by the surnames of biographees, it contains approximately 1,800 biographical sketches. Valuable biographical source.

2162.   **Ukraine: A Concise Encyclopedia**. Edited by Volodymyr Kubijovych. Toronto, Canada: University of Toronto Press, 1963-1971. 2 vols. $45.00 (v.1); $60.00 (v.2). (10-12, T)
The most comprehensive reference source in English on the Ukraine and Ukrainians. Covers history, culture, religion, demography, literature, ethnography, education, social, and economic life and other aspects of Ukrainian historical development. A

special section deals with Ukrainians in the United States. Most articles include comprehensive bibliographies. Indispensable reference tool.

2163.   Weres, Roman. **Ukraine: Selected References in the English Language.** 2nd ed. Chicago: Ukrainian Research and Information Institute, 1974. 312p. $10.00pa. (10-12, T)
A comprehensive listing of references, including bibliographies, catalogs, union catalogs, indexes, abstracts, and periodical publications. Ukrainian history, geography, socioeconomic information, demography, culture, language and litera-ture, and other topics are covered. Some references pertain to Ukrainians in the United States.

2164.   Wertsman, Vladimir, ed. **The Ukrainians in America 1608-1975: A Chronology & Fact Book.** Dobbs Ferry, N.Y.: Oceana, 1976. 140p. $6.00. (6-12)
According to the editor, "Ukrainian-Americans comprise an ethnic community of about 2,000,000 people spread all over the United States" (Foreword). This volume consists of chronology, documents, and bibliography. The Documents section includes a comprehensive study on Ukrainian Americans by Yaroslav J. Chyz, *The Ukrainian Immigrants in the United States* (Scranton, Pa., 1940).

Non-Fiction Titles: History, Culture, Sociology, Biography

2165.   Dmytriw, Olya, comp. **Ukrainian Arts.** Rev. ed. New York: Ukrainian Youth League of North America, 1955. 217p. (7-12)
A series of articles by various authors on different aspects of the Ukrainian arts, including music, ceramics, folk dances, Easter eggs, wood carving and other topics.

2166.   Dragan, A. **Ukrainian National Association, Its Past and Present (1894-1964).** Jersey City. N.J.: Svoboda Press, 1964. 162p. $2.00pa. (9-12)
This history of the Ukrainian National Association describes the role of this major fraternal organization of the Ukrainian community in America. The author is also editor of a large Ukrainian daily newspaper, *Svoboda*, in New York.

2167.   Halich, Wasyl. **Ukrainians in the United States.** Chicago: University of Chicago, 1937; repr. ed., New York: Arno, 1970. 174p. $7.50. (10-12)
A history of the Ukrainian-American experience, including the reasons for leaving the homeland, the trip across the ocean, and settlements in the United States. Problems of adjustment, acculturation, and assimilation are also described. Data on Ukrainian churches, schools, and other organizations are provided; the Ukrainian press in America is also covered, and there is a comprehensive bibliography.

2168.   Karshan, Donald H., ed. **Archipenko: International Visionary.** Washington: Smithsonian Institution Press, 1969. 116p. $10.00. (8-12)
An illustrated biography of world-famous Ukrainian sculptor Alexander Archipenko (1887-1964). Contains facsimiles of his art, drawings, sculpture, and many of his portraits. A newer work by Karshan is *Archipenko: The Sculpture and Graphic Art* (Western Press, 1975. $27.50).

2169.   Kuropas, Myron B. **The Ukrainians in America**. Minneapolis, Minn.:
        Lerner, 1972. 86p. $3.95. (6-10)
Presents four major areas of emphasis: 1) background history of the Ukraine; 2)
Ukrainian immigration to the United States; 3) the Ukrainian-American community
and its religion, education, organizations, and experience; and 4) contributions by
Ukrainians in various fields, arts, and professions. Another popular survey of
Ukrainian history is by M. Kuropas, *The Saga of Ukraine: An Outline of History*
(Chicago: MUN Enterprises, 1961. 2 vols.).

2170.   Luciow, Johanna, Anna Kmit, and Loretta Luciow. **Eggs Beautiful: How
        to Make Ukrainian Easter Eggs**. Minneapolis, Minn.: Ukrainian Gift Shop,
        1975. 96p. $7.00. (6-12)
Includes colored illustrations and clear instructions on how to prepare Ukrainian
Easter eggs ("pysanky"). A number of diagrams and designs make this "how to do
it book" on Easter eggs a welcome addition to school libraries. (May be ordered
from Ukrainian Gift Shop, 2422 Central Ave., N.E., Minneapolis, Minn. 55418). A
general introduction to Ukrainian art was published by Olya Dmytriw, *Ukrainian
Arts* (see item 2165).

2171.   Luciw, Theodore. **Father Agapius Honcharenko: First Ukrainian Priest in
        America**. New York: Ukrainian Congress Committee of America, 1970.
        223p. $7.50. (9-12)
Biographical study of the first known Ukrainian priest in the United States. Father
Honcharenko was the editor of the *Alaskan Herald* (1868-1874). Another study on
Honcharenko was published by Theodore Luciw and Wasyl Luciw, *Ahapius
Honcharenko and the Alaskan Herald* (Stamford, Conn.: Slavia Library, 1963;
repr. ed., San Francisco: R&E Research Associates, 1973. 120p. $7.00).

2172.   **Music and Song of Ukraine**. Text by Sr. Christine Opalinski. Weston, Ont.:
        Demetrius Ukrainian Catholic Church, 1975. 36p. $1.00. (Ordering
        address: 135 Le Rose Ave., Weston, Ont., Canada M9P 1A6.) (6-12)
Brief introduction to Ukrainian songs and music, folk music instruments. Although
in many instances the information is very brief, this brochure will be useful in
school libraries.

2173.   **The Story of the Ukrainian Congress Committee of America (1945-1951)**.
        New York: Ukrainian Congress Committee of America, 1951. 64p.
        $0.50. (6-12)
This history of the Ukrainian Congress Committee includes a brief summary of conditions in the Ukraine and the Ukrainians' struggle for independence prior to its
inception. Also covers the Ukrainian immigration to America and the major
Ukrainian-American organizations that sponsored the first Ukrainian Congress.
Subsequent congresses are also discussed, and the tenth anniversary of the UCCA
is described.

2174.   **Ukrainians Abroad**. Toronto, Canada: University of Toronto Press for the
        Ukrainian National Association, 1971. 172p. $3.50pa.
An offprint from *Ukraine: A Concise Encyclopedia*, this publication covers the

experiences of Ukrainians in the United States, Canada, Latin America, Europe, Asia, and Australia. General topics include Ukrainian history, distribution, demographic trends, and social problems. The section on the United States describes the Ukrainian immigrants and settlements, religion, organizations, politics, education, economic life, and cultural and community life.

Literature and Fiction Titles

2175.   Bloch, Marie Halun. **Aunt America**. New York: Atheneum, 1963, 1969. 149p. $3.50. (8-12). New York: Aladdin, 1972. $0.95pa.
When Lesya, a girl living in present-day Ukraine, learns that an American aunt is coming to visit, she looks forward to the great event with eagerness and hope. But the promise of her aunt's visit and its fulfillment are two different things. It is a strange and disturbing visit, causing Lesya's ideas and views of people to change. Based on the author's personal observations and knowledge of the Soviet Union, it is a story of the value of freedom everywhere.

2176.   Bloch, Maria Halun. **Marya of Clark Avenue**. New York: Coward-McCann, 1957. 190p. $2.75. (8-12)
Marya Palenko is a small Ukrainian-American girl who finds conflicts between her parents' Old Country customs and the new ways of her friends and classmates in the United States. The story, set in Cleveland in the 1930s, provides a portrait of many Ukrainian holiday traditions, foods, and customs.

2177.   Bloch, Maria Halun, ed. and trans. **Ukrainian Folk Tales**. Illus. by J. Hnizdovsky. New York: Coward, 1964. 76p. $3.86. (4-8)
A collection of 12 popular Ukrainian folk tales, including animal tales and other stories for children translated from the original collections of Ivan Rudchenko and Maria Lukiyanenko. Other titles by the author are *Bern, Son of Mikula* (Atheneum, 1972. $5.50; 8-12) and *The Two Worlds of Damyan* (Atheneum, 1966. $3.95; 8-12).

2178.   Čyževs'kyj, Dmytro. **A History of Ukrainian Literature: From the 11th to the End of the 19th Century**. Tr. by D. Ferguson, D. Gorsline, and U. Petyk. Ed. with a foreword by George S. N. Luckyj. Littleton, Colo.: Libraries Unlimited, 1975. 696p. $25.00; $15.00pa. (10-12, T)
Dmytro Čyževs'kyj's *A History of Ukrainian Literature* is the first comprehensive survey of the subject in English. It encompasses all periods of Ukrainian literature up to the end of the nineteenth century. It combines several approaches but emphasizes the literary value of the works discussed. Čyževs'kyj's erudition is evident throughout and his judgment is always well documented. A selective, up-to-date bibliography and extensive index complete this outstanding work. The present volume is a revised and enlarged edition of the work published in Ukrainian in 1956.

2179.   **The Flying Ship and Other Ukrainian Folk Tales**. Trans. by Victoria Symchych and Olga Vesey. Toronto, Canada: Holt, Rinehart and Winston of Canada, 1975. 93p. $8.95. (3-5)

A collection of 13 Ukrainian folk tales on supernatural power, magic, and the wisdom of Ukrainian peasants. A few stories are by the outstanding Ukrainian writer Ivan Franko.

2180.   Franko, Ivan. **Poems and Stories**. Trans. by John Weir. Toronto, Canada: Ukrainska Knyha, 1956. 341p. $3.50. (8-12)

Ivan Franko is one of the most acclaimed Ukrainian writers and poets. The present volume consists of his short stories, poems, and excerpts from his novels. Other English translations of Franko's works include *Boa Constrictor and Other Stories* (Moscow: Foreign Languages Publishing House, 1957. 293p. $3.00); *Ivan Franko: The Poet of Western Ukraine* (New York: Philosophical Library, 1948. 265p.); *Moses and Other Poems* (New York: Shevchenko Scientific Society, 1973. 164p. $10.00); *Stories* (Kiev: Ukrainian Academy of Science, 1972. 163p. $1.75).

2181.   Khvylovy, Mykola. **Stories from the Ukraine**. New York: Citadel Press, 1960. 234p. $1.65pa. (8-12)

A collection of five short stories ranging from romance to satirical comments on the communist bureaucracy.

2182.   Kulish, Mykola. **Sonata Pathetique**. Trans. by George S. N. Luckyj and Moira Luckyj. With an introduction by Ralph Lindheim. Littleton, Colo.: Libraries Unlimited, 1975. 112p. $7.50. (Ukrainian Classics in Translation, No. 3). (10-12)

Written in 1930, this play, which was a great success in Moscow, was later condemned as "nationalist." The play allegorically depicts the Revolution of 1917. The central character of Maryna is an almost classical tragic heroine, personifying the heroic struggle of Ukrainian national liberation. The play also deals with the universal theme of love. Mykola Kulish was the most prominent Ukrainian dramatist of the modern era. His collaboration with the director-producer Les' Kurbas in the *Theatre Berezil'* represents the high point of Ukrainian theatre in this century. Kulish perished in a Russian concentration camp in 1937.

2183.   Kulish, Panteleimon. **The Black Council**. Abridged and trans. from Ukrainian by George S. N. and Moira Luckyj. With an introduction by Romana Bahrij Pikulyk. Littleton, Colo.: Libraries Unlimited, 1973. 125p. $7.50. (Ukrainian Classics in Translation, No. 2). (8-12)

The Black Council, written in the middle of the last century, was the first novel in modern Ukrainian literature. Its author, Panteleimon Kulish, was, after Taras Shevchenko, the most prominent representative of Ukrainian Romanticism and the Ukrainian national revival. In the novel he is preoccupied with the Cossack era of Ukrainian history in the 17th century, and he depicts internal strife in Ukraine in terms of social forces and political rivalries. Underlying this, however, is a quest for moral values.

2184.   Luckyj, George S. N., ed. **Modern Ukrainian Short Stories**. Littleton, Colo.: Libraries Unlimited, 1973. 228p. $8.50. (8-12)

For the last seven decades some Ukrainian writers have tried to break the bonds of the populist and realist tradition and to write in a new style. Among them are Stefanyk, Kotsyubynsky, Vynnychenko, Hutsalo, Vinhranovsky, and Shevchuk.

They are all represented in this collection, which offers Ukrainian texts with parallel English translations. A suitable purchase for libraries of all types.

2185.   Manning, Clarence A. **Ukrainian Literature, Studies of the Leading Authors.** Jersey City. N.J.: Ukrainian National Association, 1944; repr. ed., New York: Books for Libraries Press, 1971. 126p. $9.50. (9-12)
A history and criticism of Ukrainian literature including studies of the most outstanding authors. A bibliography for further reference is also included.

2186.   Pidmohylny, Valerian. **A Little Touch of Drama.** Trans. from Ukrainian by George S. N. and Moira Luckyj. With an introduction by George Shevelov. Littleton, Colo.: Libraries Unlimited, 1972. 191p. $7.50. (Ukrainian Classics in Translation, No. 1). (10-12)
As George Shevelov indicates in the Introduction, "Pidmohylny's novel is not directed against the Soviet regime as such but against a much wider phenomenon, of which the Soviet system is a part. It is directed against the technological civilization of our time. It is anti-Soviet because it has an independent spirit, because it is full of irony about the religion of reason and of progress. It demonstrates the limitations of reason and the absence of progress and to these two new religions opposes its own bitter agnosticism."

2187.   Rudchenko, Ivan. **Ivanko and the Dragon.** Trans. by Marie Halun Bloch. Illus. by Yaroslava. New York: Atheneum, 1970. unp. $4.95. (4-8)
A childless old couple make a stick doll named Ivanko. They care for it tenderly and with such love that it turns into a real little boy. While Ivanko is fishing he is kidnapped by a dragon and how he gets safely home to his parents is an exciting favorite Ukrainian folk tale.

2188.   Shevchenko, Taras. **The Poetical Works of Taras Shevchenko—the Kobzar.** Trans. from Ukrainian by C. H. Andrusyshen and Watson Kirkonnel. Toronto, Canada: University of Toronto Press, 1964. 563p. $12.50. (8-12)
Taras Shevchenko (1814-1861) is the most widely acclaimed Ukrainian poet in world literature. This is the first complete English translation of his poetical works in *Kobzar.* Other works that are available in English are *Taras Shevchenko: The Poet of Ukraine*, translated by Clarance Maning (Jersey City, N.J.: Ukrainian National Association, 1945); Taras Shevchenko, *Poems* (Munich: Molode Zyttia, 1961. $5.00); Taras Shevchenko, *Selected Works, Poetry and Prose* (Moscow: Progress Publishers, 1964). For Shevchenko's relationship with America, see Roman Smal Stocki, *Shevchenko Meets America* (Milwaukee, Wisc.: Marquette University Slavic Institute, 1964. 71p.).

2189.   Struk, D. S. **A Study of Vasyl' Stefanyk: The Pain at the Heart of Existence.** Littleton, Colo.: Libraries Unlimited, 1973. 200p. $8.50. (10-12, T)
This penetrating study of one of the most prominent and unusual literary figures of modern Ukrainian literature provides for the first time in English an introduction to Stefanyk's prose. An analysis of Stefanyk's work reveals that he was a master of the psychological novella—a short, highly dramatic work of prose that captures single moments in the life of a hero. The moments chosen by Stefanyk were those

that produced an inner agony. Struk adds historical background and a literary biography to his translations of some of Stefanyk's best novellas.

2190. **The Ukrainian Poets, 1189-1962**. Selected and translated into English verse by C. H. Andrusyshen and Watson Kirkonnel. Toronto, Canada: University of Toronto Press, 1965. 500p. (10-12)
A representative collection of poetical works by noted Ukrainian poets. Covers all periods of Ukrainian literature. Recommended for all schools.

2191. Ukrainka, Lesya. **Spirit of Flame: A Collection of the Works of Lesya Ukrainka**. Trans. by Percival Cundy. New York: Bookman Associates, 1950. 320p. (10-12)
Selected poems and excerpts from one of the prominent Ukrainian writers. Other publications by and on Lesya Ukrainka (1871-1913) include *Lesya Ukrainka: Life and Works*, by C. Bida, translated by Vera Rich (Toronto: University of Toronto Press, 1968. $10.00); *In the Catacombs: Dramatic Poem*, translated by John Weir (Kiev: Ministerstvo Publishers, 1971. $1.35).

2192. Yaroslava, R. **Tusya and the Pot of Gold**. New York: Atheneum, 1971. unp. $5.50. (K-3)
The traditional Ukrainian style of reverse glass painting is used to illustrate this folk-tale about a farmer who goes to great lengths to keep the pot of gold he found.

Audiovisual Materials

2193. **Inside the Golden Door: Ethnic Groups in America**. 1 filmstrip, 1 record (or cassette). Westinghouse Learning Corporation, 1975. $45.50. (7-12)
Ukrainian religious holidays and ceremonies are described—e.g., Holy Saturday, Epiphany and "Providna Nedilia." Various Ukrainian churches in New York and New Jersey are pictured. Ukrainian young people doing traditional Easter dances, a Ukrainian wedding, and a Ukrainian-American family at a Christmas Eve supper are also some of the scenes.

2194. **My Mother Is the Most Beautiful Woman in the World: A Ukrainian Folk Tale**. 1 filmstrip. Film Associates, 1968. (4-8)
A presentation of a traditional Ukrainian folk tale which depicts Ukrainian customs and cultural values. Designed for the intermediate grade level.

2195. **Pysanka**. 16mm film, 10 min., sd., color. Marco Pereyma, 1975. $150.00. (K-12)
The tradition of decorating Easter eggs in the Ukraine has been continued by Ukrainian Americans. The technique is demonstrated by Irma Osadsa. Illustrations of ancient Ukrainian Easter egg customs are by an outstanding Ukrainian artist, William Kurelek, whose works are in the Museum of Modern Art in New York City. Narration is by Carl Clausen of Ohio State University. The film was produced with the support of the Ohio Arts Council at the Ohio State University.

WELSH AMERICANS

See also **British Americans.**

Non-Fiction Titles: History, Culture, Sociology, Biography

2196.   Conway, Alan, ed. **Welsh in America: Letters from the Immigrants.**
Minneapolis: University of Minnesota Press, 1961. 341p. $6.00. (9-12)
A collection of 197 letters written by Welsh immigrants to the editors of Welsh
periodicals. Arrangement is chronological. The author has added comments of
analysis to each group of letters. The letters describe the conditions and experience
of the Welsh immigrants and indicate their struggles for socioeconomic success and
their acculturation problems. Attention is also given to the impact of these letters
on the people in the homeland who were to later become immigrants.

2197.   Hartmann, Edward G. **Americans from Wales.** North Quincy, Mass.:
Christopher Publishing House, 1967. 291p. $6.50. (7-12)
The Welsh in America are described with respect to the reasons for their coming to
a new country, the voyage, their struggles and hardships in the new land, and their
outstanding contributions. Welsh religious and social activities, and the Welsh press
are also included. A classified bibliography of writings on the Welsh Americans is
presented.

2198.   Jones, Alexander. **Cymry of '76; or Welshmen and Their Descendants of
the American Revolution.** 2nd ed. New York: Sheldon, Lamport & Co.,
1855; repr. ed., Baltimore, Md.: Genealogical Publishing Co., 1968. 132p.
$7.50.
An address delivered in the Welsh Congregational Church of New York on the eve
of St. David's Day, February 28, 1855. It provides insight into the history of the
Welsh experience in the United States and their participation in the Revolutionary
War. The appendix and notes provide sketches and names of Welsh Americans. A
brief history of St. David's Benevolent Society, a major Welsh-American organization, is included.

2199.   Shepperson, Wilbur S. **Samuel Roberts: A Welsh Colonizer in Civil War
Tennessee.** Knoxville: University of Tennessee Press, 1961. 169p.
$7.50. (10-12)
Describes the Welsh Colony founder by Samuel Roberts, a Congregationalist
minister, editor, and social reformer. The problems of these early immigrants and
the failure of the colony are described in this historical biography of a Tennessee
colonizer during the Civil War.

2200.   Todd, Arthur C. **Cornish Miner in America.** Glendale, Calif.: A. H. Clark,
1968. 279p. $10.00. (9-12)
Covers the immigrants who came from the mining regions of West Devon and
Cornwall in Great Britain to the mining districts of the Midwest and California in
America. Mining history is included in this discussion of immigrant skilled labor and
other contributions that made mining a prosperous industry in their new homeland.

Literature and Fiction Titles

2201.   Jones, Gwyn. **Welsh Legends and Folk-Tales.** New York: Walck, 1955.
230p. $6.00. (4-7)
Welsh legends about giants, princes, and princesses blend heroism, magic,
gallantry, and violence in fascinating tales for intermediate and junior high
students.

2202.   Parry, Thomas. **Oxford Book of Welsh Verse.** New York: Oxford University Press, 1962. 577p. $6.50. (7-12)
A collection of Welsh poetry for introduction in language arts, literature, or social
science class. Welsh traditions, customs, and values are revealed in this comprehensive selection of Welsh verse.

2203.   Pugh, Ellen. **Tales from the Welsh Hills.** New York: Dodd, 1968. 143p.
$4.50. (3-7)
Twelve folktales from Welsh literature are retold here for the intermediate grade
level. Stories range from slapstick humor to those of eerie suspense.

2204.   Thomas, W. Jenkyn. **More Welsh Fairy and Folk Tales.** Mystic, Conn.:
Lawrence Verry, Inc., 1957. 95p. $2.50. (5-9)
A collection of Welsh stories designed for reading at the intermediate level, but useful for reading aloud to primary children as well. Includes traditional folk tales as
well as imaginative and magical fairy tales.

2205.   Williams, Gwyn, ed. and trans. **Welsh Poems: Sixth Century to 1600.** Los
Angeles: University of California Press, 1974. 128p. $6.95. (9-12)
A variety of Welsh poetry is presented, including love poems, religious verse, poems
of a military and nationalistic nature, and others. The introduction is a brief history
and description of the scope of Welsh poetry.

Audiovisual Materials

2206.   **America America.** 1 filmstrip, teacher's guide. Modern Learning Aids,
1968. (3-6)
Part 1 tells the story of a Welsh immigrant who comes to the United States and
saves his money to buy a farm. The second part describes his life in America. It also
describes his return to Wales in later years, and his realization that his home is now
in the New World of America. Captions are included.

2207.   **Wales.** 16mm film, 17 min., sd., b&w. International Film Bureau, 1958.
(5-12)
A good background film showing how the Welsh people live and work. Their lifestyle in Wales can be compared to the mining and farming occupations typical of
the Welsh immigrants in America.

2208.   **Wales and the Welsh Borderlands.** 16mm film, 21 min., sd., color.
Boulton-Howker Films, England, in association with Educational

Foundation for Visual Aids, 1969. Distributed in the United States by International Film Bureau.
Portrays Welsh geography, including population distribution and industrial development.

YUGOSLAV AMERICANS
(includes Croatian Americans, Serbian Americans, and Slovenian Americans)

See also **Slavic Americans.**

Reference Sources

2209.   Eterovich, Adam S. **A Guide and Bibliography to Research on Yugoslavs in the United States and Canada.** San Francisco: R&E Research Associates, 1975. 187p. $7.00. (9-12, T)
A resource guide of value to the student, teacher, and professional researcher studying the Yugoslavs in the United States and Canada. Another directory by the same author is *Biographical Directory of Scholars, Artists, and Professionals of Croatian Descent in the United States and Canada*, 3rd ed. (Cleveland, Ohio: Institute for Soviet and East European Studies, John Carroll University, 1970. 203p. $10.00pa.).

2210.   Eterovich, Adam S., ed. **Jugoslav-American Immigrant History Series 1492-1900, Jugoslav Immigrant Bibliography 1965.** San Francisco: Adam S. Eterovich, 1965. 25p. (9-12)
A bibliography of books and articles on Yugoslav immigrants to the United States, with emphasis on Croatian, Serbian, and Slovenian peoples. Includes a listing of the Yugoslav press in the United States. An expansion of this work is provided in the author's *Jugoslav Immigrant Bibliography 1968* (R&E Research Associates, 1968. $3.00).

2211.   Lockwood, Yvonne R. **Yugoslav Folklore: An Annotated Bibliography of Contributions in English.** San Francisco: R&E Research Associates, 1976. $8.00. (9-12)
Traces the historical development of interest and research into Yugoslav folklore by the English-speaking reader and scholar. Part 1 surveys research from the earliest period to the present; Part 2 is an extensive annotated bibliography of publications in English on Yugoslav folklore through 1974.

2212.   Markotic, Vladimir, comp. **Biographical Directory of Americans and Canadians of Croatian Descent.** Calgary: Research Centre for Canadian Ethnic Studies, 1973. 204p. $10.00. (7-12)
This biographical directory includes the institutions, organizations, officers and press of the Croatians in America and Canada. Arrangement is alphabetical in the main listing; other lists are by occupation or geographic location. Institutions and

organizations are listed by state (or province) under the following categories: Churches, Clubs and Halls, Lodges, Political Organizations. Periodicals include brief publishing information.

2213. Prpic, George J. **Croatia and Croatians: An Annotated and Selected Bibliography in English.** Cleveland, Ohio: John Carroll University, 1972. 15p. (9-12, T)

A selected bibliography of books, reprints, pamphlets, and dissertations on Croatians, including materials on Croatians in America. Includes 115 entries, some of which are annotated. Other publications by the author include the more scholarly *Croatian Books and Booklets Written in Exile* (Institute for Soviet and East European Studies, John Carroll University, 1973. $5.00pa.) and *The Croatian Publications Abroad after 1939* (John Carroll University, 1969. $5.00), in which the bulk of the entries cover Croatians in foreign countries.

Teaching Methodology and Curriculum Materials

2214. Kolar, Walter W. **Croatians.** Pittsburgh, Pa.: Duquesne University, Tamburitzans of Folk Arts, 1975. Free. (2-6)

Developed and funded under the Ethnic Heritage Studies Act of 1974, this educational kit for Croatians consists of the following brochures: *Songs They Sing; Arts Crafts–Customs*; *Costumes They Wear*; *Instruments They Play*; *Dances They Dance*; *Christmas in Croatia*; *Croatians: Who They Are.* Illustrated.

Non-Fiction Titles: History, Culture, Sociology, Biography

2215. Adamic, Louis. **Laughing in the Jungle.** New York: Harper, 1932. 335p.

An autobiographical account of a Slovenian immigrant and his impressions, reactions to, and experiences in his new homeland. Other titles by the author are *From Many Lands* (Harper, 1940) and *Dynamite, the Story of Class Violence in America* (Harper, 1931). A bibliography of Adamic's works was compiled by Henry A. Christian, *Louis Adamic: A Checklist* (Kent, Ohio: Kent State University, 1971. 164p. $6.50).

2216. Beckhard, Arthur J. **Electrical Genius: Nikola Tesla.** New York: Messner, 1959. 192p. $3.34. (7-12)

A secondary-level biography of the Croatian-American immigrant who became such a successful inventor and experimenter in the field of electricity.

2217. Bresson, Mary A. **Contemporary Iowa Opinions Regarding the Influence of Croatians in Waterloo and Vicinity, 1907-1949.** San Francisco: R&E Research Associates, 1971. 46p. $7.00. (9-12)

A brief regional study of Yugoslavs from Croatia who had immigrated to the area of Waterloo, Iowa, in the first half of the twentieth century.

2218. Christowe, Stoyan. **My American Pilgrimage.** Boston, Mass.: Little, Brown, 1947. 264p.

Story of a young man from Macedonia and his early years as a factory worker. Another title, the author's autobiography and story of his years as an immigrant, is *This Is My Country* (Carrick & Evans, 1938).

2219.   Colakovic, Brando Mita. **Yugoslav Migrations to America**. San Francisco: R&E Research Associates, 1973. 190p. $9.00. (9-12)
Patterns of Yugoslav settlement in the United States based upon census data and 500 oral interviews. The reasons for Yugoslav immigration from their homeland, the voyage and arrival, and the distribution of Croatian, Serbian, Slovenian, and other South Slavs in America are described. Bibliography included.

2220.   Eterovich, Adam S. **Dalmatians from Croatia and Montenegrin Serbs in the West and South 1800-1900**. San Francisco: R&E Research Associates, 1971. 127p. $7.00. (9-12)
Describes the Yugoslav immigrants—from the pioneers in California in the 1840s and the Croatians who fought on the Confederate side during the Civil War to the Slovenian communities in urban areas at the turn of the century. Includes lists of names of Yugoslav individuals, with cities of origin and business or occupation in the United States. Other regional studies by the author are *Jugoslav California Marriages: 1880-1948* (R&E Research Associates, 1968. $3.00); *Jugoslav Census of Population–California 1850-1880* (R&E Research Associates, 1968. $3.00pa.); *Jugoslavs in Los Angeles: 1733-1900* (R&E Research Associates, 1968. $3.00pa.); *Jugoslavs in San Francisco: 1870-1875* (R&E Research Associates, 1968. $3.00pa.); *Yugoslav Survey of California, Nevada, Arizona and the South 1830-1900* (R&E Research Associates, 1971. $7.00); *Yugoslavs in Nevada, 1859-1900* (R&E Research Associates, 1973. $7.00); *Jugoslavs in the Wild West: 1840-1900* (R&E Research Associates, 1968. $5.00pa.).

2221.   Gobetz, Giles Edward. **From Carniola to Carnegie Hall**. Wickliffe, Ohio: Euram Books, 1968. 103p. (7-12)
A biographical portrait of Anton Schubel, a famous singer and musician who directed choirs in the Cleveland area and other parts of the United States. Schubel was a Slovenian immigrant.

2222.   Govorchin, Gerald G. **Americans from Yugoslavia**. Gainesville: University of Florida Press, 1961. 352p. $10.00. (8-12)
A history of the immigration of Yugoslavs to America, including statistical tables that give data on their socioeconomic progress and situation. Also included are their social, cultural, and other organizations. Particular attention is paid to their contributions in various areas.

2223.   Green, Roger H., Jr. **South Slav Settlement in Western Washington: Perception and Choice**. San Francisco: R. D. Reed, 1974. 111p. $9.00. (9-12)
Provides a social and economic history of the South Slavs in the state of Washington, as well as some broader coverage of the Yugoslavs in the United States. Emphasis is on economic opportunity. Also covers much of the history of the Western region of Washington.

2224. Nikola Tesla Museum. **Centenary of the Birth of Nikola Tesla, 1856-1956.** Hackensack, N.J.: Vanous, 1959. 240p. $10.00. (9-12)

An illustrated biographical sketch of a famous Croatian-American inventor and experimenter in the field of electricity and electronics. Another salute to him prepared by the Museum is entitled *Nikola Tesla—Tribute* (Vanous, 1961. $20.00). The texts are in English and Serbocroatian.

2225. O'Neill, John J. **Prodigal Genius: The Life of Nikola Tesla.** New York: Washburn, 1944; repr. ed., New York: McKay, 1964. 326p. $6.95; $2.95pa. (7-12)

A biography of a Yugoslav immigrant who gave America many contributions in the field of electrical inventions and electricity.

2226. Parmenter, Mary Fisher, *et al.* **The Life of George Fisher.** Jacksonville, Fla.: H. W. D. Drew, 1959; repr. ed., San Francisco: R&E Research Associates, 1974. 299p. $8.00. (9-12)

A history of a Slavic pioneer family in Texas and the Southwest known to be of Croatian or Serbian background. George Fisher, one of the first well-known Yugoslavs in America, became a judge in San Francisco. His life story reflects the Yugoslav customs and cultural heritage.

2227. Prisland, Marie. **From Slovenia—to America.** Chicago: Slovenian Women's Union of America, 1968. 171p. $4.00. (6-12)

A popular-style and interesting account of the Slovenian Americans who immigrated to this country. The adjustments they made, their problems, contrasts with their homeland, and the conditions and families they left behind are all described. Their contributions to the United States are also emphasized.

2228. Prpic, George J. **The Croatian Immigrants in America.** New York: Philosophical Library, 1971. 519p. $11.95. (9-12)

Extensive coverage is given to the history and life experience of the Croatian immigrants who came to the United States. Their background and conditions in the Old Country, their reasons for emigration, and their adjustments and socio-economic problems are all covered. Croatian contributions to the growth and development of America's industry and culture are emphasized also. A comprehensive bibliography is included.

2229. Pupin, Michael. **From Immigrant to Inventor.** New York: Scribner's, c1923, 1960. 396p. (7-12)

The story of a poor Serbian peasant boy who immigrated to America in 1874 and worked as a farm laborer and factory laborer until he saved enough money to attend Columbia University. He studied science, went on to graduate school, and became an outstanding scientist and professor.

2230. Vujnovich, Milos M. **Yugoslavs in Louisiana.** West Haven, Conn.: Pelican Press, 1974. 246p. $12.50. (7-12)

A history of the Yugoslavs in Louisiana published on the occasion of the United Slovenian Benevolent Association Centennial, 1874-1974. A bibliography is included.

Literature and Fiction Titles

2231.   Adamic, Louis. **Grandsons: A Story of American Lives**. New York:
        Harper, 1935. 370p. (7-12)
The theme centers around the impressions and sentiments of the three grandsons
of a Slovenian immigrant. The sons are well assimilated into American life. One
is a wounded war veteran, one is a gangster, and the other a member of the I.W.W.,
but their cultural heritage and customs are still evident.

2232.   Curcija-Prodanovic, Nada. **Yugoslav Folk-Tales**. Illus. by Joan Kiddell-Monroe.
        New York: Walck, 1957. 210p. $6.00. (4-6)
A collection of traditional Yugoslav folk tales retold by the author. The reading
level is somewhat difficult for young children, but they make excellent storytelling
materials or reading-aloud stories at the intermediate grades.

2233.   Glocar, Emilian. **A Man from the Balkans**. Philadelphia, Pa.: Dorrance,
        1942. 189p. (9-12)
A story about a Serbian immigrant who found prosperity and satisfaction in his
new homeland of America. His experiences and impressions are related here.

2234.   Judson, Clara Ingram. **Petar's Treasure: They Came from Dalmatia**.
        Chicago: Follett, 1945. 186p. (4-6)
Petar and his family are immigrants from Dalmatia who settle in a small fishing
and shrimp-canning region of Mississippi. Yugoslav customs and values are part of
this story of Petar's desire to become Americanized and his search for buried
treasure.

2235.   London, Jack. **The Valley of the Moons**. New York: Macmillan, 1913.
        530p. (9-12)
This novel, set in a California community of Dalmatian immigrants, portrays their
role in the development of the frontier.

Audiovisual Materials

2236.   **Croatian Calendar**. Picture calendar. Ethnic Service Company, 1975.
        $3.00. (K-12)
An annual calendar with large colored photographs of scenes from Croatia depicting the culture, physical geography, history, religion, and art of the land and heritage
of the Croatian Americans. Very useful for bulletin board displays to be used in
studying the East Europeans, particularly the Croatians. A large color photograph is
included for each month.

2237.   **Yugoslavia: The Land and People**. 16mm film, 14 min., sd., color. Coronet
        Instructional Films, 1969.
Portrays various people in Yugoslavia, their culture, and the geography of the
country.

MULTI-ETHNIC MATERIALS

(Materials pertaining to two or more ethnic groups.)

See also **General Titles on Ethnicity**, page 21.

Reference Sources

2238. Children's Music Center, Inc. **Recommended Records and Books on History and Contributions of Black Americans, Spanish-Speaking Americans, North American Indians, Living Together in the U.S. and around the World.** Los Angeles: Children's Music Center, Inc., 1969. 76p. $1.00. (T)
A list of records, books and some audiovisual kits on the history, social conditions, and contributions of various American minority groups. Emphasis is on Blacks, Puerto Ricans, Spanish, and the American Indian. Includes basic study units as well.

2239. **Interracial Books for Children.** v. 1— . Council on Interracial Books for Children, 1970— . Quarterly. (T)
A quarterly newspaper providing reviews and information on the development of Black and other minority writers for children. Works in children's literature are evaluated for bias, treatment, degree of representation, accuracy, and authenticity.

2240. **RIF's Guide to Book Selection.** Washington, D.C.: Reading Is Fundamental, 1973. 91p. Free. (K-12)
An annotated bibliography of paperback books for children, with special emphasis on Blacks, American Indians and Spanish-speaking. Includes approximately 1,850 entries.

Teaching Methodology and Curriculum Materials

See also **Teaching Methodology and Curriculum Materials** under **General Titles on Ethnicity**, page 31.

2241. Healey, Gary W. **Self-Concept: A Comparison of Negro, Anglo and Spanish-American Students across Ethnic, Sex and Socio-Economic Variables.** San Francisco: R&E Research Associates, 1974. 85p. $8.00. (T)
This work, the author's dissertation (1969), is an in-depth study of ethnic children in American education. His conclusions and data on the self-concept of students of various ethnic groups is valuable for teachers working with Black, Anglo, and Spanish children.

2242. Santa Clara County Office of Education. **Contributions of Black Americans, Indian Americans, Mexican Americans and Asian Americans to American History.** San Jose, Calif.: Santa Clara County Office of Education, 1970. 109p. (T)
A course outline for teaching the history and contributions of Blacks, American Indians, Mexicans and Asians in the United States is included for the K-6 level and

for the 7-12 level. Arrangement is in three columns, with content in one, learning activities suggested in another, and supplementary resource materials listed in the third. The elementary section of this guide deals with ethnicity in a general way; the secondary section treats the individual ethnic groups in more detail.

2243.   Stone, James C., and Donald P. De Nevi. **Teaching Multi-Cultural Populations: Five Heritages.** New York: Van Nostrand Reinhold, 1971. 488p. $5.95pa. (T)
A collection of addresses, essays, and lectures presented on the subject of minority education in the United States.

Non-Fiction Titles: History, Culture, Sociology, Biography

2244.   Bannon, Laura. **The Gift of Hawaii.** Chicago: Albert Whitman, 1961. unp. $3.95. (K-3)
This story of a little boy, John John, who wants to buy a birthday present for his mother is also a colorful picture of Hawaii's multi-ethnic and multiracial background.

2245.   Buckley, Peter, and Hortense Jones. **Urban Social Studies Series: William, Andy, and Ramon.** New York: Holt, 1966. 70p. $3.48. (K-3)
A social studies series studying multiracial and multicultural relationships in America's urban environments. Three little children, William, Andy, and Ramon, all have different ethnic backgrounds.

2246.   Coy, Harold. **The Americans.** Boston, Mass.: Little, Brown, 1958. 328p. $5.95. (7-9)
Gives an overview of the country and its diverse peoples. A bibliography for further reading is included.

2247.   Evans, Eva Knox. **People Are Important.** Illus. by Vana Earle. New York: Golden Press, 1951. 86p. $3.95. (K-4)
An explanation of the different backgrounds and diverse customs, language, dress, housing, foods, and heritage of America's ethnic groups.

2248.   Fauset, Arthur, and Nellie Bright. **America: Red, White, Black, Yellow.** Philadelphia, Pa.: Franklin Publishing, 1969. 342p. $4.60. (5-8)
Relates the history of the role of the various ethnic minorities in the discovery, settling, and growth of the United States. Their unique contributions to American culture and society are also indicated.

2249.   Gay, Kathlyn. **Where the People Are: Cities and Their Future.** Illus. by Dan Nevins. New York: Delacorte, 1969. 148p. $4.95. (4-8)
A brief introduction to urban populations and problems with illustrations showing a diverse culture and peoples of various customs and cultural heritages.

2250.   Glanz, Rudolf. **Jew and Irish: Historic Group Relations and Immigration.** New York: Waldon Press, 1966. 159p. $7.50. (9-12)
Covers Jewish-Irish history and relations in the United States, including a collection

of anecdotes, quotations, and sketches from modern periodicals and newspapers describing these two groups. Particular attention is paid to these groups as immigrants and the importance of the timing of their arrival in America with their later interaction and relations.

2251.   Goldin, Augusta. **Straight Hair, Curly Hair.** Illus. by Ed Emberley. New York: Crowell, 1966. unp. $3.95. (K-2)
A book explaining the reasons why different peoples have different kinds of hair. A valid way of incorporating cultural awareness into the science curriculum. Also available in a Spanish edition: *Pelo Lacio, Pelo Rizo.*

2252.   Gomez, Rudolph, *et al.*, eds. **The Social Reality of Ethnic America.** Lexington, Mass.: D. C. Heath Co., 1974. 412p. $7.95. (T)
Blacks, American Indians, Japanese, and Mexican-Americans are represented here in a collection of 27 essays on ethnicity.

2253.   Handlin, Oscar. **The Newcomers: Negroes and Puerto Ricans in a Changing Metropolis.** Cambridge, Mass.: Harvard University Press, 1959. 171p. $1.95pa. (9-12)
Blacks and Puerto Ricans are studied as the latest of a continuous transition of inner-city ethnic groups from Irish, German, Italian and other nationality groups. Handlin contends that the groups' cohesiveness helps them to survive and even to contribute during this adjustment stage.

2254.   Higham, John. **Send These to Me: Jews and Other Immigrants in Urban America.** New York: Atheneum, 1975. 259p. $10.00; $4.95pa. (9-12)
A study of America's treatment of, reaction to and variation of response to Jews and other ethnic groups throughout her history. Special attention is paid to political and economic circumstances.

2255.   Lauber, Patricia. **Who Discovered America?** New York: Random House, 1970. 128p. $4.95. (4-8)
A description of the settlers and explorers of the New World before the time of Columbus. Vikings, Asian traders, English and Japanese fishermen, and others are included.

2256.   Miller, Wayne, ed. **A Gathering of Ghetto Writers: Irish, Italian, Jewish, Black and Puerto Rican.** New York: New York University Press, 1972. 442p. $12.00; $3.95pa. (8-12)
An overview of the experience and history of the ethnic writers of the twentieth century including Blacks, Italians, Jews, Puerto Ricans, and Irish. Their contributions to American literature, their cultural heritages, and their social acculturation are covered in this collection.

2257.   Murphy, Sharon. **Other Voices: Black, Chicano and American Indian Press.** Dayton, Ohio: Pflaum, 1974. 132p. $5.25pa. (10-12)
This book presents journalism to high school students as a possible career choice by studying the history of the minority press in the United States. Groups included are

Blacks, Chicanos, and American Indians. A bibliography and a list of periodicals published by each of these groups are included.

2258.   Solbert, Ronni. **I Wrote My Name on the Wall: Sidewalk Songs**. Boston, Mass.: Little, Brown, 1971. 72p. $5.95. (3-6)
A photographic essay of Black, white, Asian, and Puerto Rican children and their urban environments and settings in New York City.

Literature and Fiction Titles

2259.   Alexander, Martha. **We Never Get to Do Anything**. New York: Dial, 1970. 32p. $4.95. (K-3)
A picture book showing multiracial children playing together. The story centers around a little boy who wants to swim and must convert his sandbox into a swimming pool to do so.

2260.   Bacmeister, Rhoda W. **The People Downstairs and Other City Stories.** Illus. by Paul Galdone. New York: Coward-McCann, 1964. 120p. $4.97. (K-3)
A collection of 18 short stories about immigrants, Blacks, Puerto Ricans, Orientals, Jews, and children of varying religious as well as ethnic groups. All the stories revolve around children in an urban area.

2261.   Benary-Isbert, Margot. **Long Way Home**. New York: Harcourt Brace Jovanovich, 1959. 280p. $5.95. (7-12)
The story of Chris, an orphan of World War II Germany, who is adopted by a multiracial family in America. His new sister is Italian, and his new brother is Korean. The story revolves around how they solve their cultural differences and problems of adjustment to each other.

2262.   Bethancourt, T. Ernesto. **New York City Too Far from Tampa Blues**. New York: Holiday, 1975. 190p. $6.95. (7-9)
The two main characters in this story are Tom, a Puerto Rican boy, and Aurelio, an Italian. They work up a singing act together and call themselves the Irish Griffin Brothers. Black and Jewish Americans are also cast in the story.

2263.   Binzen, Bill. **Miguel's Mountain**. New York: Coward, 1968. 48p. $4.69.
Children of multi-ethnic and multiracial backgrounds are shown climbing all over Miguel's mountain, which is a heap of soil piled up by some builders working in the area. To urban children who spend their days playing in concrete playgrounds and ghetto streets, this dirt pile is an exciting treat.

2264.   Buchan, Bryan. **Copper Sunrise**. New York: Scholastic Book Services, 1972. 112p. $0.85pa. (4-6)
A Scottish settler in the early days of the Colonies and an Indian become fast friends. The story points out their cultural differences as they made each boy feel uneasy with the other at first. Also emphasizes how the Indian's survival has been threatened.

2265. Caudill, Rebecca. **Somebody Go and Bang a Drum.** Illus. by Jack Hearne. New York: Dutton, 1974. 144p. $4.95. (2-4)
The story of the Garth family, which is comprised of seven adopted children of racially mixed backgrounds. The juvenile novel is based on an actual family case.

2266. Clark, Ann Nolan. **Summer Is for Growing.** New York: Farrar, Straus & Giroux, 1968. 180p. $3.95. (4-6)
Set on a New Mexico hacienda of the 1850s, this story centers around a young girl, Lola, her love for a little foal, and everyday life with the activities of ranch life. Indian contacts are also part of the plot.

2267. Desbarats, Peter. **Gabrielle and Selena.** Illus. by Nancy Grossman. New York: Harcourt Brace Jovanovich, c1968, 1976. 32p. $5.50; $0.95pa. (2-4)
Gabrielle and Selena are two little eight-year-old girls, one Black and one white, who decide to exchange roles and families for some unexpected fun.

2268. Deutsch, Babette, and Avrahm Yarmolinsky, eds. **More Tales of Faraway Folk.** Illus. by Janina Domanska. New York: Harper and Row, 1964. 93p. $3.79. (3-6)
A collection of 15 folktales revealing human weaknesses. This mixture of humorous stories represents a variety of ethnic backgrounds. Tales about Armenians, Finns, Estonians, Lapps, Ukrainians, and other peoples are presented for reading and retelling.

2269. Fall, Thomas. **Wild Boy.** Illus. by Henry C. Pitz. New York: Scholastic Book Services, 1965. 105p. $3.57. (3-6)
Development of the Western United States is a part of this story of an American Indian boy and a Mexican-American boy. Their cultural conflicts add to the problems of their relationship. The story is set in Texas in the 1870s.

2270. Gault, William. **Back Field Challenge.** New York: Dutton, 1967. 160p. $5.50. (7-10)
Bigoted intolerance and also mutual respect are part of this football story, in which the central characters are a Black player, a Puerto Rican player, and a white player, as well as their coach, a former All-American player from Mississippi.

2271. Ginsburg, Mirra, ed. **How Wilka Went to Sea and Other Tales from West of the Urals.** New York: Crown, 1975. 128p. $6.95. (4-8)
A collection of ten folk tales representing different cultures from the Lapps to the Mongols. Types of tales include tall tales, hero stories, and stories of imagination, magic, and sorcery.

2272. Griffith, Francis, and Joseph Mersand. **Eight American Ethnic Plays.** New York: Scribner's, 1974. 386p. $4.37. (7-12)
Ethnic groups represented here are the Irish, Scandinavians, Italians, Jews, Mexicans, Puerto Ricans, and Blacks in American culture. A discussion of the group's history and experience introduces each of the plays.

2273.   Gugliotta, Bobette. **Katzimo, Mysterious Mesa.** Illus. by Morence F.
         Bjorklund. New York: Dodd, Mead, 1974. 224p. $4.50. (4-7)
Carl is part Acoma Indian and part Jewish. His cousin, Horace, is a full-blooded
Acoma. Ethnic identities, hostilities, and customs are a major focus in this mystery
story.

2274.   Jackson, Jacqueline. **The Taste of Spruce Gum.** Illus. by Lillian Obligado.
         Boston, Mass.: Little, Brown, 1966. 212p. $4.95. (6-8)
After her father dies, 11-year-old Libby and her mother go to live with her Uncle
Charles in a rugged logging town in Vermont. The lumberjacks are a mixture of
Italian and French immigrants. Libby's impressions of them and her experiences in
her new multicultural environment are interesting reading, especially for young
girls.

2275.   Jordan, June, and Terri Bush, comps. **The Voice of the Children.** New
         York: Holt, Rinehart and Winston, 1970. 101p. $3.59; $1.95pa. (K-12)
A collection of short stories written by Black and Puerto Rican children between
the ages of 9 and 17. The young writers were participants in a creative writing
workshop. Their prose and poems reveal the problems and sentiments of the youth
of their ethnic minorities.

2276.   Joseph, Stephen M. **The Me Nobody Knows: Children's Voices from the
         Ghetto.** New York: Avon, 1969. 144p. $0.95pa. (5-12)
Writings by children in New York's inner-city public school classes reflect the
experience of the Blacks and Puerto Ricans. Poems, stories, letters, and personal
narratives are included.

2277.   Kaufman, Michael. **Rooftops and Alleys: Adventures with a City Kid.**
         New York: Knopf, 1973. 87p. $5.57. (4-7)
A story of a half-Black boy whose mother is part Indian. His funny adventures living
in various communal families in New York City are related.

2278.   Levoy, Myron. **The Witch of Fourth Street and Other Stories.** Illus. by
         Gabriel Lisowski. New York: Harper and Row, 1972. 110p. $4.95. (4-7)
This collection of short stories recaptures the flavor of the ethnic neighborhoods of
New York's immigrant population during the period of 1919 to 1933. A social
history of the lower East Side is also presented through these narratives.

2279.   McCarthy, Agnes. **Room 10.** Illus. by Ib Ohlsson. Garden City, N.Y.:
         Doubleday, 1966. 72p. $2.50; $0.75pa. (2-3)
A story centered around the children and activities in an integrated classroom,
written by a third-grade teacher.

2280.   Mann, Peggy. **When Carlos Closed the Street.** Illus. by Peter Burchard.
         New York: Coward-McCann, 1969. 70p. $3.86. (2-4)
West 94th Street is divided both by a fire hydrant and by loyalties between the
Black Young Kings and the Spanish Angels. Carlos closes the street in honor of
a big stickball game.

2281.   Mayerson, Charlotte L. **Two Blocks Apart**. New York: Holt, Rinehart
        and Winston, 1965. 126p. $3.95. (7-12)
An Anglo and a Spanish Boy in New York City live in two entirely different
worlds that are only two blocks apart. A story of contrasting socioeconomic and
cultural environments.

2282.   Murray, Michele. **The Crystal Nights**. New York: Seabury Press, 1973.
        310p. $6.95. (7-12)
Elly rejects her family because she hates living on a farm and wants to become an
actress. Her mother is Russian, her father is Jewish, and her cousins are refugees
from Germany. Eventually she comes to understand and appreciate her parents'
sense of values and accepts their love.

2283.   Myers, Walter M. **Where Does the Day Go?** Illus. by Leo Carty. New
        York: Parents' Magazine Press, 1969. unp. $4.95. (K-3)
Black, Spanish, and Asian children are the central characters of this story about a
day's activities in the park.

2284.   Sawyer, Ruth. **Roller Skates**. New York: Viking, 1936. 186p. $6.95.
        (2-4)
A ten-year-old girl roller skates around New York in the days when most of the
city's occupants were foreign-born. She makes friends with an Italian produce seller,
an Irish policeman, and others.

2285.   Shotwell, Louisa R. **Adam Bookout**. Illus. by W. T. Mars. New York:
        Viking, 1967. 256p. $3.77. (4-8)
An exciting mystery story centers around 11-year-old Adam, who doesn't like
living with his great-aunt in Oklahoma after his parents die. He runs away to live
with some cousins in a multi-ethnic neighborhood of Brooklyn. He and his
three friends, a Black, a Jew, and a Puerto Rican, solve a neighborhood crime
involving a stolen dog, and in the process Adam learns that he most cope with his
problems and not run away from them.

2286.   Weaver, Robert G. **Nice Guy, Go Home**. New York: Harper and Row,
        1968. 180p. $3.95. (7-9)
This baseball story centers around a young pitcher for the St. Louis Cardinals farm
team who is from an Amish background. His long hair is responsible for his being
taken for a Northern civil rights worker. A multi-ethnic story of young people's
personal problems and cultural conflicts.

Audiovisual Materials

See the **Audiovisual Materials** section under
General Titles on Ethnicity, page 47.

DIRECTORY OF PRODUCERS AND DISTRIBUTORS OF AUDIOVISUAL MATERIALS

The following names and addresses include those of producers and distributors whose catalogs were consulted for this project.

ABC Media Concepts
c/o Xerox Films
245 Long Hill Rd.
Middletown, Conn. 06457

ACI Films
35 W. 45th St.
New York, New York 10036

AEVAC, Inc.
1604 Park Ave.
South Plainfield, New York 07080

AIMS Instructional Media Services
5420 Melrose St.
Hollywood, Calif. 90028

Afro-American Heritage House
24 Whittier
Englishtown, N.J. 07726

Afro-American Publishing Co., Inc.
1727 S. Indiana Ave.
Chicago, Ill. 60616

American Educational Films
132 Lasky Dr.
Beverly Hills, Calif. 90212

American Jewish Historical Society
2 Thornton Rd.
Waltham, Mass. 02154

Amy Uno Ishii
1801 N. Dillion St.
Los Angeles, Calif. 90026

Anti-Defamation League of B'nai B'rith
315 Lexington Ave.
New York, New York 10016

Appalshop Productions
P.O. Box 743
Whitesburg, Kentucky 41858

Applause Productions, Inc.
85 Longview Rd.
Port Washington, New York 11050

Armenian National Choral Society
Boston, Mass.

Artisan Productions
Box 1827
Hollywood, Calif. 90028

Asia Society
112 E. 64th St.
New York, New York 10021

Asian American Studies
Berkeley Unified School District
1414 Walnut
Berkeley, Calif. 94709

Associated Press
50 Rockefeller Plaza
New York, New York 10020

Association Films
866 Third Ave.
New York, New York 10022

Association for the Study of Negro Life
   and History
1407 14th St. N.W.
Washington, D.C. 20005

Atlantis Productions
850 Thousand Oaks Blvd.
Thousand Oaks, Calif. 91360

Audio-Lingual Educational Press
217 Laurel Rd.
East Northport, New York 11731

Audio-Visual Dept.
Board of National Missions
United Presbyterian Church
475 Riverside Dr.
New York, New York 10027

Audio Visual Associates
805 Smith St.
Baldwin, New York 11510

Audio-Visual Enterprises
911 Laguna Rd.
Pasadena, Calif. 91105

Audio-Visual Narrative Arts
P.O. Box 398
Pleasantville, New York 10570

Augsburg Publishing House
426 S. Fifth St.
Minneapolis, Minn. 55415

Avco Corp.
2385 Revere Beach Parkway
Everett, Mass. 02149

BFA Educational Media
2211 Michigan Ave.
Santa Monica, Calif. 90404

Bailey Film Association
2211 Milk Ave.
Santa Monica, Calif. 90404

Baker & Taylor
1 Gladiola Ave.
Momence, Ill. 60954

George Ballis Association
4696 N. Millbrook
Fresno, Calif. 93726

Barr Films Productions
3490 E. Foothill Blvd.
Pasadena, Calif. 91107

Biograph
P.O. Box 109
Canaan, New York 12029

Bowmar Co.
12 Cleveland St.
Valhalla, New York 10595

Bowmar Records
622 Rodier Dr.
Glendale, Calif. 91201

Brigham Young University
Dept. of Motion Picture Production
291 HRCB
Provo, Utah 84601

Bureau of Indian Affairs
Dept. of the Interior
Washington, D.C. 20242

CMS Records, Inc.
14 Warren St.
New York, New York 10007

Caedmon Records, Inc.
Div. Houghton Mifflin Co.
110 Tremont St.
Boston, Mass. 02107

Carman Educational Associates, Inc.
P.O. Box 205
Youngstown, New York 14174

Carousel Films
1501 Broadway
New York, New York 10036

Cathedral Films
2921 West Alameda Ave.
Burbank, Calif. 91505

Center for Mass Communication of
  Columbia University Press
440 W. 110th St.
New York, New York 10025

Centron Corp.
1621 West Ninth St.
Lawrence, Kans. 66044

Chelsea House Educational
Communications
70 West 40th St.
New York, New York 10018

Childrens Press
Jackson Blvd. & Racine Ave.
Chicago, Ill. 60602

The Child's World
P.O. Box 681
Elgin, Ill. 60120

Churchill Films
662 N. Robertson Blvd.
Los Angeles, Calif. 90069

Civic Ed. Service
1733 K St., N.W.
Washington, D.C. 20006

Class National Publishing, Inc.
3815 Bucker Hill Rd.
Brentwood, Md. 20722

Classroom Film Distributors, Inc.
5610 Hollywood Blvd.
Hollywood, Calif. 90028

Classroom Materials Co.
93 Myrtle Dr.
Great Neck, New York 11021

Coleman Productions, Inc.
75 West 45th St.
New York, New York 10036

Colorado Dept. of Education
201 E. Colfax Ave.
Denver, Colo. 80203

Columbia Pictures Corp.
711 5th Ave.
New York, New York 10022

Columbia Records
799 Seventh Ave.
New York, New York 10019

Communications Group West
6335 Homewood Ave.
Suite 204
Hollywood, Calif. 90028

David C. Cook Pub. Co.
850 N. Grove
Elgin, Ill. 60120

Coronet Instructional Media
61 East South Water
Chicago, Ill. 60601

Council on Interracial Books
CIBC Resource Center
1841 Broadway
New York, New York 10005

County Sales
309 E. 37th St.
New York, New York 10016

Creative Visuals
P.O. Box 1911
Big Spring, Tex. 79720

Current Affairs Films
24 Danbury Rd.
Wilton, Conn. 06897

Czech Ethnic Heritage Studies
Kirkwood Community College
Cedar Rapids, Iowa 52406

Danska Films
498 3rd Ave.
New York, New York 10016

Decca
445 Park Ave.
New York, New York 10022

Denoyer-Geppert Audiovisuals
355 Lexington Ave.
New York, New York 10017

Denver Public Schools for
ETV on Channel 6 KRMA
Denver, Colo. 80219

Desto
c/o CMS Records
14 Warren
New York, New York 10007

Dimension Films
733 N. La Brea Ave.
Los Angeles, Calif. 90038

Documentary Photo Aids
Box 2237
Phoenix, Ariz. 85002

Doubleday
Educational Systems Division
Garden City, New York 11530

Doubleday Multimedia
Box C-19518
1371 Reynolds Ave.
Irvine, Calif. 92713

Dynamic Films, Inc.
405 Park Ave.
New York, New York 10022

EAV (Educational Audio Visual, Inc.)
29 Marble Ave.
Pleasantville, New York 10570

EBEC (Encyclopaedia Britannica Educational Corp.)
425 N. Michigan Ave.
Chicago, Ill. 60611

Ealing Corp.
2225 Massachusetts Ave.
Cambridge, Mass. 02140

Education Unlimited
13113 Puritan
Detroit, Mich. 48227

Educational Design, Inc.
47 W. 13th St.
New York, New York 10011

Educational Development Corporation
202 Lake Miriam Dr.
Lakeland, Fla. 33803

Educational Dimensions Corp.
P.O. Box 126
Stamford, Conn. 06904

Educational Film Libraries
17 West 60th St.
New York, New York 10023

Educational Filmstrips
1401 19th St.
Huntsville, Tex. 77340

Educational Projections Corp.
3070 Lake Terr.
Glenview, Ill. 60025

Educational Record Sales
157 Chambers St.
New York, New York 10007

Educational Resources, Inc.
47 W. 13th St.
New York, New York 10011

Educational Services, Inc.
1730 Eye St. N.W.
Washington, D.C. 20006

Ethnic Service Co.
P.O. Box 38507
Los Angeles, Calif. 90038

Extension Media Center
Film Distribution
University of California
Berkeley, Calif. 94720

Eye Gate House, Inc.
146-01 Archer Ave.
Jamaica, New York 11435

Federation of Jewish Philanthropies of New York
130 E. 59th St.
New York, New York 10022

Field Educational Publications
2400 Hanover St.
Palo Alto, Calif. 94304

Film Associates
2211 Michigan Ave.
Santa Monica, Calif. 90404

Film Wright
Diamond Heights
Box 31348
San Francisco, Calif. 94131

Films, Inc.
1144 Wilmette Ave.
Wilmette, Ill. 60091

Filmstrip House
432 Park Ave. South
New York, New York 10016

Filmways
540 Madison
New York, New York 10010

Folkways Records
FSR
165 W. 46th St.
New York, New York 10036

Folkways/Scholastic
50 W. 44th St.
New York, New York 10036

Friendship Press, Inc.
475 Riverside Dr.
New York, New York 10027

Globe Filmstrips
320 Irwin Ave.
Albion, Mich. 49224

U.S. Government Printing Office
Washington, D.C. 20402

William Greaves Productions, Inc.
1776 Broadway
New York, New York 10019

Greenwood Press, Inc.
Educational Film Division
51 Riverside Ave.
Westport, Conn. 06880

Guidance Associates
757 Third Ave.
New York, New York 10017

Guggenheim Productions
3121 South St.
Washington, D.C. 20007

Handel Film Corp.
8730 Sunset Blvd.
West Hollywood, Calif. 90069

Hearst Metrotone News
450 W. 56th St.
New York, New York 10019

T. N. Hubbard Scientific Co.
2855 Shermer Rd.
Northbrook, Ill. 60062

Hulton Educational Publications
Ranns Rd.
Amersham, Bucks
England

Imperial Educational Resources
4900 S. Lewis Ave.
Tulsa, Okla. 74105

Imperial Film Company, Inc.
4404 S. Florida Ave.
Lakeland, Fla. 33803

Imperial International Learning Corp.
P.O. Box 548
Kankakee, Ill. 60901

Indian House
Gallup, New Mexico

Indiana University Audio-Visual Center
Division of University Extension
Bloomington, Ind. 47401

Institute of Texas Cultures
P.O. Box 1226
San Antonio, Tex. 78294

Instructo Corp.
Cedar Hollow & Matthews Rds.
Paoli, Pa. 19301

Instructor Publications, Co.
Division of Harcourt, Brace Jovanovich
    World, Inc.
Bank St.
Dansville, New York 14437

International Film Bureau
332 S. Michigan
Chicago, Ill. 60604

Louis M. Irigary
155 Juniper Hill
Reno, Nev. 89502

Jam Handy Organization
c/o Scott Graphics
104 Lower Westfield Rd.
Holyoke, Mass. 01040

Japanese American Citizens League
22 Peace Plaza
Suite 203
San Francisco, Calif. 94115

Japanese American Curriculum Project
P.O. Box 367
414 East Third Ave.
San Mateo, Calif. 94401

Jewish Education Committee of
    New York
426 W. 58th St.
New York, New York 10027

Jewish Federation Council of Greater
    Los Angeles
590 North Vermont Ave.
Los Angeles, Calif. 90004

Joshua Tree Productions
15 West 46th St.
New York, New York 10036

Journal Films, Inc.
909 West Diversey Parkway
Chicago, Ill. 60614

June Appal Records
P.O. Box 743
Whitesburg, Ken. 41858

KOMO Television
Seattle, Washington 98102

KPFA Division of Documentaries
Pacifica Tape Library
Berkeley, Calif. 94701

Key Records
P.O. Box 46128
Los Angeles, Calif. 90046

King Screen Productions
320 Aurora Ave. North
Seattle, Wash. 98109

Kosciuszko Foundation
15 E. 65th St.
New York, New York 10022

Learning Corporation of America
1350 Sixth Ave.
New York, New York 10019

Library Filmstrip Center
3033 Aloma St.
Wichita, Kans. 67211

Lyceum Productions, Inc.
P.O. Box 1226
Laguna Beach, Calif. 92652

McGraw-Hill Contemporary Films
1221 Avenue of the Americas
New York, New York 10020

Macmillan Films, Inc.
34 MacQuesten Parkway, South
Mount Vernon, New York 10550

Marco Pereyma, Inc.
3225 E. St., Route 55
Troy, Ohio 45373

Media Materials
409 W. Cold Spring Lane
Baltimore, Md. 21210

Midwest Educational Materials
P.O. Box 706
Kansas City, Mo. 64141

Miller Brody Productions
342 Madison Ave.
New York, New York 10017

Modern Learning Aids
P.O. Box 302
Rochester, New York 14603

Monroe-Williams Productions
3940 Douglas Rd.
Coconut Grove, Fla. 33133

Multi-Media Productions
Box 5097
Stanford, Calif. 94305

NBC Educational Enterprises
30 Rockefeller Plaza
New York, New York 10020

NBC News
30 Rockefeller Plaza
New York, New York 10020

National Academy for Adult Jewish
   Studies
United Synagogue of America
218 East 70th St.
New York, New York 10021

National Audiovisual Center
General Services Administration
Washington, D.C. 20409

National Center for Audio Tapes
Bureau of Audiovisual Instruction
University of Colorado
Boulder, Colo. 80902

National Communications Foundation
1040 North Las Palmos Ave.
Hollywood, Calif. 90034

National Educational Television Film
   Service
Audio-Visual Center
Indiana University
Bloomington, Ind. 47401

National Federation of Temple
   Sisterhoods
838 Fifth Ave.
New York, New York 10003

National Film Board of Canada
6th Floor
1251 Avenue of the Americas
New York, New York 10020

National Geographic Society
17th and M St., N.W.
Washington, D.C. 20036

National Jewish Welfare Board
15 E. 26th St.
New York, New York 10010

New Line Cinema
121 University Place
New York, New York 10003

New York Times/Arno Press
229 West 43rd St.
New York, New York 10036

Newbery Award Records
342 Madison Ave.
New York, New York 10017

Oakland Unified School District
Oakland, Calif. 94601

Official Films
Grand & Linden Avenues
Ridgefield, N.J. 07657

Olcott Forward, Inc.
234 N. Central Ave.
Hartsdale, New York 10530

Oxford Films
1136 North Las Palmas
Hollywood, Calif. 90038

Pathescope Educational Films, Inc.
71 Weyman Ave.
New Rochelle, New York 10802

Penn State AV Services
Willard Bldg.
University Park, Pa. 16802

Perspective Films
369 W. Erie St.
Chicago, Ill. 60610

Photo Lab, Inc.
3825 Georgia Ave., N.W.
Washington, D.C. 20011

Pitman Publishing Corp.
10 East 43rd St.
New York, New York 10017

Popular Science Co.
Popular Science Audio-Visuals
355 Lexington Ave.
New York, New York 10017

Prentice-Hall Media
Educational Book Division
Englewood Cliffs, N.J. 07632

Pyramid Films Producers
P.O. Box 1048
Santa Monica, Calif. 90406

RCA Victor
RCA Educational Service
RCA Service Co.
Camden, N.J. 08108

RMI Film Productions
701 Westport Rd.
Kansas City, Mo. 64111

Random House
201 East 50th St.
New York, New York 10022

Readers' Digest Services, Inc.
Educational Division
Pleasantville, New York 10570

Rediscovery Productions Inc.
2 Halfmile Common
Westport, Conn. 06880

Rockwell Company
233 Broadway
New York, New York 10007

Rounder Records
65 Park St.
Somerville, Mass. 02143

Roy Productions
Pennsylvania Folklore Society
R.D. No. 1
Breinigsville, Pa. 18031

San Francisco Newsreel
450 Alabama St.
San Francisco, Calif. 94110

Sandak
180 Harvard Ave.
Stamford, Conn. 06902

Sandia Corp.
Div. of American Telephone &
    Telegraph
195 Broadway
New York, New York 10007

Joseph Schlitz Brewing Co.
43 George
Brooklyn, New York 11201

Scholastic Audiovisuals
906 Sylvan Ave.
Englewood Cliffs, N.J. 07632

Scholastic Book Services
904 Sylvan Ave.
Englewood Cliffs, N.J. 07632

Scholastic Magazines
50 West 44th St.
New York, New York 10036

Shalom Productions
2007 Vista del Mar Ave.
Hollywood, Calif. 90068

Silver Burdett
250 James St.
Morristown, N.J. 07960

Singer Education Systems
3750 Monroe Ave.
Rochester, New York 14467

Social Science Education Consortium, Inc.
Boulder, Colo. 80902

Social Studies School Service
10000 Culver Blvd.
Culver City, Calif. 90230

Society for French American
Cultural Services and Educational
Aid
972 Fifth Ave.
New York, New York 10021

Society for Visual Education
1345 West Diversey Parkway
Chicago, Ill. 60614

Solfilm International
R.R. No. 1, Box 30
Kopaa, Kanai, Hawaii 96746

Southwest Film Center
169 Franklin Ave.
San Gabriel, Calif. 91775

Spoken Arts
310 North Ave.
New Rochelle, New York 10801

State Historical Society of
Wisconsin
816 State St.
Madison, Wisc. 53706

Sunburst Communications
Hemlock Hill Rd.
Pound Ridge, New York 10576

John Sutherland Learning Associates
8425 West Third St.
Los Angeles, Calif. 90048

Synchro Films
43 Bay Drive West
Huntington, New York 11743

Tandem Press, Inc.
Box 2190
Philadelphia, Pa. 19103

Tapes Unlimited
13113 Puritan
Detroit, Mich. 48227

Teaching Resources Films
Station Plaza
Bedford Hills, New York 10507

Thorne Films, Inc.
934 Pearl
Boulder, Colo. 80302

Time-Life Films
Time-Life Bldg.
Rockefeller Center
New York, New York 10020

Tricontinental Film Center
Box 4430
Berkeley, Calif. 94704

Troll Associates
320 Route 17
Mahwah, N.J. 07430

Tweedy
208 Hollywood Ave.
East Orange, N.J. 07018

Union of American Hebrew
Congregations
Dept. of Audio-Visual Aids
838 Fifth Ave.
New York, New York 10021

United Learning
6633 W. Howard St.
Niles, Ill. 60648

Universal Education and Visual Arts
100 Universal City Pl.
Hollywood, Calif. 91608

University of Michigan
Audio-Visual Education Center
416 Fourth St.
Ann Arbor, Mich. 48103

University of Washington
School of Music Archives
University of Washington Press
1416 NE 41st St.
Seattle, Wash. 98195

Urban Media Materials
212 Mineola Ave.
Roslyn Heights, New York 11577

Valiant Instructional Materials Corp.
237 Washington Ave.
Hackensack, N.J. 07601

Vedo Films
85 Longview Rd.
Port Washington, New York 11050

Vignette Films
981 S. Western Ave.
Los Angeles, Calif. 90006

Viking Press
625 Madison Ave.
New York, New York 10022

Visual Aids Section
State Library
Harrisburg, Pa. 17101

Visual Education Consultants
Box 52
Madison, Wisc. 53701

Visual Education Corp.
364 Nassau St.
Princeton, New York 08540

Voice Over Books
200 Park Ave.
New York, New York 10003

Vought Aeronautics
P.O. Box 5907
Dallas, Tex. 75222

WDEM (Walt Disney Educational
Materials Co.)
800 Sonora Ave.
Glendale, Calif. 91201

WGBH-TV
WGBH Educational Foundation
125 Western Ave.
Boston, Mass. 02134

WKYC-TV
1403 East Sixth St.
Cleveland, Ohio 44114

J. Weston Walch
Box 1075
Portland, Maine 04104

Warren Schloat Productions
150 White Plains Rd.
Tarrytown, New York 10591

Westinghouse Learning Corporation
100 Park Ave.
New York, New York 10017

Weston Woods
Weston, Conn. 06880

Westwood Educational Productions
701 Westport Rd.
Kansas City, Mo. 64118

H. Wilson Corp.
555 W. Taft Dr.
South Holland, Ill. 60473

Wisdom Co.
1727 Vine St.
Philadelphia, Pa. 19103

Wollensak
1697 Broadway
New York, New York 11377

Wombat Productions, Inc.
77 Tarrytown Rd.
White Plains, New York 10607

Xerox Education Publications
245 Long Hill Rd.
Middletown, Conn. 06457

Yasutomo & Co.
24 California
San Francisco, Calif. 94111

AUTHOR INDEX

TITLE INDEX

Bibliography of Negro History and Culture for Young Readers, 589

Bibliography of Nonprint Instructional Materials on the American Indian, 199, 204

Bibliography of Selected Childrens' Books about American Indians, 198

Bibliography of Spanish Materials for Children K-6, 7-12, 2068

Bibliography on Hispano America History and Culture, 2074

Big Star Fallin' Mama: Five Black Women in Black Music, 743

Bilingual/Bicultural Education Models. Final Report, 1668

Bilingual Bicultural Materials: A Listing for Library Resource Centers, 19

Biographical Dictionary of Early American Jews: Colonial Times through 1800, 1524

Biographical Directory of Americans and Canadians of Croatian Descent, 2212

Biographical Directory of Scholars, Artists, and Professionals of Croatian Descent in the United States and Canada, 2209

Birthday Visitor, 1482

Black Almanac, 627

Black American: A Documentary History, 707

Black American Fiction since 1952: A Preliminary Checklist, 610

Black Americans in Autobiography: An Annotated Bibliography of Autobiographies and Autobiographical Books Written since the Civil War, 580

Black American in Books for Children: Readings in Racism, 643

Black American in United States History, 801

Black American Leaders, 813

Black American Literature: A Critical History of the Major Periods, Movements, Themes, Works, and Authors, 809

Black American Music: Past and Present, 644

Black American Writers Past & Present: A Biographical & Bibliographical Dictionary, 618

Black Americans, 776

Black Americans: A Study Guide and Source Book, 640

Black Athlete: His Story in American History, 771

Black B C's, 683

Black, Black, Beautiful Black, 823

Black Book, 721

Black College Sport, 676

Black Cop, 712

Black Council, 2183

Black Courage, 785

Black Crusaders for Freedom, 806

Black Culture Collection Catalog: United States Section . . . The Black Experience in America since the 17th Century, 574

Black Culture: Reading and Writing Black, 789

Black Defenders of America: 1776-1973, 615

Black Drama: The Story of the American Negro in the Theatre, 767

Black Experience and the School Curriculum; Teaching Materials for Grades K-12: An Annotated Bibliography, 576

Black Experience in America, 685

Black Experience in American Politics, 730

Black Experience in Children's Audiovisual Materials, 598

Black Experience in Children's Books, 575, 602

Black Families and the Struggle for Survival, 664

Black Families in White America, 664

Black Family and the Black Woman, A Bibliography, 591

Black Folktales, 753

Black Frontiersmen: Adventures of Negroes among American Indians, 733

Black Heroes in Our Nation's History, 696

Black History: Events in February, 763

Black History Past & Present, 652

Black Image: Education Copes with Color: Essays on the Black Experience, 641

Black Image on the American Stage: A Bibliography of Plays and Musicals 1770-1970, 587

Black in America—A Fight for Freedom, 741

Black Information Index, 578

Black Is Brown Is Tan, 814

Black List: The Concise Reference Guide to Publications, Films & Broadcasting Media of Black America, Africa and the Caribbean, 622

Black Literature in America, 821

Black Man in America, 739

Black Man on Film: Racial Stereotyping, 758

Black Man's Burden, 859

Black Means, 728

Black Migration, 727

Black Mountain Boy: A Story of the Boyhood of John Honie, 252

Black Music in America, 782

Black Music in Our Culture: Curricular Ideas on the Subjects, Materials & Problems, 638

Black Muslims in America, 755

Black Nationalism in America, 667

Black on Black, 650

Black Out Loud, 815

Black Pilgrimage, 705

Black Pioneers of Science and Invention, 729

Black Poets of the United States: From Paul Laurence Dunbar to Langston Hughes, 877

AUDIOVISUAL INDEX

The following code explains the abbreviations used in this index to designate media type:

cal = calendar

cass = cassette

ch = chart

8mm f = 8mm film

16mm f = 16mm film

fl = film loop

fs = filmstrip

foldouts = foldouts

kit = multimedia kit

map = map

post = posters

prts = study prints

rec = record

sl = slides

t = tape

trans = transparencies

vid = videotape